ASPEN PUBLISHE

INTELLECTUAL PROPERTY

Second Edition

Margreth Barrett

Professor of Law

University of California

Hastings College of the Law

The *Emanuel Law Outlines* Series

Wolters Kluwer

Law & Business

AUSTIN   BOSTON   CHICAGO   NEW YORK   THE NETHERLANDS

© 2008 Aspen Publishers. All Rights Reserved.
http://lawschool.aspenpublishers.com

No part of this publication may be reproduced or transmitted in any form or by any means, electronic or mechanical, including photocopy, recording, or any information storage and retrieval system, without permission in writing from the publisher. Requests for permission to make copies of any part of this publication should be mailed to:

Aspen Publishers
Attn: Permissions Department
76 Ninth Avenue, 7th Floor
New York, NY 10011-5201

To contact Customer Care, e-mail customer.care@aspenpublishers.com, call 1-800-234-1660, fax 1-800-901-9075, or mail correspondence to:

Aspen Publishers
Attn: Order Department
PO Box 990
Frederick, MD 21705

Printed in the United States of America.

1 2 3 4 5 6 7 8 9 0

ISBN 978-0-7355-6297-4

This book is intended as a general review of a legal subject. It is not intended as a source of advice for the solution of legal matters or problems. For advice on legal matters, the reader should consult an attorney.

Siegel's, Emanuel, the judge logo, Law in a Flash and design, CrunchTime and design, Strategies & Tactics and design, and The Professor Series are registered trademarks of Aspen Publishers.

About Wolters Kluwer Law & Business

Wolters Kluwer Law & Business is a leading provider of research information and workflow solutions in key specialty areas. The strengths of the individual brands of Aspen Publishers, CCH, Kluwer Law International and Loislaw are aligned within Wolters Kluwer Law & Business to provide comprehensive, in-depth solutions and expert-authored content for the legal, professional and education markets.

CCH was founded in 1913 and has served more than four generations of business professionals and their clients. The CCH products in the Wolters Kluwer Law & Business group are highly regarded electronic and print resources for legal, securities, antitrust and trade regulation, government contracting, banking, pension, payroll, employment and labor, and healthcare reimbursement and compliance professionals.

Aspen Publishers is a leading information provider for attorneys, business professionals and law students. Written by preeminent authorities, Aspen products offer analytical and practical information in a range of specialty practice areas from securities law and intellectual property to mergers and acquisitions and pension/benefits. Aspen's trusted legal education resources provide professors and students with high-quality, up-to-date and effective resources for successful instruction and study in all areas of the law.

Kluwer Law International supplies the global business community with comprehensive English-language international legal information. Legal practitioners, corporate counsel and business executives around the world rely on the Kluwer Law International journals, loose-leafs, books and electronic products for authoritative information in many areas of international legal practice.

Loislaw is a premier provider of digitized legal content to small law firm practitioners of various specializations. Loislaw provides attorneys with the ability to quickly and efficiently find the necessary legal information they need, when and where they need it, by facilitating access to primary law as well as state-specific law, records, forms and treatises.

Wolters Kluwer Law & Business, a unit of Wolters Kluwer, is headquartered in New York and Riverwoods, Illinois. Wolters Kluwer is a leading multinational publisher and information services company.

This edition is dedicated to my husband,
Ken Louden,
and my sons,
Andrew Vinson Louden
and
Robert Barrett Louden

Margreth Barrett
January 2008

Summary of Contents

Table of Contents	ix
Preface	xxxi
Casebook Correlation Chart	xxxiii
Capsule Summary	C-1
Chapter 1. Introduction to the Study of Intellectual Property	1
Chapter 2. The Law of Trade Secrets	5
Chapter 3. Patents	27
Chapter 4. The Law of Undeveloped Ideas	93
Chapter 5. Copyright Law	101
Chapter 6. Trademark Law	223
Chapter 7. Unfair Competition	309
Chapter 8. The Right of Publicity	327
Chapter 9. The Relationship Between Federal and State Law	335
Essay Exam Questions and Answers	349
Table of Cases	383
Table of References to the Copyright Act of 1976 (17 U.S.C. §101 *et seq.*)	387
Table of References to the Lanham Act (15 U.S.C. §1051 *et seq.*)	389
Table of References to the Patent Act (35 U.S.C. §101 *et seq.*)	391
Subject Matter Index	393

Table of Contents

Preface xxxi
Casebook Correlation Chart xxxiii
Capsule Summary C-1

CHAPTER 1
INTRODUCTION TO THE STUDY OF INTELLECTUAL PROPERTY

I. Scope of the Term "Intellectual Property" 2
   A. Generally 2
II. Primary Policy Issues 2
   A. An incentive to create 2
   B. Promotion of competition 2
   C. Potential conflict 2
   D. Reaching a balance 2
   E. Trademark law and related doctrines 3
III. Sources of Authority to Regulate Intellectual Property 3
   A. Federal regulation 3
   B. State regulation 3

Quiz Yourself on INTRODUCTORY ISSUES 3

Exam Tips on INTELLECTUAL PROPERTY GENERALLY 4

CHAPTER 2
THE LAW OF TRADE SECRETS

I. The Purpose, Nature, and Source of Trade Secret Law 6
   A. Generally 6
   B. The Restatement and the Uniform Trade Secrets Act 6
   C. The elements of a trade secret misappropriation cause of action 6
II. Status of Ideas or Information as Trade Secret 7
   A. General definition 7
      1. Continuous use 7
   B. Six factors considered in determining trade secret status 7
      1. How widely is the idea or information known outside the claimant's business? 7
      2. Who within the claimant's company knows the idea or information? 7

3. What measures has the claimant taken to ensure that the idea or information remains secret? 7
4. How difficult would it be for others properly to acquire or duplicate the idea or information? 8
5. How valuable is the idea or information to the claimant and its competitors? 8
6. How much effort or money has the claimant expended in developing or acquiring the idea or information? 8

III. When Acquisition, Use, or Disclosure of a Trade Secret Constitutes an Actionable Misappropriation 8
  A. Disclosure or use of a trade secret in breach of confidence 8
    1. Special relationships 8
    2. Express contracts to retain confidentiality 9
    3. Implied contracts to retain confidentiality 9
  B. Disclosure or use of a trade secret learned from a third party with notice 10
    1. Notice 10
  C. Disclosure or use of a trade secret learned by mistake with notice 10
    1. Notice 10
  D. Continued disclosure or use of a trade secret after receipt of notice of trade secrecy and breach of duty 10
    1. The Restatement of Torts 11
    2. The Uniform Trade Secrets Act 11
  E. Continued disclosure or use of a trade secret after receipt of notice that it is a trade secret and was acquired by mistake 11
  F. Acquisition, disclosure, or use of a trade secret acquired through improper means 11
    1. Illegal conduct 12
    2. Conduct below generally accepted standards of commercial morality 12
  G. Disclosure or use of a trade secret with notice that the provider acquired it through improper means 12
    1. Notice 13
  H. Defendant's modification of plaintiff's trade secret 13

IV. Private Owners' Rights in Trade Secret Information Submitted to Government Agencies 13
  A. Freedom of information acts 13
    1. Exemptions in freedom of information acts 13
  B. An unconstitutional "taking" 14
    1. The standard for finding a taking 14
    2. The standard applied 14

V. Use and Disclosure by Employees and Former Employees 14
  A. In the absence of an express agreement 14
    1. Preexisting trade secrets disclosed to the employee 14
    2. Trade secrets created by the employee 14
  B. In the case of an express agreement 15
    1. Non-disclosure agreements 15

2. Advance assignment agreements 15
3. Non-competition agreements 16
C. The doctrine of inevitable disclosure 17
VI. Remedies for Trade Secret Misappropriation 17
A. Injunctions 17
1. Duration limited to the life of the trade secret 18
2. Unlimited duration 18
B. Damages 18
C. Criminal prosecution 18

Quiz Yourself on TRADE SECRETS 19

Exam Tips on TRADE SECRETS 25

CHAPTER 3

PATENTS

I. Utility Patents 29
A. The nature of a utility patent 29
B. The term of a utility patent 29
C. Constitutional limitations 29
D. Implementation of the limitations 30
E. Enforcing the limitations 30
1. Summary of the P.T.O. examination process 30
2. Routes of appeal 31
3. Reissue 31
4. Reexamination 31
II. Statutory Subject Matter of a Utility Patent 32
A. Process 32
1. New use of a known process, machine, manufacture, or composition of matter 32
B. Machine 32
C. Manufacture 33
D. Composition of matter 33
E. Naturally occurring vs. man-made articles 33
F. Live vs. inanimate matter 33
G. Laws of nature and abstract ideas 33
1. Specific applications of laws of nature and abstract ideas 33
2. Applicability of the rule to computer programs 34
H. Business methods 35
I. Medical procedures 35

III. The Novelty Standard 36
A. Subsection 102(a) 36
1. When an invention is "known by others" in this country 36
2. When an invention will be deemed "used by others" in this country ... 37
3. When an invention will be deemed described in a printed publication in this or a foreign country 37
4. When an invention will be deemed patented in this or a foreign country ... 38
B. Subsection 102(e) 39
C. Subsection 102(g) 40
1. Determining who is first to invent 40
2. Abandonment, suppression, and concealment 40
3. Interferences 41

IV. The Statutory Bar and Inventor Requirements 42
A. The §102(b) statutory bar 42
1. A statute of limitations 42
2. When an invention will be deemed "in public use" in this country 43
3. When an invention will be deemed "on sale" in this country 45
4. When an invention will be deemed patented or described in a printed publication ... 46
B. Subsection 102(c) 46
1. Express abandonment 46
2. Implicit abandonment 46
C. Subsection 102(d) 46
D. Subsection 102(f) 46
1. Who is the inventor? 46
2. Joint inventors 47

V. The Non-Obviousness Standard 47
A. The pertinent prior art 47
1. Determining which prior art is "pertinent" 48
B. The level of skill in the pertinent art 48
C. The legal determination of obviousness 48
D. Secondary considerations 48
1. Commercial success 49
2. Long-felt need 49
3. Commercial acquiescence 49
4. Additional considerations 49
5. The necessity of a nexus 49
E. Combination patents 49
1. The *KSR* decision 50
F. Section 103(c)—Secret prior art in collaborative situations 51
G. Biotechnological process patents 51
H. Obviousness as a trigger for the §102(b) statute of limitations ... 51

VI. The Utility Standard 52
A. A significant benefit to society 52
1. The utility requirement for pharmaceuticals 52
B. Inoperability as lack of utility 52

VII. The Disclosure Requirement 52
A. The claiming requirement 52
B. The enablement requirement 53
C. The best mode requirement 53
1. The subjective inquiry 53
2. The objective inquiry 53
D. The written description requirement 53

VIII. Infringement of Utility Patents 54
A. Suits to enforce patents 54
1. Infringement 54
2. Claim interpretation 54
3. Literal infringement 55
4. The doctrine of equivalents 55
B. Direct infringement 58
1. "Making" the patented invention in the case of combination patents 58
2. Selling the patented invention 60
3. Offering to sell the patented invention 60
4. Importing the patented invention 61
C. Inducement to infringe 62
1. Active solicitation or assistance 62
2. Knowledge and intent 62
3. Corporate officers, directors, and majority shareholders 62
D. Contributory infringement 62
1. Knowledge 63
2. The component sold, offered for sale, or imported 63
3. Recent amendments 63
E. Importing, selling, offering to sell, or using a product made through a process protected by a U.S. patent 63
1. Made by a patented process 63
2. Scope of §271(g) 63
3. Burden of proof 64
4. Exceptions 64
F. Supplying components of a U.S.-patented invention to be assembled abroad 64
1. Supplying a material component of a U.S.-patented invention 64
2. Supplying software 65
G. Provisional rights prior to patent issuance 65
1. Publication 65
2. The provisional rights 66

H. Defenses to infringement claims 66
1. Patent invalidity 66
2. Patent misuse 66
3. Inequitable conduct 68
4. The experimental use defense 69
5. Prior use 69

IX. Remedies for Patent Infringement 70
A. The proper measure of damages 70
1. The reasonable royalty measure of damages 70
2. The lost-profits measure of damages 71
3. Attorney fees 72
4. Double or treble damages 72
5. Prejudgment interest 73
B. Injunctive relief 73
1. Preliminary injunctions 73
C. Remedies for infringement through performance of "medical activities" 74
1. The caveat 74

X. Comparison of Utility Patent and Trade Secret Protection for Inventions 74
A. Duration of protection 74
B. Breadth of protection 75
C. Cost 75
D. Risk of losing protection 75
E. Licensing 75

XI. Design Patents 75
A. The nature of design patents 75
1. Articles of manufacture 75
2. The duration of design patents 75
B. Standards for design patents 75
1. Novelty and statutory bars 76
2. The non-obviousness standard 76
3. The ornamentality standard 76
C. Infringement of a design patent 77
1. The Federal Circuit's additional requirements 77
2. Comparing the standard for design patent infringement with the standard for utility patent infringement 77
D. Defenses and remedies for infringement of design patents 77
E. Double patenting 77
F. The success of design patents 78

XII. Plant Patents 78
A. The nature of a plant patent 78
1. Scope of plant patents 78
B. Standards for plant patents 78

1. Asexual reproduction	78
2. Novelty and statutory bars	78
3. The distinctiveness requirement	79
4. The non-obviousness requirement	79
C. Infringement of a plant patent	79
1. Independent discovery	79
2. Taking seeds	79
3. Plant parts	79
D. Other considerations	79
E. Other methods of obtaining property rights in new varieties of plants	80
1. Utility patents for plants	80
2. Plant Variety Protection Act	80
XIII. Key International Patent Treaties	80
A. The Paris Convention	80
1. National treatment	80
2. Filing priority	81
3. Common rules	81
4. Criticisms of the Paris Convention	81
B. The Patent Cooperation Treaty	82
1. Procedure	82
C. The Agreement on Trade-Related Aspects of Intellectual Property Rights	82
D. The Patent Law Treaty	83
Quiz Yourself on PATENTS	83
Exam Tips on PATENTS	91

CHAPTER 4

THE LAW OF UNDEVELOPED IDEAS

I. The Nature of the Law of Undeveloped Ideas	93
A. Miscellaneous accumulation	93
B. The express contract theory	94
1. Lack of consideration	94
2. Implied condition	94
C. The contract-implied-in-fact theory	95
D. The contract-implied-in-law theory	95
E. The confidential relationship theory	95
F. The property theory	95
II. The Novelty and Concreteness Requirements	96
A. The novelty requirement	96
1. New York law regarding novelty	96
B. The concreteness requirement	96

C. The general policy reasons for imposing novelty and concreteness requirements 96
D. Treating idea claims as claims for the value of services rendered 97

Quiz Yourself on RIGHTS IN UNDEVELOPED IDEAS 97

Exam Tips on RIGHTS IN UNDEVELOPED IDEAS 99

CHAPTER 5

COPYRIGHT LAW

I. The Purpose and Nature of Copyright Law 103
  A. The purpose of copyright law 103
  B. The nature of copyright law 103
    1. Copyright gives rights in "works of authorship" 104
    2. Property right vs. personal right 105
    3. Rights in the intangible 105
  C. Federal vs. state law 106
    1. 1976 Act vs. 1909 Act 106
  D. The Copyright Office 106

II. The Subject Matter of Copyright 106
  A. Section 102 106
  B. The "originality" requirement 107
    1. Copyright Office rule regarding words, short phrases, slogans, etc 107
    2. *Scenes a faire* 108
    3. "Sweat of the brow" 108
  C. The fixation requirement 108
    1. The meaning of "fixation" 108
    2. Common-law copyright protection for unfixed works 109
  D. Exclusion of ideas, procedures, processes, etc. 109
    1. The *Baker v. Selden* case 110
    2. Copyrightability of facts and research 111
  E. Categories of protectible works of authorship 112
    1. The literary works category—copyrightability of computer programs 112
    2. The pictorial, graphic, and sculptural works category 117
    3. The architectural works category 120
    4. The sound recordings category 122
  F. Other problem areas 122
    1. Copyright for fictitious characters 122
    2. Copyright protection for immoral or obscene works 123
    3. Protection for semiconductor chips 123
  G. Compilations 124
    1. Collective works 124
    2. Other compilations 124

  3. Copyright protection is limited to the compilation author's
   original expression 124
  4. Unauthorized use of copyrighted material 125
 H. Derivative works 125
  1. Originality and derivative works 125
  2. Concern about the effect of derivative work copyrights 126
 I. Government works as copyrightable subject matter 126
  1. No copyright for works of the U.S. government 126
  2. Copyright in state and local government works 127

III. **The Rights Afforded by Copyright Law** 127
 A. **The exclusive economic rights of copyright** 127
 B. **Moral rights in works of visual art** 128
 C. **Ownership of rights** 128

IV. **The "Copyrighted Work"** 128
 A. **The *Arnstein* copying and unlawful appropriation test** 129
  1. Copying 129
  2. Unlawful appropriation 129
 B. **The Ninth Circuit's variation on the *Arnstein* approach to finding
  "unlawful appropriation"** 132
  1. An evolving standard 132
 C. **Other approaches to evaluating unlawful appropriation** 133
  1. The "abstraction, filtration, comparison" standard 133
  2. The "more discerning" standard 133
  3. The "thin copyright" standard 133

V. **The Exclusive Right to Reproduce the Work** 133
 A. **The act of reproduction** 133
  1. "Reproduction" in the random access memory of a computer 134
 B. **Limitations on the exclusive right to reproduce—sound recordings**...135
  1. Digital sampling 135
 C. **Exception to the exclusive right to reproduce—computer programs** ...136
  1. First exception—reproduction as an essential step in using 136
  2. Second exception—reproduction for archival purposes 136
  3. Third exception—reproductions made in the course of computer repair 136
  4. The limitation to "owners" of lawful copies of programs 136
 D. **Exception to the exclusive right to reproduce—pictorial, graphic,
  and sculptural works** 137
 E. **Exception to the exclusive right to reproduce—architectural works** 137
 F. **Exception to the exclusive right to reproduce—libraries and archives** ...138
 G. **Exception to the exclusive right to reproduce—the ephemeral recordings
  provisions** 138
 H. **Exception to the exclusive right to reproduce—home audiotaping** ...138
  1. MP3 files 138

I. Exception to the exclusive right to reproduce—compulsory licenses to record nondramatic musical works 138
    1. Nonsubject musical works 139
    2. The rights afforded pursuant to a compulsory license 139
    3. Voluntary licenses 139
J. Exception to the exclusive right to reproduce—specialized formats for the visually impaired or otherwise disabled 139

VI. The Exclusive Right to Prepare Derivative Works 139
  A. Overlap with the right to reproduce or publicly perform 140
    1. The relevance of the prerequisites for copyrighting derivative works: 140
  B. The adaptation right and computer program enhancements 140
    1. A subsequent limitation on enhancement programs 141
    2. The Family Entertainment and Copyright Act of 2005 141
  C. Limitations on the exclusive right to adapt in the case of sound recordings 142
  D. Exception to the exclusive right to adapt—computer programs 142
  E. Exception to the exclusive right to adapt—architectural works 142

VII. The Exclusive Right to Distribute to the Public 142
  A. Transfer of a material copy 142
  B. The doctrine of first sale 143
    1. The doctrine only applies to lawful copies and phonorecords 143
    2. Exception for record and computer program rentals 143
    3. The *droit de suite* 144
    4. Imports 144
    5. The doctrine of first sale on the Internet 145

VIII. The Exclusive Right of Public Performance 145
  A. The meaning of "performance" 146
  B. When a performance is "public" 146
    1. A place open to the public 146
    2. A place where a substantial number of persons outside of the normal circle of a family and its social acquaintances is gathered 147
    3. Transmitted to the public, regardless of whether members of the public can receive the performance at the same place or time 147
  C. Performing rights societies 147
  D. The new limited performance rights in sound recordings 148
    1. Numerous limitations 148
  E. Rights in live musical performances 148
  F. Exception to the exclusive right of public performance—nonprofit performances of nondramatic literary or musical works 149
  G. Other exceptions to the exclusive right of public performance 149
  H. Exceptions to the exclusive rights of public performance and display 149

IX. The Exclusive Right to Display the Copyrighted Work Publicly 150
  A. When a display is public 150
  B. Exception to the exclusive right of public display—owners of lawfully made copies ... 150

C. Exception to the exclusive rights of public performance *and* display—transmissions received on home-style receivers..........150
1. A broader exception for public performances and displays of nondramatic musical works 151
D. Exception to the exclusive rights of public performance *and* display—face-to-face nonprofit instruction..........151
E. Exception to the exclusive rights of public performance *and* display—instructional and "distance learning" transmissions..........152
F. Exception to the exclusive rights of public performance *and* display—religious services..........152
G. Exception to the exclusive rights of public performance *and* display—electronic video games..........152
H. Exceptions and compulsory licenses—secondary transmissions..........152
I. Exception to the exclusive rights of public performance *and* display—compulsory licenses for noncommercial broadcasting..........153

X. Moral Rights..........153
A. The nature of moral rights..........153
1. The right of attribution..........153
2. The right of integrity..........153
B. The Visual Artists' Rights Act of 1990..........153
1. Works of visual art..........153
2. The rights of attribution and integrity..........154
3. Works of visual art incorporated into buildings..........155
C. Indirect protection of moral rights under the Copyright Act..........155
D. Other federal sources for protecting moral rights—Lanham Act §43(a)..........156
E. State causes of action that may vindicate moral rights..........156

XI. Direct and Indirect Copyright Infringement..........156
A. Direct infringement..........156
B. Three forms of indirect infringement liability..........157
1. Contributory infringement..........157
2. Vicarious infringement liability..........158
3. The *Grokster* "intentional inducement" theory of indirect infringement liability..........159
C. Infringement liability on the Internet..........160
1. Safe harbors for Internet service providers..........160

XII. Fair Use and Other Defenses to Infringement..........162
A. The nature of the fair use defense..........162
B. Section 107..........162
1. The examples..........162
2. The four listed factors..........162
3. Four factors not exclusive..........164
4. No factor is conclusive..........165
C. Special considerations in parody cases..........165
1. Parody of the copyrighted work itself or of something else?..........165

2. The amount of copyrighted material taken 165
3. Effect on the plaintiff's market 165
D. Educational and library copying 166
E. Reverse engineering 166
F. Market failure and fair use 166
1. The implications of the market failure line of reasoning for fair use on the Internet 167
G. Copyright misuse 167

XIII. Anticircumvention and Digital Rights Management Provisions 168
A. Anticircumvention provisions 168
1. Two kinds of "technological measures" and three causes of action 168
2. Liability for circumventing access controls 168
3. Liability for manufacturing, distributing, or trafficking in circumvention devices or services 169
4. Early decisions construing the "anti-trafficking" provisions 169
5. Exceptions 172
B. Copyright management information 172

XIV. Ownership of Copyright 172
A. Determining the initial owner of copyright in a work 172
B. Ownership of copyright in joint works 172
1. Emphasis on intent 172
2. Contribution of copyrightable expression 173
3. Other requirements 173
C. Works for hire 173
1. Work prepared by an employee within the scope of his employment 173
2. Specially ordered or commissioned works 175
D. Ownership of copyright in collective works 175
1. Presumed privileges 176
2. Limitation on the presumed privileges 176
E. Divisibility of ownership 176
F. The requirement of a writing to transfer 177
1. Recordation of documents 177
G. Beneficial ownership of copyright 177

XV. Notice of Copyright 177
A. The history of notice requirements in the United States 177
B. The Copyright Act of 1909 177
1. Publication under the 1909 Act 177
C. The Copyright Act of 1976—January 1, 1978 to March 1, 1989 178
1. Publication under the 1976 Act 178
2. Notice on visually perceptible copies 178
3. Notice on phonorecords 178
4. Savings provisions 179
5. The effect of an error in the notice 179

- D. The Berne Convention amendments—March 1, 1989 to the present 179
- E. Foreign copyright restoration 180
  - 1. Effective date and term of restoration 180

XVI. Deposit and Registration 180
- A. Deposit requirements 180
- B. Registration requirements 181
  - 1. Certificate as *prima facie* evidence 181
  - 2. Registration as a prerequisite to a copyright infringement action 181
  - 3. Registration as a prerequisite to certain remedies 181
  - 4. Registration is not a prerequisite to a claim of moral rights violation 182

XVII. The Duration of Copyright Protection 182
- A. Commencement of federal copyright 182
- B. Congressional extensions of the copyright term 182
  - 1. Extensions held constitutional 182
- C. Duration of copyright for works created on or after January 1, 1978 182
  - 1. Works of joint authorship 183
  - 2. Anonymous and pseudonymous works 183
  - 3. Works made for hire 183
- D. Duration of the copyright for works created but not published before January 1, 1978 184
  - 1. A trade 184
  - 2. Additional term for publication 184
- E. Duration of the copyright for works already protected by federal copyright on January 1, 1978 184
- F. Duration of the rights of attribution and integrity in works of visual art 185
- G. Rule for calculating the end of the term 185

XVIII. Renewals of Pre-1976 Act Federal Copyrights 185
- A. Renewal of federal copyrights in their first term on January 1, 1978 185
- B. The rationale for renewable terms 185
- C. Ownership of the renewal right 186
- D. Transfer of expectancy of renewal right 186
  - 1. The problem with permitting transfer 187
- E. Exceptions to the rule that the author and his statutory successors have the right to renew 187
- F. The process of renewal 187
  - 1. Encouragement to file 188
- G. Renewals and derivative works 188
  - 1. The effect of 1992 amendments 189
  - 2. The effect of failure to renew copyright in a derivative work 189

XIX. Termination of Transfers of Copyright 189
- A. Maintaining the author's "second chance" under the 1976 Act 189
- B. Transfers executed on or after January 1, 1978 189
  - 1. Transfers subject to termination 189

  2. Persons entitled to terminate 189
  3. In the case of joint authors 190
  4. Time for termination 190
  5. Notice 190
  6. No waivers 191
  7. Effect of termination 191
  8. Derivative works 191
 C. Transfers executed prior to January 1, 1978 191
  1. Grants subject to termination 191
  2. Persons entitled to terminate 192
  3. Time for termination 192
  4. Notice 192
  5. Effect of termination 192
  6. Further grants 193
  7. Other provisions 193

XX. Remedies for Infringement 193
 A. Injunctions 193
 B. Damages and/or profits 193
  1. Damages and/or profits 193
  2. Statutory damages 194
 C. Costs and attorney fees 195
  1. Costs 195
  2. Attorney fees 195
 D. Criminal penalties 195

XXI. International Copyright Treaties 195
 A. The Berne Convention 195
  1. Works protected under the Berne Convention 195
  2. Prerequisites to protection 196
  3. Duration of protection 196
  4. Extent of protection 196
  5. Protection based on country of origin of the work 196
  6. United States adherence to the Berne Convention 196
 B. The Universal Copyright Convention 197
  1. Substantive provisions—duration of protection 197
  2. Rights 197
  3. Notice and other formalities 197
  4. Application of the U.C.C 197
  5. Relationship to the Berne Convention 197
 C. The Agreement on Trade-Related Aspects of Intellectual Property Rights 197
  1. Computer programs and database expression 197
  2. Additional rights 198
  3. Necessary changes to U.S. law 198
 D. The WIPO Copyright Treaty 198

1. A general right of distribution to the public 198
2. The "right of communication to the public" 198
3. Anticircumvention and rights management provisions 199

Quiz Yourself on COPYRIGHTS 199

Exam Tips on COPYRIGHTS 218

CHAPTER 6
TRADEMARK LAW

I. The Nature of Trademark Law 225
   A. The purpose of trademarks and trademark law 225
   B. The relationship of state and federal law 226
   C. The Lanham Act 226
      1. Lanham Act §43(a) 226
      2. The Lanham Act registration provisions 226

II. Types of Marks 227
   A. Four types of marks 227
   B. Trademarks 227
      1. Word, name, symbol, or device 227
      2. Indicating source, even if the source is unknown 227
   C. Service marks 228
      1. There must be a sufficiently separate service to identify 228
   D. Certification marks 228
      1. Federal restrictions on certification marks 228
   E. Collective marks 229
      1. Collective membership marks 229
      2. Collective trademarks and service marks 229
      3. Similarity of collective trademarks and service marks to certification marks 229

III. Distinctiveness 229
   A. Marks must be distinctive 229
   B. Arbitrary and fanciful marks 230
   C. Suggestive marks 230
      1. Tests for determining whether a mark is descriptive or suggestive 230
   D. Descriptive marks 230
      1. "Appear" to describe 231
      2. The justification for withholding protection for descriptive marks, absent a showing of secondary meaning 233
      3. Secondary meaning 233
      4. Evaluating distinctiveness (or descriptiveness) 233
      5. Abstract designs and other nonverbal marks 234
   E. Generic words and symbols 235

  1. The standard for determining whether a mark is generic 235
  2. Descriptive vs. generic marks 236
  3. Nonverbal generic marks 236

IV. The Content of Marks 236
 A. The sky is the limit 236
 B. Words and numbers as marks 237
  1. Slogans 237
 C. Scents and sounds 237
 D. Drawings and other forms of art or design 237
 E. Composite marks 237
 F. Trade dress 237
  1. Trade dress rights in color alone 238
  2. Trade dress and the distinctiveness requirement 238
  3. The non-functionality requirement for trade dress 239

V. Other Limitations on the Registration and Protection of Marks 241
 A. The Lanham Act and common law 241
 B. Scandalous or immoral marks 241
 C. Matter that may disparage another 241
 D. Matter that may falsely suggest a connection with persons, living or dead, institutions, beliefs, or national symbols 242
 E. Deceptive marks 242
  1. Deceptive vs. "primarily deceptively misdescriptive" marks 242
  2. "Deceptively misdescriptive" marks vs. "geographically deceptively misdescriptive" marks 243
 F. Marks in prior use 243
  1. Concurrent use 244
 G. Additional Lanham Act prohibitions 244

VI. Acquiring Ownership of Marks 244
 A. Use of the mark in trade 244
  1. Token uses are insufficient 245
  2. Approaches to determining when use is sufficient 245
  3. Simultaneous or near-simultaneous use 245
  4. The affixation requirement 246
 B. Marks that are not inherently distinctive 246
 C. Use in interstate commerce 246
  1. Use of a mark abroad 246
 D. Protection of foreign "well-known marks" 247

VII. Federal Registration of Marks 247
 A. Ownership and registration 247
 B. Advantages of registration on the Principal Register 247
 C. Two paths to registration on the Lanham Act Principal Register 248
  1. "Use applications" 248
  2. "Intent-to-use" applications 248

- D. Constructive use 249
- E. The certificate of registration 249
- F. Registration on the Lanham Act Supplemental Register 249
    1. Types of marks registerable on the Supplemental Register 250
    2. Use prior to filing 250
    3. Advantages of registration on the Supplemental Register 250
    4. Later registration on the Principal Register 250

VIII. **Cancellation of Registration** 250
- A. During the first five years of registration 250
- B. After five years of registration 250
    1. Precluded grounds 251

IX. **Geographic Boundaries** 251
- A. Geographic rights at common law 251
    1. Good faith 251
    2. Remote geographical area 251
    3. The zone of natural expansion 252
- B. The Lanham Act 252
    1. Registration removes the good-faith defense 252
    2. Registration on applications filed after November 16, 1989, provides constructive use 253
- C. A likelihood of consumer confusion about the source of goods or services 254
    1. Some movement away from the majority rule 254

X. **Infringement of Marks** 254
- A. The injury to be protected against 254
- B. The infringement determination 255
- C. The "trademark use" requirement 255
    1. Courts' construction of the "trademark use" requirement outside of the Internet context 255
    2. Courts' construction of the "trademark use" requirement in the Internet context 256
- D. The likelihood of confusion requirement 259
    1. No side-by-side comparison 259
    2. Factors to consider in determining a likelihood of confusion 259
    3. The effect of a disclaimer 262
    4. Post-sale confusion 262
    5. Initial interest (pre-sale) confusion 263
- E. Reverse confusion 264
- F. Trademark parodies 264
    1. First Amendment considerations 265
- G. Collateral use of marks 265
    1. Resale of goods lawfully bearing a mark 265
    2. Gray market goods 266
    3. Competitors' use of marks for comparison purposes 267

- H. Trademark counterfeiting 267
- I. Contributory infringement 267
  1. Inducing infringement 267
  2. Knowingly aiding infringement 268
  3. Vicarious liability 268

XI. Trademark Dilution 268
- A. The state dilution cause of action 268
  1. "Blurring" the uniqueness of the plaintiff's famous mark or trade name 268
  2. Tarnishment 269
  3. The fame requirement 270
  4. First Amendment limitations 270
- B. The Lanham Act §43(c) cause of action for dilution 271
  1. Famous marks 271
  2. Dilution by blurring 272
  3. Dilution by tarnishment 272
  4. Exclusions 272
  5. Registration preempts state dilution claims 273
  6. Dilution claims and trade dress 273
  7. Federal dilution claims in the Internet context 274

XII. Defenses to Infringement and Dilution Claims 275
- A. The fair use defense 275
  1. The manner in which the defendant uses the mark 275
  2. Is the defendant using the mark in good faith? 275
  3. Is the defendant's use likely to confuse? 276
- B. Nominative fair use 276
  1. Three factors 276
  2. The Third Circuit's version of nominative fair use 277
  3. Nominative fair use differs from "descriptive" or "classic" fair use 277
- C. Abandonment 277
  1. Acts by the registrant that cause the mark to lose its significance as a mark 278
- D. Challenges to the validity of the mark and to the plaintiff's ownership rights 279
- E. Federal registration incontestability status 279

XIII. Trademark Cybersquatting 279
- A. The Anticybersquatting Consumer Protection Act 279
  1. Factors to consider in determining whether the defendant registered, trafficked in, or used the domain name with a bad-faith intent to profit 280
  2. *In rem* jurisdiction 282
  3. Remedies and limitation of liability 282
- B. Personal names 282
- C. The Uniform Domain Name Dispute Resolution Policy—an administrative alternative 282
  1. Bad faith under the UDRP 283
  2. Remedies under the UDRP 283

XIV. Remedies for Lanham Act Violations 283
A. Injunctions 283
B. Monetary recovery 283
1. Actual damages 284
2. The defendant's profits 284
C. Attorney fees 284
D. Special remedies for use of counterfeit marks 284
1. Definition of "counterfeit" 285
2. Special civil remedies 285
E. Special remedies in anticybersquatting cases 285

XV. International Trademark Treaties 285
A. The Paris Convention 285
1. National treatment 285
2. Registration of marks 285
3. Filing priority 287
4. Criticisms of the Paris Convention 287
B. The Trademark Law Treaty 288
C. The Madrid Protocol 288
1. Eligibility 288
2. The perceived benefits of the Madrid Protocol 288
3. The perceived drawbacks of Madrid Protocol filings 288
D. The Agreement on Trade-Related Aspects of Intellectual Property Rights 288

Quiz yourself on TRADEMARK LAW 289

Exam Tips on TRADEMARK LAW 305

CHAPTER 7
UNFAIR COMPETITION

I. The Nature of the Law of Unfair Competition 309
A. The nature of the law of unfair competition 309
B. The origin of the law of unfair competition 310

II. Passing Off 310
A. The nature of the "passing off" cause of action 310
1. A direct false representation 310
2. An indirect false representation 310
B. Lanham Act §43(a) 311
1. Relationship to the Lanham Act registration provisions 311
2. Construing §43(a) 311
C. Trade names 312
1. Incorporation under a particular trade name 312
2. Special sensitivity to use of personal names 312

D. Use of the passing off claim to fill the gaps left by other intellectual property doctrines 312
   1. Use of Lanham Act §43(a) to vindicate the moral rights interest in attribution 313
   2. The Supreme Court limits the scope of §43(a) 314

III. False Advertising 314
   A. The common-law false advertising cause of action 314
      1. The difficulty of satisfying the ascertainable loss requirement 315
      2. Additional requirements 315
   B. State statutes 315
   C. Lanham Act §43(a) 315
      1. Injury 316
      2. Falsity and materiality 316
      3. Intent 316

IV. Commercial Disparagement 317
   A. The common-law commercial disparagement cause of action 317
      1. False representation 317
      2. Intent 317
      3. The special damages requirement 317
   B. State statutory provisions 317
   C. The Lanham Act §43(a) product disparagement cause of action 318
      1. Differences between §43(a) and the common law 318
      2. "Commercial advertising or promotion" 318
   D. First Amendment considerations in disparagement actions 318
      1. The *Blue Cross* decision 319

V. Misappropriation 320
   A. The nature of the misappropriation cause of action 320
      1. Plaintiff's substantial investment of time, money, skill, or effort to create intangible trade value 320
      2. The defendant has appropriated the trade value 320
      3. The plaintiff is thereby injured 320
   B. Limitations on the misappropriation cause of action 321

VI. International Treaties Regarding Unfair Competition 322
   A. The Paris Convention 322
      1. National treatment 322
      2. Article 10*bis* 322
      3. Protection for trade names 322
   B. The TRIPs Agreement 322

Quiz Yourself on UNFAIR COMPETITION 323

Exam Tips on UNFAIR COMPETITION 326

Chapter 8

THE RIGHT OF PUBLICITY

I. The Nature and Purpose of the Right of Publicity 327
   A. The nature of the publicity cause of action 327
      1. Publicity and privacy 328
      2. Common law vs. statute 328
   B. The purpose of the right of publicity claim 328

II. The Scope of the Right of Publicity 329
   A. Appropriation of the plaintiff's identity for commercial purposes 329
      1. Commercial purposes 329
      2. Ways in which the plaintiff's identity may be appropriated 329
   B. First Amendment concerns 330
      1. The transformative nature of the defendant's use 331
      2. Other approaches to balancing publicity and First Amendment interests in cases involving noncommercial speech 331
   C. Descendability of the right of publicity 332
      1. Common-law solutions 332
      2. State statutes 332
   D. Applicability of the doctrine of first sale 332
   E. Remedies for violation of the right 332
   F. Possibility of preemption 333

Quiz Yourself on THE RIGHT OF PUBLICITY 333

Exam Tips on THE RIGHT OF PUBLICITY 334

Chapter 9

THE RELATIONSHIP BETWEEN FEDERAL AND STATE LAW

I. The Supremacy Clause 335
   A. Federal law prevails over conflicting state law 335
   B. Examination of state causes of action in light of the federal Patent and Copyright Acts 336
      1. The *Sears* and *Compco* cases 336
      2. The *Goldstein* case 336
      3. The *Kewanee* case 337
      4. The *Aronson* case 338
      5. The *Bonito Boats* case 338
      6. Where do we stand now? 339

II. Copyright Act §301 340

 A. Uniform system of copyright 340
  1. Preemption reaches beyond literal "copyright" claims 340
  2. Dual test for preemption 340
 B. Works of authorship 341
  1. Ideas, procedures, processes, etc. as the subject matter of copyright 341
 C. Equivalent rights 342
  1. The "extra elements" test 342
  2. The meaning of "qualitatively different" 342
  3. A review of certain state causes of action 344
 D. Express exceptions to §301 preemption 344
 E. The relationship between §301 and Supremacy Clause preemption 345

Quiz Yourself on THE RELATIONSHIP BETWEEN FEDERAL AND
STATE LAW 345

Exam Tips on THE RELATIONSHIP BETWEEN FEDERAL AND
STATE LAW 347

Essay Exam Questions and Answers 349
 Essay Exam Questions 351
 Sample Essay Exam Answers 361
Table of Cases 383
Table of References to the Copyright Act of 1976 (17 U.S.C. §101 *et seq.*) 387
Table of References to the Lanham Act (15 U.S.C. §1051 *et seq.*) 389
Table of References to the Patent Act (35 U.S.C. §101 *et seq.*) 391
Subject Matter Index 393

Preface

This book was written to assist students who are taking intellectual property survey courses, but you are likely to find it useful for individual courses in patents, copyrights, or trademarks and unfair competition, as well.

The book covers the key substantive points of patent law, copyright law, trademarks and unfair competition, as well as state trade secret, publicity, and undeveloped idea laws. Because survey courses vary greatly in their scope and coverage, you may find that the book covers some issues that your professor did not include in your course. The **Casebook Correlation Chart** makes it easy to identify the sections of this book that correlate to your casebook assignments.

You can use this book in a variety of ways. First, you might read the relevant portion of this book along with your casebook in preparing for class. This book will help you to identify and understand the issues set forth in your assigned cases, and thus get more from the cases and class discussion. Alternatively, you might read the relevant portion of this book after each class, for closure and reinforcement. Note also that the **Quiz Yourself** section at the end of each chapter provides a number of short essay problems that you can use to test your understanding of the subject matter as you go along. Compare your responses to the **Sample Answers** that are provided.

This book also provides a good means of reviewing for your final exam. The book summarizes the black-letter law in outline form, with lots of useful examples. Of course, the very best way to study is to go through the process of making your own outline that incorporates material from this book, as well as material from your class notes. (Professors' examples and the policy considerations that are brought out in class discussion often find their way, directly or indirectly, into exams.) The **Quiz Yourself** questions at the end of each chapter, as well as the longer, multi-issue **Essay Exam Questions** at the end of the book, provide a great opportunity to check your comprehension, while perfecting your exam writing technique. Compare your answers to the **Sample Answers** that are provided. Finally, the night before your exam, you may find it useful to review the **Capsule Summary**, which restates the key rules in each subject area, but leaves out much of the detail.

I should emphasize that this book is not a substitute for reading your casebook, attending class, and taking good notes of class discussions. Class discussions are likely to emphasize and illuminate the policies underlying and driving the substantive rules of law that are summarized in this outline, and bring the rules to life. The case decisions in your casebook provide an important context for the rules, as well as exposure to the essential process of legal reasoning.

Good luck with your intellectual property course! I hope you find this book helpful.

Margreth Barrett
University of California, Hastings College of the Law
January 2008

Casebook Correlation Chart

(**Note:** General sections of the Outline are omitted for this chart. **NC** = not directly covered by this casebook.)

Barrett: Intellectual Property Emanuel Law Outline *(by chapter and section heading)*	Barrett: *Intellectual Property: Cases and Materials* (Third Edition, 2007)	Dreyfuss & Kwall: *Intellectual Property: Cases and Materials on Trademark, Copyright and Patent Law* (Second Edition, 2004)	Goldstein: *Copyright, Patent, Trademark and Related State Doctrines: Cases and Materials on the Law of Intellectual Property* (Revised Fifth Edition, 2004)	Merges, Menell, & Lemley: *Intellectual Property in the New Technological Age* (Revised Fourth Edition, 2007)
CHAPTER 1 INTRODUCTION TO THE STUDY OF INTELLECTUAL PROPERTY				
I. Scope of the Term "Intellectual Property"	2	1	NC	24-30
II. Primary Policy Issues	2-3, 15-20	2-5	14-16	2-6, 10-24
III. Sources of Authority to Regulate Intellectual Property	20	2-5	1-16	28-30
CHAPTER 2 THE LAW OF TRADE SECRETS				
I. The Purpose, Nature, and Source of Trade Secret Law	40-41	882-885	119-130	33-39
II. Status of Ideas or Information as Trade Secret	41-47, 61-67	882-885, 921-922	131-141	39-58, 74-80
III. When Acquisition, Use, or Disclosure of a Trade Secret Constitutes an Actionable Misappropriation	47-51, 80-90	882, 906-924	141-144	62-70
IV. Private Owners' Rights in Trade Secret Information Submitted to Government Agencies	NC	931-933	142-144	38, 61
V. Use and Disclosure by Employees and Former Employees	57-79, 90-102	886-906, 933-935	144-162	80-100
VI. Remedies for Trade Secret Misappropriation	88-89	924-925	142-143	105-115
CHAPTER 3 PATENTS				
I. Utility Patents	104-110, 224-236	564-567	397-403, 476-484	124-125, 144-169, 173-185
II. Statutory Subject Matter of a Utility Patent	110-140	567-582, 589-619	403-415	128-143, 1065-1070
III. The Novelty Standard	149-165	635-665	415-442	185-195, 206-210, 372, 733-734, 1075-1081
IV. The Statutory Bar and Inventor Requirements	165-181, 215-217	714-740	415-442, 485-486	192-212

Barrett: Intellectual Property Emanuel Law Outline *(by chapter and section heading)*	Barrett: *Intellectual Property: Cases and Materials* (Third Edition, 2007)	Dreyfuss & Kwall: *Intellectual Property: Cases and Materials on Trademark, Copyright and Patent Law* (Second Edition, 2004)	Goldstein: *Copyright, Patent, Trademark and Related State Doctrines: Cases and Materials on the Law of Intellectual Property* (Revised Fifth Edition, 2004)	Merges, Menell, & Lemley: *Intellectual Property in the New Technological Age* (Revised Fourth Edition, 2007)
V. The Non-Obviousness Standard	181-205	666-713	442-476	124-125, 212-250, 372-373
VI. The Utility Standard	141-149	620-634	476-484	124, 144-158
VII. The Disclosure Requirement	206-215	566-567	487-492	163-185
VIII. Infringement of Utility Patents	236-315	765-811	550-584	250-348, 359, 1065-1074
IX. Remedies for Patent Infringement	315-334	842-881	533-550	348-370
X. Comparison of Utility Patent and Trade Secret Protection for Inventions	343-344	NC	NC	NC
XI. Design Patents	366-378	618-619	964-977	371-376
XII. Plant Patents	344-360	618	414-415	135, 376-381
XIII. Key International Patent Treaties	20-31, 217-224	582-588	15-16	211, 343-348
CHAPTER 4 **THE LAW OF UNDEVELOPED IDEAS**				
I. The Nature of the Law of Undeveloped Ideas	380-399	927	36-43	882, 891-892, 894-901
II. The Novelty and Concreteness Requirements	391-399	927-928	43-67	882-894
CHAPTER 5 **COPYRIGHT LAW**				
I. The Purpose and Nature of Copyright Law	402-410	212-217	585-586, 618-623	383-390, 399
II. The Subject Matter of Copyright	410-506	223-291, 364-382	604-618, 623-637, 674-766, 770-775, 828-864, 955-962, 999-1002	55, 392-405, 411-446, 482-486, 500-506, 675, 987-1023
III. The Rights Afforded by Copyright Law	506-508	292-295	674-695	446, 474-475, 519-522
IV. The "Copyrighted Work"	508-527	359-364, 402-410	612-618, 637-665, 764-768	474-500
V. The Exclusive Right to Reproduce the Work	528-539	248-255, 488-489	635-636, 674-675	475-482, 488-489, 1024-1034
VI. The Exclusive Right to Prepare Derivative Works	539-552	345-350	675-676, 679-684	500-514, 1034-1038
VII. The Exclusive Right to Distribute to the Public	552-568	473-483	676, 685-692	389, 510-514
VIII. The Exclusive Right of Public Performance	568-577	483-484, 488-489	676-678, 692-695	389, 514-518
IX. The Exclusive Right to Display the Copyrighted Work Publicly	577-583	484-485	676-678, 693	514-518
X. Moral Rights	583-595	294, 345-350	795-816	519-522
XI. Direct and Indirect Copyright Infringement	506-595, 595-617	359-410	767-795	536-538, 569-580
XII. Fair Use and Other Defenses to Infringement	618-642	411-491	702-733	522-569

CASEBOOK CORRELATION CHART

Barrett: Intellectual Property Emanuel Law Outline *(by chapter and section heading)*	Barrett: *Intellectual Property: Cases and Materials* (Third Edition, 2007)	Dreyfuss & Kwall: *Intellectual Property: Cases and Materials on Trademark, Copyright and Patent Law* (Second Edition, 2004)	Goldstein: *Copyright, Patent, Trademark and Related State Doctrines: Cases and Materials on the Law of Intellectual Property* (Revised Fifth Edition, 2004)	Merges, Menell, & Lemley: *Intellectual Property in the New Technological Age* (Revised Fourth Edition, 2007)
XIII. Anticircumvention and Digital Rights Management Provisions	614-616, 642-658	412-413, 478-483, 488-489	749-750	580-615
XIV. Ownership of Copyright	659-676	304-345	637-774	446-465
XV. Notice of Copyright	676-684	215-216	586-597	405-408, 410-411
XVI. Deposit and Registration	684-686	214-215	597-604	409-410
XVII. The Duration of Copyright Protection	687-700	212-214, 297-304	1-12, 656-673	408, 465-469, 568
XVIII. Renewals of Pre-1976 Act Federal Copyrights	687-689, 700-702	325-333, 354-355	671-673	471-474
XIX. Termination of Transfers of Copyright	703-705	352-354	673-674	470-474
XX. Remedies for Infringement	678, 685-686, 706-717	492-522	754-767	625-632
XXI. International Copyright Treaties	20-33, 406-408, 590-591, 676-679, 682-686, 688	217-222, 294-295	15-16, 813	616-624
CHAPTER 6 **TRADEMARK LAW**				
I. The Nature of Trademark Law	720-725	6-10	220-222	633-640
II. Types of Marks	726-730	59-68	267-281	640-50
III. Distinctiveness	750-800	25-59	240-267	650-676, 704
IV. The Content of Marks	730-748, 790-800, 809-829	25-68	281-294	642-650, 674-676, 798-808
V. Other Limitations on the Registration and Protection of Marks	800-809	74-81	250-267, 376-387	664-676, 686-687
VI. Acquiring Ownership of Marks	829-844	11-16	222-240, 299-310	676-695, 686-687
VII. Federal Registration of Marks	844-852	69	222-240, 299-300	695-708
VIII. Cancellation of Registration	848, 883-884	15-16	NC	707-708
IX. Geographic Boundaries	854-870	10, 77-79	299-310	686-688, 813-819
X. Infringement of Marks	885-970, 1020-1031, 1031-1039	82-100	355-375	715-786, 835-837
XI. Trademark Dilution	976-1005, 1020-1031	101-108	310-322	737-755, 770
XII. Defenses to Infringement and Dilution Claims	870-885, 970-976, 1020-1031	114-120, 139-177	322-334	787-833
XIII. Trademark Cybersquatting	1005-1020, 1030	131-134	334-337	759-777
XIV. Remedies for Lanham Act Violations	761-762, 788-789, 898-899, 909-910, 994-995, 1005-1006, 1011, 1039-1045	178-211	337-355	838-851
XV. International Trademark Treaties	849-854	16-24	15-16	833-838
CHAPTER 7 **UNFAIR COMPETITION**				
I. The Nature of the Law of Unfair Competition	720-725, 1046-1049	9	68-69	NC
II. Passing Off	749-750, 1031-1039, 1046-1048	9, 84, 342, 523	69-76	521-522, 650, 674-676

Barrett: Intellectual Property Emanuel Law Outline *(by chapter and section heading)*	Barrett: *Intellectual Property: Cases and Materials* (Third Edition, 2007)	Dreyfuss & Kwall: *Intellectual Property: Cases and Materials on Trademark, Copyright and Patent Law* (Second Edition, 2004)	Goldstein: *Copyright, Patent, Trademark and Related State Doctrines: Cases and Materials on the Law of Intellectual Property* (Revised Fifth Edition, 2004)	Merges, Menell, & Lemley: *Intellectual Property in the New Technological Age* (Revised Fourth Edition, 2007)
III. False Advertising	1049-1063	NC	74-76	778-787
IV. Commercial Disparagement	1064-1081	NC	74-76	NC
V. Misappropriation	1081-1097	523-537, 554-556	92-101	854-866, 882-901
VI. International Treaties Regarding Unfair Competition	1048-1049	16-24	15-16	344, 620
CHAPTER 8 **THE RIGHT OF PUBLICITY**				
I. The Nature and Purpose of the Right of Publicity	1098-1111	523-526	196-197	901-904
II. The Scope of the Right of Publicity	1111-1133	527-563	178-201	904-933
CHAPTER 9 **THE RELATIONSHIP BETWEEN FEDERAL AND STATE LAW**				
I. The Supremacy Clause	1136-1170	523-527, 914-921, 929-932	1, 12-14, 61-67, 107-118, 162-177, 1022-1031	947-957, 968-969
II. Copyright Act §301	1176-1186	523-563	816-825	957-967

Capsule Summary

This Capsule Summary is intended for review after studying the main outline. Reading it is not a substitute for mastering the material in the main outline. Numbers in brackets refer to the pages in the main outline where the topic is discussed.

Chapter 1
INTRODUCTION TO THE STUDY OF INTELLECTUAL PROPERTY

I. GENERALLY

A. Policy considerations: Intellectual property law seeks to benefit the general public by providing a rich, diverse, efficient, and competitive marketplace. Most intellectual property doctrines are crafted to balance two potentially conflicting goals: (1) to provide an incentive to create by giving creators property rights in the products of their creativity, and (2) to provide the greatest possible competitor and public access to products of creativity in order to promote a competitive marketplace. Therefore the property rights provided under these doctrines are carefully limited. In the case of trademark and related unfair competition doctrines, the law provides businesses limited property rights in their indications of origin and/or business good will not as an incentive to create, but in order to promote marketplace competition and efficiency, and to protect consumers from deception. [2-3]

B. Jurisdiction: Article 1, Section 8, Clause 8 of the U.S. Constitution authorizes Congress to enact patent and copyright laws. The Commerce Clause (Article 1, Section 8, Clause 3) is the basis for Congress's regulation of trademarks and unfair competition. The states retain concurrent jurisdiction to regulate intellectual property under the Tenth Amendment to the Constitution. [3]

Chapter 2
THE LAW OF TRADE SECRETS

I. STATUS OF IDEAS OR INFORMATION AS TRADE SECRET

A. General definition: A trade secret is information that (1) derives actual or potential economic value from the fact that it is not known or readily ascertainable by others, and (2) is subject to reasonable efforts to maintain its secrecy. The Restatement of Torts definition limits trade secret status to information or ideas used continuously in the plaintiff's business. However, the Uniform Trade Secrets Act has dropped this requirement. [7-8]

B. Factors considered in determining trade secret status: In determining whether information constitutes a trade secret, courts will consider: (1) how widely the information is known outside the claimant's business; (2) who within the claimant's company knows the information; (3) whether the claimant has taken reasonable measures to ensure that the information remains secret; (4) how difficult it would be for others properly to acquire or duplicate the information; (5) whether the information gives the claimant a commercial, competitive advantage over others who do not know it; and (6) how much effort or money the claimant expended in developing or acquiring the information. [7-8]

II. WHEN ACQUISITION, USE, OR DISCLOSURE OF A TRADE SECRET CONSTITUTES AN ACTIONABLE MISAPPROPRIATION

A. Disclosure or use of a trade secret in breach of confidence: If the defendant's unauthorized disclosure or use of a trade secret was in breach of a duty of confidence, then it is actionable. A duty of confidentiality, which requires the defendant to refrain from disclosing or using the claimant's trade secret without permission, arises when the parties are in a special relationship, such as the agent-principal relationship, a partnership relationship, or a fiduciary relationship such as lawyer-client or doctor-patient. The parties may also create a duty of confidentiality by express or implied contractual agreement that the recipient will not disclose or use the secret without permission. An implied agreement to this effect may be found if the recipient has notice that the trade secret owner is about to disclose the secret to her in confidence and agrees to hear it. [8-9]

B. Disclosure or use of a trade secret learned from a third party with notice: If A reveals a trade secret to B under circumstances that impose a duty of confidentiality on B, and B breaches the confidence by revealing the secret to C, C will have a duty not to use or disclose the secret (and will be liable if he does so) if he has notice that the information is a trade secret that is being revealed to him in breach of B's duty. C will be deemed to have notice of this if a reasonable person under similar circumstances would know it or if the reasonable person would be led to make further inquiry and a reasonable inquiry would reveal it. [*Note:* This reasonable person standard is applied in many other situations, *infra.*] [10]

C. Disclosure or use of a trade secret learned by mistake: If A reveals his trade secret to B by accident or mistake and B has notice that the information is a trade secret and is being revealed by mistake, then B has a duty of confidence to refrain from using or disclosing the trade secret without permission, and will be liable if he does so. The same reasonable person standard governs the issue of notice as in section B, *supra*. [10]

D. Continued disclosure or use of a trade secret after receipt of notice: If C learns A's trade secret from a third person who was breaching his duty, or if C learns the trade secret by mistake, but at the time C has no notice of the secrecy or breach, or of the mistake, then C will not be liable for subsequent disclosure or use of the trade secret. The Restatement of Torts provides that if C later receives such notice, she must stop all further disclosure or use at that time unless she can demonstrate either: (1) that she paid value for the secret in good faith; or (2) that she otherwise has so changed her position in reliance on the secret that to require her to refrain from further disclosure or use would be inequitable. The Uniform Trade Secrets Act differs somewhat from the Restatement provisions in the case of trade secrets learned through breach of confidence, providing that good-faith users who have materially changed their position or paid value will not enjoy absolute immunity for use or disclosure after notice, but courts may permit their continued use upon payment of a reasonable royalty for the use. [10-11]

E. **Disclosure or use of a trade secret acquired through improper means:** B will be liable for acquisition, disclosure or use of A's trade secret if she acquired A's trade secret through "improper means." "Improper means" includes illegal conduct and conduct that is below generally accepted standards of commercial morality. [11-12]

F. **Acquisition, disclosure, or use of a trade secret with notice that the provider acquired it through improper means:** Acquisition of a trade secret through improper means is itself an actionable misappropriation under the Uniform Trade Secrets Act if the acquirer has reason to know that the means are improper. Moreover, if X acquires Y's trade secret through improper means and gives it to Z, Z will be liable for subsequent disclosure or use if he has notice that it is a trade secret and has been obtained through improper means. The reasonable person standard applies to determine when the defendant will be deemed to have notice. [11-12]

G. **The effect of the defendant's modification of the plaintiff's trade secret:** The fact that the defendant modified or improved the plaintiff's trade secret before using or disclosing it will not relieve the defendant from liability as long as the plaintiff can demonstrate that the information the defendant used or disclosed was "substantially derived" from the plaintiff's trade secret. [13]

III. PRIVATE OWNERS' RIGHTS IN TRADE SECRET INFORMATION SUBMITTED TO GOVERNMENT AGENCIES

A. **Government agency disclosure of trade secrets and the takings clause:** Many different statutes on the state and federal level require government agencies to publicly disclose trade secret information submitted to them by private parties. Such a disclosure will only be deemed an unconstitutional "taking" if, at the time the private party submitted the trade secret, he had a reasonable, investment-backed expectation of confidentiality. He is unlikely to be deemed to have had such an expectation unless, at the time he submitted the trade secret to the agency, there was a statute expressly prohibiting the agency from disclosing the trade secret. [13-14]

IV. USE AND DISCLOSURE BY EMPLOYEES AND FORMER EMPLOYEES

A. **In the absence of an express agreement:** An employee owes a duty of confidentiality to his employer, which prohibits him from using or disclosing trade secrets that the employer discloses to him within the scope of his employment. Moreover, if the employee was especially hired to create information of the type involved for the employer, and the employer has placed time and resources at the employee's disposal for that purpose, then an implied agreement will be found between the parties that any resulting trade secrets developed by the employee will belong to the employer. The employee will have a duty not to disclose or use them without the employer's permission. [14-15]

1. **When the trade secret belongs to the employee:** If the employee was not hired to create information of the type involved, but nonetheless creates a trade secret during the course of employment, the trade secret will be deemed to belong to the employee, and the employee will be entitled to use or disclose it as he will. However, if the employee used the employer's work time, facilities, or supplies to develop the trade secret, then the employer will have a "shop right" in it—a nonexclusive license to use the employee's trade secret. [15]

B. **In the case of an express agreement:** An employer and employee may expressly agree that the employee will not disclose the employer's trade secrets and/or that the employee will assign all his inventions in advance to the employer. In addition, an employer may require the employee to sign a covenant not to compete with the employer for a specified time in a specified geographical area after leaving the employer. However, courts are less likely to enforce agreements not to compete because they are against public policy. Generally, courts will only enforce such covenants if the employer demonstrates that the employee has the employer's trade secrets or other confidential proprietary information. Even then, courts will hesitate to enforce the agreement unless: (1) it is reasonably necessary in order to protect the employer; (2) the agreement is reasonable as to the time and geographical area in which the employee is restricted from competing; (3) the restrictions are not harmful to the general public; and (4) the restrictions are not unreasonably burdensome to the employee. [15-17]

C. **The doctrine of inevitable disclosure:** Under the doctrine of inevitable disclosure, which has been adopted in some jurisdictions, the court will enjoin a plaintiff's former employee (at least temporarily) from taking a new position if: (1) the former employee knows the plaintiff's trade secrets; (2) the former employee's new job duties are similar or related to those of his former position, and it would be difficult for him not to rely on or use the plaintiff's trade secrets in the new position; and (3) there is evidence that the former employee or his new employer cannot be relied on to avoid using the trade secrets. [17]

V. REMEDIES FOR TRADE SECRET MISAPPROPRIATION

A. **Injunctions:** A defendant may be enjoined from using or disclosing the plaintiff's trade secret. Jurisdictions differ regarding the appropriate length of such injunctions. Most limit the length of the injunction to the duration of the secrecy. [17-18]

B. **Damages:** Damages may be measured by: (1) the profits the plaintiff lost as a result of the defendant's misappropriation; (2) a reasonable royalty for the defendant's use of the trade secret; or (3) the amount of the profits the defendant made as a result of the misappropriation. [18]

C. **Criminal prosecution:** Many states have made theft of trade secrets a criminal offense. The Economic Espionage Act of 1996 makes it a federal crime in many situations. [18]

CHAPTER 3

PATENTS

I. UTILITY PATENTS

A. **The nature and term of a utility patent:** A utility patent gives its owner exclusive rights in an invention for a limited term. For many years the term lasted 17 years from the date the patent was issued. However, for patents issued on applications filed after June 8, 1995, the term begins on the date the patent issues and lasts for 20 years from the date the application for patent was filed. [29]

B. **Limitations on patents:** Patents are only available for those inventions that are non-obvious, novel and useful, and are fully disclosed. If the Patent and Trademark Office (P.T.O.) grants a patent, this creates a legal presumption that the invention meets these criteria. However, a patent may be challenged in court, either through a declaratory judgment action or through an invalidity defense in an infringement suit. All appeals in patent cases go to the Court of Appeals for the Federal Circuit. Reissue and reexamination procedures provide means to obtain P.T.O. review of issued patents. [29-32]

II. STATUTORY SUBJECT MATTER OF A UTILITY PATENT

Patent Act §101 authorizes utility patents for "any new and useful process, machine, manufacture, or composition of matter, or any new and useful improvement thereof." A newly discovered use for a known process, machine, manufacture, or composition of matter may qualify as a patentable process. [32-33]

A. Naturally occurring vs. man-made things: Patents may only be granted for "man-made" things, not for naturally occurring things. However, patents are not restricted to inanimate matter—a patent may be granted for living matter that has been altered by the applicant to have characteristics it would not have had naturally. [33]

B. Laws of nature and abstract ideas: The Supreme Court has held that laws of nature and abstract ideas may not in themselves be the subject of a patent. Because of this rule, the Court reasoned, computer programs, which are comprised of mathematical algorithms, are not patentable by themselves. However, a process or apparatus that incorporates a computer program as one step or element may be patentable. In recent case decisions, the Court of Appeals for the Federal Circuit has held that claimed inventions that incorporate mathematical algorithms—both machines and processes—constitute patentable subject matter as long as the claimed mathematical algorithm is applied to produce a useful, concrete, tangible result and doesn't preempt other uses of the mathematical principle. [33-35]

C. Business methods: Recent case law has established that business methods are patentable subject matter. It is not necessary that the claims associate the method with technology or technological elements, like computer hardware. Patentability is not restricted to the "technological arts." [35]

D. Medical procedures: Medical procedures are patentable, but infringement remedies against medical practitioners and related health care entities are limited in some cases. [35]

III. THE NOVELTY STANDARD

The novelty standard generally ensures that the first person to make an invention (rather than a subsequent inventor) gets the patent. The novelty provisions are set forth in §§102(a), (e), and (g) of the Patent Act. [36]

A. Subsection 102(a): Subsection 102(a) says that a patent must be denied if: (1) the applicant's invention was known by others in the United States before the applicant for patent invented; (2) the applicant's invention was used by others in the United States before the applicant invented; (3) the applicant's invention was described in a printed publication in the United States or a foreign country before the applicant invented; or (4) the applicant's invention was patented in the United States or a foreign country before the applicant invented. The focus is on the actions of persons other than the inventor/applicant, prior to the date the inventor/applicant made the invention. [36-37]

1. **When an invention is "known by others":** To have been "known by others" in the United States prior to the applicant's invention date, the invention must have been: (1) "reduced to practice," actually or constructively, or otherwise described in a writing sufficiently to enable a person with ordinary skill in the relevant art to make it without undue experimentation; and (2) accessible to the public. [36-37]

2. **When an invention will be deemed "used by others":** To be "used by others" in the United States prior to the applicant's invention date, the invention must have been: (1) reduced to actual practice; and (2) used in the manner for which it was intended by its inventor. Also, (3) its use must have been accessible to the public. [37]

3. **When an invention will be deemed described in a printed publication:** To find a "printed publication" that anticipates an applicant's invention, several considerations are relevant. First, the publication must have been "printed." This requirement will generally be satisfied if it was reduced to a discernible, tangible, permanent form. Second, there must have been a "publication." A publication generally will be found if an interested American, exercising reasonable diligence, could obtain the information. Third, the alleged printed publication must have set forth sufficient information about the invention to enable a person with ordinary skill in the art to make it without further experimentation. The Federal Circuit has held that when printed matter is not distributed or indexed, several factors should be considered in determining whether it was sufficiently accessible to the public to constitute a "printed publication": (1) the length of time the matter was displayed or exhibited; (2) the expertise of the targeted audience; (3) the existence of reasonable expectations that the displayed material would not be copied; and (4) the simplicity or ease with which the displayed material could have been copied. [37-38]

4. **When an invention will be deemed patented:** In order for an invention to be anticipated by a prior patent under §102(a), it must appear that: (1) the applicant's invention was the actual subject of the patent monopoly; (2) the patent effectively granted rights in the invention before the §102(a) applicant invented; and (3) the patent disclosure was available to the public before the §102(a) applicant's invention date. [38-39]

B. **Subsection 102(e):** Subsection 102(e) denies a patent to an applicant if: (1) before she invented, the same invention was described in an application for patent that was pending in the P.T.O.; and (2) the pending application was ultimately published or granted. [39]

C. **Subsection 102(g):** Subsection 102(g) prohibits B from obtaining a patent if A made the same invention in the United States before B did, and A did not abandon, suppress, or conceal the invention prior to B's invention date. [40]

1. **Identifying the first to invent:** Invention entails (1) an inventive concept, and (2) reduction of the inventive concept to actual or constructive practice. It is presumed that the first person to reduce the concept to practice is the first to invent, but this presumption can be rebutted. If the second person to reduce to practice can demonstrate that she was the first to conceive of the invention and was diligent in reducing the concept to practice from a time prior to the other's conception date, she will be found to be the first inventor. [40]

2. **Abandonment, suppression, and concealment:** A (the first inventor) will not be deemed to have abandoned, suppressed, or concealed the invention as long as she was engaged in reasonable efforts to bring the benefit of the invention to the public. It is not necessary for A to file for a patent. She may bring the benefit of the invention to the public by introducing it to the market or by writing about it. If A did abandon, suppress, or conceal her invention, but resumed

activity with regard to it before B invented, A can rely on her date of resumption as her date of invention, and still prevent B from obtaining a patent. [40-42]

3. **Earlier invention abroad:** Section 102(g) also prohibits a patent for B if A's invention was made before B's in a foreign country and was not abandoned, suppressed, or concealed—if A establishes the earlier foreign invention date in a patent interference proceeding consistent with Patent Act §104. [42]

IV. THE STATUTORY BAR AND INVENTOR REQUIREMENTS

The statutory bars ensure that inventors apply for a patent in a timely fashion. The statutory bar provisions are set forth in Patent Act §§102(b), (c), and (d). The inventor requirement is set forth in §102(f). [42]

A. Subsection 102(b): Subsection 102(b) provides that a patent must be denied if, more than one year before the application was filed: (1) the invention was in public use in the United States; (2) the invention was on sale in the United States; (3) the invention was described in a printed publication anywhere in the world; or (4) the invention was patented anywhere in the world. Thus, the focus in this section is on the actions both of the inventor/applicant and others more than one year before the application was filed. Subsection (b) may be viewed as a form of statute of limitations that requires an inventor to apply for a patent with a year after the invention enters the public domain in one of the 4 listed ways. The meanings of "printed publication" and "patented" in this context are similar to the meanings in subsection 102(a). [42-43]

1. **When an invention will be deemed "in public use":** A "public use" in the United States will be found when a person other than the inventor/applicant uses the completed, operable invention in the way the invention was intended to be used, and is under no restriction or obligation to keep the invention secret. [43]

   a. **Experimental use:** A public use that is primarily experimental will not trigger the subsection 102(b) the statute of limitations. However, the primary purpose of the use must be experimental—to test the invention from a technological standpoint—not commercial exploitation or development of a market. It is important that the inventor control the use, test aspects of the inventions that are covered in the patent claims, and systematically collect test results. Courts may also inquire whether it was necessary to test the invention publicly and whether the inventor imposed confidentiality requirements. [43-44]

   b. **Indirect public use:** If an invention is put to a commercial use that does not reveal it directly to the public (e.g., the invention is used to produce products sold to the public, but the products do not reveal the invention), courts will nonetheless find a public use that starts the one-year statute running, as long as it is the applicant who is making this use. [44]

2. **When an invention will be deemed "on sale":** An invention will be deemed "on sale" in the United States if it is offered for sale, regardless of whether it is in fact sold or delivered. While the invention need not be "reduced to actual practice" in order to be found "on sale," the Supreme Court has held that it must be the subject of a commercial offer to sell, and at the time of the offer, it must be "ready for patenting." The Court specified that the invention may be "ready for patenting" if it has been reduced to actual practice or if the inventor has prepared drawings or other descriptions of the invention that are sufficiently specific to enable a person skilled in the art to make or practice the invention. A commercial offer to sell for this purpose

is an offer that satisfies the formal standards for an offer under the Uniform Commercial Code. [45]

   a. **Experimental sale:** A sale that is primarily for experimental purposes will not trigger the §102(b) statute of limitations. However, for a sale to be "experimental" for this purpose, the inventor must tell the purchaser that the sale is for purposes of experimentation, and maintain control over the purchaser's use. [45]

B. **Subsection 102(c):** Subsection 102(c) prohibits a patent if the applicant abandoned his invention. However, the focus is on whether he abandoned his right to a patent, rather than his invention. Abandonment of the right to a patent may be express or implied through conduct that indicates an intent to forego a patent. In some cases, refraining from applying for a patent for a long period of time may be sufficient evidence of an intent to abandon a patent. [46]

C. **Subsection 102(d):** Subsection 102(d) prohibits a patent if: (1) the applicant filed a patent application in a foreign country more than 12 months before he filed his U.S. application; and (2) the foreign patent was granted before the U.S. filing date. [46]

D. **Subsection 102(f):** Subsection 102(f) requires that the applicant for patent be the inventor—the person who conceived of the specific invention claimed (as opposed, for example, to that person's employer, who may have directed him to conceive of the invention). If more than one person makes a mental contribution to the final invention concept, then each is a joint inventor. [46-47]

V. THE NON-OBVIOUSNESS STANDARD

Patent Act §103 provides that an invention is not patentable if, at the time it was made, it would have been obvious to a person having ordinary skill in the pertinent art. To make this determination, a court must ascertain: (1) the scope and content of the prior art; (2) the differences between the pertinent prior art and the invention; and (3) the ordinary level of skill in the pertinent art. [47]

A. **The prior art:** The person with ordinary skill in the art, from whose perspective the obviousness determination is made, is presumed to have knowledge of all the relevant prior art existing when the invention was made. Prior art must satisfy the requirements of Patent Act §§102(a), (e), (f), or (g). Prior art is "pertinent" if it is in the same field of endeavor as the invention, regardless of the problem to be solved, or if it is reasonably related to the particular problem with which the inventor was concerned. While novelty, under §102, can only be defeated by a single prior reference that includes all the elements of the invention in the same arrangement, obviousness can be demonstrated by combining two or more prior art references. [47-48]

B. **Secondary considerations:** In determining obviousness, a court may also consider objective factors, including: (1) the commercial success of the invention; (2) the length of time that the need for the invention had been felt before the invention was made; (3) the level of acquiescence of others to the patent; (4) movement of persons skilled in the art in a different direction from that taken by the inventor; (5) the existence of skepticism on the part of experts regarding the approach taken by the inventor; and (6) the fact that the defendant copied the invention, rather than existing alternatives. These factors may provide circumstantial evidence of obviousness. However, a nexus must be demonstrated between the objective factor and the issue of obviousness. [48-49]

C. **Combination patents:** A "combination patent" is a patent for an invention that combines old, known elements in a new way. In such cases, it is the combination that is the invention. In determining the obviousness of such inventions it may be relevant to ask whether there is something in the pertinent prior art to suggest the desirability, and thus the obviousness, of making the combination. However, it is not necessary to show precise or explicit prior art teachings that are directed to the specific subject matter of the claims. Courts should adopt an "expansive and flexible" approach to determining obviousness and recognize that market demand, as well as scientific literature, may lead an inventor to try a new combination. The Supreme Court has provided several principles as guidance:

- When a patent "simply arranges old elements with each performing the same function it had been known to perform and yields no more than one would expect, the combination is obvious.

- If a technique has been used to improve one device, and a person of ordinary skill in the art would recognize that it would improve similar devices in the same way, using the technique is obvious unless its actual application is beyond his or her skill.

- When a work is available in one field of endeavor, design incentives and other market forces can prompt variations of it, either in the same field or a different one. If a person of ordinary skill can implement a predictable variation, it is likely to be obvious.

- When there is a design need or market pressure to solve a problem and there are a finite number of identified, predictable solutions, a person of ordinary skill has good reason to pursue the known options within his or her technical grasp. If this leads to the anticipated success, it is likely to be obvious. (In such case, a combination that was "obvious to try" will be deemed obvious).

- When prior art teaches away from combining certain known elements, discovery of a successful means of combining them is more likely to be non-obvious. [49-50]

D. **Section 103(c): Secret prior art in collaborative situations:** Section 103(c) limits the use of "secret prior art" under §102(e)(f)and (g) to evaluate obviousness if that prior art was developed by a person in a collaborative relationship with the applicant. Such a relationship will be deemed to exist if the applicant's invention and the secret prior art were owned by the same person, subject to an obligation to assign to the same person, or generated pursuant to a written joint research agreement between two or more separate research entities. [51]

E. **Biotechnological process patents:** Patent Act §103(b) provides that a claim for a biotechnological process will not have to undergo a separate review of non-obviousness if the process uses or produces a composition of matter that is itself patentable. If the applicant meets the specified qualifications, he can elect to have the biotechnological process deemed non-obvious on the ground that the composition of matter that it uses or produces is non-obvious. If a process claim is granted under this provision, it will cease to enjoy a presumption of non-obviousness that normally accompanies claims granted by the P.T.O. if the claim to the composition of matter to which the process claim is linked is held invalid. [51]

F. **Obviousness as a trigger of the subsection 102(b) one-year period:** The §102(b) one-year statute of limitations will begin to run once information enters the public domain that, while not anticipating the invention, renders it obvious. It is not necessary that the information be found all in one place. It is sufficient that the new information, when combined with other, already existing, information and/or ordinary skill in the art, renders the invention obvious. [51]

VI. THE UTILITY, or "USEFULNESS" STANDARD

An invention will be "useful" (or "have utility") if there is a current, significant, beneficial use for the invention or, in the case of a process, the product of the process. An invention may be denied a patent for lack of usefulness if it fails to operate as claimed in the application. The Court of Appeals for the Federal Circuit has applied the utility standard liberally in the case of pharmaceutical patents. [52]

VII. THE DISCLOSURE REQUIREMENT

Patent Act §112 requires the patentee to fully disclose his invention as the price of obtaining a patent. The disclosure requirement consists of four parts. First, the applicant must include one or more claims that clearly and distinctly describe the invention. (This is called the "claiming" requirement—the claims are the official definition of the invention and establish the scope of the patent monopoly.) Second, the applicant must describe how to make and use the invention with sufficient clarity and detail to enable a person with ordinary skill in the relevant art to make and use it without undue experimentation. (This is called the "enablement" requirement.) Third, the applicant must set forth the best mode that he contemplates for carrying out his invention as of the application filing date. (This is known as the "best mode" requirement.) Finally, the applicant must demonstrate that he had possession of the invention, as ultimately claimed, at the time he filed his application. (This is called the "written description" requirement.") The enabling, best mode, and written descriptions take place in the patent specification. [52-53]

VIII. INFRINGEMENT OF UTILITY PATENTS

A. **Suits to enforce patents:** Suits to enforce a patent or to challenge its validity may be brought in any U.S. district court where venue is proper. Appeals from the district courts must be brought to the U.S. Court of Appeals for the Federal Circuit. From there, review may be sought in the U.S. Supreme Court. Claims that infringing goods are being imported into the United States may be taken to the International Trade Commission (I.T.C.). Appeals from the I.T.C. are also taken to the Federal Circuit, and then to the Supreme Court. [54]

1. **Infringement:** Persons may be liable: (1) for directly infringing a patent; (2) for inducing another to infringe a patent; (3) for contributory infringement; (4) for importing, selling, offering to sell, or using a product made through a process protected by a U.S. process patent; or (5) for manufacturing or selling certain components of a patented invention to be assembled abroad. [54]

2. **Claim interpretation and literal infringement:** To determine whether a defendant's product or process infringes the plaintiff's patent, one must look to the patent claims, which describe the scope of the invention. The meaning and scope of the claims is an issue of law, to be decided by the court. (To interpret claims, courts may look at definitions and drawings provided by the applicant in the specification, or to the written prosecution history. Such "intrinsic evidence" is favored over "extrinsic evidence," such as dictionaries, treatises, expert witnesses or technical journals.) If the defendant's product or process literally falls within the description in a patent

claim, containing all the elements set forth in the claim, it literally infringes the patent. However, if the defendant has made a change, so that his product or process does not literally fall within the wording of any claim, he may still be liable for direct infringement under the doctrine of equivalents. [54-55]

3. **The doctrine of equivalents:** The doctrine of equivalents prevents a defendant from avoiding liability through insubstantial changes that take his device or process outside the literal language of the patent claims. In order to find infringement in these cases, it must be determined that the defendant's device or process contains an element that corresponds (is either identical or equivalent) to each element described in the patent claim. Equivalency is an objective determination made on an element-by-element basis from the perspective of a person with ordinary skill in the art as of the time of the infringement. The inquiry may be framed as (1) whether the defendant's differing element performs substantially the same function in substantially the same way to obtain the same result as the claimed element, or (2) whether the difference between the defendant's element and the claimed elements is "insubstantial." Important considerations in making this evaluation include: (1) whether persons reasonably skilled in the art would have known that the differing elements were interchangeable at the time of the infringement; (2) whether finding the defendant's invention equivalent, and thus infringing, would give the patentee rights that she would not have been able to obtain initially, in the P.T.O., through broader claim language; and (3) how great a departure the patentee's invention is from the prior art. [55-56]

4. **The doctrine of prosecution history estoppel:** The doctrine of prosecution history estoppel (or file wrapper estoppel) requires that the scope of the patent claims be interpreted in light of what happened in the application process in the P.T.O. If the applicant took a position with regard to the scope of coverage of the claims, he will not be permitted in a later infringement action to take an inconsistent position. (For example, he may not use the doctrine of equivalents to bring an element relinquished in the course of prosecution back within the scope of the patent's protection.) The Supreme Court has held that any narrowing amendment that the applicant made to satisfy any statutory requirement of the Patent Act will give rise to prosecution history estoppel. When the purpose of the amendment is not clear, it will be presumed to have been made to satisfy a statutory requirement unless the applicant can bear the burden of proving otherwise. [56-57]

   a. **The extent of the estoppel:** The Supreme Court has held that when narrowing claim amendments are made in order to satisfy the statutory requirements for patentability, it will be presumed that all equivalence arguments are barred as to the narrowed claim element. However, the patentee may rebut that presumption by showing that: (1) the equivalent at issue was unforeseeable at the time the narrowing amendment was made; (2) the rationale underlying the amendment bears no more than a tangential relation to the equivalent in question; or (3) there is some other reason suggesting that the patentee could not reasonably be expected to have described the insubstantial substitute in question in the amended claim language. The ultimate question is whether, at the time of the amendment, one skilled in the art could reasonably be expected to have drafted a claim that would have literally encompassed the alleged equivalent. If so, then the equivalent will be barred. [57-58]

   b. **An additional ground for limiting the doctrine of equivalents:** The Court of Appeals for the Federal Circuit has held that when a patent applicant discloses subject matter in his specification, but does not include it in the claims, he dedicates it to the public, and may not rely on the doctrine of equivalents to hold a defendant liable for incorporating that subject matter in the place of claimed elements. [58]

B. Direct infringement: Under Patent Act §102(a), as amended in 1996, a person who makes, uses, sells, offers to sell, or imports the patented invention in the United States during the patent term without the patentee's authorization will be liable for direct infringement. [58]

  1. "Making" the patented invention in the case of combination patents: While there is no official category of patents known as "combination patents," the Supreme Court has explained that a combination patent is a patent for an invention whose individual components are already known but are combined in a novel, non-obvious fashion. In such cases it is the combination (as opposed to the individual elements) that is the subject of the patent protection. Supreme Court precedent provides that in order to demonstrate an infringing "making" of the patented invention in such cases, the patentee must prove that the defendant made an operable assembly of all the claimed components. However, the U.S. Court of Appeals for the Federal Circuit has found a "making" in a case in which the defendant: (1) entered into a contract to sell the patented invention; (2) manufactured all the components; (3) subassembled the components; (4) tested the operation of the various parts in subassembled form; and (5) delivered the subassembled components to its customer in the United States during the patent term. [58-59]

  2. Repair vs. reconstruction as a "making": In the case of a combination patent, since there are no monopoly rights in the individual components, mere replacement of individual components—even key components—is permissible repair, and does not constitute "making." Only reconstruction constitutes an impermissible "making" of the patented invention. Reconstruction generally occurs when the entire machine is spent and the owner thus essentially makes a whole new combination. The Court of Appeals for the Federal Circuit has provided four factors to consider in deciding whether a defendant's activities constitute permissible repair or infringing reconstruction: (1) the nature of the defendant's actions (whether complex or simple); (2) the nature of the patented device and its design (are the replaced parts expected to have a shorter useful life than the whole?); (3) whether a market has developed to manufacture or service the part at issue; and (4) objective evidence of the patentee's intent. [59-60]

  3. Selling the patented invention: The Supreme Court has specified that for purposes of subsection 271(a) infringement liability, a patented invention cannot be "sold" until it is "made." Moreover, under the doctrine of exhaustion (or doctrine of first sale), once the patentee authorizes the initial sale of a product incorporating the invention, she loses the right to control subsequent resales and uses of it, absent an express contractual restriction. [60]

  4. An offer to sell the patented invention: An offer to sell is one in which the sale will occur prior to the expiration of the patent term. Courts must employ traditional rules of contract law to determine whether an "offer to sell" the patented invention has been made. [60-61]

  5. Importing the patented invention: The Court of Appeals for the Federal Circuit recently held that the doctrine of exhaustion only applies to the patentee's sales of patented products in the United States. Accordingly, if the patentee sells the patented invention abroad, it may assert rights to prevent the importation, use, or sale of that foreign-sold good in the United States by subsequent owners, even in the absence of contractual restrictions. [61-62]

C. Inducement to infringe: Patent Act §271(b) imposes liability for inducing infringement if the defendant actively and knowingly solicited or assisted a third party to infringe a patent, and the third party did so infringe. The defendant must take some initiative. Merely complying with the request of a third party who directly infringes is insufficient. Moreover, generally the defendant must know that direct infringement is likely to occur as the result of his acts. [62]

D. Contributory infringement: Under Patent Act §271(c), a person who sells, offers to sell, or imports a material component of the patented invention, which has no substantial use other than use in the patented invention, will be liable for contributory infringement if: (1) he knows that the component he sold was especially made or adapted for use in the patented invention and has no other substantial use; and (2) the buyer in fact uses the component to infringe directly. The defendant must know of the patent and that the buyer's use is likely to constitute infringement. [62-63]

E. Importing, selling, offering to sell, or using a product made through a process protected by a U.S. patent: Patent Act §271(g) provides that the unauthorized import, sale, or offer to sell of a product made by a U.S. patented process constitutes infringement of the process patent unless the product: (1) has been materially changed by subsequent processes; or (2) has become a trivial or nonessential component of another product. Some exceptions and limitations are made to shelter innocent infringers, noncommercial users, and retail sellers from liability. [63-64]

F. Manufacturing or selling components of a patented invention to be assembled abroad: Subsection 271(f) prohibits persons in the United States from supplying all or a substantial portion of the components of a patented invention in a manner that induces combination of the components abroad. It also prohibits persons in the United States from supplying a material component of a U.S.-patented invention that has no substantial use aside from use in the invention if: (1) the person knows that the component is especially adapted for use in the patented invention and has no substantial non-infringing use; and (2) the person intends that the component will be combined with other components abroad in a manner that would infringe the patent if such combination occurred within the United States. However, supplying master disks of software that foreign purchasers then copy and install into the U.S.-patented invention abroad will not constitute infringement under §271(f). [64-65]

G. Provisional rights prior to patent issuance: In 1999, Congress amended the Patent Act, directing the P.T.O. to publish most patent applications 18 months after their filing date. (An exception is made when the applicant requests not to be published and certifies that the invention has not and will not be the subject of an application filed in another country, or under a multilateral international agreement, that requires publication of applications prior to patent issuance.) Congress further provided patentees with provisional rights against third parties who make, use, sell, offer to sell, or import the invention (or in the case of a process, the product of the claimed process) in the United States during the period between publication and patent issuance. However, the defendant must have actual notice of the published application, and the claims in the published application must also be substantially identical to those in the issued patent. Recovery is limited to a reasonable royalty. [65-66]

H. Defenses to infringement: There are a number of defenses to a claim of patent infringement. Five that are specific to patent litigation are patent invalidity, patent misuse, inequitable conduct, the experimental use defense, and the prior user defense. [66]

    1. Patent invalidity: A patent is presumed valid. However, the defendant may overcome this presumption by proving with clear and convincing evidence that a condition of patentability was not satisfied. If the defendant succeeds, the court will not enforce the patent. Patent licensees are not estopped from challenging the validity of the patent under which they took a license.

Patent assignors are estopped from challenging the validity of a patent they assigned to another. [66]

2. **Patent misuse:** The patentee will be deemed to have misused his patent if he uses it unreasonably to extend his market power beyond what Congress intended. If the defendant is able to demonstrate patent misuse, the patentee will be denied enforcement of his patent until the misuse ceases and the patentee no longer enjoys any benefits from his prior misuse. A patent owner who commits a violation of the antitrust laws through use of the patent generally will be subject to the misuse defense. However, the misuse defense is not expressly limited to antitrust violations. [66-67]

   a. **Tying arrangements:** Conditioning a license to make, use, sell, or import the patented invention (or conditioning sale of the patented invention itself) on the licensee/purchaser's agreement to purchase another good or license from the patentee will generally constitute patent misuse unless: (1) the good the purchaser/licensee is required to purchase is a material component of the invention, and has no substantial non-infringing use; (2) the patentee lacks market power in the relevant market for the patented invention; or (3) in the case of package licensing, the first patented invention cannot be practiced without infringing the second patented invention. [67-68]

   b. **Activities that will not constitute patent misuse:** Patent Act §271(d) expressly provides that it does not constitute patent misuse for the patentee to: (1) derive revenue from acts that would constitute contributory infringement if performed by another without the patentee's consent; (2) license or authorize others to perform acts that if performed without the patentee's consent would constitute contributory infringement; (3) seek to enforce his rights against infringement or contributory infringement; or (4) refuse to license or use any rights in the patent. [68]

3. **Inequitable conduct:** The inequitable conduct defense renders a patent unenforceable when the defendant proves, with clear and convincing evidence, that the patentee intentionally made a representation or withheld material information about the patentability of the invention during patent prosecution. The defendant must show: (1) prior art or information that is material to patentability; (2) knowledge chargeable to the applicant of the prior art or information and its materiality; and (3) failure of the applicant to disclose the prior art or information resulting from an intent to mislead the P.T.O. [68-69]

4. **The experimental use defense:** A person may make or use a patented invention without authorization if her purpose is only to satisfy her scientific curiosity or to amuse herself as an intellectual exercise and she has no commercial or other practical motivation. [69]

   a. **Subsection 271(e):** Patent Act §271(e) permits persons, under limited circumstances, to make, use, sell, offer to sell, or import certain patented inventions in the course of developing information to submit to federal agencies regulating manufacture, use, or sale of drugs or veterinary biological products. [69]

5. **Prior use:** Patent Act §273 provides a defense to a claim that the defendant infringed a patented business method. To succeed in the defense, the defendant must prove by clear and convincing evidence that it (1) actually reduced tha patented business method to practice, in good faith, at least one year before the effective filing date of the plaintiff's patent application, and (2) commercially used the patented business method before the effective filing date of the patent application. This defense is separate from an invalidity defense. [69-70]

IX. REMEDIES FOR PATENT INFRINGEMENT

Both damages and injunctions are available for patent infringement. If the patentee fails to give proper notice of the patent on its products, it may only be able to recover damages for infringement that takes place after the defendant receives notice of the infringement claim. [70]

   A. The proper measure of damages: Courts may measure infringement damages by calculating a reasonable royalty for the defendant's use of the patented invention (the amount a willing licensee wanting to make, use, sell, or import the patented invention would pay and a reasonable patentee would accept for a license, when negotiating at arms' length) or by calculating the patentee's lost profits attributable to the infringement. Courts may use the incremental income approach in calculating lost profits. Under the entire market value rule, courts may award lost profits on unpatented components sold with a patented apparatus if the patented and unpatented components are considered to be parts of a single assembly, or constitute a functional unit, operating together to achieve a result. Courts may also award lost profits on products that do not embody the patented invention if the patentee can demonstrate: (1) that it would have sold the unpatented device but for the defendant's infringement; (2) the lost sales were reasonably foreseeable by the infringing competitor; and (3) the unpatented device directly competes with the defendant's infringing product. However they are calculated, damages may be doubled or tripled upon a showing of willful infringement or bad faith on the part of the defendant. [70-71]

   B. Other monetary relief: The Patent Act authorizes awards of reasonable attorney fees to the prevailing party in exceptional cases. In addition, prejudgment interest is awarded to prevailing plaintiffs as a routine matter. [71-73]

   C. Injunctive relief: Courts may permanently enjoin further infringement under the usual four-factor test: (1) has plaintiff suffered irreparable injury?; (2) are remedies at law inadequate to compensate for the injury?; (3) given the balance of hardships between the parties, is a remedy at equity warranted?; and (4) will the public interest be disserved by a permanent injunction? Preliminary injunctions also are available upon a clear showing of irreparable harm and likelihood of success on the merits. [73-74]

   D. Remedies for infringement through performance of "medical activities": Patent Act §287(c) provides that there can be no infringement remedies against medical practitioners and related health care entities that directly infringe or induce infringement of a patent through performance of a medical activity. As a general matter, this exception to liability only applies when the defendant performs a patented surgical or medical procedure that does not involve drugs or patented devices, such as the Heimlich maneuver or CPR. However, the exception will apply if the patent claim cites a drug (composition of matter), but use of the drug does not directly contribute to achievement of the objective of the claimed medical or surgical procedure. [74]

X. DESIGN PATENTS

   A. The nature and requirements of design patents: A design patent gives its owner a 14-year monopoly in the design (appearance) of an article of manufacture. To qualify for a design patent, a design must be novel, non-obvious, and ornamental. The novelty standard is essentially the same for design patents as for utility patents.

1. **Non-obviousness:** Non-obviousness is determined from the perspective of the professional designer of ordinary skill, comparing the overall appearance of the design with the prior art. The Court of Appeals for the Federal Circuit has held that, in order for a claimed design to be obvious, there must be a primary reference whose design characteristics are basically the same as the claimed design, and the prior art, market trends, or other factors must suggest making the modifications to the primary reference in order to produce the claimed design. [76]

2. **Ornamentality:** With regard to the ornamentality requirement, the design must be primarily ornamental, not dictated by functional considerations alone. The Federal Circuit has provided the following list of considerations in evaluating the ornamentality of a claimed design: the existence of alternative designs; whether the protected design represents the best design; whether alternative designs would adversely affect the utility of the specified article; whether there are any concomitant utility patents; whether the advertising touts particular features of the design as having specific utility; and whether there are any elements in the design or overall appearance clearly not dictated by function. [76-77]

B. **Infringement of a design patent:** Patent Act §271, defining the various ways a patent may be infringed, applies equally to utility and design patents. However, design patents are not published prior to issuance, and thus give rise to no provisional rights between publication and issuance. The standard for judging infringement of a design patent is whether, in the eye of an ordinary observer, giving such attention as a purchaser usually gives, the two designs are substantially the same, i.e., similar enough to deceive such an observer and induce him to purchase one supposing it to be the other (the *Gorham* "eye of the ordinary observer" test). The similarity to the ordinary observer must arise from the novel aspects of the design (the "points of novelty" requirement). Moreover, when the patented design is comprised both of functional and ornamental features, the ordinary observer must be deceived by reason of the common ornamental features ("common ornamental features" requirement). [77]

C. **Defenses and remedies for infringement of design patents:** Defenses and remedies available for infringement of utility patents are also available for infringement of design patents. In addition, the Patent Act provides for recovery of the defendant's profits or an alternative minimum statutory damage amount for certain types of design patent infringement. [77-78]

XI. PLANT PATENTS

A. **The nature of plant patents:** Plant patents are available to persons who discover or invent a distinct and new variety of plant and asexually reproduce it. Cultivated sports, mutants, hybrids, and newly found seedlings may qualify for a plant patent, but tuber-propagated plants and new plants found in an uncultivated state do not. To qualify for a plant patent, a new variety must be novel, distinct, and non-obvious, and it must have been asexually reproduced. [78]

1. **The novelty requirement:** To be novel, a variety of plant must not have existed before in nature. A plant will not be deemed to have existed in nature unless it existed in a form that was capable of naturally reproducing the new characteristics that set it apart from preexisting varieties. Patent Act §102 applies to plant patents. A "printed publication" may be found, for purposes of subsections 102 (a) and (b), if the inventor published a written description of the new plant variety's characteristics, or a photograph, and also made the new variety available on foreign markets. (These acts, combined, will effectively put knowledge of the new variety in to the possession of persons of ordinary skill in the art.) [78]

2. **The distinctiveness and non-obviousness requirements:** To be distinctive, the new plant variety must have characteristics that are clearly distinguishable from those of existing varieties. In order for the plant to be non-obvious, the new characteristics must be significant. [79]

B. **Infringement of a plant patent:** A plant patent grants the owner the right to exclude others from (1) asexually reproducing the patented plant; (2) selling or using a plant so reproduced or any of its parts; and (3) importing a plant so reproduced or any of its parts. [79-80]

C. **Utility Patents and the Plant Variety Protection Act:** Utility patents are available for new varieties of plants that are "man-made" and meet the other utility patent requirements. The Plant Variety Protection Act gives patent-like protection to persons who breed new plants by use of seeds (sexual reproduction). Sexually reproduced and tuberpropagated plants other than fungi and bacteria are eligible. To qualify, the new variety must be new, distinct, uniform, and stable. A certificate of plant variety protection, granted by the Department of Agriculture, gives the owner the right to exclude others from selling the variety, offering it for sale, reproducing it, importing or exporting it, or using it in producing (as opposed to developing) a hybrid or different variety. [80]

XII. INTERNATIONAL PATENT TREATIES TO WHICH THE UNITED STATES ADHERES

A. **The Paris Convention:** The Paris Convention for the Protection of Industrial Property (Paris Convention) requires each member country to grant patent protection to applicants from other member nations on essentially the same basis that it grants protection to its own domestic inventors. (This is known as "national treatment.") It also provides for filing priority: Qualified applicants who file an application for patent in one member nation receive the benefit of their filing date in that nation for all subsequent filings in other member nations made within the next 12 months. With these and a few other exceptions, members of the Paris Convention generally are free to determine the nature and extent of substantive patent protection they will provide for inventions. [80-81]

B. **The Patent Cooperation Treaty:** The Patent Cooperation Treaty (P.T.C.) provides a centralized filing system to assist inventors applying for patents in a number of different countries simultaneously. An inventor's patent application can be filed, searched, and examined in a centralized fashion, prior to prosecution in the various individual countries' patent offices. [82]

C. **The Agreement on Trade-Related Aspects of Intellectual Property Rights:** The World Trade Organization's TRIPs Agreement incorporates the provisions of the Paris Convention and builds on them. Among other things, TRIPs imposes minimum disclosure requirements for patent applications, prescribes the subject matter for which WTO members must provide patent protection, the rights they must provide to patentees, and the minimum term of protection. [82]

D. **The Patent Law Treaty:** The Patent Law Treaty undertakes to harmonize application filing procedures among its members, thus further reducing the complexity and cost of obtaining international patent protection. [83]

Chapter 4
THE LAW OF UNDEVELOPED IDEAS

I. THE NATURE OF THE LAW OF UNDEVELOPED IDEAS

The law of undeveloped ideas is a miscellaneous accumulation of state common-law opinions addressing a claimed right to compensation for a defendant's unauthorized use of the plaintiff's idea. Five theories of recovery have been recognized. [93-94]

A. The express contract theory: Express contracts to pay for an idea have been enforced. However, some jurisdictions have required that the plaintiff demonstrate that the idea was novel. Some also require that the idea be concrete. [94-95]

B. The contract-implied-in-fact theory: Courts have found and enforced implied contracts to pay for ideas based on the parties' actions and surrounding circumstances, which indicate that they intended to make a binding contract to pay. However, many courts will not find or enforce an implied contract to pay for an idea if the idea was not novel (and in some jurisdictions, concrete). [95]

C. The contract-implied-in-law theory: A contract implied in law (or "quasi-contract") is not based upon the intentions of the parties but on a court's finding of unjust enrichment—that the defendant received a benefit for which equity and justice require him to pay. Most jurisdictions will not find that the defendant was unjustly enriched by receipt and use of a plaintiff's idea unless the idea was novel and concrete. [95]

D. The confidential relationship theory: Some courts have found a right to recover for an idea if, when the plaintiff revealed her idea to the defendant, the parties were in a confidential relationship in which the plaintiff reposed trust and confidence in the defendant's good faith. The confidential nature of the relationship imposes a duty on the defendant to refrain from taking advantage of the plaintiff's disclosure without plaintiff's permission. Again, some courts have added the requirement that the idea disclosed by the plaintiff be novel (and in some jurisdictions, concrete). [95]

E. The property theory: Some courts and commentators have suggested that a plaintiff may have a right to recover for a novel, concrete idea on the same general basis as a person could recover for the unauthorized taking of an item of personal property, or for infringement of a copyright. This is an extreme theory and has rarely if ever been relied on as a sole basis of recovery. [95]

II. THE NOVELTY AND CONCRETENESS REQUIREMENTS

A. The novelty requirement: Three views of the novelty requirement can be identified in the case law: (1) the idea must be original to the plaintiff (that is, the plaintiff must have conceived of the idea himself); (2) the idea must be innovative and creative in nature; or (3) the idea must be both original to the plaintiff and innovative in nature. In some cases, courts may differ in their construction of the novelty requirement, depending on the plaintiff's theory of recovery. [96]

B. The concreteness requirement: Three views of concreteness can be identified in the case law: (1) the idea must be reduced to tangible form; (2) the idea must be fully developed—in a detailed form ready for immediate use with little or no additional work on the user's part; or (3) the idea must be both reduced to tangible form and fully developed. [96-97]

CHAPTER 5
COPYRIGHT LAW

I. THE PURPOSE AND NATURE OF COPYRIGHT LAW

A. **The nature of copyright law:** The ultimate purpose of copyright law is to stimulate the creation and dissemination of as many works of authorship as possible, in order to benefit the public. It does this by giving creators of works of authorship *limited* rights in their works. Copyright protection is limited to an author's particular method of expressing an idea. Copyright never gives rights in the idea being expressed, or in facts or other elements of the public domain that the author may have incorporated into the work. [103-105]

1. **Property right vs. personal right:** U.S. copyright law traditionally has focused on granting authors *economic rights* in their works. U.S. authors have relied on other areas of law, such as the law of defamation, unfair competition, and contract, to protect their personal interests in being identified as the author and in protecting their reputation as an author. By contrast, many countries have fashioned their copyright (or authors' right) laws to extend such personal rights, along with economic rights. After ratifying the Berne Convention, Congress amended the U.S. Copyright Act to provide personal rights ("moral rights") in the narrow category of "works of visual art." [105]

2. **Rights in the intangible:** The common law of personal property protects rights in tangible embodiments of works of authorship, such as manuscripts and canvases. Copyright, by contrast, protects the *intangible expression itself.* A transfer of the physical embodiment of a work of authorship does not transfer the copyright. A separate writing is required to transfer copyright. [105-106]

3. **Federal vs. state law:** Prior to the effective date of the Copyright Act of 1976 (January 1, 1978), the United States had a dual system of copyright. Unpublished works of authorship were protected by state common-law copyright. Once a work was published, common-law copyright ended. Federal statutory copyright was available to works published with proper notice of copyright. In the Copyright Act of 1976, Congress made federal statutory copyright available upon the fixation of a work in tangible form, regardless of publication, and provided that the federal copyright law would preempt state copyright protection for works of authorship fixed in tangible form. [106]

II. THE SUBJECT MATTER OF COPYRIGHT

A. **The statutory definition:** The 1976 Act provides that copyright subsists "in original works of authorship fixed in any tangible medium of expression, now known or later developed, from which they can be perceived, reproduced, or otherwise communicated, either directly or with the aid of a machine or device." [106]

B. **The originality requirement:** A work of authorship must be *original* in order to qualify for copyright protection. This means: (1) that the author must have engaged in some intellectual endeavor, and not just copied from a preexisting source; and (2) that the work must contain a minimal amount of creativity. Under this rule, *de minimis* "works" such as words, short phrases, slogans, and the like, are not protected. Because facts are "discovered" rather than "created," they are not proper subject matter for copyright. Only the author's original means of expressing the facts can be protected. [107-108]

  1. **Scenes a faire:** An author may not obtain copyright in *scenes a faire*: incidents, characters, settings, or other elements that are indispensable, or at least standard, in the treatment of a given topic. [108]

C. **The fixation requirement:** Federal copyright attaches to the intangible work of authorship, not the physical manifestation of it, but the work only qualifies for federal copyright protection once it has been fixed in a tangible form. Fixation may take many forms. The Copyright Act of 1976 provides that a work is fixed in a tangible medium of expression "when its embodiment in a copy or phonorecord, by or under the authority of the author, is sufficiently permanent or stable to permit it to be perceived, reproduced, or otherwise communicated for a period of more than transitory duration." [108-109]

  1. **Copies and phonorecords:** All copyrightable works of authorship are fixed either in copies or phonorecords. Phonorecords are "material objects in which sounds, other than those accompanying a motion picture or other audiovisual work, are fixed. . . ." All other material objects in which works of authorship are fixed are copies. [108]

D. **Exclusion of ideas, procedures, processes, etc.:** Copyright protection never gives rights in ideas, procedures, processes, systems, methods of operation, concepts, principles, or discoveries. When use of an idea *requires copying the plaintiff's expression,* the expression will not be protected. Indeed, under the merger doctrine, when the subject matter of a work is so narrow and straightforward that there are only a *limited number* of ways to express it, there may be no copyright in any one form of expressing it. To provide otherwise might enable a person to obtain a *de facto* monopoly in the subject matter, or idea, by obtaining copyright in all the alternative forms of expressing it. [109-111]

  1. **Thin copyright:** An alternate way some courts deal with situations in which there are relatively few ways to express an idea is to recognize copyright protection, but refuse to find infringement unless the defendant's copying is nearly exact. This is called "thin copyright." [111]

  2. **Blank forms:** Courts deny copyright protection to blank forms that are designed for recording information and do not in themselves convey information. [111]

E. **Categories of protectible works of authorship:** The 1976 Act provides that "works of authorship" include the following categories: (1) literary works; (2) musical works, including any accompanying words; (3) dramatic works, including any accompanying music; (4) pantomimes and choreographic works; (5) pictorial, graphic, and sculptural works; (6) motion pictures and other audiovisual works; (7) sound recordings; and (8) architectural works. This list is not meant to be exclusive. [112]

  1. **The literary works category—copyrightability of computer programs:** The 1976 Act, as amended, expressly protects computer programs, which it defines as "a set of statements or

instructions to be used directly or indirectly in a computer in order to bring about a certain result." Copyright protection extends both to programs in source code and programs in object code and to both application and operating system programs. Likewise, copyright extends to programs regardless of the medium in which they are encoded, such as chips. [112-113]

   a. Copyright in the structure of programs: Computer programs are considered "literary works" for purposes of copyright, and their authors are entitled to copyright protection not only in their literal expression but also in nonliteral elements of expression, such as aspects of the program's structure or organization. In the *Altai* case, the Second Circuit adopted the "abstraction-filtration-comparison" test for determining which, if any, elements of a program's structure are copyrightable. This test has been widely adopted. [113-114]

      i. The abstraction, filtration, comparison test: In the abstraction phase, the program is broken down into its structural components, at increasing levels of abstraction, or generality. In the filtration phase, the court identifies those components that (1) constitute an idea; (2) are required in order for the program to perform its functions efficiently; (3) are required by factors external to the program itself; or (4) were taken from the public domain. These components are uncopyrightable and must be removed from consideration at each level of abstraction. In the comparison phase, the court evaluates the remaining structural components, which constitute copyrightable expression. [114-115]

      ii. Selection and arrangement expression: The Second Circuit has clarified that a programmer's original selection and arrangement of uncopyrightable elements may be protected under the *Altai* abstraction-filtration-comparison test. However, some circuits have held that when the plaintiff is relying on selection and arrangement expression, it must demonstrate "bodily appropriation of expression" or "virtual identicality" of expression in the defendant's alleged infringing program. [115]

   b. Copyright in the user interface: A program's user interface is comprised of the visual and aural elements through which the program communicates with the user. Aspects of a screen display may be protected if they are sufficiently original and do not merge with the underlying idea. In the *Lotus* case, the First Circuit held that the menu command hierarchy of a program did not constitute copyrightable expression, but rather, constituted an uncopyrightable *method of operation*. The *Lotus* court reasoned that even if the method of operation contained expressive elements, they would be uncopyrightable because they were part of the method of operation. The Tenth Circuit has subsequently disagreed that expressive elements *incorporated into* a method of operation are uncopyrightable. [115-117]

2. The pictorial, graphic, and sculptural works category: Pictorial, graphic, and sculptural works include two-dimensional and three-dimensional works of fine, graphic and applied art, photographs, prints and art reproductions, maps, globes, charts, diagrams, models, technical drawings, and "works of artistic craftsmanship insofar as their form but not their mechanical or utilitarian aspects are concerned." [117]

   a. Copyright in the design of useful articles: A useful article is "an article having an intrinsic function that is not merely to portray the appearance of the article or to convey information." Pictorial, graphic, or sculptural features of useful articles may be copyrighted if they are physically or conceptually separable from the utilitarian aspects of the useful article. [117-118]

i. Evaluating conceptual separability: The prevailing test for conceptual separability focuses on the design process. If the design features were *significantly influenced by utilitarian considerations,* then the features are "inextricably intertwined" with the utilitarian function of the article and are not conceptually separable. If the design features were not influenced by the utilitarian function of the article, but reflect purely aesthetic choices, then the design features are conceptually separable. While the Second and Seventh Circuits have adopted the "design process" standard described above, the Fifth Circuit has adopted a "likelihood of marketability" standard, at least in the case of costumes or clothing. Under this standard, conceptual separability will be found if there is a substantial likelihood that even if the article had no utilitarian use, it would still be marketable to some significant segment of the community simply because of its aesthetic qualities. [118-119]

b. Copyright in technical drawings: Technical drawings and blueprints are protected by copyright. However, unauthorized use of copyrighted plans to build the useful article depicted in them generally does not in itself constitute infringement of the plans. [119-120]

c. Semiconductor chips: Semiconductor chips, or "integrated circuits" are a collection of transistors, in a single structure, that work together to perform an electronic function. Because semiconductor chips are useful articles, and their design is not physically or conceptually separable from their function, they generally do not qualify for copyright protection. However, Congress did enact a form of *sui generis* protection for semiconductor chips in the Semiconductor Chip Protection Act of 1984 (SCPA). While the SCPA has rarely been used, it is an important precedent for enactment of specially designed *sui generis* protection for works that do not fit within the parameters of copyright. [123-124]

3. The architectural works category: Copyright Act §101, as amended by the Architectural Works Copyright Protection Act (AWCPA), defines an architectural work as the design of a building, as embodied in any tangible medium of expression, including a building, architectural plans, or drawings. The work includes the overall form as well as the arrangement and composition of spaces and elements in the design, but does not include individual standard features. The legislative history indicates that, in enacting the AWPCA, Congress intended to prohibit unauthorized copying of the two-dimensional architectural plans, unauthorized use of the plans to build a three-dimensional building, and unauthorized direct copying of the building. However, only those original design elements that are *not dictated by functional considerations* will be protected "expression" within the work. [120]

a. The design of a "building": The AWCPA defines a protectible "architectural work" as "the design of a building." "Buildings" are humanly habitable structures that are intended to be both permanent and stationary, such as houses, office buildings and other structures designed for human occupancy. Stores built inside an enclosed shopping mall are not "buildings" for this purpose. [120]

b. Pre-AWCPA works: The AWCPA only applies to architectural works created on or after December 1, 1990, or that were unconstructed and embodied in unpublished plans or drawings on that date. *Architectural works that do not qualify for protection under AWCPA can only be protected as pictorial, graphic, or sculptural works.* The plans are treated as graphic works, and the buildings are treated as useful articles. [121-122]

4. The sound recordings category: Sound recordings are "works that result from the fixation of a series of musical, spoken, or other sounds," but do not include the sounds accompanying a motion picture or other audiovisual work. The sound recording copyright is separate from any copyright that may exist in the work that is the subject of the recording. Domestic sound recordings fixed before 1972 are not protected by federal copyright. Forms of state protection may be available for them, however. [122]

5. **Copyright for fictitious characters:** Under the more widely accepted rule, fictitious characters are entitled to separate copyright protection, apart from the work in which they appeared, if the characters were very distinctly delineated in the author's work. When the character has a visual aspect as well as personality characteristics described by word and story line, courts have been more willing to find copyright protection. (The less widely applied standard that would be applied only in the case of characters without a visual aspect, if then, is the "story being told" standard: The character will only be separately protected if he constitutes the story being told, and is not just the vehicle for telling the story.) [122-123]

6. **Compilations:** Compilations are works formed by collecting and assembling preexisting materials or data. Compilations include collective works (such as periodical issues, anthologies, or encyclopedias) that compile a number of separate, independently copyrightable works. Compilations that are *not* collective works include directories, catalogs, or automated databases that compile material, such as facts, that is not separately copyrightable. [124]

   a. **The protectible expression in compilations:** The copyrightable expression in a compilation is that expression contributed by the compilation author—usually the selection, coordination and arrangement of materials, along with any original explanatory matter. Compilations, like other categories of copyrightable subject matter, must be original. The compiler's selection and arrangement must entail a minimum threshold of creativity: If the act of compiling was merely rote, obvious, or clerical in nature, with no meaningful exercise of judgment or intellect, the originality requirement will not be satisfied. [124-125]

7. **Derivative works:** Derivative works are works based upon one or more preexisting works, such as translations, musical arrangements, dramatizations, fictionalizations, motion picture versions, art reproductions, abridgments, etc. Derivative works are within the subject matter of copyright, but copyright protection extends only to the original material contributed by the derivative author, not to the preexisting material. In order to constitute a separately copyrightable derivative work, an adaptation of a preexisting work must contain substantial, not merely trivial, variations from the preexisting work on which it is based. The Ninth Circuit has recently added the provision that a derivative work may not be copyrighted if doing so will affect copyright protection in the underlying work. This may occur if the derivative work copyright will enable the recipient to interfere with the ability of the person holding copyright in the preexisting work to license additional derivative works. [125-126]

8. **Government works as copyrightable subject matter:** Copyright is not available for any work of the U.S. government. Works of the U.S. government are works "prepared by an officer or employee of the U.S. government as part of that person's official duties." Government agencies that arrange for independent contractors to create works for the U.S. government may require independent contractors to waive their right to copyright in some cases, when it is in the public's interest that they do so. [126-127]

   a. **State government works:** The Copyright Act does not prohibit state and local governmental entities from claiming copyright in works of authorship created by their officials or employees. However, case law indicates that judicial opinions, statutes, city ordinances, and other government laws and regulations must be accessible to the public because of due process considerations. This is generally understood to mean that these works, which have the force and effect of law, may be subject to copying by the public. When a governmental entity adopts a model code that was drafted by non-governmental entities, the model code loses copyright protection in its capacity as the law of the adopting governmental entity. [127]

III. THE RIGHTS AFFORDED BY COPYRIGHT LAW

A. The exclusive rights of copyright: The *owner of copyright* in a work has the exclusive right to do or authorize the following: (1) reproduce the copyrighted work; (2) prepare derivative works based upon the copyrighted work; (3) distribute copies or phonorecords of the copyrighted work to the public; (4) publicly perform the work (this right applies in the case of all the types of copyrightable works except pictorial, graphic and sculptural works, architectural works, and sound recordings); (5) publicly display the work (this right applies in the case of all the types of copyrightable works except architectural works and sound recordings); and (6) in the case of sound recordings, to perform the copyrighted work publicly by means of digital audio transmission. [127-128]

B. Moral rights in works of visual art: In the case of works of visual art, the *artist* has the right: (1) to claim authorship in the work; (2) to prevent use of her name as the author of works she did not create; (3) to prevent use of her name as the author of her own work if the work has been distorted, mutilated, or otherwise modified so that the use would be prejudicial to her honor or reputation; (4) to prevent any intentional distortion, mutilation, or other modification of her work that would be prejudicial to her name or reputation; and (5) to prevent the intentional or grossly negligent destruction of the work if the work is of recognized stature. [128]

IV. THE COPYRIGHTED WORK

To demonstrate that a defendant infringed any of the exclusive economic rights, it must appear that; (1) the defendant's work was copied from the plaintiff's; and (2) that the works are substantially similar in their *expression*, so that the copying amounts to an unlawful appropriation. [128-129]

A. Copying: Copying may be demonstrated by direct evidence or by circumstantial evidence that: (1) the defendant had access to the work and the defendant's work is similar to the plaintiff's; or (2) the defendant's work is strikingly similar to the plaintiff's work. In determining similarity for this purpose, all similarities—both in copyrightable and uncopyrightable elements of the works—may be considered. [129]

B. Unlawful appropriation: To ascertain whether the defendant's copying amounted to an unlawful appropriation, it must be determined whether the defendant's work is substantially similar to the copyrightable expression in the copyright owner's work. This evaluation usually is made from the standpoint of the average member of the intended audience for the copyrighted work. Under the *Arnstein* "audience" test, the evaluation is a *subjective* one, based on the *overall impression* of the average member of the intended audience. Similarities in uncopyrightable elements cannot support a finding of unlawful appropriation/substantial similarity, although similarities in the selection and arrangement of uncopyrightable elements can. The fact that the defendant's allegedly infringing work contains expression that the copyright owner's lacks, or varies from the copyright owner's in some aspects, does not in itself excuse the defendant from liability. [129-130]

  1. **The Ninth Circuit's approach:** The Ninth Circuit has adopted a two-part "extrinsic/intrinsic" test to determine whether a defendant's copying amounts to an unlawful appropriation. The extrinsic test constitutes an *objective* evaluation of the similarities of expression through use of dissection and expert witnesses. The intrinsic test constitutes a *subjective* evaluation, based on the overall impression of the average member of the intended audience, without analytic dissection or expert testimony, as in the *Arnstein* audience test. The Ninth Circuit has held that a copyright infringement plaintiff must demonstrate substantial similarity under *both* the extrinsic and the intrinsic tests in order to prevail. [132]

  2. **Other approaches:** Courts have used other standards for assessing infringement when the work at issue includes numerous uncopyrightable elements. These include the *"more discerning"* standard and the *"abstraction, filtration, and comparison"* standard. When the plaintiff is relying on "selection and arrangement" expression in a "thin copyright" situation, courts may impose a "virtual identicality" or "a bodily appropriation of copyrighted expression" standard. [133]

C. **Literal vs. nonliteral similarity:** There are two types of substantial similarity that may lead to a finding of infringement: (1) literal similarity; and (2) nonliteral similarity (similarity in the works' underlying structure or arrangement). In the case of *literal similarity,* the *amount* of copying that is necessary to find infringement depends on how important the copied material is. The more important the material, the less must be copied. The main problem in determining substantial similarity in the case of *nonliteral copying* is drawing the line between what is an uncopyrightable idea and what is protectible expression. As a general matter, the more *detail* that is copied, the more likely it is that copyrightable expression has been taken. Judge Hand's "abstractions" test is often used in drawing the line between idea and expression in this context. [131-132]

V. THE EXCLUSIVE RIGHT TO REPRODUCE THE WORK

The copyright owner has the right to prevent others from making *material copies* or phonorecords of the copyrighted work

A. **The meaning of "reproduction":** The right of reproduction is the right to reproduce the work in material copies or phonorecords. To infringe, a defendant must fix all or part of the copyrighted work in a material object in a manner that is sufficiently permanent or stable to permit the work to be perceived, reproduced, or otherwise communicated for a period of more than transitory duration. Several courts have held that bringing a work into the random access memory of a computer constitutes a reproduction for purposes of the Copyright Act, because the work can be perceived in RAM for a period of more than transitory duration. However, some courts have made exceptions for Internet Service Providers, whose computers make RAM or other temporary duplicates of works posted or transmitted by Internet users. For example, in the *CoStar* case, the Fourth Circuit held that whether a RAM duplicate is "of more than a transitory duration" should be judged both on a quantitative and qualitative basis: If the temporary RAM duplicate *serves* the ISP or other computer owner's purposes, it should be deemed to be "of more than transitory duration" and thus a "reproduction." On the other hand, if the RAM duplication does not serve the ISP or other computer owner's purposes (and the ISP or computer owner is indifferent as to its content), than it is not of more than transitory duration and thus does not constitute a reproduction. In an alternative line of reasoning, several courts have determined that although copyright infringement is a form of strict liability, there must be some element of volition or causation on the defendant's part. Thus, an Internet Service Provider that provides the automatic means for users to post or transmit (and thereby reproduce) materials, but does not otherwise participate in making a reproduction, lacks the necessary volition/causation and is not liable as a direct infringer. [133-135]

B. **Limitations on the exclusive right to reproduce—sound recordings:** The exclusive right to reproduce sound recordings only extends to the mechanical reproduction of sounds from the plaintiff's copyrighted recording. Simply mimicking the sounds in the plaintiff's recording does not constitute infringement. The Court of Appeals for the Sixth Circuit has held that mechanical reproduction *alone* is enough to demonstrate infringement of the reproduction and/or adaptation right in a sound recording—it is not necessary to demonstrate that the defendant's work is substantially similar to the plaintiff's copyrighted expression. However, it is not clear whether other circuits will follow this precedent. [135-136]

C. **Exception to the exclusive right to reproduce—computer programs:** Under Copyright Act §117, the lawful owner of a copy of a copyrighted computer program will not be liable for infringement if he copies the program, as long as it is done as an essential step in utilizing the program in a computer or is for archival purposes only. A recent amendment to §117 provides that the owner or lessee of a computer may copy a computer program if: (1) the copy is made solely by virtue of activating the computer; (2) the computer lawfully contains an authorized copy of the program; (3) the only purpose of making the copy is maintenance or repair of the computer; and (4) the new copy is destroyed as soon as the maintenance or repair is completed. [136]

   1. **Ownership of copies:** The Ninth Circuit has held that the §117 restriction to "owners" of copies of software disqualifies rightful possessors who obtained their rights under a license agreement, rather than through a transfer of title. The Federal Circuit has held that licensees may be deemed "owners," and thus entitled to the §117 exemptions, if the transaction giving them lawful possession *resembles* a transfer of title. Relevant considerations in determining whether this is the case include: (1) whether the possessor obtained its rights in the software through a single payment; (2) whether the rightful possession is perpetual; and (3) whether the rightful use of the software under the license is heavily encumbered by restrictions that are inconsistent with the status of an owner. [136-137]

D. **Exception to the exclusive right to reproduce—compulsory licenses to record nondramatic musical works:** Recording a copyrighted nondramatic musical composition and distributing the recording to the public will not constitute infringement if the §115 provisions for compulsory licenses are observed. The musical composition must already have been recorded and distributed to the U.S. public in phonorecords pursuant to the copyright owner's authorization. The compulsory licensee's primary purpose must be to make phonorecords to be distributed to the public for private use, and he must serve proper notice of his intention to take a compulsory license on the copyright owner. The compulsory licensee must pay royalties as set forth in §115 of the '76 Act. [138-139]

E. **Other exceptions to the exclusive right to reproduce:** The Copyright Act contains a host of other narrowly drawn exceptions to the right of reproduction, including: (1) an exception allowing broadcasters of programs containing performances or displays of copyrighted works to make a limited number of copies of their programs (Copyright Act §112); (2) an exception allowing persons to reproduce, distribute, or display useful objects portrayed in copyrighted pictorial, graphic, and sculptural works (§113); (3) an exception allowing people to make, distribute, and display pictures or photographs of useful articles incorporating copyrightable works of art for purposes of advertising sale of the useful articles, news reporting, etc. (§113); (4) an exception allowing persons to make, distribute, and publicly display pictures, paintings, photographs, or other representations of a copyrighted architectural work, as long as the building in which the work is embodied is located in or is visible from a public place (§120); (5) exceptions allowing public libraries and archives to reproduce works under certain circumstances (§108); (6) provisions for authorized nonprofit and government organizations to reproduce and/or distribute previously published nondramatic literary works in specialized formats for use by persons with disabilities (§121); and (7) provisions allowing people to make noncommercial or "home" digital and analog audiotapes of sound recordings and the musical works recorded on them (§§1001-1010). [137-139]

VI. THE EXCLUSIVE RIGHT TO PREPARE DERIVATIVE WORKS

A. The right to make derivative works: The right to make derivative works is also known as the right to *adapt* the copyrighted work. A derivative work is "a work based upon one or more preexisting works, such as a translation, musical arrangement, dramatization, fictionalization, motion picture version, sound recording, art reproduction, abridgement, condensation, or any other form in which a work may be recast, transformed, or adapted." In most cases in which the right to adapt is infringed, either the right to reproduce or the right to publicly perform will be infringed as well. [139-140]

1. **Relevant considerations in determining whether a defendant's acts constitute "adaptation":** Some courts have suggested that a defendant's changes must constitute a "substantial variation" from the original before an *infringement* of the adaptation right can be found. (Another way to say this is that the defendant's alleged infringing work must be one that would have *qualified for a derivative work copyright* if it had been authorized.) However, other courts have rejected such a requirement. Courts may undertake to assess the *economic impact* of the defendant's acts on potential markets for the plaintiff's work in deciding whether the defendant's acts constitute actionable adaptation. [140]

B. The adaptation right and computer program enhancements: The Ninth Circuit has held that even though one need not reproduce a copyrighted work in order to infringe the owner's adaptation right, a defendant's work must *incorporate the underlying work in a concrete or permanent form*. However, in the digital works context, a defendant's creation of an "exact, down to the last detail description of an audiovisual display" will constitute incorporation of the audiovisual display in a concrete or permanent form for this purpose, just as sheet music, which describes in precise detail the way a copyrighted melody should sound, constitutes incorporation of the melody in a concrete and permanent form. [140-141]

C. Limitations on the exclusive right to make derivative works—sound recordings: The right to adapt a sound recording, like the right to reproduce it, is only infringed if the defendant mechanically recaptures or "lifts" sounds from the copyrighted phonorecord, then alters or mixes them with other sounds. (Copyright Act §114). [142]

D. Limitations on the exclusive right to make derivative works—computer programs: The owner of an authorized copy of a computer program may make an adaptation of the program, if it is done as an essential step in utilizing the program in a computer or is done for archival purposes. However, the altered program may not be transferred to someone else unless the owner of the copyright in the program consents, and the altered copies must be destroyed as soon as the owner no longer has a lawful right to possess the original program. (Copyright Act §117). [142]

E. **Limitations on the exclusive right to make derivative works—architectural works:** The owner of a building embodying a copyrighted architectural work may make or authorize alterations to or destruction of the building. (Copyright Act §120.) [142]

VII. THE EXCLUSIVE RIGHT TO DISTRIBUTE TO THE PUBLIC

A. **The right of distribution:** Copyright includes the exclusive right to distribute copies or phonorecords of the work to the public by sale or other transfer of ownership, or by rental, lease, or lending. Traditionally, to violate the exclusive right to distribute a copyrighted work, a person had to make an unauthorized physical transfer of a material copy or phonorecord to a member of the public. However, recent case law suggests that it is not always necessary to demonstrate physical transfer of a material copy. Transmission of an electronic (digital) copy is likely to suffice. Likewise, some precedent indicates that posting a copyrighted work on a web site, where it is readily available for download, or holding an unlawful copy of a work, indexed and available in a public library collection, can be an infringing distribution of the work to the public. However, the Ninth Circuit has held that providing an html link to a file residing on another web site does not constitute distribution of that file. One must first have the file in his own possession (in this case, on his own computer hard drive) before he can distribute it to others. [142-143]

B. **The doctrine of first sale:** The doctrine of first sale provides that once the copyright owner authorizes transfer of title to a copy or phonorecord of the copyrighted work, the transferee and his successors in interest are entitled to retransfer or otherwise dispose of that copy or phonorecord without returning to the copyright owner for authorization. However, the doctrine of first sale only applies to *lawful* copies and phonorecords. A person who acquires a pirated copy of the work will infringe the copyright by reselling or otherwise distributing it to the public. Moreover, the doctrine of first sale does not authorize the owner of a lawful copy to reproduce it or to distribute the unauthorized reproductions. [143]

1. **Exception to the doctrine of first sale for record and computer program rentals:** Owners of copyright in computer programs, in sound recordings of music, and in the musical compositions that are recorded in sound recordings, may prevent purchasers of program copies and phonorecords from renting out the phonorecords and program copies commercially, or may charge a royalty for granting them the privilege to do so. [143-144]

2. *Droit de suite***:** The *droit de suite* doctrine gives the author of a work of fine art the opportunity to share in its appreciation in value when it is resold by subsequent transferees. Congress has not adopted the *droit de suite* as an exception to the doctrine of first sale, but the state of California has enacted a statute in the nature of the *droit de suite*. [144]

3. **Imports:** Copyright Act §602 provides that unauthorized importation of copies or phonorecords of a work into the United States infringes the copyright owner's exclusive right of distribution to the public. The Supreme Court has held that the doctrine of first sale is applicable to the importation right. Thus, if a copyright owner manufactured goods incorporating the copyrighted work in the United States and exported them, it could not, absent an enforceable contractual restriction, prevent foreign purchasers from bringing the goods back into the United States to resell in competition with it. While the Supreme Court's decision could be read to

apply the doctrine of first sale to *all* copies and phonorecords originally sold by or under the authorization of the U.S. copyright owner, regardless of where they were manufactured, the Court did not directly address the case of copies or phonorecords that the U.S. copyright owner manufactured abroad. Some lower courts have construed the doctrine of first sale as only applying to copies and phonorecords that are *manufactured in the United States.* [144-145]

4. **The doctrine of first sale on the Internet:** Because Internet transmissions generally entail *reproducing* the sender's copy and sending the reproduction, the doctrine of first sale will seldom apply to permit purchasers of digital works to transfer them to others via the Internet. [145]

VIII. THE EXCLUSIVE RIGHT TO PERFORM PUBLICLY

A. **The meaning of "performance":** To perform a work is "to recite, render, play, dance, or act it, either directly or by means of any device or process or, in the case of a motion picture or other audiovisual work, to show its images in any sequence or to make the sounds accompanying it audible." The initial rendition and any further act by which that rendition is transmitted or communicated or made to recur is a performance. [145-146]

B. **When a performance is "public":** There are four ways in which a performance may be "public": (1) if the performance occurs at a *place open to the public;* (2) if the performance occurs at any place where a *substantial number of persons* outside the normal circle of a family and its social acquaintances is gathered; (3) if the performance is transmitted or otherwise communicated to a place open to the public or where a substantial number of persons outside the normal circle of a family and its social acquaintances is gathered; or (4) if the performance is *transmitted* or otherwise communicated *to the public* by means of any device, regardless of whether the public receives it in the same or separate places or receives it at the same or different times. [146-149]

C. **Exception to the exclusive right of public performance—nonprofit performances of nondramatic literary or musical works:** It does not constitute infringement to publicly perform a nondramatic literary or musical work if the performance is direct (not transmitted), there is no purpose of direct or indirect commercial advantage, the performers, promoters and organizers are not paid specifically for the performance, and there is no direct or indirect admission charge (or, if there is such a charge, the proceeds, after deducting costs of the performance, are used exclusively for charitable purposes). Other exceptions to the exclusive right of public performance also apply to the exclusive right of public display, and are discussed in the next section. [149]

D. **The right to perform sound recordings publicly by means of a digital audio transmission:** The general right of public performance is not accorded to sound recordings. Pursuant to recent amendments, sound recordings enjoy "the right to perform the copyrighted work publicly by means of a digital audio transmission." This is a more limited performance right than the general public performance right enjoyed by other categories of copyrightable subject matter. It does not extend to FCC-regulated over-the-air radio or television broadcasts to the public (though it does apply to Internet "webcasts"). Nor does it apply to digital transmissions of *audiovisual* works such as music videos, or to forms of digital performances that do not constitute transmissions, such as playing sound recordings on a compact disc player. There are numerous further limitations on the digital audio transmission performance right, including compulsory licenses for performances in the case of some non-interactive digital transmissions, under which the sound recording copyright owner is compensated for performances, but has no right to prohibit the performances. [146-147]

E. **Rights in unfixed performances:** Pursuant to the United States's TRIPs Agreement obligations, Congress has enacted anti-bootlegging provisions giving "neighboring rights" in live musical performances. These provisions prohibit unauthorized broadcasts of live musical performances, unauthorized fixations of such performances, and reproduction, distribution, offers to distribute, and trafficking in unauthorized fixations. Violators are subject to civil copyright infringement remedies. [148]

IX. THE EXCLUSIVE RIGHT TO DISPLAY THE COPYRIGHTED WORK PUBLICLY

A. **What constitutes a public display:** To *display* a work is to show a copy of it, either directly or by means of a film, slide, television image, or any other device or process or, in the case of a motion picture or other audiovisual work, to show individual images nonsequentially. A computer operator who stores an image as electronic information and then serves that information directly to Internet users displays that information. However, it does not constitute a display merely to link to or frame electronic information that resides on a different computer. A display is *public* under the same circumstances in which a performance is public. [150]

B. **Exception to the exclusive right of public display—owners of lawfully made copies:** The owner of a lawfully made copy of a work may display that copy publicly either directly or by the projection of no more than one image at a time, to viewers present at the place where the copy is located. (Copyright Act §109(c).) [150]

C. **Exception to the exclusive rights of public performance and display—transmissions received on home-style receivers:** Under Copyright Act §110(5), performance or display of a copyrighted work *by transmission* to a place open to the public or where the public is gathered, on a single receiving apparatus of a kind commonly used in private homes, will not infringe unless a direct charge is made to see or hear the transmission. Congress recently amended this §110(5) exception to give commercial establishments *greater leeway to perform nondramatic musical works* by public reception of radio and television transmissions to the general public. Under the amendment, stores that are smaller than 2,000 square feet and restaurants and bars that are smaller than 3,750 square feet may play radio and television transmissions of nondramatic musical works, regardless of the type of receiver or number of speakers they use. Establishments that are larger than the specified square foot limitations are also exempt from liability if they use no more than 6 speakers or 4 televisions with screens smaller than 55 inches. (There are further limitations on the placement of the speakers and televisions.) A World Trade Organization dispute resolution panel has subsequently held the amendment described above to be in violation of the United States' international treaty obligations. [150-151]

D. **Other exceptions to the exclusive rights of public performance and display:** Additional exceptions to the exclusive rights of public performance and public display permit such things as: (1) performances and displays of works by instructors or pupils in the course of face-to-face teaching activities in a classroom or similar place devoted to instruction (Copyright Act §110 (1)); (2) performance and display of certain works by transmission as a regular part of the systematic instructional activities of a government body or nonprofit educational institution (§110(2)); (3) certain performances and displays of works in the course of religious services (§110(3)); and (4) a variety of forms of retransmission of transmitted broadcast signals. The Copyright Act also provides for compulsory licenses to enable cable systems and satellite companies to make secondary transmissions of broadcast signals. In addition, there is a compulsory license to enable public broadcasting entities to make public performances and displays of certain kinds of works. [151-153]

X. MORAL RIGHTS

A. The nature of moral rights: Many countries recognize rights that are *personal* to authors, apart from the economic rights discussed thus far. These personal rights are known as moral rights and are based on the view that a work of authorship is an extension of the author's personality and should be protected as such. Generally, moral rights include the *right of attribution* and the *right of integrity*. The Berne Convention requires member countries to protect these rights. [153]

B. The Visual Artists' Rights Act of 1990: Congress enacted the Visual Artists' Rights Act of 1990 ("VARA") to comply with the Berne Convention requirement. The Act, however, is very limited in scope, because it only provides moral rights in works of visual art. Works of visual art include paintings, drawings, prints, or sculptures that exist in a single copy or in a limited edition of 200 or fewer signed, numbered copies. Still photographs are also included, if produced for exhibition purposes only and existing in a single, signed copy or in a limited edition of 200 or fewer signed, numbered copies. Works made for hire or that do not qualify for copyright are excluded. Authors of qualifying works of visual art are given the rights of attribution and integrity in their works. These rights *attach to the single or limited edition copies, as described above*. They do not attach to the intangible work of authorship, as manifested in mass-produced or other copies other than the single and limited edition copies described above. [153-154]

  1. The right of attribution: The right of attribution gives the author the right to be identified as the author of a work, the right to prevent attribution to him of works that he did not create, and the right to prevent use of his name in connection with a work that has been modified in a way that will injure his honor or reputation. [154]

  2. The right of integrity: The right of integrity gives the author the right to prevent any intentional distortion, mutilation, or other modification of her work that would be prejudicial to her honor or reputation as an author and, in the case of works of "recognized stature," the right to prevent intentional or grossly negligent destruction of the work. [154-155]

  3. Ownership, transfer, and duration of the rights: The moral rights are granted to the author and retained by the author even after she transfers the copyright in the work to someone else. The author may not assign her moral rights, but may expressly waive them in writing in a particular instance. In the case of works created on or after the effective date of VARA (June 1, 1991), the rights of attribution and integrity last for the life of the author, or in the case of joint authors, for as long as any author survives. In the case of works created earlier than the effective date, the moral rights will endure as long as the economic rights in the work, assuming that the author retained title to the work June 1, 1991. If the author did not retain title on June 1, 1991, the work carries no moral rights. [155]

  4. Exception to moral rights: The owner of a building into which a work of visual art is incorporated may, *under limited circumstances*, remove the work from the building even though removal will destroy, distort, mutilate, or otherwise modify the work (Copyright Act §113(d)). [155]

C. Other sources of protection for moral rights: Other, more indirect methods of protecting moral rights may be available in the case of works other than works of visual art. For example, the author may assert the copyright right of adaptation to prevent mutilation of the work, if he retains copyright. In addition, unfair competition laws may sometimes be used to prohibit false designations of the origin or false representations about the work. In addition, state contract and defamation law, and specialized *state* moral rights statutes may assist an author. [155-156]

XI. DIRECT AND INDIRECT INFRINGEMENT

A. Direct infringement: Anyone who makes an unauthorized reproduction, adaptation, distribution to the public, public performance or public display may be liable for direct infringement to the owner of the copyright in the work. Lack of intent to infringe or lack of knowledge of the copyright will not avoid liability, but may affect the remedy available to the plaintiff. Anyone who violates the moral rights of attribution or integrity in a qualifying work of visual art is liable to the *author* of the work. [156-157]

B. Contributory infringement liability: One who knowingly induces, causes, or materially contributes to the infringing conduct of another is liable for contributory infringement. Generally, two elements must be demonstrated: (1) the defendant must know or have reason to know of the other person's infringing activity; and (2) the defendant must actively participate by inducing, materially contributing to, or furthering the other person's directly infringing activity. [157]

    1. The *Sony* rule: In the *Sony* decision, the Supreme Court held that a person will not be liable for providing products that *could* be used to infringe but are also capable of substantial non-infringing uses, merely because he has constructive notice that some purchasers may use the products to infringe. The Ninth Circuit has subsequently held that if the provider *learns of specific acts of infringement through use of its products or services*, it then incurs a duty to act to stop further infringement. Failure to act will constitute contributory infringement with respect to any direct infringement that occurs thereafter. However, to incur this duty to act, the provider must have the actual knowledge of infringement *at a time in which he is in a position to stop it*. If the provider no longer has any substantial interaction with the direct infringer at the time he learns of the infringement, he will have no duty to act to stop the infringement. [157-158]

    2. The *Grokster* "inducement" cause of action: The Supreme Court held, in the *Grokster* case, that the *Sony* rule does not apply to shelter the provider of products used to infringe (even if the products are capable of substantial, noninfringing uses) if the defendant distributed the product with the *clear object of promoting its use to infringe* copyright, as shown by clear expression or other affirmative steps taken to foster infringement. Relevant evidence of bad intent in *Grokster* included: 1) the defendants' attempts to capture an audience known to want the means to infringe; 2) the defendants' failure to develop filtering tools or other mechanisms to diminish infringing use of the product; and 3) the defendants' adoption of a business model that depended on user infringement. The court stressed that neither 2) nor 3), on its own would suffice to demonstrate bad intent, but that the three forms of evidence, in combination, could suffice. [159-160]

C. Vicarious infringement liability: Vicarious liability may be found whenever the defendant has 1) the right and ability to control or supervise the direct infringer; and 2) a direct financial interest in the infringement. It is not necessary that the defendant know of or participate in the direct infringement. [158]

D. Infringement on the Internet: Due to special concerns about copyright infringement on the Internet, and the possibility of Internet service providers being held liable for their users' infringement, Congress enacted Copyright Act §512, which provides a series of safe harbors from infringement liability for Internet service providers. [160-161]

XII. THE FAIR USE AND OTHER DEFENSES TO INFRINGEMENT

A. The nature of the fair use defense: The fair use defense is available once a *prima facie* showing of copyright infringement or violation of the moral rights in a work of visual art has been made. It is founded on notions of equity and common sense, and must be applied on a case-by-case basis to identify and permit unauthorized uses of copyrighted works that further the purposes of copyright law without significantly undercutting authors' incentive to create. Examples of uses that may be found fair (listed in Copyright Act §107) include uses "for purposes such as criticism, comment, news reporting, teaching (including multiple copies for classroom use), scholarship or research." [162]

B. The four factors: Copyright Act §107 provides four factors that courts should consider in determining whether a defendant's use was fair: (1) "The purpose and character of the use, including whether such use is of a commercial nature or is for nonprofit educational purposes"; (2) "the nature of the copyrighted work"; (3) "the amount and substantiality of the portion used in relation to the copyrighted work as a whole"; and (4) "the effect of the use upon the potential market for or value of the copyrighted work." No one factor is dispositive, though the Supreme Court has indicated that the fourth factor (the effect of the use on the plaintiff's potential market) is the most important. Courts have sometimes augmented these four factors with additional considerations. [162-165]

C. Special considerations in parody cases: A parody based on a copyrighted work is more likely to be excused as a fair use if the parody is at least in part aimed at the copyrighted work itself. If it is, the defendant generally may copy to the extent necessary to "conjure up" the copyrighted work in the audience's mind, so that the audience will understand the parody. This may involve taking the "heart" of the plaintiff's work. The amount the parodist can copy beyond that may depend on whether or not his sole purpose was to parody the copyrighted work. [165-166]

D. Reverse engineering object code: The intermediate copying of object code that takes place in the course of reverse engineering (decompiling) a computer program may be excused as a fair use when reverse engineering is the only means of gaining access to unprotected ideas and functional elements embodied in the object code, and the defendant has a legitimate interest in gaining such access to those ideas and elements. [166]

E. Copyright misuse: The copyright misuse defense is an equitable defense that renders a copyright unenforceable if the copyright owner has engaged in misconduct in licensing or enforcing the copyright, thereby broadening the scope of his monopoly right beyond that intended by Congress. Under the misuse doctrine, the owner's copyright will be unenforceable until the misuse ends and its effects have dissipated. The misuse doctrine may apply even in the absence of an antitrust violation. [167]

XIII. ANTI-CIRCUMVENTION AND DIGITAL RIGHTS MANAGEMENT PROVISIONS

A. **Anti-circumvention provisions:** The Digital Millennium Copyright Act makes it illegal to *circumvent* a technological measure that effectively controls *access* to a work protected under the Copyright Act. It also makes it illegal to manufacture or traffic in devices or services to defeat technological protection measures (both measures to *control access* to the work and measures to *control exercise of the exclusive rights of the copyright owner*, once access is gained). However, the devices or services must be: (1) primarily designed or produced for the purpose of circumventing; (2) have only limited commercially significant purposes or uses other than to circumvent; or (3) be marketed for use in circumventing. [168]

1. **Circumvention:** To circumvent a technological measure is to descramble a scrambled work, decrypt an encrypted work, or otherwise avoid, bypass, remove, deactivate, or impair a technological measure without the authority of the copyright owner. [169-170]

2. **Technological measure:** A technological measure effectively controls *access* to a work if, in the ordinary course of its operation, it requires the application of information or a process or treatment, with the authority of the copyright owner, to gain access to the work. [170]

3. **Unauthorized use of passwords:** Courts have split over whether unauthorized use of a password that was issued to someone else constitutes circumvention of a technological measure that controls access to a copyrighted work.

4. **Relationship of anticircumvention violation to infringement of copyright:** The Circuits appear to differ over what, if any, relationship there is between copyright infringement and violation of the anticircumvention provisions. The Second Circuit has suggested that the DMCA targets circumvention and does not concern itself with what is done with copyrighted material after circumvention has occurred. Thus, it is essentially irrelevant whether the circumvention results in copyright infringement. The Federal Circuit, by contrast, has held that the anticircumvention provisions were not intended to provide a new property right to copyright owners, but only to provide a new means of protecting existing rights created under the Copyright Act. Thus, §1201 only prevents trafficking in access control circumvention devices or services (and presumably, access control circumvention itself) if the use of the device (or the circumvention) will infringe or facilitate infringement of copyright. Trafficking in access control circumvention devices or the that enable product owners to *use* software control embedded in consumer products (as opposed to copy, adapt, distribute, perform, or display the software) thus will not violate §1201(a).

5. **Exceptions:** There are some specific exceptions to DMCA liability to accommodate reverse engineering of software to achieve interoperability, law enforcement activities, good-faith encryption research, and security testing of computer systems or networks. [172]

B. **Copyright management information:** Copyright management information includes information that identifies the work, or its creators or copyright owner; terms or conditions for use of the work; and any identifying numbers or symbols. The Digital Millennium Copyright Act prohibits persons from intentionally removing or altering copyright management information, or knowingly distributing copies or phonorecords with illegally modified copyright management information. 17 U.S.C. §1202. [172]

XIV. OWNERSHIP OF COPYRIGHT

A. **Initial owner of copyright:** The author of a work is the initial owner of the copyright in it and may either exploit the work herself or transfer some or all of the rights to others. Unless the work is a work for hire, the author is the person who conceives of the copyrightable expression and fixes it or causes it to be fixed in a tangible form. [172]

  1. **Ownership of copyright in joint works:** The authors of a joint work are co-owners of a single copyright in the work. A joint work is "a work prepared by two or more authors with the intention that their contributions be merged into inseparable or interdependent parts of a unitary whole." (Copyright Act §101) To have a joint work, each author must have intended to contribute a part to a unitary whole at the time she created her portion. Each joint author must also have contributed copyrightable expression, not just ideas or facts. The Ninth Circuit requires that a party have *decision-making authority* over the work before he will be deemed a joint author. The Second and Seventh Circuits have focused on whether the participants *intended* for an individual to be a joint author. Evidence that the individual had decision-making authority is relevant to that determination, along with other circumstantial evidence of the parties' intent. [172-173]

  2. **Works for hire:** If a work is "made for hire" within the meaning of the Copyright Act, the employer or other person who ordered and financed the work is deemed the author for copyright purposes and is the initial owner of the copyright. There are two ways in which a work may be found to be a work for hire. First, it is a work for hire if it was prepared by an employee within the scope of his employment. Common-law agency principles should be used to determine whether someone is an employee for this purpose. If the hiring party has the right to control the manner and means by which the work is accomplished, then the worker probably is an employee. Second, works created by independent contractors (rather than employees) may be works for hire if: (1) the work fits into one of nine enumerated categories of works; and (2) the parties have expressly agreed in a written, signed instrument that the work will be considered a work made for hire. [174-175]

  3. **Ownership of copyright in collective works:** In the absence of an express assignment of copyright, the author of each separate contribution in a collective work retains copyright in that contribution. The author of the collection owns copyright in the expression he or she contributed—usually the selection and arrangement of the individually copyrightable contributions. Copyright Act §201(c) provides that in the absence of a writing to the contrary, the author of the collective work will have the following privileges with regard to the individual works he has collected: the privilege to reproduce and distribute the individual contributions as part of the collective work; the privilege to reproduce the individual contributions as part of later revisions of the same collective work; and the privilege to reproduce the individual contributions in a later work of the same series. The Supreme Court has ruled that this privilege does not permit the collective work author to make the individual contributions available in expansive database collections, such as NEXIS. However, courts have held that the §201(c) privilege allows the collective work author to reproduce and distribute CD-ROM collections of all their past editions. [175-176]

B. **Divisibility of ownership:** Copyright ownership is divisible. The copyright owner may transfer some or all of her exclusive rights. Any person who receives an exclusive right under the copyright is considered a copyright owner and has the right to sue to enforce the right she owns against others. A person who has only a non-exclusive right is a licensee and has no standing to sue for infringement. [176]

C. **Transfer of copyright:** All transfers of exclusive rights must be in writing and signed by the transferor, unless the transfer is by operation of law. Transfers of non-exclusive rights (licenses) need not be in writing. The Copyright Act provides that transfers and other documents pertaining to copyright may be recorded in the Copyright Office. Proper recordation of a transfer serves as constructive notice of the transfer to others. [177]

XV. NOTICE OF COPYRIGHT

A. **The Copyright Act of 1909:** Prior to January 1, 1978, the United States had a dual system of copyright protection. Common-law copyright protected works prior to publication. When the work was published, common-law protection ceased. Upon publication, federal statutory copyright protection began if all the authorized published copies carried proper notice of copyright. Failure to include notice on even a few published copies, or failure to give notice in the proper form or location, generally lead to forfeiture of all copyright in the work. [177]

1. **Publication under the 1909 Act:** The fact that a work had been made public or commercially exploited did not necessarily mean that it had been "published," for purposes of copyright protection. As a general matter, publication required physically distributing tangible copies of the work to members of the public without restriction. Courts sometimes distinguished between investive and divestive publications. In the case of divestive publications, they found that a "limited publication"—a distribution of copies to a selected group of people for a limited purpose—would not divest the owner of common-law copyright. [177-178]

B. **The Copyright Act of 1976:** When Congress enacted the Copyright Act of 1976 (which became effective January 1, 1978), it did away with the dual system of copyright, providing that federal statutory copyright *commences upon fixation* of a work in tangible form. Congress preempted state copyright protection in fixed works. The 1976 Act provided that notice of copyright must be placed on all visually perceptible copies that were publicly distributed, and that notice of copyright in sound recordings must be placed on all publicly distributed phonorecords. [178-179]

1. **Savings provisions:** Copyright Act §405 provides that if authorized copies or phonorecords were publicly distributed without copyright notice, the copyright in the work will be invalidated unless one of three conditions was satisfied: (1) only a relatively small number of copies or phonorecords was distributed to the public without notice; (2) the work is registered with the Copyright Office within five years of the public distribution without notice and the owner makes reasonable efforts to add notice to all of the copies distributed to the public in the United States after the omission is discovered; or (3) notice was omitted in violation of an express, written agreement conditioning authorization to publish on provision of notice. [179]

C. **The Berne Convention amendments:** When the United States joined the Berne Convention, it had to eliminate notice requirements in order to comply with the Berne Convention prohibition against subjecting enjoyment of copyright to "any formality." The Berne Convention Implementation Act amended the Copyright Act of 1976 to provide that compliance with the notice provisions would be voluntary, rather than mandatory, for copies and phonorecords distributed to the public *after March 1, 1989*. However, the Berne Convention Implementation Act did not restore copyrights that had already been lost due to lack of notice under either the 1909 or the 1976 Copyright Act. [179-180]

1. **Foreign copyright restoration:** As a general matter, the status of copyright in a work is determined pursuant to the notice provisions that were applicable at the time that copies or phonorecords were distributed without notice. If copyright was forfeited under those provisions, it remains forfeited. However, Congress enacted an important *exception to this rule* in the Uruguay Round Agreements Act. As amended, Copyright Act §104A restores (or, in the case of sound recordings fixed prior to February, 1972, creates) copyright in works originating in foreign countries belonging to the Berne Convention or the World Trade Organization that have fallen into the U.S. public domain for reasons other than the normal expiration of their term of protection. The Act restored (or created) copyright in qualifying foreign works automatically, and the restored copyright will endure for the remainder of the term the work would have enjoyed had copyright not previously been denied or forfeited under U.S. law. The restored copyrights are enforceable against persons having notice of the owner's intent to enforce. However, the Uruguay Round Agreements Act limits the circumstances in which restored copyrights can be enforced against "reliance parties." [180]

XVI. DEPOSIT AND REGISTRATION

A. **Deposit requirements:** The owner of copyright or the publication rights in a published work must deposit two copies or phonorecords of the best edition of the work with the Copyright Office within three months of publication. The Copyright Office has made some exceptions to this rule. Failure to comply with the deposit requirements is punishable by fine, but not by forfeiture of copyright. [180-181]

B. **Registration requirements:** A copyright owner may register copyright in a work (published or unpublished) at any time during the copyright. If a work is registered before or within five years after first publication, the certificate of registration will constitute *prima facie* evidence of the validity of the copyright and the facts stated in the certificate. In the case of works whose "country of origin" is the United States, the owner of copyright *must* register her copyright or show that she attempted to register and was refused, before she can bring suit for infringement. (A work's country of origin is the United States if it was first published in the United States, was simultaneously published in the United States and another country, or in the case of unpublished works, was created entirely by U.S. authors.) Regardless of a work's country of origin, failure to register before infringement began (in the case of unpublished works) or within three months after first publication will result in a denial of statutory damages and attorney fees. (The author of a work of visual art is not required to register the work in order to enjoy or enforce her subsection 106A moral rights in it.) [181-182]

XVII. THE DURATION OF COPYRIGHT PROTECTION

A. **Commencement of federal copyright:** Under the Copyright Act of 1909, federal copyright in most cases commenced upon publication of the work with proper notice of copyright. Under the Copyright Act of 1976, which became effective on January 1, 1978, federal copyright commences upon *creation* of the work. A work is "created" when it is first fixed in a copy or phonorecord. [182]

B. **Duration of copyright for works created on or after January 1, 1978:** For works created on or after January 1, 1978, the duration of copyright is the life of the author plus 70 years. For works of joint authorship, the copyright endures for the life of the last of the joint authors to die plus 70 years. In the case of anonymous and pseudonymous works, and works made for hire, the duration of copyright is 95 years following first publication or 120 years following creation of the work, whichever period expires first. [182-183]

C. **Duration of the copyright for works created but not published before January 1, 1978:** Works that were created but unpublished on January 1, 1978 (and thus were protected by state common-law copyright) became protected by federal copyright on that date. The copyright will last for the life of the author plus 70 years or until December 31, 2002, whichever is longer. If the work was published on or before December 31, 2002, the copyright will not expire before December 31, 2047. [184]

D. **Duration of the copyright for works already protected by federal copyright on January 1, 1978:** Under the Copyright Act of 1909, federal copyright consisted of a term of 28 years. The copyright could be renewed at the end of that (first) term for a second term of 28 years, giving a total of 56 years of copyright protection. If the copyright was not renewed at the end of the first 28-year term, it expired. The 1976 Act retained the two-term arrangement for copyright for works that were protected by federal copyright at the time the 1976 Act became effective, but provided that the second term would be extended an additional 19 years (to a total of 47 years). The Sonny Bono Copyright Term Extension Act, enacted in 1998, further extended the second term of pre-1976 Act copyrights that were still in existence on its effective date (October 27, 1998). The Sonny Bono Act extended the Second Term an additional 20 years (to a total of 67 years). Thus, copyrights that *came into existence* before the effective date of the 1976 Act and *continued to exist* on that date enjoyed an initial term of 28 years and a second term of 47 years, for a total of 75 years. If they continued to exist on October 27, 1998, they enjoy a second term of 67 years, for a total term of 95 years. [184-185]

E. **Duration of moral rights in works of visual art:** In the case of works of visual art created on or after the Visual Artists' Rights Act's effective date (June 1, 1991), the author's moral rights of attribution and integrity will endure for the life of the author (or, in the case of joints works, the life of the last author to die). For those works of visual art created before the Act's effective date, but to which the author retained title on June 1, 1991, the rights will last as long as the economic rights of copyright. [185]

F. **Rule for calculating the terms:** Under the 1976 Act, all terms of copyright run to the end of the calendar year in which they are due to expire. [185]

XVIII. RENEWALS OF PRE-1976 ACT FEDERAL COPYRIGHTS

A. **Ownership of renewal right:** The Copyright Act of 1976 retained the renewal term system for federal copyrights already in existence on January 1, 1978, so that federal copyrights in their first term on that date still had to be renewed in order to extend beyond the initial 28-year term. Like the earlier law, the 1976 Act specifies that the *author* of the copyrighted work owns the right to renew copyright in the work at the end of the first term (thus taking title in the renewal term of up to 67 years), if she is still living. If the author is not living at that time, her renewal rights pass to her *surviving spouse and children,* if there are any. If there is neither a surviving spouse nor children, the renewal right passes to the *author's executor,* who takes the right as the personal representative of the author's legatees under her will. If there is no executor, then the renewal right passes to the *author's next of kin*. The time to renew is the last (28th) year of the first term. Upon proper renewal, the person who is entitled to renew takes the renewal term free of assignments and licenses executed in connection with the first term. [186]

B. **Transferability of expectancy of renewal right:** Any of the persons enumerated in subsection A, *supra*, may convey their expectancy of renewal to a third party, if they clearly indicate their intent to do so in writing. However, the most that any of them can convey to the third party is what they have—merely a contingent future interest. If the conveyor does not in fact qualify to renew at the time to renew, the third party/transferee takes no rights in the renewal term. [186-187]

C. **Exceptions to the rule that the author and his statutory successors have the right to renew:** The person owning the copyright at the time to renew (rather than the author or his statutory successors) is entitled to renew if: (1) the work is a periodical, encyclopedia or other composite work and the copyright originally was secured by the proprietor rather than the author; (2) the work originally was copyrighted by an employer for whom the work was created for hire; or (3) the work was a posthumous one (one for which no copyright assignment or other contract for exploitation had been made during the author's life). [187]

D. **The process of renewal:** Prior to the Copyright Amendments Act of 1992, renewal term claimants had to file an application to renew with the Copyright Office during the last year of the first term of the copyright. Failure to make a proper filing cast the work into the public domain at the end of the first term. Congress amended the Copyright Act in 1992 to eliminate the filing requirement and provide that *renewal would be automatic for all remaining first-term copyrights*. The 1992 amendment nonetheless sought to encourage authors and their successors to continue filing for renewal on a voluntary basis: It provided that registration resulting from a properly filed application to renew would constitute *prima facie* evidence of the validity of the copyright during its renewal and extended term and of the facts stated in the certificate of registration. In addition, if a person who is entitled to renew registers the renewal term by filing an application, the renewal interest will *vest in that person as of the date of application.* By contrast, if the renewal occurs automatically, without filing, *the interest will vest in the person entitled to renew at the end of the first term.* [187-188]

E. **Renewals and derivative works:** When a license has been granted to make a derivative work based on a copyrighted original during the first term of copyright in the original, and the licensee has obtained no rights in the renewal term, reproducing, adapting, publicly distributing, publicly performing, or publicly displaying the derivative work made pursuant to the license will constitute an infringement of the second-term copyright in the original work. However, 1992 amendments to the Copyright Act provide that if an author fails to file for renewal, merely relying on the automatic renewal provisions to obtain a second term, derivative works made under first-term licenses can continue to be exploited. [188-189]

XIX. TERMINATION OF TRANSFERS OF COPYRIGHT

A. **Transfers executed on or after January 1, 1978:** All assignments and licenses of copyright executed by the author *after January 1, 1978,* are subject to termination under §203 of the Copyright Act of 1976 unless the work was a work for hire or the transfer was by will. It does not matter when the work that was the subject of the assignment or license was created. [189]

1. **Persons entitled to terminate:** In the case of transfers by a single author, the author may terminate. If the author is dead, persons who have succeeded to more than one-half of the author's termination interest may terminate in the author's place. The persons succeeding to the author's termination interest are the author's surviving widow or widower and children (grandchildren stand in the place of deceased children). If the author leaves both a surviving spouse and surviving children or grandchildren, then the surviving spouse owns one-half of the author's interest and the surviving children or grandchildren share the other one-half. The rights of the author's surviving children and grandchildren are divided and exercised on a *per stirpes* basis. When the grandchildren take a deceased child's interest, they can only act as a unit. If there is no surviving spouse, children, or grandchildren, the author's executor, administrator, or trustee will own the author's entire termination interest. [189]

    a. **Joint authors:** In the case of transfers by more than one author of a joint work, termination may be accomplished by a majority of the authors who made the transfer. If any of the original transferring authors is dead, his or her termination interest may be exercised as a unit by the statutory successors described above. [190]

2. **Time for termination and notice:** An assignment or license may be terminated at any point during a 5-year period of time that begins in the 36th year after the date the assignment or license was executed. (If the grant includes publication rights, the 5-year window of time begins in the 36th year after publication or the 41st year after the assignment or license was executed, whichever is sooner.) To terminate, the author or his successors must give notice to the assignee/licensee or her successor in writing two to ten years before the date on which the grant is to be terminated. The author's right to terminate may not be waived or relinquished by agreement. [190-191]

3. **Effect of termination and further grants:** On the date that notice of termination is given, the rights that will revert at termination vest in the author or the successors to his termination interest. When the termination date occurs, all rights that were terminated revert to the persons in whom they have vested or, if they died after the notice was given, to their next of kin or legatees. Further grants and agreements to grant the terminated rights may only be made after the effective date of the termination (with an exception for agreements for further grants to the party whose rights are being terminated). [191]

4. **Derivative works:** A derivative work prepared before termination of the assignment or license that authorized it may continue to be exploited after the termination. [191]

B. **Transfers executed prior to January 1, 1978:** Copyright Act §304 applies to *all assignments and licenses of rights in the renewal copyright term* executed before January 1, 1978, by either the author or the persons designated to take the author's renewal rights if he is dead at renewal time. It does not matter whether the grant of rights in the renewal term was made during the first or the second term of the copyright, as long as it was made *before January 1, 1978,* and gives rights during the renewal term. Assignments and licenses of works made for hire may not be terminated and dispositions by will may not be terminated. [191]

1. **Persons entitled to terminate:** The persons entitled to terminate differ according to whether the *author* made the grant or his *statutory successors to renewal rights* made the grant. Grants by the author must be terminated by the author. If the author is dead, then the same persons are entitled to terminate as in the case of post-1978 transfers, and in the same fashion. In the case

of grants by persons other than the author, all the persons who made the grant who are still surviving must join in the termination. [192]

2. **Time for termination and notice:** Under Copyright Act *§304(c)*, an assignment or license may be terminated at any point during the five-year period of time beginning at the later of the following two dates: (1) the end of the 56th year of the copyright; or (2) January 1, 1978. Section *304(d)* provides that if the copyright is still in its renewal term on the effective date of the Sonny Bono Act (October 27, 1998), but the termination right set forth in §304(c) has *expired without being exercised,* then the author or his successors will have a *new opportunity* to terminate during a 5-year period commencing at the end of 75 years from the date the copyright was originally secured. In either case, written notice must be served on the assignee/licensee or his successors two to ten years prior to the date of termination. [192]

3. **Effect of termination:** As in the case of §203, the terminated rights vest in all the persons entitled to terminate as soon as the notice of termination is filed. As with terminations under §203, no regrant or agreement to make a regrant can be made until the termination is effective, except that an agreement to regrant may be made with the party holding the rights to be terminated. [192-193]

4. **Other provisions:** Authors and their successors may not waive or contract away their termination rights. Persons who have made derivative works pursuant to assignments or licenses that have since been terminated may continue to exploit the derivative works. [193]

XX. REMEDIES FOR INFRINGEMENT

A. **Injunctions and disposal of infringing articles:** Preliminary and permanent injunctions may be awarded against copyright infringement and violation of the author's moral rights in works of visual art. The Copyright Act also provides for the impounding and eventual destruction of infringing copies and phonorecords and/or articles used to make them. [193]

B. **Damages and/or profits:** The copyright owner, or author of a work of visual art, is entitled to recover the actual damages that she suffered as a result of the infringement or violation, plus any of the defendant's profits attributable to the wrongdoing that were not taken into account in determining actual damages. However, there can be no double recovery. With regard to the defendant's profits, the plaintiff bears the burden of proving the defendant's gross revenues. The burden then shifts to the defendant to prove what, if any, amounts should be deducted as expenses or costs of producing the infringing work and what, if any, portion of his profits is attributable to factors other than his infringement. [193-194]

1. **Statutory damages:** The copyright owner/author may elect to recover an award of statutory damages, instead of actual damages and profits. The court may award damages of not less than $750 or more than $30,000, as it considers just. If the plaintiff proves that the defendant willfully infringed or violated her rights, the court may, in its discretion, *increase the award* of statutory damages up to $150,000. If the defendant proves that she was not aware and had no reason to believe that her acts constituted infringement or violation of an author's rights, the court may, in its discretion, *reduce the award* of statutory damages to not less than $200. Statutory damages are not available to copyright owners who did not register their works within the time frame set forth in the 1976 Copyright Act. [194-195]

C. Costs and attorney fees: Courts may, in their discretion, award costs against either party to an infringement suit, though generally costs are only awarded against a party who acted in bad faith. Attorney fees are routinely awarded to the prevailing party, regardless of whether it is plaintiff or defendant. [195]

XXI. INTERNATIONAL COPYRIGHT TREATIES

A. The Berne Convention: The Berne Convention, to which the United States adheres, is based on the doctrine of national treatment. In addition, the Berne Convention establishes minimum levels of substantive copyright protection that member nations must afford. Among other things, the Berne Convention requires members to protect a wide range of works (although sound recordings and the design of useful articles are not mandated), and to do so without the imposition of formalities as a prerequisite. The Berne Convention also prescribes a liberal term of protection, and specifies that member nations must protect a range of rights, including the right of reproduction, the right of translation, the right of adaptation, the right of public performance, the right of public recitation, the right of broadcasting, and the film right. The Berne also provides that member nations must protect the moral rights of attribution and integrity. Works first published in a Berne Convention member, or simultaneously in a member and non-member, and works created by nationals of Berne Convention members, must be protected. [195-196]

B. The Universal Copyright Convention: The Universal Copyright Convention (U.C.C.), to which the United States also adheres, is likewise based on the doctrine of national treatment. It protects "literary, scientific and artistic works" of nationals of member nations and of non-nationals who first publish in a member nation. "Literary, scientific and artistic works" has been interpreted to include most of the works protected under U.S. copyright law except photographic works, works of applied art, and sound recordings. The U.C.C. imposes fewer substantive requirements on member nations than the Berne Convention does. The U.C.C. prescribes shorter minimum terms of protection, and only specifically provides that the rights of reproduction, public performance, and broadcasting must be protected. The U.C.C. permits members to impose notice requirements and other formalities, and does not require that moral rights be protected. [197]

C. The TRIPs Agreement: The Agreement on Trade-Related Aspects of Intellectual Property Rights (TRIPs) is based on national treatment and requires World Trade Organization (WTO) members to comply with the provisions of the Berne Convention (with the exception of protecting moral rights). In addition, TRIPs specifies that computer programs and compilations must be protected as literary works, and that members must protect performers against unauthorized broadcast or fixation of their live performances, protect producers of sound recordings against unauthorized reproduction, and protect broadcasters or the owners of copyright in broadcast subject matter against unauthorized fixation, reproduction, and rebroadcasting. TRIPs also requires members to provide copyright owners with rights to prevent commercial rentals of sound recordings, computer programs, and cinematographic works. [197-198]

D. The WIPO Copyright Treaty: Ratified by the United States in 1998, the WIPO Copyright Treaty upgrades the Berne Convention by providing a general right of distribution for all works of authorship, and a specific right of communication to the public by online transmission. The WIPO treaty also requires that member nations provide protection against circumvention of effective technological measures used by copyright owners to protect their rights in copyrighted works. In addition, members must prevent persons from tampering with rights management information, or knowingly trafficking in copies or phonorecords of works with altered or deleted rights management information. [198-199]

CHAPTER 6
TRADEMARK LAW

I. THE NATURE OF TRADEMARK LAW

A. **The purpose of trademarks:** Trademark law ensures that consumers can rely on marks to identify the source of goods or services (and thus exercise their purchasing preferences) by prohibiting competitors from using marks in a way that confuses consumers about the source, sponsorship, or affiliation of goods or services. This makes a more efficient, competitive, and productive marketplace. [225-226]

B. **The relationship of state and federal law:** Trademark law developed as one of a number of related doctrines comprising the *common law of unfair competition.* Later, Congress enacted the Lanham Act, which draws on the common-law trademark doctrine and builds on it. Lanham Act §43(a) provides federal relief for infringement of unregistered indications of origin. The Lanham Act also provides a means of *registering marks,* through which traditional common-law rights can be enhanced. [226-227]

   1. **Administrative issues:** The P.T.O. handles registration of marks on the Lanham Act's Principal Register. In-house administrative appeals from examiners' registration decisions go to the Trademark Trial and Appeal Board. From there, dissatisfied parties can seek review on the record in the Court of Appeals for the Federal Circuit, or seek *de novo* review in a U.S. District Court. [227]

II. TYPES OF MARKS

A. **Trademarks:** A trademark is a word, name, symbol or device, or any combination thereof, that is used to distinguish the goods of one person from goods manufactured or sold by others, and to indicate the source of the goods. [227-228]

B. **Service marks:** Service marks are the same as trademarks except that they identify and distinguish *services* rather than products. To register a service mark on the Lanham Act Principal Register, an applicant must provide a *service that is sufficiently separate* from the sale of goods. This will not be the case if the service is normally expected and routinely rendered in furtherance of the sale of goods. [228]

C. **Certification marks:** Certification marks are words, names, symbols, or devices used by one person to certify that the goods or services of others have certain characteristics. Since consumers rely on certification marks for information about the products or services that bear them, the Lanham Act imposes restrictions on certification marks registered on the Principal Register. First, while the owner of a certification mark may use the mark to advertise or promote the certification program or the goods or services of others that meet its certification standards, it *may not use the mark in* *connection with its own goods or services.* Second, the owner must *police use of the mark* and prohibit others from using it for purposes other than certifying and from falsely certifying the existence of characteristics that their products or services lack. Third, the owner may *not discriminatorily refuse to certify goods* or services that satisfy its stated, objective standards for certification. [228-229]

D. Collective marks: Collective marks fall into two categories. First, *collective membership marks* are marks adopted for the purpose of indicating membership in an organization. Neither the organization nor its members use the mark to identify and distinguish goods or services. Second, *collective trademarks and service marks* are trademarks or service marks adopted by a collective organization, such as a co-op, for use by its members in selling their individual goods or services, and distinguishing their goods or services from those of non-members. [229]

III. DISTINCTIVENESS

A. Marks must be distinctive: Before a word, name, symbol, or device can be recognized and protected as a mark it must be *distinctive*—consumers must understand that it indicates source. Marks are often categorized according to their distinctiveness. Highest in the hierarchy are arbitrary or fanciful marks and suggestive marks, which are deemed *inherently distinctive.* Lower in the hierarchy are common, descriptive and surname marks, which are not viewed as inherently distinctive, and can only be protected *upon acquiring distinctiveness* through use in the marketplace. At the bottom of the hierarchy are generic "marks," which are *incapable of becoming distinctive* and cannot be the subject of ownership rights. [229-230]

1. Arbitrary or fanciful marks: Fanciful marks are marks that are made up, and have no meaning other than their trademark meaning. Arbitrary marks are those that have a meaning, but in no way describe the particular product or service they identify. [230]

2. Suggestive marks: Suggestive marks are marks that *indirectly describe* the product or service they identify. Two tests have been used to determine whether a particular mark is suggestive or merely descriptive. The first, called the *"degree of imagination" test,* holds that the more imagination the consumer must use to get a description of the product or service, the more likely the mark is suggestive. The second test looks to see if the mark is one that *competitors are likely to need* in order to describe their own products or services. If not really needed, the mark is more likely to be deemed suggestive. [230]

3. Descriptive marks: The descriptive mark category includes: (1) marks that *appear to describe the product or service* they identify; (2) marks that appear to describe the *geographical location* from which the goods or services emanate; (3) marks that are primarily merely a *surname*; and (4) other marks that are *commonly used* in connection with the relevant type of goods or services. In determining whether marks fall into the "descriptive" category, one must consider what consumers encountering the mark are likely to think. If they are likely to think that the mark describes the product or its geographic origin, it is descriptive regardless of whether it does in fact provide accurate information. Highly laudatory and very common marks are often included in this "descriptive" category. These marks are not considered inherently distinctive, and cannot be the subject of ownership rights unless they have attained secondary meaning. [230-231]

a. **Geographically descriptive and misdescriptive marks:** A mark is considered to be *geographically descriptive* or *deceptively misdescriptive* if: (1) it conveys to a meaningful segment of the purchasing public primarily or immediately a geographical connotation; and (2) those persons are likely to think that the goods or services in fact come from that place. The second condition may turn on the nature of the claimant's goods or services, and whether the indicated place is known to produce those kinds of goods or services, or at least would be a likely point of origin. Geographically deceptively misdescriptive marks cannot be registered unless they attained secondary meaning prior to December 8, 1993. The Federal Circuit has held that marks may not be deemed geographically deceptively misdescriptive unless the misdescribed geographical origin would be material to consumers' purchase decision. [231-232]

b. **Surname marks:** A mark is primarily merely a surname if its *overall impact* on the consuming public is a surname meaning and nothing more. If the mark has *no meaning* to the public, surname or otherwise, then it is not primarily merely a surname. If the mark has *both a surname meaning and some other reasonably known meaning in the language,* then it generally will not be deemed primarily merely a surname. [232-233]

c. **Evaluating descriptiveness:** Marks must always *be evaluated in light of the particular good or service that they identify.* In determining whether a mark is descriptive or inherently distinctive, it is essential to consider the overall commercial impression the mark would make on the average prospective customer. If the mark is a *composite mark,* one must consider the impression that the mark makes *as a whole* and not break it down into its constituent elements. *Misspelled* words must be treated as though they are properly spelled, as long as the phonetic identity between the misspelled word and the descriptive word is clear. *Foreign words* are generally translated into English and then evaluated to determine if they are descriptive of the product or service. [233-234]

4. **Secondary meaning:** Secondary meaning is attained when, due to exposure to the mark in the marketplace, the relevant consuming public views the mark not in its primary, common, descriptive, or surname sense, but as an indication of the source of the product or service. The Lanham Act provides that proof of substantially exclusive and continuous use of a descriptive mark for five years in connection with the product or service can be *prima facie* evidence that the mark has attained secondary meaning. [233]

5. **Abstract designs and other nonverbal marks:** Many marks, such as abstract designs and packaging shapes, cannot readily be characterized as arbitrary, fanciful, suggestive, or descriptive. As a general rule, common, basic designs, such as circles, squares, or stripes, are viewed as *merely capable of becoming distinctive,* so that secondary meaning must be demonstrated. Design or symbol marks that are *striking or unusual* are more likely to be found inherently distinctive. [234-235]

6. **Generic marks:** A generic "mark" is a word or symbol that the public associates with all products of a particular type or genus. A generic name or representation of a good or service cannot serve as a valid mark for that good or service. The standard for determining whether an alleged mark is or has become generic is whether its *primary significance to consumers* is an indication of the class or genus of product or service, or an indication of origin. [235]

a. **Determining the relevant "genus":** When a producer introduces a product that differs from an established product class in a significant, functional characteristic, and uses the common descriptive name of that characteristic as the name of the product, the new product becomes its own genus, and the term denoting the genus becomes generic if there is no commonly used alternative that effectively communicates the same information. [235-236]

b. Descriptive marks as generic: There is a difference of opinion among the circuit courts over whether a highly descriptive word like "tasty" or "delicious" should be treated as generic, and thus denied protection as a matter of law, even though it is not the common name for the type or genus of product or service. [236]

IV. THE CONTENT OF MARKS

A. **As used, the mark must create a separate impression:** To qualify as a mark, a word, name, symbol, or device must be used in a way that creates a separate commercial impression on the viewer or listener, apart from the other material used with it, and its impact on the consumer must be primarily to identify or distinguish the goods or services, and not merely to serve as decoration or to serve some other function. [236]

B. **Words, numbers, designs, etc. as marks:** Recognizable words and combinations of words (slogans), arbitrary combinations of letters, combinations of letters and numbers, and numbers alone may serve as marks. Drawings and other forms of art or design, scents, and sounds may serve as marks as well. A mark may be comprised of two or more of these various elements. Such composite marks must be evaluated as a whole for distinctiveness. [237]

C. **Trade dress:** Trade dress may be protected as a mark if it identifies and distinguishes the claimant's product or service. Under the modern view, color alone, such as the pink color of residential insulation, may be protected as a mark if secondary meaning is demonstrated. Trade dress typically falls into one of two categories: product packaging and product feature. A third, hybrid form of trade dress is the overall image of a business. In order for any feature of trade dress to be protected, it must be non-functional and distinctive. [237]

1. **The distinctiveness requirement for trade dress:** In *Wal-Mart Stores, Inc. v. Samara Bros.*, the Supreme Court distinguished between product packaging and product feature trade dress, and held that *product feature trade dress can never be inherently distinctive*. The claimant of trade dress rights in product features must always demonstrate secondary meaning. *Product packaging trade dress can be inherently* distinctive, as long as the combination of elements as a whole is not descriptive of the product, commonplace for that type of product, or a trivial variation on a combination that is commonplace. [238]

2. **The non-functionality requirement for trade dress:** Trade dress must be nonfunctional. In a §43(a) suit for infringement of trade dress, the plaintiff bears the burden of proving nonfunctionality. If product features are encompassed in the claims of a utility patent, this adds great weight to the statutory presumption that the product features are functional, and the trade dress claimant must carry the heavy burden of showing that the features are not functional, for instance, by showing that they are merely an ornamental, incidental, or arbitrary aspect of the product. [239]

a. **A two-part test for functionality:** In the *TrafFix* case, the Supreme Court set forth a two-part test for functionality. First, the court must apply the *Inwood Laboratories* test: Is the feature essential to the use or purpose of the article, or does it affect the cost or quality of the article? If the answer is yes, the product feature is functional and cannot be the subject of trade dress protection. If the answer is no, then the court must then apply the *Qualitex* standard: Would the exclusive use of the feature "put competitors at a significant, non-reputation-related disadvantage? If so, there is "aesthetic functionality," and the feature may not be protected. Only if the product feature is *nonfunctional under both tests* can it be protected as trade dress. The circuit courts of appeals have disagreed over whether it is appropriate to consider the availability of alternative product features in applying the *Inwood Laboratories* test. [239-241]

V. OTHER LIMITATIONS ON THE REGISTRATION AND PROTECTION OF MARKS

A. Scandalous or immoral marks: Marks that are scandalous or immoral will not be enforced or registered. Marks are scandalous or immoral if they give offense to the conscience or moral feelings or are shocking to the sense of decency or propriety. [241]

B. Matter that may disparage another: Under Lanham Act §2(a), a mark may not be registered or protected if it consists of matter that may *disparage persons,* living or dead, institutions, beliefs, or national symbols, or bring them into contempt or disrepute. The Trademark Trial and Appeal Board has held that whether a mark disparages persons, or brings them into contempt and disrepute, should be evaluated from the standpoint of a substantial component of the persons who allegedly are disparaged, not from the standpoint of the general public. [241-242]

C. Matter that may falsely suggest a connection with persons, living or dead, institutions, beliefs, or national symbols: Lanham Act §2(a) provides that matter that falsely suggests a connection with persons, living or dead, institutions, beliefs, or national symbols may not be registered. To disqualify a mark under this provision, it must be *clear that consumers will associate the mark with the person or institution at issue.* However, it is not necessary to demonstrate that consumers will be misled to think that the identified person is the source of the marked goods, or sponsors or is otherwise affiliated with them. This provision may be *used to protect state publicity interests,* enabling celebrities to prevent the unauthorized commercial exploitation of their identities. [242]

D. Deceptive marks: Under Lanham Act §2, deceptive marks will not be enforced at common law or registered. A mark is deceptive if it: (1) falsely indicates that the product or service has a characteristic; (2) prospective purchasers are likely to believe that the misdescription correctly describes the product or service; and (3) the misrepresented characteristic would be a *material factor to a reasonable consumer* in deciding whether or not to purchase the product or service. [242]

1. **Deceptive vs. "primarily deceptively misdescriptive" marks:** Deceptive marks (that cannot be registered or protected under §2(a)) and deceptively misdescriptive marks (that can be registered or protected with a showing of secondary meaning under §2(e) and (f)) can be distinguished on the basis of materiality. If the misrepresented characteristic would be *material* to consumers in making their purchasing decision, the mark is deceptive. If it would not, then the mark is deceptively misdescriptive. [242]

2. **"Deceptively misdescriptive" marks vs. "geographically deceptively misdescriptive" marks:** While Lanham Act §§2(e) and (f) permit deceptively misdescriptive marks to be registered and protected with a showing of secondary meaning, they do not permit "primarily geographically deceptively misdescriptive" marks to be registered, unless they obtained secondary meaning prior to December 8, 1993. The Court of Appeals for the Federal Circuit has held that

a geographic mark will not be either deceptive or primarily geographically deceptively misdescriptive, for purposes of Lanham Act §§2(a) or (e) and (f), unless the misdescribed geographical origin would be material to consumers in making their purchase decision. [243]

E. **Marks in prior use:** Lanham Act §2(d) prohibits registration of any mark that, when used in connection with the applicant's goods or services, is confusingly similar to a mark or trade name that *another began using before the applicant and has not abandoned.* However, an applicant's mark can be registered if the P.T.O. determines that *both* the earlier mark or trade name and the applicant's mark can be used *concurrently* without causing a likelihood of consumer confusion—for example, if each party restricts his use to a portion of the country that is remote from the other. [243-244]

VI. ACQUIRING OWNERSHIP OF MARKS

A. **Use of the mark in trade:** To acquire ownership rights in a mark at common law one must be the first to *use it in trade* (and make continuous use in trade thereafter). To use the mark in trade is to use it in a way that allows consumers to rely on it for its ultimate purpose—to identify the user's goods or services and distinguish them from other producers' goods or services. The use must be "in the ordinary course of trade"—not merely a token use made for the purpose of reserving the mark. [244-245]

1. **"Four-factor test" for determining if use is sufficient:** Jurisdictions have varied in the *quantity of use* they will require of a mark claimant before recognizing ownership rights. Some courts have held that a mark claimant need only make a single use, as long as the use is systematic and ongoing thereafter. Others have held that the unregistered claimant's use must be sufficient to notify competitors of his claim. Still other jurisdictions have held that a mark claimant must achieve sufficient market penetration to pose a meaningful risk of consumer confusion if a competitor commences use of a similar mark. Some apply a four-factor test to evaluate whether the claimant's market penetration was sufficient to warrant recognition of rights: (1) the volume of sales of the trademarked product; (2) the growth trends (both positive and negative) in the area; (3) the number of persons actually purchasing the product in relation to the potential number of customers; and (4) the amount of product advertising in the area. [245-246]

2. **Affixation:** In order to use a mark in trade and obtain ownership rights in it, one must also satisfy the *affixation requirement.* In the case of *goods,* the mark will be deemed "affixed" if it is: (1) placed on the goods themselves; (2) placed on their containers; or (3) placed on tags or labels attached to the goods or containers. Under federal law, the affixation requirement may also be satisfied by prominently featuring the mark in a conspicuous display associated with the goods. If the nature of the goods makes all the above impracticable, use on documents associated with the goods or their sale may suffice. In the case of *services,* use or display of the mark in connection with the sale or advertising of the services is sufficient, as long as the mark is used in direct, explicit reference to the services rendered. [246]

B. **Use in the case of descriptive marks:** In order to obtain ownership rights in descriptive, geographically descriptive, surname, or other marks that are not inherently distinctive, one must demonstrate that he or she was the *first user to obtain secondary meaning in the mark.* [246]

C. **Use in commerce:** To assert rights in a mark under the Lanham Act, a claimant must demonstrate that it has used the mark in interstate commerce, or in a manner that affects interstate commerce.

A party may qualify for Lanham Act protection if it uses its service mark to advertise its services in the U.S. but only renders its services abroad, as long as it renders the services in "foreign trade" (that is, trade between subjects of the U.S. and subjects of a foreign nation). This will qualify as use in commerce for *service* marks. [246]

D. **Protection of foreign "well-known" marks:** The Paris Convention requires the U.S. to protect marks owned by nationals of other member nations if the marks are "well-known" in the U.S. However, the circuit courts have split over whether the Lanham Act implements this requirement, thus enabling a foreign mark owner who does not use its well-known mark in the U.S. to bring Lanham Act infringement claims against domestic entities using confusingly similar marks. [247]

VII. FEDERAL REGISTRATION OF MARKS

A. **The significance of registration on the Lanham Act Principal Register:** Ownership of marks is automatic under the common law as soon as the mark is first used in trade (or, in the case of marks that are not inherently distinctive, as soon as the claimant obtains secondary meaning). No registration or other administrative process is necessary to acquire ownership rights. However, federal law provides that mark owners may register them on the Lanham Act Principal Register. Registration provides additional rights beyond those that would be available under the common law. [247]

B. **Advantages of registration on the Principal Register:** Only persons who have obtained ownership rights in marks by using them in trade may obtain federal registration. Registration on the Principal Register provides: (1) a right to assistance from U.S. Customs in preventing infringing goods from entering the country; (2) presumptions of mark ownership and validity and, after five years of registration, preclusion of certain challenges or defenses to the mark; (3) rights in the mark in a greater geographical area than often would be possible under the common law; and (4) immunity to dilution claims brought pursuant to state law. [247-248]

C. **Registration:** There are two alternative routes a person may follow in applying to register. First, a person who has already satisfied the use in trade and use in commerce requirements may file application papers with the Patent and Trademark Office (P.T.O.). The P.T.O. will examine the application and publish it for opposition. If there is no successful opposition, the P.T.O. will then register the mark and issue a certificate of registration. Second, a person may file application papers with the P.T.O. alleging a *bona fide* intention to use the mark in trade and interstate commerce. The P.T.O. will make an initial examination of the application and publish it for opposition. If there is no successful opposition, the applicant will have up to three years to make the necessary use in trade and commerce and file a statement of use with the P.T.O. After the statement of use is filed, the mark can be registered and a certificate of registration can be issued. The certificate of registration provides *prima facie* evidence of the validity of the registered mark, the registration of the mark, and the registrant's ownership of the mark and exclusive right to use it in connection with the goods or services specified in the certificate. [248-249]

1. **Constructive use:** Once the mark is registered, Lanham Act §7(c) provides that the registrant will enjoy "constructive use" throughout the country, commencing from his application filing date. This permits the registrant to assert priority (rights as the first user) over persons who make their first use of the mark after the filing date. [249]

D. The Supplemental Register: Marks that are *capable of* distinguishing an applicant's goods or services but are not registerable on the Principal Register due to lack of distinctiveness may be registered on the Supplemental Register. The primary benefit of registration on the Supplemental Register is that it may assist the registrant in obtaining registration of the mark abroad. [249-250]

VIII. CANCELLATION OF REGISTRATION

A. During the first five years of registration: During the first five years of a mark's registration, a person who believes himself injured by the registration may file a *petition to cancel* the registration on any ground that would have precluded registration in the first place. [250]

B. After five years of registration: If the mark has been registered for over five years, the Lanham Act *narrows the available grounds for cancellation*. The three important grounds for cancellation that are precluded after five years of registration are: (1) that the mark is not inherently distinctive and lacks secondary meaning; (2) that the mark is confusingly similar to a mark that someone else used prior to the registrant and continues to use; and (3) that the mark is dilutive of a senior user's mark. [250-251]

IX. GEOGRAPHIC BOUNDARIES

A. Geographic rights at common law: Under the common law, the first person to use a mark (or in the case of a mark that is not inherently distinctive, the first to obtain secondary meaning in the mark) is the owner of it. However, if a second person later uses (or acquires secondary meaning in) a confusingly similar mark in good faith in a remote geographic area, the second person will have superior rights in the mark *in that remote area*, by virtue of the *remote, good faith user defense*. [251]

   1. Remote geographical area: For purposes of determining whether the second party's use is "remote" from the first person's, the first person's geographic area is deemed to include not just the area in which it sells goods or services through use of the mark, but also those areas in which its mark has a presence by virtue of advertising or general reputation. [251]

   2. Good faith: Under the majority rule, a remote user acts in "good faith" if it has no notice that another person has made an earlier, similar use that is ongoing in the United States. [251]

   3. The zone of natural expansion: Under the zone of natural expansion doctrine, a senior user of a mark may assert seniority not just in his market, as defined above, but also in his "zone of natural expansion." He may prohibit a later user from using a confusingly similar mark in that zone even though the later user was the first actually to use the mark or have a presence there. The senior user's zone of natural expansion is that geographic area into which, at the time the other user entered, the senior user logically and foreseeably would eventually expand, given the nature of the senior user's business and the history of his prior expansion. [252]

B. The Lanham Act: Federal registration of a mark on the Lanham Act Principal Register expands the registrant's geographic rights in a mark beyond those he would enjoy at common law by giving *constructive notice* of his use of the mark, and/or *constructive use*. [252]

   1. Constructive notice: Lanham Act §22 provides that registration of a mark provides constructive notice of the registrant's use. Anyone who begins using a confusingly similar mark after the registration date is thus charged with notice of the registrant's prior use and *cannot claim to have begun his own use in good faith*. This deprives the subsequent user of the remote, good-faith use defense, and prevents him from obtaining superior rights in his remote geographic area. The practical result is that registration gives the registrant superior rights not only in her actual market area (as defined above) but also in all other areas of the country where the mark was not in use at the time of her registration. [252-253]

2. **Constructive use:** In the case of marks registered on applications filed on or after November 16, 1989, Lanham Act §7(c) provides that registration gives rise to constructive use by the registrant, throughout the country, as of its application date. This "constructive use" means that the registrant will be treated as though he used the mark in connection with the registered goods or services *in every part of the country on his application* date. This gives him priority over every person who commences use anywhere in the country after that date. (Except, of course, for persons who *applied* to register even earlier, and thus have an even earlier constructive use date.) [253-254]

C. **A likelihood of consumer confusion:** Under the majority rule, even if a mark owner has superior rights in a mark in a particular geographic area by virtue of federal registration, he will not be entitled to *enjoin another's use* in that area unless the defendant's use is likely to cause consumer confusion about the source, affiliation, or sponsorship of the parties' goods or services. This will only be likely if the registrant is also using the mark in the same area or has concrete plans to begin using it there in the near future. A minority of courts have rejected this rule (sometimes called the "*Dawn Donut* rule") as outdated. They have ruled that the geographic proximity of the parties should be just one factor in their multifactor test for likelihood of confusion. [254]

X. INFRINGEMENT OF MARKS

A. **The injury to be protected against:** Trademark protection addresses two major concerns. First, it protects the public's interest in being able accurately to ascertain the source of goods and services in the marketplace. Second, it protects a trademark owner's business good will against the lost sales and damage to reputation that may occur if others are permitted to use its mark in a manner that is likely to confuse consumers about the source of the parties' goods or services. [254-255]

B. **The infringement determination:** To demonstrate infringement, the plaintiff mark owner must demonstrate that the defendant 1) made a trademark use that 2) created a likelihood that an appreciable number of consumers would be confused about the source, sponsorship, or affiliation of the parties' goods or services. [255]

1. **Trademark use:** Under the language of Lanham Act §§32(1)(a) and 43, the defendant must make a "use in commerce" of the allegedly infringing mark, that is in connection with the sale or advertising of goods or services. This generally means that the defendant must closely associate the mark with goods or services that it is advertising or offering for sale (make a "trademark use"), so that consumers have an opportunity to rely on the use for information about the source of the defendant's goods or services. Generally speaking, courts have held that trademark law is not meant to prevent all forms of free riding on a mark owner's business good will. Thus, a finding of free riding, or of predatory intent, in itself, will not suffice. [255]

a. **Trademark use in the Internet context:** In the Internet context courts have reached a host of conflicting decisions concerning what constitutes a "trademark use." Thus, in cybersquatting cases, some courts have found that registering a domain name that incorporates a person's mark, with the intent to sell the registration to the mark owner, gave rise to infringement liability (even though the defendant did not use the mark to identify the source of any goods or services it was advertising or offering for sale). Likewise, in metatagging and contextual advertising cases, some courts have held that hidden uses of marks in metatags, or to trigger contextual advertising infringed even though the defendants did not use the marks to identify the source of any goods or services they were offering for sale, or even expose consumers to the marks. Finally, in cases in which the defendant adopted a domain name that was confusingly similar to the plaintiff's mark, some courts have found the requisite "use in commerce" "in connection with the sale or advertising of goods or services" even though the defendant did not sell or advertise any goods or services on his web site. These courts found that the Lanham "use" requirement was satisfied because the defendant linked to other sites that sold goods or services, engaged in acts that affected the *plaintiff's sale of goods or services*, or by holding that the defendant's gripe site provided an "information service" within the meaning of the Lanham Act. However, a number of other courts have rejected arguments that these kinds of actions constitute the requisite Lanham Act "use." [256]

2. **The likelihood of confusion requirement:** Courts have set forth a number of factors to consider in determining whether a defendant's mark is likely to confuse consumers. They include: (1) similarity of the marks (in sight, sound, and/or meaning); (2) similarity of purchasers; (3) similarity of marketing channels; (4) the sophistication of prospective purchasers and the cost of the goods or services; (5) evidence of actual confusion; (6) the manner of presenting the mark; (7) the strength of the plaintiff's mark; (8) the similarity of the parties' products or services; (9) the defendant's good faith; and (10) the plaintiff's interest in entering the defendant's market with the mark. In determining the likelihood of confusion, the court will not assume that consumers would have the opportunity to make a side-by-side comparison of the marks. A defendant's disclaimers of affiliation with the plaintiff are unlikely to avoid a finding of likely confusion unless the court is convinced that the disclaimers will be effective. [259]

   a. **Post-sale confusion:** The traditional focus of trademark law has been the likelihood of purchaser confusion *at the point of sale*. Many courts, however, have held that a likelihood of post-sale confusion may suffice to impose infringement liability. [262-263]

   b. **Initial interest (pre-sale) confusion:** Some courts have based a finding of infringement on evidence of initial consumer confusion that is dissipated prior to the actual purchase. This doctrine has been particularly controversial in the Internet context. [263]

   c. **Reverse confusion:** Most trademark infringement cases involve a subsequent user of a mark who causes purchasers to think that his goods or services come from the prior user. However, infringement can also be found when the subsequent user causes purchasers to think that the prior user's goods or services come from it (the subsequent user). [264]

C. **Trademark parodies:** In many cases the trademark infringement cause of action will not provide relief against a trademark parody because a successful parody depends on consumers realizing that the marks are not the same. The First Amendment protects parodies that do not constitute commercial speech. In such cases (as in all cases involving non-commercial speech) the court must balance the trademark interests against the First Amendment interests at stake. [264-265]

D. Collateral use of marks: Trademark law does not give mark owners absolute rights in their marks. Generally, unauthorized uses of a mark that *do not create a likelihood of confusion* will not infringe. [265]

   1. Resale of goods lawfully bearing a mark: The trademark doctrine of exhaustion (also known as the doctrine of first sale) provides that once a mark owner sells or authorizes goods to be sold bearing its mark, it cannot prevent subsequent owners from *reselling the goods with the mark* even if the goods have been used or changed. However, subsequent owners' use of the mark must be truthful, and not misleading, and must not lead to a likelihood of confusion about the immediate source or nature of the goods. [265-266]

   2. Gray market goods: Gray market goods are goods that are manufactured abroad for sale in foreign markets, that the foreign manufacturer properly, legally marks with a trademark that is registered in the United States. After these goods are released in foreign markets, parties buy them and import them into the United States for resale in competition with the U.S. owner of the same mark. As a general matter, the import and sale of gray market goods will not constitute infringement of the U.S. registrant's mark if the imported goods are *the same* as those sold by the U.S. registrant (do not materially differ) and the *U.S. registrant and the foreign manufacturer are the same or related entities*. However, if the gray goods are materially different from the goods sold domestically by the U.S. mark registrant, they will infringe, even if the U.S. mark registrant is related to the foreign manufacturer. (The reason for this is that consumers who rely on the mark to indicate that the goods are consistent with those they purchased in the past will be misled.) If the U.S. registrant and the foreign manufacturer are not related entities the gray goods will infringe, even if identical. [266-267]

   3. Competitors' use of marks for comparison purposes: A mark owner's competitors may use its mark in selling their own goods and services—for example, as a means of informing consumers that the goods are comparable—as long as their use is truthful and does not create a likelihood of consumer confusion about the source, sponsorship, or affiliation of their goods or services. [267]

E. Trademark counterfeiting: Trademark counterfeiting entails *intentional, knowing use of a spurious mark that is identical* to (or substantially indistinguishable from) a registered mark, on the *same kind of goods or services* for which the mark is registered. U.S. trademark law provides special civil remedies against counterfeiting, and criminal sanctions against persons who intentionally traffic or attempt to traffic in goods through use of marks they know to be counterfeit. [267]

F. Contributory infringement: A defendant will be held liable for contributory infringement if: (1) he intentionally suggests, directly or by implication, that another person infringe the plaintiff's trademark, and the other does so infringe; or (2) he sells goods to another knowing or having reason to know that the buyer will use the goods in a direct infringement of the plaintiff's trademark. The Seventh Circuit has held that parties can be liable for contributory infringement if they assist the direct infringer, knowing or having reason to know that she or he is infringing. However, the defendant has no duty to seek out infringement by others, or to take precautions against it. [267-268]

G. Vicarious liability: A person may be vicariously liable for another person's infringement if he is the infringer's employer, if he and the infringer have an apparent or actual partnership, have authority to bind one another in transactions with third parties, or exercise joint ownership or control over the infringing product. [268]

XI. TRADEMARK DILUTION

A. **The nature of the dilution cause of action:** Dilution statutes provide rights in highly distinctive, famous marks and trade names that are much broader than the rights available to mark owners under the trademark infringement cause of action. Liability for dilution may arise even though the defendant's use of its mark causes no likelihood of confusion, and even though the parties do not compete. (Often, the parties use their marks in connection with very different products or services.) About half the states have dilution statutes. These state jurisdictions have differed over whether the plaintiff's mark must be nationally famous or whether locally famous marks are protected from dilution. They have also differed over whether marks must be famous with the general public or whether "niche" fame is sufficient. The state dilution statutes create two causes of action for dilution: blurring dilution and tarnishment dilution. [268]

   1. **Blurring dilution:** Blurring dilution occurs when the defendant's use of a similar mark whittles away or "dilutes" the strong, immediate association consumers have between the famous mark and the plaintiff. [268-269]

   2. **Tarnishment dilution:** Tarnishment dilution occurs when the defendant's use of a similar mark casts the plaintiff's famous mark or trade name in a bad light and thus "tarnishes" the luster of the plaintiff's commercial image or reputation. [269]

   3. **First Amendment limitations:** The First Amendment may limit application of the state dilution cause of action when the defendant has used its mark outside of the context of commercial speech (speech that does no more than propose a commercial transaction). [270]

B. **The Lanham Act §43(c) cause of action for dilution:** Congress enacted a federal dilution cause of action in 1995, and extensively revised it in 2006. As revised, Lanham Act §43(c) enables the owner of a *famous* mark that is distinctive (either inherently or through acquisition of secondary meaning) to enjoin a defendant's *use in commerce* of a similar mark or trade name that is *likely to cause dilution by blurring or tarnishment*, if the defendant first used its diluting mark in commerce *after* the plaintiff's mark became famous. Relief is available regardless of the presence or absence of actual or likely confusion, competition between the parties, or any actual economic injury. However, relief is limited to an injunction unless the plaintiff can demonstrate that the defendant used its diluting mark in commerce after the Trademark Dilution Revision Act of 2006 was enacted, and that the defendant's acts were willful. [271]

   1. **Fame:** The revised federal dilution cause of action is only available for *famous* marks that are widely recognized by the general U.S. consuming public as a designation of source of their owner's goods or services. In deciding whether a mark enjoys the requisite fame, courts must consider all relevant factors, including: (1) the duration, extent, and geographic reach of advertising and publicity of the mark; (2) the amount, volume, and geographic extent of sales of goods or services offered under the mark; (3) the extent of actual recognition of the mark; and (4) whether the mark is registered. [271-272]

   2. **Dilution by blurring:** Under revised Lanham Act §43(c), dilution by blurring is "the association arising from the similarity between a mark or trade name and a famous mark that impairs the distinctiveness of the famous mark." In deciding whether a defendant's mark blurs a plaintiff's, courts should consider all relevant factors, including: (1) the degree of similarity between the mark or trade name and the famous mark; (2) the degree of inherent or acquired distinctiveness of the famous mark; (3) the extent to which the owner of the famous mark is engaging in

substantially exclusive use of the mark; (4) the degree of recognition of the famous mark; (5) whether the user of the mark or trade name intended to create an association with the famous mark; and (6) any actual association between the mark or trade name and the famous mark. [272]

3. **Dilution by tarnishment:** The revised §43(c) provides that dilution by tarnishment is "association arising from the similarity between a mark or trade name and a famous mark that harms the reputation of the famous mark." [272]

4. **Exclusions:** As revised, §43(c) provides several *express exclusions* from the dilution cause of action. First, it excludes "any fair use" of a famous mark "other than as a designation of source for [the user's] own goods or services," including nominative fair use, descriptive fair use, use of a mark in comparative advertising, and use of a mark in identifying, parodying, criticizing or commenting about the mark owner or its goods or services. Second, §43(c) excludes uses of marks in news reporting and commentary. Finally, §43(c) excludes "any noncommercial use" of a famous mark. Courts have construed this provision to confine the federal dilution cause of action to uses of marks in *commercial speech*, as that concept has been defined in the Supreme Court's First Amendment jurisprudence. The Supreme Court has defined core "commercial speech" as "speech that does no more than propose a commercial transaction." [272]

5. **Registration preempts state dilution claims:** Federal registration is a complete bar to dilution claims brought pursuant to state law. [273]

6. **Dilution claims and trade dress:** The federal dilution causes of action apply to all forms of marks, including trade dress. The Lanham Act specifies that when unregistered trade dress is claimed to be diluted, the plaintiff bears the burden of proving that the trade dress is nonfunctional. If the trade dress incorporates marks that are registered, the claimant must prove that the unregistered portion of the trade dress, taken as a whole, is famous separate and apart from any fame of the registered marks. [273-274]

XII. DEFENSES TO INFRINGEMENT AND DILUTION CLAIMS

A. **The fair use defense:** Use of a mark that has the capacity to describe a defendant's product, or its geographic origin, or that constitutes the defendant's name, in its strictly descriptive capacity, is protected by the fair use defense. In determining whether a defendant's use is a protected fair use, a court will consider the manner in which the defendant used the mark, whether the defendant acted in good faith, and the extent to which the defendant's use is likely to confuse consumers. If it appears that the defendant used the descriptive, geographically descriptive, or surname word or symbol in good faith strictly for the purpose of describing his own product, the court will be more likely to overlook at least a moderate chance of confusion that it otherwise would find actionable. [275-276]

B. **Nominative fair use:** The Court of Appeals for the Ninth Circuit has developed a doctrine of "nominative fair use" that is to be applied when a defendant has used the plaintiff's mark to describe or refer to the plaintiff's product. It applies the doctrine in both infringement and dilution cases. In order for the nominative fair use framework to apply: (1) the plaintiff's product must not be readily identifiable without use of the mark; (2) the defendant may only use so much of the mark as is reasonably necessary to identify the plaintiff's product; and (3) the defendant must do nothing that would, in conjunction with use of the mark, suggest sponsorship or endorsement of its product by the plaintiff. The Ninth Circuit has explained that when a defendant raises a nominative fair use claim this three-factor test should be applied instead of the regular eight-factor test for likelihood of confusion. [276]

1. **The Third Circuit's version of nominative fair use:** Under the Third Circuit's version of nominative fair use, the plaintiff must first prove that the defendant's use causes a likelihood of confusion under a "modified version" of the traditional multi-factor test that ignores the strength of the plaintiff's mark and the similarity of the marks, and emphasizes the degree of consumer care, length of time the defendant has used the mark without evidence of actual confusion, defendant's intent in adopting the mark, and evidence of actual confusion. If the plaintiff is able to prove a likelihood of confusion, the burden then shifts to the defendant to demonstrate fairness under a three pronged-test: (1) is the use of the plaintiff's mark necessary to describe both the plaintiff's product or service and the defendant's product or service?; (2) does the defendant use only so much of the plaintiff's mark as is necessary?; and (3) does the defendant's conduct or language reflect the true and accurate relationship between plaintiff and defendant's products or services? [277]

C. **Abandonment:** Under the Lanham Act, a plaintiff may be found to have *abandoned* its mark in two ways. First, when the registrant has discontinued use of the mark throughout the country in connection with the particular good or service, and has no intent to resume use in the reasonably foreseeable future, it will be deemed to have abandoned it. As amended, the Lanham Act provides that *nonuse for three consecutive years* is *prima facie* evidence of an intent to abandon. Second, a plaintiff may abandon its mark through acts or omissions that cause the mark to lose its significance as a mark. Such acts and omissions include: assigning the mark "in gross," apart from the business good will that the mark symbolizes; and licensing others to use the mark without adequately supervising their use to ensure consistency. [277-278]

D. **Challenges to the validity of the mark and to the plaintiff's ownership rights:** If the plaintiff has registered the mark on the Lanham Act Principal Register, the registration will serve as *prima facie* evidence of the validity of the mark and the registrant's claim to it. This shifts the burden to the defendant to disprove these matters as a defense to the infringement claim. At least until a registered mark attains incontestability status, the defendant may challenge the plaintiff's mark for failing to comply with *any requirement of common law or the Lanham Act*. If the defendant successfully challenges the validity of the plaintiff's mark, it cannot be liable for infringing it. [279]

E. **Federal registration incontestability status:** A person whose mark has been registered for five years and is in continuous use may obtain "incontestability" status by filing an affidavit to that effect, along with other information. Incontestability status eliminates two important grounds for challenging or defending against the mark: (1) that the mark is not inherently distinctive and lacks secondary meaning; and (2) that the challenger/defendant used the mark before the registrant (but this challenge/defense can still be asserted in connection with the geographical area the challenger/defender occupied prior to the registrant's registration and has continuously occupied since). [279]

XIII. TRADEMARK CYBERSQUATTING

A. **The Anticybersquatting Consumer Protection Act:** The Anticybersquatting Act amended Lanham Act §43 by adding a new subsection (d), that prohibits the registration, trafficking in, or use of a domain name that is identical or confusingly similar to, or dilutive of, another person's mark. There are two important limitations to the cause of action. First, the mark must have been distinctive (i.e., enjoyed trademark status) at the time the domain name was registered (or, if the claim is that the domain name dilutes, the mark must have been famous at the time the domain name was registered). Second, the plaintiff must demonstrate that the defendant acted with *a bad-faith intent to profit from the business good will of the mark.* Many courts have held that Congress's purpose in enacting the Anticybersquatting Act was to prohibit registration of mark-encompassing domain names for the purpose of commercial exploitation. [279-280]

1. **Factors to consider in determining whether the defendant registered the domain name with a bad-faith intent to profit:** Subsection (d) provides courts with a non-exclusive list of nine factors to consider in deciding whether a defendant acted with the requisite bad faith intent to profit from the business good will of the mark. These include:

    1. whether the domain name registrant has trademark or other intellectual property rights in the name;
    2. whether the domain name is the same as the registrant's own legal name or established nickname;
    3. the domain name registrant's prior use of the name, if any, in connection with the bona fide offering of goods or services;
    4. the domain name registrant's bona fide noncommercial or fair use of the mark in a web site that is accessible under the domain name;
    5. whether, in registering or using the domain name, the registrant intended to divert consumers away from the trademark owner's web site to a web site that could harm the good will of the mark (either for purposes of commercial gain or with the intent to tarnish or disparage the mark) by creating a likelihood of confusion as to the source, sponsorship, affiliation, or endorsement of the site;
    6. whether the domain name registrant, while failing to use the name itself in the bona fide offering of goods or services, offered to sell the domain name to the mark owner or to a third party for financial gain;
    7. whether the domain name registrant intentionally provided material and misleading false contact information in her application for the domain name registration application, or failed to maintain accurate contact information, and has engaged in a pattern of such conduct;
    8. whether the domain name registrant acquired multiple domain names that he or she knows to be identical, confusingly similar, or dilutive of, others' marks; and
    9. the extent to which the mark at issue is distinctive and/or famous within the meaning of Lanham Act §43(c). [280-282]

2. *In rem* **jurisdiction:** The Anticybersquatting Act provides *in rem* jurisdiction, permitting the mark owner to file an action against the domain name itself. To qualify, the mark owner must demonstrate that he exercised diligence in trying to locate or obtain personal jurisdiction over the domain name registrant, and was unsuccessful. The relief available in *in rem* actions is limited to an injunction ordering the forfeiture, cancellation, or transfer of the domain name. The Court of Appeals for the Fourth Circuit has held that this *in rem* jurisdiction is applicable in the case of §43(a) and §43(c) claims, as well as §43(d) claims. However, courts have held that *in rem* claims must be filed in the judicial district where the domain name registrar, registry, or other authority is located. [282]

3. **Remedies and limitation of liability:** Traditional trademark remedies are available under the Act, including injunctive relief, recovery of the defendant's profits, actual damages, and costs. The court may, in any case, order the forfeiture, cancellation, or transfer of a domain name to the owner of the mark. The Act also provides for statutory damages in cybersquatting cases, ranging from $1,000 to $100,000 per domain name. The Act limits domain name registrars' liability if they suspend, cancel, or transfer domain names pursuant to a court order or in the implementation of a reasonable policy prohibiting cybersquatting. [282]

B. **Personal names:** The Anticybersquatting Act also prohibits the registration of a domain name that is, or is substantially and confusingly similar to, the name of another living person. However, this action is a narrow one: It is limited to situations in which the registrant's specific intent in registering the domain name incorporating the plaintiff's name is to profit by selling the registration to the plaintiff or a third party for financial gain. Remedies for violation are limited to injunctive relief, including ordering the forfeiture or cancellation of the domain name or the transfer of the domain name to the plaintiff. [282]

XIV. REMEDIES FOR LANHAM ACT VIOLATIONS

A. **Injunctions:** Courts regularly grant injunctions against further trademark infringement. Preliminary injunctions may be available, as well. Plaintiffs in §43(c) dilution cases may *only* receive injunctive relief unless they are able to demonstrate (1) that the defendant first used its mark after the effective date of the Trademark Dilution Revision Act of 2006; and (2) that the defendant's acts were willful. [283]

B. **Monetary recovery:** The Lanham Act authorizes two measures of monetary recovery. First, the plaintiff may recover *actual damages* for injury to business reputation and lost sales. The Lanham Act authorizes courts to increase the actual damages the plaintiff is able to prove up to three times, if necessary, in order adequately to compensate the plaintiff. Second, the plaintiff may recover the amount of the *defendant's profits*, if the defendant has been unjustly enriched, the plaintiff has sustained damages from the infringement, or an accounting is necessary to deter a willful infringer from infringing again. Courts sometimes permit plaintiffs to recover *both* the actual damages they can prove and the defendant's profits, as long as they do not thereby recover twice for the same sales to consumers. To recover the defendant's profits, the plaintiff must prove only the amount of the defendant's gross sales in connection with the infringing mark. The burden then shifts to the defendant to prove whatever amounts he contends should be deducted in determining the final award. [283-284]

C. **Attorney fees:** In *exceptional cases* the Lanham Act authorizes a court to award reasonable attorney fees. This usually is not provided under common law. [284]

D. **Special remedies for use of counterfeit marks and for cybersquatting cases:** Federal law provides special, enhanced civil remedies for certain use of counterfeit marks and for violations of the Lanham Act §43(d) anticybersquatting provisions. There are also criminal penalties for certain uses of counterfeit marks. [284-285]

XV. INTERNATIONAL TRADEMARK TREATIES

A. The Paris Convention: The Paris Convention undertakes to ensure that each of its member countries grants protection to the nationals of other member countries against unfair competition in commercial and industrial matters, including mark infringement. It bases its protection on the concept of *national treatment*. Each member nation must provide as strong protection to nationals of other member nations as it would to its own. [285]

1. **Registration of marks:** The Paris Convention provides that a national of a member nation may register his trademark in any other member nation through *two alternative routes*: (1) by satisfying all the nation's registration requirements on the same basis as domestic applicants; or (2) by registering its mark in its home country and relying on that registration in its application to register abroad ("*telle quelle*" registration). In the case of *telle quelle* registration, registration in the foreign applicant's home country entitles the applicant to registration in the other member country, even if the applicant's mark otherwise would not qualify. However, a country may refuse *telle quelle* registration to a mark that is confusingly similar to a mark already owned by another in that nation, to a mark that has no distinctive character, or to a mark that is deceptive or contrary to morality or public order. [285]

2. **Effect of the *telle quelle* provision in the United States:** The Paris Convention's *telle quelle* provision dictates that the United States treat foreign applications more favorably than it treats domestic applications, since marks registered in other member nations must be registered in the United States regardless of whether they have been used in trade or commerce. However, this advantage is minimized by the availability of the U.S. intent-to-use registration process, the difficulty of demonstrating a likelihood of confusion in the absence of use, and Lanham Act provisions providing for cancellation of the registration of unused marks for abandonment. [286-287]

3. **Filing priority:** The Paris Convention provides that once a mark owner applies to register her mark in member nation A, she obtains filing priority (the benefit of her application date in nation A) in other member nations during the next six months. [287]

B. The Trademark Law Treaty: The Trademark Law Treaty simplifies international filings by harmonizing and simplifying the member countries' trademark registration standards and procedures. [288]

C. The Madrid Protocol: The Madrid Protocol provides an international system for centrally filing trademark applications in its over 80 member nations. A person owning a trademark registration or application in his home country can file one Madrid application that designates any number of other member countries in which the owner wishes to register. The applicant's home Trademark Office forwards the Madrid application to the International Bureau of the World Intellectual Property Organization, which processes it, provides an international registration, publishes the mark, and forwards the application to each of the countries the applicant has designated for territorial extension of the international registration. Each designated country then has 18 months to evaluate the application based on its domestic laws and either extend the international registration or refuse extension. Registrations under the Madrid Protocol have the same scope as the registrant's domestic registration, and are dependent on the validity of the domestic registration for the first five years. [288]

D. The Agreement on Trade-Related Aspects of Intellectual Property Rights: The WTO Uruguay Round TRIPs Agreement builds upon the Paris Convention and augments international trademark protection by imposing procedural and substantive standards for protection. [288-289]

CHAPTER 7
UNFAIR COMPETITION

I. THE NATURE OF THE LAW OF UNFAIR COMPETITION

A. An umbrella term: The law of unfair competition provides redress for various forms of improper marketplace behavior by businesses. While the law of unfair competition originated in common law, Congress has provided a federal cause of action in Lanham Act §43(a) that tracks the common-law unfair competition doctrines of passing off, false advertising, and commercial disparagement. [309-310]

II. PASSING OFF

A. The nature of the "passing off" cause of action: Passing off occurs when the defendant directly or indirectly makes a false representation that is likely to mislead consumers about the source, sponsorship or affiliation of goods, services, or businesses. Indirect misrepresentation includes use of a mark, trade dress, or trade name that is confusingly similar to the plaintiff's. Under modern law, a showing of intent to confuse consumers or actual consumer confusion is unnecessary to recover, at least in the case of passing off claims involving use of confusingly similar marks, trade dress, or trade names. The law of trademarks, covered in Chapter 6, is derived directly from the common law of passing off. Rules regarding distinctiveness, functionality, ownership, priority, common-law geographic rights, and infringement, discussed in that previous chapter, apply equally to claims of unregistered mark infringement, trade name infringement, and trade dress infringement, regardless of whether the claim is brought pursuant to Lanham Act §43(a) or state law. [310-311]

B. Lanham Act §43(a): Lanham Act §43(a) prohibits use of "false designations of origin" in connection with goods or services that are "likely to cause confusion, to cause mistake, or to deceive as to the affiliation, connection, or association of [the maker] with another person, or as to the origin, sponsorship, or approval of his or her goods, services, or commercial activities." This provides a federal cause of action for passing off claims involving infringement of unregistered marks, trade dress, and trade names. Because Congress relied on its Commerce Clause powers to enact §43(a), plaintiffs must establish federal jurisdiction by showing that the prohibited activities they complain of took place in or affected commerce. Plaintiffs in §43(a) cases enjoy the same generous remedies that are available for infringement of registered marks. Moreover, the courts, in construing §43(a), look to Lanham Act registration provisions for guidance in determining eligibility for protection, and to case law defining the likelihood of confusion determination in registered mark infringement cases. [311-312]

C. **Trade names:** In modern usage, a trade name is the name of a company, partnership, or other business and its good will. Even though the Lanham Act differentiates trade names from marks, permitting registration only of the latter, both the common law of passing off and Lanham Act §43(a) protect trade names on the same general basis that they protect unregistered marks. [312]

D. **Use of the passing off claim to fill the gaps left by other intellectual property doctrines:** Because the passing off cause of action (particularly under Lanham Act §43(a)) is very flexible, it is often used to protect interests that fall within the general subject matter of copyright, the right of publicity, and other areas of intellectual property. However, the Supreme Court's opinion in the *Dastar* case has set some limits on this practice, prohibiting construction of the Lanham Act in ways that undermine restrictions that Congress has placed on copyright and patent protection. [312-314]

III. FALSE ADVERTISING

A. **The common-law false advertising cause of action:** The common-law false advertising cause of action is available to redress a defendant's misrepresentations about the nature or characteristics of his own goods or services. The plaintiff may be required to demonstrate that it lost customers as a result of the misrepresentation (which often is difficult or impossible to do), but the modern trend is away from strict application of this requirement. In addition, it must appear that the defendant's representation was *likely to deceive or mislead prospective purchasers*. Statements that are not literally false, but are misleading or constitute "half-truths," may suffice to support liability. However, the misrepresentation must concern a factor that is *material*, or likely to influence consumers' purchasing decisions. Though it is not necessary under modern law to prove that the defendant *intended* to deceive, evidence of an intent to deceive may be relevant to support a finding that he succeeded in doing so. [314-315]

B. **State statutes:** Many states have enacted statutes prohibiting false advertising, and many of them provide a cause of action to competitors, as well as to consumers. These statutes often relax the common-law requirement of demonstrated loss of customers in the case of suits for injunctive relief. [315]

C. **Lanham Act §43(a):** Lanham Act §43(a) prohibits use of a "false or misleading description of fact, or false or misleading representation of fact" in commercial advertising or promotion that "misrepresents the nature, characteristics, qualities, or geographic origin of . . . goods, services, or commercial activities." The elements of the §43(a) false advertising cause of action for an injunction are:

1. a defendant's false or misleading statement of fact in advertising about its own product;
2. the statement actually deceived or had the capacity to deceive a substantial segment of the audience;
3. the deception was material, in that it was likely to influence the purchasing decision;
4. the defendant caused its goods to enter interstate commerce; and
5. the plaintiff has been or is likely to be injured as a result.

Because the Lanham Act §43(a) false advertising cause of action is limited to "commercial advertising or promotion," it is limited to false representations in commercial speech. Courts have also found that "commercial advertising or promotion" entails speech that is intended to influence consumer purchase decisions and that is widely disseminated. [315-316]

1. **The injury requirement:** To enjoin false advertising, the §43(a) plaintiff need only demonstrate that she is *likely to be damaged* as a result of the defendant's false representations. She can do this by demonstrating (1) that the plaintiff and defendant compete, directly or indirectly, in the same market; and (2) that there is a logical causal connection between the alleged false advertising and the plaintiff's sales position. Injury will be presumed for purposes of injunctive relief when a defendant falsely compares its product with the plaintiff's product by name. [316]

   a. **Injury for purposes of monetary relief:** To obtain money damages for false advertising, the §43(a) plaintiff must demonstrate *actual consumer reliance* on the false advertisement and a resulting *measurable economic impact* on the plaintiff's business. However, the impact may take a form other than lost customers. [316]

2. **Other requirements:** The defendant's representation must be *material*, but it need not be false in the literal sense. Representations that are literally true but misleading, due to innuendo, omission, or ambiguity, may be deemed "*implicitly false*" and give rise to liability. In the case of implicitly false representations, the plaintiff must prove that consumers in fact understood the advertisement to convey the alleged false message. The §43(a) plaintiff need not demonstrate that the plaintiff's misrepresentation was intentional. However, proof of deceptive intent may shift the burden to the defendant to prove an absence of consumer deception. [316]

IV. COMMERCIAL DISPARAGEMENT

A. **The common-law commercial disparagement cause of action:** The disparagement cause of action imposes liability for a defendant's false or deceptive representation about the quality or characteristics of a plaintiff's goods or services. While the elements differ somewhat, depending on the jurisdiction, three common elements are:

   1. a false or misleading representation about the plaintiff's goods or services;
   2. an intent to harm on the defendant's part; and
   3. specific economic loss, or "special damages" to the plaintiff.

   The defendant's statement may be any manner of communication, as long as it directly or indirectly communicates a false and disparaging message to consumers, and does not constitute mere puffing. While some jurisdictions will base liability on a false statement of *opinion*, most require a false statement of fact. A false statement of fact purports to give specific facts, or at least implies that the maker has specific facts to back up his assertion. While jurisdictions differ, the Restatement (Second), of Torts suggests that the defendant must have had knowledge that his statement was false or have acted in reckless disregard of its truth or falsity. [317]

   1. **The special damages requirement:** To obtain damages relief under the common law, the plaintiff must demonstrate actual monetary loss resulting from the defendant's disparaging statement, and this requirement generally has been interpreted to mean that the plaintiff must demonstrate an *actual, specific loss of customers*. Jurisdictions differ over whether special damages must be demonstrated in the case of suits seeking only injunctive relief. [317]

B. **State statutory provisions:** The Uniform Deceptive Trade Practices Act provides injunctive relief against false or misleading statements of fact that disparage the goods, services, or business of another, if the plaintiff demonstrates that it is " likely to be damaged" by the statements. The Act specifies that proof of monetary damage and intent to deceive will not be required. [317-318]

C. **The Lanham Act §43(a) disparagement cause of action:** Lanham Act §43(a) extends to disparaging misrepresentations about a plaintiff's goods or services. While this cause of action is similar to the common-law disparagement claim, it is more liberal. The elements include:

1. a defendant's false or misleading statement of fact in commercial advertising or promotion about the plaintiff's product, services, or commercial activities;
2. the statement actually deceived or had the capacity to deceive a substantial segment of the audience;
3. the deception was material to the purchasing decision;
4. the defendant caused its goods or services to enter interstate commerce; and
5. the plaintiff has been or is likely to be injured as a result.

Intent or knowledge on the defendant's part is not required. The plaintiff need not plead or prove special damages, at least in order to obtain an injunction. [318]

D. **First Amendment considerations in disparagement actions:** Under the *New York Times v. Sullivan* rule, developed in libel cases, *plaintiffs who are public figures* must show with convincing clarity that the defendant's libelous statement was made with *actual malice*—with knowledge that the statement was false or with reckless disregard of whether it was false or not—before they will be permitted to recover. The Court of Appeals for the Third Circuit has held that the *New York Times* rule will not apply in a commercial disparagement suit when the alleged disparaging statements constitute *commercial speech*. (The court defined commercial speech as " expression related to the economic interests of the speaker and its audience, generally in the form of a commercial advertisement for the sale of goods and services.") The Lanham Act §43(a) causes of action for false advertising and disparagement are expressly limited to statements made in commercial speech, Therefore, under the Third Circuit's rule, the *New York Times* rule will not apply in federal disparagement causes of action. The Third Circuit also suggested that a corporation engaged in commercial speech might not constitute a public figure, for purposes of the *New York Times* rule. [318-319]

V. MISAPPROPRIATION

A. **The nature of the misappropriation cause of action:** To state a cause of action for misappropriation, the plaintiff must demonstrate three things: (1) the plaintiff has made a substantial investment of time, money, skill, or effort to create an intangible trade value in which the court can justify finding a property right; (2) the defendant has appropriated the intangible trade value in a manner that constitutes "reaping where he has not sown" or "taking a free ride"; and (3) the plaintiff has suffered competitive injury as a result. In a few cases, courts have dispensed with the requirement that the plaintiff demonstrate competitive injury (or any injury at all) upon determining that the public interest would be promoted by granting relief. [320-321]

B. **Limitations on the misappropriation cause of action:** Because of the potential breadth of the misappropriation claim, courts are cautious in applying it, and generally will seek to avoid applying it in a way that will undermine the limitations imposed on other, more narrow, causes of action. The Court of Appeals for the Second Circuit has relied on preemption grounds to severely limit the misappropriation cause of action. [321-322] For more information regarding preemption, see Chapter 9.

VI. INTERNATIONAL TREATIES REGARDING PROTECTION AGAINST UNFAIR COMPETITION

A. The Paris Convention: The Paris Convention for the Protection of Industrial Property requires member nations to provide protection against passing off, false advertising, and commercial disparagement types of activities. While it does not require members to maintain a system of registration for trade names, they must provide basic protection against infringement of trade names. By virtue of the Paris Convention's national treatment provision, member nations must provide essentially as great unfair competition protection for the nationals of other member countries as for their own nationals. [322]

B. The TRIPs Agreement: The TRIPs Agreement incorporates the Paris Convention provisions on unfair competition, making them binding on all World Trade Organization members. [322]

CHAPTER 8
THE RIGHT OF PUBLICITY

I. THE NATURE AND PURPOSE OF THE RIGHT OF PUBLICITY

A. The nature of the right of publicity: The publicity cause of action recognizes that an individual has a right to control others' use of his identity for commercial purposes. While some states continue to view the right of publicity cause of action as one branch of the right of privacy, the publicity and privacy causes of action generally vindicate separate interests. While privacy vindicates the personal interest in avoiding unwanted intrusions, the right of publicity primarily vindicates an economic interest in the ability to commercially exploit one's identity. Some states have found a right of publicity in the common law, but others have enacted statutes that undertake to create and regulate the right. [327-329]

II. THE SCOPE OF THE RIGHT OF PUBLICITY

A. Commercial invocation of the plaintiff's identity: In order to recover for a violation of the right of publicity, the plaintiff must clearly demonstrate that the defendant has *invoked the plaintiff's identity* in the public mind. A defendant's use of the plaintiff's nickname, a cartoon image of the plaintiff, a phrase associated with the plaintiff, an impersonator, or other devices may suffice to identify the plaintiff to the public and give rise to a cause of action. A use of the plaintiff's identity may be deemed commercial for purposes of a right of publicity cause of action even if it would not qualify as "commercial speech," as that concept has been developed under the First Amendment. [329]

B. First Amendment concerns: Unauthorized use of the plaintiff's identity in contexts such as news reporting and entertainment may be deemed "commercial," but frequently will be protected by the First Amendment. The Supreme Court has held that in cases where "noncommercial" speech of this type is involved, the individual's personal interest and the state's interest in providing the publicity cause of action must be balanced against First Amendment interests to determine whether the use exceeds the bounds of First Amendment privilege. [330-331]

1. **Differing standards for evaluating the balance:** When a defendant makes an unauthorized use of a plaintiff's identity for commercial purposes, but the use does not constitute commercial speech, the court is likely to consider the extent to which the defendant's use of the plaintiff's identity is *transformative*—whether the work contains significant creative, expressive elements beyond the mere celebrity likeness or imitation. The more transformative the work, the more likely the First Amendment interests in a free marketplace of ideas and individual self-expression outweigh the plaintiff's and states' interest in protecting the plaintiff's economic publicity interest. Some courts evaluate the balance between privacy and First Amendment interests by considering whether the defendant used the plaintiff's identity in a work *related to* the plaintiff, or by considering whether the defendant's *predominate purpose* was commercial or expressive. [331-332]

C. **Descendability of the right of publicity:** Jurisdictions differ about whether and how long a person's right of publicity endures after his death. [332]

D. **Applicability of the doctrine of first sale:** The doctrine of first sale is applicable in connection with the right of publicity. [332]

E. **Remedies for violation of the right:** Defendants may be enjoined from violating a plaintiff's right of publicity. Monetary damages generally consist of the fair market value of the defendant's use of the plaintiff's identity. Injury to the plaintiff's reputation that may lead to loss of future publicity revenues may be compensated. Some jurisdictions have permitted the plaintiff to recover the defendant's profit attributable to unauthorized use of the plaintiff's identity, as long as it does not lead to double recovery. Punitive damages may be granted in extreme cases. [332-333]

CHAPTER 9

THE RELATIONSHIP BETWEEN FEDERAL AND STATE LAW

I. THE SUPREMACY CLAUSE

A. **Federal law prevails over conflicting state law:** The U.S. Constitution's Supremacy Clause provides that state causes of action are preempted if they stand as an obstacle to the accomplishment and execution of Congress's purposes and objectives in enacting a federal statue. [335-336]

B. **The *Sears* and *Compco* cases:** In the *Sears* and *Compco* cases, the Supreme Court held that state unfair competition causes of action that would prohibit the defendants from copying the unpatentable appearance of articles of commerce were preempted. The Court reasoned that, in enacting the patent laws, Congress attempted to balance two competing interests: (1) providing an incentive to invent by giving property rights in inventions and designs; and (2) fostering free competition by allowing freedom to copy others' inventive ideas and designs and build on them. Congress determined that the proper balance was to give limited monopoly rights in inventions and designs meeting the high standards of patentability and relegate those inventions and designs not qualifying for a patent to the public domain, free for others to copy. The state unfair competition causes of action, by prohibiting the copying of the latter types of inventions and designs, interfered with Congress's purpose. [336]

C. **The *Goldstein* case:** In *Goldstein*, the Supreme Court found that in omitting sound recordings from copyright protection (as the Copyright Act did at that time), Congress did not specifically intend to leave them in the public domain. Thus, the states were free to protect sound recordings from copying. The Court stressed that the state law at issue only prohibited lifting recorded sounds: It placed no restraint on the use of ideas or concepts found in the sound recording. [336-337]

D. **The *Kewanee* and *Aronson* cases:** In *Kewanee*, the Supreme Court applied a threefold purpose test in the place of the balancing language of the earlier *Sears* and *Compco* decisions. The Court described the purposes of Congress in enacting the patent laws as: (1) to provide an incentive to invent; (2) to promote public disclosure of inventions, so as to inform the public; and (3) to ensure that information already in the public domain would remain there. The Court found that a state trade secret cause of action did not interfere unduly with accomplishment of these purposes and that whatever interference there might be was counterbalanced by the interest of the states in exercising their traditional police powers to prohibit commercially unethical behavior and invasions of privacy through trade secret doctrine. The Court later applied the same threefold purpose test in upholding the application of state contract law to enforce a contract to pay for an unpatentable idea in *Aronson*. In *Aronson*, the Court stressed that the state contract cause of action gave no monopoly rights in the idea. [337-338]

E. **The *Bonito Boats* case:** In the *Bonito Boats* case, the Supreme Court found that the Patent Act preempted a state statute that prohibited the use of a direct "plug molding" process to duplicate unpatented boat hulls. The Court returned to its original "balancing" concept in *Sears* and *Compco*, but also purported to reaffirm its threefold purpose test, as well. The Court stressed that the plug molding statute removed ideas from the public domain and gave patent-like protection to the design ideas of boats. Moreover, the state was not pursuing any traditional police power goal apart from encouraging invention, which is a key purpose of the patent law. [338]

F. **Where do we stand now?** One way the cases discussed above can be reconciled is as follows: In enacting the patent laws, Congress intended that ideas not meeting the high standards for patentability would remain in the public domain, free for the public to use. However, a state law that prohibits or restricts copying may be tolerated if: (1) the protection is limited in scope, so that the level of interference with Congress's purpose can be characterized as slight; (2) ideas that are already in the public domain are not withdrawn; and (3) the state law is intended to promote a legitimate state police power goal outside the sphere of Congress's concern when it enacted the patent laws. [339]

II. COPYRIGHT ACT §301

A. **A uniform system of copyright:** In enacting the Copyright Act of 1976, Congress *intended to unify* copyright protection and *federalize it*. Thus, it enacted §301, which expressly preempts state causes of action that duplicate copyright protection. To be preempted under §301, a state cause of action must protect matter that is *"within the subject matter of copyright"* as set forth in §§102 and 103 of the Copyright Act. In addition, the state cause of action must *provide rights that are "equivalent" to the economic rights specified in §106* of the Copyright Act. More recently, in the Visual Artists' Rights Act of 1990, Congress amended §301 to add that state causes of action giving rights equivalent to the moral rights of attribution and integrity in works of visual art, as defined in Copyright Act §101, would also be preempted. [340]

B. **Subject matter of copyright:** Questions have arisen whether ideas, procedures, processes, systems, methods of operation, concepts, principles, and discoveries (facts) that are described in or incorporated into works of authorship are within the "subject matter of copyright" as set forth in §102, so that state causes of action protecting them may be preempted. There is case precedent and legislative history to support arguments on both sides of the issue, but the majority of judicial opinions have held that the ideas, procedures, processes, etc., *are within the subject matter of copyright* for purposes of §301. [341-342]

C. **Equivalent rights:** To be preempted, the state cause of action must provide rights that are equivalent to the exclusive rights of copyright (e.g., the rights to reproduce, adapt, publicly distribute, publicly perform, and publicly display a work of authorship) or are equivalent to the moral rights of attribution and integrity in works of visual art. The meaning of "equivalent" has been the subject of some disagreement in the courts, but *most courts have adopted what may be called an "extra elements" test for equivalency.* Under this test the court looks to see if the mere act of reproduction, adaptation, public distribution, public performance, public display, misattribution, or violation of integrity will in itself give rise to the state cause of action, or whether some additional element, that is not required for copyright infringement, must also be alleged. If no other element must be alleged, then the state cause of action is "equivalent" to copyright. If other elements are required, many courts will look to *see if the additional element is "qualitatively different" from copyright.* If not, preemption may still be found. The tests for qualitative difference include: (1) determining whether the element indicates a state purpose that differs from the purpose of copyright; (2) determining whether the extra element goes to the *scope* or to the *nature* of the state-created right; and (3) determining whether the "essence" of the state claim is one for copyright infringement or violation of an author's rights of attribution or integrity in a work of visual art. [342-343]

D. **Express exceptions to §301 preemption:** Copyright Act §301 expressly provides that states may protect unfixed works, and it preserves local landmark, historic preservation, zoning, and building codes relating to architectural works. In addition, §301 permits states to continue protecting (until Feb. 15, 2067) sound recordings fixed prior to Feb. 15, 1972. [344]

CHAPTER 1
INTRODUCTION TO THE STUDY OF INTELLECTUAL PROPERTY

ChapterScope

This chapter gives a very brief introduction to the various intellectual property doctrines, the source of the federal and state power to enact intellectual property laws, and to the public policies that intellectual property laws are meant to promote. Here are the main points to be addressed:

- **Federal law:** Federal law provides for patents and copyrights, provides rights in trademarks and other indications of a product or service's origin, and prohibits three forms of unfair competition: passing off, false advertising, and product disparagement.

- **State law:** State law provides rights in trade secrets, undeveloped ideas, and the commercial exploitation of an individual's identity. Also, concurrent with federal law, the states provide rights in trademarks and other related indications of origin, and prohibit a number of other forms of unfair competition.

- **Limited property rights in intangibles:** All of these intellectual property doctrines provide limited property rights in intangible products of investment, creative intellect, or labor.

- **Ultimate purpose of intellectual property laws:** The ultimate, overall purpose of the intellectual property laws is to ensure a rich, diverse, efficient, and competitive marketplace for the benefit of the general public.

  - **Providing financial incentives:** Most of the intellectual property doctrines (copyright, patent, trade secret, publicity rights) provide rights in intangible creations (inventions, original forms of expression, collections of information, celebrity personas) in order to provide a financial incentive to produce more of these intangibles and make them available to the public. These property rights are limited in many important ways, however, to ensure as much competitor and public access as is possible, short of undermining the creators' financial incentive to create.

  - **Promoting a competitive and efficient marketplace:** Rights in trademarks and related indications of a product or service's origin, and other rights against unfair competition, are not meant to provide an incentive to create, but to ensure that the marketplace is highly competitive and efficient, to promote product quality, and to protect consumers against deception.

- **Sources of federal and state power to regulate:** Congress is empowered to provide for patents and copyrights under the U.S. Constitution, Article 1, Section 8, Clause 8, and to regulate trademarks and unfair competition under Article 1, Section 8, Clause 3. The states retain power to create and regulate intellectual property interests unless Congress intended to preempt the field or enforcement of state-created interests would interfere with the accomplishment of Congress' purposes in enacting the federal intellectual property provisions.

I. SCOPE OF THE TERM "INTELLECTUAL PROPERTY"

A. Generally: The term "intellectual property" is used to identify a collection of distinct but related legal doctrines. These doctrines are created by both federal and state law. Federal law creates patents and copyrights, and provides rights in trademarks, general rights against passing off, and rights against false advertising and product disparagement. State laws create rights in trade secrets, undeveloped ideas, and the publicity value of an individual's identity. In addition, like the federal law, state laws protect interests in trademarks and related indications of product or service origin, and provide other rights against unfair competition (including rights against false advertising, product disparagement, and misappropriation). Each of these federal and state "intellectual property" doctrines is related to the others because it provides a limited form of property right in intangible products of investment, creative intellect, or labor. In some cases the doctrines overlap to provide alternative forms of protection for the same creation.

II. PRIMARY POLICY ISSUES

The predominant public policy concern underlying U.S. intellectual property law is to ensure a rich, diverse, competitive marketplace for the benefit of the general public. Note that this is a highly pragmatic goal. It contrasts with the philosophy underlying the intellectual property laws of many other countries, which place greater emphasis on the "natural rights" authors and other creators have in the product of their labor. In the United States, as a general matter, authors and other creators of intangible products or trade values enjoy no "natural right" in their creations. Any rights they enjoy are granted for the ultimate purpose of benefiting the general public.

A. An incentive to create: Most of the intellectual property doctrines seek to promote creativity, so that there will be a greater variety of products, services, and expressive works in the marketplace. These doctrines do this by giving inventors, writers, artists, business persons, and others limited property rights in their intangible creations. The granting of property rights protects creators' opportunities to recoup their investment in the creative process and earn a profit, and thus encourages them to invest their time and efforts in the development of new products, services, and expressive works.

B. Promotion of competition: Intellectual property doctrines also seek to ensure a competitive marketplace, which generally requires the freest possible public access to the new products, services, and expressive works that are created.

C. Potential conflict: The two goals described in paragraphs A and B, above—providing an incentive to create and ensuring public access—may conflict, since granting property rights in a creation may hinder others' access to it. First, it may permit the owner of the rights directly to prohibit competitors and/or the general public from using the creation. Second, it may indirectly limit public access by putting the owner of the rights in the position to charge monopoly prices.

D. Reaching a balance: To address this potential conflict, each area of intellectual property law strives to reach the optimum balance of interests, fashioning the property rights given to creators in a way that provides a sufficient inducement to create while preserving competitor and public access to the creation to the greatest extent possible. Property rights in intellectual property are always limited.

E. **Trademark law and related doctrines:** Trademark law and related unfair competition causes of action vary somewhat in their purpose from the other intellectual property doctrines because they do not specifically provide rights as an incentive to create new products, services, or expressive works. Rather, they provide limited property rights in words, symbols, or devices that indicate the origin of products and services to consumers, or (in the case of the false advertising and product disparagement causes of action) they protect the plaintiff merchant's business good will. Indicia of origin play a vital role in ensuring marketplace competition because they enable consumers to identify the source of products and services and exercise their purchasing preferences among competing brands. This, in turn, enables businesses to develop and retain business good will. By providing rights in a business's indications of origin and the intangible business good will they represent, trademark and unfair competition laws also provide businesses with the incentive to produce superior products and services, and promote marketplace efficiency. They also protect consumers' interests in avoiding deception.

III. SOURCES OF AUTHORITY TO REGULATE INTELLECTUAL PROPERTY

There are several sources of governmental authority to regulate intellectual property.

A. **Federal regulation:** The U.S. Constitution, Article 1, Section 8, Clause 8, expressly authorizes Congress to grant patents and copyrights. It provides: "The Congress shall have power... To promote the Progress of Science and useful Arts, by securing for limited Times to Authors and Inventors the exclusive Right to their respective Writings and Discoveries...." The Commerce Clause (Article 1, Section 8, Clause 3) authorizes Congress to regulate trademarks and acts of unfair competition in or affecting interstate commerce.

B. **State regulation:** Under the U.S. Constitution's Tenth Amendment and Supremacy Clause (Article VI), the states retain a concurrent power to regulate intellectual property. State regulation is only preempted by the federal law if Congress intended to preempt the field or if the state law stands as an obstacle to the accomplishment and execution of the full purposes and objectives of Congress in enacting federal law. (See THE RELATIONSHIP BETWEEN FEDERAL AND STATE LAW, *infra*, Chapter 9.)

Quiz Yourself on
INTRODUCTORY ISSUES

1. How might intellectual property laws accommodate the potential conflict between the goals of providing an incentive to create, and ensuring the freest possible public access to the new products, services, and expressive works that are created? _____

Sample Answer

1. Intellectual property laws generally try to tailor the property rights they convey, providing only those rights that are deemed necessary to induce creators to engage in the creative process. For example, most intellectual property rights are granted for a limited duration. When the term of the rights has expired, the public may have full access to the creation. Moreover, intellectual property rights often are limited in their scope so that some public uses of creations are permitted, even while the rights are in effect. In addition, some intellectual property doctrines are designed to encourage disclosure of the creations to the public so that the public may benefit from the knowledge underlying or conveyed by the creations, and use that knowledge for other, non-infringing purposes.

Exam Tips on *INTELLECTUAL PROPERTY GENERALLY*

☛ **Public policy:** Legislative bodies and courts frequently consider the public policies underlying the provision of intellectual property rights in drafting and construing the laws in this field. Especially when you encounter an exam question on an issue for which the law is unsettled, it is useful to consider whether a particular construction of the law would further or hinder accomplishment of the underlying public policies, and discuss this consideration in your exam answer.

☛ **Multiple forms of protection:** Sometimes more than one area of intellectual property law may be relevant to resolve the problems raised in an exam question. For example, trade secret law, copyright law, and patent law all prohibit unauthorized copying of computer software under some circumstances. Thus, it might be appropriate to discuss all three legal doctrines in answering a question concerning software.

However, it is important to read the call of the exam question carefully, and to evaluate the facts to ensure that discussion of all of these doctrines is warranted. For example, patent law provides protection only when the creator of the software applied for a patent within a year of the time the software was made available to the public, and ultimately was granted a patent. If the facts make no mention of an application or a patent, then discussing patent law may exceed the scope of the question. Likewise, if the question only asks for an evaluation of copyright infringement, discussion of patents is not relevant. Because many professors do not read discussions that go beyond the scope of the question, and you are likely to have time and/or page limitations in answering the exam questions, discussion of patent law may be counterproductive.

Chapter 2
THE LAW OF TRADE SECRETS

ChapterScope

This chapter reviews trade secret law, a state cause of action that has been shaped and unified by the Restatement of Torts §§757 and 758, and (in most states) is codified through adoption of the Uniform Trade Secrets Act. Trade secret protection promotes **two public policies:** (1) it gives an incentive to businesses to invest in the development of technical "know-how," ideas, and compilations of information by prohibiting certain unauthorized uses by others; and (2) it promotes state interests in promoting and maintaining marketplace morality. On the other hand, it has the **potential to interfere with competition and employee freedom** to advance in their professions if applied too strictly to prevent employees from moving from one place of employment to another. Generally, a trade secret cause of action consists of **two primary inquiries:** first, does the information or idea at issue qualify to be deemed a "trade secret," and second, if so, do the defendant's actions constitute an unlawful "misappropriation" of the trade secret.

- **Definition of "trade secret":** To constitute a "trade secret," the information must be *substantially secret* and have *commercial value* to the claimant that can be attributed to the fact that the claimant has it and its competitors do not. (Factors used to determine whether these conditions are satisfied are discussed in Section II.)

- **Misappropriation of trade secrets:** Trade secret protection is not absolute. Acquisition, disclosure or use of trade secrets through "proper means," such as independent creation or reverse engineering the claimant's finished product, will not constitute actionable misappropriation. Liability for misappropriation of a trade secret arises under the following circumstances.

  - The defendant discloses or uses the trade secret in *breach of a duty of confidence* that he owes to the claimant. (The circumstances in which the defendant will be deemed to owe the claimant a duty of confidence are discussed in Section IIIA, below.)

  - The defendant discloses or uses a trade secret that he learned from a third party with *notice* that the information is a trade secret and was revealed to him in breach of the third party's duty of confidence. (The circumstances under which the defendant will be deemed to have the requisite notice are discussed at various points in Section III, below.)

  - The defendant discloses or uses a trade secret that he *learned by mistake*, if he has notice that the information is a trade secret and was revealed to him by mistake.

  - The defendant receives the trade secret information from a third party *without the requisite notice* that it was a trade secret and was revealed in breach of the third party's duty of confidence, commences use or disclosure of it, later *receives the requisite notice, but continues* to use or disclose it. (An exception to this rule, described in the Restatement of Torts §758, is discussed in Section IIID, below.)

  - The defendant receives the trade secret information by mistake but, *without notice* of the trade secret status or mistake, commences use or disclosure of the trade secret, later *receives the requisite notice, but continues* his use or disclosure. (In this situation, the defendant will not be liable if he can demonstrate that he paid value for the secret in good faith or otherwise so changed his position in reliance on the secret that to require him to refrain from further use or disclosure would be inequitable.)

- The defendant acquires, uses or discloses the trade secret through *"improper means."* (The standards for judging whether the defendant's means were "improper" are discussed in Section IIIF, below.)

- The defendant acquires the trade secret from a third party with *notice* that it is a trade secret and was acquired through improper means.

This chapter also discusses private trade secret owners' rights when they submit their trade secret information to **government agencies** (Section IV); **ownership** of trade secrets developed by employees within the scope of their employment (Section V); three kinds of **express agreements** that employers might use to create and/or protect trade secret interests from former employees (Section VB); the doctrine of **inevitable disclosure** (Section VC); and **remedies** for trade secret misappropriation (Section VI).

I. THE PURPOSE, NATURE, AND SOURCE OF TRADE SECRET LAW

A. **Generally:** Businesses often develop valuable ideas and information, or "know-how," such as manufacturing processes, specialized customer lists, computer programs, or business methods, which give them a competitive advantage in producing or selling their goods or services effectively. Much of the value of this know-how arises from the fact that the creator's competitors do not have access to it. If a business's know-how is found to be a "trade secret," the business may prohibit its employees and business associates from divulging it to others, and prohibit competitors from using improper means to learn it (or from disclosing or using the information once learned). Trade secret protection may be available regardless of whether other forms of intellectual property protection, such as copyright, are also available. In addition to providing an incentive to create and use valuable know-how (which may ultimately benefit the public), trade secret protection discourages improper conduct on the part of business competitors and assists states in maintaining minimum standards of "commercial morality" in the marketplace.

B. **The Restatement and the Uniform Trade Secrets Act:** Protection for trade secrets arose under state common law, which was greatly influenced by the Restatement of Torts §§757 and 758. The large majority of states have subsequently adopted the Uniform Trade Secrets Act (drafted by the National Conference of Commissioners on Uniform State Law in 1979 and revised in 1985). The Uniform Act mainly codified the existing common-law rules, which generally reflect the provisions of the Restatement of Torts. Accordingly, the Uniform Act and the Restatement of Torts §§757-758 are similar in most respects, and courts continue to look to the Restatement in interpreting and applying the Uniform Trade Secrets Act.

C. **The elements of a trade secret misappropriation cause of action:** Most trade secret cases focus on two elements: (1) whether the plaintiff's information qualifies as a trade secret; and (2) if so, whether the defendant's acquisition, use, or disclosure of the information is an actionable misappropriation.

II. STATUS OF IDEAS OR INFORMATION AS TRADE SECRET

A. General definition: The Uniform Trade Secrets Act defines a trade secret as "information, including a formula, pattern, compilation, program, device, method, technique or process" that (1) derives actual or potential economic value from the fact that it is not known or readily ascertainable by others; and (2) is subject to reasonable efforts to maintain its secrecy. The Restatement of Torts §757, comment *b,* provides that a trade secret is "any formula, pattern, device or compilation of information which is used in one's business, and which gives him an opportunity to obtain an advantage over competitors who do not know or use it."

  1. **Continuous use:** Restatement of Torts §757 comment *b* specifies that to be a trade secret, the information or idea at issue must be used "continuously" in the claimant's business. Thus, "one shot" information, such as the terms of a secret bid for a contract or the date of an upcoming announcement of a new product, would not qualify because it is not used continuously or repeatedly in the business. The Uniform Trade Secrets Act does not impose this "continuous use" requirement. This is one of the few ways that these two authorities differ.

B. Six factors considered in determining trade secret status: Courts have widely adopted a six-factor test for determining whether information or an idea is a trade secret. (These six factors are also drawn from the first Restatement of Torts §757, comment *b.*) These factors focus on two primary issues: (1) is the information or idea "secret"; and (2) does the information or idea have competitive value?

  1. **How widely is the idea or information known outside the claimant's business?** This first factor considers how well known the information is to the public or to others in the same business as the claimant. It is not necessary for the claimant to demonstrate that no outsiders know the information. Others may know of it as long as their numbers are not too great and they take measures to keep the information secret. Stated another way, the information must be "substantially secret."

  2. **Who within the claimant's company knows the idea or information?** Under this factor the claimant/employer is permitted to disclose the information to employees and others connected with its business. However, it must exercise some reasonable precautions. For example, generally the claimant should limit disclosure to those employees who actually need to know the secret in order to perform their jobs, and restrict access by others. The claimant may be required to take some measures to ensure that those who know the secret retain it in confidence. (For example, it may be required to notify workers that the information is secret, have employees sign confidentiality agreements, or screen research papers to be presented by company researchers at conferences.) The extent of these required measures will differ from case to case, depending on what is reasonable under the circumstances. A form of cost/benefit analysis may be used to determine whether a particular precaution should be deemed reasonable and thus be required.

  3. **What measures has the claimant taken to ensure that the idea or information remains secret?** The claimant should take reasonable precautions to ensure that the information remains a secret. It should anticipate ways in which others might be expected to obtain the information and take reasonable measures to prevent access. For example, if the secret can be ascertained by observing the production process in the claimant's factory, the claimant may be required to restrict public access to that part of the factory. However, the claimant will not be required to make unreasonable expenditures to protect secrecy.

Example: In *E.I. Dupont deNemours & Co. v. Christopher,* 431 F.2d 1012 (5th Cir. 1970), *cert. denied,* 400 U.S. 1024 (1971), the owner of a methanol manufacturing plant was not required to foresee that during construction of its new plant, before the roof was erected, a competitor would charter a low flying airplane and take aerial photographs of the construction (which would provide clues about the claimant's secret manufacturing process). Any measures that the claimant could have taken to prevent this "school-boy prank" (such as erecting a huge tent over the construction site) would have been unreasonably expensive.

4. **How difficult would it be for others properly to acquire or duplicate the idea or information?** For example, has the idea or information ever been published, so that persons engaged in library or Internet research could find it? If so, it probably will not qualify as a trade secret.

   a. **Reverse engineering:** A related issue is whether the information could easily be ascertained by reverse engineering—that is, through examination, analysis, or decompilation of the finished product placed on the market. If it would be *easy* to learn the information by reverse engineering, it may not qualify as a trade secret. However, the fact that the information *could* be determined through complex reverse engineering requiring significant effort and expertise will not destroy trade secret status or the owner's ability to enforce rights against persons who obtained the information through means *other than* reverse engineering.

5. **How valuable is the idea or information to the claimant and its competitors?** The idea or information must be valuable to the claimant and give it an advantage over competitors who do not have it. The value to the claimant must be commercial in nature. Religious or spiritual value, for example, will not suffice.

6. **How much effort or money has the claimant expended in developing or acquiring the idea or information?** The greater the claimant's investment in developing the know-how, the more likely the know-how has real value to the claimant and to the public generally. The greater the know-how's value, the greater the justification for providing protection as an incentive for its development.

III. WHEN ACQUISITION, USE, OR DISCLOSURE OF A TRADE SECRET CONSTITUTES AN ACTIONABLE MISAPPROPRIATION

A. **Disclosure or use of a trade secret in breach of confidence:** If the defendant's disclosure or use of a trade secret was in breach of a duty of confidentiality that he owed to the plaintiff, the disclosure or use is actionable. A duty of confidentiality—which requires the defendant to refrain from disclosing or using the claimant's trade secret without permission—will arise under several scenarios, which are discussed below.

   1. **Special relationships:** Parties will be found to be in a confidential relationship with the claimant (and thus have a duty not to disclose or use the claimant's trade secret learned within the scope of that relationship without permission) if they are in an agent-principal relationship (including employer-employee relationship), if they are partners or joint venturers, or if they are in some other fiduciary relationship such as the attorney-client relationship or the doctor-patient relationship.

2. **Express contracts to retain confidentiality:** Parties may expressly contract to maintain a trade secret in confidence. Disclosure or use of the trade secret in breach of the contract will then be actionable.

   a. **Shrink-wrap licenses for software:** Many computer software distributors have attempted to impose a contractual confidentiality obligation on mass-market software purchasers through use of "shrink-wrap licenses." The distributor packages the software in a manner that notifies the purchaser that the purchaser's use of the software will be restricted. One of the most common restrictions prohibits the purchaser from reverse engineering, decompiling, or disassembling the program's object code (the machine-readable code in which most software is distributed to the public). Such reverse engineering would entail translating the machine-readable object code into human-readable source code, and thus permit the purchaser to learn the producer's program trade secrets. The notification of the restrictions provides that the purchaser's use of the software will signify acceptance of the restrictions.

   b. **The validity of shrink-wrap licenses:** While use of shrink-wrap licenses is widespread, their value and enforceability are open to some question. They may be deemed unenforceable under established rules of contract law—for example, they might be deemed unenforceable for lack of consent, lack of consideration (because the restrictive terms were imposed after the sale), on the ground that they constitute adhesion contracts, or for other public policy reasons. State enforcement of shrink-wrap licenses may also be deemed preempted by federal law. (See Chapter 9, *infra.*) Currently, there is some difference of opinion among the U.S. Circuit Courts of Appeals over the extent to which shrink-wrap licenses are enforceable.

   c. **Click-wrap licenses:** In Internet sales of computer programs, distributors may employ "click-wrap" licenses, which serve the same purpose as shrink-wraps, but may be more easily enforced. In this case, the distributor provides the restrictions to the purchaser on the purchaser's computer screen and requires the purchaser to "click" his consent to them before he can complete the purchase transaction and have the desired software sent to him electronically. In the case of click-wrap licenses, there is no basis for objection that the restrictive terms are being imposed on the purchaser (or that the purchaser is being notified of the restrictive terms) after the sale has already taken place. However, some of the other potential objections to shrink-wrap licenses listed above may still be raised.

3. **Implied contracts to retain confidentiality:** If the defendant has notice that the plaintiff is about to disclose information to her in confidence and agrees to hear it (or at least fails to take an opportunity to protest), then the defendant may be deemed implicitly to have agreed to retain the information in confidence and thus to have acquired a duty not to use the information or disclose it to others without the plaintiff's permission.

   a. **Notice:** The defendant will be deemed to be on notice of the confidential nature of the disclosure if a reasonable person under similar circumstances would have understood that the plaintiff was making the disclosure in confidence.

      Example: A and B are negotiating a contract under which A is to sell widgets to B. In order to convince B to buy his widgets, A tells B that A has a secret manufacturing process which renders a better quality widget than that sold by A's competitors. A then proceeds to explain what the process is and why it renders a better widget. B listens to A's disclosure without protest. In some (but not all) jurisdictions, this would be sufficient to place B in a confidential relationship with A for purposes of the secret process, so that B has a duty not to use the process or disclose it to others without A's permission.

B. Disclosure or use of a trade secret learned from a third party with notice: If A reveals a trade secret to B under circumstances which impose a duty of confidentiality on B, and B breaches the duty of confidence by revealing the secret to C without A's permission, C will have a duty not to use or disclose the secret if he has notice that: (1) the information is a trade secret, and (2) it was revealed to him in breach of B's duty.

1. Notice: C will be on notice of these facts if a reasonable person under similar circumstances would know them or if the reasonable person would be led to make further inquiry and a reasonable inquiry would reveal that the information was a trade secret and was being revealed in breach of B's duty of confidentiality. C will also be on notice if A actually tells C that the information is a secret that was revealed in breach of a duty (for example, via a warning letter).

Example: A and C are competitors in the widget business. A has a trade secret process for manufacturing widgets. She reveals it to her employee, B, within the scope of B's employment, so that B has a duty of confidentiality to A and may not use or disclose the trade secret without A's permission. B later approaches C and offers to tell him a secret process for making widgets if he will employ B as a vice president in his firm. C knows that B is A's employee and that A has a secret process, though he does not know what it is. It would be appropriate for a court to find that C has the necessary notice and thus has a duty not to disclose or use the process. If C does so, C (as well as B) will be liable to A for trade secret misappropriation.

C. Disclosure or use of a trade secret learned by mistake with notice: If A's trade secret is revealed to B by mistake and B has notice that the information (1) is a trade secret and (2) was revealed by mistake, then B has a duty to refrain from using or disclosing the trade secret without A's permission, and will be liable if she does so.

1. Notice: B will be deemed to have notice of these facts if a reasonable person under similar circumstances would have known them or would have been led to make further inquiry, and a reasonable inquiry would have revealed the facts. B will also have notice if A tells him.

Example: A, the president of a company that uses a trade secret process for manufacturing widgets, finds it necessary to reveal the trade-secret process to the president of a subsidiary corporation. A dictates a letter to the subsidiary corporation's president which reveals the trade secret, and instructs her secretary to address the letter to the subsidiary president and type the word "confidential" at the top. After this is done A signs the letter and tells the secretary to send it to the subsidiary president. By mistake, the secretary addresses the envelope to B, A's competitor. When B opens the letter she sees that it is from A to the subsidiary corporation's president and that it is marked "confidential" and describes a manufacturing process with which B is not familiar. It would be appropriate for a court to find that B is on notice that the process is a trade secret and that it was revealed to her by mistake. Under these circumstances, she is under a good faith duty not to take advantage of the mistake by disclosing the trade secret to others or using it for her own benefit.

D. Continued disclosure or use of a trade secret after receipt of notice of trade secrecy and breach of duty: If B learned A's trade secret from a third party who was breaching his duty by disclosing it, but at the time B had no notice of the secrecy and breach, then B will not be liable for his subsequent disclosure or use of the trade secret. However, if he later receives notice but continues his use or disclosure, he may become liable for the disclosure or use that occurred after his receipt of notice. On this issue, the Restatement of Torts and the Uniform Trade Secrets Act differ.

1. **The Restatement of Torts:** Under Restatement of Torts §758, if B later receives notice of the secrecy and breach, he must stop all further disclosure or use *unless* he can demonstrate either: (1) that he paid value for the secret in good faith; or (2) that he otherwise has so changed his position in reliance on the secret that to require him to refrain from further disclosure or use would be inequitable. However, continued use *in the absence of* such a showing will render B liable to A for all disclosure and use that occurs after his receipt of notice.

2. **The Uniform Trade Secrets Act:** Under the Uniform Trade Secrets Act, a defendant who continues to disclose or use the trade secret after receiving notice will be liable for his continued disclosure or use, regardless of his payment of value or material change. However, the Commissioners' Comment to §2 of the Uniform Act suggests that a court may take a defendant's good faith payment or material change of position into account in determining the proper remedy for his continuing (now infringing) use or disclosure.

   Example: C sells A's trade secret manufacturing process to B for a substantial sum of money, in breach of a duty of confidentiality C owes to A. At the time, B has no notice of the trade secret status or C's breach of confidence. Later, B receives notice that the manufacturing process was A's trade secret and that C was breaching a duty of confidentiality by selling it to him. Under the Uniform Act, given B's good faith payment, a court may refuse to enjoin his further use of the secret, but condition his further use upon payment of a reasonable royalty to A.

E. **Continued disclosure or use of a trade secret after receipt of notice that it is a trade secret and was acquired by mistake:** If B learned A's trade secret by mistake, but at the time of learning it he had no notice that the information was A's trade secret and was revealed by mistake, then B will not be liable for his subsequent disclosure or use of the trade secret. If, however, he later receives such notice, he must stop all further disclosure or use unless he can demonstrate: (1) that he paid value for the secret in good faith; or (2) that he otherwise has so changed his position in reliance on the secret that to require him to refrain from further disclosure or use would be inequitable. Continued use in the absence of such a showing will render B liable to A for any disclosure or use of the secret that occurs after his receipt of notice.

   Example: B receives a copy of A's trade secret manufacturing process by mistake, but at that time he has no notice of the trade secret status or mistake. B expends a substantial amount of money altering his factory to implement the manufacturing process and begins using the process. At that point he receives notice that the process was A's trade secret and of the mistake. Given B's substantial expenditures in reliance on the process, which were made in good faith, a court may decide not to require him to discontinue use or to pay damages to A.

F. **Acquisition, disclosure, or use of a trade secret acquired through improper means:** Under the Uniform Trade Secrets Act, the *acquisition* of a trade secret, in itself, may constitute misappropriation if the acquisition was achieved through improper means and the acquirer had reason to know that it was. Moreover, both the Restatement and the Uniform Trade Secrets Act prohibit *disclosure or use* of a trade secret acquired through improper means. "Improper means" includes illegal conduct and conduct that is below generally accepted standards of commercial morality. (Note that the Restatement treats breaches of confidence and "improper means" separately. The

Uniform Trade Secrets Act, however, treats breaches of confidence as one type of "improper" conduct, which will render a defendant liable.)

1. **Illegal conduct:** A defendant's means of acquisition generally will be deemed "improper" for this purpose if they are independently illegal. Thus, for example, B will be deemed to have engaged in "improper means" or "improper conduct" if, in acquiring A's trade secret, she engaged in fraud, or if she trespassed or broke and entered A's place of business.

2. **Conduct below generally accepted standards of commercial morality:** Even if B's means of acquisition were not technically illegal in themselves, they may nonetheless have been "improper" for purposes of trade secret liability if they fell below reasonably accepted standards of commercial morality. In *E.I. Dupont deNemours & Co. v. Christopher,* the Fifth Circuit held that if the plaintiff did not voluntarily reveal its trade secret to the defendant, and the plaintiff took reasonable measures to keep its trade secret a secret, reasonably accepted standards of commercial morality required that the defendant refrain from acquiring the trade secret in a manner that gave him a "free ride."

   a. **The meaning of "free ride":** The *Dupont* court stated that as long as the plaintiff has taken reasonable measures to keep his information secret, the defendant should be required to make the same kind of investment that the plaintiff did in originally acquiring the trade secret information. Thus, if the defendant acquired the trade secret through independent research, his means would be proper—i.e., the defendant would have made the same basic type of investment of research and effort that the plaintiff did in originally developing the trade secret. Likewise, if the defendant learned the secret by reverse engineering a finished product that A voluntarily placed on the market, his means would be proper, since A made the product available and B made his own investment in the reverse engineering process. However, if the defendant acquired the secret in a manner that allowed him to avoid such expenditures, this would constitute a "free ride," and his means would be improper. The *Dupont* court held that flying over the plaintiff's half-constructed plant and taking aerial photographs in order to obtain the plaintiff's secret constituted an improper "free ride."

   b. **Taking advantage of the plaintiff's vulnerability:** In considering whether the defendant had engaged in conduct below generally accepted standards of commercial morality, the *Dupont* court also considered indications that the defendant had taken undue advantage of a temporary vulnerability that the plaintiff could not reasonably have avoided. In *Dupont,* the defendant had acquired information about plaintiff's secret process by chartering an airplane to fly low over the plaintiff's half-constructed plant and take photographs of the configuration of plaintiff's plant and its interior before the roof could be erected. The court characterized this as taking advantage of a temporary vulnerability on plaintiff's part. It would have been unreasonable to require the plaintiff to take the extraordinary measures necessary to prevent it. Thus, failure to take these measures did not render the plaintiff's exposure a voluntary one. By contrast, if the plaintiff had voluntarily placed a finished product on the market and the defendant had bought it and learned the plaintiff's secret process of manufacture by reverse engineering, there would be no grounds for liability. In that case the plaintiff voluntarily would have taken the risk of discovery.

G. **Disclosure or use of a trade secret with notice that the provider acquired it through improper means:** If B acquires A's trade secret through improper means and turns it over to C, C has a duty not to disclose or use it if he has notice that it is a trade secret and was obtained through improper means.

1. **Notice:** C will be deemed to have notice if a reasonable person under similar circumstances would know or would be led to inquire further, and a reasonable inquiry would uncover these facts.

   Example: A Co. has a trade secret manufacturing process, which is written on two 8½" × 11" pages. Each page is marked "Confidential" at the top, along with A Co.'s name. B breaks into the A Co. safe and photographs the two pages. He later approaches C, a competitor of A Co., and offers to sell C a valuable secret manufacturing process. He shows C the photograph of the first page. It would be appropriate for a court to find that C has notice that the process is a trade secret and was acquired by improper means, so that his subsequent disclosure or use of it would be actionable.

H. **Defendant's modification of plaintiff's trade secret:** The fact that the defendant modified or improved the plaintiff's trade secret before using or disclosing it will not relieve the defendant from liability, as long as the plaintiff can demonstrate that the information the defendant used or disclosed was *substantially derived* from the plaintiff's trade secret.

   Example: A has a secret manufacturing process which involves four steps. B learns the process from C, with notice that it is a trade secret and that C is breaching a duty of confidence in revealing it. After studying the process, B alters it by reversing the order of steps 1 and 2 and adding a fifth step. He then implements the improved five-step process. B probably will be liable to A because even though the process B implemented differed from the original, it was substantially derived from A's original trade secret. The fact that B improved the process might be taken into account in determining the amount of money damages to be paid to A as a remedy for B's trade secret misappropriation. For example, the proportion of B's profits to be paid to A might be reduced because some of the profits are attributable to B's improvement. If the court bases A's damages on lost sales, the court might decide that not all of B's customers represent lost sales to A—because of differences in A's and B's processes, some of B's customers would not have bought from A under any circumstance.

IV. PRIVATE OWNERS' RIGHTS IN TRADE SECRET INFORMATION SUBMITTED TO GOVERNMENT AGENCIES

A. **Freedom of information acts:** Private entities often find it useful or necessary to submit confidential trade secret information to government regulatory agencies or government agencies awarding contracts or grants. However, broad-sweeping "freedom of information acts," as well as narrower, more specialized statutes, which exist on both the state and federal level, require government agencies to disclose documents used in the course of agency decision-making to any members of the public who request them. If a government agency discloses a party's trade secret in response to a statutorily-authorized request from a member of the public, then the secrecy, and thus the value of the trade secret, may be lost.

   1. **Exemptions in freedom of information acts:** Many freedom of information acts contain an exemption from their public disclosure requirements for trade secret and other confidential, commercial or financial information. However, these exemptions may be construed narrowly to exclude information that the submitter considers to be trade secret. Moreover, the exemptions may only give agencies the *discretion* to withhold trade secret information from disclosure, rather than require withholding.

B. An unconstitutional "taking": When a government agency publicly discloses a submitted trade secret without the owner's authorization, the owner may have a cause of action against the government agency for an unconstitutional taking of private property for a public use without just compensation, in violation of the Fifth or Fourteenth Amendments of the U.S. Constitution, or a comparable state constitutional provision.

1. **The standard for finding a taking:** In *Ruckelshaus v. Monsanto Co.,* 467 U.S. 986 (1984), the U.S. Supreme Court held that the proper standard for determining whether government disclosure of a trade secret constituted an unconstitutional "taking" was whether the owner/submitter of the trade secret had a "reasonable, investment-backed expectation of confidentiality" at the time it submitted the trade secret to the government agency.

2. **The standard applied:** The *Monsanto* Court held that a trade secret submitter would only have a reasonable, investment-backed expectation of confidentiality if, at the time it submitted the trade secret to the agency, there was a statute expressly prohibiting the agency from disclosing the trade secret to others. If, by contrast, at the time of submission there was a statute *requiring* disclosure, then the submitter would be charged with notice of it and could not have had a reasonable investment-backed expectation that the trade secret would remain confidential. In such a case, subsequent disclosure pursuant to the statute would not constitute an unconstitutional taking.

   a. **When there is no express statutory provision:** If the trade secret was submitted when there was no express statutory provision either requiring or prohibiting disclosure, the *Monsanto* Court indicated that, at least in the case of highly regulated industries that are the subject of considerable public concern, there could be no reasonable, investment-backed expectation of confidentiality, and thus no taking through disclosure. In such cases, the Court reasoned, the submitter should be charged with notice that the government might find it desirable to disclose the submitted information to the public.

V. USE AND DISCLOSURE BY EMPLOYEES AND FORMER EMPLOYEES

A. **In the absence of an express agreement:** Even in the absence of an express agreement to retain trade secrets in confidence, an employee has a duty not to use or disclose her employer's trade secrets without permission if the employee learned them within the scope of her employment. The employee, as agent, owes a duty of confidentiality to her employer, the principal. This duty will continue to bind the employee to retain the employer's trade secrets in confidence even after leaving the employment.

1. **Preexisting trade secrets disclosed to the employee:** If the employer discloses a preexisting trade secret to the employee within the scope of her employment, a duty will be found on the employee's part not to use or disclose the trade secret without the employer's permission.

2. **Trade secrets created by the employee:** When the employee creates the trade secret herself, the employee will have a duty not to disclose or use the trade secret without the employer's permission if the trade secret is the property of the employer. If the trade secret is the property of the employee, no such duty exists.

a. **When the trade secret belongs to the employer:** A trade secret created by an employee will nonetheless be the property of the employer if the employee was hired especially to do research of the type that leads to the creation of the trade secret and the employer has put substantial resources at the employee's disposal for development of the trade secret. Under those circumstances the employee will be deemed to have impliedly assigned her on-the-job creations to the employer.

   Example: X Co., a leading manufacturer of widgets, employs A as a chemist in its research and development department. A is told that there is a problem with a chemical compound presently being used in the company's manufacturing process, and is assigned to try to find a solution to the problem. A works in the X Co. labs with X Co. equipment and supplies for three months, experimenting with various alternative compounds, and finally finds one that works. The new compound should be found to be the trade secret of X Co. because A was specifically hired and directed to do this kind of research and X Co. devoted its labs, supplies, and three months of A's time on the job to the project.

b. **When the trade secret belongs to the employee:** The trade secret created by the employee will belong to the employee if the conditions set forth in subparagraph a, *supra*, do not exist. If the employee is the owner, he owes no duty to the employer to refrain from disclosing or using the trade secret.

   Example: X Co., a leading manufacturer of widgets, hires A as a salesman for its finished widgets. During his spare time on the job and after hours at his home, A invents a new, improved method of manufacturing widgets. A court should find that this trade secret belongs to A, since X Co. did not hire A to engage in research concerning new manufacturing methods, and did not devote much of its valuable resources to the project.

c. **Shop right in the employer:** If the employee was not specifically hired to do research or development of trade secrets, but nonetheless created a trade secret related to the employer's business during working hours or with the employer's equipment or materials, the employee will be the owner of the trade secret, and will have no duty to refrain from using or disclosing it, but the employer will have a "shop right" in the trade secret. A shop right is an irrevocable, non-exclusive, non-assignable right, or license, to use the trade secret in the employer's business without paying the employee a royalty.

B. **In the case of an express agreement:** There are three types of express contractual provisions an employer may use to protect its trade secret interests against employees. These may be used individually or in combination.

1. **Non-disclosure agreements:** An employer may require an employee expressly to agree not to use or disclose trade secrets belonging to the employer. This is called a "nondisclosure agreement." While the employee is likely already to owe a common-law duty of confidentiality to the employer, the express non-disclosure agreement is useful because it indicates that the employee, who signs the agreement, is aware of the secret status of the information. Moreover, courts may be more inclined to find that information on the borderline of trade secret status is protectible if there is an express agreement to that effect between the employer and the employee.

2. **Advance assignment agreements:** The employer may require an employee to sign an agreement assigning all trade secrets that the employee may develop in the course of her employment to the employer in advance. Courts generally will enforce such "advance assignment"

agreements as long as they are not unconscionable and are supported by consideration (as will be the case if the advance assignment agreement is signed at the time the employee is hired).

3. **Non-competition agreements:** The employer may require the employee to sign a more general agreement not to compete with the employer for a specified time in a specified geographical area after leaving the employment. However, courts are less likely to enforce such agreements not to compete.

   a. **Public policy considerations surrounding agreements not to compete:** Public policy disfavors enforcement of agreements that restrict an individual's ability to earn a livelihood or inhibit competition in the provision of technology, products, or services to the public. For these reasons many jurisdictions hold covenants not to compete in this context presumptively invalid.

   b. **Factors courts will consider in evaluating covenants not to compete:** Generally courts will not enforce an employee agreement not to compete unless: (1) it is reasonably necessary in order to protect the employer from injury; (2) it is reasonable as to the time and geographical area in which the employee is restricted from competing; (3) the restrictions are not harmful to the general public; and (4) the restrictions are not unreasonably burdensome to the employee.

   c. **The employer's interest:** In order to satisfy the first factor, courts frequently require the employer to demonstrate that its trade secret or other confidential proprietary information is imperiled. The employee's possession of sensitive, confidential, proprietary information that does not rise to the level of a trade secret may suffice to justify an injunction to enforce a non-competition agreement against the employee.

      i. **Customer information:** Lists of the employer's customers, their addresses, and other information relevant to their business needs may qualify as a trade secret if the six factors of Restatement of Torts §757 are satisfied. (*See* pp. 7-8, *supra*.) Even if this information is not trade secret, it still may qualify as confidential proprietary information and support enforcement of a non-competition agreement. However, the employer may have to demonstrate to the court that the information is not readily available from other sources and that the employee engaged in wrongful conduct in obtaining it. Wrongful conduct will be found for this purpose if the employee stole a copy of the information, or deliberately memorized it for her own use. If the employee merely remembers the information as the result of properly using it while employed, her acquisition is unlikely to be deemed wrongful.

      ii. **The employee's general knowledge of the field and the employer's business:** Courts will not permit an employer to enjoin a former employee from simply using his skills or general background knowledge of the trade and the employer's business, even if he learned these things from the employer. Such general knowledge and skill rightfully belong to the employee, and the employer has no legitimate interest in enjoining its use.

   d. **The advantage of a general agreement not to compete:** While there is considerable overlap between the protection an employer enjoys through the trade secret law and the protection it can obtain through enforcement of an express agreement not to compete, the latter method does offer some advantages. The scope of protection is slightly larger, since employees may be enjoined from using some confidential proprietary information that does not qualify as a trade secret.

C. **The doctrine of inevitable disclosure:** Most court decisions involving former employees express concern about applying trade secret rights in a manner that impairs the employee's ability to move freely from one job to another. However, trade secret laws may sometimes be applied to inhibit free employee movement, not only through enforcement of reasonable non-competition or non-disclosure agreements, but also through application of the "doctrine of inevitable disclosure." This doctrine provides that if (1) a former employee knows the former employer's trade secrets; (2) the former employee's new job duties are so similar or related to those of his former position that it would be difficult for him not to rely on or use those trade secrets; and (3) the former employee or his new employer cannot be relied on to avoid using the trade secrets, then the former employee may be enjoined from taking the new job, at least until the threat to the trade secrets is dissipated. While this doctrine has not been universally adopted, it received a considerable boost in status through the Court of Appeals for the Seventh Circuit's decision in *Pepsico, Inc. v. Redmond*, 54 F.3d 1262 (7th Cir. 1995) (applying Illinois law).

Example: In *Pepsico,* the plaintiff producer of sports beverages sued to enjoin Redmond, the former California general manager of one of its subsidiaries, from taking an executive position with a competing producer of sports beverages. The new position primarily entailed marketing. Plaintiff alleged that Redmond knew the details of its own pricing and marketing strategies for the next year, by virtue of his former position, and that Redmond would inevitably use that trade secret pricing and marketing information in his new position directing the marketing of the competitor's beverage. The district court issued a preliminary injunction preventing Redmond from assuming the new position for a period of six months, as well as preventing him from ever using or disclosing the plaintiff's trade secrets. The Seventh Circuit affirmed, noting that the Uniform Trade Secrets Act (adopted in Illinois) authorized injunctive relief against "actual or threatened misappropriation" of a trade secret.

The Seventh Circuit noted that threatened misappropriation could be demonstrated when a defendant's new employment would inevitably lead him to rely on the plaintiff's trade secrets. In *Pepsico,* the plaintiff was not seeking to enjoin Redmond from using the general skills and knowledge he acquired during his time with the plaintiff company, but rather the particularized trade secret marketing plans that plaintiff had disclosed to him. The nature of Redmond's new job made it inevitable that he would use the information: The secret marketing plans would enable him to anticipate and counter plaintiff's marketing moves in devising the marketing plan for the plaintiff's competitor. Moreover, evidence of evasiveness and dishonesty in Redmond's leave-taking from his former employer convinced the court that he could not be relied on to refrain from using the information if permitted to take the position.

VI. REMEDIES FOR TRADE SECRET MISAPPROPRIATION

A. **Injunctions:** A defendant may be enjoined from using or disclosing the plaintiff's trade secret. In order to obtain an injunction, the plaintiff must demonstrate irreparable injury and an inadequate remedy at law. Usually these requirements are easily satisfied, because the defendant's disclosure or use of the trade secret may significantly reduce its value or destroy it, and the monetary loss may be difficult to measure. Courts have differed concerning the appropriate length of injunctions in this context.

1. **Duration limited to the life of the trade secret:** Under one view, the injunction should not endure beyond the life of the trade secret. Courts following this view will either limit the period of injunction to the time that the information can be expected to remain secret, or they will grant an injunction of indefinite length, allowing the defendant to petition the court to terminate the injunction once the secret has become generally known or could have been reverse engineered.

2. **Unlimited duration:** The other view is that, given the defendant's breach of confidence or improper conduct, a perpetual injunction against use of the trade secret is justified. Thus the defendant may be prohibited from using the secret information long after it has become generally known in the industry and is available to other competitors. This view is less generally accepted.

B. **Damages:** Courts have used a variety of measures in determining the proper amount of damages to award a successful trade secret plaintiff. The court may award: (1) the profits the plaintiff has lost as a result of the defendant's misappropriation of the trade secret; (2) a reasonable royalty for the defendant's use of the trade secret during the time at issue (the amount to which reasonable parties would have agreed if they had willingly negotiated for a license to use the trade secret); or (3) the amount of the profits the defendant made as a result of the misappropriation. A court may award both the amount of the plaintiff's loss and the defendant's profit, to the extent that these awards are not duplicative. When the plaintiff seeks to recover the defendant's profits, he need only demonstrate that the defendant made gross profits in connection with its use of the trade secret. At that point, the burden shifts to the defendant to prove what portions of the profits should be deducted for production costs or which portions should be deducted because they are attributable to other factors than use of the plaintiff's trade secret. The Uniform Trade Secrets Act authorizes punitive damage awards in the case of willful and malicious trade secret misappropriation. In addition, unlike the common law, the Uniform Act provides an award of attorney fees in cases of willful misappropriation or bad faith.

C. **Criminal prosecution:** Some states have enacted statutes specifically imposing criminal sanctions for theft of a trade secret. In 1996, Congress enacted legislation making theft of a trade secret a federal crime under a number of circumstances. This legislation, known as the Economic Espionage Act of 1996, prohibits a variety of acts amounting to the knowing, unauthorized taking or communication of trade secrets when the actor (1) intends or knows that the acts will benefit a foreign government, instrumentality, or agent; or (2) intends or knows that they will injure the owner of the trade secret to the benefit of another. The Act's criminal penalties extend to persons who attempt or conspire to do the prohibited acts, and they also expressly extend to conduct outside the United States in some circumstances. The Economic Espionage Act does not provide private causes of action, but it does authorize the U.S. government to institute civil proceedings to enjoin violation of the statute.

Quiz Yourself on
TRADE SECRETS

2. Wong was formerly a laboratory scientist with Acme Co. When he first took employment with Acme, he signed a non-disclosure agreement in which he agreed not to use or disclose Acme's trade secrets without Acme's authorization. Wong lawfully knows the Acme Co. trade secret method for manufacturing ethanol because Acme revealed it to him to use in the course of his duties.

After leaving the Acme Co., Wong accepts a job with Bennet Co., which produces ethanol in competition with Acme. Wong will be the Director of Bennet's Research and Development Department. Acme wants to enjoin Wong from taking the job on the ground that his taking the job will "threaten" misappropriation, within the meaning of the Uniform Trade Secrets Act. How likely is Acme to succeed? _____

3. Assume that in each of the situations described below, Alice, who is employed by the Ace Company, gives Ace Company Brown Company's trade secret information. Ace and Brown are competitors.

  a. Alice meets Joe Blow, whom she knows to be one of Brown Co.'s chief chemical engineers, at a national chemical engineers' conference and offers to buy him drinks at a nearby bar. Alice does not hide the fact that she works for Ace. (In fact, early in the conversation, Blow laughingly remarks that Brown Co. warned him not to socialize with competitors' employees at conferences.) After several drinks, Alice manipulates the conversation, employing flattery to lead Blow to divulge more than he should about the secret chemical processes Brown Co. uses in producing its products. When Alice provides this trade secret information to Ace, she explains how she got it. Ace later uses the information in its own manufacturing process. Should Ace be found liable for trade secret misappropriation? _____

  b. Alice buys Brown Co.'s product and takes it to the Ace Company's state-of-the-art laboratory. She uses the laboratory's highly sophisticated equipment to ascertain the components of the product and the relative amounts of each component, thus discovering Brown's trade secret product formula. When Alice provides this trade secret information to Ace, she explains how she got it. Ace later uses the information to produce a competing product. Should Ace be found liable for trade secret misappropriation? _____

  c. Prior to joining Ace's research and development department, Alice interviewed for a job with Brown Co. During the course of the interview, the supervisor of Brown's research and development department tried very hard to convince Alice to join the Brown team. The supervisor told her that she would be on the "cutting edge" of the industry working for Brown. Alice then asked, "Can you give me an example?" The supervisor responded, "Well, this is strictly confidential, you understand, but Brown is developing a revolutionary new product, which will be introduced to the market next year." Alice asked for details and the supervisor provided them. After taking her job with Ace, Alice provided the Brown trade secret information to Ace and explained the circumstances in which she received it. Ace began immediately to develop its own version of the product and got it onto the market at nearly the same time as Brown. Should Ace be liable for trade secret misappropriation? _____

4. Acme Corp. creates and markets software that enables the user to more efficiently manage and track business inventory. Acme only provides the software to the public in object code form (machine-readable code that is not capable of being read by humans). It keeps the source code (which can be read by humans) locked away. X, a graduate student in computer science, purchases a copy of the software through Amazon.com. The software, which is encoded on a disk, arrives by mail. The packaging contains a shrink-wrap license that provides that the purchaser is the owner of the disk, but a mere licensee of the software encoded on the disk, and sets forth a number of things that the purchaser (as licensee) is prohibited from doing in connection with the software. Among other things, the purchaser/licensee is prohibited from reverse engineering the software, and publishing or otherwise communicating the results of any reverse engineering.

X proceeds to reverse engineer the software in order to study the underlying mathematical algorithms. He then posts the algorithms (but none of the code) on his web site, along with his commentary on the methodology Acme used. Y, a competitor of Acme, finds the algorithms on X's web site, downloads them, and uses them in devising his own software for tracking and managing business inventory.

Please evaluate what, if any rights Acme has against either X or Y for trade secret misappropriation.

---

5. MegaLabs Corp. operates a large number of medical laboratories throughout the United States to which doctors send their patients for various medical tests. (These laboratories take various kinds of specimens from patients, analyze and perform tests on the specimens, and report their findings back to the referring doctor for assistance in diagnosing and treating patients' medical problems.) MegaLabs also operates its own Research and Development Division, which employs over 100 scientists who devote their time to developing and perfecting new testing methods and improved methods of interpreting test data.

In 2005, MegaLabs entered into a written joint research agreement with University, in which each party agreed to share information and resources and to collaborate in developing, among other things, a more effective method of testing patient blood samples for AIDS. (Hereafter, the "AIDS Project.") The agreement provided that any new laboratory tests developed as a result of the joint research agreement would be owned and exploited by MegaLabs, but that MegaLabs would pay a stated portion of its profits to University.

Appleton is a PhD in biochemistry who began work as a research scientist for MegaLabs in 1999. At the time he was employed he signed the following "Employment and Nondisclosure Agreement":

> Neither during the period of employment nor at any time thereafter will Appleton disclose to anyone any confidential information or trade secrets concerning the business affairs of MegaLabs, including but not limited to information relating to the experimental and research work of MegaLabs, its methods, processes, tools, machinery, formulae, drawings or appliances imparted or divulged to, gained or developed by or otherwise discovered by Appleton during his employment with MegaLabs.

In early 2006, Appleton was assigned primary responsibility for a project to develop a more efficient method of testing for parasites in human intestines. (This was another project covered by the MegaLabs/University joint research agreement.) In the course of his work he visited some laboratories at University to consult with Professor Bee on the parasite project. While there he encountered one of his old professors (Professor Cohen) who was presently working on the joint MegaLabs/University AIDS project. The two went to lunch and in the course of conversation, Prof. Cohen described one of his experiments to discover the AIDS virus in blood samples that had failed. After his meeting with Cohen, Appleton thought about Cohen's experiment and realized that if it was altered somewhat, it might work. In his spare time, he set up his own experiment (based on Cohen's but altered in the way he had envisioned) and succeeded in identifying the AIDS virus in a blood sample.

Appleton told his MegaLabs Supervisor about his experiment, and the Supervisor arranged for him to spend more time refining his experiment and testing the new method. For six months Appleton split his time 50-50 between the parasite project and his work on the new AIDS test. Then Appleton left MegaLabs and, in partnership with several other persons, set up a new medical laboratory that would compete with MegaLabs's individual patient testing laboratories. He took his notes on the new AIDS test experiment with him and continued to work on it in his spare time. MegaLabs, meanwhile, assigned McGee to continue work on the AIDS test and later filed an application for patent, naming Appleton and McGee as the inventors, and naming itself as the owner of the invention. At all relevant times, both Cohen's original experiment and Appleton's and McGee's later work on the AIDS test were kept in confidence, shared only among the persons working on the projects.

The patent subsequently issued and Appleton, upon learning of it, sued MegaLabs, seeking a declaratory judgment that he is the rightful owner of the invention. Please evaluate this claim.

Sample Answers

2. There is a strong public policy against interfering with the ability of employees to move to new employment within their field. This policy is likely to lead a court to find against Acme, under the facts of this case.

Wong has a duty (both by virtue of his agency relationship with his employer and by virtue of the nondisclosure agreement he signed) not to use or disclose the trade secret formula without Acme's permission. However, he has not signed a covenant not to compete with Acme. (Even if he had, it is not clear that it would be enforceable because such agreements are disfavored by the law.) Moreover, there is nothing in the facts to suggest that Wong is about to disclose the secret in violation of this duty.

Acme might argue that it has a right to enjoin Wong under the doctrine of inevitable disclosure. The theory is that in the position he has accepted, it is inevitable that Wong will use the secret information. However, this case can be distinguished from the *Pepsico* case, which adopted and applied the doctrine of inevitable disclosure. Unlike the marketing strategies in *Pepsico,* the Acme secret formula can be readily "compartmentalized." Wong probably can avoid using it in the course of performing his new duties. Moreover, unlike in the *Pepsico* case, there are no facts here to suggest that either Wong or his new employer are untrustworthy or have schemed to acquire the secret formula. Finally, unlike in *Pepsico,* an injunction against Wong would probably have to be a long-term injunction, since the trade secret at issue—the formula—will not dissipate in value and importance in a matter of months.

Under these circumstances the rather extreme remedy of enjoining Wong from taking the job is unwarranted, as a matter of policy. It would damage his career and would be contrary to the public interest in allowing him free movement. The risk of harm to Acme does not warrant this. Wong could be enjoined from disclosing or using the trade secret method while employed by Bennett Co. if there were grounds to believe that he plans to do so.

3a. A good argument exists that Ace is liable for trade secret misappropriation. Both the Restatement of Torts §757 and the Uniform Trade Secrets Act prohibit use or disclosure of trade secret information obtained through improper means. If Alice's means of obtaining the information were improper, then Ace will be liable for subsequent use of the information because it clearly had notice that the information was secret and that Alice had obtained it through improper means.

In the *DuPont* case, the court held that "improper means" encompasses not only conduct that is independently illegal, but also conduct that is below generally accepted standards of commercial morality. The court suggested that when the plaintiff is taking reasonable measures to protect the information, the defendant has a duty not to take the information under circumstances that permit it to avoid making the same kind of investment as the plaintiff did in developing it. The court also suggested that it is below generally accepted standards of commercial morality to take advantage of a temporary vulnerability on the plaintiff's part that the plaintiff could not reasonably have avoided.

Here, Alice deliberately got Blow drunk in order to induce him to breach his duty of confidentiality to his employer. This would likely be deemed below generally accepted standards of commercial morality. It appears that Brown Co. had warned its engineers not to socialize with competitors' employees at conferences, presumably to avoid the very mishap that occurred in this case. It thus had taken reasonable measures to protect the information. It would be unreasonable to require Brown Co. to take further measures, such as sending bodyguards with its engineers, or prohibiting the engineers from participating in what may be highly useful conferences. Alice could also be characterized as taking advantage of a temporary vulnerability, as in the *DuPont* case. (Indeed, X *created* the vulnerability—the engineer's drunkenness—and then capitalized on it.) Certainly Alice's actions allowed Brown Co. to obtain the information without making the kind of investment that Ace Co. made.

An alternative approach would be to argue that Alice (and through Alice, Ace) received the trade secret information with notice that it was a trade secret and that it was being disclosed in breach of Blow's duty to Brown Co. Under both the Restatement of Torts and the Uniform Trade Secrets Act, this would impose a duty on Alice (and on Ace because it knew what Alice knew) not to disclose or use Brown Co.'s secret information without Brown's permission. As a Brown employee, Blow clearly had a duty not to disclose Brown's trade secrets. Alice was aware of the engineer's status and was likely to know, or at least have inquiry notice, that the information being divulged was trade secret. After all, Alice deliberately set out to obtain confidential information and knew enough about the business to ask the right questions.

3b. Ace should not be liable for trade secret misappropriation under these facts. The courts have made it clear that obtaining trade secret information through reverse engineering a competitor's finished, publicly available product does not constitute improper conduct.

3c. Ace may be liable. Alice was on notice of the trade secret status of the information (the supervisor notified her that it was "confidential") and asked to hear it. Under these circumstances, in many jurisdictions, she would be deemed impliedly to consent to the supervisor's terms that the information be kept in confidence. This would give rise to an implied contractual duty of confidence that Alice breached in revealing the information to Ace. Because Ace (presumably) had notice of the confidential status of the information, and that Alice was breaching her duty of confidence, Ace incurred its own duty to Brown, which it breached when it used the information to develop a competing product.

4. **Acme v. X:** The first issue is whether the program (and its algorithms) enjoy trade secret status. Clearly the program provides commercial, competitive value to Acme. X might argue, however, that the program is not substantially secret because Acme sold the program to the general public. This argument should be rejected because Acme only provided the program to the public in unreadable object code form, and it appears that Acme took precautions to keep the human-readable source code secure. Acme's actions are comparable to those of a company that makes a product through use of a secret formula and then sells the product to the general public. Assuming that the product does not itself reveal the formula, the act of selling the product does not destroy the trade secrecy of the process. In the present case it is possible for persons possessing the object code to reverse engineer it back into source code and thus learn the program's secrets, but this is a difficult, time-consuming task that only programming experts are able to accomplish with special decompilation programs. It has long been understood that the ability to reverse engineer a product's secret formula by subjecting the product to complex scientific experimentation using sophisticated, expensive laboratory equipment does not destroy the trade secret status of the formula. Likewise, the ability to reverse engineer a computer program's object code should not, in itself, destroy the trade secret status of the software and its algorithms.

However, even though the software algorithms are protectible trade secrets, X acquired them through reverse engineering of a lawfully purchased copy. This generally is considered "proper means" and does not constitute trade secret misappropriation. Acme will argue that the shrink-wrap license imposed an express contractual duty of confidentiality on X, which he breached by engaging in the reverse engineering and disclosure, in violation of the shrink-wrap prohibitions. Whether Acme could prevail with this argument depends on whether the shrink-wrap license is enforceable. There is mixed case authority on this point. X might challenge the shrink-wrap license under contract principles, arguing that the restrictions are attempts to change the terms of his purchase transaction after the transaction has been completed (X never learned of the restrictions until after he paid his money and Amazon.com sent the software), and thus are unsupported by consideration. He might also argue that enforcement of the terms would be unconscionable. On another track, Y might argue that enforcement of state contract law in this case is preempted by federal patent law (enforcing universal prohibitions against reverse engineering frustrates Congress's purpose in enacting the patent law, and relegating unpatented inventions to the public domains). (See Chapter 9, *infra*.) Only if the shrink-wrap is enforceable could Acme prevail against X since X had no other relationship with Acme that would impose a duty of confidence to Acme.

Acme v. Y: Y could only be liable for misappropriation of the program trade secrets if X disclosed them in breach of a duty of confidentiality (successfully imposed by the shrink-wrap license) and Y had notice that the information was trade secret and was being disclosed in breach of a duty of confidence. There are insufficient facts to determine whether X had the requisite notice.

Even if it were found that X breached an enforceable duty of confidentiality and that Y had the requisite notice, Y might argue that the information was no longer a trade secret when he acquired and used it—rather, the earlier trade secret status was lost when X made the algorithms available to the general public on the web.

5. The rules for determining ownership of an invention (as between employer and employee) are the same, regardless of whether the invention is to be protected as a trade secret or patented. Under the

common law, if the inventor (here, Appleton) was hired especially to create inventions of the type involved, and the employer placed time and resources at the employee's disposal for that purpose, then an implied agreement will be found between the parties that any inventions developed by the employee in connection with this work will belong to the employer. If, on the other hand, the employee was not hired to create inventions of the type involved, but nonetheless creates an invention during the course of employment, or the employer placed no special resources at the employee's disposal for development of the invention, the employee will be deemed the owner of the invention. However, if the employee used the employer's work time, facilities, or supplies to develop the trade secret, then the employer will likely have a shop right in it.

Here, Appleton was hired to make medical-testing-related inventions generally, but he was not hired or expressly assigned to work on the AIDS testing invention involved here. Whether MegaLabs gave him resources for that purpose, at least initially, is arguable. Appleton could argue that MegaLabs provided few resources in the beginning, and only authorized him to spend half his time on the project after he had made the basic invention and was testing it. This would suggest that Appleton should be deemed the owner. On the other hand, MegaLabs might argue that by virtue of the Joint Research Agreement, Cohen's failed experiment (which was itself a trade secret) belonged to it, and that in using the failed experiment as a starting point, Appleton used valuable MegaLabs trade secrets in producing his own test. (Indeed, MegaLabs might go further to argue that since Appleton "substantially derived" his test from Cohen's test, and MegaLabs owned Cohen's test, Appleton could not use or disclose his own test without misappropriating the Cohen test, in violation of MegaLabs' ownership rights.)

If the court found ownership in Appleton, it would then be necessary to consider the effect of the employee nondisclosure agreement Appleton signed. As a general matter, an employee nondisclosure agreement only prohibits the employee from disclosing or using trade secrets that the common law or some other express contractual provision would allocate to the employer. However, the language of the purported "nondisclosure" agreement in this case is so broad that it might be construed to prohibit disclosure of trade secret information that the common law would otherwise allocate to Appleton. (The agreement provides that Appleton will not disclose any confidential information concerning the business affairs of MegaLabs "developed by" Appleton.) This would have the practical effect of a contractual advance assignment of all trade secrets created by Appleton to MegaLabs. Such a construction of the contractual language, however, could be criticized as contrary to public policy. Courts generally prefer to construe employee nondisclosure, assignment, and non-competition agreements narrowly because all three may impair the employee's opportunities to move to new employment and/or set up independent, competing businesses. Thus, while the agreement purports to prohibit Appleton from disclosing confidential information about MegaLabs's experimental and research work "developed by" Appleton during his employment, a court might be inclined to construe this language narrowly to apply only to confidential experimental and research information developed by Appleton *and to which the common law would assign ownership rights to MegaLabs.*

Thus, a liberal construction of the nondisclosure agreement language would possibly assign rights in the AIDS test to MegaLabs even though the common law would otherwise allocate ownership to Appleton. A narrower, more conservative construction of the agreement would find that the agreement only bound Appleton to avoid disclosing information that MegaLabs otherwise would own under the common-law rule, rather than finding that the agreement itself served as an assignment of

Appleton's rights in the AIDs invention. In the latter case, Appleton would continue to own the AIDS invention (though MegaLabs might possess a shop right to practice the test since Appleton used its resources in developing the test).

Another approach might be to argue that the AIDS test was jointly invented by Appleton and Cohen (Cohen having contributed to the inventive concept) and thus, by virtue of the Joint Research Agreement, MegaLabs owns a half interest in the invention as Cohen's assignee.)

If the court were to find either that the common law allocates ownership to MegaLabs or that the non-disclosure agreement assigns Appleton's common-law rights to MegaLabs, Appleton would be prevented from disclosing or using the AIDS test at least as long as it remains a trade secret or confidential. (Note that the facts say that the AIDS test was retained in secrecy throughout, and it undoubtedly gave its owner a competitive advantage. Thus, it probably qualified as a trade secret.) However, once the patent application (or the final issued patent) was published by the Patent Office the secret would be generally disclosed to the public, and Appleton could argue that he is no longer bound to keep the test in confidence.

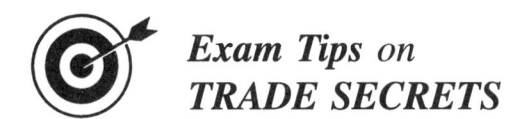

Exam Tips on TRADE SECRETS

☞ Trade secret exam questions often require that you evaluate whether information qualifies as a trade secret. To provide a thorough evaluation, state the Uniform Trade Secrets Act definition, and then think about the six factors discussed on pp. 7-8, *supra*. One way to organize your discussion effectively is to recognize that the six factors essentially ask two basic questions:

☞ Is the information secret? (factors 1, 2, 3, and 4); and

☞ Does the information have competitive value? (factors 5 and 6).

Be sure to consider each question.

☞ **Ownership issues:** If the exam question involves an employer-employee situation, there may be an ownership issue. If the employee created the trade secret, apply the standards discussed on p. 15, *supra,* to evaluate whether the employer owns the trade secret, and thus has rights to assert against the employee. Also remember that even if the employer is not the owner of the employee-made trade secret, and thus has no right to prevent the employee's use or disclosure, it may have a shop right, which permits it to continue to use the trade secret itself, without liability to the employee.

☞ **Public policy:** Trade secret law serves two basic purposes. First, it provides an incentive to businesses to develop and use innovative business know-how, which ultimately benefits the public. Second, it promotes the state's traditional police power interest in preventing dishonesty and immorality in commercial conduct. At the same time, strong enforcement of trade secret interests may be detrimental because it can interfere with marketplace competition and the ability of employees to move from one job to another and build their careers in their chosen fields. Courts are influenced by these potentially conflicting interests in deciding whether the facts in a given case give rise to liability for trade secret misappropriation.

In resolving a close case, it may be useful to evaluate how the interests enumerated above would be promoted or hindered by the recognition of trade secret rights. For example, if the alleged trade secret is not highly innovative, then there is not as great an interest in providing trade secret rights as an incentive to create. Likewise, if the defendant's acts were not strongly objectionable from a moral standpoint, the police power interest in assuring a moral marketplace will not be undermined if the court declines to find a cause of action. On the other hand, if the information is highly innovative, or the defendant's actions involve "dirty tricks" or a blatant betrayal of the plaintiff's trust, the court is more likely to find enforceable trade secret rights. Finally, if recognition and enforcement of trade secret rights would interfere with the free movement of an employee, a court is less likely to find a cause of action.

CHAPTER 3
PATENTS

ChapterScope

This chapter provides an overview of what constitutes patentable subject matter, the standards that inventions must meet to merit a patent, the process of applying for a patent, patent claim construction, the various rights of patentees, special defenses that can be raised to a claim of patent infringement, and infringement remedies. It also compares the advantages and disadvantages of patents and trade secret protection, and discusses some of the key international patent treaty provisions that affect U.S. patent practice. It does not go into the niceties of patent claim drafting and P.T.O. procedure, which are generally not encompassed in a survey course. While the chapter focuses primarily on utility patents, there are also short sections on design and plant patents. Here are the highlights:

- **The nature of patents:** A patent can be viewed as an agreement between the inventor and the public that in return for making and fully disclosing the invention to the public, the inventor obtains the exclusive right to exploit the invention for a limited period of time. Patents provide the strongest rights available under intellectual property law, but are also the hardest to get and last for the shortest period of time (generally, 20 years from the date the patent application is filed.) For details, an overview of *P.T.O. procedures*, and a discussion of the *judicial bodies* that review P.T.O. patent decisions and try patent infringement claims, see Section I, *infra*.

- **Patentable subject matter:** Utility patents are available for "any new and useful *process, machine, manufacture, or composition of matter*, or any new and useful improvement thereof." They are not available for *naturally occurring matter, laws of nature, or abstract ideas*. For elaboration, and particular discussion of patents for *computer programs, living matter, business methods,* and *medical procedures*, see Section II, *infra*.

- **The novelty requirement:** The novelty requirement essentially requires that the patent applicant's invention be "new." Patent Act §102(a), (e), and (g) work together to ensure that in most cases, American patents go to the *first person to invent* (as opposed to the first inventor to file, as is done in most countries). These three statutory subsections and the standards courts have developed to apply them are discussed in Section III.

- **The statutory bar:** Patent Act §102(b), (c), and (d) are meant to ensure that the U.S. public gets the benefit of new inventions as soon as possible by requiring that inventors *apply for a patent in a timely manner*. Section 102(b) also provides inventors a one-year *"grace" period* in which they can test the market for their inventions before making a financial commitment to patenting them. These important provisions, and the issue of who is an *"inventor,"* are discussed in Section IV.

- **The nonobviousness requirement:** To qualify for a patent, the applicant's new process, machine, manufacture or composition of matter must demonstrate *"invention"*—that is, it must represent more than ordinary skill in the art. Thus, to obtain a patent, an inventor must demonstrate that the invention *would not have been obvious to a person having ordinary skill in the pertinent art as it existed when the invention was made*. For discussion of what this showing entails, see Section V. Section V also discusses obviousness as a trigger for the §102(b) statutory bar.

- **Utility:** An invention must also be "useful," or have utility, to qualify for a patent. Generally, it will be useful if there is a *current, significant beneficial use for the invention*, or, in the case of a process, the product of the process. See Section VI.

- **Disclosure:** Patentees must fully disclose their inventions to the public as the price of obtaining a patent. This requirement can be broken down into four parts: the *claiming* requirement, the *enablement* requirement, the *best mode* requirement, and the *written description* requirement. See Section VII, *infra*, for details.

- **Claim interpretation:** Patent infringement occurs when the defendant's product or process falls within one or more of the patent claims. The product or process may infringe either *literally*, or pursuant to the *doctrine of equivalents*. Section VII discusses literal infringement, the doctrine of equivalents, and how the *doctrine of prosecution history estoppel* limits the doctrine of equivalents. It also discusses how courts construe the language of patent claims.

- **Infringing acts:** A person may be liable for: 1) *directly infringing* a patent (which entails making, using, offering to sell, selling, or importing an infringing product or process); 2) *inducing* another's infringement of a patent; 3) *contributing* to another's infringement of a patent; 4) importing, selling, offering to sell, or using a *product made abroad by means of a U.S.-patented process*; or 5) manufacturing or selling certain *components* of a patented invention *to be assembled abroad*. These actions are defined and discussed in Section VII, along with related issues such as the *doctrine of exhaustion* and *provisional rights*.

- **Defenses to infringement claims:** This chapter discusses five defenses that are specific to patent infringement cases: *patent invalidity, patent misuse, inequitable conduct,* the *experimental use* defense (and Patent Act §271(e)), and the *prior user* defense.

- **Infringement remedies:** A prevailing patentee can obtain *injunctive relief* and recover *damages* in the form of *lost profits* or a *reasonable royalty*, along with interest and costs. The Patent Act also provides for *attorney fees* and *enhanced damages* in the case of a defendant's bad faith or willful infringement. The rules for applying these provisions, along with the special provisions governing recovery against doctors and related health care entities in the case of medical procedure patents, are discussed in Section IX.

- **Patents and trade secrets compared:** Even though trade secret protection is much more limited than patent protection, it may have advantages in certain situations. The *costs and benefits* of each of these two forms of protection are compared in Section X.

- **Design patents:** Design patents protect the *ornamental designs of articles of manufacture*, in order to foster the decorative arts. To qualify, a product design must be *novel, non-obvious* and *ornamental*. Standards for determining infringement differ considerably from those for determining utility patent infringement. In some instances, a product may merit both a utility patent and a design patent, as long as the award does not constitute "*double patenting*." For details, see Section XI.

- **Plant patents:** Plant patents are also available to persons who discover and invent a *novel, non-obvious*, and *distinctive* variety of plant, and then *asexually reproduce* it. Asexual reproduction of the new plant variety is the key to finding "invention" on the discoverer's part, and is also the key to finding infringement. Today, new varieties of plants may be protected not only by plant patents, but also by *utility patents* and *certificates of plant variety protection*. See Section XII.

- **International treaties:** International patent treaties are very important to U.S. inventors because they provide the means to gain patent protection in other nations. These treaties have also played an important role in shaping U.S. patent law, and will continue to do so as nations seek to harmonize their patent laws to make global patent protection feasible. The chapter's last section discusses key provisions of the Paris Convention, the TRIPs Agreement, the Patent Cooperation Treaty and the WIPO Patent Law Treaty. See Section XIII.

PLEASE NOTE: At the time this chapter is being published, Congress is considering revisions to the Patent Act that would significantly change the way that U.S. patent law operates. The publisher has established a web site, at www.aspenlawschool.com/ip_outline, that will update this chapter if and as that becomes necessary. Please check the web site to see if Congress has enacted revisions to the Patent Act.

I. UTILITY PATENTS

Congress has provided for three kinds of patents: utility patents, design patents, and plant patents. Utility patents preceded the other two kinds of patents and are by far the most prevalent and economically important of the three. Most of this chapter will focus on utility patents. See pp. 75-80, *infra*, for brief discussions of design and plant patents.

A. **The nature of a utility patent:** A utility patent gives its owner exclusive rights in an invention. It can be viewed as an agreement between the inventor and the public (as represented by the federal government) that in return for making and fully disclosing the invention to the public, the public grants the inventor the right to prevent others, for a limited period of time, from making, using, selling, or offering to sell the invention in the United States, or from importing it into the United States.

B. **The term of a utility patent:** For many years the patent monopoly term was 17 years, commencing on the date the patent was issued. Today patents granted on applications filed after June 8, 1995, have a term that commences on the date the patent is *issued*, but the term is measured from the date the patent application was filed. The patent lasts 20 years from the date the application was filed. (There are some provisions for extending this term when the application process was subject to administrative delays. There are also some cases in which limited protection may commence prior to the issuance of the patent—this will be discussed later.) Under a transition provision, patents in existence on June 8, 1995 or subsequently granted on applications filed prior to that date will endure for the longer of 17 years from issuance or 20 years from the application date, whichever is longer. After the limited patent term elapses, the public has full access to the invention and may make, use, sell, offer to sell, or import it in competition with the inventor.

C. **Constitutional limitations:** Article I, Section 8, Clause 8 of the U.S. Constitution provides Congress with the power "to promote the Progress of Science and useful Arts, by securing for limited Times to... Inventors the exclusive Right to their... Discoveries." An important limitation is built into this provision: Congress may only grant an exclusive right (e.g., a monopoly) to an inventor when doing so "promotes progress in the useful arts." This will occur only when the value of having the invention made and disclosed to the public outweighs the negative impact of a monopoly on the public. Thus, an inventor has no natural rights in his or her invention. To qualify for a patent, an invention must meet patentability standards imposed by Congress.

D. Implementation of the limitations: Congress has implemented this constitutional limitation by providing that a utility patent will only be granted for fully disclosed inventions that are "novel," "non-obvious," and "useful." These standards will be discussed further below.

E. Enforcing the limitations: Applications for a patent are made to the U.S. Patent and Trademark Office (P.T.O.). The P.T.O. examines each application to determine whether the invention it claims is novel, non-obvious, and useful, and has been fully disclosed. If the P.T.O. finds that these requirements are all satisfied, it issues a patent. However, if the recipient (patentee) seeks to enforce the patent against another in a patent infringement action, the defendant may raise patent invalidity as a defense. Moreover, the validity of the patent may be challenged in a declaratory judgment action in some cases.

The P.T.O.'s issuance of a patent provides a *presumption* of patent validity, but if the defendant or declaratory judgment plaintiff can bear the burden of proving by clear and convincing evidence that the invention in fact did not satisfy the novelty, non-obviousness, or usefulness standards, or was not sufficiently disclosed to the public, the court will hold the patent invalid and unenforceable. The novelty, non-obviousness, usefulness, and disclosure standards are strong standards. Many applications are rejected by the P.T.O., and a significant percentage of the patents granted are later invalidated by courts for failure to meet these standards.

1. **Summary of the P.T.O. examination process:** Applicants for a patent must file: (1) a written specification, which describes the invention and sets forth patent claims, as required by Patent Act §112; (2) an oath or declaration stating that the applicant believes herself to be the original and first inventor of the subject matter; (3) drawings, where required; and (4) the filing fee. The applicant's filing date is the date on which the P.T.O. receives the specification and any required drawings. The application is assigned to an examiner with expertise in the invention's area of technology, who searches U.S. and foreign patent documents and other available published literature to determine whether the claimed invention is novel and non-obvious, as required under Patent Act §§102 and 103. The examiner also reviews the application for compliance with other requirements, and then notifies the applicant in writing of his initial decision (this is known as the "first office action"). In many cases, this first office action will reject some or all of the applicant's claims. The applicant can then request reconsideration, explaining why the examiner's decision was wrong, or amend the application, explaining why the amended claims cure any perceived deficiencies. The examiner will then issue a second office action granting or denying a patent. If a patent is granted, the P.T.O. makes the patent prosecution file available to the public. The patentee must pay an issuance fee and periodic maintenance fees to retain the patent in force.

    a. **Provisional applications:** Applicants who want to obtain an early filing date, but who are not ready to make a full filing, may file a "provisional application." To do this, the inventor must file a written description of the invention and drawings with the P.T.O., but need not submit claims or an oath. Once the provisional application is filed, the applicant has up to 12 months to file a regular, full application, complete with claims. The application only proceeds to examination once this subsequent filing is made. However, the full application gets the benefit of the earlier, provisional application date.

    b. **Publication:** The P.T.O. holds patent applications in confidence. However, under Patent Act §122 as recently amended, the P.T.O. generally publishes non-provisional utility patent applications 18 months after their earliest filing date. The applicant can avoid publication under certain circumstances. For details, see *infra*, pp. 65-66.

2. **Routes of appeal:** If a patent examiner finds that an invention is not patentable, the applicant may file a "continuation application" (to obtain consideration of different claims or further evidence) or take an administrative appeal to the P.T.O. Board of Appeals. If the Board provides no relief, the applicant may take an appeal on the administrative record directly to the U.S. Court of Appeals for the Federal Circuit. Under the Administrative Procedure Act, the Federal Circuit may set aside P.T.O. findings of fact if they are arbitrary, capricious, an abuse of discretion, or unsupported by substantial evidence. Alternatively, the disappointed applicant may file suit against the Commissioner of Patents and Trademarks in the U.S. District Court for the District of Columbia, where a *de novo* review of patentability will be made. Any appeal from the district court will be taken to the Court of Appeals for the Federal Circuit. In that case, the Federal Circuit will review the district court's findings of fact under the stricter "clearly erroneous" standard.

   a. **The Federal Circuit has exclusive appellate jurisdiction in patent cases:** Prior to 1982, appeals from U.S. district court decisions in patent cases were taken to the regional U.S. Circuit Courts of Appeals, and appeals from decisions of the P.T.O. went to the Court of Customs and Patent Appeals. In 1982 Congress created a new court—the Court of Appeals for the Federal Circuit—and gave it jurisdiction over all the cases that had gone to the U.S. Court of Claims and the Court of Customs and Patent Appeals in the past (these latter two courts were discontinued). In addition, Congress provided that the new Court of Appeals for the Federal Circuit would have exclusive jurisdiction over appeals from district courts in patent cases. (Appeals from final judgements in which the only patent issue was raised in the defendant's answer—as opposed to the plaintiff's complaint—still go to the regional circuit courts.) Accordingly, except when the Supreme Court grants *certiorari* in a patent case, the Court of Appeals for the Federal Circuit is practically the only appellant authority on patent law.

3. **Reissue:** If a patent issues but is defective, the defects may be cured through a reissue proceeding in the P.T.O., as long as the defects are not the result of the applicant's deceptive conduct. For example, a patent claim (the language that describes and defines the invention, and sets the official "metes and bounds" of patent monopoly protection) may be worded too broadly, encompassing things that are not novel or non-obvious. An overbroad claim renders the patent vulnerable to challenge and invalidation in court. The patentee may wish to have the P.T.O. reissue the patent with narrower claim language. In the alternative, a claim may inadvertently be worded too narrowly, thus failing to protect the whole of the patentee's invention. In this case, the applicant will want to have the claims broadened. He may do so, if he applies for reissue within two years of the original grant.

4. **Reexamination:** Pursuant to the Patent Act, any person, including the patentee, may ask the P.T.O. to reexamine the validity of an issued patent in light of preexisting patents or printed publications that may cast light on the patented invention's novelty or obviousness. If the P.T.O. determines that the request raises a substantial issue of patentability that was not previously considered, it will undertake a reexamination to resolve the issue. Upon conclusion of the reexamination, the P.T.O. may cancel claims found to be unpatentable, confirm claims found to be patentable, incorporate amendments to the existing patent claims or add newly drafted claims.

a. *Inter partes* **reexamination procedure:** Prior to passage of the Optional Inter Partes Reexamination Procedure Act in 1999, all reexaminations were *ex parte*, so that third parties (that is, persons other than the patentee) who requested that a patent be reexamined were not entitled to participate after initiating the proceedings. The 1999 Act provided third parties requesting reexamination an option to elect an *inter partes* proceeding. Under this option, the third-party requester is entitled to receive copies of materials submitted by either the P.T.O. or the patentee during the course of the reexamination and provide written comments on these materials. In addition, the third-party requestor can appeal to the P.T.O. Board of Patent Appeals and Interferences from an examiner's determination that the reexamined patent is valid. Amendments enacted in 2002 now enable third-party requestors to appeal an adverse decision by the Board of Patent Appeals and Interferences to the Court of Appeals for the Federal Circuit, and to be a party to any appeal brought by the patentee. This new procedure is meant to provide a more meaningful, less expensive alternative to a court challenge to the validity of a patent. It has not proven popular, however, because once the patentability issues raised by a third-party requestor have been resolved against the requestor, he is estopped from raising them (or other issues that might have been raised in the reexamination) in a subsequent civil action. This is perceived as a significant drawback, since reexamination proceedings provide no opportunity for discovery, or cross-examination, which are routinely available in judicial proceedings.

PLEASE NOTE: Congress is considering amendments to the patent reexamination provisions, and is also considering enactment of a new post-grant opposition procedure. Please check the web site for updates: www.aspenlawschool.com/ip_outline.

II. STATUTORY SUBJECT MATTER OF A UTILITY PATENT

Patent Act §101 provides for utility patents for "any new and useful process, machine, manufacture, or composition of matter, or any new and useful improvement thereof." In defining "process," "machine," "manufacture," and "composition of matter," the courts have tended to rely on the ordinary dictionary meaning of these terms. There is some overlap—many inventions could be characterized as falling into more than one of these categories.

- **A. Process:** A process has been defined as "a mode of treatment of certain materials to produce a given result. It is an act, or series of acts, performed upon the subject-matter to be transformed and reduced to a different state or thing." *Cochrane v. Deener*, 94 U.S. 780 (1877). The novelty in a process may be found either in its steps or in its particular combination of known steps.

    1. **New use of a known process, machine, manufacture, or composition of matter:** A process patent may be available for a new manner of using a known process or thing.

        Example: Turpentine has existed for a long time and is used to remove paint. X discovers that a small dose of turpentine once a month for dogs kills heart worms without hurting the dog. X may be entitled to a process patent for his new method of using turpentine. Note, however, that this patent does not give the patentee a monopoly in turpentine, as such, because X did not invent it, and it has been in the public domain for a long time. X only has rights in his method of using the turpentine to control heart worms in dogs.

- **B. Machine:** Courts have defined a machine as an instrument that consists of parts or elements that are organized to cooperate, when set in motion, to produce a definite, predetermined result. The terms "apparatus," "mechanism," "device," or "engine" are interchangeable with the term "machine." The novelty in a machine may lie in its particular components or in its particular arrangement of components.

C. **Manufacture:** The term "manufacture" refers to an article of manufacture. The Supreme Court has defined manufacture as "'the production of articles for use from raw or prepared materials by giving those materials new forms, qualities, properties or combinations, whether by hand labor or by machinery; also, anything made for use from raw or prepared materials.'" *American Fruit Growers, Inc v. Brogdex Co.*, 283 U.S. 1 (1931) (quoting from *Century Dictionary*). This is a residual category, encompassing many patentable inventions that fail to fall into one of the other categories.

D. **Composition of matter:** The Supreme Court has defined compositions of matter as "all compositions of two or more substances and all composite articles, whether they be the results of chemical union or of mechanical mixture, or whether they be gases, fluids, powders or solids." *Diamond v. Chakrabarty*, 447 U.S. 303 (1980).

E. **Naturally occurring vs. man-made articles:** Naturally occurring articles may not be patented, even by the person who is the first to discover them in nature. However, a naturally occurring article may become the subject of a patent if the applicant has changed it in a significant way, giving it characteristics that it would not develop naturally. In that case it has been transformed into a man-made article.

Example: X discovers that the bark of a certain kind of tree can be used successfully to treat malaria. X cannot get a patent on the bark, as such, because it is naturally occurring. However, if X is able to extract the chemical compound having the medicinal value from the tree bark and purify it, he may get a patent for the purified chemical compound, because the compound does not exist in nature in a purified state. Likewise, X might get a patent for a synthesized version of the chemical compound. (Note that, in addition, X might get patents for his process of extracting and purifying or synthesizing the chemical compound, and for the process of applying the compound to treat malaria patients.)

F. **Live vs. inanimate matter:** In *Diamond v. Chakrabarty, supra*, the U.S. Supreme Court rejected arguments that Congress intended to limit utility patents to inanimate matter. The Court found that Congress had intended to make utility patents available for "everything under the sun that is made by man." Thus, genetically engineered life forms that had characteristics that they would not have had in nature could be the subject of a utility patent. In *Chakrabarty*, a patent was authorized for a genetically engineered bacterium that could be used to consume oil in oil spills. The P.T.O. has subsequently construed *Chakrabarty* as authorizing patents for higher life forms, such as genetically engineered mice, sheep, and cows.

G. **Laws of nature and abstract ideas:** The Supreme Court has stated that laws of nature and abstract ideas may not in themselves be the subject of a patent. There are two reasons generally given for this rule. First, a person does not create these things—they exist independently in nature and are discovered. Second, granting exclusive rights in such basic building blocks of invention would pose an undue roadblock to further invention by others. Thus, for example, Albert Einstein would not be entitled to a patent on his formula $E = mc^2$, because it is a law of nature. It is easy to see how granting a monopoly in it might unduly block further invention by others.

1. **Specific applications of laws of nature and abstract ideas:** Specific applications of laws of nature, mathematical formulas, and other abstract ideas may be the subject of a patent. Thus,

for example, a machine whose operation depends in part on the law of gravity is not disqualified from a patent simply because it incorporates that law of nature within its specific context. Granting a patent in such a case will not give the patentee exclusive rights in the law of gravity—only in one specific application of it.

2. **Applicability of the rule to computer programs:** The Supreme Court has held that a mathematical algorithm (a procedure for solving a given type of mathematical problem) is like a mathematical formula or law of nature, and thus cannot be patented. Since computer programs consist of mathematical algorithms, they may not constitute patentable subject matter in and of themselves. However, incorporating a computer program as a step in a process or as a component of a physical apparatus does not render the claimed process or apparatus unpatentable.

Example: In *Diamond v. Diehr*, 450 U.S. 175 (1981), the Court upheld a patent for a process comprised of steps to (1) load synthetic rubber into a mold; (2) monitor the internal temperature of the mold; (3) use a computer program to repeatedly recalculate the time needed to cure the rubber, given variations in the temperature; and (4) open the mold when the proper time for curing had elapsed. The Court reasoned that the patent would not give the patentee a monopoly in the computer program or mathematical algorithm that it contained, but only in the use of that program or algorithm in connection with the rest of the steps in the process. This constituted a specific application of a mathematical algorithm or "law of nature."

   a. **The Federal Circuit's expansion and clarification of rules regarding when mathematical algorithms are patentable subject matter:** Since the Supreme Court's decision in *Diamond v. Diehr,* the Court of Appeals for the Federal Circuit has rendered a number of decisions about the patentability of algorithm (or software)-related inventions, and has expanded patent protection for these inventions to the point that most of them now constitute patentable subject matter.

      i. *Alappat*: In *In re Alappat,* 33 F.3d 1526 (Fed. Cir. 1994), the Federal Circuit held that a claim for a known, general-purpose computer programmed with a new mathematical algorithm states patentable subject matter. According to the court, new programming creates a new machine because a general-purpose computer in effect becomes a special-purpose computer once it is programmed to perform particular useful functions pursuant to instructions from a computer program. Accordingly, a person wishing to obtain patent protection in new software can claim the software algorithm in connection with standard, known hardware. The resulting patent will permit the patentee to prevent others from using the combination of elements described in the claim—the algorithm in conjunction with the hardware.

      ii. **Algorithms and a storage medium:** It is also now established that a claim to an algorithm in connection with a storage medium, such as a floppy disk, will state patentable subject matter. Because the storage of the program on the disk changes the physical features of the disk, the storage creates a new article of manufacture.

      iii. *State Street*: In *State Street Bank & Trust Co. v. Signature Financial Group, Inc.,* 149 F.3d 1368 (Fed. Cir. 1998), *cert. denied,* 525 U.S. 1093 (1999), the Federal Circuit held that the ultimate question, for purposes of evaluating the patentability of mathematical algorithms, is whether the applicant is claiming an algorithm in the abstract (which would constitute an unpatentable abstract idea) or whether the claim is for a useful application of an algorithm, which results in "a useful, concrete and tangible result."

Example: In *State Street*, the applicant claimed a computer programmed with an algorithm to calculate the price of mutual fund shares. The court held that the claim stated patentable subject matter even though the invention was directly solely to crunching numbers. The court reasoned: "the transformation of data, representing discrete dollar amounts, by a machine through a series of mathematical calculations into a final share price, constitutes a practical application of a mathematical algorithm, formula, or calculation, because it produces a useful, concrete and tangible result—a final share price momentarily fixed for recording and reporting purposes...."

    iv. **AT&T:** In *AT&T Corp. v. Excel Communications, Inc.*, 172 F.3d 1352 (Fed. Cir. 1999), the Federal Circuit held that the "useful, concrete and tangible result" test used in *State Street* should apply to determine patentability not only in the case of machine claims, but also in the case of process claims. Thus, a claim that applies an algorithm to produce a useful, concrete, tangible result without preempting other uses will state a patentable process. The court rejected arguments that the claimed process must produce a physical transformation of matter, or incorporate tangible elements.

    Example: In *AT&T*, the claims were for a process to enable long-distance carriers to provide differential billing treatment for subscribers and non-subscribers. The process called for application of Boolean algebra to certain subscriber and call recipient data, and application of the resulting value to create a signal useful for billing purposes. The claims did not include any physical elements, such as computer hardware. Nonetheless, the court held that they stated patentable subject matter.

H. **Business methods:** For many years, it was believed that business methods were beyond the scope of patents. However, in the *State Street* case, discussed *supra*, the Court of Appeals for the Federal Circuit held that business methods were patentable subject matter. In that case, the court held that a programmed computer that would be used in administering a particular type of mutual fund was patentable subject matter. Since then, numerous "business methods" have been patented. Many of them constitute methods of implementing particular business practices in the Internet context, such as the "Priceline.com patent," which essentially claims the "reverse auction" or "name-your-own-price" online shopping method. Patent claims are not limited to the "technological arts." The P.T.O.'s Board of Patent Appeals and Interferences has determined that business method claims are patentable even when they do not associate the method with technology or technological elements, such as computer hardware.

I. **Medical procedures:** As a matter of public policy, many countries do not grant patents for medical or surgical procedures. However, the United States has not proscribed issuance of patents in this subject area. In 1996, after considering proposals to prohibit patents for medical procedures, Congress amended the Patent Act, not to prohibit such patents, but rather to limit infringement remedies that owners of patents for certain kinds of medical procedures would otherwise have against medical practitioners and related health-care entities. For further information about this limitation, see the section on patent infringement remedies, at p. 74, *infra*.

PLEASE NOTE: Among the proposed revisions to the Patent Act is an amendment that would prohibit patents for tax planning methods. Please check the web site for updates: www.aspenlawschool.com/ip_outline.

III. THE NOVELTY STANDARD

PLEASE NOTE: Proposed revisions pending before Congress would drastically change the U.S. patent novelty requirement. Among other things, the revisions would transform the United States from a "first-to-invent" system of priority to a "first-to-file" system of priority. Novelty would be judged as of an applicant's application date, and patent interference proceedings would no longer be necessary. Please check the web site for updates: www.aspenlawschool.com/ip_outline.

The requirement that the patented invention be novel is set forth in §102 of the Patent Act. 35 U.S.C. §102. As you will see, the §102 novelty provisions refer to events that took place prior to the patent applicant's invention date and involved the *same* invention as that claimed by the patent applicant. For purposes of the §102 novelty requirement, the invention that was involved in the earlier event must have had all the same elements as the invention that the applicant claims in the application, arranged in the same way. Three subsections of Patent Act §102 comprise the novelty requirement: §§102(a), (e), and (g). Together, they ensure that inventions that have entered the public domain prior to an applicant's invention date are not patented, and ensure that in most cases, the first person to make the invention (as opposed to the first inventor to file an application) gets the patent.

A. Subsection 102(a): Subsection 102(a) provides that a patent must be denied if "the invention was known or used by others in this country, or patented or described in a printed publication in this or a foreign country, before the invention thereof by the applicant for patent. . . ." In such case, the applicant's invention will be deemed "anticipated," and thus lacking the necessary novelty to qualify for a patent. The focus in the subsection (a) inquiry is on the *actions of persons other than the inventor/applicant prior to the date the inventor/applicant made the invention*. Prior to that date, did those other persons cause the invention to be known or used in the United States? Did they cause it to be patented or did they make it the subject of a printed publication anywhere in the world? The policy behind this provision is to prevent a second inventor from obtaining a patent monopoly if a previous inventor has already placed the invention in the public domain in any of the listed ways before the second inventor invented.

   1. When an invention is "known by others" in this country: While there has been little case law to illuminate when an invention will be deemed to have been "known by others," within the meaning of §102(a), the Court of Customs and Patent Appeals in *In re Borst*, 345 F.2d 851 (C.C.P.A.) (1965), *cert. denied*, 382 U.S. 973 (1966), set forth two criteria: (1) the invention must have been fully disclosed; and (2) the disclosed invention must have been accessible to the U.S. public.

   a. The invention must have been fully disclosed: An invention will be fully disclosed for purposes of §102(a) if it was reduced to practice. Reduction to practice can be actual or constructive. Actual reduction to practice entails building an operable prototype—building a physical embodiment of the invention (or, in the case of a process, carrying out the physical steps of the process) as described in the applicant's patent claims and ascertaining that the invention works for its intended purpose. Constructive reduction to practice entails creating and filing an application for patent. An application for patent must describe the invention with sufficient specificity to enable a person with ordinary skill in the relevant art to make the invention without undue experimentation. In *Borst*, the court held that in addition to reducing the invention to practice, as defined above, the earlier inventor may satisfy the disclosure requirement of §102(a) by creating a writing, other than a patent application, that describes the invention in sufficient detail to enable a person with ordinary skill in the art to make it without undue experimentation.

b. **The invention must have been available to the public:** The *Borst* court held that, in addition to being reduced to practice, the invention must have been available to the public. Under subsection (a), private or secret knowledge of the invention will not preclude a later inventor from obtaining a patent. While the perimeters of this second requirement are uncertain, it has been held that private intracorporate communications, army reports transmitted to a limited number of government agencies, and abandoned patent applications are not sufficiently "available to the general public" to make the invention "known by others in this country" for purposes of subsection 102(a). On the other hand, it is possible that something less than "publication," as defined below, may suffice. For example, orally describing the invention to unrelated third parties who have skill in the art, are in a position to make the invention available to the public, and are under no restriction against using the information, might suffice.

c. **The invention must have been known to others in the United States:** It is important to note that the invention must have been known or used by others *in the United States*. Evidence that the invention was known or used by others in other parts of the world before the U.S. applicant invented will not preclude the granting of a U.S. patent under subsection 102(a).

2. **When an invention will be deemed "used by others" in this country:** The invention has been "used by others" in the United States prior to the applicant's invention for purposes of §102(a) if it was reduced to actual practice and used in the manner and context for which it was intended. The use must have been *accessible* to the public, but it is not necessary that affirmative steps were made to familiarize the public with the invention. Nor is it necessary that the case be enabling—that is, that the use provide sufficient information to enable a person with ordinary skill in the art to make or practice the invention.

   Example: A, the applicant, invented a type of cash register on January 1, 1989. In January, 1984, X had invented the same cash register and had made a physical embodiment of it. During the same year, X installed the cash register in his store and used it in selling goods to customers. He only used it for four months. However, these facts should be sufficient to preclude A from obtaining a patent under subsection 102(a), because the cash register was "used by others" in the United States prior to the date of A's invention.

   Example: X invents an airline reservation system, which, by 1970, is used by over a thousand travel agencies to make travel reservations for members of the public. Although system terminals are provided to the travel agents, X retains the essential algorithms of the system software in confidence, so that those aspects of the system that are apparent to agents and the public are not sufficient to enable one skilled in the art to duplicate the system. The system nonetheless is deemed "used by others," and qualifies as prior art which may anticipate a system invented after X's distribution to travel agents. *Lockwood v. American Airlines, Inc.*, 107 F.3d 1565 (Fed. Cir. 1997).

3. **When an invention will be deemed described in a printed publication in this or a foreign country:** To find a "printed publication" which anticipates an applicant's invention under subsection 102(a), several considerations are relevant. First, the publication must have been "printed." Second, there must have been a "publication." Third, the alleged printed publication

must have set forth sufficient information about the invention to enable a person with ordinary skill in the art to make it without undue experimentation. Note that a printed publication *anywhere in the world* may anticipate an applicant's invention under subsection 102(a), and thus render it unpatentable for lack of novelty.

   a. The "printed" requirement: While earlier decisions interpreted the "printed" requirement strictly, the more recent trend is to interpret it broadly, to give effect to ongoing advances in the technologies of data storage, retrieval, and dissemination. Thus, more modern decisions have deemed such things as microfilm and photocopies to be "printed." The chief consideration is whether the information was reduced to a tangible, permanent form that was discernible by the public.

   b. The "publication" requirement: In this context the "printed" information will be deemed a publication if, as a practical matter, the information was accessible to the public. It will be deemed accessible if an interested American, exercising reasonable diligence, could obtain the information.

   Example: One copy of a masters thesis has been found to be a printed publication for subsection 102(a) purposes when lodged in a public library and properly indexed. If not properly indexed, however, it would not constitute a printed publication, because persons searching for it could not reasonably be expected to find it.

   Example: Circulating a limited number of copies of a document to experts in the field at a conference has been found a sufficient publication, as long as there was no secrecy requirement imposed on the recipients. (If the printed publication is alleged to have occurred outside the United States, courts have been somewhat stricter, seeking to determine whether, as a practical matter, Americans might be expected to have access.)

   Example: The Federal Circuit recently found a printed publication when the inventors of a method of preparing foods containing extruded soy cotyledon fiber prepared a slide presentation that fully disclosed their invention, and then printed the 14 slides onto poster boards and displayed them at a meeting of the American Association of Cereal Chemists and at a university agriculture experiment station. The inventors did not provide a disclaimer or notice to the intended audience prohibiting note-taking or copying of the presentation. On the other hand, they did not disseminate any copies of the presentation. In finding a printed publication, the Federal Circuit rejected arguments that printed matter must be either disseminated, indexed at a library, or cataloged in a database in order to be deemed "published." The court reiterated that public accessibility is the key to finding a printed publication, and reasoned that in the absence of distribution or indexing, several factors should be considered to determine whether the printed matter was sufficiently publicly accessible: 1) the length of time the matter was displayed or exhibited; 2) the expertise of the target audience; 3) the existence (or lack thereof) of reasonable expectations that the displayed material would not be copied; and 4) the simplicity or ease with which the displayed material could have been copied. *In re Klopfenstein*, 380 F.3d 1345 (Fed. Cir. 2004).

4. **When an invention will be deemed patented in this or a foreign country:** In many cases patents are published, and thus serve as "printed publications," disclosing any inventions described in the patent. In such cases the issue of whether the invention was "patented" for purposes of subsection 102(a) need not be determined. However, in some countries patents are

not published, or are published only some time after they are granted. In such cases, the question of whether the invention was "patented" before the applicant's invention date becomes important. There are two issues that must be considered: (1) was the applicant's invention the actual subject matter of the earlier patent; and if so, (2) at what point in time was the invention actually "patented"?

   a. **Was it the applicant's invention that was "patented"?** Only material that was included in the patent claims or was otherwise the subject of exclusive rights under the earlier patent is "patented" for purposes of subsection 102(a). Thus, if the applicant's invention was disclosed in the earlier patent but was not included in the patent's monopoly grant, then the applicant's invention was not "patented."

   Example: In *Carter Products v. Colgate-Palmolive Co.*, 130 F. Supp. 557 (D. Md. 1955), *aff'd*, 230 F.2d 855 (4th Cir.), *cert. denied*, 352 U.S. 843 (1956), the U.S. applicant filed an application to patent an aerosol shaving cream, claiming an exact mixture of soap and gas propellant which remained separate in the can but generated foam when released under pressure. An unpublished Argentine patent did not give monopoly rights in this mixture, but the mixture was discussed in the patent specification (the specification is the written disclosure that explains how to make or practice the claimed invention). The court found that the U.S. applicant's patent was not anticipated under subsection 102(a).

   b. **The date of patenting:** For purposes of subsection 102(a), an invention generally is deemed "patented" on the date the patent becomes effective to grant exclusive rights to its recipient, as long as the contents of the patent are at least minimally available to the public (whether or not a "printed publication") at that point.

B. **Subsection 102(e):** Subsection 102(e) denies a patent to B if: (1) at the time B invented, the same invention was described in an application for patent pending in the P.T.O.; and (2) that application was ultimately published under Patent Act §122(b) or granted. The policy behind this provision is related to that behind subsection 102(a). The second person to invent should not obtain monopoly rights if the first to invent has taken steps that ultimately lead to public disclosure. (Most U.S. patent applications are published 18 months after they are filed. Even when the application is not published at this time, the patent claims and accompanying disclosure will be published at the time the patent is granted. Either form of publication makes the invention, and information about how to make or practice it, fully available to the public.) The information contained in the earlier, pending application will be deemed prior art as of the date the earlier application was filed.

Example: A describes a new type of widget in an application for patent which he files with the P.T.O. on January 1, 1987. B invents the same widget on July 1, 1987. If A's application ultimately is published or granted, B will be precluded from obtaining a patent, even though A's earlier widget may not have been "known or used in the U.S." or the subject of a patent or printed publication prior to B's invention date, as provided under subsection 102(a). (A's widget may not have been known, used, or disclosed in a printed publication within the meaning of subsection (a) because, under U.S. law, pending patent applications are maintained in secrecy until they are published (18 months after their filing date) or granted. Note that even though A's pending application is not in fact published or granted until after B invents, the ultimate publication or grant makes A's widget "prior art," for purposes of evaluating the novelty of B's invention, as of A's filing date—Jan. 1, 1987.)

C. **Subsection 102(g):** Subsection 102(g) prohibits B from obtaining a patent if A made the same invention in the United States before B, and A did not abandon, suppress, or conceal it prior to B's invention date. Thus, an earlier U.S. invention by A may preclude B from obtaining a patent even though the provisions of neither subsection 102(a) nor 102(e) have been satisfied. Subsections 102(a), (e), and (g), taken together, demonstrate the general U.S. policy of reserving a patent for the first person to invent in most cases, with exceptions when necessary to ensure that inventions are made available to the public. Essentially, when an earlier inventor invented in the United States, the second inventor may obtain a patent only when the first abandoned, suppressed, or concealed the invention, thereby denying the public the benefit of the invention.

1. **Determining who is first to invent:** Invention requires: (1) an inventive concept; and (2) reduction of the inventive concept to practice. It is presumed that the first person to reduce the concept to practice is the first to invent, but this presumption can be rebutted. *If the second person to reduce to practice can demonstrate that he was the first to conceive of the invention and was diligent in reducing the conception to practice from a date prior to the other's date of conception, he will be found to be the first inventor.*

    a. **The inventive concept:** An inventor will be deemed to have conceived of the invention when he perceives a specific result and a particular means of accomplishing that result, so that no more than ordinary skill in the art is needed to build or carry out the invention.

    b. **Reduction to practice:** For purposes of subsection 102(g), an invention may be either actually or constructively reduced to practice, as defined on p. 36, *supra*.

    c. **Reasonable diligence in reducing to practice:** Reasonable diligence in reducing the invention to practice requires that the inventor continually apply himself to reducing the conceived invention to actual or constructive practice. Gaps in time in which no effort is expended toward reduction to practice will be excused only if reasonable—for example, if due to illness or poverty. Delays due to the inventor's efforts to commercially exploit the invention or to his doubts about the value of the invention generally are not excused.

    Example: Assume that there are two independent inventors, A and B.

    - A is the first to conceive of the invention and the first to reduce it to practice. A is the first to invent. Diligence is irrelevant.

    - A is the first to conceive of the invention but the second to reduce it to practice. (B conceived of the invention after A but reduced it to practice before A.) A will be deemed the first inventor only if she was diligent in reducing the invention to practice from a date prior to B's conception.

    - A was the second to conceive of the invention and the second to reduce it to practice. A is not the first to invent.

    - A and B conceive of the invention simultaneously but A is the first to reduce it to practice. A is the first to invent. Diligence is irrelevant.

2. **Abandonment, suppression, and concealment:** Even if B was the second to invent, he may be favored over A, an earlier U.S. inventor, and granted a patent if A abandoned, suppressed, or concealed the invention prior to B's invention date. This is because the patent laws are

intended to encourage people not only to make inventions but also to make their benefit available to the public. To this end, the terms "abandonment," "suppression," and "concealment" are construed to ensure that an earlier U.S. inventor is diligent in bringing the invention to the public—either by applying for a patent or by taking other steps necessary to make the invention or its product available to the public—before he can preclude a later inventor from obtaining a patent.

    a. **Failure to file for a patent:** The fact that the first inventor has failed to apply for a patent does not in itself mean that he has abandoned, suppressed, or concealed within the meaning of subsection 102(g), if he has worked diligently to bring the invention to the public through means of commercialization or publication.

    b. **Commercializing the invention:** Courts have suggested that the first inventor's maintenance of the invention as a trade secret is not necessarily an abandonment, concealment, or suppression for purposes of subsection 102(g), as long as the public receives the benefit of the invention—for example, if the invention is a manufacturing process, the public receives access to a product made through use of the invention. In *Checkpoint Systems, Inc. v. U.S. Int'l Trade Comm.*, 54 F.3d 756 (Fed. Cir. 1995), the Court of Appeals for the Federal Circuit held that a finding of abandonment, suppression, or concealment can be avoided by showing that the first inventor engaged in reasonable efforts to bring the invention to market. The key issue was whether the nature and tempo of activities between the initial invention date and ultimate market distribution were in accord with reasonable business practices. If so, the first inventor would not be deemed to have abandoned, suppressed, or concealed the invention, even if it took several years following the invention date to get the invention on the market.

    c. **Resumption of activity prior to second inventor's invention date:** If A, the first inventor, abandoned, suppressed, or concealed his invention, but resumed activity to bring it to the public before B (the second inventor) invented, A can rely on his date of resumption as his date of invention. Because that date is prior to B's date of invention, B will not be entitled to a patent.

    Example: A invents in 1986. He abandons, suppresses, or conceals the invention until July, 1989. In July, 1989, he returns his attention to the invention, and applies for a patent. If B invented in 1987, B should win. Even though B was the second inventor, A, the first inventor, abandoned, suppressed, or concealed, and did not resume his efforts to bring the invention to the public until after B's invention date. However, if B invented in October, 1989, B should lose. A should have the benefit of his July, 1989, resumption date as his date of invention. Thus, even with this new invention date, A is still the "first inventor," and he has not abandoned, suppressed, or concealed since July, 1989, a date prior to B's invention.

3. **Interferences:** While issues of priority of invention are sometimes litigated in lawsuits in which the validity of an issued patent is challenged, more frequently the issue of priority is litigated before the P.T.O. in a proceeding known as an "interference." The P.T.O. may declare an interference between an issued patent and an application or between two pending applications, when both claim rights in the same invention, and it is necessary to determine which was first, and thus has priority.

a. **Earlier invention abroad:** In addition to the provision discussed in §§C and C2 above, section 102(g) also provides that a second inventor will be denied a patent if the invention has already been made *abroad*, and has not been abandoned, suppressed, or concealed. However, the earlier foreign invention will only preclude the later U.S. inventor from getting a patent if the first (foreign) inventor is able to establish his earlier invention date in a patent interference proceeding. Patent Act §104 limits a foreign inventor's ability to make such a showing.

IV. THE STATUTORY BAR AND INVENTOR REQUIREMENTS

PLEASE NOTE: Proposed revisions pending before Congress would significantly change the current statutory bar requirements. Please check for updates on the web site: www.aspenlawschool.com/ip_outline.

The statutory bar provisions, set forth in Patent Act §§102(b), (c), and (d), are primarily aimed at encouraging patentees to file their patent applications (and thus disclose their inventions to the public) in a timely manner. Section 102(f) ensures that the patent applicant is the inventor.

A. **The §102(b) statutory bar:** While subsections 102(a), (e), and (g) are meant to ensure that patented inventions are novel, and that patents generally go to the first person to make the invention, subsections 102(b), (c), and (d) are meant to ensure that inventors file their applications for patent in a timely manner. Subsection 102(b) provides that a patent must be denied if "the invention was patented or described in a printed publication in this or a foreign country or in public use or on sale in this country, more than one year prior to the date of the application for patent in the United States." Thus, the focus in this section is on *the actions both of the inventor/applicant and others more than one year before the application was filed*. (Note that the date of application may differ from the date of invention, which is the focus in subsections 102(a), (e), and (g).)

1. **A statute of limitations:** Subsection (b) may be viewed as a form of statute of limitations—regardless of when the invention is made, once the invention becomes accessible to the public through one of the means enumerated in subsection (b), the inventor has one year in which to file her application for a patent. If she fails to do so, she will lose any right to a patent she otherwise would have had.

   a. **Policy considerations:** The Court of Appeals for the Federal Circuit has identified four policy considerations behind this provision.

   i. **Early disclosure:** First, §102(b) encourages inventors to apply for a patent (and thus disclose the invention and the way to make or practice it to the public) as soon after the invention as possible. Early disclosure to the public facilitates use and improvement of the inventive concept and cuts short wasteful duplicative work by other inventors.

   ii. **Public reliance:** Second, §102(b) insures that inventions in the public domain for more than one year remain there and are not removed by the granting of a patent monopoly. This allows members of the public to rely on the continued availability of the invention and invest accordingly.

   iii. **Inventor's interest in testing the market:** Third, §102(b) acknowledges and accommodates the inventor's legitimate interest in having a limited time (one year) to test the market's reaction to the invention to see if its chances of commercial success justify the effort and expenditure of a patent application. (This one-year period is known as the "grace period.")

 iv. **Prevention of over-extended monopolies:** Finally, the one-year statute of limitations prohibits the inventor from *de facto* extending his monopoly too far beyond the period of time authorized by Congress. For example, in the absence of this provision, an inventor might market his invention for six years before any competitor is in a position to enter the market and mass-market it in competition with him, and then apply for a patent. This effectively would give the inventor five more years of exclusivity than Congress intended in enacting the limited patent term.

2. **When an invention will be deemed "in public use" in this country:** Under §102(b), if the invention is in "public use" in the United States for more than a year prior to the filing of the patent application, no patent may issue. A "public use" will be found if persons other than the inventor/applicant use the completed, operative invention in the way the invention was intended to be used, and are under no limitation, restriction, or obligation to keep the invention secret. Even one such use will be sufficient to start the one-year statutory period running. For example, in *Egbert v. Lippmann,* 104 U.S. 333 (1881), the inventor of a new corset gave a prototype to his girlfriend to use, imposing no express restrictions on her use. The girlfriend used the corset as intended, though (due to the nature of the invention) she did not expose it to general public view during use. While an extreme case, this was found a sufficient "public use" to trigger the running of the statutory period.

 Example: The Court of Appeals for the Federal Circuit has held that travel agents' use of an airline reservation system to make travel reservations for the public put the system into "public use" for purposes of §102(b), even though the creator of the system retained the essential algorithms of the system software in confidence, so that the aspects of the system that were apparent to agents and the public were not sufficient to enable one skilled in the art to duplicate the system. *Lockwood v. American Airlines, Inc., supra,* p. 37.

 a. **The inventor's private, personal use:** The inventor/applicant can make a private, personal use of the invention without triggering the one-year statutory period.

  Example: A, the applicant for patent, invented his new can opener in January, 1986. He used it in the privacy of his kitchen to open the cans that he used in the course of preparing his own meals. This use should not trigger the running of the §102(b) one-year statute of limitations.

 b. **Experimental use:** A public use that is primarily experimental in purpose will not trigger (commence) the running of the one-year statutory period. However, the primary purpose of the use must be experimental—to test the invention from a technological standpoint—rather than to test or develop a market. Factors that courts have considered in determining whether a use was primarily experimental include:

- Whether the experimentation was for the benefit of the inventor/applicant or of the user. If for the benefit of the user, the use probably is commercial, not primarily experimental.

- Whether the features being tested are part of the actual invention as claimed in the patent application or are peripheral to the part of the product or process that constitutes the novel invention. If the latter, the experimental use exception will not apply.

Example: The inventor of a new carpet cleaner allows 50 homemakers to take a can of the cleaner home and use it. Half of the cans are scented with a floral scent and the other half have a pine scent. A week later, the inventor contacts the homemakers to ask how they like the scent. Based on his findings, he decides to market the cleaner with the pine scent. Assuming that scent is not part of the claimed invention (an innovative chemical compound for cleaning), the use will not be excused as experimental. The inventor was testing the market, not the invention.

- Whether the inventor/applicant acted like he was conducting a scientific test: Did he keep strict control over the third parties' use of the invention, restricting and monitoring the third parties' actions, imposing confidentiality requirements, systematically collecting the results of the use, keeping records, taking back any of the invention that was left after the use?

- Whether the third-party use was necessary in order to test the invention. If the tests could readily have been conducted by the inventor/applicant in a laboratory, the court may find that the purpose of the use was commercial rather than experimental.

- How far along the invention was in the developmental process when the alleged experimental use was made. The more fully developed, the less likely the use was experimental rather than commercial.

c. **Commercial use that does not reveal the invention to the public:** An invention may be put to a commercial use that does not reveal it to the public. For example, if the invention is a machine or process, the inventor/applicant may use it to manufacture products for public sale. Examination of the products placed on the market may not reveal the nature of the process or machine. In this situation it has been argued that the use of the invention is not a "public use." The Court of Appeals for the Federal Circuit, however, has indicated that *such a use by the inventor/applicant* will trigger the running of the one-year statutory period. If the inventor does not apply for a patent within the year, he will be disqualified. The Federal Circuit has also indicated that the one-year statute *will not be triggered against an applicant when a third party, who is unrelated to the applicant, makes such a secret use* of the patented invention.

Example: A invents a manufacturing process on January 1, 1985, but he does not put it to use. On January 1, 1987, A begins to use the process to manufacture products for sale to the public. In order to obtain a patent under subsection 102(b), A must file his application by January 1, 1988. It does not matter whether inspection of the products would reveal the process to the public.

Example: A invents a new manufacturing process on January 1, 2002. While A is preparing to implement the new process, B independently invents the same process and begins using it on July 1, 2002. B's use is secret, and the products he provides to the public do not reveal the process. B's use will not trigger the one-year statute of limitations against A. A can still apply after July 1, 2003, and (assuming that the other requirements of patentability are met) receive a patent. Note that if B's use had revealed the invention to the public, it would have triggered the §102(b) statute of limitations, forcing A to apply before July 1, 2003.

3. **When an invention will be deemed "on sale" in this country:** Under §102(b), if the invention is "on sale" in the United States more than one year before the patent application is filed, no patent may issue. In *Pfaff v. Wells Electronics*, 525 U.S. 55 (1998), the Supreme Court held that an invention will be deemed "on sale" if it: (1) has been the subject of a commercial offer to sell; and (2) is "ready for patenting."

   a. **A commercial offer to sell:** The Federal Circuit has held that actions will only constitute a "commercial offer to sell" for purposes of §102(b) if they satisfy the formal standards of an offer under the Uniform Commercial Code, allowing another party to create a binding contract for sale with a simple acceptance and consideration. Thus, not all commercial activity in connection with the invention will trigger the §102 statute of limitations.

   b. **Ready for patenting:** In *Pfaff*, the Supreme Court specified that the invention may be "ready for patenting" if: (1) it has been reduced to actual practice (that is, an actual physical prototype has been built that incorporates all the elements set forth in the patent claim and that works for its intended purpose); or (2) if the inventor has prepared drawings or other descriptions of the invention that are sufficiently specific to enable a person skilled in the art to practice the invention.

      Example: In *Pfaff*, Pfaff, the inventor, commenced work on a new computer chip socket in November, 1980, at the request of Texas Instruments, a prospective customer. Pfaff prepared detailed engineering drawings that described the design, the dimensions, and the materials to be used in making the socket, and sent the drawings to a manufacturer in February or March, 1981. Prior to March 17, 1981, Pfaff showed a sketch of his socket concept to representatives of Texas Instruments. On April 8, 1981, Texas Instruments provided Pfaff with a written confirmation of a previously placed oral purchase order for a substantial quantity of the new sockets. As was his general practice, Pfaff never made or tested a prototype of the socket before offering to sell it in commercial quantities. The manufacturer completed and shipped the sockets to Texas Instruments in July, 1981. Pfaff filed an application to patent the socket on April 19, 1982, and the application was later granted. In a subsequent challenge to the patent, the Supreme Court held that the patent was invalid under the §102(b) "on sale" provision. The Court reasoned that when Pfaff accepted the purchase order from Texas Instruments his invention was ready for patenting. This was demonstrated by the fact that he had created detailed drawings that enabled the manufacturer to produce the socket, and the drawings contained every element of the patent claims. Pfaff accepted the purchase order more than a year before he filed his patent application.

   c. **Exception for sales that are primarily for experimental purposes:** If a sale is primarily for experimental purposes rather than for commercial purposes, it will not trigger the running of the subsection 102(b) statutory period. The considerations for determining whether a sale is experimental are similar to those for considering whether public use is experimental. In particular, the Federal Circuit has stressed that in order for a sale to be deemed "experimental," the inventor must communicate to the purchaser that the sale is for purposes of experimentation and maintain control over the purchaser's subsequent use of the invention.

   d. **Offer to sell rights in the inventive concept, patent or patent application:** An offer to assign the patent or rights in the inventive concept or patent application does not trigger subsection 102(b). The offer must be to sell physical embodiments of the patented invention. In the case of inventions that are processes, the §102(b) statute of limitations will only be triggered when the *product of the process* is offered for sale. Offering to sell or license the process itself will not commence the running of the one-year period.

4. **When an invention will be deemed patented or described in a printed publication:** Subsection 102(b) also provides that no patent may issue if the invention was patented or the subject of a printed publication (anywhere in the world) more than a year prior to the filing of the application. The considerations for determining whether an invention has been patented or described in a printed publication for the purposes of subsection 102(b) are similar to those discussed in connection with subsection 102(a). See pp. 37-39, *supra*.

B. **Subsection 102(c):** Subsection 102(c) denies a patent if the applicant abandoned his or her right to a patent. While the language of subsection 102(c) refers to abandonment of the *invention*, the case law clarifies that the focus is actually on abandonment of the right to a patent. The policy behind this provision is to encourage inventors to file an application for patent, and thus make enabling disclosure to the public, as quickly as possible. Abandonment will be found when the inventor expressly or impliedly manifests an intention to relinquish his right to a patent.

1. **Express abandonment:** The inventor may expressly abandon by openly disclaiming any intent to obtain a patent, thus dedicating the invention to the public.

2. **Implicit abandonment:** The inventor may impliedly abandon his invention through conduct that indicates an intent to forego a patent. In some cases, refraining from applying for a patent for a long period of time may be sufficient evidence of an intent not to obtain a patent. For example, one court found that a failure to apply for a patent for six years after the invention was made created a *prima facie* case of implied abandonment, which shifted the burden of proof to the inventor to show that he did not intend to abandon. Another court held that failure to apply for eight years constituted an abandonment as a matter of law. It is not necessary that the inventor have intended to abandon the invention itself during this time. For example, he may have intended to use it as a trade secret without patenting it.

C. **Subsection 102(d):** Subsection 102(d) denies a patent to an applicant if: (1) the inventor filed a patent application in a foreign country more than 12 months before he filed his U.S. application; and (2) the foreign patent was granted before the U.S. filing date.

Example: A invents a new mousetrap on January 1, 1987. She files an application for a patent in France on July 1, 1987. The French patent is granted on May 1, 1988. A files for a patent for the same mousetrap in the United States in August, 1988. A will be barred from obtaining a U.S. patent. Note, however, that if the French patent had not been granted at the time A filed her U.S. application, she would not be barred. Similarly, if A had filed in France in September, 1987, she would not be barred, even if the French patent had been granted before she filed in the United States.

D. **Subsection 102(f):** Subsection 102(f) provides that only the *inventor* is entitled to a patent in the invention. Subsection (f) does not prevent an inventor from assigning rights in an invention, or to a patent in the invention, to someone else. However, when such an assignment is made prior to the granting of a patent, the assignee must pursue the patent application in the inventor's name. For example, if the inventor has assigned his right to the invention to his employer, the employer must pursue the patent application in the inventor/employee's name.

1. **Who is the inventor?** The inventor is the person who *conceived* of the specific invention claimed. A person (for example, an employer) who merely directs another (an employee) to

solve a problem or make an invention is not an inventor unless he also told the other actually how to do it, as well.

2. **Joint inventors:** Parties working together on a problem will be joint inventors if each makes a mental contribution to the final invention concept. It is not necessary that their contributions be equal or that they be made simultaneously, as long as the parties were collaborating with one another. Nor must each joint inventor contribute to every aspect of the invention. When there are joint inventors, the application must be made jointly, in all the inventors' names. Absent an assignment of rights, all the joint inventors will own an equal interest in the resulting patent.

V. THE NON-OBVIOUSNESS STANDARD

PLEASE NOTE: Proposed revisions currently pending before Congress would, if enacted, significantly change the non-obviousness evaluation. Please check for updates on the web site: www.aspenlawschool.com/ip_outline.

The non-obviousness standard is set forth in §103 of the Patent Act, 35 U.S.C. §103. It provides that an invention is not patentable if it would have been *obvious to a person having ordinary skill in the pertinent art as it existed when the invention was made*. The Supreme Court, in *Graham v. John Deere Co.*, 383 U.S. 1 (1966), held that to make this legal determination, three factual issues must be determined: (1) the scope and content of the pertinent prior art; (2) differences between the pertinent prior art and the invention at issue; and (3) the ordinary level of skill in the pertinent art.

A. **The pertinent prior art:** The issue is whether the person with ordinary skill in the art would have thought the applicant's invention obvious in light of the prior art. Therefore, it is necessary to identify the "pertinent" prior art. In making the obviousness determination, we assume that the "ordinary person," from whose perspective the evaluation is made, is aware of all the pertinent prior art, and considers it in deciding whether the invention is obvious. Patent Act §102 identifies prior art for purposes of the §103 obviousness evaluation. Thus, in order for an earlier invention, publication or patent to constitute "prior art," it must fall within the provisions of §§102(a), (e), (f), or (g). More specifically:

- If the information or earlier invention was revealed in a patent or printed publication anywhere in the world, or was known or used in the United States within the meaning of §102(a) prior to an applicant's invention date, then it will qualify as prior art in evaluating the obviousness of the applicant's invention.

- Under §102(g), an earlier invention that was made in the United States and not abandoned, suppressed, or concealed prior to the applicant's invention date will be deemed prior art in evaluating the applicant's invention. (It is irrelevant whether the applicant could reasonably have learned of the earlier invention—"secret prior art" may be considered under §102(g) in evaluating the obviousness of a later invention.) Likewise, an earlier invention made abroad may constitute prior art pursuant to §102(g) if its earlier invention date has been established in an interference proceeding and it had not been abandoned, suppressed, or concealed, at the time of the applicant's invention.

- Under §102(e), information contained in a patent application that was pending in the P.T.O. at the time of the later applicant's invention will qualify as prior art in evaluating the obviousness of the later application if the pending patent application is eventually published or granted.

(The Supreme Court ruled in *Hazeltine Research, Inc. v. Brenner*, 382 U.S. 252 (1965), that the information in the pending application should be deemed to have entered the public domain for purposes of evaluating the obviousness of later inventions as of the pending application's filing date, even though the public had no access to it at that time.)

- Under §102(f), an earlier invention or information that was *actually revealed to the applicant* prior to the applicant's invention date will be deemed prior art in evaluating the obviousness of that applicant's invention. This will be the case even if the information was not available to other members of the public or through any means described in other parts of §102, and would not be deemed prior art against an applicant who did not know of it. *Oddzon Products, Inc. v. Just Toys, Inc.*, 122 F.3d 1396 (Fed. Cir. 1997).

While an invention can only be *anticipated* (shown to *lack novelty*) through a single prior art reference that includes all the elements of the invention in the same arrangement, *obviousness* can be demonstrated by combining two or more prior art references. Thus, an earlier invention (under §102(g)) and a printed publication (under §102(a)), neither of which fully revealed the applicant's invention, might be used in combination to show that a person with ordinary skill in the art would have found the applicant's invention obvious. However, only "pertinent," or "analogous," prior art should be considered in determining whether an invention is obvious.

1. **Determining which prior art is "pertinent":** The Court of Appeals for the Federal Circuit, which determines appeals in all patent disputes, has stated that prior art is pertinent, or analogous, if: (1) it is from the same field of endeavor, regardless of the problem to be solved; or (2) even if not from the same field, it is reasonably related to the particular problem with which the inventor is involved. In the latter case, for example, if the same problem arises in different fields, prior art addressing the problem in one field of endeavor is pertinent to assess the obviousness of the inventor/applicant's attempt to address the same problem in another.

B. **The level of skill in the pertinent art:** Non-obviousness is measured from the perspective of the person with ordinary skill in the pertinent art. Thus, it is necessary to determine what level of skill this ordinary person would have. The Court of Appeals for the Federal Circuit has stated that several factors should be considered: (1) the educational level of the inventor; (2) the educational level of active workers in the field; (3) the type of problems encountered in the art; (4) prior art solutions to those problems; (5) sophistication of the technology; and (6) rapidity with which inventions are made. It is important to bear in mind that even though the fictitious "person with ordinary skill in the art" has only ordinary skill, he has extraordinary knowledge: He is deemed for purposes of the non-obviousness determination to have knowledge of *all* the pertinent prior art, even though, in reality, it is unlikely that a person with ordinary skill would be so all-knowing.

C. **The legal determination of obviousness:** The non-obviousness determination requires consideration of whether the prior art: (1) would have suggested to the person of ordinary skill that she should pursue the invention; and (2) would have revealed that she had a reasonable chance of success. The determination must be made *as of the date the applicant's invention was made*. This evaluation may not be made with the benefit of hindsight.

D. **Secondary considerations:** In the *John Deere* case, the Supreme Court suggested that the P.T.O. or court may also entertain "secondary considerations" in determining non-obviousness, such as: the commercial success of the invention; evidence that the need for the invention had been long-felt; and commercial acquiescence to the patent. These matters may provide circumstantial evidence of obviousness.

1. **Commercial success:** The commercial success of the invention may demonstrate non-obviousness because it indicates that the market deems the invention to be an important advance in the field. Moreover, if the invention was successful, we can assume that it was not obvious because if it were obvious, persons seeking monetary gain would already have invented it. Persons in the marketplace are vigilant to seize upon obvious ways to obtain commercial success.

2. **Long-felt need:** If the need for the invention was felt long before it was made, then the chances are that the invention was not obvious. Otherwise it would have been made sooner.

3. **Commercial acquiescence:** If competitors have been willing to pay for a license from the inventor before using the invention, or if they have expended effort to "invent around" the patented invention in order to avoid infringement liability, this is circumstantial evidence that they believe that the patent is valid, and thus, that the invention is non-obvious. On the other hand, if competitors have blatantly made, used, and sold the invention despite the patent, this suggests that they do not believe that the invention qualifies as non-obvious.

4. **Additional considerations:** The Court of Appeals for the Federal Circuit has emphasized the importance of these "secondary considerations," and to emphasize their importance, prefers to call them "objective factors," rather than "secondary considerations." The Federal Circuit has added additional objective factors to the Supreme Court's initial list, including: (1) movement of persons skilled in the art in a different direction from that taken by the inventor; (2) the existence of skepticism on the part of experts regarding the approach taken by the inventor; and (3) the fact that the defendant copied the invention rather than existing alternatives. Again, these considerations may provide circumstantial evidence of non-obviousness.

5. **The necessity of a nexus:** The Federal Circuit has also stressed the necessity of demonstrating a *nexus* between the objective factor (secondary consideration) and the issue of obviousness. For example, evidence of commercial success is only relevant as circumstantial evidence of non-obviousness if it can be shown that the commercial success resulted from the innovative aspects of the invention rather than from heavy promotion, or from other features of a finished product that are not part of the patented invention.

E. **Combination patents:** A combination patent has been defined as a patent granted for an invention that combines old, known elements in a new way. In such cases it is the new combination that is the invention. The U.S. Supreme Court, in *Sakraida v. Ag Pro Inc.*, 425 U.S. 273 (1976), held that when a combination patent is at issue, non-obviousness may be demonstrated by the existence of *synergism*: The newly combined, known elements should perform some new function or give a new result that would not have been predicted, given the known elements. Thus, the question is whether a person with ordinary skill in the art would have predicted that the combination of these known elements would produce the result that the applicant's invention produced.

Example: In the *Sakraida* case, the invention was a method for cleaning the floors of dairy barns. Its elements consisted of a smooth, paved barn floor that sloped downward toward a drain, and a tank for holding water that would be dumped out at the top of the sloping floor. The water would run as a sheet down the sloped floor, moving cow offal toward the drain. All the elements of this invention were old and well known. This method was deemed more effective than prior flush systems, which had used pipes or hoses instead of a tank, because the abrupt release of a large volume of water from a tank caused a "rolling action," which had a stronger cleaning effect. The Supreme Court found that the invention did not satisfy the non-obviousness standard, stating that the invention "simply arranges old elements with each performing the same function it had been known to perform, although perhaps producing a more striking result than in previous combinations.... Exploitation of the principle of gravity adds nothing to the sum of useful knowledge where there is no change in the respective functions of the elements of the combination."

1. **The *KSR* decision:** The Court of Appeals for the Federal Circuit has long held that in cases assessing the obviousness of new combinations of known elements, the P.T.O. or court should focus on whether there is something in the pertinent prior art to suggest the desirability, and thus the obviousness, of making such a combination. In *KSR International Co. v. Teleflex, Inc.*, 127 S. Ct. 1727 (2007), the Supreme Court held that, while this standard may provide helpful insights in determining obviousness, it is inappropriate to *require* a showing of precise, explicit prior art teachings that are directed to the specific subject matter of the claims in order to demonstrate obviousness. Such a requirement is too formalistic and rigid, places too much emphasis on published articles and the explicit content of issued patents, and improperly deemphasizes the knowledge and creativity of the person with ordinary skill in the art. The Court also recognized that "market demand, rather than scientific literature," may "drive design trends" in a given context. (In the present case, the Court found that the inventor was influenced by the recent transition from mechanical gas pedals to electronic throttle controls in the automotive industry to make his invention, which consisted of the combination of a pre-existing adjustable pedal assembly with an electronic throttle control.) The Supreme Court called for an "expansive and flexible approach" to evaluating obviousness. The *KSR* Court provided several important principles to guide the obviousness inquiry:

   - When a patent "simply arranges old elements with each performing the same function it had been known to perform and yields no more than one would expect from such an arrangement, the combination is obvious."

   - "If a technique has been used to improve one device, and a person of ordinary skill in the art would recognize that it would improve similar devices in the same way, using the technique is obvious unless its actual application is beyond his or her skill."

   - "When a work is available in one field of endeavor, design incentives and other market forces can prompt variations of it, either in the same field or a different one. If a person of ordinary skill can implement a predictable variation, §103 likely bars its patentability."

   - "When there is a design need or market pressure to solve a problem and there are a finite number of identified, predictable solutions, a person of ordinary skill has good reason to pursue the known options within his or her technical grasp. If this leads to the anticipated success, it is likely the product not of innovation but of ordinary skill and common sense. In that instance the fact that a combination was obvious to try might show that it was obvious."

   - "When prior art teaches away from combining certain known elements, discovery of a successful means of combining them is more likely to be non-obvious."

F. **Section 103(c)—Secret prior art in collaborative situations:** Section 103(c) limits the use of "secret prior art" (inventions and information that would only enter the prior art through sections 102(e), (f), or (g)) for purposes of evaluating obviousness if that prior art was developed by a person in a collaborative relationship with the applicant. Such a relationship will be deemed to exist if the applicant's invention and the secret prior art were owned by the same person, subject to an obligation to assign to the same person, or generated pursuant to a written "joint research agreement" between two or more separate research entities. This provision was necessary in light of today's large corporate and university research operations, where a range of different researchers may be working on similar or related projects for the same business or academic entity. As long as the invention has not reached the public through §102(a), the work of one researcher within an organization will not be used as prior art against another, and research entities can more readily enter into partnerships in which participants share confidential information about their work.

G. **Biotechnological process patents:** Patent Act §103(b), as amended in 1995, provides that a claim for a biotechnological process will not have to undergo a separate review of non-obviousness if the process uses or produces a composition of matter that is itself separately patentable. Rather, if the applicant elects, the biotechnological process will automatically be deemed non-obvious if the composition of matter that it uses or produces is found to be novel and non-obvious. To take advantage of this provision, the applicant for the process patent must satisfy several conditions:

   1. the claims for the process and the patentable composition of matter to which the process is linked must be contained in the same application or in applications having the same effective filing date;
   2. the composition of matter invention and the process invention must be owned by the same person or be subject to an obligation of assignment to the same person; and
   3. the composition of matter must itself be patentable on its own merits.

If a process claim is granted under this provision, and the claim to the composition of matter to which the process claim is linked is held invalid, the process claim will cease to enjoy the presumption of non-obviousness that normally accompanies claims granted by the P.T.O.

H. **Obviousness as a trigger for the §102(b) one-year statute of limitations:** In *Application of Foster*, 343 F.2d 980 (1965), *cert. denied*, 383 U.S. 966 (1966), the Court of Customs and Patent Appeals (predecessor to the Court of Appeals for the Federal Circuit) established that the §102(b) one-year statute of limitations will begin to run once information enters the public domain that, *while not anticipating* the invention, *renders it obvious*. It is not necessary that the information all be found in a single embodiment, or reference, such as a new publication, patent, or invention. It is sufficient that the new information, when combined with other, already existing information and/or ordinary skill in the art, renders the applicant's invention obvious.

   Example: X invents a new mousetrap on January 1, 1987. At the time of her invention the mousetrap is novel (within the meaning of §§102(a), (e), and (g)) and non-obvious (within the meaning of §103) and thus qualifies for a patent. However, on July 1, 1988, the Journal of Mousetrapology publishes an article which, when combined with other information existing in the public domain, renders her mousetrap obvious. X must file her application for patent within one year after the article is published (by July 1, 1989) or else she will be barred from obtaining a patent under subsection 102(b).

VI. THE UTILITY STANDARD

Patent Act §101 authorizes patents for "new and useful" processes, machines, manufactures, compositions of matter, or improvements thereof. The utility requirement for utility patents is derived from this provision and its predecessors.

A. A significant benefit to society: Utility will be found when *there is a current, significant, beneficial use for the invention or, in the case of a process, the product of the process*. Merely demonstrating that the invention may lead to further invention or that the invention fills space is insufficient. However, while there must be a present, beneficial use, it is not necessary to demonstrate that the invention works better than alternative methods of accomplishing its particular goal or function. Nor is it necessary to demonstrate that the invention has commercial value.

Example: In *Brenner v. Manson*, 383 U.S. 519 (1966), the applicant had invented a process for making a chemical compound. There was no current known use for the compound, although the compound might prove useful in future scientific research. The Supreme Court held that under these circumstances, the process lacked utility for purposes of §101, and did not qualify for a patent.

  1. **The utility requirement for pharmaceuticals:** Notwithstanding the Supreme Court's decision in *Brenner v. Manson*, described *supra*, the Court of Customs and Patent Appeals and its successor, the Court of Appeals for the Federal Circuit, have applied the utility standard liberally to pharmaceutical inventions. Those courts have held that evidence that the claimed pharmaceutical invention is safe and effective in laboratory test animals is sufficient to establish utility even though the pharmaceutical invention is claimed as useful for humans. It is not necessary for patent applicants to meet the high standards of FDA approval in order to satisfy the utility standard and get a patent. As the Court of Appeals for the Federal Circuit has held: "Usefulness in patent law, and in particular in the context of pharmaceutical inventions, necessarily includes the expectation of further research and development. The stage at which an invention in this field becomes useful is well before it is ready to be administered to humans." *In re Brana*, 51 F.3d 1560 (Fed. Cir. 1995).

B. Inoperability as lack of utility: An invention that fails to operate as claimed in the patent application may be denied a patent for lack of usefulness. For example, an application claiming a perpetual motion machine would be denied for lack of usefulness because it will not in fact operate to generate more usable energy than it consumes.

VII. THE DISCLOSURE REQUIREMENT

The Patent Act requires that patentees fully disclose their invention to the public as the price of obtaining a patent. Failure to make that disclosure, as required in §112 of the Patent Act, results in a denial of patent, or if a patent is granted, subsequent invalidation. There are several different aspects to the disclosure requirement, which may be referred to as the claiming requirement, the enablement requirement, the best mode requirement, and the written description requirement.

A. The claiming requirement: A patent must include one or more claims that clearly and distinctly describe the invention, setting forth its constituent elements. The claims are the official definition of the invention, and establish the "metes and bounds" of the patent monopoly. Novelty, non-obviousness, and usefulness are judged by reference to the claims, as are assertions that defendants' products or processes infringe the patent.

B. **The enablement requirement:** The patent applicant must describe how to make and use the invention with sufficient clarity, precision, and detail to enable a person skilled in the relevant art to make and use it without undue experimentation. The enabling disclosure (with illustrations) is made in the patent specification, which precedes the claims. (It is often stated that the claims *define* the invention, while the specification *describes* it.) Because it may be impossible to enable others through means of a written description in the case of inventions involving living materials, the patent applicant may be required to deposit a sample of the living materials in a recognized depository in order to satisfy the enablement requirement.

C. **The best mode requirement:** The applicant must set forth (in the specification) the best mode that he contemplates of carrying out his invention as of the application filling date. The best mode issue has two components.

   1. **The subjective inquiry:** First, it must be established whether, at the time the inventor filed his patent application, he knew of a mode of practicing his claimed invention that he considered to be better than any other. This is a subjective inquiry, going to the inventor's state of mind, to determine whether the inventor must disclose anything beyond what is required for enablement.

      Example: If the inventor knows (at the time of application) that his claimed process works with ordinary water, but works more efficiently with distilled water, he must disclose this, even though others skilled in the art might figure this out through their own experimentation.

      PLEASE NOTE: Proposed amendments currently pending before Congress, if enacted, could change the current law regarding best mode disclosure. Please check the web site for updates: www.aspenlawschool.com/ip_outline.

   2. **The objective inquiry:** If the inventor did contemplate a preferred mode, the second issue is whether he disclosed the preferred mode adequately to enable one skilled in the art to practice it. Assessing the adequacy of the disclosure, as opposed to its necessity, is largely an objective inquiry that depends upon the level of skill in the art. Since adequacy of disclosure is measured by what persons skilled in the art would know or understand, it is not necessary for the inventor/applicant to explain things that would be self-evident to such persons.

D. **The written description requirement:** Finally, the applicant must demonstrate (through the specification) that he had possession of the invention, as ultimately claimed, at the time he filed his application. This requirement typically becomes relevant when the applicant later seeks to amend his original claims or adds new claims during the course of prosecution. The added claim material can only receive the benefit of the applicant's original filing date if the specification demonstrates that the inventor knew of the additional material on his original filing date. Without this requirement, applicants could use the amendment process to gain their original filing priority date for their later discoveries and technological advances.

VIII. INFRINGEMENT OF UTILITY PATENTS

A. **Suits to enforce patents:** Suits to enforce a patent or to challenge its validity may be brought in any U.S. district court where venue is proper. Appeals from the district courts go to the U.S. Court of Appeals for the Federal Circuit, in Washington, D.C. From there review may be sought in the U.S. Supreme Court. In addition, claims that infringing goods are being imported into the United States may be taken to the International Trade Commission (I.T.C.), which determines the issue of infringement, as well as any defense that a patent is invalid, in an administrative hearing pursuant to §337 of the Tariff Act of 1930. Determinations by the I.T.C. are also reviewed by the Court of Appeals for the Federal Circuit. (Claims that imported goods infringe upon U.S. trademarks and copyrights may also be taken to the I.T.C.)

1. **Infringement:** Persons may be liable for doing the following things in the United States: (1) directly infringing a patent; (2) inducing another to infringe a patent; (3) contributorily infringing a patent; (4) importing, selling, offering to sell, or using a product made abroad through a process protected by a U.S. process patent; or (5) manufacturing or selling certain components of a patented invention to be assembled abroad. Before examining these various infringement causes of action, however, it is useful to consider when a particular product or process will be deemed to infringe a patent.

2. **Claim interpretation:** Infringement occurs when the defendant's product or process falls within one or more of the patent claims. The court must construe the patent claims, including terms of art within the claims, to determine the scope of the patentee's exclusive nights. This construction takes place in a "*Markman*" hearing. Once the court construes the claims, the finder of fact determines whether the defendant's product or process falls within the scope of those claims. *Markman v. Westview Instruments, Inc.*, 517 U.S. 370 (1996).

    a. **The patent claims:** The patent claims are equivalent to the "metes and bounds" description in a deed to real property. They set forth the scope of the invention, which is the subject of the patent rights.

    b. **Claims contrasted with the specification:** The patent specification must provide sufficient information to enable a person with ordinary skill in the art to practice or make the invention, and set forth the best mode contemplated by the inventor of carrying out his invention. The specification is not intended to define the scope of the invention. That is the purpose of the claims. However, the specification may sometimes be consulted in the course of construing the claims. Inventors may provide express definitions of claim terms in the specification and specification drawings may illuminate the meaning of claim terms. Pursuant to Patent Act §112, a patent claim may describe a particular element of an invention as a "means for" performing a particular function. In such a case, the court will determine the nature and scope of the element by referring to structures, materials, or actions described in the specification.

    c. **Sources of evidence for claim construction:** There are a number of sources judges may draw on to construe claims. Apart from the specification, the patent's prosecution history may be helpful. (A patent's prosecution history consists of the various communications between the patent examiner and the patentee during the course of the patent prosecution, in which the parties may discuss the intended meaning of particular terms used in the claims and prior art that may shed light on their meaning.) The specification and prosecution history are considered to be "intrinsic evidence" of claim meaning. Courts may also resort to "extrinsic evidence," such as dictionaries, encyclopedias, scientific treatises, technical journals, expert testimony, or the testimony of the inventor himself, for evidence of the meaning of claim terminology. However, in *Phillips v. AWH Corp.*, 415 F.3d 1303 (Fed. Cir. 2005), *cert. denied*, 126 S. Ct. 1332 (2006), the Court of Appeals for the Federal Circuit, sitting *en banc*, expressed a preference for use of "intrinsic evidence" in claim construction. The court reasoned that extrinsic references, such as dictionaries or technical texts, are less reliable because they are not created with the specific patent in mind, may not be written for an audience having ordinary skill in the relevant art, or may define the terms in very general or abstract ways. In such cases they may shed little light on what the applicant and P.T.O. actually understood and meant the terms to encompass. Moreover, because there may be a wide range of extrinsic references, parties are likely to select those that are most favorable to their cause, skewing the construction process, and possibly leading to systematic patent overbreadth and anticompetitive effects.

3. **Literal infringement:** If the defendant's product or process literally falls within the language of one of the claims, then there is literal infringement. Claims incorporate a series of elements (also called "limitations"), which, in combination, form the invention. In order to literally infringe, a defendant's process or product must have every element ("limitation") set forth in the claim. The fact that the defendant's product or process contains additional elements will not necessarily avoid infringement liability.

   Example: The claim for A's patented machine consists of seven elements: A, B, C, D, E, F, and G. Defendant's machine has elements A, B, Z, D, E, F, and G. It does not literally infringe because it lacks element C.

   Example: The claim for A's patented machine consists of five elements: A, B, C, D, and E. The defendant's machine has elements A, B, C, D, E, F, and G. Defendant's machine probably literally infringes.

4. **The doctrine of equivalents:** If the defendant has made a change so that his product or process does not literally fall within the language of the claims, he may still be liable for infringement under the doctrine of equivalents. This doctrine is meant to prevent the unscrupulous copyist from avoiding liability by making only colorable changes. In order for the defendant's device or process to infringe under the doctrine of equivalents, it must contain each of the elements in the patent claim, or an equivalent element. This is sometimes called the "all elements" rule. *Warner-Jenkinson Co., Inc. v. Hilton Davis Chemical Co.*, 520 U.S. 17 (1997).

   Example: The patent claim sets forth six elements: A, B, C, D, E, and F. The defendant's product has elements A, B, C, X, E, and F. Defendant's product may infringe the patent only if element X is *equivalent* to element D.

   Example: The patent claim sets forth six elements: A, B, C, D, E, and F. The defendant's product has elements A, B, C, E, and F. The defendant's product does not infringe either literally or under the doctrine of equivalents, because it lacks element D or any element equivalent to D.

   a. **Evaluating equivalency:** The equivalency of one element to another is an objective determination made from the perspective of a person with ordinary skill in the art at the time of the infringement. In evaluating whether a defendant's element is equivalent to a claimed element, the inquiry may be framed as: (1) whether the defendant's element performs the same function in substantially the same way to obtain the same result as the claimed element; or (2) whether the difference between the defendant's element and the claimed element is "insubstantial." The Court of Appeals for the Federal Circuit holds that the equivalency determination is a question for the jury. Important considerations in making this evaluation include:

- Whether persons reasonably skilled in the art would have known that the differing elements were interchangeable at the time of the infringement.

- Whether finding the defendant's invention equivalent, and thus infringing, would give the patentee rights that she would not have been able to obtain initially, in the P.T.O., through broader claim language. In *Wilson Sporting Goods Co. v. David Geoffrey & Associates*, 904 F.2d 677 (Fed. Cir.), *cert. denied*, 498 U.S. 992 (1990), the Federal Circuit held that courts evaluating infringement claims under the doctrine of equivalents should visualize a hypothetical patent claim sufficient in scope to literally cover the accused product. The court should then ascertain whether that hypothetical claim would have been allowed by the P.T.O. in light of the prior art. If not (because the claim would cover matter that is not novel or that is obvious), then it would be improper to permit the patentee to obtain that coverage in an infringement suit under the doctrine of equivalents.

- How important a breakthrough the patentee's invention is. If it is a pioneering invention, or one that makes a considerable advance in the field, a wider range of differences will be deemed "insubstantial" than if the invention is a relatively minor one in a crowded field.

b. **Policy objections to the doctrine of equivalents:** Some authorities have objected to the doctrine of equivalents, or to a liberal application of the doctrine, because it makes patent coverage uncertain, undermining the ability of the public to rely on claim language to determine whether their intended actions will be found to infringe. This may lead competitors to be excessively cautious, thus chilling competition. The Supreme Court addressed this concern in *Warner-Jenkinson, supra*, and determined that the important notice function of the patent claims would not be unduly undermined as long as the doctrine of equivalents is limited to situations in which the defendant's product or process contains an element identical or equivalent to each claimed element of the patented invention.

c. **Reverse doctrine of equivalents:** When a defendant's product or process literally falls within the language of the patent claims, but is so far changed in principle from the patented product or process that it performs the same or a similar function in a substantially different way, the doctrine of equivalents may be used in the defendant's favor to restrict the claim and defeat the patentee's action for infringement. This doctrine is only rarely applied.

d. **The doctrine of prosecution history estoppel:** The doctrine of prosecution history estoppel (also called "file wrapper estoppel") requires that the scope of the patent claims be interpreted in light of what happened in the application process in the P.T.O. If the applicant took a position with regard to the scope of coverage of the claims, he or she will not be allowed in a later infringement action to take an inconsistent position. The doctrine of prosecution history estoppel thus limits the doctrine of equivalents.

Example: The patentee's application claims a process for filtering dyes through a specified type of membrane at a specified pressure. The P.T.O. examiner objects that the claim, as worded, will encompass an earlier patented process, and thus is unpatentable under Patent Act §102. The applicant then amends his claim, limiting the process to filtration "at a pH under 9.0" in order to get a patent. In a later infringement action, the patentee cannot rely on the doctrine of equivalents to prevail against a defendant who engages in the process at a pH over 9.0, even if he otherwise could demonstrate that the defendant's pH element was "equivalent" to the "pH under 9.0" element set forth in the patent claim, for purposes of the process.

i. **The purpose of a claim amendment:** In the *Warner-Jenkinson* case, the Supreme Court held that not all claim amendments will give rise to prosecution history estoppel. Prosecution history estoppel will depend on the *reason* the amendment was made. In *Festo Corp. v. Shoketsu Kinozuku Kogyo Kabushiki Co., Ltd.*, 535 U.S. 722 (2002), the Supreme Court elaborated that *any amendment made to satisfy any statutory requirement of the Patent Act, which narrows the scope of the claim*, will give rise to prosecution history estoppel. (This would include amendments made in response to P.T.O. objections that the original claim language failed to satisfy the usefulness, novelty, nonobviousness, or disclosure requirements, or made to avoid the possibility that the P.T.O might raise such objections.)

ii. **When the purpose of a claim amendment is unclear:** When it is not clear why a claim amendment was made, the burden is on the patentee to establish the reason for the amendment. When no explanation is established, the court should presume that the P.T.O. had a substantial reason related to patentability for requiring the amendment, and the doctrine of prosecution history estoppel should apply.

iii. **The extent of the estoppel:** When prosecution history estoppel applies with regard to a claim element, it does not necessarily raise a complete bar to a finding that a different element is equivalent. In *Festo, supra,* the Supreme Court held that when narrowing claim amendments are made for a reason related to patentability, it will be presumed that all equivalence arguments are barred as to the narrowed claim element. However, the patentee may rebut that presumption by showing that:

- The equivalent at issue was unforeseeable at the time the narrowing amendment was made (so that it cannot be assumed that the applicant expected to give it up when he made the amendment). This might be the case, for example, if the defendant's allegedly equivalent element was not disclosed in the prior art in the field at the time of the patentee's invention (for example, because it had not yet been developed).

- The rationale underlying the amendment bears no more than a tangential relation to the equivalent in question. For example, the original claim called for a "plate" above the membrane. The applicant later amended the claim to provide for a "plate being differentially spaced above the membrane." The defendant's device has a dome that is differentially spaced above the membrane. The patentee may assert that the defendant's dome is equivalent to the claimed "plate" because the purpose of the amendment was to limit the claim to ensure that the plate was "differentially spaced." The claim that a differentially spaced dome is equivalent to a differentially spaced plate has only a tangential relationship to the amendment.

- Some other reason suggesting that the patentee could not reasonably be expected to have described the insubstantial substitute in question in the amended claim language.

The *Festo* Court explained that, in order to overcome the presumption against equivalents, the patentee must show that, "at the time of the amendment one skilled in the art could not reasonably be expected to have drafted a claim that would have literally encompassed the alleged equivalent." If he could have been expected to draft such a claim, but failed to do so, then the equivalent is barred. If he could not have known to draft the claim in a manner that would include the equivalent, the equivalent may be considered as a basis of infringement liability.

iv. **An additional ground for limiting the doctrine of equivalents:** In *Johnson & Johnston Associates, Inc. v. R.E. Service Co.,* 285 F.3d 1046 (2002), the Court of Appeals for the Federal Circuit held (*en banc*) that when a patent applicant discloses subject matter in his specification, but does not include it in the claims, he dedicates it to the public, and may not rely on the doctrine of equivalents to hold a defendant liable for incorporating that subject matter in the place of claimed matter.

Example: X owns a patent related to the fabrication of printed circuit boards. The claim at issue calls for "a sheet of aluminum." The patent specification explains that "other metals, such as stainless steel or nickel alloys, may be used." Y makes printed circuit boards with a sheet of steel. X may not argue that steel is the equivalent of aluminum, and thus that Y's circuit boards infringe under the doctrine of equivalents. By disclosing steel in his specification, but failing to claim it, X dedicated this variation of his invention to the public.

B. **Direct infringement:** Section 271(a) of the Patent Act, as amended by the Uruguay Round Agreements Act, provides that a person who makes, uses, sells, or offers to sell the patented invention in the United States, or who imports the patented invention into the United States, during the patent term without the patentee's authorization will be liable for direct infringement. The prohibitions of offering to sell and importing the invention were added by the Uruguay Round amendments, which became effective January 1, 1996.

1. **"Making" the patented invention in the case of combination patents:** The Supreme Court has used the term "combination patents" to describe patents for inventions whose novelty lies not in their individual components, which are already known, but in their new combination of known elements. In such cases it is the combination—the interrelationship of the known components—that is the subject of the patent protection. The patentee obtains no monopoly rights in the individual components themselves. Therefore, in order to demonstrate a "making" of the patented invention in such cases, the patentee must prove that the defendant actually combined all the components in the manner described in the patent claims ("made the patented combination").

Example: In *Deepsouth Packing Co., Inc. v. Laitram Corp.*, 406 U.S. 518 (1972), the Supreme Court held that a defendant who manufactured the individual components of a patented combination (a shrimp deveining machine) and shipped the subassembled components to foreign countries, along with instructions for assembly, did not "make" the invention in the United States and thus directly infringe the patent, because at no time did the defendant actually combine the components into a completed machine. Merely making the components did not infringe, because the combination patent did not give the patentee a monopoly in the individual components. Presumably, if the defendant had combined the components into a complete machine in the United States, even temporarily to test them, then it would have "made" (and in testing, "used") the patented invention and directly infringed. Assembly of the components outside of the United States constituted a "making" of the patented invention, but it was not a making within the United States, and thus did not itself infringe.

- a. **A "constructive" making:** The U.S. Court of Appeals for the Federal Circuit, in *Paper Converting Machine Co. v. Magna-Graphics Corp.*, 745 F.2d 11 (Fed. Cir. 1984), found a "making" in the case of a combination patent when the defendant did the following acts in the United States during the patent term: (1) entered into a contract to sell the patented invention; (2) manufactured all the components; (3) subassembled the components; (4) tested the operation of the various parts in subassembled form; and (5) delivered the subassembled components to its customer, with instructions not to make the final assembly *until after the patent expired*. While the defendant had never, as a technical matter, fully assembled all the claimed elements during the patent term, the court reasoned that, given its elaborate subassembly and testing procedure, it had nonetheless "made" an "operable assembly" of the patented invention. The *Magna-Graphics* court stated that when "significant unpatented assemblies of elements are tested during the patent term, enabling the infringer to deliver the patented combination in parts to the buyer, without testing the entire combination together as was the infringer's usual practice, testing the assemblies can be held to be in essence testing the patented combination, and hence infringement." 745 F.2d at 231-232.

- b. **Repair vs. reconstruction as a "making":** When the patentee sells or authorizes sale of a physical embodiment of the patented invention, his rights in that particular embodiment are "exhausted." Unless the patentee has imposed enforceable contract restrictions on the purchaser, the purchaser may freely use, modify, and resell the embodiment. (This rule is sometimes called the "doctrine of exhaustion," or the "doctrine of first sale.") The purchaser is also free to repair the embodiment to prolong its life. However, if the "repair" is so extensive that it constitutes "reconstruction," it will be deemed a "making" of the patented invention and thus a direct infringement.

    - i. **Reconstruction for combination patents:** Since most patents are "combination patents," and grant rights in the inventor's particular *combination* of known elements rather than in the individual elements themselves, mere replacement of individual elements of a product embodying the invention—even key components—will generally be deemed permissible repair, not infringing reconstruction. The Supreme Court has held that reconstruction occurs only when the entire embodiment is spent and the owner replaces so much of it as essentially to make a whole new combination.

        Example: In *Aro Manufacturing Co. v. Convertible Top Replacement Co., Inc.*, 365 U.S. 336 (1961), the plaintiff owned a combination patent for a convertible top for an automobile, consisting of a metal frame and fabric that stretched over the frame. Purchasers of automobiles featuring the patented top found that the fabric wore out long before the frame did. The Court held that the automobile owners could replace the fabric, even though it was a key component of the invention. This merely constituted permissible repair, not an impermissible reconstruction or "making" of the patented top.

ii. **The Federal Circuit's four-factor test for determining whether acts constitute repair or reconstruction:** In *Sandvik Aktiebolag v. E.J. Co.*, 121 F.3d 669 (Fed. Cir. 1997), *cert. denied*, 523 U.S. 1040 (1998), the Court of Appeals for the Federal Circuit identified four factors that should be considered in determining whether a defendant's acts constitute reconstruction or repair. These elements assist in determining the legitimate expectations of the parties regarding the useful life of the patented product.

1. The nature of the defendant's actions. (How complex is the defendant's undertaking? The more complex and difficult, the more likely it constitutes reconstruction.)
2. The nature of the patented device and how it was designed. (Particularly, does one of the components of the patented combination have a shorter useful life than the whole? If so, replacing it is more likely to constitute repair.)
3. Whether a market has developed to manufacture or service the part at issue. (If so, then the replacement is more likely to constitute repair.)
4. Objective evidence of the intent of the patentee. (For example, if the patentee itself sells the replacement parts or offers the service at issue, that suggests that the patentee intended for the part to be replaced or serviced to prolong the life of the article, and that replacement constitutes repair.)

Example: In *Sandvik*, the Federal Circuit found that replacing the tip of plaintiff's patented drills constituted infringing reconstruction, rather than repair. The court noted that the retipping process was difficult and complex (the defendant removed the worn or damaged tip by heating the tip to 1300 degrees Fahrenheit using an acetylene torch, brazed a rectangular piece of new carbide onto the drill shank, then recreated the patented geometry of the cutting edges by machining the carbide). Moreover, this was not a case where the replaced part clearly had a much shorter useful life than the rest of the drill. There was no substantial market for drill retipping and no companies other than the defendant were known to offer the retipping service. Finally, the patentee itself did not make or sell replacement tips or provide a retipping service, indicating that it had not intended for the tip to be replaced.

2. **Selling the patented invention:** The Supreme Court has specified that for purposes of §271(a) infringement liability, a patented invention cannot be the subject of an infringing "sale" until it is "made," as defined *supra*. Note that this definition of "sale" differs somewhat from the definition of "sale" for purposes of the §102(b) statutory bar. See p. 45, *supra*.

Example: In the *DeepSouth* case, where the defendant made parts, subassembled them, and sold the subassemblies to foreign buyers, there was no infringing sale of the patented invention because the subassembled parts did not constitute the patented invention (the claimed combination). The sale was of subassembled unpatented parts only.

3. **Offering to sell the patented invention:** A defendant will only infringe the patent by "offering to sell" the patented invention if the sale will occur prior to the expiration of the patent term. One question that has arisen is whether an offer to sell the patented invention, made in the United States, will infringe if the sale is to occur abroad. While the case opinions to date are mixed, at least a couple of district courts have held that such an offer will not infringe the patentee's exclusive right to "offer to sell" the patented invention. Their reasoning was that an offer to sell cannot infringe unless the contemplated sale would itself infringe. A sale outside the United States will not infringe the patentee's exclusive right of sale.

Example: X approaches Y in New York during the patent term and offers to sell Y the patented invention the day after the patent expires. X has not made an infringing offer to sell the patented invention. The result would probably be the same if the contemplated sale would take place in Iran, during the patent term.

    a. **What constitutes an "offer to sell"?** The Court of Appeals for the Federal Circuit has held that courts should employ traditional rules of contract law to determine whether an "offer to sell" the patented invention has been made.

4. **Importing the patented invention:** Although patentees have long enjoyed the exclusive right to make, use, and sell the patented invention in the United States, Congress only recently added an express importation right, to bring the United States into compliance with U.S. multinational treaty obligations. One very important question that Congress did not expressly address in the course of adding the right was whether the doctrine of exhaustion would apply to imported goods.

    a. **The doctrine of exhaustion:** The doctrine of exhaustion (also known as the "doctrine of first sale"), discussed *supra*, at p. 59, provides that once the U.S. patentee sells or authorizes sale of a product embodying the patented invention, he "exhausts" his rights in that particular product, leaving the purchaser and his successors in interest free to use, repair, and resell the product free from the patentee's interference. This rule acknowledges the long legal tradition of avoiding restraints on alienability of goods, and facilitates free movement of goods in the marketplace. Courts have also pointed out that the patent is meant to provide the opportunity for the patentee to profit from his invention and recoup his investment in research and development, and that the opportunity to control the first sale of the product should be adequate to achieve this goal. Courts have, however, been willing to enforce express contractual restrictions that the patentee imposes on purchasers' subsequent use or resale of patented products.

    b. **The applicability of the doctrine of exhaustion to goods sold abroad by the patentee and imported to the United States without the patentee's authorization:** Traditionally, courts have held that the doctrine of exhaustion applies to all patented products sold by the U.S. patentee or under his authorization, regardless of whether the products were first sold in the United States or abroad. Absent an express contractual restriction imposed by the patentee, foreign purchasers of the patented product were free to import the product into the United States and to sell it in competition with the U.S. patentee. (This rule is sometimes called the doctrine of "international exhaustion.") Goods sold by the U.S. patentee abroad and later imported into the United States are know as "parallel imports."

        i. **A dramatic change in the law:** In *Jazz Photo Corp. v. International Trade Commission*, 264 F.3d 1094 (Fed. Cir. 2001), *cert. denied*, 536 U.S. 950 (2002), the Court of Appeals for the Federal Circuit recently changed the traditional rule, holding that the doctrine of exhaustion will only apply to patented goods originally sold in the United States. (This is sometimes called the doctrine of "territorial exhaustion.") The Federal Circuit made the change even though the legislative history associated with the amendments adding the importation right indicated that Congress did not intend to change the law regarding parallel imports. The Federal Circuit provided no explanation for its decision to change the law.

Example: U.S. patentee sells its patented widget domestically and abroad. U.S. patentee sells a large quantity of the widgets to Y, in France, imposing no contractual restriction on use or resale of the widgets. Y subsequently sells the widgets to Z, who imports them into the United States for use and resale there. While this traditionally would have been deemed legal under the doctrine of exhaustion, under the *Jazz Photo* ruling, Z will be liable for infringing the U.S. patentee's importation right, and also for use, offer to sell, and sale of the widgets in the United States.

C. **Inducement to infringe:** To be liable for inducement to infringe pursuant to 35 U.S.C. §271(b), the defendant must have actively, intentionally, and knowingly solicited or assisted a third party to infringe a patent. Moreover, it must be demonstrated that the third party did indeed engage in direct infringement.

   1. **Active solicitation or assistance:** The defendant must take some initiative. Merely complying with the request of a third party who directly infringes is insufficient. Thus, for example, merely selling a component of the invention to someone who initiates the transaction by asking for it will not render the seller liable for inducement, even if the seller knows that the buyer plans to use the component to infringe.

      Example: X manufactures and sells a chemical solution which, when mixed with a certain solid chemical compound, results in A's patented invention. X sells the solution, along with a brochure telling the buyer how to mix it with the compound in order to make A's invention. X also advertises in the newspaper that he sells the solution, and that it can be mixed with the compound to make the invention. Y, a consumer, reads X's ads and buys the solution from X. Y reads the brochure that accompanies the solution and then uses the solution to make the patented invention. X will probably be liable for inducing Y's direct infringement. X's brochure, advertising, and sale of a component of the invention, actively solicit and assist Y's infringement.

      Example: The patentee has licensed X Co. to manufacture 100 of its patented widgets per year. Y convinces X Co. to manufacture 50 more of the patented widgets than the license allows, and purchases these extra widgets. Y is likely to be liable for inducing X Co.'s direct infringement (which arises from the unlicensed manufacture and sale of the 50 widgets). Y encouraged X Co.'s infringement and provided a market for the infringing widgets.

   2. **Knowledge and intent:** Although some Federal Circuit decisions have found inducement liability on a showing of "general intent" (where the defendant merely intends to cause the acts that constitute the infringement generally) the defendant must know that direct infringement is likely to occur as the result of his acts. That is, he must be aware of the patent, the nature of his acts, and their likely consequences.

   3. **Corporate officers, directors, and majority shareholders:** Corporate officers, directors, and majority shareholders may be liable for their company's direct infringement under two theories. First, they may be liable if the requisite elements for "piercing the corporate veil" under corporate law can be demonstrated. Second, they may be liable under an inducement theory if it can be shown that they deliberately and knowingly used the corporation as an instrument to infringe; personally and knowingly initiated the infringement; or participated in the manufacture, sale, and promotion of the infringing article.

D. **Contributory infringement:** A person who sells, offers to sell, or imports a material component of the patented invention that has no substantial use aside from use in the patented invention will be liable for contributory infringement if: (1) he knows that the component he sold was especially made or adapted for use in the patented invention, has no other substantial use, and is likely to be used to infringe the patent; and (2) his actions in fact do contribute to another's direct infringement. 35 U.S.C. §271(c).

1. **Knowledge:** In *Aro Manufacturing Co. v. Convertible Top Replacement Co., Inc.*, 377 U.S. 476 (1964), a majority of five Supreme Court Justices held that the alleged contributory infringer must know the use to which the material component will be put and that there is no substantial non-infringing use. He must also know of the patent and realize that the purchaser's use of the component is likely to infringe.

2. **The component sold, offered for sale, or imported:** The item the defendant sold, offered for sale, or imported must be a *material component* of the patented invention that is *not a staple item and has no substantial non-infringing use*. Thus, selling a standard article of commerce that has various uses cannot constitute contributory infringement, even if the seller/defendant knows of the patent and the buyer's plan to use the item to infringe. (Such a sale might constitute actionable inducement if the seller actively solicited the purchase or otherwise assisted the infringing use.) Whether a component is a staple item or a commodity suitable for substantial non-infringing use is a question of fact. However, an alleged non-infringing use cannot be far-fetched, impractical, or merely theoretical.

   Example: The P Company has a patent for a process of applying a specified chemical to growing rice crops to kill weeds without harming the crops. The chemical itself is not patented, but it has no substantial known use other than in the patented process. X sells the chemical, knowing that it has no substantial non-infringing use and that buyers will apply it in a way that directly infringes the P Company's patented process. X will be liable for contributory infringement.

3. **Recent amendments:** The prohibitions against importing or offering the material component for sale were added by the Uruguay Round Agreements Act, becoming effective on January 1, 1996. Prior to then, only the sale of a material component could lead to contributory infringement liability.

E. **Importing, selling, offering to sell, or using a product made through a process protected by a U.S. patent:** Patent Act §271(g) prohibits importing into the United States, or selling, offering to sell, or using in the United States, a product made by a U.S. patented process.

1. **Made by a patented process:** A product is not deemed to be made by a patented process if: (1) it has been materially changed by subsequent processes; or (2) it has become a trivial and nonessential component of another product.

2. **Scope of §271(g):** Congress enacted this provision primarily to thwart businesses who avoided U.S. process patents by using the patented process abroad to manufacture products, then imported the products into the United States to sell or use in competition with the U.S. patentee. Use of the process outside of the United States would not infringe the U.S. process patent, and if the U.S. patentee did not have a patent on the finished product, this practice would undermine the value of the process patent. However, note that subsection (g) is not limited to products manufactured abroad. When products are made through unauthorized use of the patented process domestically, the process patent owner will have the right (via §271(g)) to prohibit sale and use of the resulting products, even if they are not themselves patented.

3. **Burden of proof:** Patentees may have difficulty proving that their process was used to create the defendant's product, especially if the manufacturer is not subject to discovery under the Federal Rules of Civil Procedure. Accordingly, Patent Act §295 creates a presumption: If the plaintiff "has made a reasonable effort to determine the process actually used," and the court finds that "a substantial likelihood exists that the product was made by the patented process," the product will be presumed to have been made with the patented process, and the burden will shift to the defendant to prove that it was not.

4. **Exceptions:** Congress recognized that it may be difficult for retailers and others to avoid infringing §271(g) because it is often hard to ascertain whether products were made by patented processes. To avoid inequitable results, Congress channeled infringement claims toward persons practicing the patented process and those controlling them, and persons having prior knowledge of infringement. Patent Act §287(b) limits remedies against innocent infringers, and allows them to sell off or use any inventory that they accumulated prior to notice that the inventory infringes. Section 271(g) also withholds a remedy against noncommercial users or retail sellers unless no remedy is available against importers or commercial users or sellers.

   Example: A has a U.S. process patent for producing widgets. Widgets, however, have been around for a long time and are unpatented. B uses A's patented process in China to make widgets and sells some of its widgets to C. C imports them into the United States and resells them to D, who was unaware that the widgets were made through A's patented process. D then resells the widgets retail to non-commercial users. Under these facts, B will not be liable to A because his acts took place outside of the United States. C will be liable for importing and selling the widgets in the United States. Since §271(g) prohibits a remedy against noncommercial users or retail sellers if there is an adequate remedy against the importer or others, A probably will not have a cause of action against either D or D's retail purchasers.

F. **Supplying components of a U.S.-patented invention to be assembled abroad:** Section 271(f) provides that a person who supplies from the United States all or a substantial portion of the components of a patented invention in a manner that actively induces combination of the components abroad will be liable as an infringer.

   Example: X Co. manufactures all the parts of a machine that is covered by a valid U.S. patent. The manufacturing is done in the United States. Rather than combine the parts to make the finished machine in the United States (which would infringe §271(a)), X Co. sells the unassembled parts to foreign buyers. It advertises to prospective foreign buyers that the parts can be very easily assembled within one hour, and ships the parts to the overseas buyers with detailed instructions for assembly. If the assembly were done in the United States, there would be a direct infringement by the buyer, and X Co. would be liable for inducement to infringe, and possibly for contributory infringement. However, since assembly takes place abroad, as a technical matter, there is no direct infringement by the buyer, and thus X Co. cannot be liable under subsection 271(b) or (c). Subsection 271(f) nonetheless makes the X Co. liable for infringement under the facts set forth above.

   1. **Supplying a material component of a U.S.-patented invention:** Subsection 271(f) also imposes liability on a person who supplies from the United States a material component of a U.S.-patented invention that has no substantial use aside from its use in the invention, if: (1) the person knows that the component is especially adapted for use in the patented invention and has no substantial non-infringing use; and (2) the person intends that the component will be combined with other components abroad in a manner that would infringe the patent if such combination occurred within the United States.

Example: X Co. has a patent on an invention that incorporates a size 3 widget. The size 3 widget is custom-made for this invention. There is no other substantial use for widgets of that particular size. Y custom-makes size 3 widgets and sells them to a Korean buyer, who combines them with other components in Korea to make X Co.'s patented invention. Y knows and intends that this will be done. Since the assembly takes place abroad, there is no direct infringement by the Korean buyer under §271(a), and Y cannot be liable for contributory infringement under subsection 271(c). However, under subsection 271(f) he will be liable for infringement to X Co.

2. **Supplying software:** In *Microsoft Corp. v. AT&T Corp.*, 127 S. Ct. 1746 (2007), the Supreme Court held that supplying software on master disks to overseas computer manufacturers, thus enabling them to make individual copies of the software to install on the computers they manufactured and sold, did not infringe under Patent Act §271(f). In that case, AT&T held a patent for an apparatus that digitally encoded and compressed recorded speech. Microsoft's Windows operating system incorporated code that, *when installed*, enabled a computer to process speech in a manner that infringed the AT&T patent. But when it was uninstalled, the Windows software did not infringe. Rather than send individual copies of its Windows software to foreign purchasers to install on the computers they manufactured and sold, Microsoft sent master disks, from which the purchasers made the individual copies they needed. While this enabled the foreign purchasers to make the patented invention, the Court found that Microsoft's actions did not fall within the statutory language of subsection (f). The Supreme Court reasoned that, under the statutory language, a defendant must supply a material "component" that is amenable to "combination." Microsoft would be liable if it provided material copies of its software that foreign purchasers could install in their computers. However, enabling them to make their own copies was not sufficient. (The Court viewed the Windows software itself as an abstract set of instructions without physical embodiment. Thus, the abstract software itself could not be deemed a "component" capable of being combined with other components, and providing the intangible software, in itself, would not constitute supplying a "component," as required under subsection (f).) The Court found it irrelevant that the software was very easily copied. Noting the presumption against extraterritorial application of U.S. laws, the Court refused to read the statutory language broadly.

G. **Provisional rights prior to patent issuance:** The P.T.O. maintains patent applications in confidence. However, in 1999, Congress amended the Patent Act, directing the P.T.O. to publish many applications 18 months after their filing date. Though patent rights traditionally have only commenced on the date a patent issues, Congress also provided that when applications are published in advance of issuance, the patentee will have *provisional rights* against infringement between the date of publication and the date of issuance.

1. **Publication:** As a general matter, U.S. patent applications are now published 18 months after their earliest claimed filing date. However, there are some exceptions. U.S. applications that have been withdrawn (are no longer pending) at 18 months from filing, or that are the subject of a government secrecy order will not be published. Also, an applicant can prevent her application from being published if she certifies that her invention has not and will not be the subject of a patent application in another country that publishes applications prior to issuance. Since most other countries do publish applications at 18 months, as a practical matter, this last exception essentially allows persons who are only filing in the United States to retain the invention as a trade secret until a U.S. patent issues. (All patents are published when issued — even if the applicant is not filing abroad.)

PLEASE NOTE: You should check the web site (www.aspenlawschool.com/ip_outline) for possible revisions concerning publication of U.S. patent applications.

2. **The provisional rights:** Congress added a new subsection (d) to Patent Act §154, which grants patentees a provisional right to recover a reasonable royalty against persons who, during the period between publication of the application and issuance of the patent:

- make, use, offer for sale, or sell the invention in the United States, or import the invention into the United States; or

- if the invention is a process, make, use, offer for sale, sell, or import a product made by that process into the United States.

However, there are *two important limitations* on the provisional rights.

a. **Actual notice:** First, the alleged infringer must have actual notice of the published application (and receive a translation of the application into English, if it was not published in English).

b. **Same claims:** Second, the claims in the published application that are alleged to give rise to provisional rights must be substantially identical to the claims in the issued patent.

H. **Defenses to infringement claims:** There are a number of defenses to a claim of patent infringement. Five that are specific to patent litigation are patent invalidity, patent misuse, inequitable conduct, the experimental use defense, and the prior user defense.

1. **Patent invalidity:** An issued patent is presumed valid. However, the defendant may overcome this presumption by proving with clear and convincing evidence that the invention lacks novelty or utility, is obvious, is not fully disclosed as required under Patent Act §112, or does not constitute patentable subject matter. If the court holds the patent invalid, the defendant will not be held liable for infringing it.

a. **Estoppel:** Under *Lear, Inc. v. Adkins,* 395 U.S. 653 (1969), patent licensees are not estopped from challenging the validity of the patent under which they took a license, notwithstanding the fact that their license agreement implicitly acknowledges the patent's validity. (The Federal Circuit, however, has held that in such cases the licensee may be liable for royalties under the licensing agreement up until the time that it asserts its claim that the patent is invalid.) In *MedImmune, Inc. v. Genentech*, 127 S. Ct. 764 (2007), the Supreme Court held that the licensee did not have to terminate or breach the license agreement (and thus risk damages for patent infringement) prior to seeking a declaratory judgment of patent invalidity. In contrast to licensee challenges, the Federal Circuit has held that *a patent owner who subsequently assigns* the patent to another *will be estopped* from later challenging the patent's validity.

2. **Patent misuse:** The patentee may be deemed to have misused his patent if he used it as leverage to obtain more market power than Congress intended to convey through the grant of a patent. The doctrine works somewhat like the equitable doctrine of unclean hands. If the defendant is able to demonstrate patent misuse, the patentee will be denied enforcement of his patent until the misuse ceases and the patentee no longer enjoys any benefits from his prior misuse. The defendant will escape liability for infringement, regardless of whether he actually infringed the patent, and regardless of whether he himself was injured by the defendant's misuse. A number of different activities have been held to constitute patent misuse.

a. **Relationship to antitrust law:** Use of a patent in a manner that violates the antitrust laws generally constitutes patent misuse. However, the patent misuse doctrine has not been expressly limited to antitrust violations.

b. **Tying arrangements:** The most common form of patent misuse claim involves a tying arrangement. A tying arrangement arises when the patentee conditions a license to make, use, sell, or import the patented invention on the licensee's agreement to purchase goods or another license from the patentee. In such situations, the patentee may be using the market power conveyed by the patent to gain an advantage in a market for goods falling outside the scope of the patent monopoly.

  i. **Material components of the patented invention with no substantial non-infringing use:** Patent Act §271 expressly authorizes some tying arrangements. For example, the patentee may condition a license to make, use, sell, or import the patented invention on the licensee's purchase of a material component of the invention that has no substantial non-infringing use.

  Example: The patentee has a patent on a process for applying a chemical to growing rice crops to kill weeds. The chemical itself is not patented, but it has no substantial non-infringing use—its only use is as a material component in the patented process. The patentee may condition a license to use the patented process on purchase of the chemical from it, refusing to grant a license to persons who buy the chemical from someone else. While this is a form of tying arrangement, it will not constitute misuse.

  ii. **Goods with substantial non-infringing uses:** The patentee may condition a license to make, use, sell, or import the patented invention (or he may condition sale of the patented product itself) on the licensee/purchaser's purchase of some other product from the patentee that has substantial uses other than in the patented invention, *but only if* the patentee lacks market power in the relevant market for the patented invention that is the subject of the license or sale. 35 U.S.C. §271(d). If the patentee has market power, then the tying arrangement will have an anticompetitive effect and should be found to constitute misuse.

  Example: X has a patent for a new type of cigarette lighter. X will only grant a license to Y to make and sell the lighter if Y buys lighter fluid wholesale from X. The lighter fluid is a staple item that has many uses apart from use in the patented lighter. X will be subject to the misuse defense only if he has market power in the market that is relevant to his patented lighter. Only if X has power in the market for lighters is his use of his patent to gain sales of lighter fluid likely to have an appreciable anticompetitive effect. Note that there may be many different types of lighters on the market. The fact that X has a patent for one particular type of lighter does not automatically mean that he has any significant power in the lighter market.

  iii. **Tie-in to another license:** Conditioning a license to make, use, or sell one patented invention on the licensee's purchase of a license for a second patented invention ("package licensing") generally will be deemed patent misuse unless: (1) the first invention cannot be practiced without infringing the patent on the second invention; or (2) the patentee lacks market power in the relevant market for the first patented invention. 35 U.S.C. §271(d).

Example: X has a patent on a new type of cigarette lighter. He also has a patent on a new type of key chain. The ABC Corp. seeks a license to manufacture and sell the lighter, and X grants it subject to the express condition that the ABC Corp. also purchase a license to manufacture and sell the key chain. It is possible to make the lighter without infringing the patent on the key chain. X will be guilty of misuse if he has market power in the lighter market.

   c. Activities that will not constitute patent misuse: In addition to authorizing tying arrangements under the circumstances described above, Patent Act §271(d) expressly permits the patentee to engage in the following acts without fear of a misuse defense:

   - Derive revenue from acts that would constitute contributory infringement if performed by another without the patentee's consent. (In other words, the patentee may herself sell a material component of her invention that has no substantial non-infringing uses.)

   - License or authorize others to perform acts that if performed without the patentee's consent would constitute contributory infringement. (In other words, the patentee may enter into an agreement providing that, in return for consideration, the patentee will refrain from exercising her right to sue the other party for contributory infringement if the party sells a material component of the patentee's invention that has no substantial non-infringing use.)

   - Seek to enforce his rights against infringement or contributory infringement. (In other words, it does not constitute misuse to bring a claim of patent infringement, as long as it is done in good faith.)

   - Refuse to license or use any rights in the patent.

   Example: These exceptions to the patent misuse defense may have the effect of allowing a patentee to "corner the market" in an unpatented item. In *Dawson Chemical Co. v. Rohm & Haas Co.*, 448 U.S. 176 (1980), the patentee had a patent on a process for applying a chemical to growing rice crops to kill weeds. The chemical itself was not patented but was a material component of the process and had no substantial non-infringing use. The patentee only granted licenses to use its process to those who purchased the chemical from it. It refused to grant a license to use the process to persons buying the chemical elsewhere or to grant a license to others to sell the chemical. It sued competitors who sold the chemical for contributory infringement. The Supreme Court found that each of these individual actions by the patentee was authorized under subsection 271(d), and that, either individually or combined, they could not constitute patent misuse, even though they had the effect of giving the patentee a monopoly in the chemical, which was not patented.

3. **Inequitable conduct:** The inequitable conduct defense, sometimes called "fraud on the Patent Office," is related to patent misuse. It renders the patent unenforceable when the defendant proves, with clear and convincing evidence, that the patentee intentionally made a misrepresentation or withheld material information about the patentability of the invention during patent prosecution (the patent application process). The Court of Appeals for the Federal Circuit has held that a defendant claiming that a patentee failed to disclose material information must show, with clear and convincing evidence: (1) prior art or information that is material to patentability; (2) knowledge chargeable to the applicant of that prior art or information and of

its materiality; and (3) failure of the applicant to disclose the art or information resulting from an intent to mislead the P.T.O.

   a. Materiality: Prior art or information is material for purposes of the inequitable conduct defense if there is a substantial likelihood that a reasonable patent examiner would have considered it important in deciding whether to allow the application to issue as a patent.

   PLEASE NOTE: You should check the web site (www.aspenlawschool.com/ip_outline) for possible statutory amendments regarding the inequitable conduct defense.

4. **The experimental use defense:** The very narrow "experimental use" defense to infringement liability permits a person to make or use a patented invention if her purpose is *only* to satisfy her scientific curiosity or to amuse herself as an intellectual exercise. However, if the defendant has a commercial motivation, or a motivation to self-convenience, the defense will not apply.

   a. Subsection 271(e): Developers of drugs and veterinary biological products must perform numerous tests of their products' safety and efficacy, and submit the results of these tests to the FDA or other regulatory agencies in order to obtain approval to put them on the market. Particularly in the case of generic drugs, the developers may need to use drugs that are still under patent to perform their tests and generate the necessary data. The Court of Appeals for the Federal Circuit held that such a use would infringe the patent: the experimental use defense would not apply because the developers using the patented drugs in their experiments have a commercial purpose. Congress enacted Patent Act §271(e) in response to the Federal Circuit's holding. Subsection 271(e) permits persons, under limited circumstances, to make, use, sell, offer to sell, or import certain patented inventions in the course of developing information to submit to federal agencies regulating the manufacture, use, or sale of drugs or veterinary biological products. The Supreme Court has construed this drug research and development safe harbor broadly, to include use of patented medical devices, as well as chemical compounds. The Court has also held that the safe harbor applies to "all uses of patented inventions that are reasonably related to the development and submission of *any* information" under the Federal Food, Drug and Cosmetics Act, regardless of the stage of the research in which they are used, and whether the information ultimately is submitted for agency review. *Merck KGAA v. Integra Lifesciences, Ltd.,* 545 U.S. 193, 201 (2005).

5. **Prior use:** Prior to the decision of the Court of Appeals for the Federal Circuit in *State Street Bank and Trust Co. v. Signature Financial Group, Inc.* (*supra* pp. 34-35), many U.S. businesses did not believe that patents were available for the methods of doing business that they developed, and thus did not apply for patents. Once it became clear that business methods may be patented, the concern arose that early developers of business methods might be held liable for infringement by later developers of the same methods who obtained patents. To address this concern, Congress enacted the First Inventor Defense Act of 1999 (part of the Intellectual Property and Communications Omnibus Reform Act of 1999) which creates a "prior user" defense against claims that a defendant has infringed a patented method of doing business. Under newly created Patent Act §273, the defense is available when a defendant proves by clear and convincing evidence that it: (1) actually reduced the patented subject matter to practice, in good faith, at least one year before the effective filing date of the patent; and (2) commercially used the subject matter before the effective filing date of the patent.

a. **Commercial use:** The legislative history explains what is meant by "commercial use": "The method that is the subject matter of the defense may be an internal method for doing business, such as an internal human resources management process, or a method for conducting business such as a preliminary or intermediate manufacturing procedure, which contributes to the effectiveness of the business by producing a useful end result for the internal operation of the business or for external sale. Commercial use does not require the subject matter at issue to be accessible to or otherwise known to the public."

b. **Separate from an invalidity defense:** The Act specifies that the successful assertion of the defense will not in itself result in a finding of patent invalidity, although the same facts used to establish the defense may also be relevant to a defense that the patent is invalid, for example, for lack of novelty, under Patent Act §102(g). (A party who invented and made commercial use of the invention in the United States before the patentee's invention date, and continues to do so, has a good chance of succeeding with an invalidity defense under Patent Act §102(g). Note that the party may not be subject to a finding of abandonment, suppression, or concealment, even if its commercial use was done in secret. See *supra*, pp. 40-41.)

c. **Exhaustion of rights in products sold by prior user:** The Act provides that when a person entitled to the §273 defense sells products of a patented business method, the sale exhausts the patentee's rights in the products. (See the doctrine of exhaustion, *supra*, at pp. 59, 61.) Thus, the prior user's purchasers have the same rights to resell or repair the product that they would have had if they had purchased from the patentee.

IX. REMEDIES FOR PATENT INFRINGEMENT

Both monetary and injunctive remedies are available for patent infringement.

A. **The proper measure of damages:** Patent Act §284 directs courts to award prevailing patentees damages "adequate to compensate for the infringement." Courts may measure infringement damages by calculating the patentee's lost profits attributable to the infringement or by calculating a reasonable royalty for the defendant's use of the patented invention, but in any event, the patentee should receive *no less* than a reasonable royalty, together with interest and costs.

PLEASE NOTE: You should check the web site (www.aspenlawschool.com/ip_outline) for possible revisions to the Patent Act's damage provisions.

1. **The reasonable royalty measure of damages:** A reasonable royalty is the amount a potential licensee seeking a license to make, use, sell, or import the patented invention would be willing to pay and a reasonable patentee would be willing to accept in arm's-length negotiations at the time of infringement. This measure is the default measure of damages, and is appropriate when lost profits are too speculative to estimate, or the patentee does not itself sell the patented invention. The fact of infringement itself is a compensable injury, because the infringement violates the patentee's right of exclusivity. Thus, the patentee is entitled to recover a reasonable royalty even if she is unable to demonstrate any actual pecuniary loss. Considerations that may be relevant in determining a reasonable royalty include:

   - The amount that other licensees have agreed to pay for comparable licenses;
   - The royalties paid by or methods for calculating royalties used by other parties in comparable situations;

- The patentee's own manufacturing and marketing capacity, and her general willingness to grant licenses with regard to the invention. (If the patentee is able to satisfy all demands for the invention herself, or follows a general policy of refusing to license inventions to competitors, she would be likely to charge a high royalty in order to make the license worth her while);

- The amount of profit or cost savings that the licensee may obtain from making, selling, using, or importing the patented invention.

2. **The lost-profits measure of damages:** The lost-profits measure of damages is preferred, when it can be determined, because it may more fully compensate the patentee. To recover under the lost-profits measure the patentee must demonstrate a reasonable probability that *but for* the defendant's infringement the patentee would have made the sales that the defendant made. To do this, the patentee generally must demonstrate several factors:

    - Sufficient demand for the patented product.

    - An absence of acceptable non-infringing substitutes. (The patentee must demonstrate that but for the infringement, the defendant's sales would have gone to her. In the case of a patent monopoly, there may be no third-party competitors selling the patented invention itself, but there may be other competitors selling *non-infringing substitutes*, which defendant's customers might have bought if the substitutes were reasonably interchangeable with the patented invention and available at a comparable price.)

        Example: Assume that X Co. sells its patented can opener. Y Co. sells a can opener that infringes X Co.'s patent. To recover lost profits, X must show with reasonable probability that, but for the infringement, Y Co.'s customers would have bought from X Co., rather than from sellers of other (non-infringing) types of can openers.

    - Manufacturing and marketing capacity to fill the demand. (In order to show that it lost sales due to the infringement, the patentee must demonstrate that it had the ability to supply enough of the patented invention to satisfy the demand of both its own customers and the defendant's.)

    - The amount of profit the patentee would have made.

    a. **The incremental income approach to calculating lost profits:** The incremental income approach recognizes that it does not cost as much to produce unit $N + 1$ if the first N units produced already have paid the fixed costs. Fixed costs are costs which do not vary with increases in production, like management salaries, property taxes, and insurance. Thus, fixed costs are not considered in determining lost profits on those units over the first N.

    b. **Lost profits on units that do not embody the patented invention:** In an *en banc* decision, a sharply divided Court of Appeals for the Federal Circuit held that, in addition to recovering lost profits from an infringer on sales of the patented device, a patentee may recover lost profits on sales of devices that do not incorporate the patented invention if the patentee can demonstrate: (1) that it would have sold the unpatented device but for the defendant's infringement; (2) the lost sales were reasonably foreseeable by the infringing competitor; and (3) the unpatented device directly competes with the defendant's infringing product. *Rite-Hite Corp. v. Kelley Co., Inc.*, 56 F.3d 1538 (Fed. Cir.), *cert. denied*, 516 U.S. 867 (1995).

Example: Assume that the patentee sells two types of can openers, only one of which incorporates the patented invention. The defendant sells a can opener that infringes the patent, which causes the patentee to lose sales on both of its can opener models. If the loss on the unpatented model was reasonably foreseeable, then the patentee can recover lost profits on both models.

c. **Entire market value rule:** The patentee may be entitled to recover lost profits on unpatented components sold with a patented apparatus under the entire market value rule. This rule applies when patented and unpatented components together are considered to be parts of a single assembly, or constitute a functional unit, operating together to achieve a result. (A court may also consider the likelihood of the defendant's selling such related unpatented items in determining a reasonable royalty.)

Example: The patentee sells a weaving apparatus that consists of three components: A frame, a weaving device, and a mechanical arm that takes completed woven fabric from the frame. Only the weaving device is patented, but it is customary for customers to buy all three components from the same source, and thus it is reasonably probable that the patentee would have sold all three but for the defendant's infringement. The patentee may be entitled to recover lost profits on the whole package, rather than just on the patented component. (If the measure of damages is a reasonable royalty, the court may consider the defendant's expectation of selling the frame and arm, along with the patented weaving device, in determining the amount that he would have paid as a reasonable royalty to the plaintiff.)

d. **Notice of patent:** Section 287 of the Patent Act requires patentees to notify the public of their patents. They may do this by causing the words "patented" or "Pat.," along with the patent number, to be marked on the articles marketed under the patent. Failure to do this will not prohibit the patentee from obtaining injunctive relief against infringers, but it will limit the availability of damages. In the absence of such marking, the patentee may only recover damages upon a showing that the defendant had notice that he was charged with infringement, and damages will be limited to infringement that occurred after the defendant's receipt of that notice. The filing of suit against the defendant will constitute notice.

3. **Attorney fees:** Section 285 of the Patent Act authorizes courts to award reasonable attorney fees to the prevailing party in exceptional cases. Courts have interpreted "exceptional cases" to include cases of willful or deliberate infringement by the defendant (when the plaintiff is the prevailing party), and bad-faith conduct by either losing party.

4. **Double or treble damages:** Section 284 of the Patent Act also authorizes the courts to increase the damages awarded to a patentee up to three times the actual damages found or assessed. The Court of Appeals for the Federal Circuit has indicated that these enhanced damages may only be awarded upon a showing of willful infringement or bad faith on the part of the defendant.

Example: X has a patent. Y, a competitor of X, is aware of X's patent and realizes that the new article he plans to manufacture and sell may infringe it. He makes an attempt to avoid infringement liability by making some superficial changes. He does not, however, consult a patent lawyer to determine whether he indeed has sufficiently changed the article. Later, X sues Y for infringement and wins. This is a likely case for a doubling or trebling of damages. When one has actual notice of another's patent, he has a duty to exercise due care to determine whether his actions will infringe. At the least, Y's actions were reckless.

Example: X has a patent. Y, a competitor of X, is aware of the patent and realizes that the new article he plans to manufacture and sell may infringe. He consults with his patent lawyer, who advises him that X's patent is likely to be invalid under the statutory bar provisions of §102(b). However, the lawyer cautions Y that victory is not certain. Y proceeds to market his new article, X sues, and Y's subsection 102(b) defense fails. Y probably will not be liable for double or treble damages because he did exercise due care by consulting with a patent lawyer and he had a substantial, good faith defense to an infringement claim. Since it promotes competition to challenge possibly invalid patents, courts generally will not penalize those who do so in good faith.

5. **Prejudgment interest:** The Supreme Court has directed lower courts to award prevailing plaintiffs prejudgment interest, calculated as of the date of infringement, as a routine matter. This is viewed as necessary to adequately compensate the patentee for the infringement, as required by §284 of the Patent Act.

Example: The court finds that Y infringed X's patent from 1992 until 1995. It assesses damages based on a reasonable royalty measure and determines that had Y in fact been licensed to use X's invention during the period of infringement, Y would have owed X a yearly royalty of $50,000 for each of the three years. To determine prejudgment interest, the court must calculate interest on each yearly payment as it would have been due. The interest will run from the date the payment would have been due until the date of the judgment. This leaves X in the position he would have been in but for the infringement. If he had received the payment when due, he could have invested it and gotten a return on his investment. The interest takes the place of that lost return.

B. **Injunctive relief:** When infringement is found, courts typically have permanently enjoined the defendant from further infringement, as well as awarded damages. However, in *e-Bay Inc. v. MercExchange*, 126 S. Ct. 1837 (2006), the Supreme Court rejected arguments that, because the Patent Act provides patentees with rights to *exclude others* from making, using, selling, or importing the patented invention, courts must always issue permanent injunctions against patent infringement absent exceptional circumstances. Rather, the *MercExchange* Court found that injunctions are a matter of equitable discretion on the part of the district court, reviewable on appeal for abuse of discretion. Thus, courts in patent cases should apply general equitable principles governing the grant of permanent injunctions, and use the usual four-factor test for injunctive relief: (1) has the plaintiff suffered irreparable injury?; (2) are remedies available at law, such as monetary damages, inadequate to compensate for that injury?; (3) considering the balance of hardships between the plaintiff and defendant, is a remedy in equity warranted?; and (4) will the public interest be disserved by a permanent injunction?

1. **Preliminary injunctions:** While courts generally have been willing to grant permanent injunctions upon a finding of infringement, they traditionally have been reluctant to award preliminary injunctions, due to concern about injury to competition: If the defendant is prohibited from marketing its allegedly infringing products for the duration of lengthy litigation, and later is found not to infringe, the defendant's position in the market may have been permanently impaired or lost altogether. Notwithstanding this traditional concern, the Court of Appeals for the Federal Circuit has liberalized the availability of preliminary injunctions considerably, finding that the movant's burden should be no different in a patent case than in other kinds of

intellectual property disputes, where preliminary injunctions may be granted on a "clear showing" of irreparable harm and likelihood of success on the merits.

C. **Remedies for infringement through performance of "medical activities":** In 1996, Congress amended Patent Act §287 to prohibit infringement remedies against medical practitioners and related health care entities (entities with whom medical practitioners have a professional affiliation, such as HMOs and hospitals) who directly infringe or induce infringement of a patent through performance of a "medical activity." As amended, §287 defines a "medical activity" as "the performance of a medical or surgical procedure on a body." However, exceptions incorporated into the provision make it clear that remedies are not precluded if the medical practitioner: (1) makes unauthorized use of a patented machine, manufacture, or composition of matter; (2) practices a patented use of a composition of matter without authorization; or (3) practices a patented biotechnology process without authorization. Thus, when these exceptions are taken into account, §287 generally only prohibits patent infringement remedies against medical practitioners and related health care entities when they infringe through performance of patented surgical or medical procedures that *do not involve drugs or patented devices*, such as the Heimlich maneuver or CPR. However, this general rule is subject to the caveat set forth below.

1. **The caveat:** Section 287 will preclude infringement remedies even though a composition of matter (generally, a drug) is cited in the patent if the use of the composition of matter does not directly contribute to the achievement of the objective of the claimed procedure.

    Example: The legislative history provides the following example: The patent claims a novel, non-obvious method of surgically transplanting a healthy heart into a patient with a diseased heart. One step involves administering a conventional anaesthetic to the patient. This should not cause the surgical procedure to be treated as a patented use of a composition of matter, and §287 should prohibit a remedy for direct infringement or inducement against a medical practitioner. In contrast, if the administration of the anesthesia entails a novel anaesthetic or dosing schedule, the use of the composition of matter (the anaesthetic) should be deemed directly to contribute to the achievement of the objective of the claimed method, and remedies for infringement should be available against the medical practitioner and related health care entities.

X. COMPARISON OF UTILITY PATENT AND TRADE SECRET PROTECTION FOR INVENTIONS

In some cases an invention may qualify both for a patent and for trade secret protection, giving the proprietor a choice. It is impossible to have both forms of protection simultaneously for the same invention, because most patent applications (which include full disclosure of the invention) are published 18 months after they are filed. Even if not published at that time, the invention will be fully disclosed to the public when the patent is granted. Moreover, secret commercial use of the invention for an appreciable time prior to filing for a patent may foreclose patent protection under Patent Act §§102(b) or (c). See pp. 44, 46, *supra*. When a choice exists, which form of protection—patent or trade secret—is most advantageous? Several factors should be considered. Their weight may differ, depending on the circumstances and the particular goals and needs of the proprietor.

A. **Duration of protection:** Pursuant to the Uruguay Round Agreements Act, a patent provides a monopoly that generally lasts twenty years from the date of application. After it expires, others are free to make, use, sell, offer to sell, and import the invention. They are assisted in doing so by the published disclosure compelled by Patent Act §112. Trade secret protection lasts as long as the invention remains a secret. Therefore, if the secret is one that can be safely kept, trade secret protection may endure longer than patent protection.

B. **Breadth of protection:** A patent gives its owner the right to prevent others from making, using, selling, offering to sell, or importing the invention, regardless of whether they copied or invented independently. Liability for patent infringement is a form of strict liability. Trade secret law only prohibits others from disclosing or using the invention in cases involving a breach of duty of confidentiality or other improper conduct. Persons who independently invent or acquire the invention by proper means, such as reverse engineering, are free to use the trade secret. Thus, patent protection, while it lasts, is much stronger than trade secret protection.

C. **Cost:** Applying for a patent is costly, complex, and time consuming. Trade secret protection, on the other hand, arises automatically as a matter of law, with no costly or lengthy application process. However, maintaining a trade secret may be costly in some cases, if it is necessary to undertake expensive security precautions to protect secrecy.

D. **Risk of losing protection:** A trade secret may be lost at any time—for example, if a third party independently discovers and publishes it. Indeed, bringing suit to enforce a trade secret may jeopardize its ongoing secrecy, notwithstanding protective orders by the court. On the other hand, a validly granted patent is secure. Of course, whenever the patentee seeks to enforce the patent he runs the risk that the defendant will successfully challenge the validity of the patent. (A significant percentage of patents, which are granted by the P.T.O. in *ex parte* proceedings, are later held invalid when challenged in litigation.)

E. **Licensing:** Licensing others to use a trade secret may be more difficult than licensing others to use a patented invention, because of the special precautions that must be taken to ensure continued secrecy. However, courts have enforced contracts to pay for use of a trade secret long after the secret has become generally known. Courts will not enforce contractual obligations to pay for use of a patented invention after the patent expires or is held invalid.

XI. DESIGN PATENTS

A. **The nature of design patents:** A design patent protects the ornamental design of an article of manufacture. Its purpose is to foster the decorative arts. In keeping with this purpose, a design will only be eligible for protection if at some point in the life of the article, its appearance is a matter of concern. This may occur while the article is in use, or prior to use, when purchasers are being attracted. For example, the ornamental design of a casket would qualify: It is a matter of concern in the showroom, and at a funeral, but probably not when put to its ultimate use.

  1. **Articles of manufacture:** For purposes of design patent protection, the term "article of manufacture" is construed broadly and includes most tangible objects that are man-made. The design patent protects the article's appearance, not its mode of operation.

  2. **The duration of design patents:** Design patent protection commences when the patent is issued and lasts 14 years. Design patent applications are not published 18 months after filing, so there are no provisional rights. (See pp. 65-66, *supra*.)

B. **Standards for design patents:** To qualify for a patent, the design of an article of manufacture must be novel, non-obvious, and ornamental. 35 U.S.C. §171.

1. **Novelty and statutory bars:** All the provisions of Patent Act §102, discussed in connection with utility patents, apply to design patents. The main difference is that the time specified in subsection 102(d) for design patents is six months, rather than one year. (See p. 46, *supra*.)

2. **The non-obviousness standard:** A design is not patentable if a designer of ordinary skill in the field of the patented design, viewing the overall appearance of the design, would consider the new design obvious in light of the pertinent prior art. As noted in connection with utility patents, to make this determination, the court must consider: (1) the scope and content of the prior art; (2) differences between the prior art and the design at issue; and (3) the level of skill in the pertinent art.

    a. **The prior art:** The pertinent prior art consists of designs of the same type of article of manufacture or of articles sufficiently similar that a designer of ordinary skill would look to them for design ideas. The Court of Appeals for the Federal Circuit has held that to find obviousness in the design patent context, there must be a "primary reference"—a pre-existing article with design characteristics that are sufficiently similar to the claimed design that the claimed design can be characterized as a variation of the primary reference. The question then becomes whether the applicable prior art, market trends, or ordinary skill in the art would suggest making the variation. If so, the claimed design is obvious. *Hupp v. Siroflex of America, Inc.*, 122 F.3d 1456 (Fed. Cir. 1997).

3. **The ornamentality standard:** To satisfy the ornamentality requirement, a design must be *primarily* ornamental. It must not be *dictated* by functional considerations. The fact that the article of manufacture serves a utilitarian function does not in itself mean that the design of the article is dictated by functional considerations. If there are a variety of ways in which the article could be designed and still effectively perform its function, then any one design is unlikely to be deemed functional. For example, the upper portion of an athletic shoe could be designed in a number of ways—in different colors, with perforations in different locations, and different styles of stitching—and still perform its basic function effectively. Such design choices are primarily ornamental—not dictated by function—and thus are protectible. However, the courts are particularly concerned to prevent design patents from being used as a back-door route to utility patent protection. If granting a design patent will have the effect of giving the patentee a monopoly in the way the article functions (as opposed to the way it looks), the courts will find that the design fails the ornamentality standard.

    a. **The Federal Circuit's list of "appropriate considerations":** The Court of Appeals for the Federal Circuit has noted that while it may be useful to analyze the individual elements of a claimed design, the determination of whether the design is primarily ornamental or dictated by the function of the article must ultimately rest on an analysis of its overall appearance. The court went on to provide a list of "appropriate considerations for assessing whether the patented design as a whole—its overall appearance—was dictated by functional considerations." The considerations include:

        1. the existence of alternative designs;
        2. whether the protected design represents the best design;
        3. whether alternative designs would adversely affect the utility of the specified article;
        4. whether there are any concomitant utility patents;
        5. whether the advertising touts particular features of the design as having specific utility; and

6. whether there are any elements in the design or overall appearance clearly not dictated by function.

Berry Sterling Corp. v. Pescor Plastics, Inc., 122 F.3d 1452 (Fed. Cir. 1997).

C. **Infringement of a design patent:** Patent Act §271 provisions governing infringement of a utility patent also apply to design patents. See pp. 58-65, *supra*. The Supreme Court has enunciated the standard for infringement of a design patent as follows: "If, in the eye of an ordinary observer, giving such attention as a purchaser usually gives, two designs are substantially the same, if the resemblance is such as to deceive such an observer, inducing him to purchase one supposing it to be the other, the first one patented is infringed by the other." *Gorham Manufacturing Co. v. White*, 81 U.S. (14 Wall.) 511 (1872).

1. **The Federal Circuit's additional requirements:** In addition to the *Gorham* standard, stated above, the Court of Appeals for the Federal Circuit has held that the allegedly infringing design must appropriate the novelty in the patented design (those features that distinguish the patented design from the prior art). This is sometimes called the "points of novelty" requirement. Also, when the patented design is comprised of both functional and ornamental features, it must appear that the ordinary observer would be deceived by reason of the common ornamental (as opposed to functional) features. This is sometimes called the "common ornamental features" requirement.

2. **Comparing the standard for design patent infringement with the standard for utility patent infringement:** The *Gorham* "eye of the ordinary observer" test looks to the ordinary observer's (generally the defendant's intended purchaser's) overall impression, without breaking the design into its constituent elements. This is different from the more precise test for utility patent infringement, which requires comparing the parties' products or processes element-by-element. However, the Federal Circuit's "points of novelty" and "common ornamental features" requirements necessitate breaking the patented and allegedly infringing designs into their constituent elements, and have the effect of narrowing the scope of design patent protection.

D. **Defenses and remedies for infringement of design patents:** The defenses and remedies available for infringement of utility patents are also available for infringement of design patents. See pp. 66-74, *supra*. In addition, Patent Act §289 provides a remedy for design patent infringement that utility patents do not convey: A person who, without permission, applies a patented design or a colorable imitation of it to an article of manufacture for purposes of sale, or sells or exposes such an article for sale, will be liable for his total profit, but in any event not less than $250.

E. **Double patenting:** A person may obtain only one patent per invention. However, this rule does not preclude more than one patent for an article of manufacture. For example, one article may contain two separate inventions that will each support a utility patent. Likewise, it is possible to obtain both a utility patent and a design patent in the same article, *if a structure embodying the mechanical invention would not of necessity embody the design, and vice versa.*

Example: The test is whether a device conforming to the written claims of the utility patent *necessarily* would have the same appearance as that depicted in the claim of the design patent, and vice versa (whether the device conforming to the design depicted in the claim of the design patent necessarily would also conform to the written claims of the utility patent). Assume that X wishes to obtain both a design and a utility patent on a new light fixture. The design patent would only consist of the outwardly visible features of the fixture. The utility patent would cover the mechanical aspects of the light, many of which may be inside the fixture—not visible when the light is in use. If a light fixture of the same appearance as X's could contain a different mechanical apparatus, and a fixture with the same mechanical apparatus could have a different outward appearance, both a design and a utility patent can issue for X's light fixture.

F. The success of design patents: The present scheme of design patents has been criticized for failing adequately to protect U.S. industry against copyists. First, it is said that the standards for patentability are high, excluding many valuable product designs from protection. Second, the application process in the P.T.O. is too lengthy, given the short life of many commercial designs. A design may have become outdated and lost its market value by the time the patent issues, but patent protection only begins as of the date the patent issues. As we will see, copyright law and the law of trademarks and unfair competition may provide alternative means of preventing others from copying the design features of a product.

XII. PLANT PATENTS

A. The nature of a plant patent: Plant patents are available to persons who discover or invent a distinct and new variety of plant and asexually reproduce it. The patent monopoly lasts for the same term as that for utility patents. See p. 29, *supra*.

1. **Scope of plant patents:** Cultivated sports, mutants, hybrids, and newly found seedlings may qualify for a plant patent. Tuberpropagated plants and new plants found in an uncultivated state do not qualify. For example, an explorer who discovers a new plant growing wild in the jungle would not qualify for a plant patent. However, a farmer who discovers a new plant (that has resulted from mutation or cross-breeding) in his fields would qualify.

B. Standards for plant patents: To qualify for a plant patent, a new variety of plant must be novel, distinct, and non-obvious, and it must have been asexually reproduced.

1. **Asexual reproduction:** Before the breeder/discoverer of a new variety of plant may obtain a plant patent she must successfully asexually reproduce the plant—that is, make a clone that preserves the new variety's novel, distinctive characteristics. This may be done, for example, by taking cuttings of the original plant and rooting them so that they grow into independent plants. It is the discoverer's recognition of the distinctive new characteristic and the preservation of that characteristic through asexual reproduction that constitutes the "invention" that is the subject of the plant patent.

2. **Novelty and statutory bars:** The novelty and statutory bar provisions of Patent Act §102 apply to plant patents.

    a. **Prior existence in nature:** To be novel, the new variety of plant must not have existed before in nature. A plant will be deemed to have existed in nature only if it existed in a form that was capable of naturally reproducing the distinctive characteristics that are the subject of the patent. Thus, for example, if the variety of plant that is the subject of the patent is a mutation, evidence that the same mutation has occurred before in nature will not indicate that the variety lacks novelty unless the earlier mutation would have been passed down naturally to subsequent generations.

3. **The distinctiveness requirement:** To be patented, the new plant variety must have at least one characteristic that is clearly distinguishable from those of pre-existing varieties. Such characteristics may include the ability to grow in a different type of soil, a different color or size or shape of fruit or flower, or a different flavor.

4. **The non-obviousness requirement:** In this context the U.S. Court of Appeals for the Fifth Circuit, in *Yoder Bros., Inc. v. California-Florida Plant Corp.*, 537 F.2d 1347 (5th Cir. 1976), *cert. denied*, 429 U.S. 1094 (1977), has held that the non-obviousness requirement merely means that the new characteristic discussed in paragraph 3, *supra*, must be significant.

C. **Infringement of a plant patent:** A plant patent grants the owner the right to exclude others from: (1) asexually reproducing the patented plant; (2) selling or using a plant so reproduced, or any of its parts; and (3) importing a plant so reproduced, or any of its parts.

1. **Independent discovery:** The Court of Appeals for the Federal Circuit has held that a plant patent only gives the patentee the right to prohibit others from reproducing, using, or selling plants that were derived through asexual reproduction from the original patented plant. To this extent, plant patents differ from utility and design patents, which prohibit not just copies, but independently conceived designs and inventions as well, when they are essentially the same as the patented invention. *Imazio Nursery, Inc. v. Dania Greenhouses*, 69 F.3d 1560 (Fed. Cir. 1995).

    Example: A discovers a new variety of chrysanthemum resulting from the mutation of an existing variety. He preserves it by asexually reproducing it and obtains a plant patent for it. The same mutation occurs again, on a chrysanthemum plant that is unrelated to A's patented plant, and B discovers and asexually reproduces it. B begins to sell his plant. Even though the chrysanthemum B is selling is exactly like A's patented chrysanthemum in terms of its characteristics, B is not infringing because he did not obtain his chrysanthemum by taking cuttings of A's plant or one of its clones. He independently discovered the new variety. By contrast, if A has a utility patent for a new mousetrap, and B independently invents a mousetrap with the same or equivalent elements, B will be liable for infringing A's utility patent if he makes, uses, sells, offers to sell, or imports his mousetrap. It will not matter that he conceived of the mousetrap on his own.

2. **Taking seeds:** Growing a plant from seeds taken from the patented plant will not infringe the plant patent. This is sexual, rather than asexual reproduction, which is not prohibited.

3. **Plant parts:** In 1998, Congress amended Patent Act §163 to specify that plant patent rights extend not only to whole plants but also to parts of patented plants, such as flowers or fruit produced by the patented plant. This amendment was necessary to close a loophole in the law that was being exploited by importers, who reproduced U.S. patented plants abroad and then imported products harvested from those plants—such as cut flowers, fruit, and harvested timber—to sell in the United States in competition with the U.S. plant patent holder.

D. **Other considerations:** It may be impossible to describe a new plant variety in the patent specification sufficiently to enable a person skilled in the art to make and use the variety. Thus, §162 of the Patent Act merely requires that the description be as complete as is reasonably possible. Apart from the special considerations set forth above, plant patents generally are governed by the same rules as are applicable to utility patents.

E. **Other methods of obtaining property rights in new varieties of plants:** There are two additional means of protecting new varieties of plants, beyond plant patents. One may obtain a utility patent if all the standards for such patents are satisfied. One may also obtain a Certificate of Plant Variety Protection, as described below.

1. **Utility patents for plants:** After the Supreme Court's *Chakrabarty* decision (discussed at p. 30, *supra*), it became apparent that new varieties of plants are eligible for utility patents, either as articles of manufacture or compositions of matter. The Supreme Court has subsequently confirmed that the availability of plant patents (and the availability of protection under the Plant Variety Protection Act, discussed below) does not preclude utility patent protection for plants when all the regular prerequisites for a utility patent are met. *J.E.M. Ag. Supply, Inc. v. Pioneer Hi-Bred International, Inc.*, 534 U.S. 124 (2001). Thus, when the inventor of a new variety of plant opts for a utility patent, eligibility and infringement will be governed by the standards applicable to utility patents. If applicants are unable to fully enable others to practice their plant invention in the patent specification, as required by Patent Act §112, they may be required to deposit a sample with an international depository (as is done in the case of patents for other types of living matter), which will make the sample available to other interested parties.

2. **Plant Variety Protection Act:** The Plant Variety Protection Act (7 U.S.C. §2321, *et seq.*) gives patent-like protection to persons who breed new varieties of plants through use of seeds (sexual reproduction). Sexually reproduced and tuberpropagated plants other than fungi and bacteria are eligible. To qualify, the new variety must be new, distinct, uniform, and stable (that is, it must appear that the new characteristics of the variety will pass uniformly and manifest themselves from one generation to the next). There is no non-obviousness requirement, though there are statutory bar provisions somewhat similar to Patent Act §102(b). A certificate of plant variety protection is awarded by the Department of Agriculture and gives the holder the right to exclude others from selling the variety, offering it for sale, reproducing it, importing or exporting it, or using it in producing (as opposed to developing) a hybrid or different variety. The term of protection recently has been increased from 18 years to 20 years (and in the case of trees and vines, 25 years) from the date of issuance. There are opportunities for protection prior to issuance of the certificate, as well. The certificate holder's rights are subject to some limited exceptions.

XIII. KEY INTERNATIONAL PATENT TREATIES

A. **The Paris Convention:** The Paris Convention for the Protection of Industrial Property (Paris Convention) is an important multinational treaty for patent protection. Organized in 1883, it has over 125 adherents, or members, including the United States and most or all other industrialized nations. The Paris Convention is administered by the World Intellectual Property Organization (WIPO), a specialized agency of the United Nations.

1. **National treatment:** The Paris Convention essentially requires each member country to grant as great patent protection to inventors from other member nations as it grants to its own domestic inventors. (Persons from countries outside the Union who are domiciled or who have real and effective industrial or commercial establishments in a member country are treated for purposes of the Paris Convention as nationals of that member country.) National treatment thus

prohibits discrimination on the basis of a patent applicant's nationality, as long as the applicant has a sufficient affiliation with another member nation.

2. **Filing priority:** The Paris Convention provides that when a patent application is filed in one member nation, additional applications for the same invention filed in other member nations over the next 12 months will have the benefit of the filing date in the first nation. The date of filing in the first country is called the "priority filing date." Having this early filing date offers U.S. inventors important advantages in other countries, most of whom award patents on a first-to-file basis and have strict novelty and non-obviousness requirements.

Example: A files an application for patent in Country X on January 1, 2003. In Country Y an invention is disqualified for a patent for lack of novelty if it is publicly disclosed anywhere in the world at any time before its inventor files an application for patent in Country Y. On August 2, 2003, A's invention is publicly disclosed. A files for a patent in Country Y on October 1, 2003. Due to the Paris Convention, his official filing date in Country Y is viewed not as October 1, but as January 1, the date he filed his application in Country X. Since this date precedes the public disclosure, A is not disqualified from obtaining a patent in Country Y.

Example: A files an application for patent in Country X on January 1, 2003. In Country Y, patents are granted to the first inventor to file, rather than to the first person to invent. In August 2003, B, who has independently made the same invention as A, files an application for patent for the invention in Country Y. A files his application in Country Y in October 2003. But for his Paris Convention filing priority date of January 1, A would lose his right to patent in Country Y to B.

3. **Common rules:** For the most part, members of the Paris Convention are free to determine the nature and extent of substantive patent protection they will provide for inventions, as long as they provide it uniformly to domestic and foreign applicants. However, the Paris Convention does impose a few minimal substantive requirements regarding the patent protection offered by its members. For example, member nations may not grant or refuse a patent on the ground that another nation has done so—they must independently evaluate their patent applications. In addition, a member nation may not refuse or invalidate a patent simply because it imposes restrictions on the sale of the invention that is the subject of the patent application (or, if the invention is a process, because it imposes restrictions on the sale of the product of the process). For example, the fact that the country restricts or prohibits sale of a particular drug cannot serve as a ground to refuse a patent for the drug or for a process for making it. Finally, the Paris Convention imposes limits on member nations' ability to impose forfeiture, compulsory licensing, or other penalties on inventors for failure to exercise their patents within the member nations' borders.

4. **Criticisms of the Paris Convention:** While the Paris Convention represents a major step toward international cooperation, it has been the subject of considerable criticism. First, it provides little real substantive protection for inventors. A member nation may decide to deny patent protection altogether for many types of inventions, or limit protection to a very short duration, as long as it does so in a nondiscriminatory fashion. Second, the Paris Convention does relatively little to alleviate the time, effort, and expense of filing separate patent applications in every nation in which patent protection is desired. Third, the Paris Convention has no effective enforcement mechanism. Thus, if a member nation violates the terms of the Convention, other members have little meaningful official recourse.

B. **The Patent Cooperation Treaty:** The Patent Cooperation Treaty (P.C.T.) became effective in 1978 and has over 100 members, including the United States and most other industrialized nations. It also is administered by WIPO. The P.C.T. provides a centralized means of filing, searching, and examining patent applications in a number of different countries simultaneously.

   1. **Procedure:** An inventor in a member nation may file in one member country a standardized international patent application, which designates all the P.C.T. member countries in which he desires patent protection. The effect of doing this is the same as if the applicant had filed a separate application in each of the designated countries on that date. The national patent office that receives the application forwards it to an international searching authority (if the national office is not itself an international searching authority), which conducts an international search of the prior art and produces a report on its findings. The applicant then has the opportunity to amend his claims in response to the search findings. The applicant may then request an optional international preliminary examination of the patentability of his invention. While the results of this examination are not binding on the designated countries, they may be influential. The application, search report, and (if requested) preliminary examination report are then sent to the national patent offices of the designated countries for consideration. The determination of whether to grant a patent is made by each designated country. The P.C.T. procedure does not permit the international applicant to avoid paying fees and prosecuting his application in each separate country, but it does streamline the process somewhat, and it permits the applicant to postpone the effort and expense of individual country prosecution for a number of months, while retaining his options. During that period he can test the market for the invention. If the market is not promising, the P.C.T. applicant can withdraw the application before it reaches the individual national patent offices, thus avoiding considerable cost and effort.

C. **The Agreement on Trade-Related Aspects of Intellectual Property Rights:** The Agreement on Trade-Related Aspects of Intellectual Property Rights, Including Trade in Counterfeited Goods (TRIPs), is a very important multinational agreement designed to strengthen and harmonize patent (and other forms of intellectual property) protection worldwide. TRIPs is administered by the World Trade Organization ("W.T.O."). It incorporates the provisions of the Paris Convention and builds on them. Among other things, the TRIPs agreement imposes minimum disclosure requirements for patent applications, and prescribes the subject matter for which patent protection must be provided, the rights that must be afforded to patentees, and the minimum term of protection. The United States' adherence to TRIPs, in December of 1994, required the U.S. to amend its Patent Act to give patentees rights against offers to sell and importation of the patented invention, and to change the basic U.S. patent term for utility and plant patents from 17 years from issuance to 20 years from application date. Moreover, TRIPs article 27 requires that "patent rights shall be available and patent rights enjoyable without discrimination as to the place of invention." While the United States grants patents to the first person to invent, rather than the first to file, it had discriminated against foreign inventors by refusing to consider evidence of inventive activity abroad. Foreign inventors applying for U.S. patents had to rely on their U.S. application date or the date on which they "introduced" their invention into the United States as their date of invention in priority contests. To comply with article 27, the United States had to amend its Patent Act to eliminate these discriminatory provisions. After January 1, 1996, inventors can rely on inventive activity in any World Trade Organization country to establish their invention date in priority contests, as long as the invention date is not prior to January 1, 1996. The United States considered these amendments worth its while in order to obtain stronger patent protection for U.S. inventions abroad. While certain developing nations have extra time to bring their laws into compliance, the TRIPs provisions promise to heighten protection of U.S. inventions abroad over the long term.

D. The Patent Law Treaty: The Patent Law Treaty (which is administered by W.I.P.O.) undertakes to harmonize patent application filing procedures among its members, thus further reducing the complexity and cost of obtaining international patent protection. Member nations accept standardized patent application forms (in the case of applications filed outside the P.C.T. system, which is already standardized), eliminate some unduly complex and expensive formalities that had been imposed on applicants, provide relief and reinstatement of rights when applicants and patentees miss certain deadlines, and otherwise conform national application procedures to international norms.

Quiz Yourself on *PATENTS*

6. Dr. Feelgood discovers that taking an antihistamine every other day is effective for treating high blood pressure in men over 50 years of age. Is this discovery patentable subject matter? _____

7. While doing research on the arctic tundra, Jim discovered a new plant that had never before been known or recorded. The plant's leaves produce a beautiful natural red dye. Can Jim obtain a utility patent for the plant? Why or why not? Can Jim obtain a plant patent? Why or why not? _____

8. In the course of research at Topeka State University, Professors Brown and Jones jointly devised a new form of widget that gave advantages over previously known widgets, and reduced the new widget to actual practice. This occurred in November, 2001. The professors made no attempt to commercialize the widget, or to apply for a patent. Instead, they undertook to write a paper for publication that would fully describe the widget and the scientific principles underlying it. They worked diligently on the paper until it was completed in November, 2002.

    Prior to August, 2002, the professors did not discuss their new widget with others. However, in August, Professor Brown sent a draft of the paper to Professor Smith, an expert in the field at Minneapolis State University, for his preliminary comments. Professor Smith read the paper and replied that the widget was an important breakthrough, congratulated Brown and Jones, and stated that he had no suggestions for improvement. In November, 2002, Professors Brown and Jones sent their completed paper to a scientific journal, which accepted it and ultimately published it in January, 2003.

    In October, 2002, Ginger Greer created a new widget design that had all the same elements as the widget invented by Professors Brown and Jones arranged in the same way. If she applies for a patent, should her invention be deemed "novel" under Patent Act §102? _____

9. Same facts as in Question 8, but instead of writing a paper, Professors Brown and Jones decide to file a patent application, and do so in January, 2002. It turns out that Dr. Gupta had invented the same widget in India in April, 2001, and had filed a U.S. patent application in September of the same year

disclosing it. Will Dr. Gupta's earlier invention prevent Professors Brown and Jones from getting a patent? _____

10. In April, 2000, Martinez (an employee of Soft, Inc., which is located in Florida) conceived of a new kind of computer program to be used by banks in administering the reinvestment of certificates of deposit for bank customers. In a memo to Jefferson (also an employee of Soft, Inc.), dated May 16, 2000, Martinez described the new program at some length, and directed Jefferson to make a prototype. Without further consultation, Jefferson went to work. He completed the coding in January, 2001. Martinez and Jefferson are both under a duty of confidentiality to Soft, Inc.

   In late November, 2000, Soft, Inc. placed advertisements in several banking trade journals announcing and promoting the new program, providing general information about what it could accomplish, stating the price, and comparing the price to that charged by competitors. Soft, Inc. began to accept and fill orders for the new program in February, 2001. It filed for a U.S. patent (as Martinez's assignee) in December, 2001.

   Assuming that a patent issues, what, if any, objections might be raised to its validity? Would the objections be likely to succeed? _____

11. X invents a new scanner for an anti-shoplifting security system in December, 2001, in New York. He does not apply for a patent, but immediately goes to work to create a commercial embodiment of the scanner and an accompanying mechanism which will be used to mark merchandise tags. X intends to sell the scanner and marking mechanism together as a package, since the scanner will be of little use without the compatible marking mechanism. X works continuously on getting the security system to the market, and ultimately places it on the market in December, 2003.

   In April, 2003, Y invents an anti-shoplifting security scanner which, while not identical to X's scanner, would be obvious to the person of ordinary skill in the art in light of X's scanner. Will Y be able to get a patent? _____

12. In August, 2001, Dr. Science invented a novel and non-obvious method of synthetically producing a medical compound formerly only extracted from tree bark. He did not immediately file a patent application, but instead worked on related projects. In September, 2002, Dr. Kato published an article in a Japanese scientific journal that, while not describing Dr. Science's method as such, rendered it obvious to a person with ordinary skill in the art when considered in combination with an earlier method of synthesizing chemical compounds that was well-known in the United States.

   Dr. Science applied for a U.S. patent in November, 2003. Should the application be granted? What if Dr. Science applied in November, 2002? What if Dr. Kato had published his article in November, 2000? _____

13. In 2000, X Co. purchased one of Y Co.'s patented machines (which was in the final year of its patent), analyzed its constituent parts, and began to manufacture the parts. X Co. placed the parts into boxes, to create "kits" for making Y's machine. Each box contained all the parts necessary to make the machine, along with instructions for assembly. The parts in the box were unassembled. X Co. did not advertise or sell any of the kits until the day after Y Co.'s patent expired. Is Y Co. likely to have a cause of action for patent infringement against X Co.? _____

14. X Co. did all the things described in Question 13, but in addition, before Y Co.'s patent expired, X Co. sold some of the kits in Canada to Canadian purchasers, who then assembled the machines. Would this render X Co. liable to Y Co. for patent infringement? _____

15. On January 1, 1996, Ace Co. applied for a patent on its new widget. The patent was granted two years later, on January 1, 1998. Lee had purchased Ace Co.'s patented widgets in the past, but felt that Ace Co. was abusing its patent by charging too much for them. In March, 2015, Lee proposed to Bell Co. that Bell Co. manufacture two widgets with the same specifications as Ace Co.'s patented widget. The parties agreed on a price, signed a contract, and Bell Co. began work. Bell Co. completed making and testing the widgets as specified in December, 2015, and delivered them to Lee in the second week of January. Lee immediately put the widgets to work in his business. Does Ace Co. have a cause of action for patent infringement against Lee? _____

16. On January 1, 1996, Acme Co. applied for a design patent on its new lamp base design. A patent was granted a year later, on January 1, 1997. Acme proceeded to manufacture lamps incorporating the new design at its New Jersey factory, and also at its factory in Mexico City, Mexico. In July, 2013, Montes purchased a number of the lamps produced by Acme's factory in Mexico City and imported them into the United States without Acme's permission. Does Acme have a cause of action against Montes for design patent infringement? _____

17. Alice was in the wholesale flower business on the east coast. One day she discovered that one of her "fufu" plants had mutated: its bloom had a pleasant "spicy vanilla" scent. Prior flowers of this species had been odorless except on very rare occasions when the mutation had appeared before briefly in the wild. Recognizing the value of this mutation, Alice took cuttings of the plant and grew additional fufu plants with the spicy scent. She applied for a plant patent, which was granted in May, 1989. She began to produce the new patented variety of fufu plant in large quantities for the market.

In January, 1998, Bill bought one of Alice's patented fufu plants. Liking the spicy scent, Bill took seeds from the plant and planted them in his window boxes.

In July, 1998, Cliff, a San Francisco flower wholesaler, noticed that one of his own fufu plants had mutated so that the flower had a pleasant spicy vanilla scent. In fact, Cliff's mutated plant was exactly like Alice's patented plant. Cliff took cuttings from his fufu plant and produced large numbers of the mutated variety and began to sell them. Is either Bill or Cliff liable to Alice for infringement of her plant patent? _____

18. The Power Company has a "combination patent" on a new kind of washing machine. The patent is now in its fifteenth year. Wong, a retiree, goes to the local junkyard and buys two of the patented washing machines, which are old and beat up. When he gets them home, he takes them apart. He then begins to assemble a new machine, using parts he has salvaged from the two old machines. He finds, however, that one key part—the agitator—is missing: neither of the agitators in the two old machines is usable. Thus, Wong goes to Yee, a machinist friend, and asks him to make a new replacement agitator. Yee knows that the agitator is specially made and adapted for use in the Power Co.'s patented washing machine and that it has no other substantial use. However, he agrees to make one for Wong, and delivers it the next week. Wong pays Yee for this work, incorporates the new agitator into the machine, and washes his dirty laundry. Is Yee liable to the Power Co. for contributory infringement of its patent? _____

19. Liu and Martinez are unrelated inventors who live and work in the United States. On January 15, 2005, Liu conceived of a new widget design. He then set the project aside until March 3, 2005, while he attended to other business. Starting March 3, he worked continuously on the project. On December 11, 2005, he built a working model of the widget. He filed a U.S. patent application on December 19, 2005.

Martinez conceived of an identical widget on March 15, 2005. She never built a working model, but filed a U.S. patent application disclosing and claiming the widget on April 4, 2005. Please explain which party is entitled to a patent and explain why. _____

20. In January, 2000, Western Pacific Co. applied for U.S., European and Japanese patents for its novel, non-obvious and useful design for a locomotive engine. Between September, 2001, and February, 2002, Zoom Corp. (which is headquartered and has its factory in upstate New York) produced twenty locomotive engines that had all the same elements, as claimed in Western Pacific's pending patent application. It immediately sold ten of the engines to an English purchaser. The following month Zoom transferred the remaining ten engines to its wholly-owned subsidiary in Mexico. In April, 2002, Western Pacific's patent issued. In June, 2002, the president of Zoom called a prospective purchaser in Pakistan from his office in New York and offered to sell the Pakistani Zoom's remaining ten engines. The offer was accepted two weeks later, and the engines were shipped from Mexico to Pakistan. Payment was made in Pakistan, upon delivery. Please explain what, if any, rights Western Pacific has against Zoom Corp. under U.S. patent law. _____

Sample Answers

PLEASE NOTE: The answer to these questions might change if Congress enacts pending revisions to the Patent Act. You should check the web site (www.aspenlawschool.com/ip_outline) for updates.

6. The use of antihistamines to treat high blood pressure falls into the "process" category of patentable subject matter. Patent Act §100(b) specifies that the term "process" "includes a new use of a known process, machine, manufacture, composition of matter, or material." While antihistamines clearly are already known, the method of taking one tablet every other day to control blood pressure is a new use of the known material.

7. Jim could not obtain a utility patent for the plant itself, because it is a natural phenomenon. Utility patents can only be granted for things that are "man-made." A genetically engineered plant can be deemed man-made because man has given it characteristics it would not have had in nature. However, this plant, though never before known, developed in nature.

   Jim could not obtain a plant patent for the plant because (so far as we know) he has not asexually reproduced it, and it is not novel (to be novel, it must not have existed in nature in a form capable of reproducing its novel characteristics). Moreover, the Plant Patent Act only provides patents for cultivated plants, not for plants found in an uncultivated state.

   Note that Jim might get a utility patent for a process of using the plant to produce the red dye, or for an isolated and purified version of the chemical compound that dyes things red.

8. Ginger has two potential novelty problems. First, there is a possibility that the invention was "known" in the United States prior to Ginger's invention date, under Patent Act §102(a). Professors Brown and Jones, the first inventors, kept their invention to themselves until August, 2002, when they sent their draft article to Professor Smith. While there is relatively little case law to indicate what it takes to

make an invention "known" within the meaning of §102(a), it appears that the invention must be (1) fully disclosed; and (2) the disclosure must be available to the public. Assuming that the draft paper "fully discloses" the new widget, one could argue that providing the draft to Professor Smith made it available to the public. There is nothing to suggest that Professor Smith was subject to any duty of confidentiality that would prohibit him from discussing the content of the paper with others. Because Smith is an expert in the field, one might reason that he is in a good position to further disseminate and possibly use the new widget, thus bringing the benefit of it to the public. (It is less likely that sending the draft to Professor Smith constituted a "printed publication" for purposes of §102(a): generally, before finding a printed publication, courts require that a written disclosure be accessible to an interested American exercising reasonable diligence to find it. In this case, to constitute a printed publication, the paper would probably have to be posted and properly indexed in a library collection, or disseminated to a larger group of people in the field—perhaps at a conference. It is likely that the standard for finding that an invention is "known" is lower than the standard for finding that the invention is the subject of a "printed publication.")

If the disclosure to Professor Smith makes the new widget "known in the U.S." in August, 2002, then Ginger's invention in October, 2002 will be disqualified under §102(a). Note that the subsequent journal publication (in January, 2003) would not affect the novelty of Ginger's invention because it occurred after her invention date. It would, however, serve as a "printed publication" that triggers the §102(b) statute of limitations, requiring Ginger to file a patent application within one year of the paper's publication date.

Ginger's second (and probably more serious) novelty problem arises under Patent Act §102(g), which prohibits a patent if the applicant's invention had already been made in the United States and not abandoned, suppressed, or concealed at the time of the applicant's invention. Here, Professors Brown and Jones clearly made the invention prior to Ginger, in the United States. The only issue is whether they had abandoned, suppressed, or concealed it. Recent case law suggests that to avoid a finding of abandonment, suppression, or concealment, the first inventor must work diligently to bring the benefit of his invention to the public. Here, it appears that Brown and Jones did this. Even though they decided not to pursue a patent or commercialize their invention, they worked diligently to produce and publish a paper that would fully disclose and make the benefit of the invention available to the public. Thus, they probably did not abandon, suppress, or conceal the invention, and §102(g) would bar Ginger from obtaining a patent.

9. Patent Act §102(e) provides that Brown and Jones's application for patent must be denied if their invention was disclosed in a U.S. patent application that was pending at the time of their invention and later published or granted. Accordingly, Dr. Gupta's earlier invention can disqualify Professors Brown and Jones under Patent Act §102(e) if his U.S. application is subsequently published or granted. Even though the publication or patent issuance may occur after Brown and Jones's invention date, the publication or granting of Dr. Gupta's application makes the information disclosed in it "prior art" as of Gupta's application date, which is prior to Brown and Jones's invention date.

Note that Dr. Gupta's earlier invention may prevent Brown and Jones from obtaining a patent under §102(g), as well, if Gupta is able to establish his earlier invention date in India in an interference proceeding. It is clear that he has not abandoned, suppressed, or concealed the invention.

10. One possible objection to a patent for the program would be that a patent is barred under Patent Act §102(b), which provides that a patent must be denied if the invention was on sale in the United States more than a year before the patent application was filed. In the *Pfaff* case, the Supreme Court held

that an invention will be on sale if it is "ready for patenting" and is the subject of a commercial offer for sale. It will be ready for patenting if it has been described in sufficient detail to enable a person with ordinary skill in the art to make it.

Under this standard it appears that the new program was "ready for patenting" more than a year before Soft's application date. Martinez's memo, dated May 16, 2000, appears to have provided the enabling information, since Jefferson was able to create the program without further consultation.

The only other question is whether the program was the subject of a commercial offer for sale more than a year before the application date. It will only have been if the November, 2000 advertisements constituted a commercial offer for sale. The Court of Appeals for the Federal Circuit has held that a commercial offer for sale must be one that would give a right to accept and form a binding contract under the Uniform Commercial Code. Generally, advertisements do not rise to this level. Therefore, it is unlikely that §102(b) would apply to disqualify or invalidate the patent.

Neither the advertisements nor Martinez's memo to Jefferson is likely to constitute a "printed publication" for purposes of the §102(b) statutory bar. The advertisements are not likely to be sufficiently detailed to enable a person of ordinary skill in the art to make the program. While the memo was enabling, it was not accessible to the public. The recipient was bound by a duty of confidentiality.

One other objection might be that the invention is a computer program or mathematical algorithm, which is not, in the abstract, patentable subject matter. However, the Court of Appeals for the Federal Circuit has made it clear that computer programs can be patented as processes or (in combination with hardware) machines, or (in combination with a storage medium) articles of manufacture. The only requirement is that the patent claim a useful application of the algorithm, which results in "a useful, concrete and tangible result."

11. The question is whether Y's scanner should be rejected as obvious under Patent Act §103. The facts state that Y's scanner would be obvious to the person of ordinary skill in light of X's scanner. Therefore it is necessary to determine whether X's scanner will be deemed a part of the pertinent prior art in evaluating what the person of ordinary skill would think. (That is, whether the person of ordinary skill would be deemed aware of X's scanner.) X's scanner would probably be deemed pertinent, since it is from the same field of endeavor. It will come into the prior art if it falls within the provisions of Patent Act §§102(a), (e), (f), or (g). The best bet is subsection (g). X's scanner was invented in the United States prior to Y's invention date, and X has not abandoned, suppressed, or concealed it (since he has worked diligently to bring the benefit of his scanner to the public through marketing). Assuming that X's scanner is considered part of the prior art, then Y's application should be rejected pursuant to Patent Act §103 for obviousness.

12. If Dr. Science applies in November, 2003, his application should be denied. Dr. Kato's publication triggered the §102 statute of limitations because (in combination with the earlier prior-art method) it rendered Dr. Science's method obvious. Dr. Science had to file within a year of the article's publication, and he failed to do so.

If Dr. Science applies in November, 2002, then his patent should be allowed: he will have filed within a year of Dr. Kato's publication.

If Dr. Kato had published his article in November, 2000, then Dr. Science's application should be denied not only due to his failure to file within one year of the publication, but also because the article would have rendered his invention obvious at the time it was made. (Kato would be the prior inventor, and his publication would come into the prior art under Patent Act §102(a) in evaluating the obviousness of Dr. Science's method as of August, 2001, pursuant to Patent Act §103.)

13. The issue is whether X Co. directly infringed Y Co.'s patent within the meaning of Patent Act §271(a), which prohibits (among other things) making, using, offering to sell, and selling the patented invention in the United States during the patent term. Presumably, Y's patent is a "combination patent," meaning that the invention is in Y's unique combination of known elements, not in the individual elements themselves. According to the Supreme Court, to directly infringe such a patent, someone must combine the elements into an operable assembly (which constitutes a "making") or use, sell, offer to sell, or import the operable assembly. Merely making, using, or selling the individual parts of the patented machine, as X Co. does, in the United States, will not constitute infringement. Note that X Co. apparently did not test subassemblies of the patented machine's parts, which probably distinguishes this case from the Federal Circuit's decision in *Paper Converting v. Magna-Graphics*.

    Since X Co. did not sell the kits to anyone during the patent term, it appears that nobody combined the parts into an operable assembly during the patent term, so that X Co. cannot be held liable for others' direct infringement through a contributory infringement or inducement claim, either. There can be no liability for contributory infringement or inducement to infringe unless the defendant's actions lead to a direct infringement by someone else.

14. Under these additional facts, X Co. would be probably liable under Patent Act §271(f), which prohibits persons: (1) from supplying all or a substantial portion of the uncombined components of a patented invention from the United States in order to actively induce combination of the components outside the United States; and (2) from supplying from the United States an uncombined component of a U.S.-patented invention that is especially made or adapted for use in the invention, knowing that the component is so made or adapted and intending that it will be combined outside of the United States into the patented invention.

15. The term for Ace's patent is measured from the date the patent issued and lasts for a period of 20 years from Ace's application date. Thus, the patent endured through December 31, 2015. Under the facts in this problem, Bell Co. would be directly liable for patent infringement under Patent Act §271(a) because it made the patented invention in December, 2015, before the patent expired. Since testing constitutes using the patented invention, Bell would be directly liable for using the invention, as well. (An argument might be made that Bell Co. sold the patented invention during the patent term, too, but we are given insufficient facts to determine exactly when the sale took place.)

    Lee only took delivery after the patent expired, so any use or subsequent sale he might have made will not directly infringe. However, Lee is likely to be liable for inducing Bell Co.'s direct infringement during the patent term, pursuant to Patent Act §271(b). It appears that Lee actively, intentionally solicited and assisted Bell's infringement by asking Bell to make the widget and agreeing to pay Bell for its work. Moreover, it appears from the facts that Lee had knowledge that Bell's actions would infringe the patent.

    It is not a defense to patent infringement that the patentee charges too much for the patented invention.

16. The term for design patents is 14 years from the date the patent issued, as specified in Patent Act §173. Therefore Montes's importation occurred after the patent had expired (the patent only endured through December 31, 2010) and cannot constitute infringement. If the term had not expired, it appears, under the Federal Circuit's recent ruling in the *Jazz Photo* case, that the importation would

infringe. Even though the U.S. patentee made the first sale of the patented lamp bases, it did so outside of the United States so that the doctrine of exhaustion does not apply to them.

17. Bill would not be liable for plant patent infringement. A plant patent grants the holder the right to prevent others from asexually reproducing the patented plant or selling or using a plant produced asexually from the patented plant. Bill would not be liable because he reproduced the patented plant sexually (i.e., by seed) rather than asexually.

    Cliff would not be liable because he did not asexually reproduce Alice's patented plant, but another plant that was unrelated to Alice's plant and its clones. A plant patent does not prohibit someone from discovering an independent mutation that is the same as the patented one and asexually reproducing it.

    The fact that the same mutation had occurred before in nature would not invalidate Alice's patent on novelty grounds, as long as the mutated plant was unable naturally to reproduce and pass the distinctive characteristics that are the subject of the patent on to future generations. The statement that the mutation had appeared "briefly" before suggests that when the scent appeared in the wild it was not reproduced in subsequent generations.

18. Yee is not liable to the Power Co. for contributory infringement even if he sold a material component of the patented invention with the requisite knowledge. In order for Yee to be liable for contributory infringement, it must be shown that Wong, to whom he sold the material component, directly infringed the patent. However, merely taking apart two old washers and reassembling the parts—even when one of the key parts is replaced with a new one—constitutes permissible repair of an existing machine that was sold under Power Co.'s authorization, rather than the unauthorized reconstruction or "making" of a new machine, which would infringe the patent.

19. The patent goes to the first to invent, which is Liu. The first to reduce the invention to practice (Martinez, who made a constructive reduction to practice in April, 2005) is presumed to be the first to invent, but the first to conceive of the invention (Liu) can rebut that presumption and prevail if he was diligent in reducing the invention to practice from a time prior to Martinez's conception date. Here, although Liu was not diligent in reducing to practice at first, the facts say that he worked continuously on the project starting on March 3, which is a couple of weeks prior to Martinez's conception date. Liu gets the benefit of his resumption date. Thus, he was the first to conceive (effectively, March 3, 2005) and was diligent in reducing to practice from a time prior to Martinez's conception date.

20. There are two separate sets of acts that should be considered. First (assuming that the application was for a utility patent), since Western applied for patents in both the United States and in Europe and Japan, its application was probably published by the U.S. P.T.O. 18 months after its application date. It thus had provisional rights from that point until the patent issued in April, 2002. Zoom's manufacture of 20 engines in New York occurred after the publication but before the patent issued. Thus, if Western gave Zoom actual notice of its published patent application and the claims that were published were substantially identical to the claims that ultimately issued, Western may be able to recover damages for the unauthorized manufacture, consisting of a reasonable royalty payment.

    Second, after the patent issued, Zoom called a prospective purchaser in Pakistan from New York and offered to sell ten of the engines. Even if the provisional rights approach does not work, Western might recover if this call constituted an infringing "offer to sell" the patented invention, within the meaning of Patent Act §271(a). However, this claim may not succeed. While the offer occurred in the United States, the actual sale probably occurred outside of U.S. territory and thus did not itself infringe. There is some case authority (reasoning from the definition of "offer to sell" in Patent Act

§271(i)) that in order to make an infringing offer to sell, the contemplated sale must also infringe. The sale in this case would not infringe because it probably occurred outside of the United States.

Exam Tips on PATENTS

☞ **Understanding novelty:** The novelty provisions (Patent Act §§102(a), (e), and (g)) exist primarily to channel patents to first inventors, and to prevent latecomers from removing inventions from the public domain. Remember that to demonstrate that an invention lacks novelty (that the invention is "anticipated"), you must be able to identify an earlier invention or disclosure (an earlier "reference") that: (1) *included all of the same elements arranged in the same way*; and (2) falls within the conditions of §§102(a), (e), or (g). An earlier invention or disclosure that lacked a claimed element, or combined the claimed elements in a different way may be relevant to demonstrate that the invention at issue is obvious, but is not relevant to demonstrate that it lacks novelty. The standard for finding that an invention lacks novelty parallels the standard for literal infringement. It has been said that "that which infringes if later, anticipates if earlier." In other words, if A's invention would literally infringe a patent on B's invention (because it literally falls within the language of B's claims), then it would anticipate B's invention (render it non-novel) if it were shown to have preceded it.

☞ **Understanding non-obviousness:** The non-obviousness requirement exists primarily to restrict patents to true "inventions"—those inventions that are worth the "public embarrassment of granting a monopoly." The inventiveness, or obviousness, of an invention is determined from the perspective of a person of ordinary skill in the art, *in light of* earlier inventions and publications. It is important to remember that in evaluating the obviousness of an invention, you can consider two or more prior inventions or publications ("references") together. However, you must demonstrate that each prior invention or publication is: (1) "pertinent" to the invention at issue; and (2) falls within the scope of Patent Act §§102(a), (e), (f), or (g).

When you are evaluating whether a reference falls within the scope of Patent Act §§102(a), (e), (f), or (g), be sure to systematically consider *all* of those provisions. Don't just ask whether the earlier invention was known or used in the United States or patented or the subject of a printed publication anywhere in the world prior to the applicant's invention date (the issues under §102(a)). *Go on to review §102(e), (f), and (g), as well.* Be thorough. In an exam, if the professor allows you to review statutory language, take the time to review the §102 provisions before writing your answer, to ensure that you have correctly remembered them all.

☞ **Distinguish Patent Act §§102(a) and (b):** Students often are confused by the superficial similarities in the statutory language of Patent Act §§102(a) and (b). It is important to remember that these two provisions serve very different purposes, and have a different focus. Subsection (a) is meant to ensure that the patent applicant's invention is novel, as discussed above. It focuses on events that occurred prior to the applicant's invention date. Subsection (b), in contrast, is meant to ensure that inventors file their patent applications in a timely manner—within a year after the invention enters into the public domain by one of the four described means (the invention is on sale or the subject of public use in the United States or the invention is the subject of a patent or a printed publication anywhere in the world). The focus thus is on events that occurred more than a year before the applicant's application date. The applicant's own actions may be relevant for purposes of §102(b), but will not be relevant for purposes of §102(a).

Consistent with the prior paragraph, note that the terms "public use" and "sale," in §102(b), do not mean the same things as "known" and "used," as those terms are used in §102(a). They represent different standards, and should not be confused.

☛ **Distinguish §103 obviousness and §102(b) obviousness:** Under Patent Act §103, one evaluates whether the applicant's invention is worthy of a patent. It is not worthy if it was obvious at the time it was invented. Under Patent Act §102(b), one evaluates whether the applicant (whose invention may have been worthy of a patent at the time it was made) has forfeited his or her right to a patent by failing to file the application within the specified time frame. Essentially, the courts have recognized that, even though A's invention was not obvious at the time it was made (and thus was worthy of a patent under §103), it may later become obvious, due to the subsequent public use or sale of a different invention in the United States, or a subsequent patent or printed publication. At that point, §102(b) requires that A file for a patent within one year. If A fails to do this, he loses his right to a patent.

☛ **Timelines can be useful:** Dates can be important in analyzing the validity of a patent, and it is important to keep them straight. It is often useful to draw a timeline to help you evaluate the facts in an exam question and determine their impact on the validity of a patent. For example, here is a sample timeline that you might draw to assist in determining the answer to Quiz Yourself, Question 12.

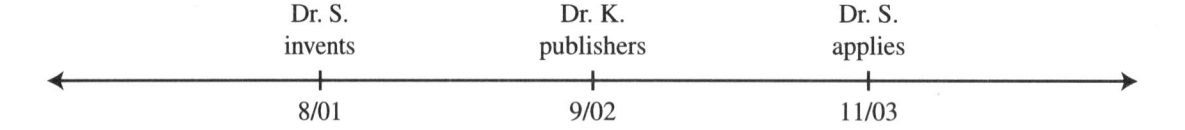

```
         Dr. S.              Dr. K.              Dr. S.
        invents            publishers           applies
    ─────┼──────────────────┼──────────────────────┼─────▶
        8/01                9/02                11/03
```

☛ **Keep the various forms of infringement straight:** Patent Act §271, which defines the various forms of infringement, is a patchwork: In addition to several broad definitions of infringement (for example, §§271(a), (b), and (c)), it contains several relatively narrow provisions, in which Congress prohibited specific practices that were not covered by the existing infringement provisions (for example, §§271(f) and (g)). When facing an exam question that asks whether a party has infringed a patent, it is important to systematically *consider all* of the various §271 provisions. If the professor allows you to review statutory language, turn to §271 and quickly review each provision to ensure that you remember the scope and limitations of each provision, and consider whether it provides a means of holding the party liable under the facts of the question.

☛ **Fitting designs and plants into the novelty and non-obviousness scheme:** Congress enacted the utility patent provisions first, and the courts developed the novelty and non-obviousness standards in connection with industry, science, and engineering-related inventions. When Congress later provided for design and plant patents, it stated that the existing standards of novelty and non-obviousness should be extended to this new subject matter. However, the fit is sometimes awkward. If you are faced with an exam question that requires you to evaluate the novelty or non-obviousness requirements in connection with an ornamental design or plant, it may be useful to think about the underlying purposes of the novelty and non-obvious requirements in determining how they should apply.

CHAPTER 4
THE LAW OF UNDEVELOPED IDEAS

ChapterScope

This chapter introduces you, briefly, to ways that courts occasionally find rights to recover for unauthorized use of ideas and information without resort to either the patent or trade secret laws. Typically these cases arise when an individual volunteers an idea to a commercial entity, and the commercial entity allegedly uses the idea but refuses to pay the individual for his disclosure. Courts are understandably wary of finding rights in ideas under these circumstances; a strong and efficient marketplace depends on the free flow of ideas and the ability of one entity to copy from another and build on what the first has done. The traditional understanding is that ideas are strictly in the public domain unless temporarily the subject of a patent monopoly. (Note that trade secret law, itself, focuses on preventing acquisition of information through *improper conduct* that falls below reasonable standards of commercial morality, or breach of a duty of confidence, and does not recognize property rights in any absolute sense.)

- **Theories of recovery:** This chapter describes five different pre-existing common-law theories that courts have employed to find rights in ideas under certain circumstances: (1) finding that the defendant has made an enforceable, express contractual agreement to pay; (2) finding that the parties' actions demonstrate a mutual intention that the defendant will pay for the idea, giving rise to an enforceable contract implied in fact; (3) finding that the defendant will be unjustly enriched under the particular circumstances of the case if allowed to use the plaintiff's idea without paying; (4) finding that the parties are in a relationship that gives rise to a duty of confidentiality on the defendant's part; and (5) (in rare cases) suggesting that novel and concrete ideas can be viewed as a form of personal property that is protected against conversion. The application of these theories is discussed in greater detail in Section I, below.

- **Novelty and concreteness requirements**: Because of their concern about interfering with the free flow of information and the competitive marketplace, courts have often conditioned the finding of rights under the common-law theories listed above on a finding that the idea at issue is "novel" (and in some jurisdictions "concrete"). This can be viewed as a means of ensuring that the plaintiff has made a sufficiently valuable contribution to justify even limited protection from the public's standpoint, and to ensure that plaintiffs are not able to tie up commonplace (or abstract) ideas. The meaning of "novelty" and "concreteness" for this purpose is discussed in Section II, below.

I. THE NATURE OF THE LAW OF UNDEVELOPED IDEAS

A. **Miscellaneous accumulation:** The "law of undeveloped ideas" is a miscellaneous accumulation of state common-law decisions addressing a claimed right to compensation for a defendant's unauthorized use of the plaintiff's idea. Following are some examples of the circumstances in which such claims may arise:

- An employee discloses an idea for a cost-saving measure to his employer, who implements the idea but refuses to pay the employee for it.

- A member of the public submits an idea for an advertising slogan to a department store, expecting compensation upon use, but gets none.

- A television screenwriter presents a comprehensive plan for a television series to a television producer, who turns it down, but allegedly copies the underlying ideas in a later series.

- An applicant for an insurance sales position discloses a system for selling insurance in the course of an interview. The insurance company implements the system, but refuses to hire the applicant/discloser or pay him for the information.

Other intellectual property doctrines often withhold relief in such cases, but, at least in some of the more extreme cases, fairness seems to mandate some possibility of recovery. The opinions addressing such claims have recognized several common-law "theories" under which redress may be provided to the claimant: the express contract theory, the implied-in-fact contract theory, the implied-in-law contract (quasi-contract) theory, the confidential relationship theory, and the property theory. For an additional approach, see the materials on Misappropriation, *infra*, in Chapter 7.

B. **The express contract theory:** Express contracts to pay for an idea have been enforced. Some (though not all) courts have required that, in addition to proving an offer, acceptance, and consideration in the traditional contract sense, the plaintiff must demonstrate that the idea at issue was "novel." Some have provided, in addition, that the idea must be "concrete." (These novelty and concreteness requirements will be discussed in Section II, below.)

1. **Lack of consideration:** In *Masline v. New York, New Haven and Hartford Railroad Co.*, 95 Conn. 702, 112 A. 639 (1920), the plaintiff told the defendant railroad company that he had an idea that, if implemented, would earn the railroad company a significant amount of money. The company's representative told the plaintiff that if he disclosed the idea, and the company decided to implement it, the company would pay the plaintiff a percentage of the profits it made as a result of the implementation. The plaintiff then suggested that the railroad company sell advertising space in or on the company's stations, depots, rights of way, cars, and fences. The company implemented the idea and earned a lot of money. It refused, however, to pay the plaintiff. The Connecticut Supreme Court refused to enforce the promise against the company, finding that there was no consideration to support it: The plaintiff's idea was not a novel one and thus was valueless. This result has been criticized because, regardless of the value of the idea, the plaintiff's agreement to disclose the idea, when he had no preexisting obligation to do so, should be sufficient consideration in itself to support the contract to pay. Notwithstanding this criticism, the *Masline* decision has been influential.

2. **Implied condition:** As an alternative to the *Masline* reasoning, courts may simply imply a term into the contract that the idea must prove to be novel and concrete before payment will be due. Some have justified this by reasoning that people would not agree to pay for an idea that was not novel and concrete, and thus that they must have intended this condition. Some have argued that this limitation is required as a matter of public policy—no individual should have enforceable rights in ideas that are commonplace or abstract, because everybody needs access to such ideas in order to compete in the marketplace.

   a. **Problems with the justifications:** The problems with these two arguments are: (1) people may be willing to pay for non-novel, non-concrete ideas because such ideas are useful to them, they have not thought of them themselves, and the plaintiff has performed a valuable service in bringing the ideas to their attention; and (2) enforcing contracts to pay for ideas does not really remove the ideas from the marketplace, since the only parties affected by enforcement are the immediate parties to the contract.

C. **The contract-implied-in-fact theory:** Courts have found and enforced contracts to pay for ideas based on the parties' actions and surrounding circumstances, which indicate that they *intended* to make a binding contract to pay, even though they did not expressly say so. To determine whether the parties have made an implied contractual obligation, courts will focus on the specific words and actions of the parties, to determine their apparent intent. They may also consider factors such as:

- whether the defendant has paid for such ideas in the past;
- whether the plaintiff customarily has been paid for his ideas; and
- whether there is an industry custom of paying for such ideas.

The answers to these questions may provide information about the parties' expectations. However, some courts will not find or enforce an implied contract to pay for an idea if the idea was not novel or novel and concrete, for the same reasons discussed in connection with express contracts, *supra*.

D. **The contract-implied-in-law theory:** A contract implied in law (or "quasi-contract") is not based upon the intentions of the parties, but on a court's finding of *unjust enrichment*—that the defendant received a benefit for which equity and justice require him to pay. For example, a court might find a company obliged to pay a plaintiff for an idea from which it profited when the plaintiff disclosed it in reliance on promises of payment made by a company official who lacked authority to bind the company. On the other hand, a court will not imply an obligation to pay a plaintiff for his idea if his disclosure was unsolicited, constituting an officious, unwanted thrusting of the idea on the defendant. Likewise, many jurisdictions will not find that the defendant was unjustly enriched by receipt and use of a plaintiff's idea, regardless of the defendant's benefit, unless the idea was novel or novel and concrete. Courts have reasoned that the plaintiff can have no property rights in a commonplace idea. If the plaintiff has no property rights in the idea, the defendant's taking it from him and using it without permission is not unjust, and justice and equity do not require payment.

E. **The confidential relationship theory:** Some courts have found a right to recover for an idea if, when the plaintiff revealed her idea to the defendant, the parties were in a confidential relationship in which the plaintiff reposed trust and confidence in the defendant's good faith. The confidential nature of the relationship imposes a duty on the defendant to refrain from taking advantage of the plaintiff's disclosure without plaintiff's permission. Again, some courts have added the requirement that the idea disclosed by the plaintiff be novel or novel and concrete before such a duty will be found.

F. **The property theory:** Some courts have suggested that a novel, concrete idea is a form of personal property. A plaintiff should be able to recover for unauthorized taking or use of such an idea in the same manner that he could recover for the taking or use of any other item of personal property. No express or implied agreement, confidential relationship, or special equitable circumstances should be required. This is an extreme theory and has rarely if ever been relied on as a sole basis of recovery.

II. THE NOVELTY AND CONCRETENESS REQUIREMENTS

A. **The novelty requirement:** Courts have not uniformly meant the same thing when they have said that an idea must be novel before the plaintiff can recover for it. Three views of the novelty requirement can be identified in the case law:

- the idea must be original to the plaintiff (that is, the plaintiff must have conceived of the idea himself);

- the idea must be innovative or creative in nature; or

- the idea must be both original to the plaintiff and innovative in nature.

1. **New York law regarding novelty:** The Court of Appeals for the Second Circuit has construed New York law as providing that the "novelty" required in the case of contract-based claims only involves a showing that the disclosed idea was novel to the *buyer* (so that the seller can be found to have provided consideration to support the buyer's agreement to pay). However, the idea must be original and novel in absolute terms in the case of "property-based claims" (such as unjust enrichment or property theory claims). The reason for this is that unoriginal, known ideas have no value as property, and so should be freely available to all as a matter of policy. Finally, an idea may be so unoriginal or lacking in novelty that, as a matter of law, the buyer is deemed to know the idea, and a right to compensation cannot be found under either a contract-based or property-based theory. *Nadel v. Play-By-Play Toys & Novelties, Inc.*, 208 F.3d 368, 380 (2d Cir. 2000).

B. **The concreteness requirement:** Not all jurisdictions that impose a novelty requirement impose a concreteness requirement. Moreover, those courts that have imposed a concreteness requirement have had differing views of what it entails. Three views of concreteness can be identified in the case law:

- the idea must be reduced to tangible form (for example, it must have been committed to writing or incorporated into a tangible product);

- the idea must be fully developed—complete, fleshed-out, reduced to a detailed form ready for immediate use with little or no additional work on the user's part; or

- the idea must be both reduced to tangible form and fully developed.

C. **The general policy reasons for imposing novelty and concreteness requirements:** Courts are concerned about the implications of recognizing legal rights—even limited rights—in ideas. People use old ideas as building blocks to make new ones. To ensure progress, existing ideas must be readily available for this purpose. Also, ideas often are developed as they are passed from one person to the next: A conceives of a raw new idea, which B develops further, and C ultimately puts in final, usable form. To give rights in the idea at an early stage—for example, to A—might interfere with fast, efficient development and implementation of new ideas. On the other hand, society needs to provide incentives to people to create new ideas and disclose them, and offering legal rights in new ideas may accomplish this. Courts impose the novelty and concreteness requirements as a compromise of these conflicting interests. It ensures that valuable new ideas reduced to usable form can be protected under the limited theories discussed above, so there is an incentive to create them. More commonplace or incomplete ideas are not protected and are left available for general use.

D. Treating idea claims as claims for the value of services rendered: It is sometimes suggested that when a plaintiff discloses an idea to a defendant, and the defendant uses the idea without the plaintiff's authorization, the plaintiff's claim should be analyzed as one for payment for services rendered, in *quantum meruit*, without regard to whether the idea is novel or concrete. The only issues should be whether there is a legal or equitable basis for requiring payment for the service of disclosing the idea and the fair market value of the service performed. Courts have done this in some cases, but generally only with regard to claims by professional idea people, like advertising agents, designers, television screenwriters, etc. Claims by amateurs, such as the average citizen who submits an idea for a new product to a company or an idea for a new television program to a network, are generally treated under the theories described above.

Quiz Yourself on
RIGHTS IN UNDEVELOPED IDEAS

21. Mary, a homemaker, decided that it would be useful to have a shopping center built on a series of vacant lots near her home. She believed that the surrounding neighborhoods would generate a great deal of business for such a shopping center. Accordingly, she made an appointment to see Cindy, a wheeler-dealer on the local real estate development scene, who had developed other shopping centers. At the meeting Mary told Cindy her idea, and then told her that if she acted on the idea and built a shopping center in the place Mary suggested, Mary expected to be paid a commission. Cindy told Mary that she wasn't interested, but two years later Cindy acquired the lots Mary had told her about and commenced building a shopping center. Is Mary likely to have a cause of action for compensation from Cindy? _____

22. Tom, the owner of a small ceramic tile business, met Jerry, a business consultant, at a cocktail party. Upon learning Jerry's profession, Tom began to discuss his business. He mentioned that he had hired a consultant to help devise a better way to keep track of his inventory, but that the consultant's suggestions had not been helpful. Tom then asked Jerry if he knew of a more efficient means of tracking his inventory. Jerry responded: "Just between the two of us, I do." Jerry proceeded to tell Tom a method. Jerry had learned about the particular method he described to Tom from a prior client, who had been using the method for a number of years. Tom implemented the inventory method that Jerry described and found it quite efficient. Later, upon learning that Tom had implemented the system, Jerry demanded compensation. Is he likely to prevail? _____

Sample Answers

21. Mary is unlikely to recover. First, there is nothing in the facts to suggest that Cindy expressly or impliedly promised to pay Mary for the information if she used it. Moreover, even if she did, arguably there was no consideration to support such an agreement. Note that Mary disclosed her idea (performed her part of the alleged agreement) before Cindy had a chance to agree to pay. Mary had nothing left to give as consideration for Cindy's promise to pay. Mary should have gotten an agreement to pay before disclosing her idea.

Likewise, there is no basis for Mary to claim a right to compensation on an unjust enrichment (quasi-contract) theory. Her disclosure was entirely unsolicited. Those officiously conferring benefits on others are not entitled to demand compensation. Mary would have a much stronger claim if Cindy had solicited her idea disclosure.

Also, if the relevant jurisdiction imposes a concreteness requirement as a prerequisite to recovering for ideas, Mary might be disqualified on this ground as well. Case precedent suggests that the plaintiff's idea will not be deemed concrete unless it is reduced to some tangible form. Moreover, some cases indicate that the idea must be developed to the point that it is ready for implementation. Clearly Mary's idea, which was unsupported by any documentation, plans, or details, would not qualify.

22. Jerry has some chance of recovering, but not a great chance. He might argue that there was a contract implied in fact that Tom would pay for use of the idea. He could argue that the parties both expected and intended that there would be payment because Tom had paid a prior business consultant for similar kinds of information. Also, Jerry, as a professional business consultant, was accustomed to being paid for his business advice. Undoubtedly, the custom is for business owners to pay business consultants for advice about inventory methods. The fact that Jerry told Tom that the information was being revealed in confidence further suggests that the parties were aware that Jerry was supplying valuable information at Tom's request, and that they intended payment. Of course, the setting in which Jerry gave the advice might undermine Jerry's argument, suggesting that the parties were not engaged in a serious business transaction. Most professionals are accustomed to having social acquaintances ask for casual advice at cocktail parties. In most instances, those acquaintances do not anticipate receiving a bill for the advice.

Jerry might also argue that he is entitled to compensation under an unjust enrichment (contract implied in law) theory. Tom did solicit the information and receive a benefit from it. Under normal circumstances, a businessman would pay for a consultant's advice about inventory methods.

However, courts generally require that information be novel before they will imply a contract to pay for it, either in fact or in law. Here the chances are good that a court would not find the inventory method novel. First, it was not original to Jerry—he learned it from a prior client. Some courts also have required that the information be innovative. Though there are not enough facts to judge for sure, the fact that Jerry's client has been using the method for years may suggest that it is not new.

Sometimes when the plaintiff is a professional idea person, as Jerry is here, courts will skip the novelty and concreteness requirement, and treat the claim as a *quantum meruit* claim for the value of services solicited and rendered. While the inventory method may not have been original to Jerry (so that he has no property rights in it), he did perform a valuable service to Tom in bringing it to his attention. This approach probably represents Jerry's best opportunity for compensation.

Exam Tips on
RIGHTS IN UNDEVELOPED IDEAS

- **Look out for preemption:** The causes of action discussed in this chapter are state causes of action, and cover subject matter that may also be subject to federal intellectual property rights. Thus, there may be a significant question of federal preemption. Preemption is covered in Chapter 9, *infra*. Whenever you encounter an exam question that asks about a cause of action under undeveloped idea law, consider whether the question also gives rise to arguments that the cause of action is preempted by federal law, and if so, discuss those arguments in your analysis.

- **Overlap with trade secret law:** Many deserving idea law cases could be resolved under a trade secret claim, especially since few jurisdictions now employ the Restatement of Torts §757, comment *b* requirement that the alleged trade secret be "continuously used" in the plaintiff's business. See p. 7, *supra*. Under the more modern approach, which is reflected in the Uniform Trade Secrets Act, "one-shot" information may qualify for trade secret protection as long as the plaintiff can demonstrate that it is substantially secret and that he derives a competitive benefit from the fact that others do not know it. Accordingly, when you encounter an exam question involving a plaintiff's attempt to recover against another's unauthorized use of his ideas, consider the relevance of both an undeveloped idea and a trade secret claim.

CHAPTER 5
COPYRIGHT LAW

ChapterScope

The purpose of copyright law is to stimulate the creation and dissemination of as many works of art, literature, music, cinema, architecture, and other forms of authorship as possible, in order to promote "science" and learning, and generally to benefit the public. A careful *balance* is needed in order to accomplish this purpose. The law must give authors exclusive rights to exploit their works in order to give them a *financial incentive* to invest in the creative process. However, the rights cannot be too broad. Monopolies are *anticompetitive* and must be limited to ensure that the market for works of authorship remains robust and efficient. Moreover, the law must ensure that the *basic building blocks of expression* (ideas, facts, and elements that are standard or routine in connection with a given kind of work) *remain in the public domain*, free from copyright owners' control, in order to ensure a continuing flow of new authorship in the future. For these reasons, copyright gives rights only in *the author's particular means of expressing* facts and ideas, never in the facts or ideas themselves. Copyright is available only for original works, and it protects only against copying: Independent creations are lawful even if similar to an existing copyrighted work. Moreover, the Copyright Act limits the duration of copyright and provides a host of exceptions to the copyright owner's rights, to permit certain kinds of unauthorized public use that are deemed beneficial, and to ensure a continuing, robust public domain from which other authors may draw. This chapter reviews these and related issues. Key topics include:

- **The nature of copyright protection:** Section I discusses how copyright provides rights in an author's *intangible work of authorship* rather than in the tangible object in which the work of authorship is "fixed" (the manuscript, canvas, or other material manifestation of the work, which is governed by state laws regarding personal property). It also explains the relative roles of the state and federal governments in providing copyright protection.

- **Copyrightable subject matter:** Copyright law provides economic rights in an author's *original, fixed "works of authorship."* Section II discusses the statutory categories of copyrightable subject matter, and the meaning of the requirements that works of authorship be "original" and "fixed" in order to qualify for federal copyright protection. It also explains the *"idea/expression dichotomy,"* the central rule of copyright, which is designed to ensure that copyright protects *an author's particular means of expressing ideas, methods of operation, systems, and facts*, but never permits authors to monopolize the ideas, systems, methods of operation, and facts that they describe or incorporate into their works. Section II then examines several specific areas of copyrightable subject matter that have proven problematic: computer programs, the design of useful articles, works of architecture, sound recordings, fictitious characters, compilations, derivative works, and works created by or for government entities.

- **Copying and unlawful appropriation:** To infringe copyright, a defendant must *copy* from the plaintiff's work and the copying must amount to an *unlawful appropriation*. It is not unlawful for members of the public to copy facts, ideas, and other uncopyrightable elements from a copyrighted work. Thus, the copyright plaintiff must demonstrate that the defendant copied the plaintiff's *copyrightable expression,* and that the copying was sufficient to create a *substantial similarity of copyrightable expression*. Section IV examines the various standards courts have adopted to determine whether the plaintiff can meet this burden.

- **The exclusive economic rights of copyright:** Copyright law provides a series of exclusive economic rights in a work of authorship: (1) the right to *reproduce* the work; (2) the right to *adapt* the work; (3) the right to *distribute* copies of the work to the public; (4) the right to *publicly perform* the work; and (5) the right to *publicly display* the work. In the case of sound recordings (which do not enjoy a general right of public performance), the Copyright Act provides an exclusive right to *perform the work by means of digital audio transmission*. Sections V-IX discuss each of these economic rights, along with the more important *statutory exceptions* to each right, as set forth in Copyright Act §§107-121.

- **Moral rights:** Many countries recognize and protect an author's *personal* interest in the identity and integrity of his work, as well as his economic interests. The United States has not traditionally recognized these *"moral rights"* as a part of copyright protection. However, in order to respond to international pressures to harmonize its laws with those of other countries, and to comply with its international treaty obligations, the United States has recently undertaken to recognize and protect the moral rights of attribution and integrity in a very narrow category of copyrightable works: works of visual art. Section X discusses the nature of moral rights, and the *Visual Artists' Rights Act of 1990*, which provides the first express U.S. moral rights protection.

- **Direct and Indirect infringement:** Anyone who reproduces, adapts, distributes, publicly performs, or publicly displays a copyrighted work without authorization may be liable for direct infringement. Copyright is a form of *strict liability*—it is not necessary that the defendant know of the copyright or intend to infringe. Defendants may also be *indirectly* liable for other people's infringement under the theories of *contributory infringement* and *vicarious liability*. In evaluating the issue of peer-to-peer file sharing over the Internet in the *Grokster* case, the Supreme Court recently adopted a new *inducement* theory of indirect liability. Section XI reviews these various avenues to finding liability as well as a series of *"safe harbor" provisions* that Congress has enacted to protect Internet service providers from liability for their users' infringement.

- **The fair use and copyright misuse defenses:** The fair use defense allows courts to avoid overly rigid application of the copyright laws and refuse to find infringement when the defendant's unauthorized use promotes the overall purposes of copyright law and does not significantly undercut authors' economic incentive to create and distribute works of authorship. Section XII discusses the fair use defense, as well as the more recent "copyright misuse" defense to infringement liability.

- **The Digital Millennium Copyright Act**: The *Digital Millennium Copyright Act* undertook to encourage copyright owners to make their works available in digital form, and to adopt *technological self-help measures* (such as password systems, encryption, and various forms of embedded code) to protect their interest in controlling access to and use of these digital works. The Act's *anticircumvention provisions* prohibit others from circumventing a copyright owner's technological access controls, and from trafficking in devices or services that facilitate circumvention of both access and use controls. The Act's *rights management provisions* prohibit others from tampering with information that the copyright owner inserts into the work to assist in exploiting it. Section XIII describes these provisions in greater depth and discusses how the courts have interpreted them.

- **Ownership of copyright:** The *author* of a work is the initial owner of copyright in it. Section XIV discusses how the author of a work is identified, *joint authorship, the work for hire doctrine*, and some special rules that apply to collective works. It also discusses how copyrights are divisible.

- **Notice and other "formalities" of copyright:** The United States has traditionally imposed a number of formal requirements on copyright owners, including one that copyright owners place *notice* of copyright on each published copy of their works, file to *renew* their copyright terms, *register* their copyrights, and *deposit* copies of the work with the Library of Congress. In order to comply with the Berne Convention and the TRIPs Agreement, the United States has had to forego or loosen many of these requirements. Sections XV and XVI discusses these "formalities" and their ongoing impact on copyright owners' rights and on infringement litigation. It also discusses U.S. compliance with the Berne Convention's requirement that it *restore foreign copyrights* that were forfeited due to failure to comply with U.S. formalities.

- **The duration of copyright:** Calculating the duration of copyright can be complex because Congress has *changed the nature of the copyright term and has retroactively extended the term* twice in recent decades. Section XVII provides the rules for calculating duration, and Sections XVIII and XIX discuss copyright renewal and the 1976 Act's provisions for terminations of transfers.

- **Remedies for infringement:** The Copyright Act provides for recovery for the *plaintiff's loss and the defendant's profit*, a *statutory damages* alternative, and other monetary relief, as well as injunctive relief. For details, see Section XX.

- **International copyright treaties:** With the advent of global trade, international copyright protection has become increasingly important to U.S. copyright industries. International *pressures to harmonize* the world's copyright laws have lead the U.S. to join a number of important multinational copyright treaties, which have in turn had a significant substantive impact on U.S. copyright laws. These treaties are briefly discussed in Section XXI.

I. THE PURPOSE AND NATURE OF COPYRIGHT LAW

A. **The purpose of copyright law:** The purpose of copyright law is to stimulate the creation of as many works of art, literature, music, and other "works of authorship" as possible, in order to benefit the public. The United States recognizes no "natural right" in an author to prevent others from copying or otherwise exploiting his work. U.S. copyright laws provide authors with *limited* property rights in their works *for the ultimate purpose* of enriching the public with as many works of authorship as possible. The author's interest is generally viewed as secondary to that of the public.

B. **The nature of copyright law:** As is the case with other intellectual property doctrines, copyright law attempts to reach an optimal balance between the potentially conflicting public interests of: (1) encouraging creativity by giving exclusive property rights in creations; and (2) fostering an efficient and competitive marketplace by giving the freest possible public access to works of authorship and the ideas they encompass. Copyright law also recognizes that granting broad rights to copyright owners today may impair the next generation of authors' expressive opportunities. Basic building blocks of expression, such as facts, ideas, and common, stock devices, must be left in the public domain to ensure a continuing flow of authorship in the future. The law thus limits property rights to the author's particular *method of expressing* an idea or information. Copyright never gives rights in the idea being expressed, or in facts or other elements of the public domain that an author may incorporate into his work. Others are free to express the same idea as the author did, or use the same facts, as long as they do not copy the author's original way of expressing the ideas or facts. In addition, even those rights granted in the author's expression are limited in duration and are subject to certain exceptions permitting public use under limited circumstances, as will be discussed *infra*.

Example: X makes an oil painting of a particular mountain. In doing so, he chooses a specific angle and lighting, and emphasizes particular colors and textures. The subject matter—the mountain—is the idea being expressed. X does not, by painting the mountain, obtain the right to prevent others from painting it, too. He does obtain the right to prevent others from copying his original means of expressing that idea—including his choice and combination of angle, lighting, color, and texture.

Example: X conceives of a new theory about how the universe was created, and describes it in detail in a published article. The theory is an idea, or an interpretation of fact, and is not itself protectible. X cannot, through copyright law, prevent others from expressing the same theory, even if they learned of the theory from X's article. Likewise, to the extent that X incorporated facts into his article, he cannot prevent others from using those facts in other writings. X may, however, be able to prevent them from copying the particular means he used to express the theory or facts in his article.

Note: Patent law gives exclusive rights in inventive concepts, or ideas, but requires that the ideas meet rigorous substantive standards as a precondition to protection. Copyright only grants rights in one particular way of expressing an idea, which is less of an intrusion on the public domain than granting rights in the idea itself. Therefore, the standards for obtaining copyright are lower than those for obtaining patents. As will be discussed in greater detail later, courts have deemed it important to prevent persons from using copyright to obtain *de facto* monopoly rights in ideas, thereby evading the strict standards of patent law. When recognition of copyright in a work would effectively give the copyright owner the right to prevent others from expressing the ideas in the work, copyright will be denied.

1. **Copyright gives rights in "works of authorship":** The Constitution authorizes Congress to give authors exclusive rights in their "writings" in order to promote the progress of science. (The term "science," as used in the Constitution, is understood to mean knowledge and learning.) Congress and the courts have construed the term "writings" broadly, to refer to much more than literary works, such as books or magazine articles. "Writing" is construed to refer to the original expression of ideas. It encompasses just about any tangible form of expression. In the Copyright Act of 1976, Congress provided copyright protection for an author's original "works of authorship," rather than in an author's "writings." (Copyright Act §102(a).) The term, "works of authorship," is also interpreted broadly, though it is understood to be slightly narrower in scope than the term "writings." In enacting the 1976 Act, Congress made it plain that it did not intend to extend protection to *every* kind of work that the Constitution authorized it to protect.

   Example: In *Burrow-Giles Lithographic Co. v. Sarony*, 111 U.S. 53 (1884), the Supreme Court found that a photograph of Oscar Wilde was a copyrightable "writing" because, even though it was a mechanical reproduction of a real person's physical features, it included original expression by the author. By posing Wilde, selecting and arranging his costume and backdrop, arranging the lighting, choosing the angle, etc., the plaintiff had imposed his own mental conception on the reproduction of Wilde's likeness. This was enough of an original contribution on the photographer's part to make the photograph a protectible "writing." Photographs are also considered to be "works of authorship" within the meaning of the Copyright Act of 1976.

Example: In *Bleistein v. Donaldson Lithographing Co.*, 188 U.S. 239 (1903), the Supreme Court upheld the copyright in a circus poster that advertised the Wallace Circus. The poster featured a combination of words and realistic drawings of circus performers. There was no question that the artist engaged in an exercise of intellect in choosing and combining words, images, design, and color. This constituted original expression. The Court rejected an argument that the poster's strictly utilitarian, commercial purpose should disqualify it from protection, holding that original expression constitutes copyrightable subject matter, regardless of whether it is of good or bad quality in the eyes of the beholder, and regardless of its commercial or noncommercial purpose. The courts should not impose their judgments about the value of works in deciding whether copyright protection is available. To do so would be a form of censorship, which is harmful to a society based on free circulation of ideas and expression.

2. **Property right vs. personal right:** U.S. copyright law traditionally has focused on granting *economic rights* to authors—rights that enable authors to reap financial rewards from their works by controlling others' use of the work. By contrast, many countries (especially civil law countries, such as France and Germany) focus on two forms of rights—economic and personal. The personal rights are called "moral rights." Moral rights (sometimes called by the French term "*droit moral*") protect the authors' personal interest in his reputation and identity as the author of a work, and in preventing others from misrepresenting or mistreating the work. While other forms of U.S. law, such as the law of defamation, contract, and unfair competition, have protected these personal interests in some instances, U.S. copyright law traditionally has not expressly undertaken to do so. When the United States ratified the Berne Convention for the Protection of Literary and Artistic Works in 1988, it became obligated to protect authors' moral rights, as well as their economic interests in their creations. See pp. 195-196, *infra*. While Congress initially found that moral rights received sufficient protection through other areas of U.S. law, it has since amended the Copyright Act of 1976 expressly to provide moral rights in a limited category of works of authorship. See pp. 153-156, *infra*.

3. **Rights in the intangible:** The common-law rules governing personal property apply to determine rights in tangible embodiments of works of authorship—e.g., the manuscript of a book, or the canvas on which a painting has been created. U.S. copyright law (with the exception of the limited moral rights mentioned above) concerns itself with the *intangible* work of authorship. So, for example, the creator of a work of authorship may pass ownership of the physical embodiment of the work (the manuscript, or the canvas, for example) without passing ownership of the copyright, and vice versa. (Copyright Act §202.) Indeed, Copyright Act §204 provides that any transfer of the copyright (other than a transfer by operation of law) must be by written instrument, signed by the transferor. Thus, sale of the physical embodiment of the work of authorship cannot serve, in itself, to pass ownership of the copyright.

Example: X paints a landscape in oils. He sells the canvas to Y, an art collector. Title to the physical object, (the canvas covered with paint) passes to Y. Y, as the new owner, may prevent others (including X) from taking or using the canvas without permission under the general laws governing personal property. Likewise, Y may resell the canvas. However, unless X has specifically transferred the copyright in writing, he retains the copyright and enjoys all the rights that are granted to an owner of copyright under the Copyright Act. For example, he may create a derivative work—a poster—based on the painting, and sell it. Y has no such right, and if he tried to make or sell a poster based on the original painting without X's permission he would be liable for infringing X's copyright.

Example: A writes and sends a letter to B. Title to the piece of stationary with writing on it passes to B under the common law of personal property. A may not take the letter back. However, unless A has specifically transferred the copyright in writing, A retains it and can exercise all the rights of a copyright owner, which may include preventing B from publishing the letter.

C. **Federal vs. state law:** Prior to January 1, 1978, the date that the Copyright Act of 1976 became effective, the United States had a dual system of copyright. Unpublished works of authorship were protected automatically under state common-law copyright. Once the work of authorship was published, state common-law copyright ended. Under the Copyright Act of 1909, federal statutory copyright was available for published works of authorship, as long as all authorized published copies bore proper notice of copyright. In the 1976 Act, Congress largely did away with the dual system. It provided that federal copyright will arise automatically as soon as a work of authorship is fixed in tangible form, thus extending federal copyright protection to unpublished works. It further provided that the federal copyright law will preempt state copyright protection for works of authorship fixed in tangible form. (Copyright Act §301. See *infra*, pp. 340-345.) Accordingly, for the most part (see p. 341, *infra*, for an exception regarding sound recordings), the only works of authorship that can still be protected by state copyright are works that are not fixed in tangible form. However, as discussed *infra*, p. 109, it is not clear to what extent the state law does protect such works.

   1. **1976 Act vs. 1909 Act:** Today, copyright in works of authorship may be governed by provisions of the Copyright Act of 1909, the Copyright Act of 1976 as originally enacted, or the provisions of the Copyright Act of 1976 as subsequently amended pursuant to the Berne Convention Implementation Act of 1988, the Agreement on Trade-Related Aspects of Intellectual Property Rights (TRIPs), or other ensuing amendments, depending on when the work was created or publicly distributed and the issues to be resolved. For the most part this outline will discuss the provisions of the Copyright Act of 1976 in their amended state, as they exist as of summer 2007. However, when it is important to do so, it will discuss earlier provisions, as well.

D. **The Copyright Office:** The U.S. Copyright Office registers copyrights and issues certificates of registration. It also keeps records of registrations, assignments and licenses of copyright and other matters, and regulates deposit of copyrighted materials. The Copyright Office's review of applications to register copyright is limited to determining whether the claimed work falls within a category of copyrightable subject matter and whether the applicant has satisfied the formal registration requirements. The review is much less detailed and substantive than that of the Patent and Trademark Office in granting patents.

II. THE SUBJECT MATTER OF COPYRIGHT

A. **Section 102:** Copyright Act §102 defines the subject matter of copyright. Section 102(a) provides that copyright subsists "in original works of authorship fixed in any tangible medium of expression, now known or later developed, from which they can be perceived, reproduced, or otherwise communicated, either directly or with the aid of a machine or device." It then lists a number of illustrative types of works that are included within the meaning of "works of authorship." Two important requirements can be taken from the quoted language. First, the work of authorship must be "original," and second, the work must be "fixed" in a tangible medium.

B. **The "originality" requirement:** A work of authorship must be "original" in order to qualify for copyright protection. This requirement has two facets: First, the author must have engaged in some intellectual endeavor of her own, and not just have copied from a preexisting source. Second, in addition to being the author's independent creation, the work must exhibit a minimal amount of creativity. This minimal creativity standard is not difficult to satisfy. For example, straightforward product descriptions and directions for using products on product labels often are sufficiently creative to satisfy the originality standard.

Example: In *Feist Publications, Inc. v. Rural Telephone Service Co., Inc.*, 499 U.S. 340 (1991), the Supreme Court found that telephone white page listings did not satisfy the originality requirement because they lacked minimal creativity. The white pages listed the names of all the telephone service subscribers in the plaintiff telephone company's area of operation alphabetically, along with the town each subscriber lived in and the subscriber's telephone number. The Court noted that the names, towns, and telephone numbers were all facts, and as such, were themselves uncopyrightable. (See *infra*, p. 111.) While facts do not constitute copyrightable expression, an author's original selection and arrangement of facts may, if original. In the *Feist* case, the Court found that the author's selection and arrangement involved no creativity and thus was not original. The Court explained that the facts need not be presented in an innovative or surprising way, but that the selection and arrangement cannot be so mechanical or routine as to require no creativity whatsoever. Rural's selection of facts—name, town, and telephone number—was "entirely obvious." Its coordination or arrangement of the facts—the listings were in alphabetical order by the subscriber's last name—was "an age-old practice, firmly rooted in tradition and so commonplace that it has come to be expected as a matter of course." In the course of its opinion, the Court found that the originality standard was constitutionally mandated, and rejected the "sweat of the brow" doctrine, adopted by some lower courts, which had justified copyright for factual compilations on the basis of the labor the author expended in collecting and cataloging the facts. While the Court accepted the proposition that such labor is valuable to the public, it stressed that labor could not be substituted for originality.

Example: In *Magic Marketing v. Mailing Services of Pittsburgh*, 634 F. Supp. 769 (W.D. Pa. 1986), the plaintiff had designed some envelopes for use in mass mailing. The envelopes were of conventional size and shape. One set had a solid black stripe running horizontally across the middle with the words "Priority Message: Contents Require Immediate Attention" on it. It also had a short black stripe in the bottom right corner with the word "Telegram" on it. The other envelope had the words "Gift Check Enclosed" above the address window, and no stripes. Even though there was no evidence that the plaintiff had copied from other envelopes, the court found the envelopes insufficiently "original" to merit copyright protection. The plaintiff's fragmentary phrases were dictated solely by functional considerations. The envelopes were generic in nature. The phrases and stripes were too trivial and insignificant to support a finding of even minimal creativity.

1. **Copyright Office rule regarding words, short phrases, slogans, etc.:** In keeping with the requirement of a minimal level of creativity, the Copyright Office has promulgated a regulation stating that the following matter will not qualify for copyright: "Words and short phrases such as names, titles, and slogans; familiar symbols or designs; mere variations of typographic ornamentation, lettering or coloring; mere listing of ingredients or contents." 37 C.F.R. §202, 1(a). The substance of this regulation has frequently been stated by courts, as well. Thus, it is generally understood that while such things as book titles and short advertising slogans may be protected as trademarks, they are not copyrightable because they are considered to be too *de minimis*.

2. ***Scenes a faire*:** Authors likewise may not use copyright to prevent others from using language that is a cliché, or matter that constitutes *scenes a faire*. *Scenes a faire* are incidents, characters, settings, or other elements that are indispensable, or at least standard, in the treatment of a given topic. For example, the Court of Appeals for the Second Circuit has held that "elements such as drunks, prostitutes, vermin, and derelict cars would appear in any realistic work about the work of policemen in the South Bronx." These elements are therefore unprotectible *scenes a faire* in such a work. Likewise, the Seventh Circuit has found that standard "maze-chase game" devices in video games, including the maze, scoring table, and tunnel exits, are unprotectible under the *scenes a faire* doctrine. Such elements are expected and routine. No single author may prevent others from using them in their own works.

3. **"Sweat of the brow":** In *Feist, supra*, the Supreme Court stressed that the originality requirement was constitutional in nature, and must be satisfied in every case. A showing that a great deal of labor ("sweat of the brow") went into the creation of the work could not serve as a substitute for originality.

C. **The fixation requirement:** As noted earlier, a protected "work of authorship" is intangible, and must be distinguished from the tangible object in which the work is "fixed." For example, a copyrightable literary work is intangible. The paper, audio tape or floppy disk on which the literary work is recorded, or "fixed," is tangible. Copyright attaches to the intangible literary work, not the tangible manifestation. However, the intangible literary work is eligible for copyright protection only once it has been fixed in a tangible form at least once. The fixation requirement is viewed as being imposed by the Constitution, since the Constitution specifically authorizes Congress to protect "writings," and "writings" is construed to entail a fixed form. Congress is not authorized to provide copyright protection for "works of authorship" that have never been fixed, such as oral statements or unrecorded musical improvisations.

1. **The meaning of "fixation":** Fixation can take many forms. A work may be reduced to words, numbers, notes, sounds, shapes, or other symbols, and placed on any type of stable, tangible medium. Copyright Act §101, the definition section of the 1976 Act, provides: "A work is 'fixed' in a tangible medium of expression when its embodiment in a copy or phonorecord, by or under the authority of the author, is sufficiently permanent or stable to permit it to be perceived, reproduced, or otherwise communicated for a period of more than transitory duration." It is important to note two things about this definition.

    a. **Copies and phonorecords:** The 1976 Act definition recognizes two categories of tangible objects in which copyrightable works of authorship can be fixed: copies and phonorecords.

    i. **Copies:** Section 101 defines "copies" as "material objects, other than phonorecords, in which a work is fixed by any method now known or later developed, and from which the work can be perceived, reproduced, or otherwise communicated, either directly or with the aid of a machine or device." The scope of qualifying "material objects" is very broad, ranging from paper and floppy disks to stone slabs, precious metals, and fabric.

    ii. **Phonorecords:** Section 101 defines "phonorecords" as "material objects in which sounds, other than those accompanying a motion picture or other audiovisual work, are fixed by any method now known or later developed, and from which the sounds can be perceived, reproduced, or otherwise communicated, either directly or with the aid of a machine or device." Thus, records, audio tapes, compact discs, MP3 files, and the like are phonorecords. All other material objects on which works are fixed are copies.

b. **Fixed by or under the authority of the author:** The statutory definition of "fixation" provides, by implication, that a work will not be deemed "fixed" unless its embodiment in a copy or phonorecord was done by or under the authority of the author. An unauthorized fixation will not qualify a work for copyright protection.

   i. **Fixation simultaneous with transmission:** Normally, an author must fix a new work —for example, by writing it down or making a sound or video recording of it—before publicly performing it in order for the work to enjoy federal copyright protection at the time of the performance. If the work is unfixed, federal copyright law will not prohibit members of the audience from copying it. (State common law may provide protection, as discussed below. Also, copying the live *performance* of a *musical work* may lead to federal liability pursuant to the "neighboring right" that performers enjoy in their live musical performances. See p. 148, *infra*). However, §101 provides that fixation simultaneous with performance will suffice to trigger copyright protection *at the time of performance* if the performance is being "transmitted"—communicated by a device or process that causes images or sounds to be received beyond the place from which they are sent. Thus, for example, live television or radio broadcasts of sports events will be protected by federal copyright as long as they are being recorded on a tangible medium (such as videotape) at the same time they are being broadcast.

c. **Interactive computer systems:** Some have argued that interactive computer systems, such as video games and their visual displays, are not fixed for purposes of copyright protection. This is because the system responds to the specific input of individual users, and thus provides a different set of responses and displays from one session to the next. Courts have rejected this argument on two grounds. First, the program that runs the game is fixed in a tangible object—a computer chip or disk. The instructions to the computer embedded on the chip or disk remain the same from one playing session to the next and can be perceived or reproduced through the assistance of a machine. Second, the audiovisual patterns themselves—what the player sees—are largely repetitive. Many aspects of the display do stay the same each time, regardless of how the player operates the controls.

2. **Common-law copyright protection for unfixed works:** Prior to enactment of the Copyright Act of 1976, unpublished works were protected under common-law copyright. Federal copyright generally only commenced when the work was published with proper copyright notice. Under the Copyright Act of 1976, federal copyright commences when the original work of authorship is fixed in tangible form, regardless of whether or when it is published. The Copyright Act permits the states to continue providing common-law copyright protection for works of authorship that are not fixed in tangible form, and therefore do not qualify for federal protection. (Copyright Act §301.) However, there is little case authority to demonstrate the extent of protection that the states will provide. A few state cases indicate that protection may be afforded for a person's extemporaneous oral statements, but only if the speaker makes it clear that he intends to claim a proprietary interest in her words.

D. **Exclusion of ideas, procedures, processes, etc.:** Copyright Act §102(b) provides: "In no case does copyright protection for an original work of authorship extend to any idea, procedure, process, system, method of operation, concept, principle, or discovery, regardless of the form in which it is described, explained, illustrated, or embodied in such work." This provision codifies the long-established understanding that copyright protection is limited to particular means of expressing ideas, methods of operation, and facts and does not give monopoly rights in the underlying ideas, methods, or facts themselves.

1. **The *Baker v. Selden* case:** *Baker v. Selden,* 101 U.S. 99 (1879), is the famous case in which the Supreme Court enunciated the rule that there can be no copyright protection in ideas. In *Baker*, the plaintiff published and claimed copyright in a book that explained a particular method of bookkeeping and included blank forms for using the method. The advantage of the method and forms was that they permitted the entire business operation of a day, week, or month to be reported on a single page, or on two opposing pages, in an account book. When the defendant published a book that included forms for use in the plaintiff's bookkeeping method, the plaintiff sued for copyright infringement. The Court denied relief, holding that when the art taught by a work of authorship cannot be used without copying some aspect of the work of authorship, then that aspect of the work will not be protected by copyright. The Court reasoned that if the plaintiff had a right to recover for infringement against persons using similar forms, and the forms were the only way of implementing the bookkeeping method, then the plaintiff would have a *de facto* monopoly in the bookkeeping method itself through copyright law. The plaintiff should not be permitted to obtain a monopoly in his useful accounting method—a form of idea or process—without satisfying the stringent requirements of the patent law. Thus, the plaintiff in this case could not assert copyright in his forms against the defendant. When use or expression of an idea requires copying the plaintiff's expression, the expression will not be deemed copyrighted for purposes of an infringement suit against the user.

    a. **Enlargement of the *Baker* rule:** The *Baker* opinion merely said that when copying expression is the *only* way to implement the idea underlying the expression, copying will not constitute copyright infringement. Arguably, this rule is a narrow one. However, lower courts and the Copyright Office have taken the underlying reasoning of *Baker* significantly further.

    i. **The merger doctrine:** In *Morrissey v. Procter & Gamble Co.*, 379 F.2d 675 (1st Cir. 1967), the court relied on the Supreme Court's reasoning in *Baker* to rule that when the subject matter of a work is so narrow and straightforward that there are only a *limited number* of ways to express it, there can be no copyright in any one way of expressing it. The court reasoned that if copyright were recognized under such circumstances, individuals could obtain copyright in all the alternative forms of expressing the underlying idea and thus effectively remove the idea from the public domain without satisfying the requirements for a patent. This reasoning gave rise to the "*merger doctrine*," which provides that when there is only one or a limited number of ways to express an idea, the expression "merges" with the idea and becomes unprotectible. For purposes of determining whether the merger doctrine should apply, courts generally will consider how many *effective* ways there are to express the idea. Far-fetched or impractical ways will not generally be considered.

    Example: In the *Morrissey* case the plaintiff claimed copyright in its sweepstakes rule. The court found that there were only a limited number of ways to express the subject matter of the rule, given its very straightforward, functional nature. It is interesting to note that the *Morrissey* court denied the plaintiff copyright protection for its rule, even though it had been shown that some alternative ways to express the subject matter existed and the defendant had shunned them and copied the language of the plaintiff's rule almost *verbatim*. This opinion makes it difficult to obtain copyright protection in highly utilitarian or functional forms of expression, such as instructions for doing something.

    ii. **The alternative of "thin" copyright protection:** Instead of finding a merger when the number of ways of expressing an idea is limited, some courts prefer to recognize copyright, but refuse to find infringement unless the defendant's copying is nearly exact. In such cases, paraphrasing that might constitute infringement in other circumstances will be permissible. This is known as affording *"thin" copyright.*

    Note: Yet a third way that courts have handled the issue of infringement claims for minimal, functional sorts of works like forms, instructions, etc., is to find that they are lacking in minimal creativity and thus fail the "originality" requirement for copyright.

b. **Blank forms:** Based on the line of cases discussed above, the Copyright Office has promulgated a regulation prohibiting copyright in "[b]lank forms, such as time cards, graph paper, account books, diaries, blank checks, scorecards, address books, report forms, order forms, and the like, which are designed for recording information and do not in themselves convey information." 37 C.F.R. §202.1(c). Under this rule (which has also been applied by courts), copyrightability of forms depends primarily on whether the form conveys significant information or merely records information to be supplied by the user. A form that includes lengthy instructions will be likely to qualify for copyright. Blank form creators sometimes argue that a form that lacks significant instructions still qualifies for copyright because the form's specification of the information to be provided by persons filling it out in itself conveys information about what information is deemed useful or relevant with regard to the issue for which the form is used. The U.S. Courts of Appeals have differed in their receptivity to such arguments.

2. **Copyrightability of facts and research:** Facts are "discoveries" and are not proper subject matter for copyright under subsection 102(b). An "author" does not create facts—they exist independently and belong to everyone. Nonetheless, advocates of broader copyright protection have argued that original research should be protected by copyright, as a matter of public policy. Their argument goes as follows: Assume that X conducts considerable research in the course of writing a non-fiction book. This research adds to the store of public knowledge and is beneficial. Y writes a book that competes with X's, but rather than doing his own research, Y "borrows" the facts from X's book, avoiding much of the cost and time that X expended in doing original research, while cutting into the market for X's work. It may be unfair to allow Y to take a free ride in this way, and if the free ride is permitted, it is possible that authors such as X will have less incentive to do original research in the future. For these reasons, advocates argue that courts should construe copyright as preventing the copying of the products of research, even though that essentially means giving the researcher property rights in facts. In the *Feist* case, discussed above at p. 167, the Supreme Court rejected these arguments. The Court stressed that only original authorship can be protected by copyright, and facts are not original to the researcher, even if she was the first to discover them. The policy arguments set forth above can also be countered with the reasoning that requiring subsequent authors to "reinvent the wheel" by duplicating research already published by others is inefficient and wasteful, and not in the public's interest. Thus, in the case of factual compilations or databases, only the author's original expression—usually her selection, coordination, and arrangement of the facts—can be protected by copyright. (And, because the copyright in databases is

"thin," often courts will require a showing of "virtual identicality" or a "bodily appropriation of expression" before they will hold a defendant liable for infringement. This is the "thin copyright" standard.) The scope of protection for nonfiction literary works, such as history books, newspaper articles, and biographies, is also relatively narrow.

- **a. The scope of the author's "original expression of the facts" in nonfiction literary works:** Copyright only protects the author's "original expression of the facts" in nonfiction literary works such as histories or biographies. Certainly the author's choice of words to describe or explain the facts can qualify as original authorship and be protected. How about her selection and arrangement of the facts? This question has given courts some difficulty. While an author's selection and arrangement of elements within her work is considered copyrightable expression in a wide range of works, protecting an author's selection and arrangement of facts in a non-fiction work may, in some cases, give a *de facto* monopoly in the author's ideas. For example, assume that in his book, X describes and advocates his theory about why an historical event occurred. To do this, he selects those facts that are most supportive of the theory, and presents them in the sequence that most persuasively suggests that the theory is correct. This is all a part of persuasive writing. However, if X's selection and arrangement of the facts is protected from copying, others may effectively be precluded from writing about the same theory, which would leave X with a *de facto* monopoly in the theory itself, contrary to §102(b). The doctrine of merger may be applicable. Moreover, the originality requirement may prevent copyright protection of "obvious" arrangements of the facts, such as a chronological arrangement in a history text.

E. Categories of protectible works of authorship: Copyright Act §102(a) provides that "works of authorship," for purposes of copyright protection, include the following categories:

- Literary works;
- Musical works, including any accompanying words;
- Dramatic works, including any accompanying music;
- Pantomimes and choreographic works;
- Pictorial, graphic, and sculptural works;
- Motion pictures and other audiovisual works;
- Sound recordings; and
- Architectural works.

Note that this list is not intended to be absolute—§102(a) merely states that protectible works of authorship *include* the listed categories. Congress left a little flexibility for the courts. If something new does not fit within any of the listed categories, it may still be protected if the court determines that Congress would have intended to include it. Several problems have arisen with respect to works in some of the listed categories, which will be discussed below.

1. The literary works category—copyrightability of computer programs: A number of questions about copyright protection for computer programs arose as the use of computers proliferated in the 1970s and 1980s. In 1980, Congress amended the Copyright Act of 1976 expressly to provide copyright protection for programs as "literary works." Section 101, as amended, defines a computer program as: "A set of statements or instructions to be used directly or indirectly in a computer in order to bring about a certain result." The key issues that courts have undertaken to resolve with regard to computer programs are discussed below.

a. **Copyright extends to programs in both source code and object code:** Source code is the language in which programmers write computer programs. It is comprised mainly of descriptive key words and common mathematical notations. Once the program has been written in source code, it is compiled, or translated, into object code which, as a general matter, only the computer can read. In its most basic form, object code is comprised of a series of 1's and 0's, that provide electronic signals to the computer. In *Apple Computer, Inc. v. Franklin Computer Corp.*, 714 F.2d 1240 (3d Cir. 1983), the U.S. Circuit Court of Appeals ruled that programs in both source code and object code are protected by copyright. The court rejected the argument that object code should not be protected because it only communicates directly with a machine and is not readable by humans.

b. **Copyright extends to programs on chips:** The program in object code is electronically or photochemically encoded onto a storage medium, which today is usually a magnetic disk or a chip. A chip, or integrated circuit, is a collection of transistors that work together to perform a particular electronic function. After programs are encoded onto chips, the chips are plugged into the computer and become a part of the computer's electronic circuitry. An argument was raised that, while programs on encoded disks were protected, programs encoded on chips were not subject to copyright protection because chips are utilitarian objects—part of the computer hardware. The court in *Franklin Computer* also rejected this argument, noting that the medium on which the program was encoded should not determine whether the program is protectible.

c. **Copyright protects both operation and application programs:** Operation programs (or operating systems) instruct the computer to perform various internal functions. They do not interact directly with human users. In contrast, application programs do interact with the user, causing the computer to perform tasks, such as word processing, at the user's command.

The copyrightability of operating systems was challenged on the ground that these programs constitute a process, system, or method of operation which, under *Baker v. Selden* and Copyright Act §102(b), cannot be the subject matter of copyright. The court in *Franklin Computer* rejected this argument, reasoning that one must distinguish between the method in which the computer operates internally and the program, which is the set of instructions the computer follows in the course of carrying out the method. The difference is the same as the difference between a method of building a model airplane and the written instructions for building the plane. The instructions are merely the expression of the method, and as expression, are within the subject matter of copyright. As long as there are sufficient alternative ways to express the same underlying method, the instructions can be protected from copying.

d. **Copyright protection for the structure of computer programs:** Computer programs are considered "literary works," and thus are in the same category of copyrightable works as novels, letters, and magazine articles. In other kinds of literary works, such as novels, copyright protects both the literal language the author uses and the underlying structure or organization of the work. The underlying structure and organization are often called "nonliteral" elements of the literary work. For example, in a novel, the author builds a framework for the novel (the plot) through his selection and arrangement of characters, settings, and sequences of action. This combination of nonliteral elements can be considered a part of the novelist's protectible expression. The question arose whether the structural elements of a computer program should be protected on the same basis, along with the programmer's literal source or object code. Courts have uniformly agreed that nonliteral elements of programs should be protected under the same principles as in other literary works. They have, however, encountered considerable difficulty in distinguishing the copyrightable wheat from the uncopyrightable chaff within a program's structure or organization.

i. **The *Whelan* opinion:** In *Whelan Associates v. Jaslow Dental Laboratory, Inc.*, 797 F.2d 1222 (3d Cir. 1986), *cert. denied*, 479 U.S. 1031 (1987), the Court of Appeals for the Third Circuit held that in utilitarian works such as computer programs, the ultimate purpose or result the work seeks to accomplish is the work's underlying idea. The court then reasoned that if a particular structure is *necessary* in order to accomplish the purpose of the computer program, then the structure merges with the purpose (idea) and is unprotectible. If the structure is not necessary—that is, if there are sufficient alternative structures that would accomplish the purpose of the program—then the structure the programmer devised is protectible expression. The court characterized the idea, or purpose, of the computer program in the *Whelan* case as "efficient management of a dental lab." The court then found that many different structural combinations could be used to accomplish that purpose. Thus, the particular structure that the plaintiff had chosen for his program constituted protectible expression. The *Whelan* court's approach provides broad copyright protection for the structure and organization of computer programs.

ii. **The *Altai* opinion:** In *Computer Associates International, Inc. v. Altai, Inc.*, 982 F.2d 693 (2d Cir. 1992), the Court of Appeals for the Second Circuit rejected the *Whelan* approach, criticizing it as overly simplistic. The court noted that a computer program is comprised of more than one idea. Each program consists of a number of interacting subprograms, which work together to perform the program's ultimate function or purpose. Each of these subprograms may represent one or more separate "ideas" in itself. Moreover, the *Whelan* approach takes no account of the fact that computer programs contain many uncopyrightable elements. The *Altai* court then set forth its "abstraction-filtration-comparison" test, which can be used to identify the copyrightable aspects of a program's structure. Most other jurisdictions have adopted this approach or a modified version of it.

Abstraction: In the first step, the court should break the program down into its constituent structural components, applying Judge Learned Hand's "abstractions" test, which the *Altai* court adapted for use with computer programs. See *infra*, pp. 131-132. The program must be conceptualized in ever-increasing levels of generality. This process begins with a conception of the program in very specific detail, describing each instruction and its organization within a hierarchy of modules. The process then progresses to increasingly generalized conceptions of the program, which leave out increasing amounts of detail. Quoting from a law review article (88 Mich. L. Rev. 867-873 (1990)), the court explained: "At a higher level of abstraction, the instructions in the lowest-level modules may be replaced conceptually by the functions of those modules. At progressively higher levels of abstraction, the functions of higher-level modules conceptually replace the implementations of those modules in terms of lower-level modules and instructions, until finally, one is left with nothing but the ultimate function of the program. . . ." Each progressively general conceptualization is a level of abstraction. "A program has structure at every level of abstraction at which it is conceptualized. At low levels of abstraction, a program's structure may be very complex. At the highest levels it is trivial."

Filtration: Once the program's levels of abstraction have been laid out, the court must examine each structural component at each level of abstraction to determine whether its inclusion at that level: (1) constitutes an "idea"; (2) is required in order for the program to perform its functions efficiently, so that it should merge with idea; (3) is required by factors external to the program itself (for example, the component is required in order to be compatible with a particular computer or with other computer programs with which it will run, is required by the industry being serviced, or constitutes a widely accepted programming practice within the computer industry); or (4) was taken from the public domain. Components falling into these categories are unprotectible and should be "filtered" out. Filtering out all these unprotectible elements serves to define the scope of the plaintiff's copyright.

Comparison: Once the court has filtered out all elements of the program that are ideas, are dictated by efficiency or external factors, or were taken from the public domain, there may remain a core of protectible expression. The court may then compare that copyrightable expression with the defendant's program to determine whether the defendant's program infringes.

iii. **The programmer's selection, coordination, and arrangement:** In expressly mandating deletion of uncopyrightable elements prior to comparing the plaintiff's and the defendant's works, the *Altai* abstraction-filtration-comparison test might be interpreted to hold that a computer programmer's selection, coordination, and arrangement of uncopyrightable elements will not be considered to be protected expression in computer programs. However, in a subsequent opinion, the Second Circuit clarified that original selection, coordination, and arrangement is protectible, explaining that individual program elements that are filtered out on one level of abstraction may nonetheless be considered and protected as part of an aggregate of elements at a higher level of abstraction. *Softel, Inc v. Dragon Medical and Scientific Communications, Inc.*, 118 F.3d 955 (2d Cir. 1997), *cert. denied*, 523 U.S. 1020 (1998). While other Circuits have followed this approach, some (particularly the Ninth and Eleventh) have been grudging in the level of protection they will afford to selection and arrangement expression in software. They have adopted a thin copyright "bodily appropriation of expression" or "virtual identicality" standard, which is higher than the "substantial similarity" standard that is normally employed in evaluating whether a defendant's work infringes the plaintiff's. Under this standard, there can be no finding of infringement unless the defendant's selection and arrangement is virtually identical to the plaintiff's.

e. **Copyright protection for a program's user interface:** A program's "user interface" is comprised of the various elements through which the program communicates with the user. The most obvious example is the program's screen display. The program's menu command hierarchy and the correspondence between particular commands and keys on the keyboard are also considered a part of the program's user interface. (Such aspects of a program may be copied without copying the program's code.) Screen displays can be protected on the same basis as audiovisual works, though highly functional, straightforward screen displays may face problems of originality, merger, and blank form status.

i. **The *Lotus* decision:** In *Lotus Development Corp. v. Borland International, Inc.*, 49 F.3d 807 (1st Cir. 1995), *aff'd*, 516 U.S. 233 (1996), the Court of Appeals for the First Circuit had to determine whether the menu command hierarchy of the Lotus 1-2-3 spreadsheet program constituted copyrightable subject matter. Users manipulated and controlled the Lotus program through a series of menu commands, such as "copy," "print," and "quit." They could choose commands either by highlighting them on the screen or by typing their first letter. In all, the Lotus spreadsheet program had 469 commands arranged into more than 50 menus and submenus. The defendant, Borland, incorporated the whole Lotus menu tree into its program as an alternative to its own menu command hierarchy, in order to make it easier for users who were accustomed to the Lotus program to switch to the Borland program. The First Circuit found that Lotus's menu command system did not constitute copyrightable expression, and thus that Borland did not infringe. The court explained that the menu command hierarchy constituted a method of operation, which cannot be protected under Copyright Act §102(b). The court defined a method of operation as "the means by which a person operates something, whether it be a car, a food processor, or a computer." The court reasoned that the Lotus menu command hierarchy provided the means by which users controlled and operated the Lotus 1-2-3 program: "If users wish to copy material, for example, they use the 'copy' command. If users wish to print material, they use the 'print' command. Users must use the command terms to tell the computer what to do." Thus, even though the menu command hierarchy could be characterized as containing elements of expression (the selection and arrangement of command terms), these elements could not be protected because they constituted part of an uncopyrightable method of operation.

Example: The *Lotus* court compared the Lotus 1-2-3 menu command hierarchy to the buttons used to control a video cassette recorder: "A VCR is a machine that enables one to watch and record videotapes. Users operate VCRs by pressing a series of buttons that are typically labeled 'record, play, reverse, fast forward, pause, stop/eject.' " The *Lotus* court explained that the fact that the buttons are arranged and labeled does not make them a "literary work," or an "expression" of the method of operating a VCR via a set of labeled buttons. Instead, the buttons are themselves the "method of operating" the VCR. The Court held that when a Lotus 1-2-3 user chooses a command, either by highlighting it on the screen or by typing its first letter, he or she effectively pushes a button. "Highlighting the 'print' command on the screen, or typing the letter 'p,' is analogous to pressing a VCR button labeled 'play.' "

ii. **Response to the reasoning in *Lotus*:** In reviewing the First Circuit's decision in *Lotus*, the U.S. Supreme Court split four-to-four, which had the effect of affirming the First Circuit by default. The Supreme Court provided no opinion. In a subsequent case, the Court of Appeals for the Eleventh Circuit applied similar reasoning to deny protection to the user interface of a program to be used in designing wood trusses for construction of roofs. The court found that the user interface constituted an unprotectible process, because the means by which it undertook to draft roof truss plans mimicked the steps a draftsman would follow in designing a roof truss plan by hand. *Mitek Holdings, Inc. v. Arce Engineering Co., Inc.*, 89 F.3d 1548 (11th Cir. 1996). On the other hand, the Court of Appeals for the Tenth Circuit rejected the *Lotus* court's reasoning. In that case, the issue was whether sets of four-digit numeric command codes used to access and use a piece of telecommunications hardware constituted an uncopyrightable method of operation. The court found that expression embodied in a method of operation may be protected. In so finding, it applied the *Altai* abstraction-filtration-comparison test (which the *Lotus* court had rejected as being inapplicable to claims of literal infringement of user interface elements), and reasoned that even though an expressive element may be part of a method of operation at a higher level of abstraction, it may nonetheless constitute protectible matter at a lower level of abstraction. *Mitel, Inc. v. Iqtel, Inc.*, 124 F.3d 1366 (10th Cir. 1997).

2. **The pictorial, graphic, and sculptural works category:** Copyright Act §101 defines "pictorial, graphic, and sculptural works" as including "two-dimensional and three-dimensional works of fine, graphic, and applied art, photographs, prints and art reproductions, maps, globes, charts, diagrams, models, and technical drawings, including architectural plans." It also includes "works of artistic craftsmanship insofar as their form but not their mechanical or utilitarian aspects are concerned. . . ." As is the case in other subject matter categories, a minimal threshold level of creativity has been required so that, for example, common geometric shapes by themselves, are unlikely to be deemed sufficiently original to merit copyright protection. However, realistic photographs, drawings, and paintings of objects, such as a realistic rendition of a product on a label, generally will qualify. The primary problem in the pictorial, graphic, and sculptural works category lies in determining the protection to be afforded to design elements incorporated into useful articles.

   a. **Copyright in the design of useful articles:** Copyright Act §101 provides that "the design of a useful article . . . shall be considered a pictorial, graphic, or sculptural work [and thus copyrightable] only if, and only to the extent that, such design incorporates pictorial, graphic, or sculptural features *that can be identified separately from, and are capable of existing independently of, the utilitarian aspects of the article*." (Emphasis added.) Thus, in the case of pictorial, graphic, or sculptural features that are incorporated into useful articles, the issue is whether the features are "separable" from the utilitarian aspects of the article. The intent of the artist to mass-produce and commercially exploit the design is irrelevant.

      i. **The definition of a "useful article":** Section 101 defines a "useful article" as "an article having an intrinsic utilitarian function that is not merely to portray the appearance of the article or to convey information." The status of an article as "useful" usually is not an issue, since it generally will be clear whether the article has an intrinsic utilitarian function other than to portray the appearance of something or to convey information. In one case, the court found that a toy airplane was not a useful article because its function was "merely to portray the appearance" of an airplane (which is a useful article). Clothing is a useful article, which means that clothing designers must satisfy the separability standard in order to obtain copyright protection. The Copyright Office considers Halloween costumes to be useful articles, as well, because they serve the dual purpose of clothing the body *and* portraying the appearance of something. However, the Copyright Office considers fanciful face masks not to be useful articles, since they have no inherent utility other than their appearance.

      ii. **The separability issue:** The legislative history states that, to be protected, the design of a useful article must contain "some element that, *physically* or *conceptually* can be identified as separable from the utilitarian aspects of the article." (Emphasis added.) Physical separability is not difficult to conceive. For example, the ornamental emblem on the hood of a car (such as the leaping jaguar on Jaguar automobiles) could physically be severed from the car and still be recognized as a work of sculpture. The notion of "conceptual separability" has given courts more difficulty.

iii. **Conceptual separability:** While some authorities have suggested that only physical separability should enable a design in a useful article to be copyrighted, the influential Second Circuit has held that either form of separability is sufficient. In *Brandir International v. Cascade Pacific Lumber Co.*, 834 F.2d 1142 (2d Cir. 1987), that court held that the question of conceptual separability should be determined by the *purpose* underlying the choice of design features at issue. If adoption of the design features was influenced by utilitarian considerations, then the features are "inextricably intertwined" with the utilitarian function of the article and are not conceptually separable. If, on the other hand, the design features were not in any respect required or influenced by the utilitarian function of the article, but reflect purely aesthetic choices, independent of the article's function, then the design features are conceptually separable.

Example: In *Carol Barnhart v. Economy Cover Corp.*, 773 F.2d 411 (2d. Cir. 1985), the useful articles at issue were display forms in the shape of human torsos. The torsos were used to display clothing in stores. The front of each torso was an anatomically correct, life-sized rendition of a human chest. The back was hollowed out so that displayed shirts could be tucked in neatly. Two of the torsos represented bare male and female chests. The other two represented male and female chests clothed in shirts, for display of jackets and sweaters. The court found that the design of the display form torsos was not conceptually separable from their utilitarian function because the features—width of shoulders, size of breasts, etc.—were dictated by the need to show clothes off to the best advantage. The features were not the result of purely aesthetic choices.

Example: In *Brandir*, the useful article at issue was a bicycle rack. The rack began as a metal sculpture, with no utilitarian function. However, the artist later discovered that the sculpture could be used as a bike rack. The artist then *altered it* so that it would be *better suited* to that function. The artist later mass produced the rack and sold it. He received design awards for it. The court, however, held that the rack was not protected by copyright because functional concerns influenced the rack's aesthetically pleasing appearance. Because of the alterations the artist adopted to make the sculpture better suited to the function of holding bicycles, the design elements did not reflect the designer's unrestrained artistic judgment exercised independently of functional considerations.

Example: In *Kieselstein-Cord v. Accessories by Pearl, Inc.*, 773 F.2d 411 (2d Cir. 1985), the useful articles at issue were belt buckles ornamented with a sculpted metal surface. These buckles, made of precious metals, were sold at jewelry and high-fashion stores, and had been accepted b the Metropolitan Museum of Art for its collection. Some purchasers had worn the belt buckles around their necks as ornamentation, rather than around their waists. The court found the sculpted metal surfaces were "conceptually separable" from the belt buckles they ornamented, and thus were copyrightable. As the court later explained, the sculpted surfaces were not in any respect required by the utilitarian function of a belt buckle, but could be conceived of as having been added to, or superimposed upon, an otherwise utilitarian article. The sculptor's choices represented purely aesthetic choices, independent of the buckles' function.

iv. **Criticism of the Second Circuit test:** The Second Circuit's test for conceptual separability has been criticized as penalizing designers who successfully merge form and function and seek aesthetic appeal through emphasis on line and shape. It has been asserted that the test favors more awkward designers, who merely decorate their utilitarian articles with independent, representational art as an apparent afterthought.

v. **Developments in other Circuits:** The Seventh Circuit purported to adopt the *Brandir* standard in *Pivot Point International, Inc. v. Charlene Products, Inc.*, 372 F.3d 913 (7th Cir. 2004), characterizing it as consistent with the "temporal displacement" standard that a dissenting Second Circuit judge had advocated. Under the "temporal displacement" standard, the issue is whether the design creates in the mind of an ordinary observer two different concepts—the artistic concept and the utilitarian object—that are not inevitably entertained simultaneously. In *Pivot Point*, the court found that the features of a mannequin head (produced for beauty school students to use to practice styling hair and applying makeup) were conceptually separable and protectible. The copyright claimant had commissioned an artist to design the head to imitate the "hungry look" of high-fashion runway models. In finding the mannequin's facial features conceptually separable, the court explained that the designer had a wide range of facial features to choose from (the shape of the eye, the shape of the nose, the cheek and jaw structure, etc.) that would serve the function of the mannequin (even a "hungry look" mannequin) equally well, so that the designer was free to exercise his artistic judgment, free from utilitarian constraints. However, the Fifth Circuit, in *Galiano v. Harrah's Operating Co., Inc.*, 416 F.3d 411 (5th Cir. 2005), declined to apply the *Brandir* standard in determining the copyrightability of flamboyant casino employee uniform designs. Rather, the court adopted Professor Nimmer's "likelihood of marketability" standard: "conceptual separability exists where there is substantial likelihood that even if the article had no utilitarian use it would still be marketable to some significant segment of the community simply because of its aesthetic qualities."

vi. **Overlap of copyright and design patents:** In some cases the design of a useful article may qualify both for copyright protection and for a design patent. (See PATENTS, *supra*, pp. 75-78, for a discussion of design patents.) It is possible to rely on both forms of protection for one design. However, many designers have complained that neither design patents nor copyright afford sufficient protection for valuable industrial designs, and have lobbied for *sui generis* statutory protection. While Congress has entertained a number of bills to provide such protection, it has only enacted protection for the design of one kind of useful article: boat hulls. See 17 U.S.C. §§1301-1332.

b. **Copyright in technical drawings:** Technical drawings are part of the pictorial, graphic, and sculptural works category of copyrightable subject matter. However, while unauthorized duplication of plans (blueprints) for a useful article constitutes infringement, unauthorized use of copyrighted plans to *build* the useful article (such as an automobile) depicted in the plans generally does not constitute an infringement of the plans. (Copyright Act §113(b).) Due to this restriction, the copyright protection afforded to technical plans for useful articles is more limited than that afforded other pictorial, graphic, or sculptural works. While building a useful article from copyrighted plans is not an infringement of the plans, transforming other types of two-dimensional pictorial, graphic, and sculptural works to a three-dimensional medium (for example, making a statue based on an oil painting) generally will infringe the copyright in the two-dimensional work. (However, see the discussion of the separate architectural works category of copyrightable subject matter, *infra*. If a building design is protected under the Architectural Works Copyright Protection Act, enacted in 1990, then unauthorized use of architectural plans to build a building may infringe the copyright in the architectural work, as opposed to copyright in the pictorial, graphic, and sculptural work (i.e., the plans).)

c. **Copyright protection in maps:** Maps qualify for copyright protection. Because they are primarily factual, much of their originality will arise from the mapmaker's selection, coordination, and arrangement of elements. The factual material for a map might be drawn either from direct observation of the terrain or from preexisting documents. The court in *Amsterdam v. Triangle Publications, Inc.*, 189 F.2d 104 (3d Cir. 1951), held that for a map to be "original," and thus entitled to copyright protection, the maker must have engaged in some direct observation or investigation of the terrain. A mere rearrangement of material from preexisting documents would not suffice. However, other courts, such as the Ninth Circuit, have rejected this higher standard of originality for maps, finding that the maker's selection, coordination, and arrangement of facts drawn from other documents in a map can be original, and thus constitute copyrightable, expression.

d. **Copyright protection for typeface:** The legislative history of the 1976 Act indicates that Congress deliberately declined to provide copyright protection for typeface designs. The Copyright Office has refused to register copyright for typeface and has been upheld by a U.S. Court of Appeals.

3. **The architectural works category:** Prior to 1990, works of architecture were only protected to the extent that they constituted "pictorial, graphic, or sculptural works," as discussed *supra*. Architectural plans were protected as graphic works. Since a building is a useful article, protection of a finished building was limited to features that were physically or conceptually separable from the utilitarian purpose of the building. In most cases, that meant that only decorative embellishments, such as friezes, were protected. However, in December of 1990, Congress amended Copyright Act §102(a) expressly to add "architectural works" as an enumerated category of copyrightable subject matter. The 1976 Act, as amended, defines an architectural work as "the design of a building as embodied in any tangible medium of expression, including a building, architectural plans or drawings. The work includes the overall form as well as the arrangement and composition of spaces and elements in the design, but does not include "individual standard features." 17 U.S.C. §101.

   a. **The design of a "building":** The amendment defines a protectible "architectural work" as "the design of a building." The Copyright Office has defined "buildings" as "humanly habitable structures that are intended to be both permanent and stationary, such as houses and office buildings and other permanent and stationary structures designed for human occupancy, including but not limited to churches, museums, gazebos, and garden pavilions." Thus, tents and bridges do not qualify. Courts have also found that stores built inside an enclosed shopping mall are not "buildings" for this purpose. The store designer did not design or construct the walls or ceiling in its store, but only designed a room within an existing building.

b. Extent of protection for architectural works: The legislative history of the amendment indicates that Congress intended to prohibit unauthorized copying of the architectural work, regardless of whether the defendant copied from building plans or the building itself. Moreover, even though a finished building is a "useful article," buildings that qualify for protection under the new architectural works category are not subject to the "physical or conceptual separability" test. The legislative history of the amendment does, however, direct courts not to overlook functionality in evaluating the copyrightability or scope of protection of works falling into the new architectural works category. It suggests a two-step analysis. First, the architectural work should be examined to determine whether there are original design elements present, including overall shape and interior architecture. If so, it should then be determined whether the design elements are "functionally required." Only design elements that are not *dictated by* function should be protected. Evidence that there is more than one method of obtaining a given functional result may be considered.

c. Effective date: The 1990 amendments protecting architectural works are prospective: They protect "architectural works created on or after the date of enactment" (December 1, 1990) and "architectural works that on the date of enactment [were] unconstructed and embodied in unpublished plans or drawings." If an architectural work does not fall within the scope of the amendments, then the only copyright protection available is that described *supra*, at pp. 117-120, under the pictorial, graphic, and sculptural works category.

Example: Architect designs an office building and draws up blueprints for it. He later oversees the construction of the building. Defendant copies the finished building in the course of creating his own set of blueprints. The building design in defendant's blueprints is substantially similar to architect's. If architect's design falls under the Architectural Works Copyright Protection Act (AWCPA), then defendant is likely to be liable for infringement. Architect's design is viewed as a "work of architecture," which is a separate subject matter category from the pictorial, graphic, or sculptural works category. It is the intangible design of the building that is protected, regardless of the form in which it is manifested—plans or completed building. Assuming that architect's design contains copyrightable elements, and defendant copied those elements, defendant may be liable for infringement.

If architect's design does not qualify for protection under the AWCPA, then it will be evaluated as a pictorial, graphic, or sculptural work. Since defendant copied the finished building, which is a useful article, the physical and conceptual separability requirement will apply. Only if architect's building has design elements that are copyrightable under this standard, and only if Defendant copied those elements, can there be infringement liability. Note that the conceptual separability test prohibits protection if architect's design elements were *influenced* by functional considerations. In contrast, the AWCPA only prohibits protection of design elements that were *dictated* by function.

Example: Architect creates plans for a house. Contractor obtains a lawful copy of the plans and, without architect's authorization, uses the plans to build the depicted house. If the AWCPA applies, and the plans contain copyrightable elements, contractor should be liable for infringement. If the AWCPA does not apply, contractor is not likely to be liable for copyright infringement. Merely using blueprints to build the useful article depicted in the blueprints is generally understood not to infringe. *Baker v. Selden* (see p. 110, *supra*) is cited for this proposition. The reasoning is that copyright in expression (the plans) cannot be used to gain rights in the underlying idea (or other uncopyrightable subject matter—in this case the useful article) that is being expressed.

4. **The sound recordings category:** Copyright Act §101 defines "sound recordings" as "works that result from the fixation of a series of musical, spoken, or other sounds, but not including the sounds accompanying a motion picture or other audiovisual work, regardless of the nature of the material objects, such as disks, tapes, or other phonorecords, in which they are embodied."

   a. **The sound recording copyright is separate from the copyright in the recorded material:** The sound recording copyright is separate from any copyright that may exist in the work (such as a literary or musical composition) that is the subject of the recording. Thus, for example, assume that X writes a musical composition, which is protected by copyright. Y performs the composition and records the performance. Of course, if Y's act is unauthorized, he will have infringed X's copyright, which gives X the exclusive right to reproduce the musical composition. However, assuming that Y has a license from X to reproduce the composition, Y may obtain a copyright in the sound recording of his particular performance of X's musical composition. The copyright will only protect against misappropriation of the *actual sounds* that have been recorded. As will be discussed *infra*, pp. 135, 145, 148, the rights afforded by a sound recording copyright are more limited than the rights afforded to other types of copyrighted works.

   b. **No federal copyright protection for pre-1972 domestic sound recordings:** In the case of domestic (U.S.) sound recordings, only those sound recordings fixed after 1972 are protected by federal copyright. Sound recordings fixed prior to that time may be protected by state common law and statutes—to the extent they exist—until February 15, 2047. For a discussion of foreign sound recordings, see *infra*, p. 180.

F. **Other problem areas:** A few additional problems regarding copyrightable subject matter deserve mention. They are: (1) copyright for fictitious characters, (2) copyright for immoral or obscene works; and (3) protection of the layout of semiconductor chips.

   1. **Copyright for fictitious characters:** Considerable uncertainty has surrounded the existence and extent of copyright protection for fictitious characters, in themselves, apart from the original work in which they were created. Today, the prevailing rule is that a character is entitled to separate copyright protection if the character was distinctly delineated in the plaintiff's work.

      a. **Distinct delineation:** The rule that characters must be distinctly delineated is meant to ensure that the character constitutes copyrightable expression, rather than merely an uncopyrightable idea. Courts have differed over how distinctly the plaintiff's character must be drawn. In the case of characters created strictly by word, e.g., in a novel or poem, the Ninth Circuit has indicated that the character must be extremely well delineated, to the point that he constitutes the story being told, rather than merely being a vehicle for telling the story. Judge Learned Hand, in *Nichols v. Universal Pictures Corp.*, 45 F.2d 119 (2d Cir. 1930), took a less rigid view, suggesting that the character must be more than just a "type" (for example, a "Falstaff" type—a drunken buffoon) and must be drawn in considerable detail. The defendant, to infringe, must copy that detail. Judge Hand's view appears to be the more widely accepted one.

      b. **Characters with a visual aspect:** In cases involving cartoon characters, or movie or television characters, where the character at issue has a visual aspect as well as personality characteristics described by word and story line, courts (including the Ninth Circuit) have been more willing to find copyright protection. The visual image, combined with conceptual qualities, gives the court something more concrete to work with, and more comfort that the character constitutes "expression" and not "idea." When the defendant has taken a combination of characters from a work, rather than just one character, there is an even greater likelihood that a court will find that the defendant has taken copyrightable expression.

Example: In *Anderson v. Stallone*, 11 U.S.P.Q. 2d 1161 (C.D. Cal. 1989), Anderson wrote a 31-page "treatment" called "Rocky IV," which he hoped to sell to Sylvester Stallone to be made into a sequel to the movie "Rocky III." The treatment used the main characters from the earlier three Rocky movies—Rocky Balboa, Adrian, Apollo Creed, Clubber Lang, and Paulie—but had a different story line. The court found that Anderson's treatment, by taking the characters, infringed Stallone's copyright protection in those characters. The court found that the characters were protected under both the standard for characters with visual aspects and the stricter "words only" standard. The court commented: "The Rocky characters are one of the most highly delineated group of characters in modern American cinema. The physical and emotional characteristics of Rocky Balboa and the other characters were set forth in tremendous detail in the three Rocky movies before Anderson appropriated the characters for his treatment. The interrelationships and development of [these characters] are central to all three movies. Rocky Balboa is such a highly delineated character that his name is the title of all four of the Rocky movies and his character has become identified with specific character traits from his speaking mannerisms to his physical characteristics. This court has no difficulty ruling as a matter of law that the Rocky characters are delineated so extensively that they are protected from bodily appropriation when taken as a group and transposed into a sequel by another author."

2. **Copyright protection for immoral or obscene works:** Congress, the Copyright Office, and the courts have made no exception to copyright for obscene or immoral works. To prohibit protection for such works would require the courts to make substantive value judgments about individual works, which they hesitate to undertake. In addition, prohibiting copyright for immoral or obscene works might undermine the goal of uniform copyright protection throughout the nation, since determinations of obscenity usually are based on local community standards and may differ from one community to another.

3. **Protection for semiconductor chips:** A semiconductor chip, or "integrated circuit," is a collection of transistors, in a single structure, that work together to perform an electronic function, such as processing, memory, or logic. Chips are used in a wide range of electric products, such as computers, automobiles, watches, and televisions. Laying out the proper pattern for transistors in a chip is highly complex and meticulous work, requiring skillful design engineering. However, copyright law does not provide a satisfactory means of protecting chips. While the technical drawings or blueprints of chips are copyrightable, the chips themselves are not. A chip is a useful article, and its design is not physically or conceptually separable from its function. Utility and design patents are also inapplicable to chips in many cases. Even when a chip otherwise qualifies for a utility patent, this form of protection may be unsatisfactory because the patent application process takes too long (a chip often will be obsolete within a year or two of its development).

   a. *Sui generis* **protection—the Semiconductor Chip Protection Act of 1984:** Because existing forms of intellectual property protection were unavailable, Congress enacted a *sui* *generis* form of protection for chips, which draws many concepts and standards from U.S. copyright law, but is custom tailored to chips. This legislation, known as the Semiconductor Chip Protection Act of 1984 (SCPA), is codified at 17 U.S.C. §§901-914. However, due to a combination of advances in technology and the Act's rather generous provisions allowing reverse engineering, the SCPA has rarely been invoked. The SCPA is nonetheless important as precedent for *sui generis* legislation to protect a narrow category of subject matter outside of the confines of the Copyright and Patent Acts.

G. **Compilations:** Copyright Act §103 specifies that compilations are copyrightable subject matter. Section 101 defines a compilation as "a work formed by the collection and assembling of preexisting materials or of data that are selected, coordinated, or arranged in such a way that the resulting work as a whole constitutes an original work of authorship." A compilation results from an author's selecting, bringing together, organizing, and arranging previously existing material of all kinds, regardless of whether the individual materials she is working with are themselves copyrightable. Compilations can be broken down into two varieties: collective works and other compilations.

   1. **Collective works:** Section 101 defines the term "compilation" as including "collective works." Section 101 defines a collective work as "a work, such as a periodical issue, anthology, or encyclopedia, in which a number of contributions, constituting separate and independent works in themselves, are assembled into a collective whole." Thus, a collective work is an assembly of separately copyrightable works of authorship. It is not necessary that the contributions emanate from different authors, though often they do. A collective work may consist of a collection of the discrete writings of one author.

   2. **Other compilations:** Compilations that do not constitute collective works include such things as business directories or automated databases, which compile facts or other materials that are unlikely to be separately copyrightable. Broadly speaking, almost all copyrightable works could be deemed compilations, for almost all works are comprised, at some level, of a number of different uncopyrightable elements.

      Example: Plaintiff's greeting card is comprised of: (1) *de minimis* text that is not sufficiently original to qualify for copyright by itself (e.g., "I wuv you," "I miss you already and you haven't even left"); (2) artwork copied from the public domain, which cannot be copyrighted; (3) a particular typeface, which is not copyrightable subject matter; and (4) a specific shade of paper and ink. The defendant sells a greeting card that has similar text, artwork, typeface, paper, and ink. The plaintiff may prevail in an infringement claim by arguing that his card is copyrightable as a compilation of uncopyrightable elements. The copyrightable expression consists of the plaintiff's selection, coordination, and arrangement of the particular text, art, typeface, paper, and ink. The defendant's copying of the selection and arrangement is an infringement, even though copying one of the individual elements would not be. Note that this selection and arrangement in artistic contexts creates a form of synergy, sometimes called "total concept and feel," which may itself be deemed copyrightable expression.

   3. **Copyright protection is limited to the compilation author's original expression:** The copyright in a compilation extends only to the compilation author's original expression. The compilation author does not obtain any rights in the preexisting works that he uses in the compilation merely by virtue of selecting, coordinating, or arranging them in the compilation. (Copyright Act §103.) For example, if X, the author of an anthology of poetry, includes Y's and Z's poems in her anthology, the inclusion gives X no copyright in those poems, as such.

Nor does inclusion affect the existence, scope, or duration of Y's or Z's copyrights in the poems.

- **a. Copyrightable elements contributed by the compilation author:** The primary copyrightable element contributed by the compilation author is her selection, coordination, and arrangement of the compiled material. Selection, coordination, and arrangement of preexisting materials may involve intellectual judgment and constitute a form of expression. (As in the *Burrow-Guiles* case, *supra*, the compiler has superimposed his own mental conception on the subject matter.) As is true for all copyrightable expression, the compiler's selection, coordination, and arrangement must satisfy a minimum threshold standard of creativity in order to be "original." See *supra*, pp. 107-108. If the act of compiling was merely rote or clerical in nature, with no meaningful exercise of judgment or intellect, the originality standard will not be satisfied.

  Example: In *West Publishing Co. v. Mead Data Central, Inc.*, 799 F.2d 1219 (8th Cir. 1986), *cert. denied*, 479 U.S. 1070 (1987), the court found that West's selection, coordination, and arrangement of case opinions in its case reporters constituted copyrightable expression because some creative intellectual effort was involved in categorizing the cases by subject matter (in the case of specialty reporters), court, and circuit. By contrast, in *Feist Publications, Inc. v. Rural Telephone Service Co., Inc.*, 499 U.S. 340 (1991), discussed on p. 107, *supra*, the Supreme Court found that the selection of all the local telephone subscribers' names, towns, and phone numbers to include in telephone directory white pages, arranged alphabetically by the subscriber's last name, was insufficiently original to satisfy the constitutionally mandated originality standard. (Note that *West* was decided before *Feist*. It is possible that the *West* case would be decided differently today.)

4. **Unauthorized use of copyrighted material:** Copyright Act §103 specifies that a compilation copyright will not extend to any portion of a compilation that incorporates a copyrighted work without the copyright owner's authorization.

H. **Derivative works:** Copyright Act §103 also provides that derivative works are within the subject matter of copyright. Section 101 defines a derivative work as "a work based upon one or more preexisting works, such as a translation, musical arrangement, dramatization, fictionalization, motion picture version, sound recording, art reproduction, abridgment, condensation, or any other form in which a work may be recast, transformed, or adapted." A work to which editorial revisions, annotations, elaborations, or other modifications have been made also qualifies as a "derivative work." As in the case of compilations, copyright protection extends only to the original material contributed by the derivative author, not to the preexisting material that he has adapted. Likewise, as in the case of compilations, copyright does not extend to portions of a derivative work in which preexisting material has been used unlawfully.

1. **Originality and derivative works:** A number of courts have held that in order to be copyrightable, a derivative work must *contain some substantial, not merely trivial, variation* from the underlying work on which the derivative work is based. *L. Batlin & Son v. Snyder*, 536 F.2d 486 (2d Cir. 1976), *cert. denied*, 429 U.S. 857 (1976). This standard of originality is higher than the standard for works that were not based on earlier works.

   Example: In the *Batlin* case, the plaintiff made a plastic version of a public domain piggy bank shaped like Uncle Sam. The original Uncle Sam bank was made of cast iron. Apart from the transfer from iron to plastic, the plaintiff's bank varied from the original in the following ways: it was shorter (in order to fit into the required price range and to accommodate the contemplated materials); Uncle Sam's umbrella was part of the one-piece mold, rather than separate; the eagle on the base of the bank held leaves instead of arrows (leaves reproduced better than arrows in plastic); and the shape of Uncle Sam's carpet bag was changed. The court found the changes to be too trivial to support a derivative work copyright. The court reasoned that the mere translation from one medium to another, in itself, was a trivial variation, and it suggested that the other changes were also trivial, in part because they were dictated by functional considerations like cost and the material being used.

2. **Concern about the effect of derivative work copyrights:** One of the primary reasons courts have given for adopting the higher "substantial variation" standard of originality is concern that if X were permitted to obtain a copyright on a derivative work that represented only a slight variation from the underlying work, then it would be hard to determine whether Y, who based his own derivative work on the same underlying work, copied from the underlying work or from X. This would give X the means to threaten or bring harassing infringement litigation against Y, and would deter Y and others like him from undertaking to make derivative works at all. A related concern is that X's attempts to enforce his copyright may interfere unduly with exploitation of the copyright in the underlying work. Based on the latter concern, the Court of Appeals for the Ninth Circuit has adopted a *"two-prong" test* for copyrightability of derivative works. First, the derivative work must have original aspects that are "more than trivial." Second, it must appear that granting copyright in the derivative work will not affect the copyright protection in the underlying work. *Entertainment Research Group, Inc. v. Genesis Creative Group, Inc.*, 122 F.3d 1211 (9th Cir. 1997), *cert. denied*, 523 U.S. 1021.

Example: The derivative works at issue in *Entertainment Research Group* were inflatable three-dimensional costumes, based on the copyrighted two-dimensional cartoon character mascots of various businesses, such as the Pillsbury Dough Boy and the Toys "R" Us Giraffe. In applying the first prong of its test, the Ninth Circuit found that these costumes did not contain a "more than trivial" variation from the original cartoon characters, because the costumes were "instantly identifiable as embodiments of the underlying copyrighted characters in yet another form." Moreover, many of the differences were dictated by functional considerations, and thus could not be protected due to the separability requirement for pictorial, graphic, and sculptural features of useful articles. The court found that the second prong was not satisfied either, because granting plaintiff a copyright in its costumes would "have the practical effect of providing [it] with a *de facto* monopoly on all inflatable costumes depicting the copyrighted characters." Any future licensee that the owners of copyright in the characters hired to manufacture costumes depicting the characters would be deterred by the potential of infringement litigation brought by the plaintiff.

I. **Government works as copyrightable subject matter:** For purposes of evaluating the copyrightability of government works, it is helpful to divide them into two categories: federal and state/local.

1. **No copyright for works of the U.S. government:** Copyright Act §105 provides that copyright is not available for any work of the U.S. government. Section 101 defines a work of the U.S. government as "a work prepared by an officer or employee of the U.S. government as part of that person's official duties." The concept of "government works" is similar to the concept of "works for hire," which will be discussed *infra*, at pp. 173-175.

a. **Works created for the U.S. government by independent contractors:** The legislative history of §105 provides that works created by independent contractors (persons other than government employees, who contract to do specific jobs for the government) may or may not be copyrighted, depending upon the circumstances. Generally, when a government agency commissions a routine work for its own use, merely as an alternative to having one of its own employees or officers create it, then measures should be taken to prevent the creator from claiming copyright in it. This may be done by promulgating narrowly drawn statutes or agency regulations specifying that there will be no copyright in such works, or by requiring independent contractors to waive their right to a copyright as a term of their work contract with the government. However, in some cases the government may find that the additional incentive of a copyright is needed in order to induce the independent contractor to create the work. In such cases, the government should not interfere with the independent contractor's ability to assert copyright in the work.

b. **Copyrights transferred to the U.S. government:** Section 105 clarifies that the U.S. government is not precluded from receiving and holding copyrights *transferred to it* by third parties.

2. **Copyright in state and local government works:** The Copyright Act contains no provision prohibiting state or local government entities from claiming copyright in works created by their officials or employees. However, case law indicates that certain kinds of state and local government works, including judicial opinions, statutes, city ordinances, and other government laws and regulations, generally may not be copyrighted. Due process requires that members of the public have access to (and the ability to copy) those things that have the force and effect of law and carry sanctions for noncompliance. Such works may be viewed as "inherently" in the public domain.

a. **Privately drafted model codes:** In *Veeck v. Southern Building Code Congress International, Inc.*, 293 F.3d 791 (5th Cir.), *cert. denied*, 537 U.S. 1043 (2002), the Court of Appeals for the Fifth Circuit considered, *en banc*, whether a model code-writing organization could prevent a web site operator from posting the text of a model code, when it identified the code only as the building code of a city that had enacted the model code as law. The court held that *as law*, the model code entered the public domain and was no longer subject to the drafter's control under copyright law. However, as a model code, the drafter's work retained its protected status. Thus, the web site operator was free to publish the model code as the law of the particular municipality even if he copied from the plaintiff's publication. The court also reasoned that when the model building code at issue was enacted into law it became fact. Moreover, because there was only one way to express the meaning of the building code, the "idea" embodied in the law merged with the model code's expression.

III. THE RIGHTS AFFORDED BY COPYRIGHT LAW

A. **The exclusive economic rights of copyright:** Copyright Act §106 sets forth the exclusive economic rights conferred by copyright. It provides that the *copyright owner* (who may be either the author or the author's transferee) has the exclusive right to do or authorize the following:

- Reproduce the copyrighted work;

- Prepare derivative works based upon the copyrighted work (this is sometimes called the right *to adapt* the copyrighted work);

- Distribute copies or phonorecords of the copyrighted work to the public;

- Publicly perform the work (this right does not apply to pictorial, graphic and sculptural works, architectural works, or sound recordings);

- Publicly display the work (this right does not apply to architectural works or sound recordings); and

- In the case of sound recordings, to perform the copyrighted work publicly by means of a digital audio transmission.

B. **Moral rights in works of visual art:** Copyright Act §106A provides that in the case of works of visual art (as defined in §101), the *author* (who may or may not be the present owner of the copyright) enjoys the "moral rights" of attribution and integrity. More specifically, the author has the rights:

- To claim authorship in the work;

- To prevent use of her name as the author of any work she did not create;

- To prevent the use of her name as the author of her work if the work has been distorted, mutilated, or otherwise modified, so that the use would be prejudicial to her honor or reputation;

- To prevent any intentional distortion, mutilation, or other modification of her work which would be prejudicial to her honor or reputation; and

- To prevent any intentional or grossly negligent destruction of the work, if the work is of recognized stature.

C. **Ownership of rights:** The means of ascertaining the author of a work (and thus the initial owner of the copyright) will be discussed at a later point. See pp. 172-177, *infra*. It is useful at this point to bear in mind that the various economic rights conferred by a copyright may be transferred altogether or individually. Whenever an exclusive right is transferred, the transferee becomes a "copyright owner." (Copyright Act §201.) Thus, there may be a number of "owners" of copyright in the same work. Each owner of an exclusive right has the right to bring suit in his own capacity to enforce the right he owns against others. The materials immediately following examine each of the exclusive economic rights of copyright, and then the moral rights.

IV. THE "COPYRIGHTED WORK"

In the case of *all* the exclusive rights, it must appear that the work the defendant reproduced, adapted, distributed, publicly performed, or publicly displayed *was the copyrighted work*. In order for this to be the case, it must appear that the defendant's work: (1) was copied from the plaintiff's work; and (2) is "substantially similar" to the plaintiff's copyrightable expression.

A. **The *Arnstein* copying and unlawful appropriation test:** The Court of Appeals for the Second Circuit, in *Arnstein v. Porter*, 154 F.2d 464 (2d Cir. 1946), *cert. denied*, 330 U.S. 851 (1947), provided the standard formula for making this determination. In that case (involving a claim that the defendant, Cole Porter, had infringed plaintiff's right to reproduce the songs plaintiff created), the court stated the rule as follows: First, it must be shown that the defendant copied from the copyrighted work. Second, it must be shown that the copying amounted to an improper appropriation (gave rise to "substantial similarity" of copyrighted expression).

1. **Copying:** Copying may be demonstrated in three ways: (1) direct evidence; (2) circumstantial evidence that the defendant had access to the work and that the defendant's work is similar to the plaintiff's; or (3) circumstantial evidence that the defendant's work is strikingly similar to the plaintiff's work. It makes no difference, for purposes of infringement liability, whether the defendant intended to copy or whether the defendant's copying was entirely subconscious and unintentional.

    a. **Direct evidence of copying:** If an eyewitness saw the defendant copy, or the defendant admits that he copied, this will constitute direct evidence of copying.

    b. **Access plus similarity:** The most common method of proving copying is to show that the defendant had *access* to the plaintiff's copyrighted work and that the parties' works are sufficiently *similar* to support an inference of copying.

        i. **Access:** Access will be proved if the plaintiff's copyrighted work was available to the public generally (e.g., it was available in libraries or stores, or broadcast over television or radio), or if it was specifically available to the defendant (e.g., because of his employment, his relationship with the plaintiff or his relationship with someone who had a copy of plaintiff's work), so that the defendant had a reasonable opportunity to copy it.

        ii. **Similarities:** If the defendant's work has similarities to the plaintiff's work that have no apparent explanation apart from copying, this, along with proof of access, will generally constitute sufficient circumstantial evidence of copying. Consequently, the burden will shift to the defendant to prove independent creation or to show that the parties both copied from a common source. For the purposes of this test of similarity (and for purposes of determining "striking similarity," described directly below), *all similarities* between the parties' works may be considered, regardless of whether the similarities involve copyrightable expression or uncopyrightable elements, such as facts or ideas. Expert testimony may be used in identifying and evaluating the similarities.

        iii. **Striking similarity:** Occasionally, the similarity between the plaintiff's and defendant's works is so striking that the *similarity alone* may give rise to an inference of copying, even without specific evidence of access. This showing will generally be possible only when the plaintiff's work is highly creative and unique, so that it is unlikely that the defendant could have independently created or copied from another source.

2. **Unlawful appropriation:** If copying is found, it must be determined whether the copying amounted to an unlawful appropriation. Copying uncopyrightable elements of a work does not constitute infringement. In order to prevail in a copyright infringement claim, a copyright owner must demonstrate that the defendant took copyrightable expression, and that the audience for whom his work was intended would perceive substantial similarities between the defendant's work and the plaintiff's protected expression. The *Arnstein* "substantial similarity"

test focuses on the *subjective response of the average member of the intended audience* and is sometimes called the "audience" test. The question is whether the average listener or viewer would recognize the alleged copy as having been appropriated from the copyrighted work. Generally, expert evidence is not admissible in assessing substantial similarity. It has been admitted, however, when the work is too technical for the fact finder to comprehend without assistance, or to assist the finder of fact to understand the perspective of members of the intended audience.

   a. **The intended audience:** In most cases, the average member of the intended audience is the average lay observer. However, sometimes the intended audience is more narrow, and possesses a perspective or specialized expertise that the average lay observer would lack. This might be true, for example, when the allegedly infringed work is a child's toy or a highly technical computer program. In such cases, the substantial similarity determination must be made from the perspective of a child, or a purchaser of such technical computer programs, respectively.

   b. **Copyrightable vs. uncopyrightable elements:** Unlawful appropriation turns on a finding of substantial similarity between the defendant's work and the copyrighted work's *protectible expression*. Similarities in uncopyrightable elements cannot support a finding of unlawful appropriation. However, an author's selection, coordination, and arrangement of uncopyrightable elements *can* constitute copyrightable expression. To ensure that the requisite substantial similarity arises from protected expression, the finder of fact may need to consider similarities in uncopyrightable elements for the limited purpose of determining whether the defendant has unlawfully appropriated the plaintiff's protected selection, coordination, or arrangement expression. Making such distinctions between expression, uncopyrightable elements, and the selection and arrangement of uncopyrightable elements may be difficult for the fact finder, and indeed, the *Arnstein* audience test is not conducive to doing so—under the *Arnstein* standard, the substantial similarity evaluation is based on the *subjective, overall reaction* of intended viewers or listeners, without the benefit of analytical dissection of the parties' works. As will be discussed later, modern cases tend to employ the *Arnstein* audience test in cases involving works that primarily consist of expression, and employ a more objective standard, which permits some level of dissection of elements, in the case of works that incorporate a substantial number of uncopyrightable elements.

   c. **Similarities in expression dictated by idea:** As discussed earlier at pp. 110-111, expression that is dictated by the underlying idea merges with the idea and is not protectible. Thus, in determining whether the defendant has unlawfully appropriated the plaintiff's protectible expression, the court must consider whether asserted similarities in expression were necessitated by the fact that the defendant was expressing the same idea as the plaintiff. If so, the similarities should be ignored. Basing infringement liability on such similarities would give the plaintiff an unwarranted *de facto* monopoly in the idea.

   Example: In *Herbert Rosenthal Jewelry Corp. v. Kalpakian*, 446 F.2d 738 (9th Cir. 1971), the plaintiff and defendant both had produced jeweled bee pins. The plaintiff's bee had been mass marketed, and the two bees were highly similar, providing circumstantial evidence of copying. However, in assessing substantial similarity/unlawful appropriation, the court found that the defendant could not have implemented the same idea as the plaintiff—a jeweled bee pin—without having the similarities that he did. Thus, the court found that the plaintiff's copyright was not infringed, because the similarities between the pins were all due to uncopyrightable elements.

d. **The existence of differences is irrelevant:** The fact that the defendant's allegedly infringing work contains expression that the plaintiff's does not, or varies from the plaintiff's in some aspects, does not in itself excuse the defendant from infringement liability. As one court has said, "No plagiarist can be excused by showing how much of his work he did not pirate." The inquiry is whether there are substantial similarities in copyrightable expression. Substantial similarity, and copyright infringement, may be found even though only a relatively small portion of the defendant's work was taken from the plaintiff.

e. **Literal vs. nonliteral similarity:** In the case of literary, dramatic, and some audiovisual works, in particular, there are two types of "similarity" that may lead to a finding of infringement: (1) *literal* similarity; and (2) *nonliteral* similarity. Either or both types of similarity may exist in a given case of infringement.

   i. **Literal similarity:** In literal infringement cases, the defendant has duplicated or paraphrased the plaintiff's literal expression—the actual language the plaintiff used to express her ideas. Substantial similarity may be gauged from both a qualitative and a quantitative standpoint. For example, even if the defendant only copied a small portion—just a paragraph or several sentences or phrases from a long article or book—he may still be found to have infringed, if the material copied was *qualitatively* an important part of the plaintiff's work that would be readily recognized as taken from the plaintiff's copyrighted work.

   ii. **Nonliteral similarity:** Nonliteral similarity exists when the defendant does not engage in *verbatim*, or literal copying of the plaintiff's language, but rather copies the fundamental essence or structure of the plaintiff's work. For example, in the case of a novel, the defendant adopts a similar plot, similar characters, and settings, but does not copy or paraphrase any of the plaintiff's actual language. The main problem in nonliteral infringement cases is determining how much of the copied material is protectible expression and how much of it is unprotectible idea. As a general matter, the more detail the defendant copied, the more likely it is that he took copyrightable expression.

   Example: Margaret Mitchell's novel, *Gone with the Wind,* involves, at its most general level, a romance between two members of southern upper-class white society during and after the Civil War. That could be described as the overall *idea* of the novel. Other works might have the same underlying idea, but would not for that reason be found to infringe. However, Mitchell's particular selection and combination of characters, events, and other plot devices are the way in which she expressed the basic idea. A work that copied a significant number of *these things* might be found to infringe. These precise character and plot details are not necessary in order to express the underlying idea of a romance between two members of southern upper-class white society during and after the Civil War, and thus go beyond the idea of *Gone with the Wind* and constitute protected expression of the idea.

   iii. **The abstractions test:** In *Nichols v. Universal Pictures Corp.*, 45 F.2d 119 (2d Cir. 1930), Judge Learned Hand enunciated the famous "abstractions" test for determining when protected expression has been copied in cases involving alleged nonliteral infringement. Judge Hand stated:

> Upon any work ... a great number of patterns of increasing generality will fit equally well, as more and more of the incident is left out. The last may perhaps be no more than the most general statement of what the [work] is about, and at times might consist only of its title; but there is a point in this series of abstractions where they are no longer protected, since otherwise the [author] could prevent the use of his "ideas," to which, apart from their expression, his property is never extended.

Under this approach, one should envision repeated descriptions of the plot of the work, each generalizing more of the detail than the last, to the point that the final description is the most basic and general description possible. At some point in this progression one must designate the boundary between the idea of the story and the author's means of expressing the idea. The more detail in the description, the more likely the description falls on the "expression" side of the line. Whether or not the defendant is liable for infringement will depend on whether he took a significant amount of the material on the "expression" side of the line.

Example: Applying Judge Hand's abstraction test to *Gone with the Wind*, if the only similarity between a defendant's and Mitchell's work was that both concerned a romance between two members of southern upper-class white society during and after the Civil War, no infringement would be found. But if, in addition, the defendant's story centered on a hot-tempered, materialistic, spoiled southern belle: (1) who had two sisters and a father who was killed while jumping his horse over a fence; (2) who was married three times but remained in love with an idealistic dreamer who was married to a generous, kindly woman who was incapable of having children; (3) whose third husband was a playboy who made his fortune running blockades during the war and ultimately left her, causing her to realize that she loved only him—then infringement might be found. At that point, using Judge Hand's terminology, the overlapping levels of abstraction are at the *level of expression*, rather than idea.

B. **The Ninth Circuit's variation on the *Arnstein* approach to finding "unlawful appropriation":** The Court of Appeals for the Ninth Circuit has adopted its own approach to determining whether a defendant's copying amounts to an unlawful appropriation. Under this approach, originally set forth in *Sid & Marty Krofft Television Prods., Inc. v. McDonald's Corp.*, 562 F.2d 1157 (9th Cir. 1977), the inquiry is divided into two parts—an "extrinsic" test and an "intrinsic" test. Both tests must be satisfied before an unlawful appropriation, and thus infringement, can be found.

1. **An evolving standard:** As initially formulated in the *Krofft* decision, the extrinsic test required that the *ideas* underlying the parties' works be substantially similar. In this part of the inquiry, analytic dissection and expert testimony were appropriate. Assuming that the *ideas* were substantially similar, the intrinsic test then measured substantial similarity of *expression* based on the audience test—the subjective, overall response of the ordinary listener or observer, without analytic dissection or expert testimony. Over the years, however, the nature of the *extrinsic* test has evolved—the Ninth Circuit now defines it as an *objective* evaluation of concrete elements of expression with the aid of expert testimony and analytic dissection. Thus, the Ninth Circuit (and some other jurisdictions that have followed the Ninth Circuit's lead) now imposes both an *objective* (analytical) and a *subjective* ("overall concept and feel") evaluation of substantial similarity, and requires that the plaintiff demonstrate substantial similarity under *both* tests in order to prevail.

C. **Other approaches to evaluating unlawful appropriation:** As noted earlier, the law requires that the defendant's work be "substantially similar" to the plaintiff's *copyrighted expression* in order to infringe. Courts seeking to evaluate this question have faced a dilemma: If they instruct the finder of fact to subjectively evaluate the overall "feel" of the works without dissection (as is done under the *Arnstein* audience test), then there is a risk of overprotection—the jury may find substantial similarity based on similarities of uncopyrightable elements. On the other hand, if the courts ask the finder of fact to dissect the works and consider only the copyrightable elements, there is a risk of underprotection—the finder of fact may ignore selection and arrangement of uncopyrightable elements, which is protectable expression. While the "overall subjective response of the ordinary viewer or listener" standard of *Arnstein* represents the *traditional* approach to determining unlawful appropriation, today courts often apply a more objective, analytical standard when faced with works that incorporate a significant number of uncopyrightable elements. The three most common of these are described below.

1. **The "abstraction, filtration, comparison" standard:** We have already reviewed the "abstraction, filtration, comparison" standard, which is now routinely applied in the case of alleged software infringement. See pp. 114-115, *supra*. Some jurisdictions have extended this standard to cases involving subject matter other than software. This approach uses analytical dissection and expert testimony to identify and filter out all the uncopyrightable elements on each level of abstraction, and then compares only the remaining copyrightable expression.

2. **The "more discerning" standard:** The Second Circuit (which is the source of both the *Arnstein* and *Altai* decisions) applies what it calls a "more discerning" standard when comparing works (other than software) containing significant quantities of unprotectible elements. According to the court, one must extract the unprotectible elements from consideration and ask whether the protectible elements, standing alone, are substantially similar. At the same time, the Second Circuit rejects use of the kind of formal dissection and filtration it employs in the abstraction, filtration, comparison approach, arguing that the finder of fact must still examine the works' "total concept and feel" in the course of its evaluation, as in *Arnstein*.

3. **The "thin copyright" standard:** Particularly in cases involving software, factual databases, or other highly utilitarian or fact-based works, some jurisdictions have stressed the "thin" status of the copyright for such works, and have required that the plaintiff demonstrate more than "substantial similarity," but rather, "virtual identicality" or a "bodily appropriation of copyrighted expression."

V. THE EXCLUSIVE RIGHT TO REPRODUCE THE WORK

The owner of the exclusive right to reproduce a work may make her own copies or phonorecords of the work and prevent others from doing so without her permission. However, this right extends only to the making of material copies or phonorecords. Merely reading a work aloud, or in the case of choreography, dancing it, would not constitute reproduction because no material copy or phonorecord is produced. (It might constitute a public performance, which would infringe a different exclusive right than the right to reproduce.)

A. **The act of reproduction:** Reproduction entails "fixing" a substantial portion of the plaintiff's work in a "copy." Note that Copyright Act §101 defines a "copy" as a material object "in which a work is fixed." A work is "fixed" in a copy "when its embodiment . . . is sufficiently permanent or stable to permit it to be perceived, reproduced or otherwise communicated for a period of more than transitory duration." As a general matter, the fixation may duplicate the copyrighted work exactly, or simply imitate it.

1. **"Reproduction" in the random access memory of a computer:** In *MAI Systems Corp. v. Peak Computer, Inc.*, 991 F.2d 511 (9th Cir. 1993), *cert. dismissed*, 510 U.S. 1033 (1994), the Court of Appeals for the Ninth Circuit held that loading software into a computer's random access memory (RAM) created a "copy," and thus a potentially infringing "reproduction" for purposes of the Copyright Act. The court reasoned that loading the program into RAM creates a material "copy" within the meaning of the Copyright Act because it duplicates the program in a material object in a manner that is sufficiently permanent or stable to permit the program to be perceived for more than a transitory duration. (The program can be perceived for as long as the computer is turned on and the user does not remove it. A program potentially could be left in RAM for a very long time.) A number of other jurisdictions have subsequently followed the *MAI* reasoning.

    a. **The implications of the *MAI* decision:** The "ramifications" of *MAI* are tremendous because to view any material on a computer one must load it into RAM, and thus "reproduce" it under the Ninth Circuit's reasoning. For persons using computers, the act of reading a digitized work constitutes a potentially infringing reproduction, even if the person makes no print copy, and never saves the material to her hard disc. Indeed, even turning the computer on constitutes a "reproduction" of the computer's copyrighted operating system software, because it is automatically loaded into RAM whenever the computer is activated. In the context of the Internet, a "reproduction" is made whenever a file is uploaded from a user's computer to a web page, whenever a digitized file is downloaded from a web site, or whenever a file is transferred from one computer network user to another.

    b. **Possible limitation on reproduction liability for automatic Internet copying:** Some courts have limited the reach of the *M.A.I.* decision somewhat in the case of Internet service providers whose computers automatically reproduce materials posted by Internet users. For example, in *CoStar Group, Inc. v. Loopnet, Inc.*, 373 F.3d 544 (4th Cir. 2004), the defendant operated a web site on which subscribers could post materials. Whenever materials were posted, the defendant's computer system automatically made digital copies of them. Some subscribers posted infringing photographs (which were automatically duplicated), and the issue was whether the defendant was directly liable for infringing the photograph copyright owners' reproduction rights. The court held that it was not. The Fourth Circuit acknowledged that copyright is a strict liability statute, but held that there must be "*some element of volition or causation* which is lacking where a defendant's system is merely used to make a copy by a third party." (Emphasis added.) The Fourth Circuit also suggested that Internet service providers may not actually make "copies," as defined in Copyright Act §101 because the duplicates their systems make are merely temporary by design, and are not capable of being perceived for more than a transitory duration. According to the court, the §101 requirement that copies be "of more than transitory duration" should be understood as both qualitative and quantitative in character. It is quantitative insofar as it describes the period during which the copy endures, and quantitative insofar as it describes the *status* of the transaction. If the copying function serves the computer or its owner (as happens, for example, when a computer automatically downloads operating system software in order to function), the copy is of more than transitory duration. However, if the computer merely copies a subscriber's infringing material and transmits it to another at the instigation of the subscriber, and the computer operator is indifferent to the content of the transmission, the automatic duplicate it is not "of more than transitory duration."

B. **Limitations on the exclusive right to reproduce—sound recordings:** Copyright Act §114 limits the scope of the sound recording copyright owner's exclusive right to reproduce his work. Pursuant to §114, the sound recording copyright only protects the copyright owner against the making of copies or phonorecords that directly or indirectly recapture the *actual sounds fixed in the copyrighted recording*. An independently recorded imitation, no matter how similar, is not an infringement. Note that this is a very substantial limitation. If one were to place an equivalent limitation on the rights of the owner of copyright in a book, the owner would be able to prohibit photocopying of the book, but would not be able to prohibit others from making their own word-for-word transcription on a personal computer or typewriter. However, no such limitation is placed on the rights of owners of copyright in books or any other works besides sound recordings.

Example: Elvis Presley makes an authorized sound recording of "Mary Had a Little Lamb," and obtains copyright in the recording. X, an Elvis impersonator, makes and sells a recording that sounds exactly like Elvis's recording. Even Elvis's most devoted fans cannot tell the difference. X is not liable for infringement of Elvis's sound recording copyright. Only if X mechanically recaptured sounds from the Elvis recording could he be liable. (Note that Elvis or his successors in interest might have a claim under the law of passing off (*infra*, Chapters 6 and 7) or under the state right of publicity (*infra*, Chapter 8).)

1. **Digital sampling:** When a musician sound samples he generally mechanically recaptures the actual sounds recorded on the sound recording and thus satisfies the §114 prerequisite for infringing the reproduction right. However, there has been significant debate about whether the act of sampling alone gives rise to liability, or whether the sound recording copyright owner must also demonstrate (as in all other infringement claims) that the defendant's resulting recording is "substantially similar" to the plaintiff's sampled recording. Note that samplers often mix sampled sounds with other sounds or alter them significantly by changing the speed, deleting certain frequencies or tones, or introducing reverberations or echoes so that the sampled sounds may no longer be recognizable as coming from the plaintiff's copyrighted sound recording. In *Bridgeport Music, Inc. v. Dimension Films*, 410 F.3d 792 (6th Cir. 2005), the Court of Appeals for the Sixth Circuit held that while the owner of copyright in a sampled *musical composition* must demonstrate substantial similarity, the owner of copyright in a sampled *sound recording* must only demonstrate the act of unauthorized digital sampling, in itself, in order to recover for infringing reproduction. The fact that the sampled sounds are *de minimis* and unrecognizable is irrelevant. The court justified this strained construction of the statutory language on the ground that a rule requiring all samplers to obtain a license would be easy and efficient to enforce, that the market would control license prices (the cost of licenses should not exceed the cost of independent fixation), and that the taking in the case of sampled sound recordings was "physical" rather than "intellectual." It is not clear whether other jurisdictions will follow the Sixth Circuit's lead on this issue.

Example: Elvis makes an authorized sound recording of "Mary Had a Little Lamb," and obtains copyright in the recording. Y, a rap singer, samples some sounds directly from the Elvis recording and includes them in his own recording, but changes them—changes the speed, adds echoes, deletes certain frequencies or tones—so that the rap recording sounds very different from the Elvis original. According to the *Bridgeport* decision, Y is liable for infringement simply because he mechanically recaptured sounds from the Elvis recording. It is irrelevant that the average listener would not find his recording substantially similar to Elvis's copyrighted sound recording.

C. **Exception to the exclusive right to reproduce—computer programs:** Copyright Act §117 provides three exceptions to the copyright owner's exclusive right to reproduce her copyrighted computer program.

1. **First exception—reproduction as an essential step in using:** Section 117 provides that the lawful owner of a copy of a copyrighted program will not be liable for infringement if he reproduces the program as an *essential step in* using it in a computer. So, for example, because it generally is necessary for the computer to copy part or all of the program into its random access memory (RAM) banks in order to use it, causing the computer to do so will not constitute infringement.

2. **Second exception—reproduction for archival purposes:** Section 117 permits the lawful owner of a copy of a copyrighted program to reproduce it for archival (back-up) purposes, as long as he destroys the reproduction once his continued possession of a program ceases to be lawful. (For example, once he transfers title to the original copy.)

3. **Third exception—reproductions made in the course of computer repair:** Under an amendment enacted in 1998, Congress provided that the owner or lessee of a computer may make or authorize others to make a copy of a computer program if:

    1. the copy is made solely by virtue of activating the computer;
    2. the computer lawfully contains an authorized copy of the program;
    3. the only purpose of making the copy is maintenance or repair of the computer; and
    4. the new copy is destroyed as soon as the maintenance or repair is completed.

    As noted in the prior section, operating system programs are loaded automatically when a computer is activated. Since the computer must be turned on in order to be serviced, under the *MAI* decision, servicing could constitute an infringing "reproduction" of the copyrighted programs if unauthorized by the copyright owner. This amendment was prompted by the outcome of the *MAI* case, in which the owner of copyright in operating system software licensed the software to users with a restrictive provision that the software could not be used by third parties. It then sued for infringement when the licensees hired third parties to service their computers. In this manner, the copyright owner was able to use its copyright in the operating system software to obtain a monopoly in servicing computers programmed with its software. The amendment was intended to prevent this.

4. **The limitation to "owners" of lawful copies of programs:** It should be noted that the first two §117 exceptions to liability are limited to the "owner" of a copy of a copyrighted program. Today most sellers of computer programs purport not to transfer title to their purchasers, but merely to "license" their programs' use. In the *MAI* case, discussed *supra*, the Ninth Circuit held that a licensee of software did not qualify as an "owner" for purposes of §117, so that the first two §117 exceptions did not apply to it. (In that case, the license authorized the licensee to reproduce the operating system programs in the course of its own internal information processing, but did not allow the use or copying of the software by third parties. Thus, when the licensee had its computers serviced by a third party, rather than by the copyright owner, the reproduction of the software in the course of servicing was not sheltered under either §117 or the license and constituted infringement.)

a. **Distinguishing owners from licensees:** In a more recent decision, the Court of Appeals for the Federal Circuit rejected the Ninth Circuit's characterization of all software licensees as non-owners, but held that the particular licensee in the case before it would not qualify as an "owner" for purposes of §117. Relevant considerations in deciding whether a rightful possessor, or licensee, should be deemed an "owner" for purposes of §117 include:

1. whether the possessor obtained its rights in the software through a single payment;
2. whether its rightful possession is perpetual; and
3. whether its right to use the software under license is heavily encumbered by restrictions that are inconsistent with the status of an owner (such as restrictions on transfer of the copy, or use of the software with particular hardware.)

DSC Communications Corp. v. Pulse Communications, Inc., 170 F.3d 1354 (Fed. Cir. 1999). Under this standard, the rightful possessor in *MAI* probably would still not be deemed an owner. Since many software licenses do impose significant restrictions on the licensee's use of the software, the Federal Circuit would probably deem §117 unavailable to many rightful possessors (or licensees) of computer programs.

D. **Exception to the exclusive right to reproduce—pictorial, graphic, and sculptural works:** Copyright Act §113 provides that owners of copyright in pictorial, graphic, and sculptural works portraying useful articles may not assert their copyright to prevent others from reproducing, distributing, or displaying the useful article that is portrayed. So, for example, while a blueprint or photograph of an automobile may be copyrighted as a pictorial or graphic work, building the automobile portrayed in the blueprint or photograph will not constitute an infringement of the right to reproduce or adapt the copyrighted blueprint or photograph. To hold otherwise would give the copyright owner a *de facto* monopoly in uncopyrightable subject matter. In addition, §113 limits the rights of owners of copyright in pictorial, graphic, or sculptural works that are *incorporated into* useful articles: They may not prevent the making or use of pictures or photographs of the useful articles for advertisements, commentaries, or news reports concerning the useful articles.

Example: X creates a teapot with an attractive design (e.g., a shape like a rooster) which is conceptually separable from the teapot, and obtains copyright in the design. X mass produces and sells teapots incorporating the design and Y, a retail merchant, buys a number of them wholesale. Y photographs one of the teapots and publishes the photograph in an advertisement of its wares. Meanwhile, Consumers' Union decides to publish a review of the merits of various teapots available on the market. It makes and publishes a photograph of X's copyrighted teapot in connection with the review. In both cases, §113 authorizes the taking of the photographs, which might otherwise infringe X's exclusive right to reproduce the copyrighted design.

E. **Exception to the exclusive right to reproduce—architectural works:** Copyright Act §120 permits making, distributing, and publicly displaying paintings, photographs, and other pictorial representations of a copyrighted work of architecture, as long as the building in which the work is embodied is located in or is ordinarily visible from a public place. So, for example, scholarly books on architecture, commercially produced postcards, posters, and the like, which depict of buildings incorporating copyrighted works of architecture, will not infringe. Note the disparity that this exception creates between protection of architectural works and protection of sculptural works (such as statues exhibited in a public park), for which no such exception exists.

F. **Exception to the exclusive right to reproduce—libraries and archives:** Copyright Act §108 provides special, limited safe harbors for public libraries, public archives, and their employees, who reproduce and distribute copyrighted works for noncommercial purposes. Subject to various limitations, these entities may reproduce unpublished works in their collection to ensure their preservation and security and to provide copies for other libraries or archives. They may also reproduce published works in their collection when necessary to replace lost, damaged, or stolen copies, if an unused replacement cannot be obtained at a fair price. Section 108 also permits public libraries and archives to reproduce certain kinds of works (excluding musical works, pictorial, graphic and sculptural works, and some kinds of audiovisual works) at the request of library or archive users, if certain conditions are met. A recent amendment permits libraries and archives to reproduce and distribute published works during the last 20 years of their copyright term for purposes of scholarship, research, or preservation, if the work is not being commercially exploited, is not available at a reasonable price, and other conditions are satisfied.

G. **Exception to the exclusive right to reproduce—the ephemeral recordings provisions:** Copyright Act §112 recognizes that broadcasters of programs lawfully containing performances or displays of copyrighted works need to reproduce their programs in the course of business operations, and gives them a narrow privilege to do so under prescribed circumstances. It also permits nonprofit religious organizations to reproduce certain copyrighted religious musical works and sound recordings in order to transmit them in religious broadcasts. In addition, §112 provides special leeway to reproduce certain instructional broadcasts and broadcasts to the handicapped. Copyright Act §118(d) permits public broadcasters to reproduce the programs they make containing published nondramatic musical works and published pictorial, graphic, and sculptural works and distribute them for rebroadcast by other public stations. It also permits nonprofit and government institutions to reproduce the transmissions of such programs for purposes of face-to-face instruction, under certain circumstances.

H. **Exception to the exclusive right to reproduce—home audiotaping:** In 1992, Congress enacted the Audio Home Recording Act (Copyright Act §§1001-1010), which permits noncommercial, or "home," digital and analog audiotaping of copyrighted sound recordings and the copyrighted musical works that are the subject of the sound recordings. The Act also prohibits contributory infringement claims against manufacturers, importers, and distributors of the equipment used to make such audiotapes, but requires manufacturers, importers, and distributors of digital audiotape recorders and blank tapes to pay royalties to designated participants in the music and sound recording business. In addition, the Act requires manufacturers, importers, and distributors of digital audiotaping machines to include serial copy management systems on their machines, to prevent the machines from recording copies from copies.

   1. **MP3 files:** The Court of Appeals for the Ninth Circuit has held that the Audio Home Recording Act does not authorize or exonerate digital copies of sound recordings made on home computers (for example, in the course of swapping MP3 files). According to the Ninth Circuit, a computer is not encompassed in the Act's provisions because it does not satisfy the Act's definition of an "audio home recording device" (the primary purpose of a computer is not to make digital audio copied recordings).

I. **Exception to the exclusive right to reproduce—compulsory licenses to record nondramatic musical works:** Copyright Act §115 provides for a compulsory license (sometimes called the "mechanical license") to make and publicly distribute sound recordings of certain copyrighted *nondramatic musical compositions.* Under this provision, a person wishing to record a copyrighted nondramatic musical work and publicly distribute the recording may do so if:

1. The copyright owner has already made or authorized a recording of the work, which has been distributed to the U.S. public;
2. The prospective licensee's primary purpose is to distribute phonorecords of her recording to the public for private, rather than commercial, use;
3. The prospective licensee serves notice of her intention to take a compulsory license on the copyright owner within a specified time of making and distributing her recording; and
4. The prospective licensee pays royalties to the copyright owner, as provided in §115.

1. **Nonsubject musical works:** The license applies only to nondramatic musical compositions. Examples of dramatic musical works, which are not subject to compulsory licenses, include operas and motion picture sound tracks.

2. **The rights afforded pursuant to a compulsory license:** The §115 compulsory license gives the licensee the right to *reproduce and publicly distribute* the musical composition in a phonorecord. ("Phonorecords" are material objects that record sounds, but not visual images, such as records, tapes, compact discs, and MP3 files.) This is only a right for a license to make its own recording—§115 conveys no right to copy preexisting recordings of the composition. Moreover, the compulsory license does not convey any right to publicly perform the musical composition. A compulsory license permits the licensee to arrange the musical work to the extent necessary to conform to the performers' style or manner of interpretation, but the arrangement may not change the basic melody or fundamental character of the work, and cannot be copyrighted as a derivative work without the consent of the owner of copyright in the musical composition. Recent amendments to §115 clarify that delivery of phonorecords to the public by digital transmission (for example, over the Internet) constitutes distribution to the public for purposes of the compulsory license.

3. **Voluntary licenses:** The §115 compulsory license provisions do not prevent parties from negotiating a *voluntary license* to record a copyrighted musical composition, and usually they do, through the auspices of the Harry Fox Agency, in New York. In practical application the §115 compulsory license provision merely induces musical composition copyright owners (usually music publishers) to license sound recordings voluntarily, and sets a royalty rate that most voluntary licenses will not exceed.

J. **Exception to the exclusive right to reproduce—specialized formats for the visually impaired or otherwise disabled:** In 1996, Congress amended the Copyright Act to permit authorized nonprofit and government organizations to reproduce and/or distribute previously published, nondramatic literary works in specialized formats (Braille, audio, or digital text) exclusively for use by persons who are visually impaired or have other disabilities. These provisions are codified at Copyright Act §121, and like most of the other statutory exceptions, are subject to a number of conditions and limitations.

VI. THE EXCLUSIVE RIGHT TO PREPARE DERIVATIVE WORKS

Copyright includes the exclusive right to prepare derivative works based on the copyrighted work. This right is also known as the exclusive right to *adapt* the copyrighted work. Copyright Act §101 defines a derivative work as "a work based upon one or more preexisting works, such as a translation, musical arrangement, dramatization, fictionalization, motion picture version, sound recording, art reproduction, abridgment, condensation, or any other form in which a work may be recast, transformed, or adapted."

A. **Overlap with the right to reproduce or publicly perform:** In most cases the right to adapt is superfluous because when this right is infringed, one of the other exclusive rights of copyright will also be infringed. For example, a person making an unauthorized screenplay from a novel will simultaneously infringe the right of adaptation and the right of reproduction. Regardless of which right the copyright owner asserts against the adaptor, he will have to prove that the defendant copied from the novel and that the screenplay is substantially similar to the novel's expression. However, the right of adaptation may be the only basis for an infringement claim if a defendant adapts an existing, authorized copy or phonorecord of the work, without reproducing or publicly performing it, or if a defendant has been authorized to reproduce or publicly perform, but not to adapt the work, and nonetheless alters it.

Example: X buys an authorized copy of a book containing Y's copyrighted prints. X cuts the prints out of the book, mounts them onto tiles, covers them with shellac, and offers them for sale as wall decorations or trivets. X has not reproduced the copyrighted prints, but he may have adapted them without authorization. The Ninth Circuit has found such actions to constitute infringement of the right of adaptation. *Mirage Editions, Inc. v. Albuquerque A.R.T. Co.*, 856 F.2d 1341 (9th Cir. 1988), *cert. denied*, 489 U.S. 1018 (1989). However, the Seventh Circuit has held in a case involving similar facts that the minor changes described above do not fall within the Copyright Act's definition of a derivative work, quoted *supra*, and are merely comparable to reframing a picture, which is non-infringing. *Lee v. A.R.T. Co.*, 125 F.3d 580 (7th Cir. 1997).

1. **The relevance of the prerequisites for copyrighting derivative works:** A work that has been based on a preexisting work will not qualify for its own derivative work copyright unless it constitutes a substantial variation from the original work on which it is based. See pp. 125-126, *supra*. The law is unsettled over whether this "substantial variation" requirement should also be applied to determine whether unauthorized alterations to a work are sufficiently substantial to constitute an infringing adaptation.

2. **An additional consideration in determining whether changes to a work should infringe the adaptation right:** In determining whether a defendant's changes to the copyrighted work infringe the plaintiff's adaptation right, courts may consider the economic impact, if any, of the changes. For example, if the defendant merely buys the copyrighted goods, alters them, and resells them in the same market, a court might be less likely to find an infringement of the adaptation right than if the changes enable the defendant to resell the copyrighted goods in a *different market*. In the latter case, the defendant's actions are more likely to interfere with the plaintiff's economic opportunity to expand into a new market.

B. **The adaptation right and computer program enhancements:** The Court of Appeals for the Ninth Circuit considered the relationship of the adaptation right to the making and marketing of software enhancement programs in *Lewis Galoob Toys, Inc. v. Nintendo of America, Inc.*, 964 F.2d 965 (9th Cir.), *cert. denied*, 507 U.S. 985 (1993). In that case, the defendant, Galoob, made and sold a physical device (the game genie) with incorporated software that plugged into Nintendo's copyrighted video game cartridges and game control deck. The game genie allowed the user to change the rules of the copyrighted Nintendo game being played: speed it up, slow it down, go immediately to the more difficult level of play, etc. The game genie did not create a separate copy of the Nintendo game and did not make permanent changes to the original game. It functioned by blocking the value for a single data byte sent by the game cartridge to the central processing unit in the control deck and replacing it with a new value. It did not alter the data that was stored in the game cartridge. The effect lasted only until the player unplugged the game or reset to start a new game. The game genie could only be used when attached to the original Nintendo game. It could not replace it. The issue was whether use of the game genie infringed Nintendo's copyrighted games by permitting users to make unauthorized derivative works. The court found that it did not, reasoning that in order to infringe, the alleged derivative work must *incorporate the underlying work in a concrete or permanent form*. Here, this did not occur: While the game genie's software was fixed in a chip, the altered images on the user's screen, which incorporated portions of the copyrighted game imagery, did not exist in a concrete or permanent form. To find infringement in such a case would suggest that copyright would be infringed whenever a viewer fast-forwarded through a copyrighted movie on a DVD or videotape, or viewed a copyrighted work of art through a kaleidoscope, which would be unacceptable. The *Galoob* Court's ruling suggests that there may be significant leeway for persons in the computer programming business to make and market a broad range of enhancements for existing copyrighted computer programs.

1. **A subsequent limitation on enhancement programs:** In a subsequent "enhancement" case, the Ninth Circuit was more willing to find an infringing adaptation. *Micro Star v. Formgen Inc.*, 154 F.3d 1107 (9th Cir. 1998). In *Formgen*, the defendant published a CD-ROM containing a number of user-created "game levels" for the popular "Duke Nukem 3D" computer game. The copyrighted game software consisted of a game engine, a source art library, and "MAP" files of instructions that told the game engine what images to take from the source art library and how to arrange them to make the screen display for a particular level of play. The MAP files themselves contained none of the copyrighted art images—all the art that appeared on the game screen came from the art library. The user-created game levels which the defendant published were MAP files for new levels of play. The Ninth Circuit found that the audiovisual displays generated when the copyrighted Duke Nukem game was run with the new MAP files constituted infringing derivative works. The court rejected arguments that the defendant's MAP files were just a more advanced version of the Game Genie in *Galoob*. The court explained that in *Galoob*, the audiovisual displays created by the Game Genie were never recorded in any permanent form. By contrast, the audiovisual displays generated by the combination of plaintiff's game and defendant's MAP files existed in a permanent and concrete form in the defendant's MAP files themselves. In *Galoob*, the audiovisual display was defined by the original game cartridge, not by the Game Genie. The data values inserted by the Game Genie did not describe the audiovisual display. In *Formgen*, the audiovisual display was described, in exact detail, by defendant's MAP file. The *Formgen* court stressed that an "exact, down to the last detail, description of an audiovisual display" in a MAP file incorporates the display in a permanent or concrete form, as required by the *Galoob* decision, just as sheet music, which describes in precise detail the way a copyrighted melody should sound, incorporates the melody in a concrete and permanent form. The court also rejected the defendant's arguments that the MAP files contained none of plaintiff's actual copyrighted expression by noting that defendant's MAP files infringed the Duke Nukem story itself, comparing the user-created MAP files to sequels to a book.

2. **The Family Entertainment and Copyright Act of 2005:** In 2005, Congress amended Copyright Act §110 expressly to permit the manufacture, sale, and use of scene-skipping technology that allows home movie viewers to skip or mute objectionable material (such as sex,

profanity or violence) in pre-recorded DVDs, as long as the technology makes no fixed copy of the altered version of the motion picture. It has been suggested that this legislation was superfluous, in light of the *Galoob* decision.

C. **Limitations on the exclusive right to adapt in the case of sound recordings:** Copyright Act §114 provides that the right to adapt a sound recording, like the right to reproduce it, is only infringed when the defendant actually mechanically recaptures, or "lifts," sounds from the copyrighted recording and then alters them or mixes them with other sounds. It is not an infringement of either the right to reproduce or the right to adapt to make a separate sound recording of independently fixed sounds, no matter how the sounds may simulate the plaintiff's copyrighted sound recording.

D. **Exception to the exclusive right to adapt—computer programs:** Copyright Act §117 permits the "owner" of an authorized copy of a computer program to make an adaptation of the program, if it is done as an *essential step in* utilizing the program in a computer or is done for archival purposes. For example, the owner may fix bugs in the software, convert the program from one programming language to another in order to facilitate use in his own computer, or add features to the program that were not present at the time that he acquired it. (Notwithstanding the "essential step" limitation in the §117 language, courts generally have construed the provision liberally to permit owner-made improvements to programs, even when they are not strictly necessary.) However, copies of the altered program may not be transferred to someone else unless the owner of copyright in the program consents, and altered copies must be destroyed as soon as the owner no longer has a lawful right to possess the original program (for example, because he has sold the original copy from which the adapted copy was made). For discussion of §117's limitation to "owners" of copies, see *supra*, p. 136.

E. **Exception to the exclusive right to adapt—architectural works:** Copyright Act §120 permits the owner of a building embodying a copyrighted architectural work to make (or authorize) alterations to the building, and to destroy (or authorize the destruction of) the building, without seeking the permission of the copyright owner.

VII. THE EXCLUSIVE RIGHT TO DISTRIBUTE TO THE PUBLIC

Copyright includes the exclusive right to distribute copies or phonorecords of the work to the public by sale or other transfer of ownership, or by rental, lease, or lending. This right is sometimes also called the exclusive right of publication. Note that the right of public distribution is separate from the right to reproduce the work. For example, if a manufacturer had a license to reproduce (manufacture) copies of a copyrighted work, but the license did not authorize the manufacturer to distribute the copies, the manufacturer's subsequent sale of the copies it manufactured to the public would constitute copyright infringement.

A. **Transfer of a material copy:** Traditionally, violation of the exclusive right to distribute a copyrighted work entailed a person actually transferring a material copy or phonorecord of the work to a member of the public without authorization to do so. However, recent case law suggests that it is no longer always necessary to demonstrate transfer of a material copy. For example, the electronic transmission of a digital file containing a copyrighted work over the Internet will constitute a distribution of the work to the public even though no "physical" or "material" copy is handed over. Likewise, there is precedent to indicate that posting a copyrighted work on a web site (where it is readily accessible to the public) is, in itself, a distribution to the public. Likewise, the Court of Appeals for the Fourth Circuit has found that when a library adds an unlawful copy of a work to its collection, lists the work in its index or cataloging system, and makes the work available to the borrowing or browsing public, it has completed all the steps necessary for distribution to the public, even absent any showing that a member of the public read or borrowed the copy. *Hotaling v. Church of Jesus Christ of Latter-Day Saints*, 118 F.3d 199 (4th Cir. 1997). However, the Ninth Circuit has held that a computer owner does not "distribute" files over the Internet when he or she provides a link to files residing on another web site. The court reasoned that distribution requires an actual dissemination of a copy. Providing HTML instructions that tell an Internet user's browser where to find copyrighted materials on a different web site does not *distribute* copies of the linked materials. It is the linked web site's computer that actually distributes copies by transmitting the materials electronically to the user's computer. *Perfect 10, Inc. v. Amazon.com, Inc.*, 487 F.3d 701 (9th Cir. 2007). The Ninth Circuit distinguished *Hotaling* on the ground that a person who links to another site does not have its own electronic file that it makes available to the public.

B. **The doctrine of first sale:** Copyright Act §109(a) sets forth the doctrine of first sale, which provides that once the copyright owner transfers, or authorizes another to transfer, title to a copy or phonorecord of the copyrighted work to a third party, the third party and his successors in interest are entitled to sell or otherwise dispose of it without obtaining the copyright owner's consent. The reasoning underlying the doctrine of first sale is that once the copyright owner has had the opportunity to profit from the initial sale of the copy, the policy goal of protecting the copyright owner's economic opportunities gives way to the policies disfavoring restrictions on the alienation of property. Thus, the copyright owner has the right to control the *initial* sale or distribution of the copy or phonorecord to the public or one of its members, but once title to that physical embodiment of the work changes hands, copyright law gives the copyright owner no right to control the transferee's subsequent resale or other transfer of title. Nor (with the exceptions noted in subsection 2 below) may he prohibit the new owner from renting or lending the copy or phonorecord to others, or (with the exceptions for works of visual art, described on p. 134, *infra*) from physically destroying it. Courts will, however, enforce contractual restrictions on a purchaser's resale or other disposal of the copy.

1. **The doctrine only applies to lawful copies and phonorecords:** The doctrine of first sale only applies to copies and phonorecords that were "lawfully made" under the Copyright Act. A person who acquires an unlawful copy of a copyrighted work will infringe the copyright in the work by reselling or otherwise distributing it to the public, regardless of whether she knows that the copy was unlawful. For example, if a merchant bought a shipment of music CDs that were made and sold pursuant to a license granted by the copyright owner, the merchant would be free to resell the CDs. If, however, the CDs were not made or sold under the copyright owner's authority, then the merchant's resale of the CDs to consumers would not be protected under the doctrine of first sale and would constitute an infringement of the distribution right, even if the merchant had no notice that the CDs were pirated.

2. **Exception for record and computer program rentals:** Copyright Act §109(b) provides an exception to the doctrine of first sale in the case of record and computer program rentals. Owners of copyright in sound recordings of music, in musical compositions, and in computer programs may prevent persons who acquire copies of the computer programs or phonorecords of the sound recordings from renting them out commercially, or may charge a royalty for the privilege of doing so. Congress deemed this exception to the doctrine of first sale to be necessary because commercial rentals of musical sound recordings and computer programs, which

enable renters to make home copies, may seriously undermine the copyright owners' opportunity to profit through sales of authorized copies and phonorecords, and thus undermine the law's ability to give a financial incentive to create such works.

    a. Exceptions to the "no rental" rule: Subsection 109(b) does not prohibit nonprofit libraries or educational institutions from lending copies or phonorecords for nonprofit purposes. In addition, computer programs embodied in consumer products that cannot readily be copied during ordinary operation of the product are excluded from the rental prohibition. For example, automobiles contain computer programs, but the programs are not readily copied in the course of operating the automobile. Thus, subsection 109(b) does not prohibit rental of automobiles. In addition, there is no prohibition against renting programs for use in limited-purpose video game computers, since these computers generally can't be used to copy the programs.

3. The *droit de suite*: The *droit de suite* is a doctrine recognized in some countries that gives the author of a work of fine art the opportunity to share in the appreciation in value of the work when it is resold by subsequent transferees. Congress has not adopted the *droit de suite* as an exception to the U.S. doctrine of first sale, though it has considered doing so from time to time. The State of California has enacted a *droit de suite* statute that entitles artists to collect 5 percent of the sales price of their works of fine art each time they are resold. Resales for a gross price of less than $1,000 or for less than the price originally paid by the seller are excluded, as are resales made more than 20 years after the artist's death. Cal. Resale Royalties Act, Cal. Civ. Code §986. Some question exists whether this California statute is preempted by federal copyright law.

Example: X, an artist, creates an oil painting, which he sells to Y, a collector, in California for $10,000. Eight years later, Y sells the oil painting to Z, in California, for $15,000. Even though the Copyright Act's first sale doctrine gives X no right to control Y's resale or to collect any share of the profit Y realizes, California's Resale Royalties Act would require Y to pay X 5 percent of the resale price ($750).

4. Imports: Copyright Act §602 provides that importing copies or phonorecords of a work into the United States without the copyright owner's authorization infringes the copyright owner's exclusive right to distribute the work to the public. Courts have experienced some difficulty in determining whether, and to what extent, the first sale doctrine applies to imports. However, in 1998, the Supreme Court provided important guidance on this issue. In *Quality King Distributors, Inc. v. L'anza Research International, Inc.*, 523 U.S. 135 (1998), the Court held that the doctrine of first sale was applicable to limit the copyright owner's rights under the §602 importation provision. The Court reasoned that §602 expressly states that unauthorized importation constitutes an infringement of the §106(3) right of distribution to the public. Section 106, in turn, expressly provides that all the exclusive rights of the copyright owner listed therein are subjected to the exceptions set forth in §§107-120. That includes the doctrine of first sale, which is codified in §109(a). Thus, under the express statutory language of the Copyright Act, the importation right is subject to the doctrine of first sale.

Example: In *L'anza*, the plaintiff manufactured hair care products in the United States, which it sold, with a copyrighted label, both domestically and abroad. It charged a considerably higher price for its products domestically than it charged abroad. The defendant purchased hair care products that plaintiff had sold abroad at low prices, and imported them for resale in the United States without the plaintiff's authorization, and outside of authorized channels. The defendant was able to resell the products at a lower price than plaintiff's standard U.S. price. The Ninth Circuit held that the plaintiff had the right to stop the importation because it infringed its rights in the copyrighted labels. The Supreme Court reversed, holding that the doctrine of first sale prevented the plaintiff from using the copyright laws to shield its discriminatory marketing scheme.

- **a. Copies and phonorecords manufactured outside the United States:** The *L'anza* decision only involved goods manufactured in the United States that were exported and then brought back to the United States. However, the Supreme Court's discussion easily could be read to suggest that the Court would reach the same result in the case of goods made and sold abroad by or under the authorization of the U.S. copyright owner. However, Justice Ginsburg filed a concurring opinion to note that "we do not today resolve cases in which the allegedly infringing imports were manufactured abroad." There is a line of decisions in the lower courts that construes the language "lawfully made under this title" in §109(a) to impose a geographic limitation on the first sale doctrine, limiting its applicability to copies and phonorecords lawfully manufactured *in the United States*. Under this view, even imported copies and phonorecords made and sold by the U.S. copyright owner abroad, or made and sold under the U.S. copyright owner's authority abroad, would be subject to the prohibition against unauthorized imports.

5. **The doctrine of first sale on the Internet:** As noted *supra*, the doctrine of first sale permits an owner of a lawfully made copy or phonorecord of a work, and her successors in title, to further transfer the copy or phonorecord without interference from the copyright owner. However, the doctrine of first sale does not permit the copy owner to make or distribute additional copies. For this reason, the doctrine of first sale may rarely apply to transfers of copyrighted works over the Internet. This is because when one transmits a work to another over the Internet, the recipient always receives a new digital copy, and the sender retains the original. Due to this technicality, it has been argued that the doctrine of first sale should never apply, even if the sender subsequently destroys her retained original.

VIII. THE EXCLUSIVE RIGHT OF PUBLIC PERFORMANCE

Copyright Act §106(4) provides that for most kinds of works of authorship, copyright gives the exclusive right to perform the copyrighted work publicly. The three major categories of works that are excluded from this right are: (1) pictorial, graphic, and sculptural works; (2) sound recordings; and (3) architectural works. Since pictorial, graphic and sculptural works, and architectural works normally would be displayed, rather than performed, the first and third exclusions have little impact. However, §106(4)'s exclusion of sound recordings from the public performance right has meant, for example, that radio and television stations may broadcast copyrighted sound recordings with no obligation to the owner of copyright in the sound recording, even though they must obtain a license from the owners of copyright in the musical works that are recorded. (Organizations such as ASCAP and BMI, that sell blanket licenses to broadcasters to play music over the air (see *infra*), represent the *owners of copyright in the music that is recorded*, not the owners of copyright in the sound recordings of the music). Very recently, Congress amended Copyright Act §§106 and 114 to provide a more limited public performance right in sound recordings. The new §106(6) provides sound recording copyright owners the right "to perform the copyrighted work publicly *by means of a digital audio transmission*." The limited scope of this new right will be discussed further, *infra*.

A. **The meaning of "performance":** Copyright Act §101 says that to perform a work is "to recite, render, play, dance, or act it, either directly or by means of any device or process or, in the case of a motion picture or other audiovisual work, to show its images in any sequence or to make the sounds accompanying it audible." So, if a singer sings a copyrighted song, that constitutes a performance of the song. If a television broadcaster transmits the singer's performance, either live or prerecorded, that constitutes a separate performance of the copyrighted song. If a cable television network picks up the broadcaster's signal over the air and transmits it to its subscribers, that constitutes yet another performance of the copyrighted song. Finally, if a person in her home turns on the television while the singer's rendition is being transmitted, that constitutes yet another separate performance within the meaning of §101. The *initial rendition and any further act by which that rendition is transmitted or communicated or made to recur is a performance.*

B. **When a performance is "public":** Only *public* performances fall within the scope of the copyright owner's control. Copyright Act §101 sets forth four situations in which a performance will be deemed "public":

- if the performance occurs at a place open to the public;

- if the performance occurs at a place in which a substantial number of persons outside the normal circle of a family and its social acquaintances is gathered;

- if the performance is "transmitted" (that is, communicated by a device or process so that images or sounds are received beyond the place from which they are sent), or otherwise communicated to a place open to the public or where a substantial number of persons outside the normal circle of a family and its social acquaintances is gathered; or

- if the performance is transmitted or otherwise communicated to the public by means of any device, regardless of whether the public receives it in the same or separate places or receives it at the same or different times.

1. **A place open to the public:** A "place open to the public" is a place to which the public is free to go. If a performance of a copyrighted work occurs, or a transmission of a copyrighted work is received at a place that is "open to the public," then the performance is a public one, regardless of the number or type of people who actually are present to perceive it. Examples of places open to the public include parks, theatres, stores, restaurants, and night clubs.

    a. **Video rental and viewing establishments:** Commercial establishments that rent videotapes and private viewing rooms to watch them in are "places open to the public," so that any performance that occurs there is a public performance. This is true even though videotapes can only be viewed in a small room, and access to the room is limited to the renter and a small number of his invitees. The courts have reasoned that these establishments are "open to the public" because any member of the public is free to rent a viewing room, even though only one member of the public can do so at a time. *Columbia Pictures Industries, Inc. v. Aveco, Inc.*, 800 F.2d 59 (3d Cir. 1986).

    b. **Hotel rooms:** In contrast to video rental establishments, the Ninth Circuit has held that hotel rooms are not places "open to the public" for purposes of the Copyright Act. Thus, if a hotel guest rents a videotape from the hotel and plays it in his room, there is a performance of the movie, but the performance is not a public performance. *Columbia Pictures Industries, Inc. v. Professional Real Estate Investors, Inc.*, 866 F.2d 278 (9th Cir. 1989). Since hotel rooms are available for rental by any member of the public, it is difficult to reconcile the *Aveco* and *Professional Real Estate* cases. The principal justification for finding that a performance in a hotel room is not public is that, unlike the video viewing rooms at video rental establishments, hotel rooms are generally not rented for the purpose of performing copyright works. Playing a videotape in a hotel room is more like playing it in a private home, which Congress clearly meant to exclude from the copyright owner's control, as long as only the normal circle of a family and its social acquaintances is present.

2. **A place where a substantial number of persons outside of the normal circle of a family and its social acquaintances is gathered:** A performance is also "public" if a substantial segment of the public that extends beyond a family and its normal circle of social acquaintances is on hand to perceive the performance, either live or via transmission. In this case, the size and composition of the audience at the time of the performance is what determines whether the performance is public or not. Even a performance in a private home may be "public" if such a group of people is present. Congress and the courts have not provided any precise numbers to demonstrate how many people must be present. However, the more there are, the more likely it is that the performance is "public."

3. **Transmitted to the public, regardless of whether members of the public can receive the performance at the same place or time:** This fourth definition of a public performance refers primarily to the act of television and radio broadcasting, which may be received by members of the public in their private homes at different times and places. It also applies to hotels that pipe music, television programming, or videos into individual rooms, where they may be received by individuals renting the rooms. Presumably, it also applies to many transmissions of copyrighted works over the Internet, such as transmissions that occur when members of the public download performances of copyrighted works from web sites. Note that under this definition it is not necessary to show that any members of the public actually tuned in and perceived the transmission. It must merely be shown that members of the public could have done so, even though at different times and places.

C. **Performing rights societies:** The public performance right is especially valuable and important to owners of copyright in *musical compositions*. However, musical compositions are performed so frequently in the United States, by broadcast and live public performance, that it would be impossible for a single copyright owner to keep track of performances of his work throughout the country and enforce his rights. Likewise, frequent performers of musical works, such as radio stations, would find it difficult or impossible to negotiate individual licenses to publicly perform all the numerous musical works that they broadcast each day. To deal with this problem, performing rights societies were formed. These societies—most notably the American Society of Composers, Authors and Publishers (ASCAP) and Broadcast Music, Inc. (BMI)—act as agents for numerous individual music copyright owners, issuing licenses and policing rights on their behalf. Because these societies can issue blanket licenses, encompassing numerous copyrighted musical works, they reduce transaction costs. For example, a radio station, upon paying a set royalty to the society, may obtain a blanket license to perform all of the musical works whose copyright owners the society represents, rather than negotiating for individual licenses to perform each work. The society, in turn, distributes the royalties it receives from these licenses to the individual copyright owners. The performing rights societies also monitor the actions of radio and television stations and other commercial establishments to ensure that they are not publicly performing copyrighted musical works without a license, in violation of the rights of the copyright owners the societies represent.

D. The new limited performance rights in sound recordings: As noted earlier, sound recordings traditionally have enjoyed no public performance right. However, in 1995, Congress enacted the Digital Performance Rights in Sound Recordings Act, which amended Copyright Act §§106 and 114 to provide a limited right against public performance of sound recordings "by means of digital audio transmission." The amendments and accompanying legislative history make it clear that Congress intended only to provide a very limited right against digital audio transmissions of sound recordings. The new right does not extend to traditional FCC-regulated over-the-air radio or television broadcasts to the public and most retransmissions of such broadcasts, though it does apply to Internet "webcasts." Nor does it extend to digital transmissions of audiovisual works such as music videos, or to forms of digital performances that do not constitute transmissions, such as playing a sound recording on a compact disc player at a night club. Congress provided the limited new right due to its concern that digital audio transmissions (via cable, the Internet, or satellite) would displace sales of records, tapes, and compact discs, on which sound recording copyright owners depend for their income. It did not find that other types of public performances, such as those by traditional over-the-air broadcasters, posed such a threat.

  1. **Numerous limitations:** The lengthy and highly complex provisions of the Digital Performance Rights in Sound Recordings Act (which were further amended in the Digital Millennium Copyright Act in 1998) provide numerous further exceptions and limitations to the digital transmission performance right. Sound recording copyright owners enjoy the greatest rights against digital transmissions by "interactive services," which are services, such as "audio-on-demand," "pay-per-listen," and "celestial jukebox" services, that enable a member of the public to request and receive digital transmission of a particular sound recording. Interactive services pose the greatest threat to the recording industry, because they enable consumers to hear their choice of sound recording at any time, undercutting their incentive to purchase a phonorecord of the sound recording from the copyright owner. In such cases, the copyright owner may authorize the digital performance under its own terms through voluntarily negotiated licenses, or may refuse to authorize the performance altogether. The copyright owner's rights in the case of many non-interactive digital transmissions are much more limited, amounting essentially to a right of compensation for performances, which are statutorily authorized under complex compulsory licensing provisions. The statute directs that 50 percent of the royalties generated from these compulsory licenses be paid to the sound recording copyright owners, and the other 50 percent be paid to the sound recording performers.

E. Rights in live musical performances: Many countries provide rights in a performer's live performance, frequently through legal doctrines closely related to copyright called "neighboring rights." While the state right of publicity cause of action has provided some protection to performers' live performances in the United States (see RIGHT OF PUBLICITY, Chapter 8), U.S. federal law has not. (Copyright protection has been limited to the *fixed works* that are being performed and to *performances that are themselves fixed* in a copy or phonorecord. An unfixed performance of a work is beyond the scope of copyright.) However, in 1994, pursuant to the TRIPs Agreement, Congress enacted a form of federal "neighboring rights" to protect live *musical* performances. (17 U.S.C. §1101.) These new federal "anti-bootlegging" provisions prohibit unauthorized broadcasts of live musical performances, as well as unauthorized fixation of live performances, and reproduction, distribution, offers to distribute, and "trafficking" in unauthorized fixations. Persons engaging in these activities are subject to civil copyright infringement remedies, and in egregious cases, to criminal penalties. These new remedies are intended to supplement, rather than replace, existing state law protection. (It is important to bear in mind that an unauthorized broadcast or fixation of a live performance may now infringe both copyright in the musical work that is being performed and the new performance rights created by the TRIPs amendments.)

F. **Exception to the exclusive right of public performance—nonprofit performances of nondramatic literary or musical works:** Copyright Act §110(4) enables persons to provide nonprofit performances of copyrighted nondramatic literary and musical works in such settings as school recitals and benefit concerts. Specifically, subsection (4) provides that it will not constitute infringement to publicly perform a nondramatic literary or musical work if the following circumstances exist:

- The performance is made directly to the public. It may not be transmitted.

- There is no purpose of direct or indirect commercial advantage. (For example, this provision would not exempt a restaurant that provided live musical performances for its patrons to enjoy without charge while dining. The performance would be deemed indirectly for commercial advantage, since it undoubtedly contributes to the popularity of the restaurant and thus to its profitability. The restaurant would need to obtain licenses to perform the musical works.)

- The performers, promoters, and organizers are not paid specifically for the performance, though they may be paid a regular salary for duties that include performing, promoting, or organizing performances. (For example, a college music professor may organize a recital that would qualify for exemption even though she is paid a salary by the college, as long as she receives no separate payment specifically for the organization of the recital.)

- There is no direct or indirect admission charge, or, if there is such a charge, the proceeds, after deducting costs of the performance, are used exclusively for educational, religious, or charitable purposes. (If there is an admission charge, the copyright owner may serve a written notice of objection to the performance seven or more days prior to the performance. Proper service of an objection will obligate the recipient to refrain from performing the copyrighted work. The apparent purpose of this last provision is to enable copyright owners to avoid making involuntary contributions to fund-raisers for causes they oppose.)

G. **Other exceptions to the exclusive right of public performance:** The Copyright Act provides a number of other narrowly drawn exceptions to the exclusive right of public performance, including an exception that permits stores to perform nondramatic musical works on their premises for the purpose of promoting sales of the musical works or the devices to play them (§110(7)); an exception permitting nonprofit broadcasts of nondramatic literary works specifically designed for hearing and sight-impaired persons (§§110(8) and (9)); and an exemption for government and nonprofit agricultural and horticultural organizations with regard to performances of nondramatic musical works in the course of fairs and exhibitions they sponsor (§110(6)).

H. **Exceptions to the exclusive rights of public performance and display:** Because many of the remaining statutory exceptions to the right of public performance apply to the right of public display as well, these exceptions will be considered in the following section on the right of public display.

IX. THE EXCLUSIVE RIGHT TO DISPLAY THE COPYRIGHTED WORK PUBLICLY

Copyright Act §106 provides that in the case of all copyrighted works other than sound recordings and works of architecture, the copyright owner has the exclusive right of public display. Section 101 states that to display a work is "to show a copy of it, either directly or by means of a film, slide, television image, or any other device or process or, in the case of a motion picture or other audiovisual work, to show individual images nonsequentially." The Ninth Circuit has recently ruled that a computer owner that stores an image as electronic information and serves that electronic information directly to Internet users (*i.e.*, physically sends electronic signals over the Internet to the user's browser) *displays* the electronic information for purposes of a copyright infringement claim. However, the owner of a computer that does not store and serve the electronic information to a user is not displaying the information, even if the owner in-line links to or frames the electronic information. The court explained that providing the HTML instructions necessary to create the link or to frame the material is not equivalent to showing a copy of the work. The HTML instructions do not themselves cause infringing images to appear on the user's computer screen. It merely gives the address of the image to the user's browser. The browser then interacts with the computer that stores the infringing image. It is this interaction that causes the image to appear on the user's computer screen. (The court called this standard for determining who "displays" information in the Internet context the "server test.") *Perfect 10, Inc. v. Amazon.com., Inc.*, 487 F.3d 701 (9th Cir. 2007).

A. **When a display is public:** Only *public* displays are under the copyright owner's control. Section 101 provides that a display is public under the same circumstances in which a performance is public. Thus, a display is public if: (1) it occurs at a place open to the public; (2) it occurs at a place where a substantial number of persons outside of the normal circle of a family and its social acquaintances is gathered; (3) it is transmitted or otherwise communicated to a place described in (1) or (2) above; or (4) it is transmitted or otherwise communicated to the public by means of any device or process, whether or not the members of the public capable of receiving the display receive it in the same place and time. See *supra*, pp. 146-147.

B. **Exception to the exclusive right of public display—owners of lawfully made copies:** Copyright Act §109(c) provides an important exception to the copyright owner's exclusive right of public display. It authorizes the *owner of a lawfully made copy* of the work (or his designee) to display that copy publicly, either (1) directly or (2) by the projection of no more than one image at a time, to viewers present at the place where the copy is located. Thus, the copy owner may display his copy by hanging it in a gallery or museum, for example, or he may display it by projection. However, if the display is by projection, there may only be one projection, and the projection may only be made to viewers present in the same location as the copy. These limitations on projection are meant to protect the copyright owner's market. A projection of multiple images—for example, on individual computer viewer screens in a large lecture room—or to a number of different sites over the Internet, could seriously undercut the copyright owner's opportunity to sell additional copies. Thus, the primary value of the public display right lies in displays of copyrighted works in television broadcasts and over the Internet, which are not subject to the §109(c) exception.

C. **Exception to the exclusive rights of public performance *and* display—transmissions received on home-style receivers:** Copyright Act §110(5) permits many businesses to play radio or television transmissions during the business day for the entertainment of customers and employees. More specifically, §110(5) (known as the "home-style-receiver exception") provides that performance or display of a copyrighted work *by transmission* in a place open to the public, or where the public is gathered, *on a single receiving apparatus of a kind commonly used in private homes*, is not an infringement of copyright unless a direct charge is made to see or hear the transmission.

Example: A, the owner of a small bar, keeps a standard home-style television set turned on so that his employees and customers can keep up with televised sports events while in the bar. A makes no direct charge for the privilege of seeing the broadcast of the copyrighted sports programs. Although this constitutes a performance of the programs, and occurs in a place open to the public, it does not constitute infringement because it falls within the §110(5) exemption.

1. **A broader exception for public performances and displays of nondramatic musical works:** In 1998, Congress expanded the §110(5) exemption to provide businesses greater freedom to perform *nondramatic musical works* by public reception of radio and television transmissions to the general public. Under the amendment, stores that are smaller than 2,000 square feet and restaurants and bars that are smaller than 3,750 square feet may play radio and television broadcasts and cable and satellite transmissions of nondramatic musical works regardless of the type of receiver or number of speakers they use. Stores that are larger than 2,000 square feet, and restaurants and bars that are larger than 3,750 square feet are also exempt from liability, if they use no more than six speakers or four televisions with screens smaller than 55 inches. (There are further limitations on the placement of the speakers and televisions.) However, businesses falling under this exemption may not make a direct charge to see or hear the transmission, and may not further transmit beyond their own establishment. This amendment frees many businesses of the necessity of obtaining a license from the performing rights societies, which have been assiduous in enforcing the rights of music copyright owners. However, business establishments that assert unsuccessful §110(5) exemption defenses without reasonable basis may be liable to the musical work copyright owners for enhanced damages.

    a. **Amendment to §110(5) in violation of U.S. TRIPs obligations:** A dispute resolution panel of the World Trade Organization has held (at the behest of the European Union) that the 1998 expansion of §110(5), described above, violates the United States' international obligations by exceeding the limitation on exceptions to copyright protection set forth in TRIPs Article 13. (Article 13 provides that WTO members must "confine limitations or exceptions to exclusive rights [of copyright] to certain special cases which do not conflict with normal exploitation of the work and do not unreasonably prejudice the legitimate interests of the right holder.") This panel ruling does not in itself invalidate or repeal §110(5)(B). The provision remains in effect until Congress acts to remove it. Until Congress takes action, the European Union is entitled to collect reparations from the United States.

D. **Exception to the exclusive rights of public performance *and* display—face-to-face nonprofit instruction:** Copyright Act §110(1) provides that performance or display of a copyrighted work by instructors or pupils in the course of face-to-face teaching activities in a classroom or similar place devoted to instruction is not an infringement. This exemption applies to all kinds of copyrighted works. However, the educational instruction must be nonprofit, by an educational institution, in a place normally devoted to instruction.

Example: A teacher in a nonprofit educational institution could have members of his drama class perform scenes from a copyrighted play for the rest of the class in the course of teaching the play or methods of interpretation. However, this exemption would not permit the class members to then perform the scenes for their parents at a P.T.A. meeting, since this would not be in the course of instruction.

E. **Exception to the exclusive rights of public performance *and* display—instructional and "distance learning" transmissions:** Copyright Act §110(2), as recently amended, authorizes *transmission* of performances and displays of copyrighted material in educational programs directed to students and governmental employees. More specifically, subsection (2) provides that performances of nondramatic literary or musical works, "reasonable and limited" performances of other works, and displays of any work by transmission will not infringe if the performance or display: 1) is made by or at the direction of an instructor; 2) is offered as an integral part of a class session; and 3) is a regular part of the systematic instructional activities of a governmental body or an accredited nonprofit educational institution. The performance or display must be directly related and of material assistance to the teaching content of the transmission. The copy or phonorecord that is used in the performance or display must be a lawful one. Works produced or marketed primarily for performance or display as part of mediated instructional activities transmitted via digital networks are excluded from the section 110(2) exception. (There are some additional qualifications and limitations.)

F. **Exception to the exclusive rights of public performance *and* display—religious services:** Copyright Act §110(3) permits performances of nondramatic literary or musical works, performances of dramatico-musical works of a religious nature (such as cantatas or choral services), and displays of any work in the course of religious services at a place of worship.

G. **Exception to the exclusive rights of public performance *and* display—electronic video games:** Copyright Act §109(e) permits owners of lawfully made copies of electronic audiovisual games intended for use in coin-operated equipment to publicly perform and display their copies in the coin-operated equipment, without seeking the permission of the owner of copyright in the game. (The only exception arises when the game contains other works of authorship, like musical compositions, whose copyright is owned by someone other than the owner of copyright in the game.)

H. **Exceptions and compulsory licenses—secondary transmissions:** Merely picking up transmitted television or radio signals and retransmitting them constitutes a separate "performance" and/or "display" of any copyrighted material that is included in the transmission, and if the transmission is "to the public," will infringe those copyrighted materials unless licensed or subject to a statutory exception. Copyright Act §§111 and 119 specifically address various types of secondary transmissions. Among other things, these sections:

- Authorize hotels, apartment houses, and similar establishments to pick up local television and radio station transmissions to the public and relay them to private guests or resident rooms, as long as they make no direct charge for the relay.

- Provide that entities such as AT&T, who merely provide wires, cables, and other means by which others pick up and carry primary transmissions to the public, are exempt from infringement liability as long as they observe specified guidelines.

- Exempt government and nonprofit organizations from infringement liability for providing translators or boosters to improve reception of transmissions to the public, as long as they make no charge for the service apart from assessments necessary to defray their actual costs.

- Provide for compulsory licenses, which enable cable systems legally to make secondary transmissions of the primary signals of broadcast stations, and specify the royalties the cable systems must pay.

- Provide for compulsory licenses, which enable satellite retransmission companies to retransmit television broadcasts to subscribing private home viewers' satellite dishes, and specify the royalties the satellite companies must pay.

I. **Exception to the exclusive rights of public performance *and* display—compulsory licenses for noncommercial broadcasting:** Copyright Act §118 provides for compulsory licenses to enable public broadcasting entities to broadcast performances and displays of published nondramatic musical works and published pictorial, graphic, and sculptural works. The statute encourages public stations and copyright owners to reach voluntary agreements, but specifies a procedure to be followed in determining royalty payments, in the absence of negotiated agreement.

X. MORAL RIGHTS

A. **The nature of moral rights:** Many nations (particularly civil-law nations) view a work of authorship as an extension of the author's personality, and expressly provide personal rights—known as "moral rights," or "*droit moral*"—in addition to economic rights, to protect that aspect of the work. There are two primary moral rights: the right of attribution and the right of integrity. Generally, moral rights are inalienable, and the author retains them even after he assigns his economic rights to another. The Berne Convention, to which the United States adheres, requires that its members protect the moral rights of attribution and integrity. See *infra*, pp. 195-196. Prior to its adherence to the Berne Convention, the United States did not expressly recognize moral rights as a part of copyright protection. Authors wishing to vindicate rights of attribution or integrity looked to other areas of law, including the Lanham Act and common-law contract, tort, and unfair competition doctrines, for assistance. In 1990, Congress enacted the Visual Artists Rights Act, which amended the Copyright Act expressly to provide moral rights in a very narrow category of subject matter, which will be described below.

   1. **The right of attribution:** The *right of attribution* ensures the author's right to be known as the author of a work, to prevent others from claiming authorship in it, and to avoid having authorship of others' works falsely attributed to him. The right of attribution also allows the author to prevent having copies of his own work that have been distorted or mutilated attributed to him.

   2. **The right of integrity:** The *right of integrity* ensures the author's right to prevent others from distorting, mutilating, or misrepresenting his work in a way that may prejudice his honor or reputation. This right may also permit him to prevent the destruction of his work.

B. **The Visual Artists' Rights Act of 1990:** The Visual Artists' Rights Act is very limited in scope, providing moral rights only in *works of visual art*, a very narrow category of works of authorship. Moreover, it applies only to those works of visual art created on or after the effective date of the Act, or to which the author retained title at the effective date (June 1, 1991).

   1. **Works of visual art:** Copyright Act §101, as amended, defines works of visual art to include: (1) a painting, drawing, print, or sculpture, which exists in a single copy or in a limited edition of 200 copies or fewer, if those copies are signed and consecutively numbered by the author; and (2) a still photographic image, if it was produced *for exhibition purposes only* and exists

in a single copy that is signed by the author or a limited edition of 200 copies or fewer that are signed and consecutively numbered by the author.

- a. **Excluded works:** Section 101 specifies that the following items *do not* qualify as works of visual art: posters, maps, globes, charts, technical drawings, diagrams, models, applied art, motion pictures, or other audiovisual works, books, magazines, newspapers, periodicals, databases, electronic information services, electronic publications, or similar publications. Merchandising items, and advertising, promotional, descriptive, and packaging materials are also excluded. Thus, protection extends to *unique and near-unique objects of fine art*, rather than to objects of utility or mass production. In addition, the definition of the protected category expressly excludes all works made for hire and all works that are not subject to copyright protection.

2. **The rights of attribution and integrity:** Copyright Act §106A provides the rights of attribution and integrity to artists creating works of visual art, as defined. These rights are independent of the exclusive economic rights of copyright, discussed in earlier sections, and are retained by the author even after she assigns her copyright. Like the economic rights, however, the moral rights are subject to the fair use defense. See *infra*, pp. 162-167. It is important to note that the Visual Artists Rights Act only protects *those physical copies qualifying as works of visual art* under the definition set forth above—that is, to the original and up to two hundred signed, numbered, limited-edition copies. The intangible work of authorship embodied in those objects is not protected as such. Thus, for example, if the author makes additional copies, beyond the protected limited edition, she will have no moral rights in those additional copies.

   Example: Author creates an original print, which she produces in a limited edition of 200 or less, properly signed and numbered. She later mass produces and sells 5,000 posters embodying the print. While the Visual Artists' Rights Act gives author the right to prevent others from misattributing or interfering with the integrity of the limited edition prints, she has no such rights with regard to the poster prints.

   - a. **The right of attribution:** The §106A right of attribution grants the author not only the right to be identified as the author of a work but also to prevent attribution of works to him that he did not create. In addition, the author may prevent use of his name in connection with a work that has been modified in a way that will injure his honor or reputation.

   - b. **The right of integrity:** Copyright Act §106A also grants the author of a work of visual art rights against: (1) any intentional distortion, mutilation, or other modification of his work that would be prejudicial to his honor or reputation as an artist; and (2) in the case of a work of "recognized stature," any intentional or grossly negligent destruction of the work. (While the Visual Artists' Rights Act does not define the requirement that works be "of recognized stature," courts have held that the requirement should be viewed as a "gatekeeping mechanism," affording protection from destruction only for those works that art experts, the art community, or society in general view as "possessing stature." This bars nuisance suits, but does not require that works be equal to a Picasso, Chagall, or Giacometti.

     - i. **Things that do not constitute a violation of the right of integrity:** Section 106A specifies that several things do not constitute a violation of the right of integrity. First, a modification due to the passage of time or to the inherent nature of the materials used by the author does not violate the author's right. (Thus, allowing an out-of-doors iron statue to rust is unlikely to violate the author's right of integrity.) Second, a modification resulting from conservation efforts or the public presentation (including lighting and placement) of the work is not a violation unless caused by gross negligence. Thus, galleries and museums continue to have normal discretion to light, frame, and place works of art.

    c. **Ownership of the rights:** The artist who creates the work of visual art is the owner of the moral rights in it. He retains these rights even if he fully assigns his copyright to another, and conveys title in the original and all copies of the work. Indeed, the moral rights cannot be assigned. If the work was created jointly by two or more authors, all the authors jointly own the moral rights.

    d. **Waiver:** The author may waive her moral rights, though waivers will be rigorously scrutinized. The author must expressly agree to the waiver in a signed writing that specifies the work and the uses of the work to which the waiver applies. The waiver will be limited to the specific uses set forth in the writing. Blanket waivers are prohibited. However, one joint author may effectively waive the rights of all the authors.

    e. **Duration of rights:** Section 106A provides that in the case of works created on or after the effective date of the Act (June 1, 1991), the rights of attribution and integrity will last for the life of the author. In the case of joint works, the rights will endure for a term consisting of the life of the last surviving author. In the case of works created earlier, to which the author retained title on the effective date, the moral rights will endure as long as the economic rights do. (See *infra*, pp. 182-185, for a discussion of the duration of the economic rights.)

3. **Works of visual art incorporated into buildings:** Copyright Act §113(d), as amended, addresses the respective rights of the parties when the work of visual art is incorporated into a building, and the building owner wishes to remove it. If the work cannot be removed without the kind of destruction, distortion, mutilation, or modification prohibited under the Act, the author's right to prevent the destruction, distortion, mutilation, or modification will not apply if either of two facts can be demonstrated: (1) the author consented to the work's installation in the building before the effective date of the Act; or (2) the author and building owner signed an agreement on or after the effective date, which consented to the installation and specified that the installation might subject the work to destruction, distortion, mutilation, or other modification, by reason of its removal. If the work can be removed without destruction, distortion, mutilation, or modification, the author's rights do apply unless: (1) the building owner diligently attempted, in good faith, to notify the author of his intent to remove the work and was unable to do so; or (2) the building owner successfully notified the author of his intent, and the author failed, within 90 days, either to remove the work or to pay for its removal. Section 113 specifies that if the author removes the work at his own expense, he regains title to it.

C. **Indirect protection of moral rights under the Copyright Act:** Authors seeking to vindicate moral rights in works that are not works of visual art must follow a more indirect route than that set forth in the Visual Artists' Rights Act. *Gilliam v. American Broadcasting Co.*, 538 F.2d 14 (2d Cir. 1976), is an example of a case in which authors were able to vindicate their moral right of integrity by asserting the economic right of adaptation. The case involved the British comedy group Monty Python. The BBC made television programs starring Monty Python, pursuant to scripts that Monty Python wrote. The parties' contract provided that the BBC could make programs and publicly perform and license others to publicly perform the programs based on Monty

Python's copyrighted scripts, but limited BBC's rights to change the scripts. The BBC licensed the defendant ABC to show some of the Monty Python programs it had made, and ABC proceeded to edit them, taking out "obscene and objectionable" material and making time for advertisements. In all, ABC chopped out about one-fourth of the material and broadcast the remainder. Monty Python was incensed at what it considered to be a mutilation of its work and sued for copyright infringement. The Second Circuit recognized that in effect Monty Python was seeking to enforce a moral right—the right of integrity—which did not exist as such under the U.S. Copyright Act. However, the court found that the economic right of adaptation could nonetheless be applied to vindicate the authors' interest. ABC, in "mutilating" the BBC programs through its editing, had made an unauthorized derivative work of the underlying scripts, to which Monty Python retained copyright. Of course, Monty Python would not have been able to rely on this theory if it had assigned its economic rights in the scripts, as many authors must do.

D. **Other federal sources for protecting moral rights—Lanham Act §43(a):** Lanham Act §43(a) (15 U.S.C. §1125(a)) has also been used to protect moral rights—particularly the right of attribution. See UNFAIR COMPETITION, pp. 311-312. Section 43(a) prohibits persons from making a false designation of the origin of goods or services or a false description or representation about goods or services in commerce. In *Gilliam* the court found, as an alternative ground, that by editing (mutilating) the work as it did and then attributing it to Monty Python, ABC had falsely indicated that Monty Python was the author of the work as edited. This constituted a false designation of origin, or a false description of the entertainment services, in violation of subsection 43(a). However, as will be discussed more fully *infra*, the Supreme Court has cut back significantly on the availability of Lanham Act §43(a) claims to substitute for moral rights protection. See pp. 313-314, *infra*.

E. **State causes of action that may vindicate moral rights:** State contract, privacy, defamation, and unfair competition doctrines may also be used to give partial effect to authors' moral rights. For example, authors who have obtained contracts specifying how a purchaser is to use their work, or how the work is to be attributed, may enforce the contracts to prevent changes to the work or misattributions that violate the contract terms. Moreover, a defendant who attributes a subsequently mutilated work to the original author may be liable to the author for defamation. A common-law passing off or false advertising or product disparagement claim might be used much in the same way as Lanham Act §43(a) has been used to prevent attribution of works that have been changed, or false representations about the nature or characteristics of the goods or services the author created (although there is some danger that such claims might be preempted under the Copyright Act). In addition, several states, including California and New York, have enacted statutes expressly designed to protect authors' moral rights of attribution and integrity in certain works of authorship (generally, works of fine art). However, to the extent that these statutes duplicate the Visual Artists' Rights Act, they may be preempted. (See FEDERAL AND STATE LAW, *infra*, pp. 340-345.)

XI. DIRECT AND INDIRECT COPYRIGHT INFRINGEMENT

A. **Direct infringement:** Copyright Act §501 provides that anyone who violates any of the exclusive rights of the copyright owner, or of the author (as provided in the Visual Artists' Rights Act), or who imports copies or phonorecords into the United States in violation of §602, is liable for direct infringement. Thus, persons engaging in unauthorized reproduction, adaptation, public distribution, public performance, public display, or importation of copyrighted works are directly liable to the copyright owner (the person who owns the exclusive economic right that has been infringed). Persons engaging in violations of an author's right of attribution or integrity in a work of visual art are directly liable to that author. In the case of direct copyright infringement liability, lack of intent to infringe and lack of knowledge of the copyright are not defenses, though they may affect the remedy afforded to the plaintiff. Copyright infringement is a form of strict liability.

B. **Three forms of indirect infringement liability:** Though the Copyright Act does not expressly provide for indirect liability for copyright infringement, the courts have long recognized claims of vicarious and contributory liability as a means of holding persons liable for the infringing acts of others. Recently the Supreme Court described a third "intentional inducement" theory of indirect infringement.

   1. **Contributory infringement:** The U.S. Court of Appeals for the Second Circuit has described a contributory infringer as "one who, with knowledge of the infringing activity, induces, causes, or materially contributes to the infringing conduct of another." *Gershwin Publishing Corp. v. Columbia Artists Mgt., Inc.*, 443 F.2d 1159 (2d Cir. 1971). Thus, two elements must be demonstrated: (1) the defendant must know or have reason to know of someone else's directly infringing activity; and (2) the defendant must actively participate by inducing, materially contributing to, or furthering the other person's directly infringing acts.

      Example: An advertising agency places advertisements to assist a client in selling infringing records, knowing or having reason to know that the records infringe the plaintiff's copyright. A radio station plays the advertisements with the same knowledge. Both the ad agency and the radio station may be contributorily liable.

      Example: Cherry Auction operated a flea market where customers came to buy various merchandise from individual vendors. The vendors paid a daily rental fee to Cherry in exchange for booth space. Cherry supplied parking, conducted advertising to promote the flea market, and retained the right to exclude any vendor for any reason, at any time. In addition to rental fees from vendors, Cherry received an entrance fee from each customer who attended the flea market, charged customers for parking, and operated a food and drink stand on the premises. The Sheriff's Department had warned Cherry that some of its vendors were selling counterfeit sound recordings at the flea market. A vendor again sold infringing sound recordings, and the Court of Appeals for the Ninth Circuit held Cherry contributorily liable for the infringement. The court reasoned that Cherry had knowledge of the infringement by virtue of the Sheriff's warning. Moreover, Cherry contributed to the infringing activity by providing space, utilities, parking, advertising, plumbing, and customers. *Fonovisa, Inc. v. Cherry Auction*, 76 F.3d 259 (9th Cir. 1996).

      a. **Sale of equipment or other products used in direct infringement:** In *Sony Corp. of America v. Universal City Studios, Inc.*, 464 U.S. 417 (1984), the U.S. Supreme Court found that a manufacturer and seller of home videotape recorders was not liable for contributory infringement, even though it had *constructive knowledge* that some of its purchasers were likely to use the recorders to make unauthorized tapes of copyrighted television programs and movies. (That is, it knew that some of its purchasers were *likely* to use the recorders to infringe, but did not specifically *intend* to cause or assist infringement.) The Court reasoned, by analogy to the contributory infringement cause of action in patent law, that a person could not be held liable simply for selling an item that could be used to infringe, but that was also capable of *substantial non-infringing uses*. To hold otherwise would extend copyright owners' monopolies beyond their copyrighted works to a wide range of reproduction and communications technology, potentially impairing progress in a number of useful technological fields, to the detriment of the public. In the *Sony* case, the defendant's videotape recorders could be used for authorized as well as unauthorized taping and for simple "time shifting," which the Court found to be a non-infringing fair use. Thus, since the recorder was capable of substantial non-infringing uses, Sony could not be held liable for contributory infringement. Constructive knowledge of potential infringement, in itself, was not a sufficient basis for imposing liability.

    b. A narrow interpretation of *Sony* by the Ninth Circuit: In *A & M Records, Inc. v. Napster, Inc.*, 239 F.3d 1004 (9th Cir. 2001), the Court of Appeals for the Ninth Circuit construed the *Sony* decision narrowly, at least in the Internet context. In that case the court found that Napster (the proprietor of an online service that provided software and other support to facilitate users' swapping of MP3 files of copyrighted music) was liable for contributory infringement *even though* its file-sharing service and software was capable of substantial, non-infringing uses. The court emphasized that the plaintiffs had expressly notified Napster of the fact that their copyrighted sound recordings were being reproduced and distributed over the Napster system without their permission. According to the Ninth Circuit, this made the situation distinguishable from *Sony*, in which the seller of video recorders had only *constructive notice* of its users' infringement. According to the Ninth Circuit: "[I]f a computer system operator learns of specific infringing material available on his system and fails to purge such material from the system, the operator knows of and contributes to direct infringement. Conversely, absent any specific information which identifies infringing activity, a computer system operator cannot be liable for the contributory infringement merely because the structure of the system allows for the exchange of copyrighted material." *Id.* at 1021-1022.

2. Vicarious infringement liability: Vicarious infringement liability is grounded in the tort concept of *respondeat superior*, although it is not limited to employer-employee settings, or even to strict agent-principal settings. The Second Circuit has held that a finding of vicarious liability is justified "[w]hen the right and ability to supervise [the infringer] coalesce with an obvious and direct financial interest in the exploitation of copyrighted materials." *Shapiro, Bernstein & Co. v. H.L. Green Co.*, 316 F.2d 304, 307 (2d Cir. 1963). A defendant who has control or supervision over the direct infringer and a direct financial interest in the infringement will be vicariously liable even if he has no actual knowledge that the infringement is taking place and does not directly participate in it.

Example: In *Shapiro*, the defendant, who operated a chain of department stores, was held liable for the infringing acts of its licensee, a phonograph record manufacturing and sales company that operated record department concessions in 23 of the defendant's department stores. The court noted that the defendant department store proprietor's license agreement with the concessionaire specifically provided that the concessionaire would "abide by, observe and obey all rules and regulations" promulgated by the department store proprietor. Moreover, the concessionaire paid the department store proprietor 10 to 12 percent of the concessionaire's gross receipts from the sale of records as its license fee. Based on these facts, the court found that the department store proprietor had the *power to police the concessionaire's conduct* and a *direct financial interest* in the proceeds of the concessionaire's infringement. This rendered the department store proprietor liable even though it had not directly participated in selling infringing records and did not know of the concessionaire's infringement. By contrast, a traditional landlord who leases space to a lessee without reserving any right to control the lessee's business activities, and charges a fixed rent that is not dependent on the extent of the lessee's sales, generally would not be vicariously liable for the lessee's infringement.

Example: In the *Fonovisa* case, discussed *supra,* the Court of Appeals for the Ninth Circuit found Cherry Auction, the flea market operator, liable for vicarious infringement, as well as contributory infringement. The court reasoned that Cherry had the right to terminate vendors for any reason, and therefore had the *ability to control* the activities of vendors on the premises. In addition, Cherry controlled access of customers to the flea market. Cherry received a *direct financial benefit* from the infringing record sales by virtue of the increased admission fees, concession stand sales, and parking fees from customers who came to the flea market to purchase infringing sound recordings. The sale of pirated recordings was a "draw" for customers, from which Cherry profited.

Example: In the *Napster* case, discussed above, the Ninth Circuit held that the defendant file-swapping service was vicariously liable for its users' infringement, as well as contributorily liable. With regard to the vicarious liability claim, the court reasoned that Napster had the *right and ability to control* its users because it could block their access to its services. In addition, Napster had an express reservation of rights policy, stating on its web site that it expressly reserved the "right to refuse service and terminate accounts in [its] discretion." Napster received a *direct financial benefit* from the infringement because the infringement drew additional users to its service, thus increasing its user base. While Napster did not charge users for its service, and had never received revenue for its service at the time of suit, the court found that it would be able to capitalize on its large user base in various ways in the future. (For example, it could sell advertising or sell data on its users to marketers.) The Ninth Circuit found that this increased opportunity for future revenue was sufficient to constitute a "direct financial benefit" for purposes of finding vicarious infringement liability.

3. **The *Grokster* "intentional inducement" theory of indirect infringement liability:** In *Metro-Goldwyn-Mayer Studios, Inc. v. Grokster*, 545 U.S. 913 (2005), the defendants provided software for a peer-to-peer file-sharing system that, unlike the *Napster* system, had no centralized server or indexing system. The only important way that the *Grokster* defendants assisted users' infringement was by providing them with the file-sharing software at the outset. The Ninth Circuit found that the defendants' software was capable of substantial, non-infringing uses, so that mere constructive knowledge that some users might use the software to infringe was insufficient to impose liability under the Supreme Court's standard in *Sony*. Although the plaintiff copyright owners notified the *Grokster* defendants of actual incidents of infringement (as they had in *Napster*), the Ninth Circuit found that receipt of this information imposed no duty to act to stop the infringement. By the time the defendants got the actual notice of infringement, they had no means of preventing it. The Ninth Circuit reasoned that the defendants must have the requisite actual knowledge of infringement *at the time* that they contributed to the infringement (here, at the time they provided the file-swapping software to the infringing users) before they would incur a duty to act. The Ninth Circuit likewise rejected the copyright owners' vicarious infringement claim because the defendants lacked the right or ability to supervise their software users' infringement at the time that the infringement occurred. On *cert.*, the Supreme Court declined the copyright owners' invitation to reconsider the *Sony* rule, and instead described a third means of indirect infringement (again, modeled on patent law) that is not subject to the *Sony* limitation, and could be applied to find the *Grokster* defendants liable. According to the Court, "one who distributes a device with the clear object of promoting its use to infringe copyright, as shown by clear expression or other affirmative

steps taken to foster infringement, is liable for the resulting acts of infringement by third parties."

    a. Differentiating *Sony:* In *Grokster*, the Supreme Court explained that the *Sony* decision only addressed the circumstances in which intent should be imputed. Evidence that the defendant was selling technology that had no substantial use other than to infringe would provide a good basis for imputing the requisite intent to assist or induce infringement. On the other hand, the *Sony* Court was unwilling to infer or impute the necessary intent for liability if the technology the defendant was selling had substantial, non-infringing uses. To do so would interfere unduly with the development of new technologies, to the detriment of the public. The *Grokster* Court explained that if the defendant could be proved to fall within the definition of the inducement cause of action, then there would be no need to impute intent, and the *Sony* rule would not apply.

    b. Evidence relevant to proving intent to induce infringement: In finding that the *Grokster* plaintiffs could prevail, the Supreme Court pointed to three kinds of evidence of the defendants' bad intent. First, the defendants clearly were attempting to capture the Napster audience, which was a known source of demand for means to infringe. Second, the defendants did not attempt to develop filtering tools or other mechanisms to diminish infringing use of their software (though the Court noted that such evidence would not be enough in itself to demonstrate intent). Third, the Court noted that the defendants' business model depended on infringement (that is, its revenues from sale of advertising depended on a large volume of software use, which would result from the ability to swap infringing files), but again, the Court noted that this evidence would not be enough in itself to prove intent. The Court explained that it was the *combination* of these three lines of evidence that was compelling under the facts in *Grokster*.

C. Infringement liability on the Internet: There has been considerable concern about infringement liability on the Internet. As discussed on p. 134, *supra*, reproductions of documents, sound recordings, artwork, or other copyrightable works may be made whenever digital files of those works are uploaded or downloaded, and Internet service providers may make numerous additional reproductions of the works as they are transmitted from computer to computer over the Internet. In the absence of express or implied consent from the copyright owner, each of these reproductions may infringe the copyright. In addition, many unauthorized transmissions of works are likely to be deemed infringing distributions to the public, particularly since the doctrine of first sale is unlikely to be deemed applicable to shelter the transmission. (See p. 145, *supra*.) Many transmissions of works may also constitute public performances or displays, such as when an Internet user downloads the work from a web site without the copyright owner's permission. (See pp. 147, 148, *supra*.) To address the potential for direct and indirect infringement liability in this context, Congress enacted the Digital Millennium Copyright Act (DMCA) in 1998. Among other things, the DMCA provides safe harbors from infringement liability for Internet service providers. 17 U.S.C. §512.

    1. Safe harbors for Internet service providers: As noted above, Internet service providers (ISPs), such as access providers, search engines, and bulletin board services, routinely reproduce works, as well as transmit them, in the course of their day-to-day operations. Thus, if users infringe copyrighted works on the Internet, the ISPs who provide the users with the means to transmit, distribute, post, or locate the infringing works may themselves be deemed liable either as direct infringers or indirect infringers. In the DMCA, Congress limited ISP liability for infringement in such cases by providing a series of "safe harbors." Each safe harbor provides a set of conditions that the ISP must meet in order to qualify for immunity from infringement liability. If the ISP qualifies, it will be shielded from liability for monetary damages and will face only limited injunctive remedies. The safe harbors are provided to augment, not displace, any defenses that the ISP might already have under copyright law, such as the fair use defense. To qualify for the safe harbors, ISPs must designate agents to receive notice of claimed infringement, adopt and inform users of a policy to terminate users who are repeat infringers, and accommodate standard technological protection measures (such as digital watermarks or encryption) used by copyright owners to protect their works. The safe harbor provisions are set forth in Copyright Act §512.

a. **The definition of "service provider" for purposes of the Act:** An ISP qualifies for the first safe harbor listed below (§XID1b) if it is "an entity offering the transmission, routing, or providing of connections for digital online communications, between or among points specified by a user, of material of the user's choosing, without modification to the content of the material as sent or received." The definition of a qualifying service provider for the other three safe harbors is broader, including any "provider of online services or network access, or the operator of facilities therefor."

b. **Safe harbor for transmission and transient storage:** This safe harbor shelters ISPs from liability for serving as a conduit: transmitting, routing or providing connections to material through their system, or temporarily storing material in the course of these activities. Several conditions apply. In particular, the transmission of infringing material must have been initiated by someone other than the ISP and have been carried out through an automatic technical process, so that the ISP did not participate in selection of the material or the recipients or alter the material's content while it was being transmitted.

c. **Safe harbor for system caching:** This safe harbor permits ISPs to "cache," or temporarily reproduce and store copies of frequently-sought materials in order to provide them to users more efficiently. Again, several conditions apply. For example, the ISP must store the cached material through an automatic technical process, comply with rules concerning updating the material, refrain from interfering with technology (such as "cookies") intended to return information about use of the work to the person placing it online, and limit access to users who meet the copyright owner's conditions for access—such as having passwords or paying fees.

d. **Safe harbor for storing materials for users:** This safe harbor limits an ISP's liability for storing its users' infringing materials (such as in web pages or chat rooms) on its system. To qualify, the ISP must not know that the stored material infringes, or be aware of facts that would make it apparent. Upon obtaining such knowledge, the ISP must expeditiously remove the materials from its system or block access to them. (There are additional conditions.)

e. **Safe harbor for information location tools:** This safe harbor limits an ISP's liability for assisting users to infringe by providing search engines, hypertext links, directories, or similar resources directing users to infringing materials. To qualify, the ISP must not know that the materials infringe, or be aware of facts that would make the infringement apparent, and must not receive a direct financial benefit from the infringement. Upon becoming aware, the ISP must remove or block access to the infringing resource.

XII. FAIR USE AND OTHER DEFENSES TO INFRINGEMENT

A. **The nature of the fair use defense:** Once the plaintiff has made a *prima facie* showing of copyright infringement (or violation of an artist's right of attribution or integrity in a work of visual art), the defendant may raise the defense of fair use. When courts accept the fair use defense they find, essentially, that though infringement may have occurred as a technical matter, it should be excused. The doctrine of fair use allows courts to avoid rigid application of the copyright laws when rigid application would inappropriately stifle creativity or the production and dissemination of useful works to the public—the very activity that the copyright law was meant to foster. The doctrine of fair use is founded on notions of equity and common sense. Because it is meant to be a sort of escape hatch to give courts flexibility, it is of necessity left somewhat vague, to be applied on a case-by-case basis in light of the specific facts of each case. As a general matter, a use will be excused as a fair use of it *promotes the purposes* of copyright law (encouraging production and dissemination of works of authorship) and *will not undercut authors' economic incentive* to create and disseminate works by seriously undermining their marketing opportunities.

B. **Section 107:** Though the doctrine of fair use had long been recognized in the case law, Congress undertook to codify it in the Copyright Act of 1976 (17 U.S.C. §107). Keeping in mind the need for flexibility, Congress did not attempt to define fair use in concrete terms. Rather, it gave some illustrative examples of uses of copyrighted material that might be deemed "fair," and listed four nonexclusive factors that courts should consider in determining whether a particular use of a copyrighted work constitutes an excusable fair use.

1. **The examples:** Section 107 lists the following examples of uses that might be found fair in a given case: uses "for purposes such as criticism, comment, news reporting, teaching (including multiple copies for classroom use), scholarship, or research." While these examples have been influential, either literally or as an indication that courts should favor "productive" uses such as those listed, *uses other than those listed* have been found to be fair. Moreover, a showing that a defendant's use *falls within* one of the listed examples by no means guarantees that it will be excused as a fair use.

2. **The four listed factors:** Section 107 lists four factors that courts *must* consider in determining whether a particular defendant's use was a fair one: (1) the purpose and character of the use, including whether the use is of a commercial nature or is for nonprofit educational purposes; (2) the nature of the copyrighted work; (3) the amount and substantiality of the portion used in relation to the copyrighted work as a whole; and (4) the effect of the use upon the potential market for or value of the copyrighted work. Each of these factors is discussed further below. The Supreme Court has stressed that courts must consider *all* of these factors in each case. Courts may consider additional factors if it appears appropriate under the specific facts of the case. While §107 does not specify how each of the factors should be weighted, it is clear that no one of them, by itself, creates a *presumption* of fair use or the lack of it.

    a. **The purpose and character of the use:** A number of considerations are relevant in evaluating the first factor—the purpose and character of the defendant's use.

        i. **Commercial or noncommercial:** In *Harper & Row Publishers, Inc. v. Nation Enterprises*, 471 U.S. 539 (1985), the Supreme Court said that a defendant's use for *commercial purposes* is less likely to be deemed fair than a use for non-commercial purposes. The Court indicated that a use is "commercial" if the *user stands to profit economically from exploiting the copyrighted material without paying the customary* *price*. In *Harper*, the Court characterized a news magazine's article (which quoted impermissibly from President Ford's memoirs) as commercial in character. Thus, even though the use of the copyrighted memoirs material was for the purpose of news reporting (one of the statutory examples of uses that can be found fair), the commercial (profit-making) nature of the article, in combination with other factors, led the *Harper* Court to reject the fair use defense in that case.

ii. **The propriety of the defendant's conduct from a moral standpoint:** The Court in *Harper* also noted that the fair use defense is an equitable one, so that the ethical propriety of the defendant's conduct should be considered. If the defendant did not act in good faith, this weighs against giving him the benefit of the fair use defense. In *Harper*, the defendant had knowingly used a stolen copy of the plaintiff's unpublished manuscript to obtain its quotes. This fact contributed to the Court's rejection of its fair use defense.

iii. **The productivity of the defendant's use:** A very important consideration is whether the defendant's use was *productive*, or "*transformative*." A transformative use is much more likely to be deemed fair than a nontransformative use. A defendant's alleged infringing work is "transformative" when the new work does not merely supersede the objects of the original creation, but rather adds something new with a further purpose or different character, altering the first with new expression, meaning, or message. A parody of the plaintiff's work is a good example of transformative use. Recent case decisions have also found a defendant's use transformative when it used the plaintiff's work for a different purpose than the plaintiff did. For example, in *Perfect 10, Inc. v. Amazon.com, Inc.*, 487 F.3d 701 (9th Cir. 2007), the plaintiff alleged that the Google search engine's "Image Search" function infringed the copyrights in its photographs because it created and displayed "thumbnail" versions of the photographs in its image search results. In evaluating Google's fair use defense, the court found its use highly transformative because while the plaintiff's use was to provide artistic expression, Google's use provided improved access to information on the Internet. The Ninth Circuit noted: "a search engine provides social benefit by incorporating an original work into a new work, namely, an electronic reference tool. Indeed, a search engine may be more transformative than a parody because a search engine provides an entirely new use for the original work, while a parody typically has the same entertainment purpose as the original work."

iv. **Incidental use:** Another issue is whether the defendant's use was *incidental*. An incidental use is more likely to be excused as fair. For example, assume that a television news team tapes on-the-scene coverage of a political demonstration in a park. The reporter happens to stand in front of a copyrighted statue while making her report, thus reproducing and publicly displaying the statue without authorization and infringing the copyright. This infringement was merely incidental to the news report, and thus may be excused under the fair use doctrine.

b. **The nature of the copyrighted work:** With regard to the second §107 factor—the nature of the copyrighted work—the Supreme Court, in *Harper & Row*, stressed that the *published or unpublished* status of the plaintiff's work was highly important. Unauthorized pre-publication use has frequently been viewed as unfair because it undercuts the author's important interest in determining the timing of publication and in being the first to publish her work. Another important consideration is whether the plaintiff's work is one of *fact or fiction*. Members of the public are entitled to copy facts or other uncopyrightable elements from a plaintiff's work, and it often benefits the public that they do so. In some cases it may be necessary for a defendant to take some of the plaintiff's expression in order to convey the underlying facts. For example, in *Harper & Row*, the Court suggested that it might be necessary for a news report about President Ford's memoirs to reproduce the term "smoking gun," which President Ford used to describe the White House Tapes, in order adequately to convey the President's professed reasons for pardoning President Nixon. The fair use defense provides defendants some leeway to do so. On the other hand, it is seldom necessary directly to quote or paraphrase fiction or other non-factual or nonfunctional works. On the whole, the law affords narrower protection for factual works (or other works containing a substantial amount of uncopyrightable public domain elements), because of other authors' need to access and use the public domain elements.

c. **The amount and substantiality of the portion used in relation to the copyrighted work as a whole:** Even though the defendant's work may be "substantially similar" to the plaintiff's, and thus infringe as a technical matter, it is still appropriate to weigh the quantity and quality (or importance) of the copied portions, to determine whether the copying should be excused. As the *Harper* decision demonstrates, a defendant who takes a short but substantively important portion (for example, a paragraph that constitutes the climax or "heart" of the work) may be denied a fair use defense. An important inquiry is whether the defendant copied *more than was necessary* to accomplish his legitimate purpose. If so, that argues against finding a fair use.

d. **The effect of the use upon the potential market for the copyrighted work:** The *Harper* Court indicated that this fourth factor is generally the most important one. Copying that does not materially impair a market for the copied work, or for derivative works based upon it, can be considered a fair use. Evidence of either *actual or potential* harm to the plaintiff's market will suffice to tilt the fair use analysis away from a finding for the defendant.

   i. **Supplanting vs. suppressing the market:** The market harm that is envisioned under the fourth factor arises when the defendant's work *supplants* demand for the plaintiff's, by serving as a substitute for it. However, if the defendant's work *suppresses* plaintiff's market (for example, by criticizing it and bringing it into public contempt), the resulting market injury will not be considered under the fourth factor. Plaintiffs should not be able to use the fourth factor as a means of *censoring criticism* of their works.

3. **Four factors not exclusive:** In construing and applying §107, courts have noted that the four enumerated factors were not intended to be exclusive. Courts have often introduced additional considerations raised by the particular facts of the case before them. For example, some courts have considered not just the amount and substantiality of the material taken from the plaintiff's copyrighted work in proportion to the copyrighted work as a whole (as required by the third factor), but also the amount and substantiality of the copied portion *in relation to the defendant's work as a whole*. Indeed, in *Harper*, the Court was impressed by the fact that while the copied portions constituted only a small proportion of the plaintiff's copyrighted memoirs, they constituted 13 percent of the defendant's total article about the memoirs.

4. **No factor is conclusive:** The Supreme Court has stressed that no single §107 factor should be deemed conclusive. There are no categories of presumptively fair or unfair uses. Courts should fully consider all of the factors in ruling on fair use defenses.

C. **Special considerations in parody cases:** Parodies of serious works of art, music, and literature are a useful, productive form of social commentary, and since copyright owners are unlikely voluntarily to license others to make parodies of their work, parody authors often must rely on the fair use defense. Several particular issues should be considered in determining whether a parody use of a copyrighted work is a fair use.

1. **Parody of the copyrighted work itself or of something else?:** To be a fair use, a defendant's purpose should be at least in part to parody the plaintiff's work. If his purpose is to parody the plaintiff's work, then he must copy at least enough of the plaintiff's material to "conjure up" the plaintiff's work in the audience's mind, and communicate his point to the audience. On the other hand, if the defendant's purpose is not to comment on the substance or style of the plaintiff's work, but to make some other social comment, then there is little or no justification for copying from the plaintiff. The defendant is not privileged to copy from the plaintiff merely to get attention or to avoid the labor of creating his own material.

2. **The amount of copyrighted material taken:** In *Campbell v. Acuff-Rose Music, Inc.*, 510 U.S. 569 (1994), involving a rap-style parody of the Roy Orbison song, "Oh, Pretty Woman," the Supreme Court stressed the interrelationship of all the §107 factors, and tied the third factor (amount and substantiality of the portion used in relation to the copyrighted work as a whole) closely to the first (the purpose of the defendant's use). The issue, the Court noted, is whether the amount of the defendant's taking is *reasonable in relation to the purpose of the copying*. In the context of parody, the amount the defendant will be justified in copying will depend on the extent to which his purpose was to parody some aspect of the plaintiff's work. The Court noted that at a minimum, a parody of the substance or style of the plaintiff's work must copy enough to conjure up the original and make the object of its critical commentary recognizable to the audience. *The best and most direct way to obtain the necessary recognition is to copy the original work's most distinctive or memorable features*, which the parodist can be sure the audience will know. Thus, the parodist may be justified in taking the "heart," or most distinctive or important part of the plaintiff's work.

3. **Effect on the plaintiff's market:** As a general matter, a parody serves a different purpose than the serious work it parodies, and will not serve as a market substitute for it: Persons seeking the original are unlikely to purchase the parody in its place. Thus, in most cases a parody is unlikely to displace demand for the original. (While a scathing parody may, like a critic's bad review, decrease public respect and demand for the original, this is not the kind of market injury that the fourth factor is concerned with.) Even though there is no displacement of demand for the original, however, the court must also consider the market for derivative works based on the plaintiff's work. In the *Campbell v. Acuff-Rose* case, the Supreme Court rejected the assertion that the defendant's use had undermined the potential market for parodies of the plaintiff's song: "The market for potential derivative uses includes only those that creators of original works would in general develop or license others to develop. [T]he unlikelihood that creators of imaginative works will license critical reviews or lampoons of their own productions removes such uses from the very notion of a potential licensing market" *Id*. at 592-93. However, there were other markets to consider. The defendant's work was not only a parody but also a piece of rap music. Thus, the Supreme Court remanded for consideration of the

effect of the defendant's rap parody on the plaintiff's market for a non-parody rap version (or for a license to make a rap version) of the plaintiff's song.

D. **Educational and library copying:** One of the most controversial issues when the Copyright Act of 1976 was enacted was the proper scope for library and educational photocopying. The special exemptions that were adopted to permit *library* copying, set forth in §108 of the Act, are discussed briefly, *supra*, at pp. 137-138. Libraries may also avail themselves of the fair use defense to justify copying that does not fit within the explicit §108 exemptions from liability. In the case of *educational* institutions, Congress enacted some specific exceptions to liability to permit performance and display of copyrighted works in face-to-face teaching and instructional transmissions, as discussed *supra*, pp. 151-152. Congress also expressly mentioned teaching (including multiple copies for classroom use), scholarship and research as examples of possible fair uses in §107. However, it declined to enact a more general exemption to permit copying for educational and scholarly purposes. Nevertheless, Congress encouraged the interested parties to discuss permissible educational uses of copyrighted materials and try to reach agreement on some practical guidelines for purposes of the fair use defense. Ultimately, educational groups, authors, and publishers were able to agree upon "Guidelines for Classroom Copying in Not-for-Profit Educational Institutions," which Congress included in the House Report that accompanied the 1976 Copyright Act. The House Report notes that the Guidelines are a reasonable interpretation of what the fair use defense would allow, as a minimum, in cases of educational copying. With regard to multiple copies for classroom use, the Guidelines specify that making multiple copies will constitute a fair use if no more than one copy is made per student, each copy contains a notice of copyright, and the copying meets specified tests for brevity (the Guidelines specify maximum lengths for various types of works), spontaneity (essentially, there must not have been time between the inspiration to use the material and the use to request permission to copy), and cumulative effect. Courts have deemed the Guidelines to be "persuasive authority" in applying the fair use defense in cases involving classroom copying.

E. **Reverse engineering:** In *Sega Enterprises v. Accolade, Inc.*, 977 F.2d 1510 (9th Cir. 1992), the defendant translated the object code of some of plaintiff's copyrighted video games into human-readable source code so that it could study the programs and identify the elements that were necessary in order to design video games that would be compatible with the plaintiff's game console hardware. The Court of Appeals for the Ninth Circuit held that the intermediate copying of code that takes place in the course of translating, or decompiling, a computer program infringes the copyright owner's exclusive right to reproduce the computer program. However, the court found that *this intermediate copying will be excused as a fair use when decompilation is the only means of gaining access to unprotected ideas and functional elements embodied in the object code, and the defendant has a legitimate interest in gaining such access to those ideas and elements*. In the *Sega* case, the court found that the defendant's need to identify the elements necessary for compatibility with plaintiff's hardware (which were themselves uncopyrightable) to be a legitimate purpose, and found that decompilation of the plaintiff's object code was the only effective way to access these unprotected elements. Under these circumstances, the intermediate copying that decompilation entailed was a fair use.

F. **Market failure and fair use:** One very prominent justification given for having a fair use defense is that it is necessary in cases of market failure—situations in which the transaction costs of obtaining a license are so great that subsequent authors may decide that they outweigh the benefit of using copyrightable expression from the plaintiff's work, and decline to do so. Even though the costs may outweigh the benefit *to the subsequent authors*, they may not outweigh the benefit of those authors' use *to the general public*. In such cases, it is to the public benefit to permit such authors to make their use without obtaining a license through provision of a fair use defense. The corollary to this reasoning is that if the transaction costs of obtaining a license are relatively low, the defendant should be required to obtain a license rather than be afforded a fair use defense. The Second Circuit famously pursued this line of reasoning in *American Geophysical Union v. Texaco*, 60 F.3d 913, 930-931 (2d Cir. 1994). In that case the Second Circuit considered the ready availability of photocopying licenses through the Copyright Clearance Center, Inc. (a large licensing agent representing a wide range of copyright owners, including owners of copyright in scientific journals) to be relevant in evaluating a scientist's unlicensed, occasional photocopying of scientific journal articles that he wanted to have handy for reference in his office and in the lab. In rejecting the scientist's fair use defense, the court held:

> [I]t is not unsound to conclude that the right to seek payment for a particular use tends to become legally cognizable under the fourth fair use factor when the means for paying for such a use is made easier. This notion is not inherently troubling: it is sensible that a particular unauthorized use should be considered "more fair" when there is no ready market or means to pay for the use, while such an unauthorized use should be considered "less fair" when there is a ready market or means to pay for the use.

1. **The implications of the market failure line of reasoning for fair use on the Internet:** The line of reasoning described above may lead to a reduction in the availability of the fair use defense in the Internet context. This is because the Internet can greatly reduce the transaction costs of locating copyright owners and obtaining licenses to use copyrighted material. Internet users seeking to use copyrighted material may automatically be confronted with a "click-wrap" license when they attempt to access the work on the Internet. The click-wrap license will state the terms on which various uses of the work will be permitted, and the Internet user will need only to click the "I agree" button to obtain the desired authorization. Or new electronic permission clearing houses may be created to represent numerous copyright owners and dispense licenses quickly and efficiently. This potential lead the President's Information Infrastructure Task Force, in its Report of the Working Group on Intellectual Property Rights (1995), to suggest that application of the fair use defense could be reduced in the Internet context.

G. **Copyright misuse:** Another court-developed defense to copyright infringement that has emerged relatively recently is copyright misuse. This is an equitable defense that renders a copyright unenforceable if *the copyright owner has engaged in misconduct in licensing or enforcing the copyright, thereby broadening the scope of his monopoly right beyond that intended by Congress.* Under the misuse doctrine, the owner's copyright will be unenforceable until the misuse ends and its effects have dissipated. Some recent court opinions indicate that acts that do not constitute an antitrust violation may nonetheless constitute copyright misuse.

Example: In licensing its copyrighted software, the copyright owner used a standard licensing agreement that prohibited the licensee and all of its employees from developing competing software for 99 years. The defendant in a subsequent copyright suit alleged copyright misuse as a defense, even though he himself was not subject to the license restriction. The Court of Appeals for the Fourth Circuit held for the defendant, finding the plaintiff's copyright unenforceable under the misuse doctrine. The court reasoned that the copyright was being used in a manner that violated the public policy embodied in the grant of the copyright. *Lasercomb America, Inc. v. Reynolds*, 911 F.2d 970 (4th Cir. 1990).

XIII. ANTICIRCUMVENTION AND DIGITAL RIGHTS MANAGEMENT PROVISIONS

The Digital Millennium Copyright Act (DMCA) encourages copyright owners to engage in technological self-help (such as digital watermarking, password systems, and encryption measures) to prevent unauthorized access and to control use of their works on the Internet. It also prevents tampering with the copyright management information that copyright owners place on their works.

A. **Anticircumvention provisions:** The DMCA makes it illegal to circumvent technological measures that copyright owners use to control others' *access* to their works. It also prohibits persons from manufacturing, distributing, or trafficking in devices or services that *enable others* to circumvent such technological access controls, as well as technological controls that copyright owners use to regulate *use* of their works once access is gained. The Act provides both civil and criminal penalties for violations. It is important to note that liability for violation of the anticircumvention provisions is separate from liability for copyright infringement, and may be imposed even if the defendant's circumvention or trafficking in circumvention devices did not result in a copyright infringement. The anti-circumvention provisions are codified at Copyright Act §§1201-1205.

1. **Two kinds of "technological measures" and three causes of action:** It is important to note that the DMCA recognizes two different kinds of "technological measures": (1) measures used to control access to the copyrighted work (for example, password systems or encryption); and (2) measures used to control use of the copyrighted work (exercise of the exclusive rights of copyright—reproduction, adaptation, distribution to the public, public performance and public display) once access is gained (for example, code embedded in a digital work that permits performance of the work, but prohibits reproduction; or embedded code that allows only a specified number of copies to be made). The DMCA then prohibits: (1) circumvention of access controls; (2) manufacturing, selling or trafficking in services or devices that enable circumvention of access controls; and (3) manufacturing, selling or trafficking in services or devices that enable circumvention of use controls.

2. **Liability for circumventing access controls:** DMCA §1201(a) provides that no person shall circumvent a technological measure that effectively controls *access* to a work protected under the Copyright Act. As is noted in the legislative history, this provision essentially prohibits the electronic equivalent of breaking into a locked room in order to obtain a copy of a book. Liability arises from the invasion, and does not depend on a showing of copyright infringement. (The DMCA directs the Librarian of Congress to investigate whether this broad prohibition will interfere unduly with people's ability to engage in legal uses of copyrighted material, such as fair uses, and to engage in rulemaking to make any exceptions to liability that may be necessary. To date, the Librarian has only made a few *very* narrow exceptions.)

    a. **"Technological measure" that controls access defined:** Section 1201 provides that "a technological measure effectively controls access to a work if the measure, in the ordinary course of its operation, requires the application of information, or a process or a treatment, with the authority of the copyright owner, to gain access to the work." *Id.* This would include password systems and encryption, among other things.

b. **"Circumvention" defined:** Section 1201 provides that to "circumvent a technological measure" means "to descramble a scrambled work, to decrypt an encrypted work, or otherwise to avoid, bypass, remove, deactivate, or impair a technological measure, without the authority of the copyright owner." 17 U.S.C. §1201(a)(3).

   i. **The definition of "circumvention" applied in the case of password systems:** Several courts have been faced with situations in which the copyright owner devised a password system to control access to its copyrighted material and issued a password to A, and B (a third party) later used A's password to gain access to the materials without the copyright owner's permission. The question was whether B's unauthorized use of the password to gain access to the materials constituted actionable circumvention of an access control. The response has been mixed. One line of cases has held that there is no actionable circumvention, reasoning that circumvention entails bypassing or avoiding the deployed technological measure in the measure's gatekeeping capacity. However, what the defendant (B) avoided and bypassed was not the technological measure itself but *permission* to engage and move through the technological measure. This reasoning thus suggests that the DMCA prohibits bypassing the gate, but not passing through it without permission. See, *e.g., I.M.S. Inquiry Management Systems, Ltd. v. Berkshire Information Systems, Inc.*, 307 F. Supp. 2d 521, 531-533 (S.D.N.Y. 2004). The other line of cases finds that B's unauthorized use of the password does constitute actionable circumvention, reasoning that unauthorized use of the password constitutes circumvention of the password system itself. See, *e.g., 321 Studios v. Metro-Goldwyn Mayer Studios, Inc.*, 307 F. Supp. 2d 1085, 1097 (N.D. Ca. 2004).

c. **Circumvention of technological measures that "effectively protect a right of a copyright owner" is not prohibited:** The DMCA does not itself prohibit circumvention of technological measures that control reproduction, adaptation, distribution, public performance, or public display of a work, once lawful access is gained. So, for example, if a person with lawful access to a copyrighted work circumvented a technological device (such as software) limiting the number of hard copies that can be made of the work, his *liability would be judged under the rules governing copyright infringement,* and he would be able to assert a fair use defense. He would not be liable for circumvention, in itself.

3. **Liability for manufacturing, distributing, or trafficking in circumvention devices or services:** The DMCA prohibits manufacturing, distributing, or trafficking in devices or services to defeat technological protection measures (both technological measures that control *access* to copyrighted works *and* technological measures that control *reproduction, adaptation, distribution, public display, and/or public performance* of the work once access is gained). Such devices and services have been referred to as "electronic crowbars" and infiltration strategies. However, to ensure that multi-purpose devices can continue to be made and distributed, the prohibition is limited to devices or services that (1) are primarily designed or produced for the purpose of circumventing; (2) have only limited commercially significant purposes or uses other than to circumvent; or (3) are marketed for use in circumventing.

4. **Early decisions construing the "anti-trafficking" provisions:** When the anticircumvention provisions were enacted, many commentators criticized them on the ground that they were far broader than they needed to be, essentially giving copyright owners a new exclusive (property) right of "access" in their works, which is not subject to a general fair use defense. There were concerns that copyright owners' new ability to lock up works in technological measures

and prohibit circumvention, and acts enabling circumvention, would enable copyright owners effectively to prohibit traditional fair uses of their works, and to monopolize their works' public domain elements. As will be discussed below, the first set of Circuit Court-level decisions generated by the §1201 provisions have varied in their construction of the scope of rights given.

> **a. The *Corley* decision:** In Universal City Studios, Inc. v. Corley, 273 F.3d 429 (2d Cir. 2001), motion picture copyright owners released their films on DVDs protected through an encryption scheme (called "CSS") that allowed the DVD only to be viewed on players or computer drives equipped with licensed technology that permitted playing, but not copying, the film. A Norwegian teenager reverse engineered a licensed DVD player and developed a decryption program (called "DeCSS") that enabled users to "rip" encrypted DVDs, play them on non-compliant computers (such as a Linux system) and copy them. The defendants maintained a web site that originally posted the DeCSS code, and later provided links to other web sites that had posted the DeCSS code. The copyright owners sued, alleging that the defendants were trafficking in an access control circumvention device (the DeCSS code), and the Second Circuit agreed, enjoining them from posting DeCSS on their web sites and from knowingly linking their web sites to any other web site on which DeCSS was posted. The court noted that "the DMCA targets the circumvention of digital walls guarding copyrighted material (and trafficking in circumvention tools), but does not concern itself with the *use* of these materials after the circumvention has occurred." It thus rejected arguments that there could be no liability absent a showing of copyright infringement resulting from the defendants' acts. The court rejected a number of additional arguments for a narrower construction, as well as constitutional challenges based on the language of the Patents and Copyrights clause and the First Amendment.
>
> **b. Cases involving use of technological measures to monopolize markets for replacement parts and aftermarket products:** Some industries saw the opportunity to use the DMCA anticircumvention provisions to monopolize the market for replacement parts and aftermarket products, by incorporating access control measures into the computer programs that operated their products. It seems clear from the legislative history that Congress did not have this kind of activity in mind when it enacted the DMCA. Both the Federal Circuit and the Court of Appeals for the Sixth Circuit have construed the anticircumvention provisions to avoid upholding the industries' actions, but as will be discussed below, the Federal Circuit's construction has a much more profound effect on the overall scope of §1201 rights.
>
>> **i. The *Chamberlain* decision:** In *Chamberlain Group, Inc. v. Skylink Technologies, Inc.*, 381 F.3d 1178 (Fed. Cir. 2004), *cert. denied,* 544 U.S. 923 (2005), the plaintiff placed a lock-out code in the software that operated the opening and closing mechanism in its automatic garage doors. The software couldn't be activated to open the door until a signal from the plaintiff's remote control unit unlocked the code. The defendant developed a universal garage door opener that "circumvented" the lock-out code, enabling owners of plaintiff's doors to control them with the defendant's remote. The plaintiff alleged that the defendant was trafficking in an access control circumvention device (its universal remote). The Federal Circuit rejected the claim, on two lines of reasoning. First, the court reasoned that consumers normally expect to have full use of the consumer goods they purchase, including the right to use the goods with aftermarket products and replacement parts manufactured by competitors. Thus, in making an *unrestricted sale* of its garage doors to consumers, the *plaintiff implicitly authorized* its

purchasers to circumvent the software access control and use other producers' door openers. Second (and more importantly) the court held that §1201 was not intended to provide a new property right (or "exclusive right of access") to copyright owners, but merely to provide *a new means of protecting existing rights* created under the Copyright Act. Thus, §1201(a) only prohibits trafficking in circumvention devices *whose use will infringe or facilitate infringement of copyright*. In the present case, the defendant's universal opener did not create an unauthorized reproduction, adaptation, distribution, performance or display of the copyrighted software. It merely permitted functional *use* of the software to open the garage door, which did not constitute infringement. The Federal Circuit concluded with a list of elements that a plaintiff alleging violation of §1201(a)(2) must demonstrate:

1. Ownership of a valid copyright in a work
2. effectively controlled by a technological measure, which has been circumvented
3. that third parties can now access
4. without authorization in a matter that
5. infringes or facilitates infringing a right protected by the Copyright Act, because of a product that
6. the defendant either: (a) designed or produced primarily for circumvention; (b) made available despite only limited commercial significance other than to circumvent; or (c) marketed for use in circumvention of the controlling technological measure.

ii. **The *Lexmark* decision:** In *Lexmark International, Inc. v. Static Control Components, Inc.*, 37 F.3d 522 (6th Cir. 2004), the Court of Appeals for the Sixth Circuit considered a claim very similar to that in *Chamberlain*: The defendant incorporated a lock-out device into the software that ran its printers so that the software would only work upon receiving an authentication sequence from a chip located on Lexmark toner cartridges. The defendant manufactured and sold a chip that mimicked the authentication sequence and allowed owners of Lexmark printers to use competitors' toner cartridges. The Sixth Circuit rejected Lexmark's "trafficking in access control circumvention devices" claim, but on much narrower grounds than the Federal Circuit did. The Sixth Circuit held that the plaintiff's authentication sequence was not an access control measure, within the meaning of the DMCA, because it did not prohibit all forms of access. It controlled the consumer's ability to *make use* of the printer software, but it did not prevent anyone from *reading* the software code or *copying* it.

c. **Construction of §1201(c)(1):** Subsection 1201(c)(1) provides that "Nothing in this section shall affect rights, remedies, limitations, or defenses to copyright infringement, including fair use, under this title." In *Chamberlain*, the Federal Circuit found that construction of §1201(a)(2) to apply to prevent all circumventions (even those that do not facilitate infringement) would be inconsistent with subsection (c)(1). In such a case, the copyright owner could, through a combination of contractual terms and technological measures, prohibit fair uses altogether. The Second Circuit, in contrast, held that subsection (c)(1) "simply clarifies that the DMCA targets the *circumvention* of digital walls guarding copyrighted material (and trafficking in circumvention tools), but does not concern itself with the *use* of those materials after circumvention has occurred." Thus, for example, a finding that a defendant violated the DMCA (and is liable for circumvention or trafficking in circumvention devices) should not in itself prevent the defendant from asserting a fair use defense in answer to a copyright infringement claim arising from his (or his device users') circumvention.

5. **Exceptions:** Although it declined to enact a general "fair use" defense to circumvention or circumvention device trafficking liability, Congress did add several *narrow exceptions* to the anticircumvention prohibitions, which permit, among other things (and under certain circumstances):

   1. software developers to reverse engineer technologically protected software in order to achieve interoperability;
   2. police and intelligence agents to circumvent for law enforcement purposes;
   3. researchers to engage in good-faith encryption research; and
   4. persons to engage in testing the security of a computer system or network.

B. **Copyright management information:** Copyright management information includes information that identifies the work or its copyright owner or (if appropriate) performers, writers, or directors of the work. It also includes terms and conditions for a license to use the work, and any identifying numbers or symbols. Congress considered it particularly important to prevent tampering with such information in the Internet context because the information will be digitally encoded in copyrighted works and used in automated licensing and tracking of the works on the Internet. The DMCA prohibits persons from intentionally removing or altering copyright management information, or knowingly distributing copies or phonorecords with illegally modified copyright management information. The DMCA includes some exceptions, particularly for broadcasting entities.

XIV. OWNERSHIP OF COPYRIGHT

A. **Determining the initial owner of copyright in a work:** The *author* of a work is the *initial owner of the copyright* in it, and may exploit the work herself or transfer some or all the rights conferred by the copyright to others. (Copyright Act §201). The author generally is *the person who conceives of the copyrightable expression and fixes it or causes it to be fixed in a tangible form.* (Thus, for example, if a business executive dictates a letter to her secretary, who then transcribes and types it, the executive is the "author" of the letter. The executive conceived of the expression and caused it to be fixed. The secretary merely fixed the expression pursuant to the executive's direction.) *"Works made for hire" are an important exception to this rule*: When a work is "made for hire," within the meaning of the Copyright Act, the employer or commissioning party, who pays for creation of the work, is deemed the author, rather than the employee or commissioned party who actually conceives and fixes the expression (or causes its fixation). There are several issues regarding determination of "authorship" and initial ownership of copyright, which will be considered below.

B. **Ownership of copyright in joint works:** The authors of a "joint work" are co-owners of a single copyright in the work. Copyright Act §101 defines a joint work as "a work prepared by two or more authors with the intention that their contributions be merged into inseparable or interdependent parts of a unitary whole."

   1. **Emphasis on intent:** In determining whether a work is a joint work, so that there is a single, jointly-owned copyright in it, the emphasis is on the *intent* of the parties at the time each made

his or her contribution to the work. While it is not necessary that all the authors work at the same time, or even that they know one another, each party must intend to contribute a part to a unitary whole, and thus create a joint work.

Example: A writes a melody, intending it to be complete as it is. A year later, he decides to have B add lyrics. While pre-1976 Act case law indicated that the combined melody and lyrics could be deemed a joint work, the Copyright Act of 1976 changed the law. Under the 1976 Act, the combined melody and lyrics cannot be a joint work because both authors must have intended, *at the time they made their respective contributions*, to be contributing to a larger, unitary work. A did not have such an intent. At the time he wrote the melody, he intended it to be a complete work in itself. The fact that he later changed his mind is irrelevant. A and B do not jointly own the copyright in a unitary work (melody and lyrics combined). Rather, each owns a copyright in his own individual creation. A has exclusive copyright in the melody. By adding lyrics to the melody pursuant to a license from A, B has created a derivative work, to which he alone owns copyright.

Note: If A and B are found to be authors of a joint work, they each own an undivided interest in the copyright. (In the absence of an agreement to the contrary, each owns an *equal* undivided interest.) They are tenants in common, and each is entitled to exercise rights in the work as a whole—*e.g.*, each may reproduce or publicly perform the whole work or license others to do so—subject to a duty to account to the other co-owner for any profits. On the other hand, if, as in the example above, A and B own separate copyrights, then any unauthorized use by one of the other's contribution will render him liable to the other for copyright infringement.

2. **Contribution of copyrightable expression:** To be a joint author, *a party must have contributed copyrightable expression*, not just facts or ideas. While one party may contribute considerably less copyrightable expression to the work than the other and still be deemed a joint author, the quantity of expression a party contributed to the work may provide circumstantial evidence regarding the parties' intent to contribute to (or create) a joint work.

3. **Other requirements:** The Ninth Circuit has held that, in addition to contributing copyrightable expression, an alleged joint author must "originate" and "superintend" the work, *imposing his or her own mental conception on it*, exercising decision-making authority with regard to the work as a whole. The Second and Seventh Circuits require that, in addition to contributing original expression, the alleged joint authors *intend for each of them to be joint authors*. Evidence of such an intent might include a showing that each participant exercised decision-making power with regard to the final form of the work, evidence that the parties portrayed themselves as joint authors in the credits or bylines, and evidence that the parties divided royalties generated through exploitation of the work.

C. **Works for hire:** If a work is "made for hire" within the meaning of the Copyright Act, the employer or commissioning party, who paid for the work and took the economic risk of it, is deemed the author for copyright purposes and is the initial owner of the copyright. Copyright Act §101 sets forth the two circumstances under which a work may be found to be a work for hire.

1. **Work prepared by an employee within the scope of his employment:** First, a work is a "work for hire" if it is prepared by an employee within the scope of his employment. In *Community for Creative Non-Violence v. Reid,* 490 U.S. 730 (1989), the Supreme Court held that the term "employee" in this context should be interpreted according to common-law agency principles. If the person doing the work is an "employee" within the meaning of the common

law, and the work was done within the scope of his employment, then the work is a work for hire and the employer is the initial owner of the copyright (even though the employee actually conceived and fixed the expression).

a. Common-law agency criteria for determining whether a person is an employee: To determine whether a person is an employee under common-law agency principles (as opposed to an independent contractor) the court must examine the *hiring party's right to control the manner and means by which the work is accomplished.* The factors that the *Reid* decision requires courts to consider in doing this are set forth below. They are taken from the Restatement (Second) of Agency, §220. In *Reid*, the Supreme Court stated that no one of these factors should be deemed determinative. However, subsequent circuit-level opinions have warned that the weight to afford each factor may differ, depending on its relevance in the particular setting at issue. For example, factors relating to the hired party's authority to hire assistants will not normally be relevant if the very nature of the work requires the hired party to work alone.

- The level of skill required to do the work (the more skill required, the more likely the worker is an independent contractor, rather than an employee);

- The source of the instrumentalities and tools used to do the work (if the worker is the source, he is more likely an independent contractor than an employee);

- The location of the work (if the work is done on the worker's premises, the worker is more likely to be an independent contractor);

- The duration of the relationship between the parties (the shorter the duration, the more likely the worker is an independent contractor);

- Whether the hiring party has the right to assign additional projects to the worker (if so, the worker is more likely an employee than an independent contractor);

- The extent of the worker's discretion over when and how long to work (the more discretion, the more likely the worker is an independent contractor);

- The method of payment (is the worker paid in the same manner as employees usually are?);

- The worker's role in hiring and paying assistants (if the worker controls the hiring of assistants and pays them himself, he is more likely to be an independent contractor than an employee);

- Whether the work is part of the regular business of the hiring party (if not, it is more likely that the worker is an independent contractor, rather than an employee);

- Whether the hiring party is in business (if not, it is more likely that the worker is an independent contractor);

- The provision of employee benefits (if employee benefits are provided, it is more likely the worker is an employee); and

- The tax treatment of the worker (does the hiring party withhold social security, income taxes, etc., as would normally be done for an employee?).

b. **Criteria for determining whether the employee made the work "within the scope of his employment":** Factors courts will consider in determining whether an employee made a work "within the scope of his employment" include:

- whether the work is the kind he was employed to prepare;

- whether the preparation takes place primarily within the employer's time and place specifications; and

- whether the work was activated, at least in part, by a purpose to serve the employer.

2. **Specially ordered or commissioned works:** Works created by independent contractors (rather than employees) can be deemed works for hire *only if* two conditions are satisfied. First, the work must fit into one of nine categories of works enumerated in Copyright Act §101. Second, the parties must expressly agree in a written, signed instrument that the work will be considered a work made for hire.

   a. **The nine categories of works:** To constitute a work for hire under the independent contractor branch of the work for hire doctrine, the work must be one specially ordered or commissioned for use:

   1. as a contribution to a collective work;
   2. as a part of a motion picture or other audiovisual work;
   3. as a translation;
   4. as a supplementary work (a work, such as a forward, afterward, index, chart, or appendix, prepared for publication as a secondary adjunct to a work by another author in order to introduce, conclude, illustrate, explain, revise, comment upon, or assist in the use of the other work);
   5. as a compilation;
   6. as an instructional text (a literary, pictorial, or graphic work prepared for publication with the purpose of use in systematic instructional activities);
   7. as a test;
   8. as answer material for a test; or
   9. as an atlas.

   Note: Even if a work is not a work for hire as defined under §101, a person commissioning a work by another may require, as a term of the contract, that the worker assign his copyright to the commissioning party. The immediate end result—copyright in the commissioning party—is the same as if the work were a work for hire. However, the work is not, by virtue of the assignment, a work for hire, and this may be important. For example, the party preparing the work has termination rights if he was the initial author and assigned the copyright to the commissioning party, but not if the copyright initially vested in the commissioning party under the work for hire doctrine. See *infra*, pp. 189-193. Likewise, the duration of the copyright may depend on whether or not the work was created as a work for hire. See *infra*, p. 183. In addition, under the Visual Artists' Rights Act, the artist who creates a work of visual art as a work for hire will not enjoy moral rights in it. See *supra*, p. 154.

D. **Ownership of copyright in collective works:** A collective work is a collection of independent, separately copyrightable works of authorship, such as a newspaper, magazine, or encyclopedia. In the absence of an express written assignment of copyright, the author of each individual work in the collection retains copyright in that work. The compiler, or author of the collection, owns copyright in the expression he or she contributed, which is primarily the selection and arrangement of the separate contributions, but may include such things as a preface, advertisements, etc., that the collective author created.

1. **Presumed privileges:** Copyright Act §20l(c) provides that in the absence of a writing to the contrary, it is presumed that the author of the collective work has the following privileges with regard to the individual works he has collected:

    1. the privilege to reproduce and distribute the individual contributions as part of that particular collective work;
    2. the privilege to reproduce the individual contributions as part of later revisions of the *same* collective work (for example, if the collective work is an encyclopedia, the collective author may reproduce individual entries in updated editions); and
    3. the privilege to reproduce the individual contributions in a later work of the *same series* (for example, if the collective work is a magazine, the author has a privilege to reproduce the individual contribution—perhaps a short story or article—in a later issue of the same magazine).

2. **Limitation on the presumed privileges:** In *New York Times Co., Inc. v. Tasini*, 533 U.S. 463 (2001), the Supreme Court found that §201(c) did not authorize newspapers to make freelance articles appearing in their daily editions available for inclusion in electronic databases, such as NEXIS, that give subscribers access to articles from a large number of periodicals. The Supreme Court found that such a database could not be considered a "revision" of the newspaper (collective work) in which an article first appeared, even though the entire content of the newspaper was contributed to the database. When viewed as part of the database, the article is divorced of the context of the original newspaper in which it appeared. The database presents the article as part of a new, much larger collective work consisting of articles from thousands of individual collective works. In contrast, courts have found a §201(c) "revision" when a newspaper or magazine publishes a CD-ROM collection of all its prior editions. In such cases, the CD-Rom preserves the original selection and arrangement, presenting the freelance works in their original context.

E. **Divisibility of ownership:** As noted *supra*, the Copyright Act of 1976 provides that copyright ownership is divisible. Each of the exclusive economic rights conferred by copyright—the right to reproduce the work, the right to prepare derivative works, the right to distribute copies to the public, the right to perform the work publicly, and the right to display the work publicly—may be assigned to others, by itself or in combination with other rights. Moreover, each of these rights may be subdivided. For example, the owner of the exclusive right to make derivative works may assign the exclusive right to *translate* the work into another language to one assignee, and the exclusive right to *adapt the work into a screenplay* to another assignee. The owner of the exclusive right of public performance in a work may assign the exclusive right to publicly perform the work *in New York* to one person, while retaining the exclusive right to perform it everywhere else. Any person who owns an exclusive right is considered a copyright owner and has the right to bring suit in his own capacity to enforce the right he owns against others. A person who has a nonexclusive right (i.e., a right that others may also have, such as a right to publicly perform a popular song pursuant to license) is a mere licensee, rather than a copyright owner, and has no independent standing to sue for infringement. (As discussed on p. 155, moral rights in works of visual art are not assignable.)

F. **The requirement of a writing to transfer:** *All* transfers of copyright ownership (that is, all transfers of exclusive economic rights in the work) must be in writing and signed by the transferor, unless the transfer is by operation of law (e.g., passage by intestate succession). (Copyright Act §204.) The transfer of non-exclusive rights is not a transfer of copyright ownership, but rather is merely a license. Licenses may be oral.

   1. **Recordation of documents:** Copyright Act §205 provides that assignments, licenses, and other documents pertaining to copyright may be recorded in the Copyright Office. Proper recordation of a document may serve as constructive notice to the world of the facts stated in the recorded document. With regard to assignments and licenses, subsection 205(d) provides a kind of recording act, similar in operation to the recording acts for transfers of real property.

G. **Beneficial ownership of copyright:** When a person assigns his copyright (or one of the exclusive rights), but retains the right to receive royalties from the assignee's exploitation of the work, the assignor is viewed as a beneficial (as opposed to legal) owner of the assigned rights. The beneficial owner has standing to sue third parties for infringement of the rights, because infringement is an injury to the beneficial owner: Infringement may dilute his royalty payments. Given that the beneficial owner has assigned away his exclusive rights, however, he may not continue to exploit them himself. Any attempt to do so may render him liable to the legal owner/assignee for copyright infringement.

XV. NOTICE OF COPYRIGHT

A. **The history of notice requirements in the United States:** Unlike most developed nations, the United States has traditionally emphasized placement of copyright notice on all published copies and phonorecords of a work. As will be discussed below, copyright notice requirements were extremely strict under the Copyright Act of 1909, and failure to comply generally lead to forfeiture of copyright. The Copyright Act of 1976 retained mandatory notice requirements, but softened their impact by including "savings provisions," under which an omission of notice might be forgiven or cured, to avoid a forfeiture. When the United States joined the Berne Convention, it was required to amend the Copyright Act to make notice optional. The Berne Convention amendments became effective on March 1, 1989. It is useful to be familiar with the prior laws regarding notice because the more recent *amendments are not retroactive*: If copies of a work were published without proper notice in the past, *the law existing at the time of the publication applies*. If the publication without proper notice rendered copyright in a domestic work invalid under the law applicable at that time, then the work remains unprotected by copyright today. (With regard to foreign works, see *infra*, p. 180.)

B. **The Copyright Act of 1909:** Prior to January 1, 1978 (the effective date of the Copyright Act of 1976), the United States had a dual system of copyright protection. State common-law copyright protected works prior to publication. When the work was published, common-law protection ceased. Upon publication, federal statutory copyright protection began, *if all the authorized published copies carried proper notice of copyright*. Failure to include notice on even a few published copies, or failure to give notice in the proper form or location, generally lead to forfeiture of all copyright in the work.

   1. **Publication under the 1909 Act:** Under the 1909 Act, publication marked the end of common-law copyright and the beginning of federal statutory protection, if proper notice was

provided. The Act left definition of "publication" to the courts, who made the issue rather complex. The fact that a work had been made public or commercially exploited did not necessarily mean that it had been "published," for purposes of copyright protection. *As a general matter, publication entailed physically distributing tangible copies of the work to members of the public without restriction on their use.* Thus, a public performance of the work, for example, by national broadcast, did not itself constitute a publication.

- **a. Divestive vs. investive publication:** A publication was deemed "*divestive*" if it would deprive a work of common-law copyright without the possibility of federal statutory copyright (due to improper provision of notice), thus thrusting the work into the public domain. A publication was deemed "*investive*" if it would have the effect of triggering federal statutory copyright for a work bearing proper notice. In the case of divestive publications, the courts tended to require a greater showing of unrestricted distribution of copies to the public.

  - **i. Limited publications:** In finding some distributions of copies to the public insufficient to constitute a divestive publication, the courts developed the concept of "limited publication," which, for practical purposes, was not publication at all. A limited publication was a distribution of copies to a selected group of people for a limited purpose. So, for example, if an author sent drafts of his work to selected scholars in his field to review and comment, and omitted copyright notice, this might be excused as a limited publication. The distribution was made for the limited purpose of scholarly review and comment. It would not forfeit common-law copyright protection.

C. The Copyright Act of 1976—January 1, 1978 to March 1, 1989: When Congress enacted the Copyright Act of 1976 (which became effective on January 1, 1978), it essentially did away with the dual system of copyright. Under the 1976 Act, federal statutory copyright commences upon fixation of a work in tangible form. State copyright protection is preempted for works that have been so fixed. See RELATIONSHIP BETWEEN STATE AND FEDERAL LAW, *infra*, pp. 340-345. While the 1976 Act retained mandatory notice requirements for all *published* copies and phonorecords of a work, and provided that failure to provide proper notice could result in forfeiture of copyright, it incorporated savings provisions which, when satisfied, would forgive notice omissions or deem the omissions cured, so that forfeiture could be avoided.

1. **Publication under the 1976 Act:** Copyright Act §101 defines "publication" as follows: "'Publication' is the distribution of copies or phonorecords of a work to the public by sale or other transfer of ownership, or by rental, lease, or lending. The offering to distribute copies or phonorecords for purposes of further distribution, public performance, or public display, constitutes publication. A public performance or display of a work does not of itself constitute publication."

2. **Notice on visually perceptible copies:** As originally enacted, Copyright Act §401 provided that notice of copyright *must* be placed on all visually perceptible copies of a copyrighted work that were publicly distributed. Proper notice consists of three elements: (1) either the letter "c" in a circle, or the word "copyright," or the abbreviation "copr."; (2) the year of first publication of the work (this could be omitted for certain types of works); and (3) the name of the owner of copyright.

3. **Notice on phonorecords:** As originally enacted, Copyright Act §402 *required* notice of copyright for sound recordings on all publicly distributed phonorecords of the sound recording. Proper notice of copyright for sound recordings consists of three elements: (1) the letter "p" in

a circle; (2) the year of first publication of the sound recording; and (3) the name of the owner of copyright.

4. **Savings provisions:** Copyright Act §405 provided that if authorized copies or phonorecords were publicly distributed without copyright notice, the copyright in the work would be *invalidated unless one of three conditions was satisfied.* (These three conditions would forgive or cure an omission, regardless of whether the omission was inadvertent or deliberate.)

   a. **Small number of copies:** Copyright would not be invalidated if only a relatively small number of copies or phonorecords was distributed to the public without notice.

   b. **Registration and effort to add notice:** Copyright would not be invalidated if the work was registered with the Copyright Office within five years of the public distribution without notice and the owner made reasonable efforts to add notice to all of the copies distributed to the public in the United States after the omission was discovered. "Reasonable efforts" generally would include adding notice to all copies left in inventory. In some cases it might be necessary for the copyright owner to add labels giving copyright notice to copies still in the hands of wholesale or retail distributors.

   c. **Omission in violation of an express agreement:** Finally, §405 provided that copyright would not be invalidated if the notice was omitted in violation of an express writing in which the copyright owner specified that notice must be included, as a condition to authorizing the public distribution.

   d. **Innocent infringement:** Even when §405 applied to excuse an omission of notice, innocent infringers who relied on the omission as an indication that the work was in the public domain were excused from paying actual or statutory damages for their infringement prior to the time that they received actual notice that the work was copyrighted. (Of course, further infringement could be enjoined, and the court could require that the innocent infringer pay over his profits attributable to the infringement.)

5. **The effect of an error in the notice:** Copyright Act §406 spelled out the effect of errors in the notice of copyright. A complete omission of the copyright owner's name was treated as an omission of notice of copyright. Misidentification of the copyright owner would not affect the validity of the notice, but could provide a defense to an infringer who was reasonably misled by the error and got an assignment or license in good faith from the person misnamed as the owner. If no year of first publication was given, §406 provided that the situation should be treated as one in which no notice of copyright was given. If a year of first publication was given, but was too early, §406 provided that the date given would be considered the actual date of publication, to the extent that date of publication was relevant. If a year of publication was given, but was more than a year later than the actual date of first publication, the work would be treated as if no notice was given.

D. **The Berne Convention amendments—March 1, 1989 to the present:** When the United States joined the Berne Convention, it had to *eliminate notice requirements* in order to comply with the Berne Convention prohibition against subjecting enjoyment of copyright to "any formality." The Berne Convention Implementation Act *amended the Copyright Act of 1976 to provide that compliance with the notice provisions discussed above is voluntary, rather than mandatory for copies and phonorecords distributed to the public after the effective date of the Act (March 1, 1989).* In order to encourage voluntary compliance, the Act provided that if proper notice was provided on the published copy or phonorecord to which a copyright infringement defendant had access, the defendant could not make an innocent infringement defense to mitigate actual or statutory damages.

E. **Foreign copyright restoration:** As noted earlier, as a general matter, *the status of copyright in a work is determined pursuant to the notice provisions that were applicable at the time that copies or phonorecords were distributed without notice.* If copyright was forfeited under those provisions, it remains forfeited. Subsequent amendment of the copyright law to eliminate notice requirements does not revive the copyright. However, Congress enacted an important *exception to this rule* in the Uruguay Round Agreements Act, which implemented the United States' obligations under the Agreement on Trade-Related Aspects of Intellectual Property Protection (TRIPs). As newly amended, Copyright Act §104A *restores copyright in works originating in foreign countries belonging to the Berne Convention or the World Trade Organization (WTO) that have fallen into the United States' public domain for reasons other than the normal expiration of their term of protection.* More specifically, the amendments restore copyright in these foreign works if the U.S. copyright was forfeited for lack of proper notice or other formalities, such as a lack of proper renewal. *The amendments also provide U.S. copyright for eligible foreign sound recordings that were fixed prior to February 15, 1972* (the date the United States first recognized federal copyright in sound recordings) and for foreign works that were denied U.S. copyright protection because their country of origin did not have copyright relations with the United States at the time they were published.

1. **Effective date and term of restoration:** The amendments automatically restore copyright in eligible foreign works effective January 1, 1996. Copyright in works from countries who were not members of the Berne Convention or the WTO on January 1, 1996, but later join, or that are later extended protection by Presidential proclamation, will be restored on the date of adherence or proclamation. *The restored term will endure for the remainder of the term the work would have enjoyed had copyright not previously been denied or forfeited* under U.S. law. Restored copyrights are enforceable against persons with *notice* of the owner's intent to enforce.

    a. **Reliance parties:** The copyright is enforceable as soon as it is restored, except against "reliance parties." A reliance party is a person who began reproducing, adapting, or publicly distributing, performing, or displaying a foreign work before its copyright was restored, and continued to engage in these acts thereafter. Under the amended §104A, a restored copyright cannot be enforced against a reliance party until the copyright owner complies with prescribed notice requirements. Upon receiving notice, reliance parties must stop reproducing the restored work, but may continue to use or sell preexisting copies of the work for the next 12 months. If the reliance party has created a derivative work based on the foreign work prior to the restoration of copyright, the reliance party may continue to exploit the derivative work beyond one year if he pays reasonable compensation to the restored copyright owner.

XVI. DEPOSIT AND REGISTRATION

A. **Deposit requirements:** Copyright Act §407 requires the owner of copyright (or the owner of publication rights) in a published work to deposit two copies or phonorecords of the best edition of that work with the Copyright Office within three months after publication. The purpose of this requirement is to enrich the Library of Congress's collections. The Copyright Office has authority to make some exceptions to this rule by regulation, and has done so. Failure to comply with the deposit requirement, as modified by Copyright Office regulations, is punishable by fine, but does not result in forfeiture of copyright.

B. Registration requirements: Copyright Act §408 provides that the owner of copyright in a published or unpublished work may, at any time during the copyright, register the work with the Copyright Office. The purpose of the registration provisions is to create as comprehensive a record of U.S. copyright claims as is possible. To register, the registrant must complete an application form and send it, along with the filing fee and copies or phonorecords of the work, to the Copyright Office. (Section 407 provides that a deposit pursuant to §407 may satisfy the registration deposit requirements, as well. The Copyright Office may require or permit the deposit of other identifying material in lieu of copies or phonorecords of the work in some cases—among other reasons, to accommodate persons wishing to register materials that they consider to be trade secret). The Copyright Office reviews applications for obvious errors or lack of copyrightable subject matter, and then issues a certificate of registration. Unlike the P.T.O.'s rigorous examination of patent applications, the Copyright Office's examination of applications to register copyrights entails no attempt to evaluate the merits of the work or to search the prior art.

1. **Certificate as *prima facie* evidence:** A certificate of registration for a work that was obtained before or within five years after the work was first published constitutes *prima facie* evidence of the validity of the copyright and of the facts stated in the certificate. 17 U.S.C. §410(c). This can be useful to the copyright claimant in litigation for copyright infringement.

2. **Registration as a prerequisite to a copyright infringement action:** Prior to the Berne Convention Implementation Act, U.S. copyright law required all copyright claimants to register their works (or show that they attempted to register and were refused) before instituting a suit for infringement. However, the Berne Convention prohibits its members from imposing formalities as a precondition to protecting works whose "country of origin" is another Berne Convention member. See *infra*, pp. 195-196. Because the United States was loath to give up mandatory registration, *it distinguished between works whose country of origin is the United States and works whose country of origin is not the United States. It retained the registration requirement for the former group of works, and made registration voluntary for the latter group*. Thus, domestic copyright owners must register their copyrights (or demonstrate that they attempted to register and were refused) before they can bring a suit for infringement. While it is necessary to register before bringing suit, it is not necessary that registration occur before the defendant's infringing activities. However, as noted below, the 1976 Act encourages early registration.

    a. **Ascertaining a work's country of origin:** As a general matter, a work's country of origin is the United States if it was first published in the United States, was simultaneously published in the United States and another country, or in the case of unpublished works, was created entirely by U.S. authors.

3. **Registration as a prerequisite to certain remedies:** Copyright Act §412 encourages early registration of both foreign and domestic works by *prohibiting awards of statutory damages or attorney fees when the copyright owner/plaintiff failed to register his work before the infringement at suit began (in the case of unpublished works) or within three months after first publication.* (See pp. 193-195, *infra*, for a full discussion of remedies for copyright infringement.)

4. Registration is not a prerequisite to a claim of moral rights violation: It is not necessary for any author to register prior to bringing suit for violation of the rights of attribution or integrity in a work of visual art, pursuant to Copyright Act §106A.

XVII. THE DURATION OF COPYRIGHT PROTECTION

A. **Commencement of federal copyright:** Under the Copyright Act of 1909, federal copyright in most cases commenced upon publication of the work with proper notice of copyright. (Prior to publication, the work was protected by state common-law copyright.) Under the Copyright Act of 1976, which became effective on January 1, 1978, federal copyright commences upon creation of the work. Copyright Act §101 provides that a work is created "when it is fixed in a copy or phonorecord for the first time."

B. **Congressional extensions of the copyright term:** Calculating the term of a copyright can be tricky because Congress has extended the term twice in the last few decades, and has given existing copyrights the benefit of the extensions. Under the Copyright Act of 1909, federal copyright lasted for an initial term of 28 years from the date of first publication. During the last year of this period, the copyright could be renewed for a second 28-year term, for a total of 56 years of copyright protection. *When Congress enacted the Copyright Act of 1976* (which became effective on January 1, 1978), it changed the means by which the terms of new copyrights would be measured (from a specific number of years to the author's life plus 50 years). It was expected that the new measurement would provide a term that was, on the average, about 19 or 20 years longer than the previous method of measurement. While Congress only applied the new method of measurement to copyrights coming into existence *after* the effective date of the 1976 Act, it added 19 years to the second term of existing copyrights, thus extending their potential duration to 75 years. *In 1998 (The Sonny Bono Copyright Term Protection Act), Congress again extended the term* of copyright by 20 years (to the life of the author plus 70 years), and provided that both new copyrights and existing ones would enjoy the extension. (The effective date of this extension is October 27,1998.) It is important to note, however, that if a copyright had already expired prior to the effective date of the 1998 extension, the extension did not revive it. Thus, for example, if an existing copyright expired on December 31, 1997, it remains expired: It does not revive to last an additional 20 years.

   1. **Extensions held constitutional:** In *Eldred v. Ashcroft*, 537 U.S. 186 (2003), the Supreme Court considered arguments that Congress's extension of existing copyrights is unconstitutional because it conflicts with the First Amendment and with the provision in the Patents and Copyrights Clause (art. I, §8, cl. 8) that limits copyright protection to a "limited" time. The Court upheld the extension against both challenges. The Court reasoned that the extension was a rational exercise of Congress' legislative authority under the Patents and Copyrights Clause, and rejected arguments that Congress' acts should be subject to heightened judicial review under the First Amendment. The Court reasoned that the copyright system already incorporates safeguards for free speech interests, and that when Congress "has not altered the traditional contours of copyright protection, further First Amendment scrutiny is unnecessary."

C. **Duration of copyright for works created on or after January 1, 1978:** Copyright Act §302 (as amended in 1998 by the Sonny Bono Copyright Term Extension Act) provides that in the case of *works created on or after January 1, 1978*, copyright endures for the life of the author plus 70 years. It makes no difference whether or when the work is published. There are some exceptions and special rules, which are discussed below.

1. **Works of joint authorship:** In the case of jointly authored works, the copyright endures for the life of the last of the joint authors to die plus 70 years.

    a. **Determining the date of the author's death:** Copyright Act §302 provides a means of safely assuming that a work has entered the public domain (i.e., that the author has died more than 70 years ago) when it is difficult or impossible to determine for certain whether or when the author has died. Section 302 directs the Register of Copyrights to maintain records to assist in determining whether an author still lives and if not, the date of his death. (These records are compiled from statements filed with the Copyright Office by "interested persons" and other sources.) Ninety-five years after a work has been published or 120 years after it was created, whichever occurs sooner, a person may inquire what these records reveal about the author of a work. If the Copyright Office certifies that there is nothing in its records to indicate that the author has been alive during the past 70 years, that *creates a presumption* that the copyright term has expired and the work is now in the public domain.

    i. **Reliance on the Copyright Office's certification:** If a person obtains a certified report from the Copyright Office as described above and relies on it in good faith (that is, without notice that the copyright is still in effect), then the presumption that the copyright term has expired will be a complete defense in an infringement action, if the copyright has not in fact expired and the copyright owner sues for infringement.

    ii. **The copyright owner's rights:** In the case set forth above, reliance in good faith on the Copyright Office's certificate will constitute a complete defense against an infringement claim, but that does not mean that the owner of the still-valid copyright has lost all rights in it. All that person has to do is file a statement with the Copyright Office demonstrating that the author has not been dead for 70 years, and then no more certified reports will issue, and no additional persons will have the benefit of the §302 good faith reliance defense.

2. **Anonymous and pseudonymous works:** Copyright for anonymous and pseudonymous works lasts for 95 years following first publication or 120 years following creation of the work, whichever period expires first. Copyright Act §101 provides that a work is pseudonymous if the copies or phonorecords in which it is embodied identify the author under a fictitious name. The fact that the general public nonetheless knows who the real author of an anonymous or pseudonymous work is does not affect its status as such for purposes of calculating the duration of the copyright. However, §302(c) provides that if, prior to the end of the copyright term, the identity of one or more of the anonymous or pseudonymous authors is revealed in the copyright registration documents on file in the Copyright Office, then measurement of the copyright term will convert to the life of the author or authors identified plus 70 years. Any person having an interest in the copyright may make a filing with the Copyright Office that reveals the author and thus convert the calculation of the copyright term to life plus 70 years.

3. **Works made for hire:** In the case of works made for hire the copyright term is 95 years following first publication or 120 years following creation of the work, whichever period expires first.

D. **Duration of the copyright for works created but not published before January 1, 1978:** Works that existed but were unpublished on the effective date of the 1976 Act (January 1, 1978) were *protected by state common-law copyright*. Common-law copyright lasted indefinitely—until the work was published. When Congress enacted the 1976 Act, it abolished common-law copyright for all works of authorship fixed in a tangible medium and provided federal statutory copyright in its place. Copyright Act §303 provides that works that were protected by common-law copyright on January 1, 1978, received a federal copyright that would last for the life of the author plus 70 years (or, in the case of a joint work, an anonymous or pseudonymous work, or a work for hire, the comparable §302 term for such works) or until December 31, 2002, whichever is longer. The work's common-law protection was extinguished.

   1. **A trade:** Simply to abolish authors' common-law copyright protection without payment and without replacing it with another form of protection might have constituted an unconstitutional "taking" of private property for public use without just compensation. Thus, Congress provided that persons having common-law copyright would receive federal copyright in its place. To ensure that the trade was meaningful, Congress ensured that even the oldest unpublished works would receive at least 25 years of federal copyright protection.

   2. **Additional term for publication:** To encourage publication of these unpublished works, §303 provides that if the work is published on or before December 31, 2002, the term of the copyright will not expire before December 31, 2047.

      Example: X created a novel in 1872, which has never been published. She died in 1898, passing her common-law copyright in the novel to her daughter, Y. Y died in 1957, passing the common-law copyright in the novel to her son, Z. On January 1, 1978, the common-law copyright in the novel was transformed into federal copyright. Z then owned federal copyright in the novel that endured until December 31, 2002. If Z published the novel before December 31, 2002, the copyright term will extend until December 31, 2047.

      Example: A created a novel in 1950. She never published it. She died in 1980, passing all her property rights to B. On January 1, 1978, A's common-law copyright became a federal copyright. It will endure until December 31, 2050.

E. **Duration of the copyright for works already protected by federal copyright on January 1, 1978:** The Copyright Act of 1909 provided for a copyright term of 28 years, which could be renewed for a second term of 28 years. If the copyright was not renewed at the end of the first 28-year term, it expired, and the work entered the public domain. If it was renewed, then the copyright lasted for a total of 56 years. When Congress enacted the Copyright Act of 1976, it provided a potentially longer term (life of the author plus 50 years, or in the case of works for hire and anonymous or pseudonymous works, 75 years from publication or 100 years from creation, whichever was shorter) for works created *after* its effective date (January 1, 1978). Congress decided to extend the term of *existing* federal copyrights (on works created *before* January 1, 1978) by a roughly equal amount. Thus, it added 19 years to the *second* term of existing, pre-1976 Act copyrights to give a second term of 47 years. In 1998, Congress again extended the copyright term for works created *after* January 1, 1978 (this time by adding 20 years). Congress provided that still-existing copyrights on works created *before* January 1, 1978, would receive another 20 years *added to the second term*. Accordingly, Copyright Act §304 *extends the second term of the pre-1976 Act federal copyrights in existence on October 27, 1998, to 67 years*. Today, for works that were created before the effective date of the Copyright Act of 1976 (January 1, 1978), but whose copyrights had not expired on October 27, 1998, the first term of copyright is

28 years. If the copyright is renewed, the second term is 67 years, giving a total copyright term of 95 years.

Example: X published a novel and obtained federal copyright for it in 1922. He renewed the copyright in 1950. The copyright expired on December 31, 1997 (the second term lasted 47 years, giving a total copyright term of 75 years). X will not get the benefit of the additional 20 years that Congress added in the 1998 Sonny Bono Copyright Term Extension Act because his term had expired prior to October 27, 1998, the effective date of that Act.

Example: X published a novel and obtained federal copyright for it in 1960. In 1988, when the first 28-year term ended, he did not renew the copyright. The copyright expired in 1988, receiving no benefit from any of Congress's generous extensions (which were added to the *second* term).

Example: X published a novel and obtained federal copyright for it in 1960. He renewed his copyright in 1988. His copyright will expire on December 31, 2055. (Because his copyright was still in existence on October 27, 1998, he got the benefit of both the 1976 Act 19-year extension to the second term, *and* the Sonny Bono Act 20-year further extension, for a second term totaling 67 years.)

F. **Duration of the rights of attribution and integrity in works of visual art:** Copyright Act §106A provides that for works of visual art *created on or after* the Visual Artists' Rights Act's effective date (June 1, 1991), the author's moral rights of attribution and integrity will endure for the life of the author (or, in the case of joint works, the life of the last author to die). For those works of visual art *created before the Act's effective date, but to which the author retained title on June 1, 1991*, the rights will last as long as the economic rights of copyright, as set forth above.

G. **Rule for calculating the end of the term:** Copyright Act §305 provides that *all terms of copyright run to the end of the calendar year in which they are due to expire.*

Example: A creates a painting in 1980. He dies on April 1, 2000. Under §302, his copyright will endure for 70 years after his death, or until the year 2070. However, his copyright will not expire on March 31, 2070, but on December 31, 2070. Thus, in this case, A's term really lasts for his life plus 70 years and nine months.

XVIII. RENEWALS OF PRE-1976 ACT FEDERAL COPYRIGHTS

A. **Renewal of federal copyrights in their first term on January 1, 1978:** As noted above, the Copyright Act of 1909 provided for an initial 28-year term that could be renewed for a second 28-year term. The Copyright Act of 1976 retained the renewal term system for federal copyrights already in existence on January 1, 1978, but extended the duration of the second term. Thus, those works in their first term of federal copyright on January 1, 1978, had to be renewed in order to prolong the copyright beyond the initial term of 28 years. This section will examine the rules regarding renewal.

B. **The rationale for renewable terms:** In the Copyright Act of 1909, Congress provided for a 28-year term that could be renewed once, rather than a single term of 56 years, in order to benefit authors. Congress recognized that authors seeking to exploit their copyrights through assignment and licenses often are in a poor bargaining position. They may be unable to obtain payment representing the true value of their works, since the works are new and untried, especially when the authors are unknown. The theory of renewable terms was that when the first term ended, all the assignments and licenses the author had made in connection with a work during the first term would come to an end. The *author would obtain a second term that was free of all earlier assignments and licenses*, and a second chance to sell rights in the work. The public's response to the work during the first term would be known, the value of the work would be more clear, and the author could negotiate royalties the second time around that would better reflect the work's real value.

C. **Ownership of the renewal right:** Copyright Act §304, which governs renewals, provides that the *author* of the copyrighted work owns the right to renew copyright in the work at the end of the first term and obtain ownership of the second term. If the author is not living at the time for renewal (the 28th year of the first term), §304 dictates the persons who are to take the renewal right and the renewal term in the author's place. It provides that if the author is dead, the right to renew passes to her *surviving spouse and children*. If there are no surviving spouse or children, the right to renew passes to the *author's executor*, who takes the right as the personal representative of the author's legatees under her will. Thus, the 1976 Act gives the rights to the deceased author's surviving spouse and children first, regardless of the author's wishes specified in her will. However, if there are no surviving spouse or children, then the author may designate who takes the right, through her will. If the author left no surviving spouse or children, and no will, the renewal right passes to the *author's next of kin*, as determined by the intestacy laws of the author's domicile at the time of her death.

D. **Transfer of expectancy of renewal right:** Prior to the time to renew the copyright (the 28th year of the first term), each of the persons potentially having renewal rights (in order of precedence, the author, then surviving spouse and children, then executor/legatees, and then next of kin) has only an *expectancy* of renewing and receiving the renewal term—a kind of contingent future interest. The author must satisfy the contingency of being alive at renewal time in order to exercise renewal rights and obtain the second term. The contingencies of surviving spouse and children are that the author must be dead and they must be alive at renewal time, and so on. The Supreme Court has held that these persons *may convey their interests in the renewal term to third parties*, if they clearly indicate their intent to do so in writing. However, the most that any of these persons can convey to the third party is what they have—an expectancy, or contingent interest. If the conveyor does not satisfy his or her contingencies for taking the right to renew, the third-party transferee gains no rights in the second term.

Example: A writes a novel and obtains federal copyright in it in 1960. She assigns her copyright to a publisher in that year, in return for royalties. The assignment states that A is "conveying all her rights" in the novel. This language probably is not sufficiently specific to convey her renewal rights, so all the publisher takes is A's first 28-year term. This first copyright term will end in 1988, and the person owning the renewal rights at that time must renew in order to obtain a second term. In 1970, A explicitly assigns all her rights in the renewal term to X. In 1980, A's husband and children assign all their rights in the renewal term to Y. If A is alive in 1988, then X, her transferee, will be entitled to renew in A's name and enjoy ownership of the second copyright term. If A dies in 1985, then X will take nothing. Assuming that husband and/or children are alive in 1988, their assignee, Y, will be able to renew in their names and take the rights in the renewal term. If neither the husband nor children are alive, then Y will take nothing and the right to renew will pass to A's executor, on behalf of A's legatees.

Example: A writes a novel and obtains federal copyright in 1960. She assigns her copyright to a publisher in that year, in return for royalties. The written assignment agreement specifies that A is assigning all her rights in both the original and the renewal term. In 1988, if A is still alive, the publisher may renew the copyright in A's name, and retain the renewal term. If A is not alive, A's surviving spouse and children may renew and obtain the second term free of any claim by the publisher.

1. **The problem with permitting transfer:** By recognizing assignments of renewal rights, the Supreme Court arguably undercut accomplishment of Congress's purpose in providing for renewals. Assuming that the author lacks bargaining power when he initially sets out to sell his rights in the first term, the buyer can insist that the author assign over his renewal rights as a part of that first transaction, thus depriving the author of the second chance to negotiate to sell rights in the work. Of course, the buyer takes subject to the risk that the author will not be alive to renew, in which case the author's statutory successors will obtain the rights in the second term. (None of the author's statutory successors will be bound by the author's assignment.) To avoid this risk, the buyer will have to get an assignment of renewal rights from both the author *and* the author's statutory successors.

E. **Exceptions to the rule that the author and his statutory successors have the right to renew:** Copyright Act §304 provides some exceptions to the rule that the author or his statutorily designated successors receive the renewal right. In a few situations the proprietor of the copyright (the person owning the copyright during the last year of the first term) has the right to renew. The proprietor has the right to renew if:

- The work is a periodical, encyclopedia, or other composite work and the copyright originally was secured by the proprietor;

- The work originally was copyrighted by an employer for whom the work was created for hire;

- The work was originally copyrighted by a corporate body (otherwise than by the corporation as an assignee or as a work for hire);

- The work was a posthumous one. (A "posthumous" work has been defined as one for which no copyright assignment or other contract for exploitation was made during the author's life.)

F. **The process of renewal:** Before the Copyright Amendments Act of 1992, renewal term claimants had to *file an application to renew* with the Copyright Office during the last year of the first term of the copyright. Failure to make a proper filing cast the work into the public domain at the end of the first term. This led to many unintended forfeitures. Moreover, the requirement of a filing failed to comply with the Berne Convention's rule that members cannot condition copyright protection on compliance with formalities. See p. 196, *infra*. For this reason, Congress amended §304 in 1992 to *eliminate the filing requirement* and provide that renewal will be *automatic* for all *remaining* first-term copyrights. Note that this amendment did not revive renewal terms that had been lost before the amendment's effective date because of a failure to file. (As discussed at p. 180, pursuant to the United States' obligations under the TRIPs agreement, Congress has restored qualifying *foreign* copyrights lost due to failure to comply with the formality of filing for a renewal. Renewal terms lost for domestic works have not been restored.)

Example: X, a U.S. author, obtained a federal copyright for his novel in 1960. He failed to file for renewal in 1988, the last year of his first term. Thus, his novel fell into the public domain and remains there. (If the country of origin of the novel was not the United States, but was a Berne

Convention or WTO member, then the copyright was restored, effective January 1, 1996). By contrast, if X first obtained copyright in 1970, his first term would end in 1998. As of 1992, all copyright renewals became automatic, with no need to file. Thus, even if X forgot to file for renewal in 1998, his copyright would be automatically renewed and would endure for an additional 67 years—until 2037.

1. **Encouragement to file:** Though the 1992 amendment provides for automatic renewal, it nonetheless seeks to encourage authors and their successors to continue filing for renewal on a voluntary basis. As amended, §304 provides that registration resulting from a properly filed application to renew will "constitute *prima facie* evidence as to the validity of the copyright during its renewal and extended term and of the facts stated in the certificate." In addition, if a person who is entitled to renew (or his assignee of renewal rights) registers the renewal term by filing an application to renew, the renewal interest will *vest in the filer as of the date of application* (during the last year of the first term). By contrast, if the renewal occurs automatically, without a filing, the interest will vest in the person entitled to renew on the last day of the first term. The following example illustrates why this may be important.

   Example: A, the author, assigns his renewal rights to B. The final year of the first term begins on January 1, 1994. B makes a voluntary filing, in A's name, to renew the copyright in January, 1994, while A is still alive. A dies in February, 1994, leaving a surviving spouse and child. Because B made a voluntary filing, the renewal interest vests as of the date of application, in January, and B will be able to take the renewal term at the end of the year. If B had not made a voluntary filing, the renewal interest would have vested at the end of 1994, after A's death, and A's surviving spouse and child would have taken the renewal right.

G. **Renewals and derivative works:** Assume that A writes a novel and grants to B the exclusive right to make a movie—a derivative work—based on the novel. B produces and begins to exploit the movie, obtaining a separate copyright for it as a derivative work. A dies, the first term of A's copyright ends, and A's statutory successor renews. The renewal term starts as a clean slate: A's statutory successor is not bound by assignments or licenses made during the first term. He can grant a license to a third person, C, to make a movie from the novel during the renewal term. The promise of exclusivity to B in the first term is not binding during the renewal term. Since B only received rights to adapt the novel during the first term of the novel's copyright, he has no right to produce another movie based on the novel after the first term has expired. *The question arose, however, whether B would have the right to continue publicly performing the movie he made under the authority of the license executed in the first term.* Note that a derivative work consists of portions of the underlying original work combined with new aspects added by the derivative author. Normally, public performance of a derivative work will infringe the exclusive right of public performance in the underlying original copyrighted work, if the performance is unauthorized. *While A's original license to B undoubtedly authorized public performance of B's movie, that license gives no rights in the renewal term.* Will termination of the first-term license terminate B's right to exploit the work he made pursuant to that license? In *Stewart v. Abend*, 495 U.S. 207 (1990), *the Supreme Court ruled that A's first-term license to B did not give B a right to continue exploiting his derivative work made pursuant to that license during the second term*: No rights granted in the first term carry over to the second term unless the grantor specifically undertook to assign rights in the renewal term and in fact was able to renew, thus consummating the assignment.

1. **The effect of 1992 amendments:** When Congress amended Copyright Act §304 in 1992 to provide for automatic renewal, it sought to encourage second-term copyright claimants to continue to file renewal applications. To this end it provided, in §304(a)(4)(A), that *if no application to renew is filed, a derivative work prepared under an assignment or license in the first term may continue to be exploited under the terms of the initial grant during the renewal and extended term* of the copyright without infringing (although the first-term assignee/licensee may not make *additional* derivative works during the second term).

2. **The effect of failure to renew copyright in a derivative work:** Assume that A grants a license to B to make a derivative work and B does so, obtaining her own copyright in the derivative work. A then renews his copyright, but B fails to renew hers. At the end of B's first term, copyright expires and B's derivative work falls into the public domain. A's work is still copyrighted. Should the public have the right to use the whole derivative work, including the parts taken from A's still-copyrighted work, or do only the parts B added become available to the public? Note that if it is the latter, as a practical matter, B's work probably will be unavailable to the public, even though its copyright has expired. The Ninth Circuit considered this issue in *Russell v. Price*, 612 F.2d 1123 (9th Cir. 1979), *cert. denied*, 446 U.S. 952 (1980), and determined that the public had no right to use the portions of the derivative work taken from A's still-copyrighted work.

XIX. TERMINATION OF TRANSFERS OF COPYRIGHT

A. **Maintaining the author's "second chance" under the 1976 Act:** When Congress enacted the Copyright Act of 1976, it eliminated the system of renewable copyright terms for works created after January 1, 1978. Congress nonetheless sought to promote the purpose underlying the renewal provisions—to provide authors a second chance to negotiate for assignments and licenses of rights (hereafter, "transfers") once the work has been published and its economic value can more readily be ascertained. Congress also decided, in augmenting the second term of existing, pre-1978 copyrights, to provide a means for authors to seize the benefit of the 19- and 20-year extensions that it was providing. Accordingly, Congress implemented a system by which authors or their statutorily designated successors can terminate earlier transfers of rights. One of two sets of rules applicable to terminations will apply, depending on when the transfer to be terminated was executed.

B. **Transfers executed on or after January 1, 1978:** Terminations of transfers executed on or after January 1, 1978, are governed by Copyright Act §203.

1. **Transfers subject to termination:** All assignments and licenses of rights in a copyrighted work executed *on or after January 1, 1978, by the author*, are subject to termination under §203, *unless the work was a work for hire or the transfer of rights was by will*. It does not matter when the work that is the subject of the assignment or license was created.

2. **Persons entitled to terminate:** In the case of transfers by a single author, *the author may terminate*. If the author is dead, §203 designates the successors to his termination rights. Successors holding over one-half of the author's termination rights may terminate in the author's place.

a. **The persons succeeding to the author's termination interest:** When the author is dead, his or her surviving spouse and surviving children and grandchildren succeed to the termination interest as follows: (1) If the author leaves a surviving spouse and no surviving children or grandchildren, the spouse owns the entire termination interest; (2) if the author leaves both a surviving spouse and surviving children or grandchildren, then the surviving spouse owns one-half of the author's interest and the surviving children or grandchildren share the other one-half; (3) if the author leaves no surviving spouse but does leave surviving children/grandchildren, then the surviving children/grandchildren own the entire termination interest. The rights of the author's surviving children and grandchildren are always divided and exercised on a *per stirpes* basis. That is, each surviving *child* gets a share. If a child is dead, but has left surviving children (the author's grandchildren), the grandchildren take the share that would have gone to their deceased parent, had he or she survived. When grandchildren take a deceased child's interest, they can only act as a unit. That is, in order to exercise their share of the termination interest, the majority must agree to the exercise. If the majority agree, then the whole share is exercised. Grandchildren do not take a share of the termination interest as long as their parent (the author's child) is still living.

Example: Author dies, leaving a widow (W), a surviving son (S) (who has a daughter, GD), and three grandchildren who are the children of a deceased daughter (GC). Their ownership interests would be as follows: W-½; S-¼; GC-¼ collectively (or ¹⁄₁₂ each). Note that GD would not own an interest, since her parent is alive. GC take their deceased parent's ¼ share, by right of representation. Section 203 says that persons entitled to exercise a total of more than one-half of the termination interest may terminate a transfer, and that the grandchildren, taking by right of representation, must act as a unit. Thus, to terminate, W must act and be joined *either* by S or by a majority of GC.

b. If there is no surviving spouse, children, or grandchildren: If the author's widow or widower, children, and grandchildren are not alive, the author's executor, administrator, personal representative, or trustee shall own the author's entire termination interest.

3. **In the case of joint authors:** In the case of transfers by more than one author of a joint work, termination may be accomplished by a majority of the authors who made the transfer. If one of the original transferring authors is dead, his or her interest may be exercised as a unit by the statutory successors described above.

Example: Originally X, Y, and Z, joint authors, executed an assignment of copyright to ABC Corp. Y has since died, leaving a widower and two surviving children (no grandchildren). X wants to terminate the assignment. He must convince Z or the persons owning more than one-half of Y's interest (widower and one child) to join him.

4. **Time for termination:** Under §203, a transfer may be terminated at any point during a 5-year period that begins in the 36th year after the transfer was executed. (If the grant includes publication rights, the 5-year window of time begins in the 36th year after publication *or* the 41st year after the transfer of rights was executed, whichever is sooner.)

Example: In 1980, the author assigns the exclusive right to adapt his novel into a screenplay to X. He may terminate during the years 2016 through 2020. If the author had assigned the right to publish the novel in 1980, and the novel was published pursuant to the assignment in 1984, then the assignment could be terminated during the years 2020 through 2024.

5. **Notice:** To terminate, the author or his successors must give notice to the transferee (or to whomever presently holds the transferred rights) in writing, two to ten years before the date

on which the transfer is to be terminated. A copy of the notice must be filed with the Copyright Office.

6. **No waivers:** The author's right to terminate may not be waived or relinquished by agreement. Thus, even if a transferee requires the author and his successors expressly to agree not to exercise termination rights, the author and his statutory successors will not be bound by that agreement and may exercise their right to terminate within the designated time frame.

7. **Effect of termination:** On the date that notice of termination is given, the rights that will revert at termination vest in the author, or the successors to his termination interest if the author is dead. When the termination date occurs, all rights that are terminated revert to the persons in whom they have vested or, if they died after the notice was given, to their legatees or next of kin.

   a. **Further grants:** A new grant (or an agreement to make a new grant) of terminated rights is valid only if made *after* the effective date of the termination. The only exception is that the terminators may enter into an agreement for regrant with the person whose interest is to be terminated after the notice of termination has been served. The agreement and new grant must be signed by the same number and proportion of the owners as are required to terminate the grant (although it need not be the same persons).

8. **Derivative works:** Section 203 specifies that a derivative work prepared under authority of an assignment or license prior to its termination may continue to be exploited under the terms of the now terminated assignment or license. This result is the opposite of the result the Supreme Court reached in the *Abend* case (*supra*, p. 188) with regard to rights in first-term derivative works during the renewal term of copyright in the original.

   Example: Author grants a license giving X Co. the right to make and publicly perform a screenplay and movie based on Author's novel. X Co. makes the screenplay and movie pursuant to the license and proceeds to exploit it. Author then terminates the license pursuant to §203. While X Co. may make no further screenplays or movies based on the novel, it may continue to publicly perform the movie it had made before the termination, without liability for infringement.

C. **Transfers executed prior to January 1, 1978:** As discussed above, the Copyright Act of 1976 added 19 years to the second term of copyrights in works created prior to January 1, 1978, but still in existence on that date. Moreover, in 1998, Congress enacted the Sonny Bono Copyright Term Extention Act, which added another 20 years to the second term, for those pre-1976 Act copyrights still in existence on the Bono Act's effective date. Copyright Act §304 allows the author or his statutory successors to *recapture these extensions* by terminating assignments and licenses giving rights to transferees in the second (renewal) term.

   1. **Grants subject to termination:** Section 304 termination applies to all assignments and licenses of rights in the renewal copyright term executed before January 1, 1978, by either the author or the persons designated in §304 to take the author's renewal rights if he is dead at renewal time ((1) surviving spouse and children; (2) executor; or (3) next of kin). See *supra*, p. 186. It does not matter whether the transfer of rights in the renewal term was made during the first or the second term of the copyright, as long as it was made before January 1, 1978, and gives rights during the renewal term. Assignments and licenses in works made for hire may not be terminated, and transfers by will may not be terminated.

2. **Persons entitled to terminate:** The persons entitled to terminate differ according to whether the *author* made the grant or his *§304 statutory successors* to renewal rights made the grant.

   a. **Grants by the author:** Grants by the author must be terminated by the *author*. If the author is dead, then the same persons are entitled to terminate as under §203, and in the same fashion.

   b. **Grants by persons other than the author:** In the case of grants by persons other than the author (author's spouse and/or surviving children, executor, or next of kin, who obtained the renewal term), *all the persons who made the grant who are still surviving must join in the termination.*

3. **Time for termination:** Under §304(c), an assignment or license may be terminated at any point during a five-year period that begins at: (1) the end of the 56th year of the copyright; or (2) January 1, 1978, whichever is later.

   Example: Artist created and published a series of drawings in 1948 and secured federal copyright in it. In 1955 Artist sold X Co. the exclusive right to make and sell posters based on five of the drawings. The exclusive license also specified that it gave rights in both the first and the renewal copyright terms. In 1976, Artist renewed the copyright in the drawings, which ensured that X Co. would continue to own rights to make and sell posters during the renewal term. (Note that if Artist had died prior to renewal time, his grant of rights to X Co. during the renewal term would not have been effective.) Artist died in 1985, survived by three children, A, B, and C (no surviving spouse). A, B, and C obtained Artist's termination rights. The earliest that they may terminate the license to X Co. under §304 is the 57th year of the copyright—2005. At least two of the three children must agree to terminate and serve notice as set forth below.

   a. **A second chance under the Sonny Bono Copyright Term Extension Act:** In enacting the Sonny Bono Copyright Term Extension Act, Congress added a new §304(d) that permits authors or their successors to recapture that Act's 20-year extension through a termination of transfer, *if they have not already terminated as provided above.* (Note that if they have already terminated pursuant to the §304(c) provisions described above, they will have retrieved the transferred rights for the entire remaining duration of the renewal term, including the Sonny Bono Act augmentation.) Section 304(d) provides that if the copyright is still in its renewal term on the effective date of the Sonny Bono Act (October 27, 1998), but the termination right set forth in §304(c) has expired without being exercised, then the author or his successors will have a new right to terminate during a five-year period commencing at the end of 75 years from the date the copyright was originally secured.

4. **Notice:** As under §203, written notice must be served on the transferee or his successors two to ten years prior to the date of termination. A copy of the notice must be recorded in the Copyright Office.

5. **Effect of termination:** The terminated rights revert to the persons entitled to terminate them. As in the case of §203, the rights vest in all the persons entitled to terminate as soon as the notice of termination is filed. If one of these persons dies after notice is given but before the actual termination occurs, he or she may pass the rights by will or through intestate succession.

6. **Further grants:** As with terminations under §203, no regrant or agreement to make a regrant may be made until the termination is effective, except that an agreement to regrant may be made with the party holding the rights to be terminated.

7. **Other provisions:** Section 304, like §203, provides that authors and their successors may not waive or contract away their termination rights. It likewise provides that persons who have made derivative works pursuant to assignments or licenses subsequently terminated may continue to exploit the derivative works.

XX. REMEDIES FOR INFRINGEMENT

A. **Injunctions:** Copyright Act §502 authorizes courts to grant both preliminary and permanent injunctions against copyright infringement and against violations of the author's rights of attribution and integrity in works of visual art. There are also provisions for impounding allegedly infringing copies, phonorecords, and other materials used to infringe, and for their ultimate destruction upon a final judgment of infringement.

B. **Damages and/or profits:** Copyright Act §504 gives the copyright owner/author a choice of recovering: (1) her actual damages and any additional profits of the defendant; or (2) statutory damages.

1. **Damages and/or profits:** The plaintiff is entitled to recover the *actual damages* that she suffered as a result of the infringement *plus any of the defendant's profits* attributable to the infringement that are not taken into account in computing the actual damages.

    a. **No double recovery:** The language of §504 prohibits double recovery. When economic rights have been infringed, the plaintiff's actual damages will generally take the form of lost sales when the defendant is a direct competitor or, if the defendant is not a direct competitor, the reasonable royalty that the plaintiff would have received if the defendant had purchased a license to engage in his otherwise infringing activity.

    i. **In cases of direct competition:** In cases in which the defendant directly competes with the plaintiff, the lost sales will often be the same as the defendant's profits from infringing sales, since the defendant is likely to have stolen customers who would otherwise have bought from the plaintiff. In such cases, the plaintiff will not be permitted to recover *both* her lost sales and the defendant's profits, because that would constitute double recovery. However, if the plaintiff can demonstrate that the defendant's profits attributable to the infringement *exceed* the amount of her own lost sales, or if the plaintiff can prove damages *beyond* lost sales, such as damage to reputation, she may recover those amounts, in addition to the amount of sales that she actually lost to the defendant.

    ii. **In infringement cases not involving direct competition:** When the plaintiff's damage is the loss of an opportunity to sell a license and obtain a royalty, she may be able to recover, *in addition to a reasonable royalty* for the defendant's infringing use, an amount representing the defendant's net profits after deducting his costs and the amount he would have paid as a reasonable royalty to the plaintiff.

    b. **The burden of proof regarding the defendant's profits:** To establish the amount of the defendant's profits, all the plaintiff must do is prove the defendant's *gross revenue*. The burden is then on the defendant to prove what, if any, amounts should be deducted from the gross revenue as expenses or costs of producing the infringing work, and what, if any, portion of his profits is attributable to factors other than his infringement.

Example: The defendant makes a movie that infringes the plaintiff's copyrighted play. The plaintiff proves that the defendant's gross revenue for the movie was $1,000,000. The defendant then bears the burden of proving what amounts should be deducted from the gross revenue before making an award of profits to the plaintiff. If the defendant is able to prove that 45 percent of his gross revenue went to paying costs of producing and promoting the movie, and that 40 percent of his gross revenue was attributable to elements that he independently created, such as changes in the plot, casting popular movie stars, promotions, etc., then only 15 percent of his revenues will remain available for award to the plaintiff.

2. **Statutory damages:** Instead of recovering actual damages and profits, the copyright owner/author may elect to recover an award of statutory damages. In such cases the court may award damages of not less than $750 or more than $30,000, as it considers just.

    Example: A Co. owns copyrights in a novel and a compilation of short stories, both written in English. X makes unauthorized translations of both works to French and sells copies of the translation in the United States. If A Co. is unable to prove how many copies were sold, or its provable damage is low and X has made no appreciable profit from making and selling his translations, A Co. may decide to ask the court for statutory damages instead of pursuing actual damages and profits. It may recover between $750 and $30,000 for infringement of its copyright in the novel and it may recover between $750 and $30,000 for infringement of its copyright in its compilation of short stories. (For purposes of calculating statutory damages, a compilation counts as only one work.) The court will determine what amount within that range is just under the circumstances. Note that A Co. is entitled to a separate recovery for each of the two works. However, it is not entitled to recover a separate amount for each separate act of infringement of that work (*i.e.*, each separate act of reproducing and publicly distributing). One award will be made to cover all the infringements of that work. Likewise, when ownership of the copyright is divided—for example, S owns the reproduction rights and T owns the distribution rights—then multiple owners may not separately recover, but must share in one award of statutory damages.

    a. **Determining what amount is just:** In determining how much in statutory damages to award within the $750 to $30,000 range, courts often consider *how much actual damage the plaintiff has suffered* (the court will have to estimate, since the plaintiff may not have introduced specific evidence about its actual loss). They also consider what amount of damages it would take to *induce* a person in the plaintiff's position to create and enforce rights in a similar work and how much it would take to *deter* defendants from similar types of infringement or violation in the future.

    b. **Willful infringement:** If the plaintiff proves that the defendant *willfully* infringed, the court may, in its discretion, increase the award of statutory damages up to $150,000 per infringed work.

    c. **Innocent infringement:** If the defendant proves that she was not aware and had no reason to believe that her acts constituted infringement, the court may, in its discretion, reduce the award of statutory damages to not less than $200. (Note that Copyright Act §§401 and 402 provide (with some narrow exceptions) that if proper notice of copyright appeared on the published copy or phonorecord to which the defendant had access, then no weight will be given to the defendant's assertion of an innocent infringement argument in mitigation of actual or statutory damages.)

   d. **No statutory damages in certain cases:** Statutory damages are not available to copyright owners who did not register their works within the time frame set forth in Copyright Act §412. See *supra*, p. 181.

C. **Costs and attorney fees:** Copyright Act §505 permits courts, in their discretion, to award costs against either party, and to award reasonable attorney fees to the prevailing party.

   1. **Costs:** Costs can be awarded to either the winning or losing party, and generally are only awarded when the other party acted in bad faith.

   2. **Attorney fees:** Unlike in patent infringement cases, attorney fees are routinely awarded to prevailing plaintiffs, even in the absence of evidence of willful infringement. (Note, however, that copyright owners who failed to register their works within the time frame set forth in §412 may not be awarded fees.) Awards are often made to prevailing defendants, as well. In *Fogarty v. Fantasy, Inc.*, 510 U.S. 517 (1994), the Supreme Court rejected a dual standard that provided attorney fee awards to defendants only when they demonstrated that the plaintiff's suit was frivolous or brought in bad faith. The Court endorsed a more evenhanded approach, reasoning that defendants who seek to advance meritorious copyright defenses should be encouraged to litigate them to the same extent that plaintiffs are encouraged to litigate meritorious claims of infringement.

D. **Criminal penalties:** In addition to the civil remedies discussed above, the Copyright Act provides for *criminal prosecution* in some cases of willful copyright infringement. See 17 U.S.C. §506. There are also criminal sanctions for fraudulent copyright notice, fraudulent removal of copyright notice, and false representations in applications for copyright registration. The Digital Millennium Copyright Act imposes criminal sanctions for certain acts of circumvention and interference with copyright management information. 17 U.S.C. §1204. See *supra*, pp. 168-172. There are no criminal sanctions for violating the rights of attribution and integrity held by the author of a work of visual art.

XXI. INTERNATIONAL COPYRIGHT TREATIES

A. **The Berne Convention:** The International Union for the Protection of Literary and Artistic Works (known as the "Berne Convention") was created in 1886 and has well over 150 member nations, including most developed nations. The United States joined, effective March, 1989. The Berne Convention is administered by the World Intellectual Property Organization (WIPO). The Convention is founded on the concept of *national treatment*. Thus, each member nation must afford essentially as strong copyright protection to works originating in other member nations as it does to its own domestic works. In addition, the Berne Convention establishes *minimum levels of substantive protection* which member nations must afford. This has required members to harmonize their national laws somewhat, though they still vary in significant aspects.

   1. **Works protected under the Berne Convention:** The Berne Convention protects *literary and artistic works*, including "every production in the literary, scientific and artistic domain, whatever may be the mode or form of its expression." As examples of protected works, the Berne

Convention cites books, pamphlets, dramatic works, cinematographic works, drawings, paintings, architecture, works of applied art, maps, illustrations, plans, and sketches. Member nations have an *option to require that works be fixed in some material form*. It is generally understood that members are *not obligated to extend copyright protection to sound recordings*. (There are other treaties that provide for copyright and/or "neighboring rights" protection for sound recordings.) Likewise, the Berne Convention *leaves copyright for works of "applied art" or "industrial design" to the discretion of each member nation*.

2. **Prerequisites to protection:** Member nations must afford automatic protection to copyrightable works originating in other member countries. *No formalities*, such as notice or registration, may be required as a prerequisite.

3. **Duration of protection:** Protection *must* be afforded in most cases for the life of the author plus 50 years, though member nations may provide for a longer term. Anonymous and pseudonymous works must be protected for at least 50 years from publication. Photographs and works of applied art (if protected) must be protected at least 25 years, and cinematographic works must be protected at least 50 years after their making.

4. **Extent of protection:** The Berne Convention requires that member nations protect the right of reproduction, the right of translation, the right of adaptation, the right of public performance, the right of public recitation, the right of broadcasting, and the film right in connection with various types of works. It also provides that member nations must protect the moral rights of paternity (attribution) and integrity. The Berne Convention *does not provide for a right of distribution to the public, as such*.

5. **Protection based on country of origin of the work:** The Berne Convention provides for protection of works based on their country of origin. If a work's country of origin is a Berne member, the work is entitled to protection in all member nations. A work's country of origin generally is the *place of its first publication*. If a work is published simultaneously in a Berne country and a non-Berne country, the Berne country is the country of origin. However, if the author is a national of a member nation, the work is protected even if it is first published outside the Berne Union. If the work is unpublished and the author is a national of a Berne country, the work is protected.

6. **United States adherence to the Berne Convention:** The United States delayed joining the Berne Convention until 1989, due to concern about the extent to which U.S. copyright laws would have to be amended in order to comply with Berne requirements. Key areas of concern included provision of moral rights and the prohibition of formalities (notice and registration) as a prerequisite to copyright protection. In ratifying the Berne Convention, Congress determined to take a *minimalist approach to compliance*. To date, it has limited the Copyright Act's express protection of moral rights to works of visual art, reasoning that other existing federal and state causes of action provide sufficient indirect protection for moral rights in other kinds of works. Congress eliminated long-standing mandatory notice requirements, and partially eliminated mandatory registration as a prerequisite to copyright infringement suits. While Berne Convention article 18 requires new members to restore copyrights in works originating in Berne member nations that went into the public domain for reasons other than the expiration of their term of protection (e.g., for lack of proper notice or renewal), the United States declined to do so until it adhered to the TRIPs Agreement, discussed below, which reiterated the requirement. Congress retained its long-established deposit requirements, reasoning that deposit is not a prerequisite to U.S. copyright protection because noncompliance is punished by fine, rather than forfeiture.

B. **The Universal Copyright Convention:** The Universal Copyright Convention (U.C.C.) was created shortly after World War II, primarily as a means of including the United States in a multinational copyright treaty. Administered by UNESCO, the U.C.C. protects *"literary, scientific and artistic works,"* which has been interpreted to include most of the works now included under U.S. Copyright Act §102 except photographic works, works of applied art, and sound recordings. Like the Berne Convention, the U.C.C. is based on the doctrine of *national treatment*. However, the U.C.C. imposes fewer substantive standards that member nations must follow.

   1. **Substantive provisions—duration of protection:** Aside from adopting the rule of national treatment, the U.C.C. requires that members provide a minimum copyright term of 25 years from the death of the author or from first publication or registration of the work.

   2. **Rights:** The U.C.C., as revised in Paris in 1971, provides that member countries shall provide "adequate and effective protection" for "the basic rights ensuring the author's economic interests, including the exclusive right to authorize reproduction by any means, public performance and broadcasting." There is no provision for moral rights.

   3. **Notice and other formalities:** The U.C.C. provides that use of a prescribed form of notice will satisfy notice requirements in all the U.C.C. member nations. This *"U.C.C. notice"* is an encircled "c," with the name of the copyright owner and the year of first publication on all copies published with the copyright owner's authorization. The U.C.C. allows each contracting state to impose procedural formalities (such as registration) as a precondition to judicial relief for infringement.

   4. **Application of the U.C.C.:** The U.C.C. protects: (1) works of nationals of member nations; and (2) works first published in a member nation, regardless of the author's nationality.

   5. **Relationship to the Berne Convention:** Because the Berne Convention requires a greater level of copyright protection, and imposes greater responsibilities on its members than the U.C.C., some were concerned that Berne Convention members might withdraw from the Berne and rely solely on the U.C.C. in their international relations. To prevent this, the U.C.C. provides that *no Berne member may withdraw from the Berne and subsequently rely on the U.C.C. in its relations with other Berne members.* (Some exceptions to this rule have been made for developing countries.) Moreover, the Berne Convention, rather than the U.C.C., will apply to relationships between Berne members, even though they may be U.C.C. members too. While Berne members cannot "regress" from their former Berne Convention level of responsibility to other Berne members by leaving the Berne Convention and joining the U.C.C., Berne Convention members may join the U.C.C., in addition to Berne, in order to establish copyright relations with U.C.C. members who are not Berne members.

C. **The Agreement on Trade-Related Aspects of Intellectual Property Rights:** The Agreement on Trade-Related Aspects of Intellectual Property Rights, Including Trade in Counterfeit Goods (TRIPs), which the United States implemented effective January 1, 1996, requires World Trade Organization (WTO) members to abide by principles of national treatment, and it *expressly requires members to comply with the provisions of the Berne Convention, with the exception of protecting moral rights.*

   1. **Computer programs and database expression:** Because the Berne Convention does not expressly list computer programs as subject matter to be protected, the TRIPs agreement specifies that "computer programs, whether in source or object code, shall be protected as literary

works under the Berne Convention." It also expressly requires WTO members to extend copyright protection to authors' original selection and arrangement of data or other materials in compilations.

2. **Additional rights:** In addition to the rights specified by the Berne convention, TRIPs requires its members to provide rights to prevent commercial rentals of computer programs, sound recordings, and cinematographic works. (Members may be excused from providing rental rights in cinematographic works if rental has not led to widespread unauthorized copying.) TRIPs also requires members, through copyright or "neighboring rights," to protect performers against unauthorized broadcast or fixation of their live performances, to protect producers of sound recordings against unauthorized reproduction, and to protect broadcasters or the owners of copyright in broadcast subject matter against unauthorized fixation, reproduction, and rebroadcasting.

3. **Necessary changes to U.S. law:** Acceptance of the TRIPs Agreement required the United States to amend its copyright laws in several respects. One of the most important amendments the United States adopted was a form of *"neighboring rights"* to protect live musical performances. See *supra*, pp. 148-149. Another very important amendment restored copyright (or recognized it for the first time) in certain foreign works from Berne Convention or World Trade Organization (WTO) nations that had fallen into the U.S. public domain for reasons other than the normal expiration of their term of protection. This amendment was necessary in order finally to bring the United States into compliance with Berne Convention article 18. Specifically, as amended, Copyright Act §104A *restores copyright in works from eligible countries* if the works fell into the public domain because (1) the copyright owner failed to comply with U.S. copyright formalities (notice or renewal); (2) the works constituted sound recordings fixed prior to February 15, 1972 (U.S. law only recognized copyright in sound recordings fixed after that date, so such foreign works will enjoy U.S. copyright for the first time); or (3) the source country did not have copyright relations with the United States at the time the work was published. See *supra*, p. 180. Note that §104A does not restore (or create) copyright in any domestic works. However, Congress contemplated that U.S. copyright owners would benefit by reciprocal restoration of copyright in U.S. works abroad.

D. **The WIPO Copyright Treaty:** The United States ratified the WIPO Copyright Treaty in 1998. The treaty is a "protocol" to the Berne Convention, a special agreement among Berne member nations that upgrades the level of protection under the Berne among the countries ratifying the protocol. A number of the WIPO Copyright Treaty's provisions simply bring the Berne up to speed with the TRIPs agreement (for instance, providing rental rights in computer programs, sound recordings, and cinematographic works; clarifying that computer programs are literary works for purposes of copyright protection; and clarifying that copyright applies to the expressive elements of databases). However, other provisions break new ground, particularly with regard to the application of copyright on the Internet.

1. **A general right of distribution to the public:** Article 6 of the WIPO Copyright Treaty mandates provision of a general right of distribution for all works of authorship, which the Berne has not mandated before.

2. **The "right of communication to the public":** Article 8 specifically addresses the Internet, requiring members to provide an exclusive right of "communication to the public by wire or wireless means, including the making available to the public of... works in such a way that members of the public may access those works from a place and at a time individually chosen

by them." This means that members must provide copyright owners a right of online transmission.

3. **Anticircumvention and rights management provisions:** The WIPO Copyright Treaty also requires that member nations provide protection against circumvention of effective technological measures used by copyright owners to protect their rights in copyrighted works. In addition, members must prevent persons from tampering with "rights management information," or knowingly trafficking in copies or phonorecords of works with altered or deleted rights management information. These provisions lead Congress to enact the anticircumvention and rights management provisions discussed at pp. 168-172, *supra*.

Quiz Yourself on COPYRIGHTS

23. Eileen published a book containing the Minnesota-style hot dish (casserole) recipes that she had created over the years. Wanda Sue made one of the recipes, but changed one of the key ingredients in the course of doing so. (She substituted grits for the canned cream of mushroom soup that the recipe called for.) Eileen would never authorize such a shocking substitution. Has Wanda Sue infringed Eileen's exclusive right of adaptation? Why or why not? _____

24. Arco, Inc., a designer and producer of heavy machinery, produces and sells a highly automated assembly-line production machine. The machine is operated through use of a series of four-digit numeric instructions, or "command codes." These command codes are used to access the computerized features of the machine and cause the machine to perform various production tasks. In creating the four-digit codes, Arco divided the production tasks to be represented by the codes into logically related categories and assigned a separate number to each category. It then reflected the category number in the first two digits of the four-digit command code for each production task. The last two digits in the command code reflect whether the particular task is a higher- or lower-level task, on a scale of 01-10.

    Arco's machine was the first of its kind and is the standard in the industry. Most workers who operate such machinery were trained on and are accustomed to using the Arco four-digit command codes. Brown Co. has begun to produce competing machines and wants to adopt the Arco command codes for operation of its own machines, so that workers will not need to be retrained to use them. If it does, will it risk liability for copyright infringement? Please provide both sides of the argument. _____

25. What is the difference between a phonorecord and a sound recording? _____

26. X has created the form of a running deer from various materials, which he uses as a mount for deerskins in his taxidermy business. He mounts a deerskin on the form, and after adding glass eyes, etc., he is able to create a very realistic looking facsimile of a living deer. He sells these facsimiles to museums of natural history, to hunters (as a hunting trophy), and other public and private collectors.

X would like to market his running deer form to other taxidermists and claim copyright in the form to prevent others from copying it without his authorization. Would the "physical or conceptual separability" test be likely to prevent him from obtaining copyright? _____

27. Acme Corp. designs and manufactures high-quality, expensive, classically styled furniture. One chair, which Acme calls "The Philadelphian," is a standard wingback chair design and has been on the market for a number of years. In the course of designing and manufacturing The Philadelphian, Acme's designers created a set of drawings, annotated with manufacturing specifications, that Acme uses in mass-producing the chair. There were four copies of the annotated drawings at the Acme plant when X, a worker at Acme, got access to one of the copies and took it without authorization. X had decided to set up his own furniture business. He used the annotated drawing to produce his own chair for sale in competition with Acme. X did not use the same fabric to upholster his chair, and he called his chair "The Bostonian" in advertising and sales literature. Is Acme likely to have a cause of action against X for copyright infringement? _____

28. Arnie composed a nondramatic musical work (a song) and registered his copyright in it. The following year Bill, a famous singer, acquired a license to record Arnie's song. Bill recorded the song shortly thereafter and sold the recording to the public. He paid royalties to Arnie in accordance with the license agreement. The following year Charles, who had learned to mimic Bill's distinctive voice and singing style, also took a license to record Arnie's copyrighted song, and proceeded to make his own recording, mimicking Bill's recording so effectively that a casual listener could not tell the difference between Bill's recording and Charles's recording. Charles advertised his recording extensively and sold a number of copies to the public. Charles paid royalties to Arnie, but not to Bill. Based on these facts, is Bill likely to have a cause of action for copyright infringement against Charles? _____

29. In 1998, Alice wrote a short novel centered upon a romantic relationship between a man and woman. At the end of the novel these characters had a disagreement and parted. Satisfied with the work, Alice made plans to publish it. Before she was able to publish, however, she was killed in an automobile accident. In her will, Alice left all her property to her husband, Tom, and her son, Jerry, in equal shares. In going through Alice's effects, Tom found the short novel and read it. Dissatisfied with the ending, Tom added four additional chapters to the end. In the new chapters, the man and woman met again after three years, were reconciled, married, and lived happily ever after. Tom then published the novel in this form. Later, Tom licensed Dizzy, Inc. to make a movie based on the novel as published. What, if any, rights does Jerry have with regard to the movie license? _____

30. Alice purchased (over the Internet) an authorized digital colorized copy of an old cowboy movie entitled "Homes on the Range," that was popular in the early 1950s. Bill, an actor who was popular in the 1950s, starred in the movie. Alice also purchased an authorized digital copy of a more modern movie starring Brad, a very popular, current movie star. Through digital manipulation, Alice substituted Brad's head for Bill's in a 20-minute segment of "Homes on the Range," and posted the altered 20-minute segment on her web site. Alice sold advertising space on her web site, and charged advertisers a fee based on the number of persons visiting the site. Cliff Enterprises is the owner of copyright in "Homes on the Range." Cliff authorized the sale of the digital copy of the movie to Alice and received a royalty from the sale. Does Cliff Enterprises have a cause of action for copyright infringement against Alice? _____

31. ZBS Corp., a nationwide broadcasting company, produced and aired a very popular soap opera called "Law School Lovelorn." The show centered around the complex love lives of several glamorous law school students. The show had a considerable following. However, many of the show's fans were lawyers, who found it necessary at times to miss the show (which was aired during the day) in order to

make court appearances and meet with clients. The Sensational Bar Journal decided to publish a weekly column that explained what had happened in the past week's episodes for the benefit of fans who had to miss them. The column generally consisted of about eight to ten paragraphs that described the events that had taken place in the particular week's episodes. The column did not quote dialog from the show, or provide photographs or other visual imagery from the show. Is ZBS, the owner of copyright in the show, likely to have a cause of action against Sensational Bar Journal for copyright infringement? _____

32. Goodreads, Ltd., a British bookseller, sets up a web page through which consumers around the world can order and pay for books. The books are then shipped to the consumer by regular mail. Among the books Goodreads, Ltd. sells is Myra Mistique's newest romance novel, *Sizzle*. Myra assigned the British copyright to U.K. Publishers, Ltd., and the American copyright to Old Glory Publishers, Inc., which is unrelated to U.K. Publishers, Ltd. The copies Goodreads, Ltd. sells over its web site were produced and originally sold by U.K. Publishers, Ltd. Old Glory Publishers, Inc., would like to prohibit Goodreads from making any further sales of the British-produced *Sizzle* to American purchasers. Would it have a cause of action for copyright infringement, on the theory that Goodreads is engaged in unauthorized importation of the book? _____

33. Artist created a highly inspiring painting of a forest with sun streaming through the trees. He sold the painting to Mr. and Mrs. Devout, who donated it to Church. Shortly thereafter, Church's pastor delivered a sermon about "The Wonders of God's Nature," and to inspire the congregation, projected the painting on an opaque projector, in a manner that created images of the painting on three different locations of the Church sanctuary walls—one in the front behind the pastor, and one on each side wall. Did this constitute infringement of Artist's copyright? _____

34. X downloaded Y's copyrighted photograph from the Internet into his computer's random access memory. He proceeded, with the assistance of some software, to alter the photographic image for his own amusement. He did not save the altered image to his hard drive or print it out. All of his work took place in the random access memory of his computer only. When he exited his computer, the original and altered images in his random access memory were destroyed. Assuming that X's actions were unauthorized, is it likely that he violated Y's exclusive right of adaptation? _____

35. DeBartolomeo, the owner of a small Italian restaurant, often brings his accordion to the restaurant and plays popular Italian tunes for the guests' enjoyment when he has a spare moment. Needless to say, he makes no separate charge for this music, and makes no recording or transmission of the performance. Assuming that some of the songs he plays are copyrighted, do his acts constitute infringement? _____

36. Compare and contrast the right of integrity granted to the author of a work of visual art under the Visual Artists' Rights Act with the exclusive right of adaptation in the same work. _____

37. Mary purchased a lawful copy of a copyrighted photograph and scanned it onto her computer's hard drive. She later posted the digitized photograph on an Internet bulletin board. Could her acts constitute a public display of the photograph? What if she had instead posted the lawful copy she bought on the cork bulletin board in her college dormitory? What if she kept the copy she bought in her room and instead printed a digitized copy and posted it on the dormitory bulletin board?

_____

38. Architect designed and built a highly innovative office building, which quickly became a famous landmark in the city. Photographer made a photograph of the building from a nearby city park, and

had it mass-produced as a post card, for sale to tourists in various local shops. Does Architect have a cause of action against Photographer for copyright infringement? _____

39. Elbert drafted a list of "The Ten Worst-Dressed Professors at Law School," in descending order of worst dress, and circulated it to the student body. Campus Newspaper obtained a copy of the list and published it without Elbert's permission. Is Newspaper likely to have infringed Elbert's copyright? _____

40. In 1995, Y, an architect, filed the plans for a house he had recently designed with the City Planner's Office, as required by local ordinance. Y built the house the following year. X admired the house, stole the plans from the City Planner's files, and built his own house from the plans without Y's permission. Is X likely to be liable for copyright infringement? _____

41. Patty purchased a new computer game on a CD-ROM. Pursuant to the instructions accompanying the game, she e-mailed the game's producer and registered her purchase. The producer then issued Patty a "personal password" that she must use to activate the game each time she wants to use it. The game cannot be used without the password. Patty later lent the game to her friend Fred, and told him her password so that he could use the game while she was away on vacation. If Fred used the password to play the game, did this violate the producer's rights? If so, on what basis? _____

42. Dr. Heckel and Dr. Jeckel, research scientists and professors, worked together on a research project. In the course of their research, they collaborated to write a paper describing the project and its results to date. Each of them wrote a substantial portion of the paper. Shortly thereafter, Heckel attended a conference. At the conference, Heckel presented the paper, but did not acknowledge Jeckel's role in writing it, suggesting instead that Heckel was the sole author.

Two years later, Heckel revised the paper, describing the latest developments in the project. He did this by himself and did not obtain Jeckel's permission to do so. Shortly thereafter, Jeckel found and reproduced the revised paper and, without Heckel's permission, distributed copies of it to participants at a conference. Jeckel named both Heckel and Jeckel as the authors, and included copyright notice.

What are Heckel's and Jeckel's respective rights against one another under the Copyright Act? _____

43. In 1963, Able completed and published a novel with proper copyright notice. The novel was a moderate success. In 1969, Able executed a license to Brown, authorizing Brown to produce and publicly perform a play based on the novel. The license expressly stated that Able conveyed the exclusive right to base a play on the novel, and to publicly perform the play, "both in the original and renewal term" of the novel's copyright.

Brown produced the play pursuant to the license and it was a great success. It ran for a number of years on Broadway and was taken on tour in the United States and in Europe. In 1975, Brown executed a license to Cohen Productions, Inc., to make a movie based on the play. The movie was produced and distributed in 1979.

Able died in 1982, and was succeeded by her son, David. In 1991, David renewed the copyright in the novel. In 2003, Brown decided to stage a revival of his play on Broadway, and Cohen Productions, Inc. decided to make its movie available for purchase on videotape. David has consulted you about his rights, if any, with regard to Brown and Cohen's activities. Please advise him. _____

44. In 1969, Allen, a staff artist employed in the Promotions Department of Gemco Films, Inc., was assigned to design a poster promoting a recently released Gemco movie. The poster Allen designed

consisted of the name of the movie, the names of the persons starring in the movie, and a watercolor sketch of one of the action scenes in the movie. Gemco printed a thousand copies of the poster and sent them to theaters featuring the movie, with a letter stating that the poster could be used to promote greater audience attendance. Notice of copyright was properly indicated on the poster and the copyright was registered in 1969. Allen died in 1984 and did not undertake to assign any rights in the poster to anyone. When will copyright protection in the poster end? _____

45. Brown was a staff artist at Ace Pictures, Inc. In that capacity, in 1982, he created paintings of various action scenes from Ace Pictures' upcoming motion picture release, which he incorporated into a poster to advertise the motion picture. Ace Pictures published the poster with proper copyright notice in 1984. Brown died in 2013. When will copyright in the poster expire? _____

46. On August 12, 1980, Allen, a freelance commercial artist and printer, entered into a contract with Brown, Inc., to produce a brochure for Brown to advertise various of Brown's products. Allen completed the work on October 25, 1980. However, Brown, Inc., only began to distribute the brochure (with proper copyright notice) to the public on February 5, 1982. Allen had a heart attack and died on November 1, 1985. When will the copyright in the brochure expire? _____

47. Joe Lee was a newspaper journalist in New York, who worked hard to support his wife and two children. In 1954, he began work on a novel during his spare time, and continued to work on it for the next six years on weekends and in the evenings after work. He and his wife were divorced in 1957. In 1960, Joe finished his novel and assigned it to a publisher that published it with proper notice of copyright the same year. The publisher immediately registered the copyright. In 1972, Joe moved in with a girlfriend and lived with her for the rest of his life. He died in 1981, devising all of his real and personal property to his girlfriend. Assuming that his girlfriend filed renewal paperwork with the Copyright Office in a timely fashion, when will the copyright expire? _____

48. Mark created a play and obtained copyright in it in 1979. The play was publicly performed and published in 1984. In 1992, Mark executed a license to XBS to produce a movie based on the play. Mark died in 1994, survived by his wife Marla, his daughters Olivia and Patricia, and two children (Randy and Steve) of a deceased son. Mark's children and grandchildren disliked the movie that XBS produced pursuant to its license, believing that it distorted the moral lesson that Mark wanted to communicate in his play. They would like to terminate the license. Under what circumstances could they do that, and would the termination take care of their concerns? _____

49. Chang was a witness to the Hindenberg explosion on May 6, 1937, in New Jersey. He was deeply moved by the experience, and wrote extensively about it in his private diary. He died 13 years later, in November 1950. His niece inherited all of his personal property. In 1960, the niece donated all of Chang's books and private papers to Archive. In 2003, Johnson was doing research on a book about the Hindenberg explosion, and came upon Chang's diary in the Archive. He would like to quote lengthy excerpts from the diary in his book—more than would be likely to be allowed under the fair use doctrine. Does he need to worry about potential copyright infringement liability? _____

50. Buildings.com is a web site that permits subscribing real estate brokers to post photographs and descriptions of buildings that they are offering for sale in major U.S. cities. The system operates automatically: A subscriber wishing to post photographs and descriptions simply follows a step-by-step automated procedure to do so. The Buildings.com system retains posted materials on the web site for two weeks and then deletes them. If the subscribing broker wants to retain them on the web site for a longer period, she must repost them. The owner of the Buildings.com web site does not itself review or select the materials being posted on its site. Whenever a visitor to the web site logs on, he or she can download posted materials, either to view on-line or to print. One of Buildings.com's subscribing brokers posts infringing photographs on the web site. Without discussing the Copyright Act §512 safe harbor provisions, please explain whether Buildings.com should be liable for direct infringement of the copyright owner's reproduction rights. _____

51. X wrote a song and made a recording of it, which was sold to the general public. Y bought a lawful copy of X's recording and took a digital sample of it, without authorization. He then incorporated it into his own recording. The sample Y took consisted of three chords of background guitar. Y speeded them up and added reverberations, so that the sampled chords produced a very different sound on Y's recording than on X's recording. It is very unlikely that anyone listening to Y's recording would recognize he sampled material as coming from X's recording. Is X likely to have a cause of action for copyright infringement against Y? Please explain your answer. _____

52. Acme Corp. created and markets software that enables the user to more efficiently manage and track business inventory. Acme only provides the software to the public in object code form (machine-readable code that is not capable of being read by humans). It keeps the source code (which can be read by humans) locked away. X, a graduate student in computer science, purchased a copy of the software through Amazon.com. The software, encoded on a disk, arrived by mail. The packaging contained a shrink-wrap license that provided that the purchaser would be the owner of the disk but a mere licensee of the software, and set forth a number of things that the purchaser was prohibited from doing. It then provided that the purchaser would manifest his/her agreement to these limitations by opening and using the software. The prohibitions included reverse engineering the software and publishing or otherwise communicating the results of any reverse engineering. X proceeded to reverse engineer the software in order to study the underlying mathematical algorithms. He then posted the algorithms (but none of the code) on his web site, along with his commentary on the methodology Acme used. Y, a competitor of Acme, found the algorithms on X's web site, downloaded them, and used them in devising his own software for tracking and managing business inventory.

    (a) Please evaluate whether Acme has a cause of action against X for copyright infringement and explain your answer. _____

    (b) Please evaluate whether Acme has a cause of action against Y for copyright infringement and explain your answer. _____

53. In 1947, Vik, a reporter for BigNews Magazine, researched and wrote an expose of government corruption. BigNews published the expose in 1948. In 1970, BigNews Magazine went out of business. In 1976, Vik filed to renew the copyright in the article. Vik died in 1989, leaving all his personal and real property by will to Friend, deliberately cutting off Son, who would otherwise have been his sole heir. In 2008, Publisher, Inc. published a book that reproduced large portions of Vik's article without authorization. Both Friend and Son want to bring an infringement action. Assuming that the year is 2008, what are their respective rights? _____

54. In 1930, Famous Poet wrote a colorful but shocking letter written to his Mistress. The Mistress saved the letter. In 1988, she showed it to Emma, who worked as her nurse. Emma observed where the Mistress kept the letter, and later "borrowed" it long enough to make a photocopy. She did not seek or receive permission to make the copy. (Famous Poet had died in 1960.) Emma later sold the photocopy to Mary, a wealthy business woman, who collected memorabilia of famous persons. Mary died in 2003, leaving her entire estate to University. The University placed the photocopy of Famous Poet's letter in its Library's documents collection, where it was indexed and made available to researchers and other members of the University community and the public. Famous Poet's Widow discovered

the letter in the Library index and has brought suit against Library for copyright infringement. There is nothing in the Library records to suggest that anyone ever checked out the letter. How would you evaluate the respective rights of the parties? Please explain your answer. _____

55. Acme, Inc., a multinational corporation, owns copyright worldwide in a sound recording. It produces phonorecords of the sound recording at its factory in Australia, and sells them all over the world, including in New Zealand and the U.S.A. DiscountCo purchases numerous phonorecords of the sound recording in New Zealand, ships them to the U.S.A. and sells them through its retail outlets in Florida, Georgia, Alabama and Mississippi. Acme brings suit against DiscountCo for copyright infringement in the U.S.A. How would you evaluate the claim? Please explain your answer. _____

56. Trucking, Inc. designs, manufactures, and sells heavy-duty trucks and trailers for log-distance hauling. It is the leading seller of trucks, but has significant competition in the market for the trailers that are to be attached to its trucks. Trucking, Inc. developed a new type of high-tech trailer hitching device, which it now attaches to all the trucks it manufactures and sells. The hitching device contains software that controls the movement of the mechanisms necessary to hitch a trailer to the truck. This software cannot be activated unless encrypted software in the trailer's hitching mechanism sends a special code to the software in the truck hitching mechanism to make a secret "handshake." Only when the handshake routine is completed will the Trucking, Inc. truck hitching device release the mechanisms needed to hitch the trailer to the truck. This effectively requires persons buying Trucking, Inc. trucks to buy Trucking, Inc. trailers.

Long-Haul, Inc., a leading manufacturer and seller of trailers for long distance hauling, and a competitor of Trucking, Inc. in the market for trailers, develops software for its trailer hitching devices that avoids the Trucking, Inc. handshake routine, allowing owners of Trucking, Inc. trucks to activate the truck's hitching software and hitch trailers made by Long-Haul to their trucks. The Long-Haul software does not reproduce any copyrightable expression from the Trucking, Inc. software.

Is Trucking, Inc. likely to succeed in a lawsuit against Long-Haul? Please explain your answer. _____

57. Alex created an original comic strip that was carried by a number of daily newspapers around the country and enjoyed significant success. Alex licensed Betty to make and sell dolls based on the leading characters in the comic strip. Several years later, Alex licensed Charles to create and sell greeting cards featuring the comic strip characters. The depictions of the comic strip characters in Charles's cards are highly similar to the dolls that Betty is marketing. Betty, accordingly, has brought suit against Charles, alleging copyright infringement. How would you evaluate the respective rights of the parties? _____

58. Dave, a veteran of years of television and radio work, decided to go into business with his wife, Becky, to make a series of low-budget children's videos. Dave and Becky wrote the scripts, directed and acted in the videos, which introduced young children to such things as firefighting, construction work, the manufacture of cars, the postal service, etc. Dave and Becky did almost everything themselves except the camera work, for which they hired an employee. Generally they just acquired a license to incorporate pre-existing recorded music into their videos, but in commencing work on a video to introduce children to airplanes, Dave and Becky decided to include some original music. They contacted Janet, an old friend of theirs, who sang and played guitar, and asked her if she would write and sing a song about flying to be used in the video. Janet did so. Because the parties were old friends, they made no written contract. Dave and Becky told Janet that she would be paid a sum constituting 5 percent of net sales of the video, to be paid yearly, for the first 10,000 videos sold.

A year after the airplane videos went on sale, Janet arranged to give a series of children's concerts. In each concert, she sang the song about flying that she had written and performed for the video. In the background on stage, she projected scenes from the video. When Dave and Becky learned that Janet had been showing the video in her performance they demanded that she stop. However, Janet refused. Please evaluate the respective rights of the parties, given the available facts. _____

Sample Answers

23. Wanda Sue has not infringed. First, Eileen's recipe may not constitute copyrightable expression. Recipes generally consist of a list of ingredients, coupled with straightforward, highly utilitarian instructions for combining the ingredients. The language of the recipe may merge with the underlying idea that is being expressed because there are a limited number of ways effectively to express the ingredients and steps of the recipe. At most, the recipe is likely to enjoy a thin copyright that protects against "virtual identicality." (While Eileen's selection and arrangement of recipes within the book is likely to be protected, Wanda Sue did not copy selection and arrangement because she only used one recipe.)

    More importantly, *Baker v. Selden* teaches that copyright never extends rights to the underlying idea or art that a literary work teaches. Here, even if Eileen enjoyed copyright in the recipe, Wanda Sue's use of the recipe to create the casserole (the underlying useful article the recipe explains) would not constitute infringement. To hold otherwise would permit copyright to be used to gain monopoly rights in things meant to be judged by the higher standards of the patent laws. The fact that Wanda Sue altered the recipe in the course of making it is irrelevant for purposes of a copyright infringement claim.

24. Brown can argue that the command codes are uncopyrightable methods of operation, under the authority of the First Circuit's opinion in *Lotus Development Corp. v. Borland International, Inc.* The command codes do not describe the method of operating the machine, but constitute the actual means by which the machine is operated, like the "record" and "play" buttons on a VCR. That being the case, Brown could argue, it does not matter whether the codes contain expressive elements, such as the selection and arrangement of numbers, and the assignment of particular numbers to categories of tasks and to represent levels of task complexity. These expressive elements should be excluded from copyright because they are part of a method of operation, as in *Lotus*.

    Brown might also argue that the command codes are uncopyrightable for lack of originality. While some intellectual judgment may have gone into the decision to begin codes with a number representing the category in which the task falls, and to assign lower numbers to simple tasks and higher numbers to more complex tasks within a category, such decisions are "obvious" and "inevitable," like the decisions to list telephone subscribers alphabetically by last name in the *Feist* case. Moreover, as a matter of policy, the courts should not construe the copyright laws to provide a cause of action in this case because of the public's interest in a competitive marketplace. It appears that Arco's machines were the first of their kind in the marketplace, and have become the *de facto* standard. The work force is trained in the Arco codes. To change to another command code system would require users to make a considerable investment in retraining. The cost of a switch thus may serve as a barrier to competitors' entering the market for this type of machinery. If Arco is permitted to use the copyright laws to prohibit competitors from using similar command codes, this may seriously deprive the public of beneficial competition.

However, Brown cannot be sure of success. Not all jurisdictions have accepted the logic of the *Lotus* decision. Based on precedent from the Tenth Circuit, a court might apply the abstraction-filtration-comparison test and find that while the numeric sequences are part of a method of operation at a high level of abstraction, their individual expressive elements may still be protected at a lower level of abstraction. Moreover, while Arco cannot claim copyright in the *idea* of assigning particular numbers to represent categories of tasks or complexity, there are practically limitless combinations of numbers that can be assigned to a particular category or level of complexity, and there is no reason (from a copyright standpoint) why Brown must use the same numbers. With regard to Brown's policy argument, a court might reply that it would undercut copyright policy to penalize a copyright claimant for being the first in the market and creating a system that is so successful that it has become the standard in the field.

25. A sound recording is a category of copyrightable expression. According to Copyright Act §101, sound recordings are "works that result from the fixation of a series of musical, spoken, or other sounds, but not including the sounds accompanying a motion picture or other audiovisual work, regardless of the nature of the material objects, such as disks, tapes, or other phonorecords, in which they are embodied.

A phonorecord is the material object upon which a sound recording is fixed. Copyright Act §101 defines phonorecords as "material objects in which sounds, other than those accompanying a motion picture or other audiovisual work, are fixed by any method now known or later developed, and from which the sounds can be perceived, reproduced, or otherwise communicated, either directly or with the aid of a machine or device."

26. No. The physical and conceptual separability tests only apply to pictorial, graphic, or sculptural works that are embodied in a useful article. A useful article has an intrinsic utilitarian function that is not merely to portray the appearance of the article. The deer form appears to have no utilitarian function other than to portray the appearance of a deer, and thus is not a useful article.

27. A chair is a useful article. Only design elements that are original, and physically or conceptually separable would be protected by copyright. Since Acme's chair is a "classic" wingback chair, it is not likely that it is either physically or conceptually separable. (The fabric in which the chair is upholstered might qualify if Acme created it or has acquired proprietary rights in it, but X did not copy the fabric.)

The two-dimensional annotated plans would be subject to copyright. However, the facts do not indicate that X copied the plans. Rather, he used the copy he stole to manufacture his competing chair. Using plans for a useful article to build the article itself does not infringe the copyright in the plans. See Copyright Act §113(b).

28. No. Bill's copyright in his sound recording cannot be infringed unless Charles mechanically reproduced sounds directly from Bill's recording, which he did not. An independent fixation of sounds will not infringe a sound recording copyright, no matter how similar. 17 U.S.C. §114(b).

29. Tom did not violate any of Jerry's rights in licensing Dizzy to make a movie. However, Jerry could demand that Tom share royalties payable under the license.

Tom and Jerry inherited equal shares in the copyright for Alice's original novel. The revised novel that Tom published was a derivative work to which Tom alone held copyright. However, Tom's derivative work copyright only gave him exclusive rights in the new material he added. Dizzy's movie undoubtedly uses expression from Alice's original novel, as well as the new material Tom added in his adaptation. Tom, as a co-owner of the copyright in Alice's original work, was entitled to license Dizzy to use material from the original, as well as from the derivative work. However, he must share the proceeds of the license that are attributable to use of the original work with Tom.

30. Cliff has a good cause of action. While Cliff authorized sale of a digital copy of "Homes on the Range" to Alice, it did not authorize the alteration, which arguably constitutes the making of an unauthorized adaptation. Alice's altered 20-minute segment incorporates the copyrighted movie in a concrete or permanent form (on her computer hard drive), as required by the *Galoob* decision, and is substantially similar to the original movie. The only question is whether her alteration (replacing Bill's head with Brad's head) is a sufficient change to constitute an infringing adaptation. It is unclear under the case law whether the change must constitute a "substantial variation" (such as is required to qualify for a derivative work copyright) in order to infringe. If the relevant jurisdiction did impose this requirement, then Alice might successfully argue that the change was not sufficient. Moreover, it is not clear whether Alice's acts interfered with any meaningful market opportunities Cliff Enterprises might have had.

Even if Alice's acts did not constitute an infringing adaptation, however, she clearly infringed Cliff's reproduction rights. She reproduced "Homes on the Range" when she uploaded the 20-minute segment to her web site, and arguably, she reproduces it every time a visitor to the site downloads it to view it on his or her computer screen. (When a user downloads the segment, Alice's server creates and transmits a digital copy of it.) While an authorized sale of a digital copy of a movie may carry with it an implied license permitting the purchaser to reproduce the movie as necessary to play it for her own personal enjoyment, that implied license probably would not be construed to authorize reproduction for other purposes, such as adaptation, posting to a web site, and transmitting to downloaders.

Moreover, Alice's posting of the segment on her web site probably constitutes a distribution to the public because she is making copies available on her web site, and her computer is transmitting copies to members of the public who visit the web site. It is important to note that the doctrine of first sale would not apply to shelter Alice's activities because the copies she is transmitting to web site visitors are not the same copy she purchased. They are new copies that she caused to be made by posting the altered segment on her web site.

Finally, Alice's posting of the segment on her web site arguably constitutes a public performance because she is essentially causing the performance to recur through a transmission "to the public," as provided in Copyright Act § 101.

Even if Alice's acts in maintaining the 20-minute segment on her web site did not constitute direct infringement, her site visitors infringe by reproducing the segment without Cliff's authorization. Pursuant to the *MAI* decision, bringing a work into the random access memory of a computer constitutes a reproduction, and downloaders must bring the segment into their random access memories in order to view it. Alice could be indirectly liable for their direct infringement under either a contributory, a vicarious, or an inducement liability theory. First, under a contributory infringement theory, Alice has assisted the visitors to infringe (indeed, has made it possible for them to infringe by making the segment available on her web site) with actual knowledge that the visitors' downloading and reproduction of the movie segment is unauthorized by the copyright owner. Second, under a vicarious liability theory, Alice has the right to control the visitors' actions (she has the power to remove the infringing material from her web site, so that visitors cannot infringe by downloading it) and stands to gain a direct financial benefit from their infringement (under the *Fonovisa* decision, the infringing material on her site constitutes a "draw" for visitors, and the more visitors she gets, the higher her advertising revenues). Finally, Alice might be liable for inducing the visitors' infringement under *Grokster* by knowingly, intentionally placing the infringing segment on her web site and inviting visitors to reproduce it by downloading it.

Alice would not enjoy the benefit of the safe harbor provisions that Congress enacted in the Digital Millennium Copyright Act (codified at 17 U.S.C. §512) to protect Internet service providers from liability for their users' infringement. Alice is not a passive, automated provider of services that others use to initiate infringement. She is directly, knowingly initiating and participating in the infringement and gaining a financial benefit that is directly attributable to the infringement.

Moreover, Alice is unlikely to enjoy a fair use defense. Her purpose is commercial, and her use does not appear to be overly transformative: It does not appear that she added much expressive content in replacing Bill's head with Brad's. She was not undertaking to produce a parody or other commentary about the "Homes on the Range" movie that would enrich the public, but rather to capitalize on Brad's popularity and show off her technical skills in digital manipulation. In addition, there is no apparent reason why Alice needed to use a substantial portion (20 minutes) of Cliff's movie to do this. She could have made her own film and manipulated it. Moreover, Alice's actions could be characterized as interfering with Cliff's potential market to make or license derivative works constituting digital remakes of the copyrighted cowboy movie (if a market for such rights can be found).

31. The Sensational Bar Journal's column is likely to infringe ZBS's rights. Even though the Journal did not take any direct quotes or any visual imagery, it engaged in nonliteral infringement. The various events, scenes, and characters in the "Law School Lovelorn" program are fictitious, and their conception, selection, and arrangement into program plots constitutes copyrightable expression. Journal's reproduction of this expression, even though paraphrased, is an unauthorized reproduction (as well as an adaptation and distribution to the public). There is little doubt that the column would be deemed "substantially similar" because it reproduces all the important developments in the plot.

32. Goodreads probably is liable for infringement. While the Supreme Court has indicated that the doctrine of first sale limits the importation right, the doctrine only applies to first sales made by or under the authorization of the U.S. copyright owner. Since U.K. Publishers, Ltd. made and sold the copies at issue, and is not related to or authorized by Old Glory (the U.S. copyright holder) there is no argument that the first sale doctrine should apply. (Moreover, it is unclear under the existing precedents whether the doctrine of first sale would apply to copies made outside of the Unites States even if made by or under the authorization of the U.S. copyright owner.)

Copyright Act §602(a)(2) provides that it will not infringe the importation right for persons to import a single copy of a copyrighted work for their own private use. Goodreads might rely on this provision to argue that its U.S. purchasers are the importers and they only import the copy for their own private reading enjoyment. Thus, the §602(a)(2) exception applies and no infringement of Old Glory's copyright occurs. However, a court might not be persuaded. The purpose of this exception appears to be to permit random, isolated acts of importation, which would not be likely to have a significant impact on the U.S. copyright owner's market. Here, there is a large, systemized importation scheme, which Goodreads creates and orchestrates through its web site, and which is likely to have a significant impact on Old Glory's market in the United States. Under the circumstances, Goodreads' actions have the same impact as if it imported a large number of the books into the United States and sold them retail through a shop located on U.S. soil. The fact that Goodreads' web site is physically located in the U.K. makes little difference in practical terms.

33. The pastor's acts would not be excused under Copyright Act §109(c) because he projected more than one image of the work. However, they probably would be excused under §110(3), which permits display of a work in the course of services at a place of worship or other religious assembly.

34. In *Lewis Galoob Toys, Inc. v. Nintendo of America, Inc.,* the Court of Appeals for the Ninth Circuit held that to infringe the adaptation right a defendant must incorporate the plaintiff's work into the alleged derivative work in a permanent or concrete manner. The court emphasized that this requirement differed from the fixation requirement.

   Here it is clear that the plaintiff's work is incorporated into the alleged derivative work because the defendant integrated his own additions into the original in RAM. The only question is whether the incorporation (which only took place in the defendant's RAM) is "permanent or concrete" as required in *Galoob*.

   When X downloaded Y's photo he "fixed" it in his random access memory (under the reasoning in the *MAI* decision). Thus, presumably, the altered version in RAM is also "fixed." One might argue that if the altered photo is "fixed" it should be deemed "permanent and concrete" too. Thus, while the *Galoob* court suggested that "incorporation in a permanent or concrete form" was not the same requirement as "fixation," a court might find fixation in RAM to be sufficiently "permanent and concrete" to satisfy the *Galoob* standard, under the facts of this case.

35. DeBartolomeo's acts constitute a public performance of the copyrighted songs, because he renders them in a place open to the public. The public performance is not excluded under any of the §110 exceptions to liability. Section 110(4) does not apply because the restaurant is a commercial enterprise and the performance augments the guests' enjoyment of the restaurant and thus provides indirect commercial advantage to DeBartolomeo. Section 110(5) does not apply because it only extends to performances by transmission, not to live performances. The fair use defense would not likely apply because (1) DeBartolomeo's purpose is commercial; (2) the songs are not useful or factual works; (3) DeBartolomeo performs the entire song; and (4) if such unauthorized performances were regularly undertaken, they would significantly interfere with the existing market for performance licenses for the musical compositions.

36. The author's right of integrity enables her to prevent intentional distortions, mutilations, or other modifications of the work that would be prejudicial to her honor or reputation. The right cannot be transferred, and remains with the author even after she has assigned her copyright in the work of visual art. The right of adaptation is an economic right that permits the owner to make or authorize others to make changes to the work. Because the right of adaptation may be assigned, the owner of the adaptation right may differ from the owner of the right of integrity. In such cases, the copyright owner's right of adaptation may be restricted by the author's right of integrity, to the extent that the adaptation the copyright owner undertakes would be deemed prejudicial to the author's honor or reputation.

37. Mary's posting of the digitized copy on the Internet bulletin board is likely to constitute a public display of the photograph. Mary's act is a display because she showed a copy of the photograph, by means of a device. The display is public because it is transmitted "to the public, by means of any device or process, whether the members of the public capable of receiving the display receive it in the same place or in separate places and at the same time or at different times." 17 U.S.C. §101.

This public display on the Internet bulletin board is likely to infringe, because there is nothing in the facts to suggest that it was authorized. Copyright Act §109(c) will not exempt Mary's acts because (even though her original copy was a lawful one) the digitized copy she posted was not lawfully made. Moreover, even if the digital copy was lawfully made, the §109(c) exception to the public display right is limited to displays that are direct or are made by projection of no more than one image at a time to viewers present at the place where the copy is located. When Mary posted the photograph on the bulletin board she caused it to be transmitted to persons who were not in the same location as the digital copy.

If Mary posted her original copy on the college dormitory bulletin board her display would fall under the §109(c) exception to the copyright owner's right of public display, and would not infringe. However, if she posted the unauthorized digital copy, §109(c) would not apply to shelter her from liability because the digital copy was not a copy that was lawfully made.

38. Architect has no cause of action, due to Copyright Act §120, which provides that "[t]he copyright in an architectural work that has been constructed does not include the right to prevent the making, distributing, or public display of pictures, paintings, photographs, or other pictorial representations of the work, if the building in which the work is embodied is located in or ordinarily visible from a public place."

39. It probably did infringe copyright. Composing the list (or database) of badly dressed professors required Elbert to exercise intellectual judgment and creativity in determining and applying the appropriate criteria, giving rise to selection and arrangement expression. While the copyright in such a list is likely to be thin, Newspaper engaged in a "bodily appropriation of expression," when it reproduced the list in its entirety, thereby meeting the higher than normal standard for infringement of works covered by thin copyright.

40. Because Y's work qualifies for protection under the Architectural Works Copyright Protection Act, it can be protected, not as a pictorial, graphic, or sculptural work, but as a "work of architecture." A work of architecture is protected from copying regardless of whether Y copied the finished building or the plans in the course of making his own building. X's unauthorized copying of the work is likely to infringe Y's rights because X's building seems to be an exact duplication of Y's design, and it is likely that Y's design contains copyrightable expression (since architectural works are not subject to the physical or conceptual separability test).

41. Fred may be liable under the anti-circumvention provisions enacted in the Digital Millennium Copyright Act. The Act prohibits the "circumvention of a technological measure that effectively controls access" to a copyrighted work. 17 U.S.C. §1201. By making the game inaccessible without a password, and restricting the password to Patty (as arguably was done in giving Patty a "personal" password), the producer implemented a technological measure that effectively controls access to the game, which is copyrightable subject matter, and probably is copyrighted. By using Patty's "personal" password, Fred arguably circumvented that measure, in violation of the Act. However, courts are divided over whether unauthorized use of a password constitutes circumvention. Some have held that to circumvent, one must bypass the technological measure, not just pass through it without permission. Other courts have held that passing through the technological measure without permission constitutes bypassing it, and thus circumventing it. If Fred is in a jurisdiction that adopts the latter line of reasoning, he will be liable. There is no fair use defense to liability for circumventing technological measures controlling access to works.

42. Heckel and Jeckel were probably joint authors of the original paper. Joint authorship requires that both authors contribute copyrightable expression with the intent that their portions be merged into inseparable or interdependent parts of a unitary whole. In this case, Heckel and Jeckel each wrote a substantial portion of the paper (which means that they each probably contributed copyrightable expression), and the size of each participant's contribution, coupled with the nature of the work (a single scholarly paper describing research they had jointly done) provides circumstantial evidence that the parties intended to merge their portions into a unitary, jointly owned whole. The only evidence suggesting otherwise is the fact that Heckel left Jeckel's name off the paper when he later presented it at a conference. Presumably, each of them had equal control over the creation and contents of the paper.

Assuming that Heckel and Jeckel were joint authors, both had the right to exploit the paper independently, subject only to the obligation to account to the other for any profits made through exploitation.

Heckel had the right to present (publicly perform) the paper, with or without Jeckel's knowledge or consent. The only issue is whether Heckel violated a right on Jeckel's part to have joint authorship attributed to him. While many countries recognize the moral right of attribution in connection with all copyrighted works, the United States only provides an express right of attribution for works of visual art. Thus, the Copyright Act would provide Jeckel no relief. He might consider avenues of legal relief outside of the Copyright Act.

Heckel had a right to revise (adapt) the paper with or without Jeckel's knowledge or consent. Because Heckel was the sole author of the revisions, he was the sole owner of copyright in the resulting derivative work (assuming that the derivative work constituted a "substantial variation" from the original and thus qualified for its own copyright), and he had the exclusive right to reproduce it and distribute it to the public. Accordingly, unless Jeckel's acts can be justified as a fair use, they will infringe. A fair use defense seems unlikely because Jeckel's actions seem to undermine Heckel's interest in first publication and may fully satisfy demand for the paper. It should also be noted that Jeckel's use is not a "productive" one (he did not further enlarge on Heckel's work), and Jeckel copied the whole work. While Jeckel's purpose was for scholarship and was not commercial, this is unlikely to outweigh the other relevant factors mentioned above.

43. David's rights against Brown: Brown's license expired in 1991, with the first term of the novel's copyright. Even though Able's grant purported to give Brown rights in the second term of the novel's copyright (and would have done so if Able had lived to renew), the grant only created a contingent interest in Brown which expired when Able failed to live to renew the copyright. David, Able's son, had the right to renew and took the renewal term free from any grants Able made during the first term of the copyright. Thus, if Brown wants to continue to exploit the play, he must negotiate a new license with David. If he publicly performs the play during the second term without doing so, he will be liable to David for infringing the copyright in the novel. (If further facts were available, it might be possible to argue that B is liable for C's infringement, discussed below, on a contributory infringement theory.)

Presumably, Cohen's movie took copyrightable expression derived from the novel, as well as the copyrightable expression that Brown added in the course of creating the play based on the novel. However, the facts indicate that Cohen only obtained a license from Brown, not from Able or David. Brown had no authority to license Cohen to adapt the novel, and his license was not binding on Able or his successors. Thus, it appears that Cohen's creation and exploitation of the movie infringed the novel's copyright during the first term, and will continue to infringe during the second term.

44. Since the poster was already protected by federal copyright on January 1, 1978, when the Copyright Act of 1976 became effective, the length of protection is determined under Copyright Act §304, as amended. That section provides that copyrights in their first term of protection on January 1, 1978 enjoy 28 years of protection, beginning on the date of publication with proper notice, the same as under the Copyright Act of 1909. However, if the copyright is renewed, it will enjoy a second term of 67 years. Here, the first term of copyright terminated on December 31, 1997 (28 years after first publication). Under recent amendments, the copyright was automatically renewed (in favor of the proprietor, since the poster was a work for hire). Thus, the protection will last through the year 2064. The date of Allen's death is irrelevant.

45. The poster is a work for hire, which was created after the effective date of the 1976 Act. Therefore its duration is governed by Copyright Act §302(c). It will endure 95 years from the date of first publication or 120 years from the date of creation, whichever expires first. Here the copyright will expire in 2079. The date of Brown's death is irrelevant.

46. Under Copyright Act §302(a), the copyright would expire on December 31, 2055. The work appears not to be a work for hire, since the facts suggest that Allen was not an "employee" of Brown, and there is no suggestion that the requirements for making an independent contractor's work a work for hire were satisfied. Thus, Brown is the "author" and initial owner of copyright, and the proper measure is 70 years from Allen's death.

47. The copyright term ended 28 years after first publication with notice. While that first term might have been renewed, it could only be renewed by the author or the next persons in line under §304—his two children. Even though author left all his personal property to the girlfriend, the law allocates his renewal rights to his children. Since the children did not renew, the second term is forfeited. (Note that automatic renewal was not yet in effect.)

48. The license could be terminated in the year 2029, but in order to do this, owners of a majority of the interest in the termination rights must give notice of intent to terminate between two to ten years prior to that date. (The children and grandchildren would have to convince Marla to join them in the termination.) Unfortunately, even if the license is terminated, XBS will be able to continue to exploit the movie without liability for infringement. Termination will only prevent XBS from making more movies based on the play.

49. Yes, he does. Since Chang never published his diary, it was protected under common-law copyright. When the Copyright Act of 1976 became effective, that copyright became a federal copyright which will endure for Chang's life plus 70 years (the year 2020) or until the end of the year 2002, whichever is longer. 17 U.S.C. §303. Depositing the diary in Archive probably does not constitute a publication of it, nor does it transfer ownership of the copyright from niece. Johnson should contact niece for a license.

50. There is precedent for holding that Buildings.com's actions should not be found to constitute direct infringement. In Costar Group v. Loopnet, the Fourth Circuit held that even though copyright is a strict liability statute, there must be some element of volition or causation, which is lacking when a defendant's automated system is merely used to make a copy by a third party. Passive ownership and management of an electronic Internet facility on which others post infringing materials thus would not lead to direct infringement liability on the system owner's part. The system owner must engage in the act that constitutes infringement to become a direct infringer. The court also suggested that an ISP does not "fix" a copy in its system for more than a transitory duration (and thus make a copy) when it provides the kind of Internet hosting service described in the problem.

51. There are two copyrights at issue here, both presumably owned by X. The first is the copyright in the musical composition. The facts indicate that Y only took three chords of background guitar. In order to demonstrate an infringing reproduction, X would have to show not only that Y copied from his work (which he clearly did) but also that the copying resulted in a substantial similarity of copyrightable expression (judged by the average lay listener's overall, subjective response). Given the very limited nature of the material taken, the changes, and the fact that listeners wouldn't recognize the inclusion of X's material, it is likely that a court would find Y's copying *de minimis* and non-infringing.

However, the second copyright for the sound recording might be infringed by the mere act of digital sampling, even in the absence of a substantial similarity of copyrightable expression. In the *Bridgeport* case, the Sixth Circuit construed the language of Copyright Act §114(b) to impose liability upon the mechanical lifting of *any* of the copyrighted recorded sounds. This is a very liberal reading of the statutory language, and contrary to the United States' long history of requiring a showing of substantial similarity of copyrightable expression (at the very least) as a prerequisite to infringement liability in all categories of copyrightable works. It is not clear whether other Circuits will follow the *Bridgeport* lead. In other circuits, the analysis regarding infringement of the sound recording copyright may entail a determination of whether the parties' recordings are substantially similar. If so, as in the case of the musical composition copyright, Y is not likely to be found liable.

52. (a) Acme v. X. Acme might argue that in reverse engineering the object code, X was circumventing an access control measure, in violation of the DMCA anticircumvention provisions. There is little precedent to indicate whether a court would read the DMCA provisions this broadly. However, since the question specifically asks about a cause of action for copyright infringement (as opposed to a cause of action for circumvention), copyright infringement will be the focus of this answer.

A copyright infringement cause of action is unlikely to be successful. X did reproduce the whole program in order to translate it from object to source code. However, this copying is likely to be excused as a fair use. Under fair use factor number 1, X made the copy for non-commercial purposes (for study and scholarship), and he did not avoid paying the customary price: he bought the copy he reverse engineered. Moreover, his ultimate creation (the posting of the algorithms, along with his critique of Acme's methodology) was transformative and beneficial to the public. Under factors 2 and 3 of the fair use analysis, the Acme program was a highly utilitarian work, with numerous public domain elements, and it was necessary for X to copy the entire work in order to obtain the mathematical algorithms, which are in the public domain. (Mathematical algorithms are most likely equivalent to the underlying idea of the program, or a system or method of operation, which would not constitute copyrightable subject matter.) Finally, under factor 4, X did not supplant demand for the Acme program by marketing an infringing substitute for it. In the *Sega* case, the Ninth Circuit held that "where disassembly is the only way to gain access to the ideas and functional elements embodied in a copyrighted computer program, and where there is a legitimate reason for seeking such access, disassembly is a fair use of the copyrighted work, as a matter of law." This rule of law would seem to fit X's actions in creating a copy in the course of reverse engineering and excuse it. (X's posting of the algorithm would not itself infringe, because the algorithm is not copyrightable expression.)

(b) Acme v. Y. Acme is unlikely to have a copyright cause of action against Y since Y only copied the Acme program mathematical algorithms, which are not likely to be deemed copyrightable expression. He appears otherwise to have independently created his program.

53. Neither Friend nor Son has any rights, because Vik's renewal was not effective. The article was most likely a work for hire, since Vik wrote it in his capacity as a reporter for BigNews. In that case, under §304, BigNews (the proprietor) had the right to renew, not Vik. Since there is nothing to suggest that BigNews or its successors in interest (if any) renewed, the article probably entered the public domain in 1977.

If Vik had had the right to renew, he would have owned the second term of the copyright, and would have been free to pass his interest by will to Friend. As long as the will was valid, Son would have no claim and (since the transfer to friend was by will) no termination right.

54. The letter was protected by common-law copyright until Jan. 1, 1978, when the copyright was converted to federal copyright. The new federal copyright will end 70 years from Famous Poet's death, and thus is still valid. The facts do not indicate who succeeded to Famous Poet's copyright interests, but assuming that it is his Widow, then her best bet would be to allege infringement of her exclusive right to distribute copies of the work to the public. Because the photocopy of the letter was unauthorized and infringing, any further distribution of it will also infringe, regardless of whether the defendant knew that the copy it distributed was unauthorized.

Distribution to the public traditionally has entailed physically handing a copy of the work to a member of the public. Here, there is no evidence to show that the Library ever loaned the photocopy to anyone. However, the Fourth Circuit has held, in the *Hotaling* case, that when a library makes an infringing work available to the public, properly indexed in its collection, this constitutes an infringing distribution. This is because the library has taken all the steps necessary for distribution of the copy to the public, and any member of the public could obtain it, if he or she tried. This decision was undoubtedly influenced by cases finding that posting an infringing copy of a work on an Internet web site constitutes a distribution to the public.

55. This case raises the question of the extent to which the doctrine of first sale applies to parallel imports. In the *L'Anza* case, the Supreme Court construed Copyright Act §§602 and 106 to provide that the doctrine of first sale applies when the U.S. copyright owner manufactures copyrighted goods in the United States for sale abroad, and permits foreign purchasers to bring the goods back into the U.S. for resale. In this case, the U.S. copyright owner (Acme) made the first sale of the sound recordings abroad, but did not manufacture the sound recordings in the United States. The *L'Anza* decision did not address this situation. Copyright Act §109(a) provides that the doctrine of first sale applies only to copies and phonorecords "lawfully made under this title." Some lower courts have construed this language to impose a geographical limitation on the doctrine of first sale—reasoning that "lawfully made under this title" means lawfully made within the United States where the Copyright Act applies. Under this construction, Acme could assert that the phonorecords purchased in New Zealand infringe its U.S. copyright under Copyright Act §602.

However, there are alternative ways to construe §109(a). A phonorecord may be "lawfully made under this title" if it is made by the U.S. copyright owner. (The key would be that the person holding rights "under this title" made the copies and authorized their sale.) This result would be consistent with the rationale (adopted by the Third Circuit) that applying the doctrine of first sale turns not on where the first sale was made but on who made it—any first sale made by or under the authority of the U.S. copyright owner triggers the doctrine of first sale, no matter where it was made. Why should the U.S. copyright owner be able to keep goods out of the country in one instance, but not the other? Parallel imports provide a means for consumers to avoid discriminatory pricing practices by multinational corporations.

56. The issue here is whether Long-Haul (LH) can be found liable under the DMCA, 17 U.S.C. §1201(a)(2), for trafficking in a device that circumvents a technological measure that effectively controls access to a copyrighted work (the software in the Trucking, Inc. trailer hitching device). The literal language of §1201 suggests that it could. However, two circuit court decisions addressing the issue of circumvention of software access measures in consumer goods have construed these provisions narrowly to prevent the plaintiffs from using the DMCA provisions in this way. The *Lexmark* decision might not be applicable because Trucking Inc. encrypted its software, as well as controlled access to its functionality. Under the reasoning in *Lexmark*, the handshake routine probably would be deemed to "effectively control access" to the software, since there would be no alternative means of access (such as simply reading or reproducing the code) available to truck owners.

However, in *Chamberlain*, the Court of Appeals for the Federal Circuit held that the DMCA only prohibits forms of circumvention that constitute a threat to rights created under the copyright law: Thus, trafficking in a circumvention device will only violate §1201(a)(2) if use of the device will infringe or facilitate infringement of a copyright. Here, it appears that it will not. All LH's software does is permit the truck owner to access the functionality (use) of the hitching software to hitch a trailer to the truck. It does not permit the user to reproduce, adapt, publicly distribute, perform or display the copyrighted software. Moreover, the *Chamberlain* Court held that when a producer sells consumer goods to a purchaser without an express restriction, the purchaser should be deemed authorized to access the software in the consumer good for purposes of using aftermarket replacement parts or accessories. The facts do not suggest that the plaintiff sold its trucks subject to an express restriction against use of the trucks with competitors' trailers. Thus, in this case, two of the factors identified by the *Chamberlain* court as necessary to a §1201(a)(2) claim are missing: 1) a lack of the copyright owner's authorization to circumvent; and 2) a showing that use of LH's device will infringe or facilitate infringement of one of the §106 rights of the copyright owner.

It is not yet clear whether other Circuits will follow the Federal Circuit's lead on this issue. If they don't, then a reasonable argument could be made that the handshake routine is a technological measure that effectively controls access to a copyrighted work (because it requires that information or a process be applied, with the authority of the copyright owner, to gain access to the software). LH's trailer software "circumvents" the measure because it "avoids, bypasses, or impairs" the technological measure without the authority of the copyright owner, and the trailer software "is primarily designed or produced for the purpose of circumventing a technological measure that effectively controls access to a" copyrighted work.

57. Normally dolls would constitute copyrightable subject matter—they would probably be considered sculptural works. However, these dolls are derivative works, based on a preexisting copyrighted work—Alex's comic strip characters. The issue is whether the dolls would qualify for their own derivative work copyright. A number of courts, including the Second, Seventh and Ninth Circuits, have imposed a higher standard of originality for derivative works: They must constitute a substantial variation from the underlying work (here, the comic strip characters). As the Seventh Circuit has explained, this higher standard is meant to deal with situations just like this. If the law makes it easy to obtain derivative work copyrights (for works that deviate little from the original), the first person to make a derivative work based on a particular preexisting work may be able to chill the making of subsequent derivative works by threatening harassing infringement claims. It is difficult to gain summary judgment in copyright cases, so the costs of litigation may be high. Since the unlawful appropriation evaluation is often subjective in nature, and it may be difficult to determine wither the defendant copied from the underlying work or from the first derivative work, the outcome of infringement litigation may be hard to predict. This may lead others to decide that the risks of making their own derivative works based on the same underlying work are too great, to the general detriment of the public. Requiring a substantial variation as a prerequisite for the derivative work copyright makes it harder for the first derivative work maker to obtain copyright, and ensures that the underlying work and the first (copyrighted) derivative work are sufficiently different that it will be easier to tell what was copied from the derivative work and what was copied from the original.

In this case there are insufficient facts to determine whether Betty's dolls constitute a substantial variation from the comic strip characters, and thus are copyrightable under the standard discussed above. Betty probably tried to make the dolls as like the comic strip characters as possible in order to capitalize on the comic strip's popularity. Moreover, the case law indicates that a mere change of medium (and changes necessitated by the new medium) often are not sufficient to constitute a substantial variation. It might be noted, too, that the Ninth Circuit, applying a similar standard, found that three-dimensional costumes based on two-dimensional cartoon characters did not constitute a substantial variation from the original and thus did not qualify for a derivative work copyright.

In addition, the Ninth Circuit has held that copyright in a derivative work that was based on a copyrighted original should only be recognized when the derivative work copyright will not interfere with the exploitation of the original copyrighted work. Under this standard, it seems clear that Betty's ability to sue Charles for infringement will interfere with Alex's ability to exploit his own copyright by licensing adaptations.

If Betty fails to demonstrate the prerequisites for a derivative work copyright, then she cannot succeed in an infringement suit against Charles.

58. The rights of the parties depend on the status of the parties' work. If the video and song together constitute a single joint work, then Janet is a joint owner along with Dave and Becky, and has the right to exploit the whole thing, subject to a duty to account to the other co-owners of copyright for the profits she makes. If the video and song together are not a single joint work, then Janet has no right to publicly perform the images from the video, and is infringing Dave and Becky's copyright. Of course, if Janet's song was a work for hire, then she has no rights in the song, either—making her performance of the song an infringement, as well.

It seems clear that Janet's song was not a work for hire because Janet is an independent contractor, not an employee. She worked for Dave and Becky for only a short time, performing only one task. Presumably a new contract would have been required to perform additional tasks. There is nothing to suggest that Dave and Becky paid employee benefits for Janet, and Janet's form of payment is somewhat contingent in nature—not the kind of payment arrangement generally made for regular employees. There is nothing to suggest that Dave and Becky provided the location or tools for Janet to write her song (though they may have provided the studio for her to record it), or controlled the hours she worked. Writing and recording songs is not a part of Dave and Becky's regular business. Thus, it does not appear that Dave and Becky controlled the manner or means of Janet's creation of the song, and that the song is not a work for hire. Moreover, even though a contribution to a motion picture created by an independent contractor can be a work for hire if the necessary written agreement is made, there is nothing in the facts to suggest that there was such a written agreement.

The chances are pretty good that the song-video combination is not a joint work, either. A joint work is "a work prepared by two or more authors with the intention that their contributions be merged into inseparable or interdependent parts of a unitary whole." (Copyright Act §101). According to the Ninth Circuit, to be a joint author, one must contribute copyrightable expression (which Janet clearly did), and have some final say regarding what comprises the finished work as a whole. Janet would not meet this second factor. According to the Seventh and Second Circuits, all the parties have to intend for each to be a joint author. Here, that is unlikely. Dave and Becky clearly are accustomed to being the only authors of the video, and did not expect that Janet would be an equal owner. They retained the final decision-making power regarding whether Janet's material would be included. Moreover, Janet's contribution was only a relatively small part of the whole video, which is circumstantial evidence that the parties did not intend equal partnership. The fact that Dave and Becky offered to pay Janet 5 percent of the net proceeds, for only the first 10,000 videos sold, also suggests that they did not intend for Janet to be the owner of a joint work. Finally, it does not appear that the parties intended for the song to be merged into the video as an inseparable part of a unitary whole. Janet clearly understood that the song could be separately performed.

Thus, it appears that Janet is the owner of the copyright in the song, and that Dave and Becky have an implied license to reproduce and perform the song in the video. Dave and Becky are the sole owners of copyright in the video images, and Janet infringes when she publicly performs them without a license.

Exam Tips on COPYRIGHTS

☞ **Remember the policies and ultimate purpose underlying copyright:** Copyright law can be vague and conceptually challenging, particularly when it is necessary to distinguish idea from expression, apply the originality standard, apply the "conceptual separability" test, or evaluate the fair use defense. It is often helpful, in the course of discussing such issues in an exam, to step back and consider how real courts might address them. Courts (who experience the same uncertainty and frustration with the law that you do) routinely consider the *underlying purposes of copyright* and try to determine *what interpretation of the precedent will best effectuate those purposes*, given the facts at hand. While the interest in protecting authors' "natural rights" in their creations sometimes surfaces in the judicial discussions, as a general matter, courts concern themselves with enriching the general public by adopting policies that will encourage the creation of as many diverse works of authorship as possible, while retaining as much public access to existing works as feasible. This entails a balancing act: the key is to find a resolution to the case that (if applied on a widespread basis) will not undercut authors' incentive to create, but will not give authors greater control over others' use of their works than is necessary to provide that incentive. It is also essential that the basic building blocks of expression—such as ideas; systems; methods of operation; facts; "functional" product features; and common, stock devices—remain in the public domain to ensure a continued flow of expressive works in the future, for the public benefit. In explaining why you would resolve an exam question in a certain way, it may be helpful to explain how your resolution would promote these goals.

☞ **The idea/expression dichotomy:** As the likes of Judge Learned Hand have acknowledged, there is no way to devise a concrete or universal black-letter rule for distinguishing idea from expression for purposes of copyright protection. Discussing and applying Judge Hand's "abstractions" test can be a useful vehicle in addressing the question in exams, but the abstractions test only gives you a framework for making what ultimately will be an arbitrary decision based on a gut instinct:

You will have to decide, as a matter of policy, where it makes the most sense to draw the line between idea and expression under the particular facts of the case, and in light of the policies underlying copyright and the distinction between copyright and patent protection. Be prepared to defend your choice in those terms.

Also, don't forget that the abstractions test itself has been used in different ways. As originally conceived by Judge Hand in the *Nichols* case, it was meant to draw a line between copyrightable expression and uncopyrightable idea, in itself. In the *Altai* "abstraction-filtration-comparison" test, often used in connection with computer software and other utilitarian works, the abstraction test is merely a means to lay out a work in preparation for a process that identifies and filters out individual uncopyrightable elements at each level of abstraction.

☛ **The originality standard:** The originality standard of copyright law is generally a very low standard—much easier to meet than the novelty or non-obviousness standards of patent law. Under the *Feist* decision, originality requires only that the work not be copied and entail some minimal exercise of intellectual judgment, even if very modest. Only decisions that are "obvious" or "expected," such as the decision to order a list of telephone subscribers alphabetically by last name, are likely to fail the test. (In such cases, it is questionable whether the alleged author really exercised any independent judgment at all.) However, courts have adopted a different (and higher) standard of originality (the "substantial variation" standard) in the case of derivative works. In evaluating originality in derivative works, it may be useful to consider the policy concerns that have driven courts to adopt the higher standard: the concern that derivative work copyrights may be used to bring harassing infringement claims against subsequent authors who make derivative works from the same underlying work, and the concern that derivative work copyrights may be used to interfere with exploitation of the copyright in the original work on which the derivative is based.

It is important to remember, too, that the Copyright Office and courts have generally withheld copyright for words, short phrases, and titles of works, on the ground that they lack originality. In such cases (and assuming that it is consistent with the call of the exam question to do so), you should consider whether protection might be available under Lanham Act §43(a), which will be discussed in the next chapter, *infra*.

☛ **Overlap with other doctrines:** Courts have had considerable difficulty applying copyright to certain kinds of subject matter, such as computer programs and the design of useful articles. Assuming that it is consistent with the call of the exam question, it is always a good idea to discuss alternative ways in which this subject matter can be protected. Aspects of computer programs may be protected under trade secret law and utility patents, and aspects of the user interface might be the subject of trade dress or design patent rights. The design of useful articles may be protectible under a design patent or under trade dress law (although the Supreme Court has cut back recently on trade dress protection for product features. See pp. 237-241, *infra*.). Notwithstanding these alternatives, producers of software and designers of useful articles have often complained that U.S. law does not provide adequate protection. There has been considerable discussion, in Congress and in the legal literature, of devising *sui generis* protection—legal protection tailored specifically for computer programs or useful articles—that borrows aspects from both patent and copyright law. If no form of existing protection seems to fit the subject of the exam question, it might be useful to discuss whether *sui generis* legislation would be appropriate, or whether public policy is better served by leaving the matter unprotected (or underprotected).

- **The varying infringement standards:** As discussed in the outline, courts have used a range of standards for evaluating infringement claims, without always explaining when the different standards should be employed. A court's decision to use one standard over another frequently turns on concern about overprotection or underprotection. When the subject matter has a large number of uncopyrightable elements, application of an "overall subjective impression of the average lay observer" standard may lead to overprotection, because the fact finder may rely on similarities of uncopyrightable elements to find an unlawful appropriation. Thus, in such cases, courts may adopt a "more discerning" standard, an "abstraction, filtration, comparison" standard, or a "virtual identicality" or "bodily appropriation of copyrightable expression" standard (at least for selection and arrangement expression), all of which make it less likely that overprotection will occur. When there are fewer uncopyrightable elements (or the work is within the creative "core" of copyright protection—works of art, music, fiction, etc.), courts are more likely to favor the traditional "overall subjective response of the average lay observer" standard. In such cases, adoption of a higher standard may lead to underprotection. If the uncopyrightable elements of the work are identified and/or filtered out, the finder of fact may overlook protectible selection and arrangement expression in evaluating whether unlawful appropriation has occurred.

- **Infringement on the Internet:** Unauthorized transactions over the Internet may implicate a number of the copyright owner's rights simultaneously. Using a work in a computer almost always involves reproducing it, and there may be multiple reproductions made in the course of transmitting the work from one place to another. Moreover, when a work is transmitted, there may be a distribution to the public, and either a public display or public performance, depending on the type of work being transmitted and the destination of the transmission. Thus, a single transaction may implicate most of the exclusive rights of the copyright owner.

    The doctrine of first sale is unlikely to shelter alleged distributions to the public over the Internet, because the computer does not transmit a sender's lawful copy, but a reproduction of that copy. The fair use defense may be particularly problematic on the Internet, as well. Click-wrap licensing and electronic rights clearinghouses are likely to reduce the transaction costs of obtaining licenses to use copyrighted works in the digital world, and some courts have already indicated that the ready availability of licensing on reasonable terms will weigh against finding that an unauthorized use is fair. Moreover, the proliferation of multimedia works on the Internet has created a growing market for small parts of works that never existed before. The existence of a market for small parts makes it harder for courts to find that unauthorized use of a small part will have no effect on the copyright owner's market opportunities. It may prove useful to discuss these considerations if the issue of fair use is raised in an Internet setting.

- **Calculating duration:** While the provisions governing the duration of copyrights may seem daunting, you can keep them straight by simply asking which of three categories the work at issue falls into: (1) works created after January 1, 1978; (2) works created before January 1, 1978 that were already published and covered by federal copyright on January 1, 1978; and (3) works that were created before January 1, 1978 and had not been published as of January 1, 1978 (and thus were protected by state common-law copyright).

    Works falling into the first category are governed by Copyright Act §302. Look to see whether the work is a work for hire, anonymous, or pseudonymous work to determine whether to apply the life + 70 term or the 95/120-year term.

    Works falling into the second category are governed by Copyright Act §304. The first term is 28 years. Check to see when the first term ends to ascertain whether a filing had to be made to renew or if renewal was automatic. (A renewal filing had to be made for all copyrights commencing before January 1, 1964. Automated renewal began in 1992.) Assuming there is a second term (because a filing was made or no filing was necessary), calculate when the second term would end if it lasted 47 years. If it would end after October 27, 1998, then add another 20 years to the end.

Works falling into the third category are governed by §303. Calculate what the term would be under §302 and compare that to the year 2002 (or if the work was published prior to December 31, 2002, the year 2047) and take the later date.

Chapter 6
TRADEMARK LAW

ChapterScope

Trademark law and related "passing off" causes of action *ensure that consumers can rely on marks and other indications of origin accurately to indicate the source of goods or services*. They do this by prohibiting marketplace participants from using marks in ways that are likely to confuse consumers about the source, sponsorship, or affiliation of goods, services, or their producers. This ensures an efficient marketplace by *lowering consumer search costs* and *encourages producers to invest in producing high quality goods and services*. Because the purpose of trademark law differs significantly from that of patent and copyright law, trademark rights are more narrowly tailored: Trademark law is not intended to give broad property rights in marks. To provide such rights in marks would likely have *anticompetitive effects* and *interfere with the free flow of useful information in the marketplace*. Thus, courts are careful to apply trademark rights in ways that will not unduly interfere with the interests of competitors and others to *describe and name* their own goods or services, *copy functional product features*, and *refer* to producers or *discuss their products* through use of the products' marks. This chapter will focus primarily on the prerequisites of trademark protection and infringement. However, it will also discuss two narrower, more recent causes of action available to mark owners. First, the *dilution* cause of action gives somewhat broader rights in highly *famous* marks in order to protect their owners' investment in developing those marks' *commercial magnetism*. Second, the *anticybersquatting* cause of action protects mark owners' interests by prohibiting bad-faith registration and use of marks as domain names.

- **The nature of trademark protection and the relationship of the federal trademark provisions to the common law:** Section I discusses the nature and purpose of trademark law more fully, and explains how trademark rights arose as part of the common law of unfair competition. It then describes how Congress, in the *Lanham Act, built on existing common-law rules to provide a system for registering marks* on the Lanham Act's Principal Register, and to provide a federal cause of action for infringement of unregistered marks and other indications of origin.

- **Types of marks:** Section II discusses four types of marks: trademarks, service marks, collective marks, and certification marks. Trademarks (which identify the source of *products*) and service marks (which identify the source of *services*) are by far the most common types of marks. Most of the rules relating to ownership and protection of these marks are the same, so this chapter will refer to them collectively as "marks." It will also use the term "indications of origin," which encompasses all words, names, symbols or devices that indicate origin to consumers.

- **The distinctiveness requirement:** Section III addresses the key requirement of trademark protection: distinctiveness. A mark is "distinctive" if prospective consumers *will understand it to indicate the source or sponsorship of the good or service* that it accompanies. Trademark law categorizes marks by their level of distinctiveness, affording more rights to marks that are *inherently distinctive* than to those that are merely *capable of becoming distinctive through acquisition of secondary meaning* (that is, through being used to the point that consumers *learn* to think of them as an indication of product or service source). Section III discusses rules for evaluating the distinctiveness of a mark and focuses on several categories of marks in the "merely capable of becoming distinctive" category. It also discusses *generic* words or symbols that are *incapable of indicating source*.

- **The kinds of things that can serve as marks and the functionality doctrine:** Marks are defined very broadly, to include "any word, name, symbol or device," or any combination of these things. Section IV discusses several types of marks and then focuses on *trade dress*. Trade dress consists of combinations of features in a *product or service's "packaging"* that may indicate source to consumers. Trade dress may also consist of one or a combination of *product features*. However, to ensure that trade dress protection does not interfere unduly with free competition, and isn't used to undermine patent law's strict standards and limited duration, trade dress may only be protected if it is *"nonfunctional."* Section IV discusses the standards for determining *functionality*.

- **Other limitations on the protection of marks:** Section V discusses some additional limitations on marks: among other things, they may not be *"deceptive"* or *"scandalous,"* they may not *falsely suggest a connection* with other persons or entities, or *"disparage"* others.

- **Acquiring ownership in marks and federal registration:** Businesses attain common-law ownership rights in marks by *using them in trade* in a manner that permits consumers to rely on them for information about source. In order to claim rights in marks under the Lanham Act, a person who uses the mark in trade must also show that the use was *"in commerce."* Section VI explains these concepts, and Section VII then explains how mark owners can *register* their marks on the Lanham Act's *Principal Register*, and thus obtain enhanced rights beyond those available under the common law. Section VIII explains how and when registrations can be cancelled.

- **Geographic boundaries of mark owners' rights:** Priority of trademark rights is based on a *"first in time, first in right"* rule. However, under the common law, a mark owner only enjoys priority over other users in its *"market area"*—the area in which it uses and advertises its mark. A person who later commences use of a confusingly similar mark for similar products *in good faith, in a remote geographic area*, may actually attain rights in *that area* that are superior to those of the first user. Section IX explains the common-law rules in more depth, and then explains how *registration* on the Lanham Act's Principal Register *enhances* the registrant's geographic rights through *constructive notice* (in the case of older registrations) and *constructive use* (in the case of more recent registrations).

- **Infringement of marks:** Section X discusses the cause of action for trademark infringement, which entails a showing that the defendant's *unauthorized trademark use* causes a *likelihood of consumer confusion about the source, sponsorship, or affiliation of the parties' products or services*. This section explains the "use" and "likelihood of confusion" standards, and discusses particular problems courts have encountered in applying them in the Internet context. It also discusses the concepts of *reverse confusion, initial interest confusion, post-sale confusion, and trademark counterfeiting,* and special problems that arise in the case of *trademark parodies*. It then turns to *"collateral uses"* of marks (including *resale* of goods lawfully bearing a mark, *gray market goods*, and use of marks in *comparative advertising*), that may not be actionable. It ends with an explanation of *indirect liability* for other's direct infringement (through the doctrines of *contributory infringement and vicarious liability*).

- **Trademark dilution:** The trademark *dilution* cause of action is a statutorily created cause of action that enables the owners of *famous marks* to prevent others' use of similar marks even if their use *does not cause a likelihood of confusion*. Section XI discusses the two traditional dilution theories: *"blurring"* (use of the famous mark that *erodes consumers' automatic association between the famous mark and its owner*), and *"tarnishment"* (use of the mark in an unwholesome or tacky context that dulls the famous mark's luster). Section XI discusses these and other concepts under state statutes, and under the recently revised Lanham Act §43(c) dilution provisions. It also discusses *First Amendment* and *statutory limitations* on application of the dilution cause of action.

- **Defenses and remedies in the case of infringement and dilution claims:** Section XII describes several important defenses to infringement and dilution claims, including the *"descriptive fair use" and "nominative fair use"* doctrines, *trademark abandonment,* and *challenges to mark validity.* It also briefly describes *"incontestability status,"* which the Lanham Act confers on marks that have been registered for over five years. Section XIV describes the remedies that are available for the various Lanham Act causes of action.

- **The Anticybersquatting Consumer Protection Act**: The Anticybersquatting Consumer Protection Act actually protects mark owners more than it protects consumers. It prevents persons from registering, trafficking in or using a domain name that is confusingly similar to or dilutive of a mark, with *bad-faith intent to profit from the mark's good will.* Section XIII discusses this relatively new Lanham Act cause of action, the factors to be used in determining whether a defendant has acted with the requisite *bad faith intent*, and the *in rem jurisdiction* provided by the Act. The section winds up with a discussion of an *administrative alternative* to litigation for victims of cybersquatting provided by the Internet Corporation for Assigned Names and Numbers (ICANN) under its *Uniform Domain Name Dispute Resolution Policy* (UDRP).

- **International trademark treaties:** The final section of this chapter discusses the key international treaties that govern and facilitate trademark protection: the *Paris Convention, TRIPs, the Trademark Treaty,* and *the Madrid Protocol.*

I. THE NATURE OF TRADEMARK LAW

A. **The purpose of trademarks and trademark law:** Trademarks play a very important role in the marketplace. They permit consumers to identify the *source* of goods or services. Since consumers assume that products or services from the same source will be consistent, trademarks enable consumers to rely on their prior experience and make meaningful choices among competing products and services—they can repeat satisfactory purchases and avoid duplicating unsatisfactory ones. The purpose of trademark law is to *ensure that consumers are able to rely* on marks in exercising their preferences by prohibiting competitors from using marks in a way that confuses consumers about the source of a product or service. Ensuring that trademarks accurately identify the source of goods or services benefits both consumers and business enterprises. Consumers benefit because they are able efficiently to identify and obtain the goods or services that they want. (Another way to say this is that accurate trademarks "lower consumers' search costs.") Also, because consumers can identify producers, assign blame for poor quality, and reward good quality through repeat patronage, trademarks encourage businesses to strive for quality. Businesses benefit because trademark law helps them create and protect business good will. Good will is the business's image, good reputation, and expectation of repeat patronage, which, while intangible, can be extremely valuable. While trademark law protects both consumer and business interests, it is important to note that trademark law gives a cause of action for trademark infringement to businesses—the mark owners and users. It does not provide a direct cause of action to confused consumers.

Example: X Co. creates and markets a new fountain pen under the trademark "Sleekpen." X Co. invests great effort and money in promoting the pen and maintains high standards of quality. Over the years, consumers come to associate the Sleekpen mark with particular product characteristics and quality and develop brand loyalty. (This is business good will.) Y Co. begins to market its fountain pen under the confusingly similar mark "Slickpen" and with similar packaging. Consumers mistakenly buy Y Co.'s pen when they mean to buy X Co.'s. The consumers are injured because they do not get the product they intended to buy. X Co. is damaged in a couple of ways. First, it has lost immediate sales that it would have gotten but for Y Co.'s deception. Second, X Co. has lost control over its product's reputation. If, for example, Y Co.'s pen is of poor quality, consumers (thinking the pen came from X Co.) will blame X Co., and X Co.'s reputation will be injured. This could result in long-term loss of sales. X Co. will have a cause of action against Y Co. for trademark infringement, which will enable it to enjoin Y Co.'s infringing use of the "Slickpen" mark and obtain damages to compensate its loss. In the process, X will vindicate consumer interests in marketplace efficiency.

B. **The relationship of state and federal law:** Trademark law originated as one of several related doctrines comprising the common law of unfair competition. Later, Congress passed a series of federal statutes (the Lanham Act) that incorporated and built upon the common-law trademark doctrine. Today, trademark owners may obtain relief for trademark infringement under the state common law of unfair competition, under state trademark statutes, or under the federal Lanham Act. Aggrieved trademark owners often bring suit in federal court pursuant to the Lanham Act, and allege alternative causes of action under state law. Federal law specifically provides pendant jurisdiction for such state claims, when brought with a Lanham Act claim.

C. **The Lanham Act:** As noted above, the Lanham Act, 15 U.S.C. §1051, *et seq.*, incorporates common-law trademark doctrine and builds on it in two ways. First, Lanham Act §43(a) (15 U.S.C. §1125(a)) provides a federal cause of action for unregistered indications of origin. Second, the Lanham Act provides a system by which mark owners *may register* their marks and thereby expand the scope of protection that they would otherwise enjoy under common-law principles.

   1. **Lanham Act §43(a):** Lanham Act §43(a) prohibits the use of "false designations of origin" in connection with goods, services, or their containers that are "likely to cause confusion, to cause mistake, or to deceive as to the affiliation, connection, or association of [the producer or seller] with another person, or as to the origin, sponsorship, or approval of his or her goods, services, or commercial activities." This provides a federal cause of action for claims of infringement of unregistered trademarks and other indications of origin.(Also known as "passing off.") While courts apply general rules of common law in construing and applying §43(a), this federal cause of action is very popular because it provides a *federal forum* for infringement claims, and Lanham Act infringement *remedies*, which are more generous than the remedies afforded under most states' laws.

      a. **"Indications of origin":** The term "indications of origin," as used in this book, includes all the kinds of marks described in the next section, and other things that indicate a product or service's origin, or a business's identity, to consumers. The Lanham Act §43(a) protects not just *marks*, but also *product and packing trade dress and business trade names*. Product and packaging trade dress will be discussed in more depth later in this chapter. Business trade names will be discussed in the next chapter. See pp. 311, 313, *infra*.

   2. **The Lanham Act registration provisions:** Persons owning marks under the common law have the option to *register* those marks on the Lanham Act's Principal Register. Registration enhances the owner's common-law rights in several important ways. For example, registration provides rights in a *broader geographic area* than the owner would enjoy under common law,

legal *presumptions of trademark validity*, and the opportunity to obtain the assistance of the Customs Service in excluding infringing imports from the country. While the emphasis in this chapter will be on the traditional common-law rules, which apply to unregistered marks, you should bear in mind that most of the same rules will apply both to registered marks and unregistered marks and other indications of origin. The chapter will specify the points where the Lanham Act registration provisions depart from the general principles of common law to enhance rights for registered marks.

   a. **Administrative issues:** Lanham Act registration of marks is handled by the U.S. Patent and Trademark Office (P.T.O.). Administrative appeals from P.T.O examiners' registration-related decisions are taken to the Trademark Trial and Appeals Board. From there, Lanham Act §21 (15 U.S.C. §1071) provides two alternative means of judicial review. A direct appeal may be taken to the U.S. Court of Appeals for the Federal Circuit, which will review the P.T.O. decision on the record. Alternatively, a dissatisfied party may seek *de novo* review of the P.T.O. decision in a U.S. district court. Appeals from the district court go to the appropriate regional circuit court of appeals, not to the Federal Circuit. Note, as well, that all appeals in Lanham Act infringement actions are taken to the regional circuit courts of appeals: Unlike in the case of patent infringement appeals, trademark infringement appeals are not centralized in the Court of Appeals for the Federal Circuit.

II. TYPES OF MARKS

   A. **Four types of marks:** There are four different types of marks: trademarks, service marks, certification marks, and collective marks. For the most part, the law governing all four is the same, both under the Lanham Act and common law. Except where specifically noted in the course of this chapter, you can assume that the rules of law being discussed would apply equally to all four categories of marks. For convenience, we will refer to all four generically as "marks" or "trademarks."

   B. **Trademarks:** A trademark is a word, name, symbol, device, or any combination thereof, that is used to distinguish the *goods* of one person from goods manufactured or sold by others, and to indicate the *source of the goods*, even if the source is unknown. (Lanham Act §45.)

   1. **Word, name, symbol, or device:** The range of things that are capable of serving as trademarks is great and includes not just words but also such things as drawings and abstract designs; slogans; distinctive features of the product's packaging; and distinctive, non-functional features of the product itself. Even sounds and scents have been registered and protected as trademarks. So, for example, the manufacturer of a soft drink might claim as trademarks not only the brand name of the drink, but also the artwork on the label, the distinctive shape of the bottle in which the drink is sold, and the slogan used on the label and in advertising.

   2. **Indicating source, even if the source is unknown:** A trademark indicates that the product comes from *a particular source*, which is the same source as that of similar products bearing the same trademark. It does not matter whether the consumer knows the identity of the source.

      Example: The mark "Ajax" on a can of bathroom cleanser tells the consumer that this can of cleanser comes from the same source as the last can of Ajax cleanser that he bought, and thus that it will have similar quality and characteristics. It does not matter whether the consumer knows the name of the company that manufactures Ajax cleanser.

C. **Service marks:** Service marks are the same as trademarks except that they identify and distinguish a business's *services* rather than its products. Thus, a service mark is a word, name, symbol, device, or any combination thereof, that is used to distinguish the *services* of one person from services rendered or sold by others, and to indicate the *source of the services*, even if the source is unknown. (Lanham Act §45.) Examples of well-known service marks include Greyhound bus services, Aetna insurance, McDonald's fast-food restaurants, and the call numbers of radio stations for radio entertainment services.

   1. **There must be a sufficiently separate service to identify:** To register a service mark on the Lanham Act Principal Register, an applicant must demonstrate a service that is sufficiently separate from the sale of goods. Services that only constitute promoting, selling, advertising, or building up good will for one's own products are not viewed as sufficiently separate to support registration of a service mark. The test is whether the service is normally expected and routinely rendered in furtherance of the sale of goods. If so, it is insufficient to support registration of a service mark.

      Example: Under the Lanham Act, a store that sold vacuum cleaners probably could not register a service mark for in-store demonstrations of how its vacuum cleaners work. Such demonstrations are normally expected and routinely rendered in the furtherance of sales of vacuum cleaners. However, if the store undertook to provide instruction on effective and safe use of *all brands* of vacuum cleaners generally, this service might be sufficiently separate to qualify as the basis for registering a service mark.

D. **Certification marks:** Certification marks are words, names, symbols, devices, or combinations thereof, used by one person or organization to certify that the goods or services of others have certain characteristics. (Lanham Act §45.) The characteristics might include such things as origin in a particular geographical region, composition from a particular material, quality, accuracy, or creation through union labor. So, for example, the State of Florida might use the mark "O.J." to certify that the orange juice of individual private producers bearing that mark is made from Florida-grown oranges. Well-known certification marks include Underwriters' Laboratories and the Good Housekeeping Seal of Approval.

   1. **Federal restrictions on certification marks:** Because consumers *rely* on certification marks for information about the products or services they identify, the law imposes restrictions on their use, as described below. Lanham Act §1064 provides that failure to observe the restrictions can result in cancellation of the certification mark's registration. (While common-law authority for certification marks is scarce, it has been suggested that courts may deny common-law enforcement of certification marks on similar grounds.)

      a. **The owner may not apply the certification mark to its own goods or services:** While the owner of a certification mark may use the mark to advertise or promote its certification program or the goods or services of others that meet its certification standards, it may not use the mark in selling its own goods or services, either as a certification mark or as a trademark or service mark. Use as a certification mark on the owner's own goods might compromise the integrity of the mark, because the owner of the certification mark cannot be relied upon to apply the certification standards objectively to its own goods or services.

Even use of the certification mark as a trademark or service mark may mislead consumers, suggesting that the owner's product or service has satisfied standards it has not.

    b. The owner must control use of the mark: The owner must oversee others' use of the mark and prohibit others from using the mark for purposes other than certifying, or from falsely certifying the existence of characteristics that their products or services lack.

    c. The owner must be objective and may not discriminate: The owner of a certification mark may not discriminatorily refuse to certify goods or services that satisfy its stated, objective standards for certification.

E. Collective marks: Collective marks can be divided into two categories: collective membership marks and collective trademarks or service marks. (Lanham Act §45.)

    1. Collective membership marks: Collective membership marks are marks adopted for the purpose of indicating membership in an organization, such as a union, a professional society, or a social fraternity. Neither the organization nor its members use the mark to identify and distinguish goods or services. The sole function of the mark is to indicate that the person displaying it is a member of the organization.

    2. Collective trademarks and service marks: Collective trademarks and service marks, in contrast, are trademarks or service marks adopted by a collective organization, such as a co-op, for use by its members in selling their individual goods or services, distinguishing their goods or services from those of non-members. The collective organization itself neither sells goods nor performs services under the mark, though it may advertise or otherwise promote the goods or services sold under the mark by its members.

    Example: A dairy co-op may adopt and register the mark "Clover," which its members may use to identify the dairy products they produce and sell, and distinguish them from those of non-members.

    3. Similarity of collective trademarks and service marks to certification marks: If an organization imposes substantive standards on its members, the collective trademark or service mark it adopts for its members' use may indirectly serve the same function as a certification mark. In that case the collective mark will indicate that the producer of the goods or services, by virtue of being a member of the organization, adheres to the organization's substantive standards. This in turn may indicate that the member's goods or services themselves have specified characteristics.

    Example: A dairy co-op adopts the word "Clover" as a collective trademark, which co-op members use to identify the dairy products they sell. The co-op requires that its members use no hormones or other chemical enhancements in their dairy operations. If that restriction is generally known, then members' use of the Clover mark in selling their milk will essentially certify to consumers that the milk contains no hormones or other chemical additives.

III. DISTINCTIVENESS

A. Marks must be distinctive: To be recognized and protected as a mark, a word, name, symbol, or device must be distinctive. Courts have categorized marks according to their level of distinctiveness. Marks in the highest category—arbitrary, fanciful, and suggestive marks—are deemed *inherently* distinctive. (Inherently distinctive marks receive protection immediately upon use, and the greatest degree of protection.) Marks in the middle category—descriptive marks—are not viewed as inherently distinctive, but they are *capable of becoming distinctive* if they are used as marks sufficiently to acquire secondary meaning. Words and symbols in the final category—generic marks—are *incapable of becoming distinctive*, and cannot be the subject of mark ownership rights. *Abercrombie & Fitch Co. v. Hunting world, Inc.,* 537 F.2d. 4 (2d Cir. 1976).

B. Arbitrary and fanciful marks: A mark is *arbitrary* if it has a meaning, but does not describe the product or service it identifies or any of its characteristics. Examples include "Blue Diamond," as a mark for nuts or "Green Leaf," as a mark for insurance. *Fanciful* marks, by contrast, convey no meaning at all, other than their trademark meaning. Examples include newly coined words, and combinations of letters and numbers, such as "Xerox," for photocopiers and "TLD-5," for fertilizer. As noted above, arbitrary and fanciful marks are considered to be *inherently distinctive*. Consumers encountering them in connection with the product or service they identify will immediately understand that they are indications of origin, because there is no other apparent function for them to serve.

C. Suggestive marks: Suggestive marks are marks that *indirectly describe* the product or service they identify. The consumer must engage in a *mental process* of his or her own in order to associate the mark with a description of the product or service. For example, the mark "Greyhound" for bus services is suggestive. The consumer must think about greyhounds and their characteristics (they run fast) in order to obtain a description of the bus service. Other examples include "Coppertone" for suntan oil, and "Roach Motel" for insect traps. Suggestive marks, like arbitrary and fanciful marks, are considered *inherently distinctive*.

    1. Tests for determining whether a mark is descriptive or suggestive: Sometimes it can be hard to determine whether a particular mark is suggestive (and thus inherently distinctive) or descriptive (thus requiring a showing of secondary meaning as a prerequisite to protection). Two tests have been used to determine whether a particular mark is suggestive or merely descriptive. The first looks to the *degree of imagination* consumers must exercise in order to obtain a description of the good or service from the mark. The more imagination the consumer must use, the more likely the mark will be found suggestive, rather than descriptive. The second test looks to see if the mark is *one that competitors really need* in order to describe their own products or services to consumers. If not really needed, the mark is more likely to be deemed suggestive.

    Example: The word "Greyhound" for bus services requires an exercise of imagination on the part of consumers in order to get a description of the services, and is suggestive. By contrast, the word "fast" requires no imagination and would be deemed descriptive. (Test #1)

    Example: The word "Greyhound" is not really needed by other bus companies to describe their rapid bus services. The word "fast" is needed, and thus would not be deemed suggestive. (Test #2)

D. Descriptive marks: The "descriptive" category of marks includes several types of marks, including: (1) marks that appear to *describe the product or service* they identify (e.g., the word "crunchy" or a realistic drawing or photograph of a cookie as a mark for cookies); (2) marks that appear to describe the *geographical location* from which the goods or services emanate (e.g., the word "California" or an outline of the state of California as a mark for almonds); and (3) marks that are primarily merely a person's *surname* (e.g., "Smith's" plumbing services).

1. **"Appear" to describe:** For purposes of the distinctiveness evaluation, it doesn't matter whether the mark accurately describes the product or not. The question is whether consumers are likely to *think* that the mark provides a description of the product or service, or of its geographic origin. If they are likely to think that, then the mark is *not inherently distinctive*, but will fall into the "descriptive" category. If protection is available, it will only be on a *showing of secondary meaning*, as described at subsection 3, *infra*. For circumstances in which a misdescriptive mark will not be protected even with a showing of secondary meaning, see pp. 242-243, *infra*.

   a. **Marks that are merely descriptive or deceptively misdescriptive of the product or service:** A mark that consumers will understand as describing the product or service, or the results of its use, is "descriptive," and can only be protected on a showing of secondary meaning. This rule includes general laudatory words, such as "best" or "first" and other words or images that are commonly used in connection with the particular type of product or service.

   Example: "Quick-wash" would likely be found descriptive as a mark for clothes washing machines. "One-minute" may *not* be descriptive, since consumers are unlikely to think that the clothes *will actually be washed in just 60 seconds*. (The "one-minute" mark might be suggestive, requiring the consumer to exercise his intellect and determine that the clothes washer will wash clothes quickly.) A drawing of a sparkling, clean stack of folded laundry may be deemed descriptive of clothes washing machines, since it depicts what the product accomplishes. Likewise, a realistic depiction of a person using a washing machine or a mass of soap bubbles would likely be deemed descriptive.

   Example: "Superior" would be deemed descriptive for a clothes washer (or just about any other product). "Platinum" is likely to be held descriptive of financial services, as it is commonly used to indicate top quality or prestige in the financial field.

   i. **Common marks:** Courts frequently also find that *highly common marks* fall into the "descriptive" category. For example, "United," "American," "National," "Allied," "Acme," or "Federated" are likely to be treated as descriptive, even if they would not be found to describe the product or its use or result.

   b. **Marks that are primarily geographically descriptive or deceptively misdescriptive:** Under the Lanham Act, a mark is considered primarily geographically descriptive or geographically deceptively misdescriptive if: (1) it conveys to a meaningful segment of the purchasing public primarily or immediately a geographical connotation; and (2) those persons are likely to think that the goods or services in fact come from that place. As will be discussed later at p. 243, Congress amended Lanham Act §2(e) and (f) to provide that marks that are primarily geographically deceptively misdescriptive may not be registered unless they obtained secondary meaning *prior to December 8, 1993*. Thus, pursuant to the amended statutory language, while deceptively misdescriptive marks may be registered on a showing of secondary meaning, most *geographically* deceptively misdescriptive marks may not. However, the Court of Appeals for the Federal Circuit has subsequently held that marks may not be deemed "geographically deceptively misdescriptive," for purposes of §2(e) and (f), unless the misdescribed geographical origin would be a *material factor* to consumers in making their purchasing decision. *See* p. 243, *infra*. The Federal Circuit did not specify how geographically misleading marks that are *not material* should be handled.

i. Means of determining whether marks are geographically descriptive or misdescriptive: The P.T.O. often relies on atlases or reference books to determine whether a word or symbol carries a geographical connotation. Whether or not the purchasing public is likely to think that the user's goods or services come from the indicated origin depends in large part on the nature of the user's goods or services. If the indicated geographic location is *noted for* producing the type of product at issue, consumers are likely to think that the mark indicates that the good comes from that place. This may also be true if, more generally, the geographic location is known to be a manufacturing region, and the product is a manufactured product. In contrast, if the place is *highly unlikely* to produce the good at issue, the public is unlikely to think that the product comes from the indicated geographic region. In that case, the mark is likely to be deemed arbitrary and inherently distinctive, rather than geographically descriptive or misdescriptive.

Example: "Dixie," "Rio Grande," "Lone Star State," and "Chicago" would all likely convey primarily or immediately a geographical connotation to a meaningful segment of the purchasing public, as would the outline of the State of Texas. Consumers would be likely to think that the use of "Lone Star State" or an outline of the state of Texas, in connection with the sale of cowboy boots or salsa, indicates that the cowboy boots or salsa come from Texas, because Texas is associated with those products and is known to produce them. Likewise, the public might think that the use of "Chicago" as a mark for shirts indicates that the shirts were manufactured in Chicago. Even though Chicago is not known for manufacturing shirts, in particular, it is a heavy manufacturing area. However, the public would not be likely to think that the use of "Galapagos" for shirts, or "Dixie" for sealskin coats indicates that these goods come from the place indicated by the mark. Under these circumstances, "Dixie" and "Galapagos" would be deemed arbitrary marks.

Example: Sometimes the public may understand that the producer has used a geographic mark to *associate the product with a particular characteristic of the geographic location,* rather than to indicate that the goods actually come from that place. For example, the public may not think that "Rodeo Drive" as a mark for perfume, or "Fifth Avenue" as a mark for cars, indicates the place where these items were manufactured. Rather, the public may understand the marks to suggest that the products share the qualities of sophistication and glamour that are associated with Rodeo Drive (Beverly Hills) and Fifth Avenue (New York City). In such cases, the mark is likely not to be deemed geographically descriptive or misdescriptive, but arbitrary or suggestive and inherently distinctive.

c. Surnames: A mark is primarily merely a surname if its overall impact on the consuming public is *a surname meaning, and nothing more.*

- If the mark has *no meaning* to the public, surname or otherwise, then it is not primarily merely a surname for purposes of the distinctiveness requirement, even if it is the user's name. (This might be true, for example, in the case of an uncommon surname such as "Posten.")

- If the mark has *both a surname meaning and some other reasonably well-known meaning* in the language (such as "Miller" or "King"), then it generally will not be deemed primarily merely a surname for purposes of the distinctiveness evaluation.

The P.T.O. often relies on telephone directories as evidence of what the public is likely to think a word means: If a word has a number of listings as a surname in telephone directories, and no dictionary meaning, it is likely to be deemed primarily merely a surname. However, mark distinctiveness is determined through evaluation of the mark as a whole. A "composite" mark consisting of a surname combined with other elements may not be deemed "primarily merely a surname."

Example: The overall impact of "Mr. Jones" or "John Jones" is probably just a surname. However, "Jones Worldwide Technology" is not likely to be primarily merely a surname.

2. **The justification for withholding protection for descriptive marks, absent a showing of secondary meaning:** There are at least two justifications for the rule that descriptive marks may not be protected absent a showing of secondary meaning.

    - First, protection may not be needed to accomplish the purposes of trademark law (preventing consumer confusion about the source, affiliation, or sponsorship of goods or services). *Consumers may not automatically think that descriptive marks indicate origin:* they may assume that the marks merely provide information about the nature or characteristics of the product or service. If consumers do not view these marks as indicating the origin of the product, competitors' use of similar marks will not lead to a likelihood of consumer confusion about the source of their goods or services, and no recognizable trademark harm will result from their use.

    - Second, competitors may legitimately need to use descriptive words and symbols in order effectively to describe their products and services to consumers, and persons having the same surname may legitimately wish to use that name as a mark for their own goods or services. If the first user of a descriptive, common, or surname mark can exclude competitors from using it, this *may impair competition and interfere with the legitimate personal interest in using one's own name in business.* As a matter of policy, we can only justify providing rights in common, descriptive, or surname marks if the public has come to recognize the mark as indicating the origin of the claimant's product or service, so that the danger of consumer confusion outweighs competitors' interest in free use of the word or symbol.

3. **Secondary meaning:** Secondary meaning arises when the relevant consuming public has been exposed to use of the descriptive mark enough to *recognize the mark not just in its primary, descriptive, or surname sense, but also as an indication of the source of the product or service.* Proof of long and extensive use of the mark in connection with a product or service, or of extensive advertising through use of the mark, is circumstantial evidence of secondary meaning—courts will assume that constant exposure to trademark use has familiarized consumers with the trademark meaning of the word, symbol, or device. Indeed, Lanham Act §2 (15 U.S.C. §1052(f)) specifies that proof of substantially exclusive and continuous use of a descriptive mark in selling goods or services for five years may serve as *prima facie* evidence that the mark has attained secondary meaning. Direct evidence that a descriptive mark has attained secondary meaning can be provided through scientifically conducted consumer surveys, in which consumers are asked about their perception of the mark.

4. **Evaluating distinctiveness (or descriptiveness):** The classification of a mark as inherently distinctive (arbitrary, fanciful, or suggestive) or descriptive can be very important because it is easier to obtain rights in inherently distinctive marks. (There is no need to demonstrate

secondary meaning). Remember that in determining which distinctiveness classification is right, you *must evaluate the mark in light of the particular good or service that it is meant to identify.* For example, the mark "brilliant" may be an arbitrary mark if it is used to identify apples, but descriptive if it is used to identify diamonds.

- **a. The overall commercial impression:** In determining whether a mark is descriptive or inherently distinctive, it is essential to consider the *overall commercial impression* the mark would make on the average prospective customer. If the mark contains more than one element (that is, if the mark is a *composite* mark), one must consider the impression that the mark makes as a whole, and not break it down into its constituent elements. Sometimes combining two descriptive elements results in an inherently distinctive mark.

    Example: The words "skin" and "invisible" may both be descriptive of transparent bandages, but the mark "skinvisible" may be deemed arbitrary or fanciful for the same product.

    Example: While the word "best" may be descriptive of household sponges, a composite mark comprised of the word "best" combined with the outline of an angel blowing a trumpet is likely not to be deemed descriptive.

- **b. Misspellings:** In evaluating whether or not a mark is descriptive, misspelled words must be treated as though they are properly spelled, as long as the phonetic identity between the misspelled word and the descriptive word is clear.

    Example: The mark "kwix-tart" for car batteries would be deemed descriptive of the batteries because even though the word is misspelled, there is phonetic identity with the phrase "quick-start," which describes the product. Likewise, "tastee" would be deemed the same as "tasty," and "lite" would be considered the same as "light."

- **c. Foreign words and abbreviations:** Foreign words are generally translated into English and then evaluated to determine if they are descriptive of the product or service. (This rule is called the "doctrine of foreign equivalents.") Recognized abbreviations are treated as though they are the abbreviated word.

    Example: "Volkswagen" means "cheap, popular car" or "people's car" in German, and thus is considered a descriptive mark for inexpensive, mass-produced cars.

    Example: "Multistate Bar Examination" is descriptive as a mark for the infamous examination for aspiring lawyers, and so is its abbreviation: "M.B.E."

5. **Abstract designs and other nonverbal marks:** Many marks, such as abstract designs and product or packaging shapes, cannot readily be characterized as "arbitrary," "fanciful," "suggestive," or "descriptive" in relation to the product or service they identify. In the case of such marks, it may be easier to think in terms of two essential categories: (1) marks that are *inherently distinctive*; and (2) marks that are *merely capable of becoming distinctive* (and thus only capable of being recognized and protected upon a showing of secondary meaning). As a general rule, common, basic designs, such as circles, squares, stars, and simple stripes, are viewed as merely capable of becoming distinctive, so that secondary meaning must be demonstrated. (Such designs on labels or packaging are very common. Consumers may not automatically assume that they are meant to indicate product origin. Moreover, competitors may legitimately need to use the designs in connection with their own products.) On the other hand, abstract designs or symbol marks that are striking or unusual, and thus likely to be recognized and

understood as an indication of origin, are likely to be found inherently distinctive. (But with regard to product features claimed as marks, see pp. 237-36.

E. Generic words and symbols: A generic word or symbol is the common descriptive name of the good or service it is used to identify, or is otherwise viewed as synonymous with the product or service. The generic name of a good or service, by definition, cannot serve as a valid mark for that good or service, because it cannot identify those goods coming from a particular merchant and distinguish them from other merchants' goods of the same kind. *It is the common name of all the goods of a particular type or genus, regardless of their origin.* Thus, for example, the word "peanuts" could not serve as a mark for peanuts, since consumers will not understand the word to identify and distinguish the peanuts of a particular producer. Likewise an unadorned, realistic likeness of a peanut is incapable of source identification and could be deemed generic. Sometimes words that originated as trademarks are taken over by the public as the common name of the product and *become generic.* When that happens, the original user loses its trademark rights in the word. At that point, all providers of the particular good or service are entitled to use it, because it has become the common name of the good or service itself. Permitting the original user to exclude competitors from identifying their products by that name would be anticompetitive. Examples of terms that were once trademarks but became the generic name of the products they identified include "thermos," "aspirin," "escalator," and "yo-yo."

1. **The standard for determining whether a mark is generic:** Whether an alleged mark is generic depends on whether its primary significance to the relevant purchasing public is: (1) the common name of a class or genus of product or service, or (2) an indication of origin. The fact that there are alternative common names is generally irrelevant, as is evidence regarding measures the person claiming the word or symbol as a mark has taken to try to prevent the public from using it as a common name.

    a. **Determining the relevant "genus":** Because a generic term is the name of a class or "genus" of products or services, it may be necessary to *define* the relevant genus of the product at issue before trying to determine whether the public views the alleged mark as the name of the genus. In many cases, the genus of the product is clear and is not an issue for the court. However, the issue can be controversial, especially in the case of *a new product or service.* The Court of Appeals for the Third Circuit has held that when a producer introduces a new product that differs from an established product class in a significant, functional characteristic, and uses the common descriptive name of that characteristic as the name of the product, the new product becomes its own genus, and the term denoting the genus becomes generic if there is no commonly used alternative that effectively communicates the same information. *A.J. Canfield Co. v. Honickman*, 808 F.2d 291 (3d Cir. 1986).

    Example: In *Honickman, supra,* the plaintiff sought protection for "chocolate fudge" as a mark for a soda. The defendant argued that the alleged mark was the generic name of the genus of plaintiff's product. The court found that the question turned on whether the relevant product genus was chocolate soda (in which case plaintiff's composite mark "chocolate fudge" soda might be descriptive or even suggestive) or chocolate fudge soda. This would depend on whether the word "fudge" denoted a separate flavor or flavor variation of chocolate. Applying the test set forth above, the court noted that the plaintiff had emphasized the difference between regular chocolate soda and chocolate fudge soda in its advertising, and found that chocolate fudge soda was a separate flavor. Accordingly, a soda tasting like chocolate fudge differed from a chocolate soda with respect to a significant, functional characteristic (its flavor), and constituted a separate product genus. The term "fudge" denoted that different characteristic, and since there was no commonly used alternative word for the flavor variation, "chocolate fudge" should be viewed as the generic name for this new genus of soda. Because it was generic, it could not be protected as a mark.

2. **Descriptive vs. generic marks:** Some authorities have suggested that *very basic, common descriptive terms* such as "delicious" or "tasty" should, as a matter of law, be held "generic" (incapable of distinguishing one producer's goods from another's) and thus incapable of becoming the mark of one competitor. Presumably this is because the word is so highly descriptive that consumers are unlikely to understand its mark significance, and because of concerns that permitting one competitor to gain exclusive rights in such highly descriptive terms would have anticompetitive effects. However, this view has not been accepted in most of the circuit courts. In those circuits, at least theoretically, even the most common descriptive terms, such as "tasty," or "delicious," can become protected marks upon a showing of secondary meaning. Of course, for such common descriptive terms, it might prove difficult to make the necessary showing of secondary meaning.

   Example: The adjective "light," when used in "light beer," is generic because it is part of the common descriptive name of a type or genus of beer. However, the term "tasty," when used in "tasty salad dressing," is not generic, at least in most circuits. Tasty salad dressing is not a particular *type or genus* of salad dressing. By contrast, the adjective "French" would be generic when used in connection with salad dressing.

3. **Nonverbal generic marks:** While most of the case opinions finding alleged marks to be generic involve words, nonverbal marks may sometimes be found generic, as well. As noted earlier, the realistic appearance of a peanut might be deemed generic for peanuts. In a recent case, the Court of Appeals for the Ninth Circuit held that grape-leaf designs are generic for wine because of their widespread use in the industry, which has led consumers to view grape-leaf designs as an earmark of wine. This is not to say that a producer could not obtain rights in a *particular, distinctive rendition of a grape leaf.* His rights, however, would be limited to the particular rendition, and would not permit him to enjoin other wine producers from using grape leaves altogether.

IV. THE CONTENT OF MARKS

A. **The sky is the limit:** A wide variety of things can serve as marks—any word, name, symbol, or device, or any combination thereof. Moreover, a number of different marks can be used to indicate the origin of a particular good or service. However, regardless of the form the alleged mark takes, it must be used in a way that *creates a separate commercial impression on the viewer or listener (or "sniffer," in the case of scents), apart from other material used with it.* For example, if used on the label of a product, the mark must stand out separately and impress the viewer as a separate element, apart from the other features of the label. In addition, as discussed above, the alleged mark must be distinctive—either inherently, or by virtue of acquiring secondary meaning. Essentially, consumers must recognize that the alleged mark indicates the origin of the product or service.

B. **Words and numbers as marks:** Words are one of the most common forms of marks. Words used as marks may be recognizable words or new, fanciful combinations of letters or letters and numbers. In some cases numbers alone have served as marks—for example, the numerical location of a radio station on the radio dial.

   1. **Slogans:** Slogans (combinations of words) also serve as trademarks. Many slogans are highly descriptive, and in such cases secondary meaning will have to be demonstrated. For example, the slogan "Extra strength pain reliever" was registered for Excedrin pain reliever, but only upon a showing of secondary meaning.

C. **Scents and sounds:** Scents and sounds have also been registered as trademarks pursuant to the Lanham Act. There are few limits on the kinds of symbols and devices that can serve as marks, as long as they are capable of becoming distinctive (that is, capable of indicating source), and are not functional.

D. **Drawings and other forms of art or design:** Drawings and other forms of art may serve as marks. A realistic drawing or photograph of the product or service being identified, or of someone making use of the product or service, generally will be found to be a descriptive mark, and will only be protected if the purported owner of the mark can demonstrate secondary meaning. In some cases, simple, realistic depictions of the product may be deemed generic. However, if a depiction of the product or service is *whimsical* rather than realistic, it may be viewed as inherently distinctive—i.e., suggestive, arbitrary, or fanciful. A famous example is the "Mr. Peanut" trademark used to identify Planter's brand nuts—a peanut with arms and legs, sporting a monocle, walking cane, and top hat. Cartoon-style renditions of the product or its uses will frequently be deemed inherently distinctive.

E. **Composite marks:** A mark may be comprised of one or a number of different elements. When a composite mark (a mark comprised of two or more elements) is claimed, it must be *evaluated as a whole*. Even though one particular element of a mark, such as a word or design, may not be sufficiently distinctive or make a sufficiently separate commercial impression to serve as a mark by itself, it may be sufficient in combination with other elements. For example, in the composite mark "Coca-Cola," one word (cola) is generic. However, when evaluated as a whole, the mark is distinctive and protectible. Likewise, a mark comprised of a strictly descriptive word combined with a whimsical design might be deemed inherently distinctive, and protectible without the need to show secondary meaning. Since rights in composite marks are rights in the mark as a whole, others will not necessarily be deprived of the use of any individual component.

F. **Trade dress:** Under the modern view, trade dress, such as a striking combination of features in a product's packaging or a feature (or combination of features) of the product itself, may be protected as a mark if its likely impact on consumers is to identify or distinguish the product's source. Trade dress is generally divided into two categories:

   1. *product packaging trade dress,* which includes combinations of packaging elements (such as color, design, artwork, and graphics) and the overall appearance of the product's packaging; and
   2. *product feature trade dress,* which may include one or a combination of features of the product itself. A product's producer may claim the overall configuration of the product as its trade dress, or individual aspects of its appearance.

   In some cases, it may be hard to determine whether a particular feature should be considered packaging or a part of the product itself. A third, hybrid form of trade dress is the *overall trade dress of a business.* The trade dress of a business is the total image of the business, which may include such things as the shape and appearance of the building, the business's interior design and decor, signs, and the workers' uniforms. While some trade dress may be registered on the Lanham Act Principal Register as a mark, more often businesses protect their interests in source-identifying trade dress under Lanham Act §43(a). Either way, to be protectible, trade dress must be distinctive, and it must also be non-functional. These requirements are discussed further below.

Example: Two distinctive bands of red and white polka dots at the top and bottom of a can of cleanser might be protected as trade dress. This combination of color and design is eye-catching, and sets the cleanser apart from other brands. Consumers may rely on it to identify the cleanser as it sits on the shelf of a grocery store. Likewise, the distinctive shape of the handle of a suitcase, or the overall shape of the suitcase might be protected because consumers may associate these features with a particular source of suitcases, and rely on their presence to distinguish suitcases produced by that source from others.

1. **Trade dress rights in color alone:** Traditionally, courts hesitated to recognize color alone as a trademark, requiring that the color be integrated into a design, like the example of the red and white polka dots mentioned above. So, for example, a merchant that always used blue labels for its products would have difficulty claiming exclusive rights in the color blue, as such. Under modern law, this view has changed. For example, in *In re Owens-Corning Fiberglas Corp.*, 774 F.2d 1116 (Fed. Cir. 1985), the U.S. Court of Appeals for the Federal Circuit held that the color pink could be registered as a trademark for fiberglass insulation upon a showing of secondary meaning. More recently, in *Qualitex Co. v. Jacobson Products Co., Inc.*, 514 U.S. 159 (1995), the U.S. Supreme Court found that the manufacturer of pads for dry cleaning presses could enforce rights in the green-gold color of its pads against a competitor. The Court reasoned that a color, while not inherently distinctive, was capable of identifying and distinguishing the goods of a particular producer, and rejected arguments that recognizing rights in color would have unacceptable anticompetitive effects. The Court noted that the Lanham Act defines marks very broadly: as "any word, name, symbol, or device, or any combination thereof." A "symbol" or "device" might encompass almost anything capable of carrying meaning to human beings.

2. **Trade dress and the distinctiveness requirement:** In *Wal-Mart Stores, Inc. v. Samara Bros., Inc.*, 529 U.S. 205 (2000), the Supreme Court distinguished between product packaging and product feature trade dress for purposes of construing and applying the distinctiveness requirement. The Court held that product packaging trade dress may be inherently distinctive, and thus protectible without a showing of secondary meaning. However, *plaintiffs claiming rights in product feature trade dress under §43(a) must always demonstrate secondary meaning as a prerequisite to relief.* The Court rejected arguments that product feature trade dress could be inherently distinctive, noting the lack of a workable standard for evaluating the distinctiveness of product features; doubts that consumers rely on product features (as opposed to labels and packaging) to indicate source; and concerns about the anticompetitive effects of making Lanham Act protection for product features readily available. The Court went on to hold that in cases in which the proper categorization of trade dress as product packaging or product feature is unclear, courts should generally categorize the trade dress as product feature, and require a showing of secondary meaning.

    a. **Evaluating the distinctiveness of product packaging trade dress:** Businesses usually have a virtually limitless selection of lettering styles, shapes, colors, art, words, and other elements that they may select and combine to make a unique label or packaging. Generally a business's total combination of such elements can be deemed arbitrary, and thus inherently distinctive, even if some of the individual elements, if used alone, would be viewed as commonplace, descriptive of the product, or even generic. *As long as the combination of elements, as a whole, is not descriptive of the product or commonplace for that particular type of product, or a trivial variation on a combination that is descriptive or commonplace, the trade dress can be deemed inherently distinctive* and protected without the need to demonstrate secondary meaning.

3. **The non-functionality requirement for trade dress:** Trade dress may not be protected or registered if it is functional. The key concerns underlying the non-functionality requirement are to avoid anticompetitive use of trademarks and to avoid undermining the strict eligibility provisions and time limits built into the patent laws. If trademark rights can be enforced in functional product or product packaging features, then competitors can circumvent the novelty and non-obviousness requirements of patent law, and obtain rights of unlimited duration in utilitarian creations that other competitors may legitimately need to copy. A recent amendment to the Lanham Act specifies that in the case of alleged infringement of unregistered trade dress, the plaintiff bears the burden of proving non-functionality.

   a. **The *TrafFix* decision:** The Supreme Court provided a *two-part test for functionality* in *TrafFix Devices, Inc. v. Marketing Displays, Inc.*, 532 U.S. 23 (2001), and also elaborated on the *relevance of a utility patent in the functionality determination.*

      i. **The relevance of a utility patent in the functionality determination:** In *TrafFix*, the Court held that a utility patent constitutes "strong evidence that the features claimed in it are functional," and adds "great weight" to the statutory presumption that product features are functional. To overcome this presumption, the person claiming trade dress rights in these patented product features "must carry the heavy burden of showing that the feature is not functional, for instance by showing that it is *merely an ornamental, incidental, or arbitrary aspect of the device."*

      ii. **The *TrafFix* Court's two-part test:** The Supreme Court held that in determining the functionality of product features, the court must first apply the *Inwood Laboratories* test:

      > Is the feature essential to the use or purpose of the article, or does it affect the cost or quality of the article?

      If the answer is yes, then the product feature is functional and cannot be the subject of trade dress protection. If the answer is no, then the court must then apply the *Qualitex* standard:

      > Would the exclusive use of the feature "put competitors at a significant non-reputation related disadvantage?"

      If so, then there is "aesthetic functionality," and again, the feature may not be protected. Only if the product feature is non-functional under *both tests* can it be protected as trade dress.

      Example: In *TrafFix*, the trade dress claimant sought to prevent a competitor from copying the dual spring mechanism that it incorporated into its outdoor sign stands to keep the sign from falling over in the wind. It had two utility patents for the mechanism, which had expired. The dual spring mechanism was visible to people observing the sign stands, and the claimant argued that prospective customers relied on it to identify the stands as coming from the claimant. The Supreme Court found that the dual spring mechanism was functional under the *Inwood Laboratories* standard, and thus unprotectible. The Court reasoned that beyond serving the purpose of informing consumers about the source of its sign stands (assuming that it did so), the plaintiff's dual-spring mechanism served the useful purpose of resisting the force of the wind. That purpose was clear from the patent specifications and prosecution history. The Court explained that it was unnecessary to speculate about the availability of other means of performing the same function. The dual spring mechanism was "essential to the use or purpose" of the sign stand, and therefore was functional.

Example: In *Qualitex Co. v. Jacobson Products Co., Inc.*, 514 U.S. 159 (1995), the Court found the green-gold color of the trade dress claimant's laundry press pads to be non-functional and protectible. In *TrafFix*, the Court explained that there had been no indication that the green-gold color of the press pads had any bearing on the use or purpose of the product, or its cost or quality. Accordingly, the color was non-functional under the *Inwood Laboratories* test. The *Qualitex* Court then went on to a second inquiry: whether the color was "aesthetically functional" or "a competitive necessity." The green-gold color would only be a competitive necessity if the granting of exclusive rights would put competitors at a significant non-reputation-related disadvantage. They would only be put to such a disadvantage if there were insufficient alternative colors available to them that would be equally aesthetically pleasing to consumers. Because it appeared that competitors could use alternative colors effectively in *Qualitex*, the trade dress claimant's green-gold color was non-functional and protectible.

b. **The circuit courts' construction of the *TrafFix* decision:** The Circuit Courts of Appeals have split in their interpretation of *TrafFix*.

   i. **The Court of Appeals for the Federal Circuit:** The Federal Circuit has long applied its *Morton-Norwich* test for functionality, which holds that trade dress features are not functional merely because they perform a useful function in a product, other than to indicate source. Rather, trade dress will only be deemed functional if competitors need to copy it in order to compete effectively. They will only need to copy *if the trade dress design is superior to the alternatives in function or economy of manufacture.* The *Morton-Norwich* test directs courts to consider evidence regarding four issues in making this determination:

   1. Is there an expired utility patent that discloses the utilitarian advantage of the design?
   2. Does the designer tout the design's utilitarian advantages through advertising?
   3. Does the design result from a comparatively simple or cheap method of manufacturing?
   4. (Since the effect upon competition "is really the crux of the matter") are there alternative ways available to competitors to accomplish the same function?

   In *Valu Engineering, Inc. v. Rexnord Corp.*, 278 F.3d 1268 (Fed. Cir. 2002), the Federal Circuit found that *TrafFix* did not alter the *Morton-Norwich* analysis. According to the Federal Circuit, *TrafFix* focused its functionality inquiry on the *effect of trade dress protection on competition,* and did not intend to prohibit courts from considering the availability of alternatives in making the *Inwood Laboratories* functionality determination. The Federal Circuit concluded that, under *TrafFix,* a product feature can still be protected as trade dress even though it plays a useful function in the product other than identifying source.

    ii. **The Court of Appeals for the Fifth Circuit:** The Fifth Circuit, in contrast, has read *TrafFix* to supersede the sort of standard embraced by the Federal Circuit. According to the Fifth Circuit, *TrafFix* recognized two separate tests for functionality, both of which must be satisfied before trade dress protection can be afforded. Under the first (*Inwood Laboratories*) test, *the question is essentially whether the product feature plays a significant, useful role in the product other than indicating source. If it does, the feature is functional.* The availability of alternative designs is irrelevant to the *Inwood Laboratories* evaluation. If product features are functional under *Inwood Laboratories,* then there is no need to move on to the *Qualitex* test, which considers whether the features are a competitive necessity (or more specifically, whether there are alternatives available to competitors). *Eppendorf-Netheler-Hinz GmbH v. Ritter GmbH,* 289 F.3d 351, 355-356 (5th Cir. 2002).

V. OTHER LIMITATIONS ON THE REGISTRATION AND PROTECTION OF MARKS

  A. **The Lanham Act and common law:** Lanham Act §2 (15 U.S.C. §1052) lists the things that specifically cannot be registered on the Lanham Act Principal Register. In *Two Pesos, Inc. v. Taco Cabana, Inc.,* 505 U.S. 763 (1992), the Supreme Court held that the §2 provisions also generally define what can be protected as an unregistered indication of origin under Lanham Act §43(a). (Since the distinctiveness and non-functionality requirements have already been discussed *supra,* they will not be discussed again here.)

  B. **Scandalous or immoral marks:** Marks that are scandalous or immoral will not be enforced or registered. Marks are scandalous or immoral if they give offense to others' conscience or moral feelings or are shocking to others' sense of decency or propriety. Most of the modern cases finding marks scandalous or immoral have involved marks that conveyed *vulgar imagery.*

    Example: Under the Lanham Act, the following marks have been rejected as scandalous or immoral:

      1. a mark for newsletters comprising a photograph of a man and woman kissing and embracing in a manner exposing the man's genitalia;
      2. "Bullshit" for handbags; and
      3. the design of a defecating dog, for shirts.

    In contrast, the Court of Appeals for the Federal Circuit held that a mark consisting of the words "Old Glory Condom Corp." and a pictorial representation of a condom decorated with stars and stripes, suggesting the American flag, was not scandalous or immoral. The court expressly rejected the argument that many citizens would be scandalized by use of the American flag in connection with the image of a condom.

  C. **Matter that may disparage another:** Under Lanham Act §2(a), a mark may not be registered or protected if it consists of matter that may *disparage* persons, living or dead, institutions, beliefs, or national symbols, or bring them into contempt or disrepute. The Trademark Trial and Appeal Board relied on this provision to cancel registration of the "Redskins" mark, owned by the Washington Redskins football team. The Board found that the mark disparaged Native Americans. According to the Board, *disparagement should be evaluated from the standpoint of a substantial component of Native Americans (rather than a substantial component of the general public) as of the time of the registration.* The Board held it unnecessary that the mark claimant intend to disparage the opposer. The Board found that the "Redskins" mark brought Native Americans into "contempt and disrepute" for the same reasons that it found that it disparaged them. (On review, a federal district court agreed with the standard as stated by the Board, but held that the Board lacked sufficient evidence to find §2(a) grounds to cancel in the Redskins case. *Pro-Football, Inc. v. Harjo,* 284 F. Supp. 2d 96 (D.D.C. 2003).)

D. **Matter that may falsely suggest a connection with persons, living or dead, institutions, beliefs, or national symbols:** The Court of Appeals for the Federal Circuit has held that this Lanham Act §2(a) provision was *intended to protect privacy interests.* In order to demonstrate that a mark falsely suggests a connection with a person or institution, it must be shown that consumers will clearly *associate* the mark with that person or institution. However, it is not necessary to demonstrate that consumers will be misled to think that the identified person is the source of the marked goods, or sponsors, or is otherwise affiliated with them. This provision may be used to protect the state law interest in publicity rights. See *infra,* Chapter 8. It permits celebrities and others to prevent the unauthorized use of their identities to sell products.

E. **Deceptive marks:** Marks that are deceptive will not be enforced at common law or registered. (Lanham Act §2(a).) A mark is deceptive if:

1. it falsely indicates that the good or service has a characteristic;
2. prospective purchasers are *likely to believe* that the misdescription correctly describes the good or service; and
3. the misrepresented fact would be *material* to a reasonable consumer in deciding whether or not to purchase the good or service.

Example: In *In re Budge Manufacturing Co., Inc.*, 857 F.2d 773 (Fed. Cir. 1988), the Court of Appeals for the Federal Circuit held that the mark "Lovee Lamb" for all-synthetic automotive seat covers was deceptive and could not be registered. The court found that the words falsely suggested that the seat covers contained wool, that prospective purchasers were likely to believe that the words were meant to be an accurate description (since sheepskin seat covers were available in the marketplace), and that the presence of wool in the seat covers would be a material factor in consumers' purchase decision.

1. **Deceptive vs. "primarily deceptively misdescriptive" marks:** As discussed at pp. 230-232, *supra,* marks that consumers understand to describe the product, but which do not describe it accurately, may be registered and protected on a showing of secondary meaning, pursuant to Lanham Act §§2(e) and (f). It is easy to confuse these §2(e) and (f) "deceptively misdescriptive" marks with §2(a) "deceptive" marks. *The key is materiality.* If consumers would not consider the misrepresented characteristic a material factor in their purchasing decision, the mark is "deceptively misdescriptive," and can be registered or protected on a showing of secondary meaning. If consumers would consider the misrepresented characteristic material in deciding to purchase, the mark is deceptive, and cannot be registered or protected, per §2(a).

2. **"Deceptively misdescriptive" marks vs. "geographically deceptively misdescriptive" marks:** While Lanham Act §§2(e) and (f) permit deceptively misdescriptive marks to be registered and protected with a showing of secondary meaning, *they do not permit "primarily geographically deceptively misdescriptive" marks to be registered or protected, unless the marks obtained secondary meaning prior to the effective date of the North American Free Trade Agreement (NAFTA),* which is Dec. 8, 1993. Congress amended Lanham Act §§2(e) and (f) to make this distinction between deceptively misdescriptive and geographically deceptively misdescriptive marks in order to bring the United States into compliance with international treaty obligations. Subsequently, the Court of Appeals for the Federal Circuit construed the amendment *not only* to prohibit registration of geographically descriptively misdescriptive marks with a showing of secondary meaning (assuming that the secondary meaning was accrued after the NAFTA date), *but also to introduce a materiality requirement* to the determination that a mark is primarily geographically deceptively misdescriptive, within the meaning of Lanham Act §§2(e) and (f). Adding a materiality requirement obliterates the distinction between primarily geographically deceptively misdescriptive marks (under §§2(e) and (f)) and geographic marks that are deceptive (under §2(a)). It also appears to undercut Congress' purpose to prohibit registration of all marks that deceive consumers about the product's geographic origin (regardless of whether the deception is material or not). *In re California Innovations, Inc.*, 329 F.3d 1334 (Fed. Cir. 2003). (For discussion of geographically descriptive and misdescriptive marks generally, see pp. 231-232, *supra*.)

   Example: X. Co. (which is headquartered in Des Moines, Iowa) commences selling men's shirts under the "Chicago" mark in 2003. The shirts are manufactured in Hong Kong and do not have any relationship to the City of Chicago. In determining whether X Co. can claim rights in the Chicago mark, the first question is whether the word "Chicago" primarily and immediately conveys a geographical connotation to a meaningful segment of the purchasing public. Clearly it does. The second question is whether the public is likely to understand the mark as indicating that the shirts are made in Chicago. If the public is *not likely* to think that the mark indicates that the shirts were made in Chicago, then the mark is suggestive or arbitrary, and inherently distinctive. There is nothing in the Lanham Act to prevent its registration or protection. However, since Chicago is a major manufacturing area, it is possible that consumers *will think* that the shirts come from that city (that is, that they will make a "goods-place association"). Assuming that they do, under the Federal Circuit's construction, the mark may be disqualified (either as geographically deceptively misdescriptive (§§2(e) and (f)) or deceptive (§2(a)) *only* if the geographic origin would be a material factor in consumers' purchase decision. If it would not be a material factor, then neither §§2(e) and (f) nor §2(a) would prohibit registration or protection (at least, if the mark has acquired secondary meaning).

F. **Marks in prior use:** Lanham Act §2(d) prohibits registration of a mark that, when used in connection with the applicant's goods or services, is confusingly similar to a mark or trade name that someone else began using before the applicant and has not abandoned. It is not necessary that the earlier mark be registered. (Since trade names—the names of businesses—cannot be registered, it is likewise unnecessary that the earlier trade name be registered.) This provision reflects the common-law doctrine that the first person to use a mark or trade name has priority over later users. See pp. 251-254, *infra*. Confusing similarity for purposes of §2(d) is essentially the *same standard* as is used to determine whether a defendant's mark *infringes* the plaintiff's mark. See pp. 259-264, *infra*.

Example: Ace Co., which manufactures and sells golf clubs, begins doing business under the "Ace" trade name and mark in 1989. It never registers its "Ace" mark. In 2003, Brown Company wants to register the mark "Ace" for its athletic equipment, including a line of golf clubs. Lanham Act §2(d) prohibits Brown from registering the mark if: (1) Ace Co. has not abandoned its own use of the "Ace" mark; and (2) Brown's use is confusingly similar to Ace's (that is, Brown's use would create a likelihood of consumer confusion over the source, sponsorship, or affiliation of Brown's and/or Ace's goods).

1. **Concurrent use:** Notwithstanding the above, §2(d) provides that an applicant's mark can be registered if the P.T.O. determines that both the earlier mark or trade name and the applicant's mark can be *used concurrently without causing a likelihood of consumer confusion*. In such cases the P.T.O. may register the applicant's mark subject to conditions or limitations calculated to minimize any chance of confusion. For example, the P.T.O. might limit the registration and use to a designated area of the country where the prior user does no business.

    Example: Same example as above, except Ace Company only sells its "Ace" golf clubs on the west coast of the United States, and Brown only plans to sell its "Ace" clubs in New England. In that case, the P.T.O. might agree to register both marks, because the concurrent use in two different geographical locations may not cause a likelihood of consumer confusion. However, the P.T.O. may impose limitations on the parties, to ensure that they do not begin using the mark in the same places, or in a manner that is likely to confuse consumers regarding the source of their respective products.

G. **Additional Lanham Act prohibitions:** In addition to the matter set forth above, Lanham Act §2 (15 U.S.C. §1052) expressly prohibits registration of marks that:

- Consist of a "geographical indication" used in connection with wines or spirits, that identifies a place other than the actual geographic origin of the goods (but only if the mark was first used in this fashion on or after January 1, 1996). A mark will constitute a "geographical indication" for this purpose if it identifies wines or spirits as originating in the territory of a member of the World Trade Organization, and the indicated territory has a reputation for wines or spirits, so that the wine or spirits at issue will be assumed to have the characteristics associated with the indicated territory;

- Consist of the flag or coat of arms or other insignia of any U.S. or foreign governmental body;

- Consist of the name, portrait, or signature of a living individual, unless the individual consents in writing;

- Consist of the name, signature, or portrait of a deceased U.S. President during the life of his widow, unless the widow consents; or

- Are likely to cause dilution under Lanham Act §43(c) (see pp. 268-275, *infra*), but the P.T.O. can only refuse registration in this case if an interested person someone files an opposition to the registration. (See p. 248, *infra*).

VI. ACQUIRING OWNERSHIP OF MARKS

A. **Use of the mark in trade:** To acquire ownership rights in a mark, *one must be the first to use it in trade, and then continue to use it on a regular basis thereafter.* To use the mark in trade is to use it in a way that allows consumers to rely on it for its ultimate purpose—to identify and distinguish the user's particular goods or services from those of other producers. Placing the mark on the goods, or on labeling, packaging, or displays associated with the goods, and making them available for sale to customers, is the most common means of using a mark in trade. In the case of services, use in trade entails using the mark in connection with sales of the service—for example, on signs, forms or letterhead used in connection with sales transactions, or in the course of rendering the services.

1. **Token uses are insufficient:** The use must be reasonably substantial and "in the ordinary course of trade"—not merely for the purpose of reserving rights in the mark. A mere internal use, such as a company's use of the mark on samples sent to its sales representatives, will not suffice. The use must be directed to the user's intended customers. Moreover, a use of the mark on *different* goods or services than those that it ultimately is intended to identify will not suffice to give ownership rights in it.

2. **Approaches to determining when use is sufficient:** Jurisdictions have varied in the *quantity of use* they will require of a mark claimant before recognizing ownership rights. Moreover, even within a jurisdiction, courts may vary the requirements to some extent to accommodate the equities and special circumstances of the case. The issue often arises when two entities claim ownership in the same (or a highly similar) mark, and the court must decide which claimant used the mark first (has "priority"). Some jurisdictions, following the Fifth Circuit in *Blue Bell, Inc. v. Farah Manufacturing Co., Inc.*, 505 F.2d 1260 (5th Cir. 1975), find that a *single use is sufficient* to give priority as long as the use is then ongoing and systematic. However, the Seventh Circuit has held that an unregistered mark claimant will only be deemed to have "used" the mark when the use is *pervasive enough to notify competitors of his claim*. *Zazu Designs v. L'Oreal, S.A.*, 979 F.2d 499 (7th Cir. 1992). Other jurisdictions have suggested that the claimant must *achieve sufficient market penetration to pose a meaningful risk of consumer confusion* if a competitor commences use of a similar mark. They may apply a *four-factor test* to evaluate whether the claimant's market penetration was sufficient to warrant recognition of rights:

    1. the volume of sales of the trademarked product;
    2. the growth trends (both positive and negative) in the area;
    3. the number of persons actually purchasing the product in relation to the potential number of customers; and
    4. the amount of product advertising in the area.

   Lucent Information Management, Inc. v. Lucent Technologies, Inc., 186 F.3d 311 (3d Cir.), *cert. denied*, 528 U.S. 1106 (2000).

3. **Simultaneous or near-simultaneous use:** The general rule is that the *first* person to use a mark in trade obtains ownership rights in it. However, when two persons begin to use a mark in trade at the same, or close to the same time, the court may consider the *equities* of the case in determining who has priority and thus is the owner. If both users made their use in good faith, and expended money in reliance on obtaining ownership rights, the court may attempt to find a way that both users may continue to use the mark if this can be done without causing undue confusion of consumers. For example, the court may allow both parties to continue using the mark on the condition that they adopt different ways of presenting the mark—e.g., through use of the company name along with the mark, different lettering and color on the

label, etc.—so that the public can distinguish their orespective goods. *Manhattan Industries, Inc. v. Sweater Bee by Banff, Ltd.*, 627 F.2d 628 (2d. Cir. 1980).

4. **The affixation requirement:** In order to demonstrate use in trade one must also demonstrate that the mark was properly "affixed" to the goods or services.

   a. **In the case of goods:** Under the Lanham Act, the mark will be deemed "affixed" in the case of goods if it is: (1) placed on the goods themselves; (2) placed on their containers; or (3) placed on tags or labels attached to the goods or containers. The affixation requirement may also be satisfied by prominently featuring the mark in a conspicuous display associated with the goods. Also, if the nature of the goods makes all of the above impracticable, use on documents associated with the goods or their sale will suffice. This might apply, for example, in connection with wholesale transactions in bulk goods, like grain or oil. See 15 U.S.C. §1127.

   b. **In the case of services:** A mark cannot be physically attached to the service it identifies, so the affixation requirement can be satisfied in the case of service marks by using or displaying the mark in the course of selling or advertising the services. However, the mark must be used in direct, explicit reference to the services rendered.

   Example: In *In re Carson*, 197 U.S.P.Q. 554 (T.T.A.B. 1977), Johnny Carson sought to register his name as a service mark for entertainment services. To prove that he had acquired ownership rights through use of the mark (his name) in trade, he submitted a poster that had been used to advertise his performance at a nightclub. The poster stated that "Johnny Carson is in the Congo Room at Del Webb's Hotel Sahara with Bette Midler." The Trademark Trial and Appeals Board held this an insufficient use to establish use in trade because it only identified the individual, not his services. To satisfy the affixation and use in trade requirements and establish mark ownership, the poster would need to refer explicitly to the services Carson would perform. For example, it would need to state that Johnny Carson would be "in concert" or "performing" at the Congo Room.

B. **Marks that are not inherently distinctive:** In order to obtain ownership rights in descriptive, geographically descriptive, surname, common, or other marks that are not inherently distinctive, but are merely capable of becoming distinctive, one must demonstrate that he or she was the *first user to acquire secondary meaning in the mark*. See pp. 230-233, supra.

C. **Use in interstate commerce:** Since Congress's jurisdiction to regulate the use of marks is based on the U.S. Constitution's Commerce Clause, a person seeking to enforce a mark under §43(a), or to register a mark, *must demonstrate not only that she has used the mark in trade, but also that she has used it in interstate commerce (or in a manner that* affects *interstate commerce)*. This requirement is usually easy to meet. The applicant may satisfy the requirement by demonstrating that its goods were shipped or its services were supplied over interstate or national boundaries. Even if the applicant only provided services within one state, it may satisfy the interstate commerce requirement by showing that the services were rendered to persons engaged in interstate travel or commerce, thus *affecting* interstate commerce.

   1. **Use of a mark abroad:** The circuit courts have differed somewhat over whether a business that is conducted only abroad, but which *advertises*, using its mark, in the United States makes a sufficient "use in commerce" of its mark to avail itself of Lanham Act protection. In *Buti v. Impressa Perosa, S.R.L.*, 139 F.3d 98 (2d Cir.), *cert. denied,* 525 U.S. 826 (1998), an Italian mark claimant promoted its "Fashion Café," a Milan restaurant, in the United States before a

domestic business began using the same mark for its U.S. restaurant, but the Second Circuit held that this did not give the Italian business priority over the domestic business. The Second Circuit explained that the restaurant *services themselves* must be rendered in U.S. commerce before the advertising could be deemed to give priority. However, in *International Bancorp, LLC v. Societe des Bains de Mer et du Cercle des Estrangers a Manaco*, 329 F.3d 359 (4th Cir. 2003), *cert. denied*, 540 U.S. 1106 (2004), the Fourth Circuit found that a Monaco casino that only did business in Monaco, but advertised, using its mark, in the United States *could* bring a Lanham Act claim for infringement. The court reasoned that under Lanham Act §45 (15 U.S.C. §1127), a mark is used "on services when it is used or displayed in the sale or advertising of services *and the services are rendered in commerce.*" (emphasis added) The court noted that the casino fell literally within this language: it had used the mark in the United States to advertise its services, *and* that it had rendered its casino services "in commerce." ("Commerce, under the Lanham Act, includes "foreign trade" or trade between U.S. subjects and subjects of a foreign nation. Here, the casino's services were rendered in foreign trade because U.S. citizens went to and gambled at the casino in Monaco.) The Fourth Circuit distinguished *Buti* on the ground that the Italian restaurant had conceded in oral argument that its restaurant services were not a part of United States-Italy trade.

D. **Protection of foreign "well-known marks":** The Paris Convention and the TRIPs Agreement (to which the United States adheres) both require the United States to protect foreign marks that are "well known" in the United States regardless of whether they are used in the United States (Paris Convention art. 6bis;, TRIPs art. 16(2) & (3).). The Ninth Circuit has held that, under this principle, a Mexican chain of stores that is well known to U.S. residents who have ties with Mexico can use the Lanham Act infringement cause of action to prevent a domestic entity from opening a U.S. store under the same name. *Grupo Gigante SA De CV v. Dallo & Co.*, 391 F.3d 1088 (9th Cir. 2004). In contrast, the Second Circuit has held that the Lanham Act provides no basis for protecting "well-known marks" that are not used in the United States. The Paris Convention and TRIPs Agreements are not self-executing and thus provide no cause of action independent from the provisions of the Lanham Act. *ITC Ltd. v. Punchgini, Inc.*, 482 F.3d 135 (2d Cir. 2007). The Second Circuit explained that under the long-established doctrine of territoriality, use of a mark in a foreign country does not give rise to ownership rights in the United States. A mark claimant must use the mark in the United States.

VII. FEDERAL REGISTRATION OF MARKS

A. **Ownership and registration:** It is important to remember that *ownership* of marks arises automatically under the common law when a mark is used in trade (or in the case of marks that are not inherently distinctive, when the claimant uses them in trade to the point that they acquire secondary meaning). No registration or other administrative process is necessary to acquire ownership rights at common law. The Lanham Act provides that persons owning trademarks, service marks, certification marks, and collective marks (under common-law rules) may *enforce them under §43(a),* or *register them* on the Lanham Act Principal Register. *Registration supplements the rights that are available under the common law.*

B. **Advantages of registration on the Principal Register:** Only persons who have obtained ownership rights in marks by using them in trade (and have satisfied the "use in commerce" requirement) may obtain federal registration. Among other things, registration provides a right to assistance from the U.S. Customs Service in preventing the importation of infringing goods, and a presumption of mark ownership and validity that eases registrants' burdens in lawsuits challenging or enforcing their rights. Indeed, after five years of registration, certain challenges or defenses to the mark may be prohibited altogether. (For more details on this advantage, see *infra*, p. 279.) Registrants are also immune to dilution claims brought pursuant to state law. Perhaps most importantly, registration allows the mark owner to acquire rights in the mark in a greater geographical area than often would be possible under the common law. See *infra*, pp. 251-254.

C. Two paths to registration on the Lanham Act Principal Register: There are two alternative routes to follow in applying to register a mark on the Principal Register.

    1. "Use applications": A person who already has used a mark in trade and interstate commerce may apply to register by filing application papers with the Patent and Trademark Office (P.T.O.) that set forth, among other things: the dates of first use in trade and use in interstate commerce; the goods or services the mark was used to identify; a drawing of the mark and specimens of the mark as used (for example, copies of the product label or posters advertising the service); and a statement that to the best of the applicant's belief, no other person has a conflicting right to use the mark. When the P.T.O. receives the application to register, an examiner reviews the application to ensure that it complies with statutory requirements, and to determine if there are any apparent grounds for rejecting the application. (Many of those grounds are discussed in the previous sections.) If the examiner approves the mark it will be published in the P.T.O.'s *Official Gazette*. At that point people who believe they may be injured by the registration (because, for example, the mark is a descriptive term that they want to use freely, or because the mark is confusingly similar to their own) may file an opposition, challenging the registration as inappropriate under the provisions of the Lanham Act. If it is discovered that someone else has made an earlier, ongoing use of a confusingly similar mark, the applicant may initiate a concurrent use proceeding to convince the P.T.O. to grant registration subject to restrictions to ensure that consumer confusion will not arise from the concurrent use. If the P.T.O. ultimately determines that registration is appropriate, it will *issue a certificate of registration*.

    2. "Intent-to-use" applications: Alternatively, a person may file application papers with the P.T.O. that, among other things, state that the applicant has a *bona fide intention* to use the mark in trade and in interstate commerce; identify the goods or services on which the mark will be used and the manner of intended use; and state that to the best of the applicant's knowledge, no other person has a conflicting right to use the mark. The P.T.O. will undertake an initial examination of the mark, and publish it for opposition. If there is no successful opposition, the P.T.O. will *issue a notice of allowance* and the applicant will then have six months in which to begin actual use of the mark. (Six-month extensions of time are available up to a total of two and a half years. The first extension is automatic upon request. Subsequent extensions are granted upon a showing of good cause.) When the *applicant actually uses the mark in trade and in commerce, it must file a statement of use*, at which point a second examination occurs. If accepted, the mark is then registered. Note that even under the intent-to-use application process, registration will not be granted until the applicant has made the requisite use in trade and interstate commerce. The advantage of the intent-to-use registration process is that it *allows the applicant to "reserve" the mark* while it gears up to introduce products to the market bearing the mark. As described below, although the mark is not actually registered until it is used, ultimate use and timely completion of the registration process gives the registrant *nationwide priority over others who commence use of the mark after the registrant's application date*.

D. **Constructive use:** Even though registration cannot occur until after the mark is *used* in the prescribed manner, the Lanham Act provides that once the mark is registered, the registration creates "constructive use" during the period between application filing and final registration. This constructive use may prove invaluable both to "use" and "intent-to-use" applicants. Since an owner's common-law rights over others depend on being the first to use a mark in a given geographic area, the constructive use provision will allow the registrant to prevail over another who *actually used* the mark *anywhere in the country* before the registration but after the date of the registrant's application to register. (Lanham Act §7(c),15 U.S.C.§1057(c)).

Example: In January, 2000, X Co. files an application to register the mark "Spiff" as a trademark for women's jeans, alleging a bona fide intent to use it in trade and interstate commerce. The application is allowed, and X Co. then has six months to commence use of the mark. At the end of that six months, X Co. files for and receives an extension of an additional six months to commence use. In March, 2001, X Co. sells jeans, with the mark affixed, to customers in interstate commerce and files a statement of use. Shortly thereafter the mark is registered. In July, 2000, Y uses the mark "Spiff" in trade on women's jeans in California. Even though Y was the first *actually to use* the mark in trade, Lanham Act §7(c) gives X Co. the benefit of *"constructive use"* as of his application date. This officially makes X Co. the "first" to use the mark, and gives it priority—superior rights over Y. (Note that while X Co. has superior rights over Y by virtue of constructive use, he has no right to a remedy for Y's use of the mark prior to X's actual use and registration. By the same token, during the period between July, 2000 and March, 2001, Y has no right to enjoin X from making his intended use and thus completing his registration and obtaining constructive use.)

Example: In January, 2000, X Co. commences use of the mark "Spiff" for cane syrup that it produces and sells in Florida, Georgia, Alabama, and Mississippi. It applies to register the mark (a "use" based application) in March, 2000. The P.T.O. publishes the mark, and an opposition is filed. X ultimately wins the opposition, and the P.T.O. registers the mark in February, 2001. Y Co. begins to use the mark "Spiff" for pancake syrup in California, Oregon, and Washington in March, 2000. The common law would recognize Y Co. as having superior rights in the "Spiff" mark on the west coast, because he was the first to use the mark, in good faith, in a geographic area that is remote from X Co's area of use. (See pp. 251-252, *infra*.) However, in this case, X has priority because he gets the benefit of constructive use as of his filing date, which means that he is viewed as the first to use the mark on the west coast.

E. **The certificate of registration:** When registration is granted, the P.T.O. issues a certificate of registration. The certificate of registration is "*prima facie* evidence of the validity of the registered mark and of the registration of the mark, of the registrant's ownership of the mark, and of the registrant's exclusive right to use the registered mark in commerce on or in connection with the goods or services specified in the certificate." 15 U.S.C. §1057(b). The registration is good for ten years, subject to the periodic filing of affirmations that the mark remains in use. Registration may be renewed for additional ten-year terms as long as the mark remains in commercial use in connection with the designated goods or services.

F. **Registration on the Lanham Act Supplemental Register:** Lanham Act §23 (15 U.S.C. §1091) provides that marks in lawful use that are *capable* of distinguishing an applicant's goods or services, but are not registerable on the Principal Register (because not inherently distinctive, and lacking secondary meaning), may be registered on the Supplemental Register.

1. **Types of marks registerable on the Supplemental Register:** Any mark that is descriptive or deceptively misdescriptive, geographically descriptive, primarily a surname, common, or otherwise not inherently distinctive, and that lacks secondary meaning, may be registered on the Supplemental Register. However, the mark must be *capable* of distinguishing the applicant's goods or services, so that generic words and their nonverbal equivalents may not be registered. Also barred from Supplemental Registration are marks that are unregisterable because they are confusingly similar to a mark or trade name in prior use by another, or because they are deceptive, or violate other provisions of Lanham Act §2.

2. **Use prior to filing:** To register on the Supplemental Register, the applicant must demonstrate that she has used the mark in trade and commerce prior to the application. There is no "intent-to-use" application process for the Supplemental Register.

3. **Advantages of registration on the Supplemental Register:** The Supplemental Register was created to assist Americans wishing to register marks abroad. (As will be discussed *infra*, registration in a party's country of origin may give rise to a right to register in foreign countries, as well. See pp. 286-287, *infra*.) The advantages of registration on the Principal Register, such as rights in a greater geographic area and presumptions of validity, are not available to marks registered on the Supplemental Register.

4. **Later registration on the Principal Register:** Registration on the Supplemental Register does not preclude an applicant from later applying to register on the Principal Register, if her mark has become sufficiently distinctive through use.

VIII. CANCELLATION OF REGISTRATION

A. **During the first five years of registration:** Since many people do not regularly review the publication of applications for registration in the *Official Gazette*, they do not know to bring an opposition to registration within the required time frame. In fairness, some means must be available to challenge a registration after it is granted. On the other hand, persons should be required to bring their challenges to a registration as early as is reasonably possible, so that the registrant may rely on the validity of his registration and feel free to invest in the mark. 15 U.S.C. §1064 provides that *during the first five years* of a mark's registration a person who believes himself injured by the registration may file a petition with the P.T.O. to cancel the registration *on any ground* that would have precluded registration in the first place.

B. **After five years of registration:** If the mark has been registered for *over five years*, the Lanham Act *narrows the available grounds for cancellation*. Challenges to the mark's validity that remain available include:

- the mark has become generic;
- the mark is functional;
- the mark has been abandoned;
- the registration was obtained through fraud;
- the mark is deceptive; or scandalous; or disparages a person, institution, belief, or national symbol, or brings it into disrepute; or constitutes a geographical indication first used on or after

January 1, 1996, that, when used on or in connection with wines or spirits, identifies a place other than the origin of the goods;

- the mark includes the insignia of a government, or includes the name, likeness, or signature of a living person without his written consent, or of a deceased U.S. President without the written consent of his or her surviving spouse;

- in the case of a certification mark, the owner has made improper use of the mark or has failed adequately to police others' use of it.

   1. **Precluded grounds:** The three important grounds for cancellation that are precluded after five years of registration are: (1) that the mark is not inherently distinctive and lacks secondary meaning; (2) that the mark is confusingly similar to a mark or trade name that someone else used prior to the registrant and continues to use; and (3) that the mark is dilutive of the challenger's senior mark.

IX. GEOGRAPHIC BOUNDARIES

A. **Geographic rights at common law:** Under the common law, *the first person to use* a mark in trade (or in the case of a mark that is not inherently distinctive, the first person to obtain secondary meaning in the mark) is the owner of it. (For convenience, we will call this first person the "senior user.") Notwithstanding this, if another person later uses the same or a confusingly similar mark in a *remote geographic area in good faith,* he (the "junior user") will have a defense against the senior user's attempt to stop him within that territory. The defense is that the junior user occupied his geographically remote area first, in good faith (the "remote good-faith user defense"). Indeed, the junior user will have *superior rights* within the area in which he was the first to use in good faith, so that if the senior user later tries to enter that area with his own confusingly similar mark, the junior user can stop him (even though the senior user was, in an absolute sense, the first to use the mark).

   1. **Good faith:** Under the *majority rule,* to use a mark in good faith is to use it with no knowledge or notice that another person has made an earlier use that is ongoing in the United States. Under the minority rule, the good-faith user may know or have notice of the senior user, as long as he did not intend to encroach on the senior user's business good will.

   2. **Remote geographical area:** For purposes of determining geographic boundaries, the area of a party's use of a mark is comprised not just of the area in which he has sold goods or services through use of the mark, but also those areas in which (while there have been no sales) the mark has a "presence" by virtue of advertising or general reputation. A "remote" geographical area is one in which the senior user's mark has no "presence" either through use or general reputation.

      Example of the common-law rule (1): In 1990, A begins to use the mark "spiffo" for hair cream, which he sells throughout New England. In 1995, B begins to use the same mark for shampoo in New England. Since A was the first to use the mark in New England, he has superior rights there. He may enjoin B's use of the mark there if B's use causes a likelihood of consumer confusion. It does not matter whether B had good faith or not, because he is not using the mark in a geographic area that is remote from A's (the senior user's).

Example of the common-law rule (2): In 1990, A begins to use the mark "spiffo" for hair cream throughout New England. In 1995, B begins to use the same mark for shampoo in Florida (which is "geographically remote" from A's New England area). B's use in Florida is in good faith. A will have no right to enjoin B's use for two reasons. First, since A herself is not using the mark in Florida, A has no right to enjoin B from using it there because B's use will not cause a likelihood of consumer confusion. Second, even if A later began to use the mark in Florida, she could not enjoin B. B has the defense that he was the first to use the mark in Florida (a remote area) in good faith. Indeed, B could enjoin A's use in Florida because, even though A used the mark before B in an absolute sense, B was the first to use it in good faith in Florida, and this gives him superior rights over A in Florida.

3. **The zone of natural expansion:** The common-law "zone of natural expansion" doctrine was developed to give a senior user some flexibility to expand his business. Under this doctrine, a senior user may assert superior rights in a *limited geographical area* that he did not occupy at the time that a junior user first used the mark in good faith. However, the senior user must demonstrate that when the junior user began to use the mark, the area in which he used it was already within the senior user's "zone of natural expansion." If it was in the zone of natural expansion, at that time, the senior user, *upon later entering* the area himself, may enjoin further use there by the junior user. (It should be noted that courts *rarely apply* the zone of natural expansion doctrine, and apply it sparingly when they do, usually confining it to a very limited geographic area.)

    a. **What constitutes a senior user's zone of natural expansion:** A senior user's zone of natural expansion is that geographic area into which, at the time the junior user began his use, the senior user logically and foreseeably would eventually expand, given the nature of the senior user's business and his history of prior expansion.

    Example: A begins using the mark "spiffo" for hair cream in New England in 1980. In 1990, though A has not yet established a presence with the mark in upstate New York, it is logically foreseeable that A will eventually expand her business and use of the mark there, given the nature of A's business and A's history of expansion. In 1990, B begins using the mark "spiffo" for hair cream in good faith in upstate New York. In 1995, A begins to use the mark in upstate New York. Since upstate New York was *within A's zone of natural expansion in 1990,* when B began using the mark there, A has superior rights in the mark in upstate New York and can enjoin B's continued use (even though B was the first to use the mark in New York and did so in good faith).

B. **The Lanham Act:** Registration of a mark on the Lanham Act Principal Register expands the registrant's geographic rights in a mark beyond those he would enjoy at common law. (Note, however, that the scope of geographic rights for *unregistered marks and other indications of origin* continue to be governed by common-law rules even when their owners sue for infringement under Lanham Act §43(a).)

    1. **Registration removes the good-faith defense:** Lanham Act §22 (15 U.S.C.§1072) provides that *registration* of a mark on the Principal Register gives *constructive notice of the registrant's use of the mark.* The constructive notice is effective *as of the registration date.* Anyone who begins using a confusingly similar mark after the effective date of the constructive notice cannot claim to have begun his own use in good faith. Since the subsequent user did not begin his use in good faith, he has no remote, good-faith defense to a suit subsequently brought by the registrant. The practical result is that the registrant enjoys superior rights not only in her

area of actual use (which she would have anyway under the common law) but also *in all areas of the country in which the mark was not already in use at the time the constructive notice took effect.*

2. **Registration on applications filed after November 16, 1989, provides constructive use:** In the case of marks registered on *applications filed after November 16, 1989,* registration gives rise to *constructive use priority throughout the country as of the registrant's application date.* 15 U.S.C. §1057(c). (See *supra*, p. 249.) Under §7(c), anyone who begins use after the date the registrant applied to register the mark cannot be deemed to have been the first to use the mark in his geographic area, even if the geographic area is "remote" from the registrant's area of actual use. Again, this effectively gives the registrant *nationwide rights, but at an even earlier date* than under §22. (Section 7(c) makes a couple of exceptions: The registrant does not get constructive use priority over persons who, at the time of the registrant's application, had pending applications of their own, or had filed foreign applications that gave them an effective U.S. filing date that preceded the registrant's. (See *infra*, p. 287.)

Example: A is the first to use the mark "spiffo" for hair cream anywhere in the United States. She begins her use in 1985 in New England. In 1988, A registers the mark on the Lanham Act Principal Register. In 1990, B begins to use the "spiffo" mark for shampoo in California, which is "geographically remote" from A's New England territory. B has no actual knowledge of A's prior use or registration. In 2003, A decides to expand sales into California and sues to enjoin B's further use of the mark in California, alleging that B's concurrent use will cause a likelihood of consumer confusion. Assuming that it will, A should win. B first used the mark after A, and he had *constructive notice* of A's prior use by virtue of A's registration, which deprives him of the remote good faith user defense.

Example: A is the first to use the "spiffo" mark for hair cream in the United States. She begins her use in 1980 in New England. In 1983, B begins using the same mark for hair cream, in good faith, in California, which is geographically remote. In 1987, A registers the "spiffo" mark on the Lanham Act Principal Register. In 2003, A decides to expand her business into California and sues to enjoin B's further use of the mark there, alleging that concurrent use will cause a likelihood of consumer confusion. Even if it does, A should lose. At the time B began using the mark in California, A had not registered and *B had no actual or constructive notice of A's prior use.* Thus B has the benefit of the remote good faith user defense (the Lanham Act calls it the "limited area defense") and, having been the first to use the mark in California—a geographically remote location—in good faith, B has superior rights in California. In fact, B can enjoin A's use of the "spiffo" mark there. However, *B's rightful area of use is restricted to the area that he occupied on the date of A's registration and has continuously occupied thereafter.* If B expanded to a new area (for example, Oregon) after the registration, he did so with notice of A's prior use, due to her registration, and thus lacks the benefit of the good faith defense as to that new area.

Example (junior user registers): A is the first to use the "spiffo" mark for hair cream in the United States. She begins her use in 1980 in New England. In 1983, B begins using the mark in sales of a similar product in good faith in Texas, a geographically remote area. *B registers* the mark on the Lanham Act Principal Register in 1987. Later, B decides to expand use of the mark to New England and sues to enjoin further use by A there, alleging that A's continued use will cause a likelihood of confusion. B should not be able to enjoin A's use in New England. Rather, A can rely on her senior use there and enjoin B. Whether A can assert superior rights in areas that she occupied for the first time *after B's registration date* depends on whether B's registration has attained incontestability status (see p. 279, *infra*). If so, then A is confined to the area she occupied at the time of B's registration. If not, the scope of A's rights will depend on the court's view of the equities, under the particular circumstances of the case.

Example: On January 1, 1998, A files an application to register the "spiffo" mark for hair cream, alleging a *bona fide* intent to use the mark in commerce. The P.T.O. allows the mark in June of 1998, and A begins use of the mark on hair cream in New England in November, 1998. A then files an affidavit of use in December, 1998, and completes her registration. B begins using the "spiffo" mark for shampoo in New England in February, 1998, several months before A's first use and actual registration. Assuming that B's use causes a likelihood of consumer confusion, A can enjoin the use. Because A filed *her application to register after November 16, 1989*, upon registration she gets the benefit of *constructive use,* dating back to her application filing date. Thus, she is viewed as commencing her use in January, 1998, a month before B began his use. A has priority over B.

C. **A likelihood of consumer confusion about the source of goods or services:** Under the majority rule, even if a mark owner has superior rights in a mark in a particular geographic area by virtue of federal registration, she will not be entitled to enjoin another's use in that area *unless* the defendant's use is likely to cause consumer confusion about the source, sponsorship, or affiliation of the parties' goods or services. This will only be the case if the registrant is also using the mark in the area the defendant is occupying (or at least has a "presence" there), or has concrete plans to begin use there in the immediate future.

Example: X has registered the mark "Yums" for cake mixes, which it sells wholesale to bakers on the East Coast. X does not do business in the Chicago area, and has no presence there. Y, a junior user with no good faith defense, begins to sell cake mixes wholesale in the Chicago area using the mark "Yums." X will not be entitled to enjoin Y's use *unless* X is able to show either that its mark already has a "presence" or reputation in Chicago or that X has immediate, concrete plans to begin using the mark in Chicago. Otherwise, Y's use there will not cause a likelihood of consumer confusion about the source, sponsorship, or affiliation of the cake mixes. Y can continue his use *until* X begins his own use there, or can demonstrate concrete plans to commence use there in the immediate future. *Dawn Donut Co. v. Hart's Food Stores, Inc.*, 267 F.2d 358 (2d Cir. 1959).

1. **Some movement away from the majority rule:** In recent years some courts (including the Sixth Circuit) have rejected the rule stated above (sometimes called the *Dawn Donut* rule) as outdated, reasoning that, given how mobile people are today, and given mass communications and the Internet, one cannot assume that people in one market area won't be exposed to the use of the mark in a different market area. Thus, instead of adopting a flat rule that there can be no consumer confusion when the plaintiff doesn't use its registered mark in the defendant's area (and lacks immediate plans to begin), these courts just treat geographic proximity as one factor in their multifactor test for likelihood of consumer confusion.

X. INFRINGEMENT OF MARKS

A. **The injury to be protected against:** As previously discussed, trademark protection addresses two major concerns. First, it protects the public's interest in being able accurately and efficiently to ascertain the source of goods and services in the marketplace. Second, it protects a business's good will, and encourages business to strive for quality. In cases in which the plaintiff and defendant directly *compete,* the defendant's use of a confusingly similar mark may cause consumers to buy the defendant's goods or services when they mean to buy the plaintiff's. However, even when there is *no direct diversion of sales,* as, for example, in the case of non-competing goods or services, the defendant's use of a confusingly similar mark may, by suggesting an affiliation with the plaintiff that does not exist, lead consumers to assign blame to the plaintiff for the defendant's mistakes and poor quality. In the long term this too may undermine the public's ability to rely on marks, damage the plaintiff's business good will, and lead to economic loss.

B. **The infringement determination:** Modern law suggests that there are two inquiries that should be made in determining whether a defendant's acts amount to trademark infringement. First, did the defendant *use* the plaintiff's mark (or one similar to it) *as a trademark*, to indicate the source of its goods or services? Second, if he did, is the defendant's use *likely to cause an appreciable number of consumers to be confused about the source, sponsorship or affiliation of goods or services?*

C. **The "trademark use" requirement:** The earliest federal trademark statutes required that the defendant "affix" his allegedly infringing mark on goods that he was offering for sale, as a prerequisite to finding infringement. Similar language was carried over into the Lanham Act. Lanham Act §32(1)(a) (providing an infringement cause of action for registered marks) requires that the defendant "*use* [the mark] *in commerce*" "*in connection with the sale, offering for sale, distribution or advertising of goods or services,*" and §43(a) (providing a cause of action for infringement of unregistered indications of origin) requires that the defendant "*use* [the mark] *in commerce*" "*on or in connection with any goods or services, or any container for goods.*" Lanham Act §45 defines "use in commerce" (in the case of goods) as placing the mark on goods or their containers, tags or labels, or on displays associated with them, and then selling or transporting the goods in commerce. (In the case of services, §45 defines "use in commerce" as using or displaying the mark in the sale or advertising of services, and rendering the services in commerce.) Thus, it seems clear that *the defendant must closely associate the mark with goods or services that it is advertising or selling.* This ensures that the defendant is *using the mark in a way that is likely to indicate source to consumers.* This is an important requirement because it limits the infringement cause of action to its purpose: preventing consumer confusion about the source of goods or services. Use of words or symbols in other (non-source-indicating) ways is not likely to interfere with the ability of trademark law to accomplish its limited purpose, and permitting trademark owners to prohibit such uses would likely interfere with the free flow of information in the marketplace, thus actually undercutting the pro-competitive purpose of trademark law.

  1. **Courts' construction of the "trademark use" requirement outside of the Internet context:** Prior to the Internet, the issue of trademark use seldom came up, and courts seldom had cause to discuss it. However, the case law made it clear that *the legal significance of marks lies in their message to consumers about the source of a product or service*—marks *have no legal existence apart from their role in identifying source.* Thus, there are *no* "rights in gross" or "rights at large" in a word or symbol that serves as a mark. Trademark law (unlike the broader patent and copyright laws) was not intended to give monopoly rights in words or symbols, as such. The cases also made it clear that a defendant's *predatory intent* (that is, his intent to free-ride on the plaintiff's business good will) could not substitute for trademark use. Trademark law is not intended to prevent all forms of free-riding.

Example: Plaintiff claimed rights in the "Holiday Inns" mark and also in a vanity telephone number, "1-800-HOLIDAY," which it featured in advertisements. Customers could dial the 1-800-HOLIDAY number to make room reservations. The defendant secured and used a number that potential Holiday Inn customers frequently dialed by mistake when attempting to reach the plaintiff. (The number essentially took advantage of the well-known fact that consumers often substitute a zero for the letter "o".) The defendant used that number in its business of making reservations for customers with a large number of hotel chains, including Holiday Inns. The Court of Appeals for the Sixth Circuit assumed that the plaintiff had trademark rights in its vanity number, and noted that the defendant's "sole purpose" in choosing its number was "to intercept calls from misdialing consumers who were attempting to reach Holiday Inns," and thus to free-ride on the plaintiff's business good will. Nonetheless, the court rejected Holiday Inns' infringement claim as a matter of law, on the ground that the defendant did not "use" the plaintiff's trademark or any variant of it. It only used a telephone number, which was neither phonetically nor visually similar to the plaintiff's mark. The court emphasized that the defendant had to advertise or otherwise expose consumers to the 1-800-Holiday mark (or something similar to it) in connection with its reservation services. *Holiday Inns, Inc. v. 800 Reservation, Inc.*, 86 F.3d 619 (6th Cir. 1996), *cert. denied*, 519 U.S. 1093 (1997).

2. **Courts' construction of the "trademark use" requirement in the Internet context:** The Internet has provided numerous creative new ways for people to utilize others' marks for their own purposes—in order to free-ride on the mark owner's business good will, in order to attract the kind of Internet users who might be seeking the mark owner, in order to comment about the mark owner, or for other reasons. These practices have put the "trademark use" requirement in the spotlight, as it had rarely been before. Because of the lack of precedent, and possible judicial confusion about the new technology, courts have split in numerous ways over the scope and purpose of the "trademark use" requirement in this new context. The main problem areas include: use of marks in cybersquatting, use of marks in metatags, use of marks in "forum site" domain names, and use of marks in contextual advertising, to trigger ads for competing businesses.

   a. **Cybersquatting as "trademark use":** In the 1990s a number of enterprising individuals registered domain names consisting of others' marks followed by ".com" or another generic top level domain, and attempted to sell the registrations at a profit to the trademark owners. When trademark owners brought Lanham Act claims, courts rejected the proposition that simply registering the plaintiff's mark as a domain name, in itself, constituted the requisite "use in commerce" to trigger infringement or dilution liability either on the part of the registrant or the registering agency. However, a line of cases held that registering a domain name comprised of a mark and generic top level domain did constitute a Lanham Act "use" *when coupled with* an *intent to sell or license the registration* to the trademark owner. The courts reasoned that even though the cybersquatter defendants did not use the domain name in connection with the sale of goods or services, their use constituted a "commercial use" because the cybersquatters made a business of registering trademarks as domain names and then selling the registrations to trademark owners, and the defendants "traded on the value of the marks," as marks. *See, e.g., Panavision International, L.P. v. Toeppen*, 141 F.3d 1316 (9th Cir. 1998). This line of cases essentially found an "in gross" right in the marks, disassociated from their role of identifying the source of goods or services. They also can be characterized as substituting the defendants' predatory intent for trademark use, contrary to prior precedent.

b. Incorporation of marks into forum site domain names: A number of cases arose in which the defendant registered a domain name that incorporated the plaintiff's mark, and then set up a "gripe site" or other "forum site" under the domain name to comment on the plaintiff mark owner, its political or religious beliefs, or its goods or services. While use of a mark in a domain name to identify a *commercial site that sells or advertises goods or services* can be deemed a Lanham Act "trademark use," the forum site cases mainly involved defendants who *did not* sell or advertise any goods or services on their site, making it difficult to characterize their domain name use as a "use in commerce" in connection with the sale or advertising of goods or services. Nevertheless, the case decisions split over whether the forum site defendants made an actionable Lanham Act "use" of the plaintiff's mark. While some courts found no Lanham Act use and thus no liability, others found the requisite use based on links from the defendant's site, an effect on the plaintiff's sales, or a finding that the defendant's site constituted an "information service," as described below.

   i. Relying on links: Some courts found the requisite "use" of the mark in connection with sale or advertisement of goods because the defendant's forum site *linked to other sites that sold or advertised goods or services*. Other courts *rejected* this approach, arguing that the this connection to the sale of goods or services was too attenuated, and reasoning that, given the interconnected nature of the World Wide Web, basing a finding of trademark use on the existence of links would essentially place every unauthorized reproduction of a plaintiff's mark on the Internet within the mark owner's control.

   ii. Relying on a finding that the defendant's use "affects" the plaintiff's sales: Other courts found the requisite use "in connection with the sale of goods or services" by reasoning that, by waylaying consumers seeking the plaintiff's site, the defendant's incorporation of the plaintiff's mark in its domain name would *affect the plaintiff's sale of goods or services*. (They thus combined the *defendant's use of the mark* with the *plaintiff's sale of goods or services*.) Other courts *rejected* this reasoning, finding that the defendant's use of the mark must be in connection with *his own* sale of goods or services. Since the defendant sold no goods or services, consumers could not possibly understand the defendant's domain name use as indicating *the source* of goods or services. Moreover, since any negative commentary is likely to *affect* the plaintiff's sales, this approach made it possible for trademark owners to censor on-line criticism of itself or its product or service.

   iii. Finding "services" and relying on predatory intent: Still other courts found the requisite Lanham Act "use" in forum site cases by characterizing the defendant's critical commentary about the mark owner as an *"information service,"* so that the use of the mark in the domain name was *"in connection with the distribution of a service."* Others seemed to be motivated to find "use" (or overlook the need for "use") because of the defendant's "predatory" motive to draw in Internet users who were seeking the plaintiff's site. Still other courts rejected these lines of reasoning, again, citing prior case precedent and policy concerns about trademark owner interference with free speech and the free flow of potentially useful information on the Internet.

c. Metatags as trademark use: Metatags consist of HTML code, integrated into a web site, that is invisible to web site visitors but can be read by search engines. Particularly during the middle and late 1990s, search engines relied on metatags to formulate and rank their search results. Web site operators realized that if they inserted a plaintiff's mark into their metatags, they could get their sites included in the search result when Internet users entered the plaintiff's mark as a search term. Most of the courts to consider Lanham Act claims in this context found for the plaintiff, but typically did not explain how they found the requisite "use in commerce" in connection with the sale or advertisement of goods or services. The most influential decision on this issue analogized metatag use to posting a sign that features the plaintiff's mark but directs consumers to the defendant's store, leading them to think that the defendant's store is the plaintiff's. *Brookfield Communications, Inc. v. West Coast Entertainment Corp.*, 174 F.3d 1036 (9th Cir. 1999). If this analogy were correct, it would probably demonstrate the requisite trademark use. However, commentators have criticized the analogy, noting, among other things, that while consumers can see signs, they are never exposed to a defendant's metatag use of the plaintiff's mark, and thus cannot rely on it for information about source. Moreover, use of metatags does not direct consumers to the defendant's site. It merely causes the defendant's site to be listed in the search result, along with the plaintiff's. While consumers may choose to visit the defendant's site, there is no reason to think that they are relying on the *presence of the site in the search result* for information about the source of any goods or services that are available on the defendant's site. Assuming that the parties' domain names are not confusingly similar, the defendant's use of the plaintiff's mark in metatags can be viewed as pro-competitive: it offers consumers a choice that they might not otherwise have realized they had.

d. Use of marks in contextual advertising: Additional lines of cases address hidden references to marks that facilitate contextual advertising. These cases can be divided into two groups: (1) the *WhenU.Com* line of cases, involving software that generates "pop-up" advertisements on computer users' screens, and (2) the search engine cases, which involve keying advertisements to users' input of marks as search terms. Courts typically have rejected Lanham Act claims against use of marks in connection with the WhenU.Com software, on the ground that there is no actionable "trademark use." Keying advertisements to marks has generated a wider range of contrasting views concerning the "trademark use" issue.

  i. The *WhenU.Com* line of cases: Computer users download the *WhenU* software from the Internet. The software tracks the user's activity on the web, examining the search terms and web site URLs the user enters. It compares these terms and URLs to its directory, which lists a large number of web addresses, keywords, and search terms, categorized in much the same way that telephone directories categorize businesses. If it finds a match for the user's search term or URL, it identifies the relevant product or service category and causes an ad to appear on the user's screen pertaining to that category. So, for example, if the computer user enters the URL "wellsfargo.com," the software would find that URL in its "financial services" category and generate a "pop-up" ad for an advertiser in the same category, like Bank of America. The ad might partially cover the computer user's screen, on which the Wells Fargo web site appears. The ads are displayed in separate, conspicuously branded windows and specifically advise the user that they are from WhenU.Com and are not sponsored by whatever web site the user might be viewing. The user can click the ad shut, or exercise a link to visit the advertiser's web site. A line of decisions, including one from the Second Circuit, rejected Lanham

Act claims against WhenU.Com on the ground that the defendant's use of the plaintiff's marks does not constitute the requisite Lanham Act "use." See *1-800 Contacts, Inc. v. WhenU.Com, Inc.*, 414 F.3d 400 (2d Cir. 2005). These courts rejected a number of arguments for finding use that the plaintiffs based on the earlier cybersquatting, forum site domain name and metatag precedent. In rejecting arguments that the software "displayed" the mark (which appeared on the plaintiff's web site) in connection with the products and services featured in the advertisements, the courts stressed the fact that the ads appeared in a separate window and were properly labeled. *"Simultaneous visibility" was not enough* to establish trademark use. Moreover, the plaintiff, rather than the defendant, had caused the mark to appear on the screen. With regard to the reproduction of the marks in the software directory, the courts stressed that *consumers were not exposed* to the marks and thus could not rely on them for information about source. Moreover, the *defendant did not use the marks to indicate the source of its advertisers' goods or services*. It merely used the marks to indicate the proper category of ad to send to the user. Finally, the directory use did not interfere with users' ability to access the mark owners' sites, and the defendant's comparative advertising was pro-competitive. The Second Circuit noted that *trademark law is concerned with source identification and is not meant to protect consumer good will in a more general sense*.

ii. **The search engine cases:** The first keying case involved Netscape, but most of the subsequent decisions have considered Lanham Act claims concerning the Google "sponsored links" program, which permits advertisers to pay to have their advertisements displayed when search engine users input a particular word (which may or may not be a trademark) as a search term. The first Google case found the requisite trademark use, relying on the metatag decisions and the forum site cases to reason that the defendant's hidden use of the plaintiff's mark might *affect* the plaintiff's sales of goods or services (by luring potential purchasers away). It seemed also to analogize Google's sale of rights to key to a mark to the sale of domain name registrations in cybersquatting cases. *Government Employees Insurance Co. v. Google, Inc.*, 330 F.Supp. 2d 700 (E.D. Va. 2004). Other courts, in contrast, have applied the Second Circuit's reasoning in the *WhenU* case to find that Google's internal use of marks is not a Lanham Act "use," because consumers are not exposed to the use, and the use is not made to identify source. *See, e.g.,* Merck & Co v. Mediplan Health Consulting, Inc., 425 F. Supp. 2d 402 (S.D.N.Y. 2006). Subsequent decisions have fallen on both sides of the divide.

D. **The likelihood of confusion requirement:** The issue in the second part of the infringement analysis is whether the defendant's unauthorized use of its mark causes a *likelihood that consumers will associate the defendant's goods or services with the plaintiff, and think that the goods or services are produced by, endorsed by, or otherwise affiliated with the plaintiff*. If so, the defendant's mark infringes the plaintiff's. (Note that it is not necessary to demonstrate *actual* consumer confusion.)

1. **No side-by-side comparison:** In determining whether the defendant's mark is sufficiently similar to the plaintiff's to be likely to cause consumer confusion, the court *cannot assume* that *the consumer would have the opportunity to make a side-by-side comparison* of the marks. Indeed, the consumer may have only a hazy recollection of the plaintiff's mark at the time he or she encounters the defendant's mark.

2. **Factors to consider in determining a likelihood of confusion:** Courts have set forth a number of factors to consider in determining whether a defendant's mark is likely to confuse

consumers about the source, affiliation, or sponsorship of goods or services, and thus infringe the plaintiff's mark. In most cases no one single factor is determinative, but the weight assigned to different factors may vary, depending on the particular circumstances of the case.

- **a. Similarity of the parties' marks:** Probably the *most important factor in most cases* is the similarity of the parties' marks. In evaluating this factor, courts consider the Restatement of Torts §729 *"sight, sound, and meaning"* test, which considers similarity from three perspectives.

    - **i. Similarity of appearance:** The similarity of appearance of the defendant's and the plaintiff's marks is important, especially in cases involving a picture or design trademark. It also is a key factor in cases involving foreign, or newly coined, or nonsense words. In making the comparison of appearance *a court will look to the overall visual impression created by each mark.* If the mark is a composite of several elements, such as a word combined with a drawing, the court will not dissect the mark in making the comparison.

    - **ii. Similarity of sound:** The similarity of sound evaluation *focuses on how the mark sounds phonetically.* It is important because in many cases *consumers may have never actually seen the mark*, but have only heard it mentioned by others, or in radio or television ads. In some cases courts may undertake a linguistic analysis, comparing the number of syllables, the stress pattern, and the acoustic similarity and placement of the letters that differ between the plaintiff's and defendant's marks.

        Example: The marks "S.O." and "Esso" do not look alike, but would be confusingly similar when only heard. After a linguistic analysis, a court found the marks "dramamine" and "bonamine" to be confusingly similar, due to the similarities in number of syllables, stress pattern, and the acoustic properties of the letters.

    - **iii. Similarity of meaning:** The *mental image* evoked by marks may overpower any differences between them in sound or appearance, and lead to a finding of a likelihood of confusion.

        Example: Courts have found the marks "Cyclone" and "Tornado" for wire fencing, and the marks "Pledge" and "Promise" for furniture wax, confusingly similar because they evoke similar images in the consumer's mind. In another case a court found that Mobil Oil's mark, consisting of an image of a horse with wings, was infringed by the defendant's word mark "Pegasus." The court reasoned that, regardless of whether the plaintiff used the name "Pegasus" itself, the public associated the plaintiff's winged horse image with the mythological horse Pegasus, and was likely to be confused by the defendant's use of that name.

        Example: The mark *"chat noir"* was held confusingly similar to the mark "black cat," because it is French for black cat. To people who understand French, the two marks would mean the same thing and be confusingly similar.

- **b. Similarity of the parties' products or services:** If the defendant and plaintiff use their marks on *the same or related kinds of products or services,* there is a much greater likelihood of confusion about source than otherwise.

    Example: If the plaintiff uses the mark "Acme" for perfume, and the defendant uses the same mark for face powder, consumers may assume that both sets of goods come from the plaintiff, or that the defendant and plaintiff are related, because even though the products are different, there is a *logical relationship between them.* On the other hand, if the plaintiff uses the mark "Acme" on women's cosmetics and the defendant uses it on heavy earth-moving equipment, consumers are much less likely to associate the sources, due to the great disparity between the products.

c. **Similarity of purchasers:** Do the *same* customers shop for both plaintiff's and defendant's goods? If so, confusion is more likely than otherwise.

d. **Similarity of marketing channels:** Are the plaintiff's and defendant's goods or services likely to be *sold in the same or the same kind of stores?* If so, this increases the likelihood of confusion. If, on the other hand, the plaintiff only sells in high-priced boutiques, and the defendant only sells in drug stores and discount stores, there is less likelihood that the defendant's use of a similar mark will lead to consumer confusion.

e. **Sophistication of purchasers/cost of goods or services:** The assumption is that *the more sophisticated the potential purchasers and the more costly the goods or services in question, the more careful and discriminating the purchasers will be,* and the less likely it is that they will be misled or confused by similarities in the plaintiff's and defendant's marks.

f. **Evidence of actual confusion:** Evidence of actual confusion is *not necessary* to prove that the defendant's use causes a likelihood of confusion. If available, however, such evidence can be highly persuasive.

g. **Manner of presenting the mark:** Some authorities have suggested that the manner or immediate context in which the marks are presented to consumers—for example, if the marks are on a label, the rest of the label—should not be considered in determining whether the marks are confusingly similar. After all, some consumers may never have seen the whole label. Nonetheless, particularly in close cases, courts do sometimes consider whether the immediate *context in which the marks are presented* is similar. If so, this augments the likelihood of confusion.

Example: In determining that the mark "Drizzle" for women's coats did not infringe the plaintiff's "Drizzler" mark for men's wind breakers, the court in *McGregor-Doniger, Inc. v. Drizzle, Inc.*, 599 F.2d 1126 (2d Cir. 1979), considered the fact that the plaintiff usually presented its mark along with the company name "McGregor" in a distinctive scotch plaid, while the defendant usually presented its "Drizzle" mark by itself. This diminished the likelihood of confusion and supported the court's ultimate finding that the defendant had not infringed the plaintiff's mark.

h. **The strength of the plaintiff's mark:** The stronger the plaintiff's mark (that is, *the greater the mark's distinctiveness and the public's recognition of it* as an indication of the origin of goods or services), the more likely it is that consumers, seeing the defendant's allegedly similar mark, will be confused about the source of the defendant's goods, believing that they are associated with the plaintiff.

i. **Distinctiveness:** In evaluating a mark's strength, courts generally consider where it falls on the *Abercrombie & Fitch* distinctiveness scale. (See p. 230, *supra.*) If the mark is arbitrary or fanciful, they deem it very strong. If it is suggestive, it is only moderately strong. If the mark falls into the "descriptive" category, it is relatively weak. This reflects the view that the more distinctive the plaintiff's mark, the more likely consumers will confuse it with a similar one. It also reflects the *general public policy that, in the interest of free competition, we provide a smaller scope of rights in words or symbols that have a surname or descriptive meaning, or are common*, because such words and symbols may legitimately be needed by competitors in order to communicate with the public about their own goods or services.

   ii. **Secondary meaning:** Courts may also consider whether and to what extent the plaintiff's mark has secondary meaning. Even though secondary meaning is not necessary to claim rights in an inherently distinctive mark, consumers who are familiar with a mark are more likely to associate a defendant's similar mark with it, and thus be confused.

   i. **The defendant's good faith:** Especially when the parties' products or services are *not directly competitive,* courts may weigh the respective equities of each party's use. If the defendant acted in good faith in adopting its mark (was not intentionally copying in order to "cash in" on the plaintiff's business good will), and has expended significant amounts in promoting its mark, a court will be more hesitant to provide relief to the plaintiff than otherwise. On the other hand, *evidence that the defendant intended to confuse the public may be taken as circumstantial evidence (or in some jurisdictions create a* presumption) *that he succeeded,* and lead to a finding of infringement.

   j. **The plaintiff's interest in entering the market:** When the parties' products or services differ, a court may consider how likely the plaintiff is to begin selling the products or services the defendant is selling with a similar mark. Even if the plaintiff has no immediate plans to sell the same kind of goods or services through use of the mark, the court may still consider *the plaintiff's interest in reserving the option* to use the mark on such goods or services in the more distant future.

3. **The effect of a disclaimer:** A disclaimer by the defendant (for example, a statement on the label that the defendant *is not affiliated* with the plaintiff) will not avoid infringement liability in most cases. Courts tend to be skeptical of a disclaimer's effect, and will consider how likely it is that consumers who see or hear the defendant's otherwise confusingly similar mark will also be exposed to the disclaimer. Is a disclaimer on the label so conspicuous that consumers are bound to read it? Is it likely that an appreciable number of customers will not see the label at all prior to purchase?

4. **Post-sale confusion:** The traditional focus of trademark law has been the likelihood of purchaser *confusion at the point of sale*. More recently, however, courts have held that a *likelihood of post-sale confusion may suffice* to impose infringement liability. Even if immediate purchasers are not confused about the source of the goods they purchase, other persons who *receive the goods from the immediate purchaser,* or *see the goods in the purchaser's possession* after the sale may be confused about their source. This post-sale confusion may lead to an injury of the plaintiff's business good will.

   Example: The defendant sells inexpensive, cheaply constructed watches with the mark "Rolex." He *tells his purchasers* that these watches are not made by the plaintiff, who makes the expensive, prestigious Rolex watches, but are merely cheap copies. There is also a written disclaimer to that effect on the box. Nonetheless, persons receiving the watch as a gift, or seeing the purchaser wear the watch may think that it is a genuine Rolex watch. If the watch appears to be poorly made, the recipient or observer may think less of Rolex watches generally, and perhaps be less likely to consider buying the plaintiff's watches in the future. Moreover, if "Rolex" watches appear on the arms of numerous lower income purchasers, this may diminish the aura of exclusivity and prestige that the mark owner has carefully cultivated, and lead to lost customers.

5. **Initial interest (pre-sale) confusion:** A number of courts have also based a finding of infringement on evidence of *initial consumer confusion that is dissipated prior to the actual purchase.* A defendant's use of a mark that is confusingly similar to the plaintiff's marks may divert consumers who are seeking the plaintiff. Once they arrive at the defendant's door, it becomes evident to them that the defendant is an independent, unaffiliated entity. Thus, *if they remain to purchase goods or services from the defendant,* they are not confused about source at the point of sale. Nonetheless, the defendant's initial use of the plaintiff's mark gave the defendant the *opportunity to make its pitch to consumers seeking the plaintiff's goods, which it would not otherwise have had.* This may enable it to divert sales from the plaintiff, thus injuring the plaintiff's business good will.

   Example: The initial interest (or pre-sale) confusion doctrine has proven to be especially important in *Internet transactions.* For example, assume that two movie rental businesses, Moviebiz and Filmaholics, operate web sites on the Internet, at which customers can rent movies. Moviebiz registers "filmaholics.com" as the domain name for its web site. Customers seeking to find the web site of Filmaholics to rent a movie are likely to enter that company's mark, followed by ".com," or to select a site with that domain name from a list of search results. When they arrive at the web site, it becomes clear that they are at the Moviebiz web site, rather than the Filmaholics web site, but they go ahead and rent a movie from Moviebiz at that point because it is easier than continuing their search for Filmaholics. The initial interest consumer confusion caused by Moviebiz's use of Filmaholics' mark in its domain name may give rise to a cause of action for infringement. The injury to Filmaholics' business good will is similar to the injury in point-of-sale confusion cases because Moviebiz has *capitalized on the consumer good will that has attached to the Filmaholics mark and attracts consumers, and has diverted sales from Filmaholics.*

   a. **Initial interest confusion in metatagging cases:** Some courts have relied on an initial interest confusion theory to find infringement when a defendant inserted the plaintiff's mark into its hidden metatags, to get search engines to list his web site in the search results of persons entering the plaintiff's mark to search for the plaintiff. However, the defendant used a *domain name* that was *not* confusingly similar to the plaintiff's mark. *See, e.g., Brookfield Communications, Inc. v. West Coast Entertainment Corp.,* 174 F.3d 1036 (9th Cir. 1999). The courts reasoned that by inserting the plaintiff's mark into its metatags, the defendant *capitalized on the plaintiff's business good will* to get its own site listed on the search results page. If consumers decided to visit the defendant's site as a result of this, the defendant could get sales that it otherwise would not have gotten, and the *plaintiff could lose sales.* Thus, use of the mark in metatags gave the defendant a *chance to make its "pitch" to consumers that it otherwise would not have had.* The *Brookfield* line of cases has been criticized as going too far, however. While the *result* of the defendant's actions was similar to the *result* in cases in which the defendant uses the plaintiff's mark to cause initial interest confusion, there was never actually any point at which consumers were likely to be confused, because consumers never saw the metatag use, and the parties' domain names were different. Arguably the courts penalized the defendant, not for causing a likelihood of consumer confusion about source, but for offering consumers a conscious choice, which might cause the plaintiff to lose sales.

b. **Initial interest confusion in cases in which the parties are not commercial competitors:** Applying the initial interest confusion theory liberally in Internet domain name cases could greatly expand the scope of mark owners' rights. Consumers may be confused strictly because of the defendant's use of a domain name that is similar to the plaintiff's mark. Because consumers do not know *what* products or services the defendant offers prior to acting on their confusion and visiting the defendant's site, differences in products or services become irrelevant to the likelihood of confusion determination, potentially allowing the plaintiff to extend his rights to a much larger range of goods or services than he traditionally could. In such cases the defendant may be free-riding on the plaintiff's business good will by diverting consumers seeking the plaintiff to his own site, and he may thereby get an opportunity to "make his pitch" that he otherwise would not have had. While the plaintiff will not lose sales to the defendant, it may lose some sales due to the fact that consumers were distracted from their search for the plaintiff's site. However, several courts have expressed concern over the potential breadth of the initial interest confusion theory in such cases, and have either decided to factor product similarity into the likelihood of confusion determination (although consideration of product similarity is somewhat artificial under the circumstances), or have declined to apply the initial interest confusion theory altogether when the parties' goods are dissimilar.

E. **Reverse confusion:** Most trademark infringement cases involve a *subsequent user* of a mark that causes purchasers *to think that its goods or services come from the prior user.* However, sometimes the subsequent user is so big and famous that it *overshadows the prior user.* In such cases, the subsequent user's use of the mark may confuse consumers into *thinking that the prior user's goods come from the subsequent user.* This is known as "reverse confusion," and may also give rise to a trademark infringement claim on the part of the prior user against the subsequent user.

Example: The plaintiff, a small company that plans conventions for science fiction buffs, begins operating under the service mark "Dream Machine" in 1990. Defendant, a major motion picture producer, begins to operate a motion picture studio under the "Dreammachine" mark in 2000. The defendant's studio produces a series of block-buster movies, and the "Dreammachine" mark for motion picture entertainment services becomes very well known to the general consuming public. At that point it becomes likely that potential patrons of the plaintiff's convention-planning services will believe that the plaintiff is, or is affiliated with, the defendant. Plaintiff should be able to recover for trademark infringement under a reverse confusion argument. Consumers' mistaken belief that the parties are the same or affiliated entities *causes plaintiff to lose control over its reputation. Consumers may hold plaintiff responsible for whatever complaints they have against the defendant.*

F. **Trademark parodies:** Trademark law only provides relief upon a showing that the defendant's use of his mark is likely to cause consumer confusion about the source, sponsorship, or affiliation of goods or services. It thus may not always provide relief against a defendant's *deliberate parody* of the plaintiff's mark. Parody, by its nature, does not seek to confuse consumers about source. If the parody is to be successful, consumers must be aware of the differences in the marks so that they can appreciate the humor of the defendant's parody. In some cases, however, where the parody was particularly vicious and harmful to the plaintiff, courts have stretched to find a likelihood of consumer confusion so that the defendant's use could be enjoined.

Example: In *Jordache Enterprises, Inc. v. Hogg Wyld, Ltd.*, 828 F.2d 1482 (10th Cir. 1987), the plaintiff, owner of the "Jordache" mark for women's designer jeans, claimed that the defendant's use of the mark "Lardashe" for its size extra-large women's jeans constituted trademark infringement. The U.S. Court of Appeals for the Tenth Circuit upheld a verdict for the defendant, finding that, as presented to the public, the defendant's mark would not cause a likelihood of confusion about source—consumers were unlikely to think that the defendant's jeans came from or were sponsored by or affiliated with the plaintiff.

Example: By contrast, in *Coca-Cola Co. v. Gemini Rising, Inc.*, 346 F. Supp. 1183 (E.D.N.Y. 1972), the court found that a parody of the plaintiff's mark constituted trademark infringement. The Coca-Cola Company customarily used a red sign with white script saying "Enjoy Coca-Cola." The defendant produced a sign that was highly similar but said "Enjoy Cocaine." In finding trademark infringement the court found, somewhat remarkably, that "some persons of apparently average intelligence did attribute sponsorship to plaintiff and discontinued their use of Coca-Cola as an expression of resentment."

1. **First Amendment considerations:** Defendants in trademark parody cases often raise a First Amendment defense to the plaintiff's attempt to hold them liable for their parody. This defense seldom prevails in the context of the typical infringement claim, such as the *Jordache* case, in which the defendant's parodying mark was used on product labels to sell goods and identify their source. This form of trademark use is *commercial speech,* which, under First Amendment law, is entitled to a lower level of protection than other forms of speech. When the parody takes place in *non-commercial speech,* such as a newspaper editorial, magazine article, or book or motion picture title, courts must give the First Amendment defense greater weight, balancing the competing trademark and First Amendment interests and construing the trademark laws narrowly to avoid interference with First Amendment freedoms. (Such balancing must be done whenever a plaintiff claims that use of a mark in non-commercial speech constitutes infringement.) For a definition of commercial speech, see pp. 270, 273, *infra*.

G. **Collateral use of marks:** Trademark law does not give mark owners absolute control over others' use of the words or symbols constituting their marks. As long as another person's use of a plaintiff's mark causes no likelihood of consumer confusion, that person will not be liable for trademark infringement. There are several *particular settings in which a defendant's unauthorized use of a mark may be found non-infringing,* which are discussed below.

1. **Resale of goods lawfully bearing a mark:** The trademark doctrine of exhaustion (sometimes called the doctrine of first sale) provides that once a mark owner sells or authorizes goods to be sold bearing its mark, it has no authority to prevent subsequent owners from *reselling* those goods with the mark. However, subsequent owners' use of the mark in the resale must be truthful, and must not lead to a *likelihood of consumer confusion about the immediate source* of the goods (for example, if the immediate seller has *changed* the goods), or *mislead consumers about the nature of the goods* (for example, *mislead* consumers into thinking that the goods are new when they are used, or that they are in their original state when they have been materially changed).

Example: In *Champion Spark Plug Co. v. Sanders*, 331 U.S. 125 (1947), the defendant brought used Champion spark plugs, reconditioned them, and placed them on the market, still bearing the original Champion mark. The Supreme Court refused to enjoin defendant's use of the Champion mark to identify the original source of the reconditioned plugs, but held that the defendant must make it clear to purchasers that its Champion plugs were reconditioned, not new, and that the defendant, not plaintiff, was the immediate source of the reconditioned plugs. The Court noted that there may be some cases in which the goods being resold are so far changed from their original state that *any* use of the original seller's mark would be misleading to consumers. However, this was not such a case.

2. **Gray market goods:** Gray market goods (also known as "parallel imports") are goods that are manufactured abroad for sale in foreign markets, that the foreign manufacturer properly, legally marks with a trademark that is registered in the United States. After these goods are released into foreign markets, parties buy them and import them into the United States for resale in competition with the U.S. mark registrant. As a general matter, the import and sale of gray market goods *will not constitute infringement of the U.S. registrant's trademark if the imported goods are the same as those sold by the U.S. registrant and the U.S. registrant and the foreign manufacturer are the same or related entities.* This rule is consistent with the doctrine of exhaustion, discussed above, and is essentially the same under both Lanham Act §§32 (a)(1) and 42 (15 U.S.C. §§1114(a)(1) and 1124), and Tariff Act §526 (19 U.S.C. §1526).

   a. **The U.S. registrant and foreign manufacturer must be the same or related entities:** As long as the U.S. mark registrant and the foreign manufacturer are the same entity or related entities, such as brother-sister corporations or parent and subsidiary corporations, the gray market goods will not infringe the U.S. mark, as long as the gray market goods do not differ materially from the goods sold by the U.S. registrant under the same mark.

   Example: X Corp., a Japanese company, manufactures cameras, which it marks with its "x-cellent" trademark. It sells the cameras bearing this mark in numerous nations. X Corp. organizes a wholly-owned subsidiary in the United States under Delaware law and designates the subsidiary to be the exclusive distributor of its cameras in the United States. It then transfers all its rights in its "x-cellent" mark in the United States to the subsidiary, which registers the mark on the Lanham Act Principal Register. Y, a third party, buys "x-cellent" cameras manufactured and marked by the X Corp. in Korea, imports them into the United States, and sells them in competition with the manufacturer's subsidiary. Because the subsidiary (which owns the U.S. rights in the mark) is related to X Corp. (the foreign manufacturer of the gray market goods), there is no infringement.

   Example: Instead of setting up a subsidiary, X Corp. enters into an arms-length transaction in which it authorizes Z Corp., an independent U.S. corporation, to serve as the exclusive distributor of X Corp. cameras in the United States. As part of the transaction, X Corp. assigns all its rights in the "x-cellent" mark in the United States to Z Corp., which then registers the mark. Third parties buy X Corp.'s cameras in Korea and import them to the United States. Z Corp., the U.S. registrant of the "x-cellent" mark, has a good cause of action for trademark infringement against the third parties who imported the Korean cameras bearing the "x-cellent" mark. *Z Corp. is not related to X Corp.,* the foreign manufacturer.

   b. **The imported goods must not be materially different from those sold by the U.S. registrant:** If the gray market product is a *different grade or quality* than the product sold under the mark by the U.S. registrant, *has different ingredients, carries a different warranty, or materially differs in some other way,* then infringement is likely to be found *even though* the U.S. registrant and the foreign manufacturer are related. Sale of such imported products in the United States is *likely to lead to consumer confusion,* since consumers will not be able to rely on the imported product's mark to indicate that the quality and characteristics of the imported product are consistent with other goods on the market that bear the same mark. A difference is "material" if it would influence consumers' purchase decision.

Example: Lever Brothers Co. owns the U.S. registration of the mark "Shield" for soap, which it sells under that mark in the United States. An affiliated company in the United Kingdom uses the same mark for its soap, but uses a different formulation for its product than Lever Brothers does, to accommodate differing tastes and conditions in the United Kingdom. (Due to the preference for showers in the United States, the U.S. Shield soap contains a higher concentration of coconut soap and fatty acids to generate lather quickly. Since the British prefer baths, which permit more time for lather to develop, the U.K. Shield has less of those ingredients.) A third party buys a large quantity of the U.K. Shield soap and imports it into the United States for resale. Even though Lever Brothers is affiliated with the producer of the U.K. product, it will have a cause of action for trademark infringement against the gray marketeer because the gray market good differs materially from the good Lever Brothers, the U.S. registrant, sells under the mark. *Note that if the sale is permitted, consumers will be misled by the similar mark on the U.K. product: They will rely on the similar mark to indicate that this product has the same qualities and characteristics as the Shield product they have purchased in the past, and they will be disappointed.*

3. **Competitors' use of marks for comparison purposes:** A mark owner's competitors may use its mark in the course of selling their own goods and services—for example, to inform consumers that their goods are comparable—as long as their use is truthful and does not create a likelihood of consumer confusion about the *source* of their goods or services.

Example: In *Smith v. Chanel, Inc.*, 402 F.2d 562 (9th Cir. 1968), the defendant manufactured a duplicate of the Chanel No. 5 fragrance, which it called "Second Chance," and offered for sale at a fraction of the price of Chanel No. 5. In advertising, the defendant gave its full name and address and stated that its perfumes duplicated the world's finest and most expensive perfumes. The ad also stated: "We dare you to try to detect any difference between Chanel #5 ($25.00) and Ta'Ron's 2nd Chance. $7.00." The Ninth Circuit denied Chanel's attempt to enjoin the defendant's use of its mark. It reasoned that one who copies an unpatented product sold under a trademark should be able to use the trademark in his advertising to identify the product he has copied, as long as the advertising does not contain misrepresentations or create a reasonable likelihood that purchasers will be confused as to the source, identity, or sponsorship of the advertiser's product. The concern that the defendant was getting a "free ride" on the plaintiff's good will was outweighed by the public's interest in free competition.

H. **Trademark counterfeiting:** Trademark counterfeiting is a particularly egregious form of trademark infringement. It entails intentional, knowing use of a spurious mark that is identical to (or substantially indistinguishable from) a registered mark, on the same kind of goods or services for which the mark is registered. To deter counterfeiting, Congress has enacted special remedies, including attorney fees, treble damages, statutory damages, ex parte orders to seize goods bearing counterfeit marks, and criminal sanctions against persons who intentionally traffic or attempt to traffic in goods through use of marks they know to be counterfeit. See pp. 284-285, *infra*.

I. **Contributory infringement:** A person may be held liable for another's trademark infringement if he assisted in the infringement.

1. **Inducing infringement:** A defendant may be liable for contributory infringement if he intentionally suggests, directly or by implication, that the other person infringe the plaintiff's trademark, and the other does so infringe.

Example: The defendant manufactures goods that are identical to the plaintiff's goods and sells them in bulk to retailers. The defendant suggests to its retailers that they can sell its goods as plaintiff's goods to those customers who ask for the plaintiff's goods by name. If some of the retailers do this, it will constitute trademark infringement and the defendant, by inducing the infringement, will be contributorily liable.

2. **Knowingly aiding infringement:** A defendant may be liable for contributory infringement if he or she sells goods to another, knowing or having reason to know that the buyer will use the goods in a direct infringement of the plaintiff's trademark.

   a. **Assisting in ways other than supplying products:** In *Inwood Laboratories, Inc. v. Ives Laboratories, Inc.* 456 U.S. 844 (1982), the Supreme Court defined contributory infringement as occurring when "a manufacturer or distributor intentionally induces another to infringe a trademark, or . . . continues to supply its product to one whom it knows or has reason to know is engaging in trademark infringement." However, the Court of Appeals for the Seventh Circuit has held that supplying products is not the only way that a person who permits or assists infringement may be held contributorially liable for the infringement. *Hard Rock Café Licensing Corp. v. Concession Services, Inc.*, 955 F.2d 1143 (7th Cir. 1992). In *Hard Rock*, the court found that the operator and promoter of a flea market at which a booth operator sold infringing tee-shirts could be liable for the booth operator's infringement *if it knew or had reason to know* of the booth operator's infringement. However, he had *no duty to seek out infringement or to take precautions against it.*

3. **Vicarious liability:** In *Hard Rock*, the Seventh Circuit noted that a defendant may bear vicarious liability for trademark infringement if the defendant and the infringer have an apparent or actual partnership, have authority to bind one another in transactions with third parties, or exercise joint ownership or control over the infringing product. (Employers may also be vicariously liable for their employees' infringement, if it is done within the scope of their employment.) However, the Seventh Circuit found that it would be inappropriate to adopt the much broader theory of vicarious liability that courts have applied in the copyright infringement context. (See pp. 158, *supra*). The *Hard Rock* court explained that secondary liability for trademark infringement should be more narrowly drawn than secondary liability for copyright infringement, because the trademark interest is not as strong as the copyright interest. The trademark interest is more like a tort interest than a property interest.

XI. TRADEMARK DILUTION

A. **The state dilution cause of action:** Unlike the trademark infringement cause of action, the dilution cause of action arose through state statutory provisions, rather than through the common law. Approximately half of the states have enacted dilution statutes, providing rights in distinctive, famous marks and trade names that go well beyond the rights provided under traditional trademark infringement and unfair competition doctrine. The state dilution statutes essentially recognize two forms of actionable dilution: (1) diminution or "blurring" of the uniqueness of the plaintiff's famous mark or trade name; and (2) "tarnishment" of the plaintiff's famous mark or trade name.

   1. **"Blurring" the uniqueness of the plaintiff's famous mark or trade name:** The quintessential claim for dilution arises when the plaintiff has a very strong, famous mark, that the public

closely associates with the plaintiff as a business or as a source of a particular good or service. The defendant uses the same or a highly similar mark on *dissimilar goods or services.* While this does not cause a likelihood of consumer confusion about the source or affiliation of the parties' goods or services (the defendant's goods or services are so dissimilar to the plaintiff's that the public is unlikely to think that they all come from the same source), the defendant's use *whittles away or dilutes the strong, immediate association consumers have between the mark and the plaintiff.* Because this strong, immediate consumer association has considerable commercial value, dilution law recognizes a property right in it, and a right to protect it against diminution. The plaintiff may enjoin the defendant's commercial use of the mark or trade name, even though its use involves no likely deception of consumers. The injury redressed is the *diminution of the uniqueness and commercial effectiveness* of the plaintiff's mark or trade name. Because this theory of trademark protection represents a radical departure from the traditional law of passing off, is of questionable benefit to consumers, and may have anticompetitive effects, courts have tended to restrict diminution relief to very strong, famous marks and trade names.

Example: The plaintiff, Tiffany's Jewelry, has a strong mark for jewelry. The public, upon hearing the name "Tiffany's," immediately thinks of the plaintiff and its prestigious jewelry. The defendant opens Tiffany's Laundromat or sells Tiffany's bobby socks. While this is unlikely to cause the public to think that the defendant's business, products, or services come from or are affiliated with the plaintiff, continued exposure to these alternative uses of the Tiffany's mark will erode the public's strong, immediate association of the Tiffany's mark with the plaintiff. Thus, the plaintiff may enjoin the defendant's use.

2. **Tarnishment:** The "tarnishment" branch of dilution provides relief when the defendant's use of a similar mark or trade name casts the plaintiff's distinctive, famous mark or trade name in a bad light and thus "tarnishes" the luster of the plaintiff's commercial image or reputation. This may occur when the defendant uses the mark or trade name in a *context that is unwholesome, or at least out of keeping with the plaintiff's high-quality image.* Again, it is unnecessary to show that the defendant's use of the mark leads to a likelihood of consumer confusion about the source or affiliation of the parties' goods, services, or business.

   a. **Use in an unwholesome context:** Examples of use of the plaintiff's mark in an unwholesome context include: (1) use of the Dallas Cowboys Cheerleaders uniform (a form of service mark or trade dress) in a pornographic movie; and (2) display of a red sign that says "Enjoy Cocaine" in white script, looking very much like the Coca-Cola Company's well-known red and white "Enjoy Coca-Cola" sign.

   b. **Use in a context that is out of keeping with the plaintiff's high-quality image:** An example of this second type of tarnishing use can be found in *Steinway & Sons v. Demars & Friends*, 210 U.S.P.Q. 954 (C.D. Cal. 1981), in which the defendant used the mark "Steinway," for clip-on handles for beer cans. Plaintiff, the owner of the prestigious Steinway mark for pianos, was able to obtain relief on the argument that the defendant's use caused consumers to associate the plaintiff's mark with a product that was incompatible with the quality and prestige attached to the plaintiff's mark. (Of course, to demonstrate injury in such cases, the plaintiff will have to demonstrate that the public is likely to *associate* the defendant's product with the plaintiff's, upon encountering the defendant's mark, even though that association does not lead to a likelihood of confusion about the source, sponsorship, or affiliation of the goods.)

3. **The fame requirement:** The dilution causes of action protect the "commercial magnetism," or "selling power" of a mark, which its owner has developed through extensive advertising and promotion. Thus, dilution protection is only available for *famous* marks that are able to evoke in consumers' minds an automatic association with the mark owner and all the favorable imagery the owner has created through extensive exposure and persuasive advertising. While all jurisdictions require a showing that the plaintiff's mark is "famous," however, jurisdictions have differed over the *scope* of the necessary fame. While some jurisdictions require that the mark be nationally famous with the general public, others have found a right to dilution relief upon a showing of "local" fame, in a very limited geographic area, or "niche" fame among a limited subset of the public.

   Example: In *Wedgwood Homes, Inc. v. Lund*, 294 Or. 493 (Or. 1983), the Supreme Court of Oregon held that a homebuilder that had operated with and extensively advertised its mark in part of Washington County, Oregon, was entitled to dilution relief against the builder of retirement residences, who used a similar mark in the same portion of Washington County. The court rejected arguments that dilution relief should be limited to nationally famous marks: "We see no reason why marks of national renown should enjoy protection while local marks should not. A small local firm may expend efforts and money proportionately as great as those of a large firm in order to establish its mark's distinctive quality. In both situations the interest to be protected and the damage to be prevented are the same."

   Example: In *Mead Data Central, Inc. v. Toyota Motor Sales, U.S.A., Inc.*, 875 F.2d 1026 (2d Cir., 1989), the Second Circuit, applying New York law, rejected the plaintiff's claim that the "Lexus" mark for cars diluted its "Lexis" mark for computerized legal research services. While the "Lexis" mark was famous with lawyers, law students and accountants, these persons constituted only about 1 percent of the total U.S. population. This "niche" fame was insufficient: "For the general public, LEXIS has no distinctive quality that LEXUS will dilute." (The court also found that "Lexus" and "Lexis" were not sufficiently similar to support a finding of dilution.)

4. **First Amendment limitations:** In *L.L. Bean v. Drake Publishers*, 811 F.2d 26 (1st Cir.), *cert. denied*, 483 U.S. 1013 (1987), the U.S. Court of Appeals for the First Circuit held that First Amendment considerations generally limit the state dilution cause of action to cases in which the defendant has used the plaintiff's mark or trade name in commercial speech. The court defined commercial speech as *speech that is related solely to the economic interests of the defendant and its audience.* Thus, the court appeared to confine the dilution cause of action to cases in which the defendant used the similar mark or trade name in the course of selling or advertising goods or services.

   a. **Policy justifications:** Giving mark owners a cause of action to prevent uses of their marks or trade names in newspaper editorials criticizing them by name, or in magazine articles parodying their mark, would interfere considerably with the First Amendment interests in free speech and press. In contrast, providing dilution relief in cases involving strictly *commercial speech* may be acceptable because commercial speech traditionally has been deemed more robust than other kinds of speech, and less likely to be chilled by government regulation. Commercial speech thus receives less protection than other forms of speech. Moreover, since the purpose of unfair competition law is to regulate unfair *marketplace* conduct, there is relatively little justification for applying an unfair competition doctrine to regulate speech outside of the *marketplace* context.

Example: Defendant opens the "Star Wars Hotdog Stand." The owner of the "Star Wars" mark for entertainment services and related toys and promotional items sues to enjoin this use in a dilution cause of action. Since the defendant is using the mark in commercial speech to sell food services, the First Amendment probably is not offended. On the other hand, if a newspaper published an article discussing the Strategic Defense Initiative, and referred to it as "Star Wars," this would not constitute commercial speech and probably would be immune to dilution attack under the First Amendment. Even though use of the term "Star Wars" in connection with the Strategic Defense Initiative may dilute the value of the mark for motion picture entertainment, prohibiting its use would interfere considerably with highly protected political speech.

Note: Although not all courts would agree that state dilution actions are strictly limited to commercial speech, their hesitance to extend such actions, in many instances, to fully protected non-commercial speech contexts limits the usefulness of the dilution cause of action as a means of preventing a mark from becoming generic. For example, the Xerox Company has long feared that rampant public use of its valuable mark, "Xerox," as a common noun for photocopy machines (as well as a noun for photocopies and a verb for the act of photocopying), may ultimately lead to a finding that the mark has become generic. The Xerox Company routinely writes letters to the editor and publishes advertisements requesting that the media and the public not use its mark generically. In such contexts the First Amendment would probably prevent the Xerox Co. from bringing a dilution suit to stop the use of its mark in these contexts.

B. The Lanham Act §43(c) cause of action for dilution: There was considerable lobbying for a *federal* dilution cause of action, which eventually led Congress to enact the Federal Trademark Dilution Act of 1995, which created a new Lanham Act §43(c), 15 U.S.C. §1125(c). The new §43(c) dilution provisions were controversial, however, and during the next decade the circuit courts of appeals differed considerably over their proper construction. Ultimately, the Supreme Court, in *Moseley v. V Secret Catalogue, Inc.*, 537 U.S. 418 (2003), construed the §43(c) dilution cause of action so narrowly that its supporters returned to Congress to seek to recover the ground they had lost in the courts. In response, Congress enacted the Trademark Dilution Revision Act of 2006, which effectively overruled the Supreme Court's holding in *Mosley*, and undertook to clarify some of the issues over which the circuit courts had differed.

The newly amended §43(c) enables the owner of a "*famous*" mark that is *distinctive* (either inherently or through acquisition of secondary meaning) to enjoin a defendant's "*use in commerce*" of a mark or trade name that is *likely to cause dilution by blurring or tarnishment*, if the defendant first used its diluting mark in commerce *after* the plaintiff's mark became famous. Relief is available regardless of the presence or absence of actual or likely confusion, competition between the parties, or any actual economic injury. However, *relief is limited to an injunction* unless the plaintiff can demonstrate that the defendant first used its diluting mark in commerce after the Trademark Dilution Revision Act of 2006 was enacted, and that the defendant's acts were willful. While there is little case law construing the revised §43(c) at this point, the following subsections will discuss the key provisions.

    1. Famous marks: As was true in the past, the federal dilution cause of action is only available for "famous" marks. The legislative history stresses that the dilution cause of action is meant to be applied "sparingly," as an "extraordinary remedy" available only for marks of "significant" fame. Newly amended §43(c)(2)(A) provides that a mark is "famous" "*if it is* *widely recognized by the general consuming public of the United States as a designation of source of the goods or services of the mark's owner."* Thus, the new statutory language makes it clear that the federal dilution cause of action *will not be available for "locally famous" marks*, like that in the *Wedgwood* case, *or for "niche famous" marks*, like that in the *Mead Data* case. Subsection (2)(A) goes on to provide that courts should consider "all relevant factors" in determining whether a mark has the requisite fame, including the following: 1) the duration, extent, and geographic reach of advertising and publicity of the mark: 2) the amount, volume, and geographic extent of sales of goods or services offered under the mark; 3) the extent of actual recognition of the mark; and 4) whether the mark is registered.

    a. **Distinctiveness:** While some of the circuits formerly held that federal dilution relief was only available for famous marks that were *inherently distinctive*, the revised §43(c) statutory language clearly rejects this limitation, specifying that the famous mark must be *"distinctive, inherently or through acquired distinctiveness."*

2. **Dilution by blurring:** Section 43(c)(2)(B) provides that dilution by blurring is the "association arising from the similarity between a mark or trade name and a famous mark that impairs the distinctiveness of the famous mark." Subsection (2)(B) provides that courts should consider *all relevant factors* in evaluating whether a defendant's mark or trade name blurs the plaintiff's mark, including: 1) the degree of similarity between the mark or trade name and the famous mark; 2) the degree of inherent or acquired distinctiveness of the famous mark; 3) the extent to which the owner of the famous mark is engaging in substantially exclusive use of the mark; 4) the degree of recognition of the famous mark; 5) whether the user of the mark or trade name intended to create an association with the famous mark; and 6) any actual association between the mark or trade name and the famous mark.

3. **Dilution by tarnishment:** Section 43(c)(2)(C) provides that dilution by tarnishment is "association arising from the similarity between a mark or trade name and a famous mark that harms the reputation of the famous mark."

4. **Exclusions:** When Congress enacted the §43(c) dilution provisions, both in 1995 and 2006, it was concerned about the harmful effect the cause of action could have on competition and on exercise of First Amendment freedoms. Thus, it *enacted several express exclusions from dilution liability*.

    a. **Fair use exclusion:** As revised, Lanham Act §43(c)(3)(A) excludes from the dilution cause of action *"any fair use"* of a famous mark, *"other than as a designation of source for [the user's] own goods or services."* Subsection (3) goes on to provide that the following uses are *"included"* in the exclusion: 1) nominative fair use (see pp. 276-277, *infra*); 2) descriptive fair use (see pp. 275-276, *infra*); 3) use of a mark in comparative advertising; and 4) use of a mark in identifying, parodying, criticizing, or commenting about the mark owner or its goods or services. The broad language of this provision suggests that the federal dilution cause of action should *only apply* against defendants *who use the plaintiff's famous mark "as a trademark," to designate the source of their own goods or services*. Uses for other purposes should not lead to liability. The exclusion also extends to persons who *facilitate* fair uses of famous marks.

    b. **Newspaper reporting and news commentary:** Section 43(c)(3)(B) also excludes all forms of news reporting and news commentary.

c. **"Noncommercial" use of a mark:** Like the original Federal Trademark Dilution Act of 1995, the revised §43(c) expressly provides that the dilution cause of action *will not apply to "any noncommercial use" of a famous mark.* Courts that have construed this provision have routinely found that it *confines the federal dilution cause of action to uses of marks in commercial speech,* as that concept has been defined in the Supreme Court's First Amendment jurisprudence. The Supreme Court has defined core "commercial speech" as *"speech that does no more than propose a commercial transaction." Bolger v. Youngs Drug Products Corp.,* 463 U.S. 60, 66 (1983). As noted *supra,* commercial speech is subject to less First Amendment protection than other forms of speech, and thus is more amenable to Lanham Act regulation. Mixed messages, that simultaneously propose a commercial transaction *and* address social, political or other issues of interest, may be deemed "commercial speech" in some instances. The Supreme Court considers three factors in determining whether mixed speech should be deemed commercial speech or fully protected speech: 1) whether it is an advertisement; 2) whether it refers to a specific product or service; and 3) whether the speaker has an economic motivation for the speech. However, the decisions have stressed that if the primary purpose of the speech is informational, as opposed to "commercial," full First Amendment protection applies.

   i. **Dilution claims confined to "core" commercial speech:** In *Mattel v. MCA Records,* 296 F.3d 894 (9th Cir. 2002), the Ninth Circuit held that the federal dilution cause of action is only available when the defendant's use of the famous mark constitutes "core" commercial speech—speech that does no more than propose a commercial transaction. It is not clear whether other jurisdictions will confine dilution claims to core commercial speech, or if they will apply dilution in cases where the defendant's speech was "mixed speech" that is deemed commercial under the three factors listed above.

   Example: In *Mattel,* the plaintiff claimed that the defendant music group's inclusion of its "Barbie" mark in the title of a song diluted the mark. The Ninth Circuit agreed that the defendant's use diluted the "Barbie" mark, but rejected the dilution claim. The court found that song titles are not purely commercial in nature, because they play a dual role—selling the song *and* communicating a message about what the song is about. Thus, use of a mark in a song title constitutes a "noncommercial use" of the mark for purposes of Lanham Act §43(c), and is outside the reach of the federal dilution cause of action.

5. **Registration preempts state dilution claims:** Congress did not intend to preempt state dilution claims in all cases. However, like the original §43(c), the revised §43(c) provides that federal *registration is a complete bar* to dilution claims brought pursuant to state statute or common law. This ability to avoid state dilution claims provides another incentive for trademark owners to register their marks on the Principal Register, since state dilution causes of action may be broader or more liberal than the federal dilution cause of action.

6. **Dilution claims and trade dress:** Section 43(c) provides dilution relief for all famous marks, including marks consisting of trade dress. However, some courts have expressed concern that dilution protection for product features may effectively provide patent-like protection for products without applying the high standards of patent law and without the limited duration of a patent. This could effectively undermine the patent laws and interfere with competition to the

detriment of consumers. In addition, the First Circuit has suggested that application of the dilution laws to permanently enjoin competitors from using product features may be unconstitutional. The Constitution's Patents and Copyrights Clause only permits Congress to grant rights to inventors for *limited times*. Arguably, in enacting the dilution provisions, Congress used its Commerce Clause power (which is the basis for its regulation of trademarks and trade dress) to trump the "limited times" restriction of the Patent Clause. However, the First Circuit found it unnecessary to make a finding on this issue, since the plaintiff in that case had not satisfied the fame and dilution standards. *I.P. Lund Trading ApS v. Kohler Co.*, 163 F.3d 27 (1st Cir. 1998). In the Trademark Dilution Revision Act of 2006, Congress provided that "[n]othing in this subsection shall be construed to impair, modify, or supersede the applicability of the patent laws of the United States." 15 U.S.C. §1225(c)(7).

    a. Burden of proof in cases of unregistered trade dress: As revised, §43(c)(4) provides that when unregistered trade dress is claimed to be diluted, the plaintiff bears the burden of proving that the trade dress is nonfunctional. Moreover, if the trade dress incorporates marks that are registered, the claimant must prove that the *unregistered portion of the trade dress, taken as a whole, is famous* separate and apart from any fame of the registered marks.

7. Federal dilution claims in the Internet context: Trademark owners made extensive use of the original §43(c) dilution provisions to enjoin unauthorized uses of their marks in domain names. As will be explained below, it is not yet clear whether this will continue under the 2006 revisions.

    a. Cybersquatting: When cybersquatters registered famous marks, followed by ".com" or another top level generic domain, and then tried to sell the domain name registrations to the trademark owners, the owners argued that this action constituted actionable "use in commerce" of the famous mark (because the defendant cybersquatter was undertaking to *sell* the registration and intended to "*trade on the value of the mark as a mark*"). (See p. 256, *supra.*) They argued that this diluted the famous mark's capacity to identify and distinguish the mark owner's goods and services on the Internet, because (since there can only be one registration of "mark.com,") the defendant's registration of the domain name *prevented the mark owner from using "mark.com" as its own domain name*. A line of decisions accepted this reasoning and enjoined the cybersquatters on federal dilution grounds. *See, e.g., Panavision International v. Toeppen*, 141 F.3d 1316 (9th Cir. 1998). In *Panavision*, the Ninth Circuit relied on the original Dilution Act's broad definition of "dilution" in Lanham Act §45 (defining dilution as "the lessening of the capacity of a famous mark to identify and distinguish goods or services"). The court explained that while cybersquatters did not fall within the traditional definitions of blurring or tarnishment, they fell within the Lanham Act's dilution definition, which was broader. It is not clear whether such claims can still be brought under the 2006 revisions, since the revisions limit the dilution cause of action to blurring and tarnishment. One could also argue that cybersquatting use of marks is not actionable under §43(c) when cybersquatters do not use the domain names to indicate the source of their own goods or services (as is often the case).

    b. Forum site domain names: Trademark owners also used dilution claims to prevent persons operating "gripe sites" and other non-commercial "forum sites" from using a domain name that incorporated their marks. As in the cybersquatter cases, the mark owners argued that such use diluted their marks: (1) by making the domain names unavailable to them;

(2) by frustrating consumers and leading them to abandon their search for the plaintiff; and (3) by offering consumers a range of different web sites under the same name, thus diminishing consumers' automatic association of the mark with the owner. However, the decisions finding dilution under such circumstances are subject to question. Use of a mark as the domain name for a forum site (that does not sell or advertise goods or services) should be deemed "noncommercial speech," and thus outside the reach of §43(c) claims. (See p. 273, *supra*.) While defendants raised the §43(c) noncommercial use exclusion under the original 1995 dilution provisions, a number of courts rejected the argument, finding that the defendant's domain name use was "commercial." However, in so ruling, these courts mistakenly confused "commercial use," or "use in commerce" (which is required in order to make a case of infringement or dilution against a defendant) with "commercial speech," as defined by First Amendment jurisprudence. In addition to retaining the "noncommercial use" exclusion, the 2006 revisions also prohibit a cause of action against defendants who make a fair use of marks for purposes of criticism, commentary or parody. (See p. 272, *supra*.). Thus, there are now two reasons for courts to reject dilution claims in the "forum site" context.

XII. DEFENSES TO INFRINGEMENT AND DILUTION CLAIMS

A. **The fair use defense:** While marks that describe a product or service describe a product or service's geographical origin, or constitute a surname may be protected, their owners' rights are limited. It must always be remembered that such marks have *two meanings*: their trademark meaning and their independent descriptive or surname meaning. Trademark law only gives rights in the trademark meaning. Owners of such marks may prohibit others from using them as a trademark if the use causes a likelihood of confusion or dilutes. They may not, however, assert rights in the descriptive or surname meaning of their mark. *A defendant is free to use the mark in its strictly descriptive capacity, to describe her own product or its geographical origin, or to identify its producer.* This is known as a "fair use," or "descriptive fair use." To determine whether a use is a fair use or an infringing use, courts will consider several factors.

1. **The manner in which the defendant uses the mark:** Courts will attempt to ascertain whether the defendant's use is strictly to describe the product or service. Circumstantial evidence of the purpose of the use can be found in the size, placement, or other physical characteristics of the use. Is the word or symbol prominently featured, as a trademark would be, or is it secondary to other words or features that clearly are meant to serve as the indication of origin of the defendant's product or service?

    Example: Plaintiff has trademark rights in the word "crunchy," which she uses to identify and distinguish the cookies she sells. She features the word prominently in large red block letters on each bag of cookies. The defendant sells cookies in a bag that features the word "delecto" in large gold letters. In somewhat smaller green script underneath, the words "They're quite crunchy!" appear. The defendant's use of the word "crunchy" in this context suggests that the use is descriptive and a fair use.

2. **Is the defendant using the mark in good faith?** Courts will look for any evidence that the defendant is intentionally using the word or symbol to try to "cash in" on the plaintiff's business good will. They will find a fair use only if it appears that the defendant is justifiably, in

good faith, using the word or symbol strictly to describe his goods or services or their producer, and not to confuse consumers.

3. **Is the defendant's use likely to confuse?** If the factors listed above indicate a fair use, the court will tolerate a greater chance of consumer confusion than it otherwise would. However, if the defendant's use is such that it is *highly likely to confuse numerous consumers about the source of his goods or services*, a court may consider this as evidence against the defendant's claimed purpose merely to describe. *See K.P. Permanent Make-Up, Inc. v. Lasting Impression I, Inc.,* 543 U.S. 111 (2004).

B. **Nominative fair use:** The Court of Appeals for the Ninth Circuit has developed a doctrine of "nominative fair use," which is to be applied when a defendant has used the plaintiff's mark to *describe or refer to the plaintiff's product*. The nominative fair use analysis acknowledges and accommodates others' interest in referring to a particular product by its identifying mark for purposes of comparison, criticism, parody, or the like. It permits unauthorized use of the plaintiff's mark *to identify or describe the plaintiff's product* as long as the use does not attempt to capitalize on consumer confusion. The Ninth Circuit has applied this doctrine in both infringement and dilution cases.

1. **Three factors:** The Ninth Circuit has identified three factors to be considered in determining whether a defendant is entitled to a finding of nominative fair use:

   - The plaintiff's product must not be readily identifiable without use of the plaintiff's mark (so that it is necessary to use the mark to identify the product);

   - The defendant may only use so much of the plaintiff's mark as is reasonably necessary to identify the product (for example, a soft drink competitor would be entitled to compare its product to "Coca-Cola" or "Coke," but would not be entitled to use Coca-Cola's distinctive lettering, as well); and

   - The defendant must do nothing that would, in conjunction with use of the mark, suggest sponsorship or endorsement of its product by the trademark owner.

   The court has explained that when a defendant raises a nominative fair use defense, this three-factor test should be applied instead of the regular multi-factor test for likelihood of confusion, because it better addresses concerns regarding the likelihood of confusion in nominative use situations.

   Example: The defendant newspapers used the service mark/name of the musical group "New Kids on the Block" in conducting opinion surveys concerning the group. The newspapers asked fans to call a "900" telephone number and state their opinion about which New Kid is the sexiest, which is their favorite, etc. The callers had to pay for the call. The newspapers planned to publish the results of the survey. The New Kids themselves provided for-profit 900 number telephone services for fans to call to listen to messages from the New Kids or talk to other fans. They sued the newspapers for trademark infringement. The Ninth Circuit found that the newspapers' use of the New Kids mark was excused as a nominative fair use. The court rejected arguments that the newspapers' use of the mark implied that the New Kids endorsed or sponsored the polls. The court held that the third factor (*supra*) looks for actions other than the mere use of the mark, which suggest the plaintiff's sponsorship or endorsement. No such actions were evident under the facts. Mere use of the mark, by itself, will not suffice to negate the third factor even if the context is one in which consumers might assume a relationship based on the use of the mark alone. The fact that the newspapers were free-riding, to some extent, on the cachet of the New Kids' mark, was not determinative. The court viewed the newspapers' uses as legitimate in purpose—news reporting and self-description. The fact that there was a commercial motivation was not determinative. *The New Kids on the Block v. News America Publishing, Inc.*, 971 F.2d 302 (9th Cir. 1992).

Example: The defendant, a former Playboy model and Playmate of the Year, used various Playboy marks (particularly "Playboy Playmate of the Year 1981") on her web site: on the masthead, in banner ads, and in metatags. The owner of the Playboy marks sued, alleging trademark infringement and dilution. Applying the three-factor nominative fair use test, the Ninth Circuit found all of these uses excused. The court reasoned that the marks truthfully identified defendant as a past "Playmate of the Year," and did not imply any current sponsorship or endorsement by the plaintiff (indeed, defendant affirmatively disavowed any sponsorship or endorsement on her web site). There was no other way that defendant could identify or describe herself and her services without using the marks. Moreover, the defendant had not emulated the font or symbols associated with the plaintiff's marks. The court noted, however, that defendant might have been found to infringe if she had used the mark so frequently that search engines searching for plaintiff's marks would rank her site *above* plaintiff's in their search results. Moreover, defendant's additional use of plaintiff's marks as wallpaper was not necessary in order to describe herself, given her other uses, and thus was not excused as a nominative fair use. *Playboy Enterprises, Inc. v. Welles*, 279 F.3d 796 (9th Cir. 2002).

2. **The Third Circuit's version of nominative fair use:** The Third Circuit has adopted its own version of the nominative fair use defense. Unlike the Ninth Circuit, the Third Circuit requires that the plaintiff first prove that the defendant's use causes a likelihood of confusion, under a "modified version" of the traditional multi-factor test. (The modified version ignores the strength of the plaintiff's mark and the similarity of the marks, and emphasizes the degree of consumer care, length of time the defendant has used the mark without evidence of actual confusion, defendant's intent in adopting the mark, and evidence of actual confusion.) If the plaintiff is able to prove a likelihood of confusion, the burden then shifts to the defendant to demonstrate fairness under a "three-pronged test" derived from the Ninth Circuit's nominative fair use standard: (1) Is the use of the plaintiff's mark necessary to describe both the plaintiff's product or service and the defendant's product or service?; (2) Does the defendant use only so much of the plaintiff's mark as is necessary in order to describe plaintiff's product?; and (3) Does the defendant's conduct or language reflect the true and accurate relationship between plaintiff and defendant's products or services? *Century 21 Real Estate Corp. v. LendingTree, Inc.*, 425 F.3d 211 (3d Cir. 2005).

3. **Nominative fair use differs from "descriptive" or "classic" fair use:** Nominative fair use (which may arise when the defendant *uses the plaintiff's mark to identify or describe the plaintiff's product* or service) should not be confused with the descriptive fair use defense, which may excuse a defendant from infringement liability when it has *used the plaintiff's mark in its original descriptive (non-trademark) capacity only to describe the defendant's own product*.

C. **Abandonment:** A defendant may raise a defense that the plaintiff has *abandoned her mark*, and thus no longer has rights to assert. Under the Lanham Act, a mark will be deemed "abandoned" *when the registrant has discontinued use of the mark throughout the country in connection with the particular good or service for which it is registered and has no intent to resume use within the reasonably foreseeable future*. For many years, the Lanham Act, 15 U.S.C. §1127, provided that nonuse for two consecutive years would be *prima facie* evidence of an intent to abandon. Pursuant to the Uruguay Round Agreements Act, this provision was amended. After January 1, 1996, nonuse for *three* consecutive years constitutes *prima facie* evidence of an intent to abandon. A trivial or token interim use is not enough to avoid a finding of abandonment.

1. **Acts by the registrant that cause the mark to lose its significance as a mark:** A *second way* in which a registrant may be found to have abandoned its mark is through *acts or omissions that cause the mark to lose its significance as a mark*.

    a. **Assignment of the mark in gross:** One way an owner can cause her mark to lose its significance as a mark is to assign the mark "in gross" to another—that is, *assign the mark without the ongoing business good will that the mark symbolizes*. Such assignments are invalid and constitute an abandonment. A mark may only be assigned along with the good will of the business, or that part of the goodwill of the business that is symbolized by the mark. The primary significance of a mark is its informative function—informing consumers that a product or service will be similar to products or services sold under the same mark that consumers have used in the past. If an assignment is made "in gross," there is no way to ensure that the mark will continue accurately to inform prospective consumers about the nature and characteristics of the product or service the mark identifies. By making that information unreliable, an assignment in gross will cause the mark to lose its significance as a mark. Rather than informing consumers, the mark may mislead them.

    i. **Assignment of good will:** More traditional case law suggested that the assignor's business good will would not be deemed assigned with the mark unless other business assets, such as plant, inventory, product formula, or know-how, were assigned along with the mark. Assignment of such things ensures that the product or service sold under the mark will have the same basic characteristics both before and after the assignment. This continuity is what the rule against assignments in gross attempts to preserve.

    ii. **The liberal view:** The more liberal, modern view will uphold an assignment of a mark even in the absence of a transfer of physical assets or product formula if the assignee *in fact* continues selling goods or services of the same basic quality and nature as the assignor did. This demonstrates that the good will has *in fact* passed with the mark. *Pepsico, Inc. v. Grapette Co.*, 416 F.2d 285 (8th Cir. 1969).

    iii. **The consequences of finding abandonment arising from an assignment in gross:** A finding that a mark owner has abandoned his mark by assigning it in gross means that the assignee will not be able to "stand in the assignor's shoes" and assert the assignor's first use or registration date to demonstrate priority of use. The assignee will be treated as though he made his first use of the mark on the date he actually began using it, and he will not get the benefit of the assignor's registration.

    b. **Licensing without adequate supervision:** Another way an owner can cause her mark to lose its significance as a mark is to license others to use the mark without taking measures to insure that the licensees' products or services retain the characteristics and level of quality that the public has come to associate with the mark. *Failure to police the licensees' use to assure continued quality and uniform characteristics may lead to public deception and cause the mark to lose its informative function.* This, in turn, will constitute an abandonment because the mark will have lost its significance as a mark.

i. **Level of supervision:** Generally, the mark owner should conduct regular inspections of the licensee's operations. The inspections should be carried out by personnel with adequate training. However, the reasonableness of licensee control measures will be judged under the particular circumstances of the case. For example, if the licensee and licensor have worked together successfully for a long time, less formal control measures may be required. The Restatement (Third) of Unfair Competition suggests that consumers' likely expectations regarding consistency, given the particular product or service, should also be taken into account in determining the necessary level of supervision. Restatement (Third) of Unfair Competition, §33, cmt. c (1995).

D. **Challenges to the validity of the mark and to the plaintiff's ownership rights:** In an infringement action, the plaintiff normally must prove ownership and validity of his mark as a part of his case against the defendant. If the plaintiff has *registered the mark* on the Lanham Act Principal Register, however, the registration will serve as *prima facie* evidence of the validity of the mark, of its registration, and of the registrant's ownership and exclusive right to use the mark in connection with the goods or services specified in the registration. This shifts the burden to the defendant to disprove these matters as a defense to the infringement claim. Until a registered mark attains incontestability status (discussed below), the defendant may challenge the validity of the plaintiff's mark for failing to comply with any requirement of common law or the Lanham Act.

E. **Federal registration incontestability status:** A mark that has been in continuous use for five consecutive years following its registration will obtain "incontestability" status upon the registrant's filing of an affidavit with the P.T.O. to that effect, that truthfully states that there has been no final decision adverse to the registrant's claim of ownership of the mark and that there is no proceeding presently pending involving the registrant's rights in the mark. Incontestability gives the registrant an advantage in an infringement action (regardless of whether the registrant is the plaintiff or the defendant), though not as great an advantage as the name might suggest. For the most part, the incontestable mark is subject to all the same challenges and defenses as a mark that has not attained incontestability status would be. However, two important challenges or defenses are precluded:

1. that the mark is not inherently distinctive and lacks secondary meaning.
2. that the challenger/defendant used the mark before the registrant (except that this challenge/defense can only be made with regard to the actual geographic area in which the challenger/defender used the mark prior to the incontestable registrant's registration or application to register).

XIII. TRADEMARK CYBERSQUATTING

A. **The Anticybersquatting Consumer Protection Act:** In 1999, Congress enacted the Anticybersquatting Consumer Protection Act, which amends Lanham Act §43 by adding a new subsection (d). Subsection (d) prohibits the registration, trafficking in, or use of a domain name that is identical or confusingly similar to, or dilutive of, another person's mark. There are two important limitations to the cause of action, however:

- First, the mark must have been distinctive (i.e., enjoyed trademark status) at the time the domain name was registered (or, if the claim is that the defendant's domain name *dilutes* the plaintiff's mark, the mark must have been famous at the time the domain name was registered).

- Second, the plaintiff must demonstrate that the *defendant acted with a bad-faith intent to profit* from the business good will of the mark.

Thus, the Act does not extend to innocent domain name registrations by persons who are unaware of the plaintiff's use of the name as a mark, or to persons who are aware of the trademark status of the word, but register it as a domain name for reasons other than to profit from the good will associated with the mark. The majority of courts to address the anticybersquatting provisions have found that Congress had very specific conduct in mind that it wished to target: registration of a mark-incorporating domain name *for purposes of commercial exploitation*. The defendant might commercially exploit the domain name by (1) selling the registration to the mark owner for an inflated price, or (2) setting up a web site under the domain name to divert consumers seeking the plaintiff: to sell the misled consumers its own products, to gain "hits" to boost its advertising revenues, or to gain some other commercial advantage. *See, e.g., Lucas Nursery and Landscaping, Inc. v. Grosse*, 359 F.3d 806 (6th Cir. 2003). Congress made it clear in the legislative history that it did not intend to interfere with others' registration of domain names in order to engage in legitimate, noncommercial expression, such as comparative advertising, comment, criticism, parody, news reporting, or fair use.

1. **Factors to consider in determining whether the defendant registered, trafficked in, or used the domain name with a bad-faith intent to profit:** The new Section 43(d) provides courts with a non-exclusive list of *nine factors* to consider in deciding whether a defendant acted with the requisite bad-faith intent to profit on the business good will of the mark. The factors include:

   - Whether the domain name registrant has trademark or other intellectual property rights in the word. (For example, does the domain name registrant have a concurrent right to use the word as a mark for its own, differing, products or services? If so, this suggests a lack of bad faith.)

   - Whether the domain name is the same as the registrant's own legal name or established nickname. (If so, this indicates an absence of bad-faith intent.)

   - The domain name registrant's prior use of the name, if any, in connection with the *bona fide* offering of goods or services. (This would indicate an absence of bad-faith intent.)

   - The domain name registrant's *bona fide* noncommercial or fair use of the mark in a web site that is accessible under the domain name. (For example, does the registrant use the plaintiff's mark in comparative advertising, comment, criticism, parody, news reporting, or similar activities on the web site? This would indicate an absence of bad-faith intent. This factor is particularly meant to protect defendants' First Amendment interests in commenting on the plaintiff or its product, and identifying the plaintiff or its product through use of the mark.)

   - Whether, in registering or using the domain name, the registrant intended to confuse consumers seeking the trademark owner's web site and thus divert them away from the trademark owner's web site to a web site that could harm the good will of the mark, either for purposes of commercial gain or with the intent to tarnish or disparage the mark. (For example, did the domain name registrant deliberately use the mark to attract consumers who are looking for the plaintiff's web site, in order to sell them inferior goods, or to defraud them into providing credit card or other personal information, or to increase the number of "hits" on his site so that he can charge more for advertising? That would indicate bad faith.)

- Whether the domain name registrant: (1) made no use of the name itself in the *bona fide* offering of goods or services, and (2) offered to sell the domain name to the mark owner or to a third party for financial gain. (If so, this is indicative of bad faith.)

- Whether the domain name registrant intentionally provided material and misleading false contact information in her application for the domain name registration, or failed to maintain accurate contact information, and has engaged in a pattern of such conduct. (This would suggest an attempt to avoid services of process and bad faith.)

- Whether the domain name registrant acquired multiple domain names that he or she knows to be identical to, confusingly similar to, or dilutive of others' marks. (If so, this suggests mark "warehousing" and bad faith.)

- The extent to which the mark at issue is distinctive and/or famous within the meaning of Lanham Act §43(c). (The more distinctive and famous the mark, the more likely the owner of the mark deserves relief.)

Example: The facts of *Panavision International, L.P. v. Toeppen,* 945 F. Supp. 1296 (C.D. Cal. 1996), *aff'd*, 141 F.3d 1316 (9th Cir. 1998), illustrate the kind of situation Congress intended to address in enacting the Anticybersquatting Act. In *Panavision*, the defendant registered over a hundred domain names that consisted of famous marks in the ".com" top level domain, and attempted to sell the registrations to the mark owners for between $10,000 to $15,000 each. In the case of the plaintiff's Panavision mark, the defendant set up a web site under the "Panavision.com" domain name that did nothing other than display a photograph of Pana, Illinois. Most of the factors listed above would weigh in favor of finding the requisite bad-faith intent to profit. (The legislative history of the Anticybersquatting Act comments that the *Panavision* defendant could not evade liability merely by setting up such a minimal web site and arguing that it was a noncommercial, fair use under factor 4.)

Example: The facts in *Lamparello v. Falwell*, 420 F.3d 309 (4th Cir.), *cert. denied*, 126 S. Ct. 1772 (2006), illustrate the kind of situation that Congress *did not intend to target* in enacting the Anticybersquatting Act. In that case, Lamparello registered the domain name "fallwell.com" and set up a web site that took issue with the Rev. Jerry Falwell's stated religious views concerning homosexuality. Falwell maintained a very popular on-line ministry at the domain name "falwell.com." Lamparello's web site expressly stated that "this website is NOT affiliated with Jerry Falwell or his ministry," and provided a link to Rev. Falwell's site. Lamparello sold no goods or services on his web site (although he provided a link to the Amazon.com web page for a book that offered interpretations of the Bible that Lamparello favored). The Fourth Circuit rejected Falwell's arguments that Lamparello acted with bad-faith intent to profit. Lamparello's web site was an earnest, good-faith expression of criticism of the plaintiff's religious teachings (religious speech, which is fully protected under the First Amendment), and fell fully within the fourth factor. The court also emphasized that the defendant did not register multiple marks, and never offered to sell the registration. Moreover, the defendant did nothing on the web site itself to confuse consumers into thinking they had really reached the Rev. Falwell's site. The court found that the link to Amazon.com did not diminish the communicative function of the defendant's site, noting that criticism or commentary, "even where done for profit" does not alone evidence a bad-faith intent to profit. Moreover, Lamparello had no financial interest in Amazon's sales of the book.

2. *In rem* **jurisdiction:** Mark owners often have difficulty locating and obtaining personal jurisdiction over cybersquatters. To address this problem, the Act provides *in rem* jurisdiction, permitting the mark owner to file an action against the domain name itself. To qualify, the mark owner must demonstrate that he exercised due diligence in trying to locate or obtain personal jurisdiction over the domain name registrant, and was unsuccessful. He will be deemed to have exercised due diligence in trying to find the domain name registrant if he sends notice of the alleged violation and his intent to bring suit to the postal and e-mail addresses that the domain name registrant provided to the registering authority, and publishes notice of the action promptly after filing the action. The relief available in *in rem* actions is *limited to an injunction* ordering the forfeiture, cancellation, or transfer of the domain name registration.

   a. *In rem* **jurisdiction is available for §§43(a) and (c) claims:** The Court of Appeals for the Fourth Circuit has held that the Anticybersquatting Act's *in rem* jurisdiction provisions apply in the case of Lanham Act §43(a) (infringement of unregistered indications of origin) and §43(c) (dilution) claims, as well as to claims under §43(d). However, several court opinions have found that *in rem* jurisdiction over a disputed domain name lies only in the judicial district where the domain name registrar, registry, or other authority is located.

3. **Remedies and limitation of liability:** The Anticybersquatting Act authorizes the court, in any case, to order the forfeiture, cancellation, or transfer of a domain name to the owner of the mark. Traditional trademark remedies are also available under the Act, including injunctive relief, recovery of the defendant's profits, actual damages, and costs. The Act also provides for statutory damages in cybersquatting cases, ranging from $1000 to $100,000 per domain name. The Act encourages domain name registrars to assist in preventing cybersquatting by limiting their liability if they suspend, cancel, or transfer domain names pursuant to a court order. However, a trademark owner who knowingly and materially misrepresents to the domain name registrar that a domain name infringes may be liable to the domain name registrant for any resulting damages.

B. **Personal names:** The Anticybersquatting Act specifies that personal names that qualify as marks under the Lanham Act are protected on the same basis as all other marks. In addition, the Act prohibits the registration of a domain name that is, or is substantially and confusingly similar to, the name of another living person (even though the name does not qualify as a mark). 15 U.S.C. §1129. However, this action is a narrow one: It is limited to situations in which the *registrant's specific intent in registering the plaintiff's name is to profit by selling it to the plaintiff or a third party for financial gain*. Remedies for violation are limited to injunctive relief, including ordering the forfeiture or cancellation of the domain name registration or the transfer of the domain name to the plaintiff. While damages are not authorized, the court may award costs and attorney fees to the prevailing party in appropriate cases.

C. **The Uniform Domain Name Dispute Resolution Policy—an administrative alternative:** A non-profit, private corporation, known as the Internet Corporation for Assigned Names and Numbers (ICANN), has taken over global administration of the Internet name and address system. It contracts with a number of competing domain name registrars, and has adopted a dispute resolution policy to assist in resolving disputes between trademark owners and people who register domain names with its authorized registrars. This policy, known as the Uniform Domain Name Dispute Resolution Policy (UDRP), is incorporated into all domain name registration agreements made by ICANN-accredited registrars. Under the policy, registrants must agree to mandatory administrative proceedings when a third party asserts that:

1. The registered domain name is identical or confusingly similar to a trademark or service mark in which the complainant has rights;
2. The registrant has no rights or legitimate interests in the domain name; and
3. The domain name has been registered and is being used in bad faith.

At least in routine cases, this administrative form of dispute resolution is likely to provide a faster and less expensive means for trademark owners to obtain redress from cybersquatting.

1. **Bad faith under the UDRP:** Under the UDRP, a registrant may be deemed to have registered in bad faith if he registered and used the domain name:

   - primarily to sell or rent the domain name for profit;
   - primarily to disrupt a competitor's business;
   - intentionally to create a likelihood of confusion with the complainant's mark and thus lure Internet users to his web site for commercial gain; or
   - in order to prevent the mark owner from registering and using the mark as its own domain name (provided that there has been a pattern of such conduct).

   A registrant can *rebut a* claim of bad faith by demonstrating that:

   - she used or prepared to use the domain name in selling goods or services prior to notice of the dispute;
   - she had been commonly known by the domain name; or
   - she is making a legitimate, noncommercial or fair use of the domain name, without intent to obtain commercial gain.

2. **Remedies under the UDRP:** Under the UDRP, a trademark owner's remedies against a bad-faith registrant are limited to cancellation of the domain name registration or transfer of the registration to the complainant. The existence of the mandatory administrative proceeding does not prevent either party from submitting the dispute to a court for independent resolution.

XIV. REMEDIES FOR LANHAM ACT VIOLATIONS

A. **Injunctions:** Courts regularly grant injunctions against further trademark infringement, once infringement has been found. Preliminary injunctions may also be granted. While courts vary somewhat, the factors most commonly emphasized in determining whether to grant a preliminary injunction against mark infringement include: (1) the plaintiff's likelihood of success on the merits, (2) the existence of irreparable injury to the plaintiff, (3) the respective hardship that the court's grant or denial will have on each party, and (4) the public interest.

B. **Monetary recovery:** Courts may also award damages, the defendant's profits, and costs. The Lanham Act damage provisions apply both in cases of infringement of registered marks and cases of infringement of unregistered marks brought pursuant to Lanham Act §43(a). (15 U.S.C. §1125(a).) Plaintiffs in §43(c) dilution cases may only recover damages if they can demonstrate

(1) that the defendant first used its diluting mark in commerce after the Trademark Dilution Revision Act of 2006 was enacted; and (2) that the defendant's acts were willful. The defendant's acts will be willful in the case of a blurring claim if the defendant "willfully intended to trade on the recognition of the famous mark." They will be willful in the case of a tarnishment claim if the defendant "willfully intended to harm the reputation of the famous mark." 15 U.S.C. §1125(c)(5). Plaintiffs in Lanham Act §43(d) anticybersquatter cases can recover damages if the defendant engaged in her cybersquatting acts after the effective date of the Anticybersquatting Act (November 29, 1999).

1. **Actual damages:** The plaintiff may suffer lost sales and/or injury to its business reputation as a result of the defendant's Lanham Act violations. These losses may be recovered, but are often difficult to prove and quantify. First, in connection with lost sales, the plaintiff will have to demonstrate that *but for* the defendant's actions the plaintiff would have made a certain number of sales that he in fact never got to make. This may be difficult, as there may be other variables that would lead customers to purchase from the defendant even in the absence of the infringement, to refrain from purchasing altogether, or to purchase from other competitors rather than from the plaintiff. Also, injury to reputation may be hard to measure or translate into dollar amounts.

   a. **Increase in actual damages:** Because of the difficulties discussed above, the Lanham Act authorizes courts to increase established actual damages up to three times, if necessary, in order adequately to compensate the plaintiff. This allows a court to increase the damages awarded in cases in which it believes that the plaintiff has actually suffered more damage than it has been able to prove. However, as a general matter, courts have been hesitant to award any damages at all when the defendant has acted in good faith. A doubling or tripling of damages is unlikely unless the defendant has acted willfully.

2. **The defendant's profits:** A monetary award in the amount of the defendant's profits may be granted if the defendant has been unjustly enriched, the plaintiff has sustained damages from the infringement, or an accounting is necessary to deter a willful infringer from infringing again. Courts sometimes permit plaintiffs to recover both the actual damages they can prove and the defendant's profits, as long as they do not thereby obtain double recovery for the same sales. For example, a plaintiff would not be permitted to recover both his own lost profit and the defendant's ill-gotten profit resulting from the same sales transaction to a customer.

   a. **Burden of proof:** To recover the defendant's profits, the plaintiff must prove only the amount of the defendant's gross sales in connection with the infringing mark. Once that is done, it is up to the defendant to prove the amounts that should be deducted from the award as costs of production and any amounts that are not attributable to the infringement.

   b. **Courts have the power to adjust:** The Lanham Act permits a court to increase or decrease an award of profits if it finds the amount either inadequate or excessive under the circumstances.

C. **Attorney fees:** The Lanham Act authorizes a court to award reasonable attorney fees to the prevailing party "in exceptional cases." An exceptional case includes one in which the trademark infringement can be characterized as malicious, fraudulent, deliberate, or willful. Attorney fees normally are not available under the common law.

D. **Special remedies for use of counterfeit marks:** Federal law provides special, enhanced civil and criminal penalties for certain uses of counterfeit marks. See p. 267, *supra*.

1. **Definition of "counterfeit":** The Lanham Act defines a counterfeit mark as a spurious mark that is identical to or substantially indistinguishable from a registered mark.

2. **Special civil remedies:** Absent extenuating circumstances, the Lanham Act directs courts to *triple the plaintiff's damages or the defendant's profits* whenever intentional, knowing use of a counterfeit mark is found. In addition, courts should award attorney fees, and they may award prejudgment interest for the period between the filing of plaintiff's pleading and the court's judgment. There are also provisions for court-ordered seizure of goods bearing counterfeit marks. In an amendment enacted in 1996, Congress provided that plaintiffs in counterfeiting cases may elect *statutory damages* in lieu of actual damages or profits. The statutory damages range from $500 to $100,000 per counterfeit mark per type of goods or services sold, offered for sale, or distributed, as the court considers just. However, if the court finds that the defendant's use of the counterfeit mark was willful, it may award up to $1,000,000 per counterfeit mark per type of goods or services.

E. **Special remedies in anticybersquatting cases:** Plaintiffs alleging violation of the Lanham Act's §43(d) anticybersquatting provisions may elect to recover an award of statutory damages in lieu of actual damages and profits. These statutory damages may range from $1,000 to $100,000 per domain name, as the court considers just.

XV. INTERNATIONAL TRADEMARK TREATIES

A. **The Paris Convention:** The Paris Convention for the Protection of Industrial Property (discussed in connection with patents at pp. 80-81, *supra*) undertakes to ensure that each of its member nations protects the nationals of other member nations against unfair competition, including trademark infringement.

1. **National treatment:** The Paris Convention bases its international protection of trademarks on the concept of *"national treatment."* Each member nation must provide as strong trademark protection to nationals of other member nations as it does to its own nationals. (Nationals of non-member nations who are domiciled in, or have real, effective industrial or commercial establishments in a member nation are entitled to treatment as nationals of that member nation for purposes of the Paris Convention.) The Paris Convention provides relatively few substantive standards for the protection that must be afforded, as long as the protection is available on an equal basis. The Convention does contemplate that members maintain a trademark registration system. However, while it requires that members afford protection for service marks, it does not require that the opportunity to register service marks be afforded.

2. **Registration of marks:** The Paris Convention provides that a *national of a member nation may register its trademark in any other member nation* through either of two alternative routes: (1) by satisfying all the registration requirements that the nation imposes on domestic applicants; or (2) by registering its mark in its home country and relying on that registration in its application to register abroad.

    a. **Satisfaction of the nation's registration requirements:** Under the concept of national treatment, each member nation must make its domestic registration process available to qualifying foreign applicants on essentially the same basis as to domestic applicants.

b. **The *telle quelle* principle:** The Paris Convention also provides that *once an applicant's trademark is duly registered in the nation in which the applicant is a national, is domiciled, or maintains a commercial establishment, it must be registered by other members of the Convention.* This prohibits member nations from refusing to register foreign marks, for example, on the ground that they *have not been used in trade* or because their physical form fails to conform to the nation's requirements (as long as if the applicant's own nation does not impose such requirements). Likewise, a member nation may not refuse registration on the ground that sales of the particular product the mark represents are restricted or prohibited. There are a few exceptions to this "*telle quelle*" principle:

   i. **Marks infringing preexisting trademarks:** A member nation may refuse telle quelle registration when the proffered mark is *confusingly similar* to a mark already owned by another in the nation in which the application has been filed.

   ii. **Non-distinctive marks:** A member nation may refuse to register a mark that has *no distinctive character.*

   iii. **Immoral or deceptive marks:** Member nations may refuse to register marks that are *contrary to morality or public order* or that are deceptive. In addition, registration must be refused for marks that include the state emblem of a member nation without its authorization.

c. **Effect of the *telle quelle* provision in the United States:** The United States' adherence to the Paris Convention arguably results in more favorable treatment for foreign (*telle quelle*) applicants for registration than for domestic applicants. While the U.S. domestic registration laws require use in trade and commerce, the laws of most countries do not. Thus, *telle quelle* applicants may obtain registration in their home countries without using the mark, and then apply for U.S. registration, based on their home country registration. The Paris Convention requires the United States to register these marks, as long as one of the exceptions described above does not apply. Thus, *foreign applicants can obtain U.S. registration without ever using their marks in trade or commerce, even though domestic applicants cannot.* (Foreign applicants must allege a bona fide *intent to use* the mark in trade and commerce.) However, the advantage to foreign applicants is very limited.

   i. **The domestic "intent to use" application process closes the gap:** One of the reasons that Congress enacted the U.S. "intent-to-use" application process (described at p. 248, *supra*) and its constructive use provisions was to close the gap between foreign and domestic registration applicants. Pursuant to the 1988 amendments, once a domestic applicant obtains registration, the registration essentially relates back (through the constructive use provisions) to the registrant's application date. Thus, assuming that the domestic applicant does eventually use its mark in trade and commerce and obtain registration, *it is in almost as good a position as if it had obtained registration on its application date, prior to using the mark.*

   ii. **Infringement relief is limited:** While the United States must register foreign marks that have not been used but are registered in their home country, it is not required to provide such marks any greater protection from infringement than is provided for domestic marks. Under U.S. law, no relief is available for trademark infringement unless the defendant's use of the same or similar mark causes a likelihood of consumer confusion about the source, sponsorship, or affiliation of goods or services. *If the* *registered foreign mark has not been used in trade in the United States, it is unlikely that a defendant's use of that mark or a similar one will cause any likelihood of consumer confusion.* Thus, while an unused foreign mark may be registered, it generally will not be enforceable against others in infringement suits.

    iii. **Cancellation for abandonment:** Registration of a mark may be cancelled for abandonment. Nonuse of a mark anywhere in the United States for three years is *prima facie* evidence of abandonment. Accordingly, *if the foreign registrant does not begin use in the United States within three years after registration, it runs the risk of a petition to cancel or a challenge in litigation.* In any event, the P.T.O. will *automatically cancel* the registration if the registrant fails to file an affidavit alleging continued use of the mark (or that nonuse is due to special circumstances that excuse nonuse) during the sixth year following registration.

    iv. **Notice:** The main advantage that most foreign registrants who have not used their mark obtain from U.S. registration without use is *notice to other U.S. businesses of their claim* to the mark, and their intent to use it, which may dissuade the others from adopting the same or a similar mark.

3. **Filing priority:** Once a mark owner registers her mark in one Paris Convention member nation, she obtains *filing priority in other member nations during the next six months*. If she files applications to register in additional member countries within that six-month period, she will have *the benefit of her initial filing date in those additional countries*. This provision is useful in the many countries that grant registration on a first-to-file basis, rather than on the basis of first-to-use. It is useful in the United States, too: Under the 1988 amendments to the Lanham Act, the earlier foreign filing date will become the applicant's constructive use date, once U.S. registration is granted. This will give the foreign applicant priority over U.S. applicants who make their first use or file an intent-to-use application between the foreign applicant's initial foreign filing date and her actual U.S. filing date.

4. **Criticisms of the Paris Convention:** While the Paris Convention does provide some substantive protection for U.S. trademark owners abroad, it has been criticized for not going far enough.

    a. **Too few substantive guarantees:** The Paris Convention, through its national treatment provisions, requires members to afford as strong protection to foreign mark owners as to domestic mark owners, but does not dictate the level of protection that must be afforded. Thus, some member nations may afford relatively little protection to U.S. mark owners against trademark infringement.

    b. **No enforcement mechanism:** There is no effective enforcement mechanism for compelling member nations' compliance with the terms of the Paris Convention. A registrant must rely on the legislature and courts of each member nation to follow the requirements of the treaty.

    c. **No centralized filing system:** The Paris Convention itself does little to ease the effort and expense required to apply for, obtain, and maintain registration in a large number of countries. A widely subscribed centralized registration system would be useful as a means of facilitating global marketing strategies.

B. **The Trademark Law Treaty:** The Trademark Law Treaty, negotiated under the auspices of the World Intellectual Property Organization, simplifies international filings by harmonizing and simplifying the member countries' trademark registration standards and procedures. The United States has ratified this treaty. However, the Trademark Law Treaty *does not provide a centralized registration system* that permits trademark registration in multiple countries with a single application.

C. **The Madrid Protocol:** In 2002, the United States officially joined the Madrid Protocol, which provides an *international system for centrally filing trademark applications* in the over 80 member nations. Under the Madrid Protocol, a person owning a trademark registration or application in his home country can file one Madrid Application that designates any number of other member countries in which the owner wishes to register. The owner pays one filing fee based on the number of countries and classes of products he designates. The home trademark office forwards the application to the International Bureau of the World Intellectual Property Organization. The International Bureau processes the application, provides an international registration, publishes the mark in the *WIPO Gazette of International Marks,* and forwards the application to each of the countries the applicant has designated for *territorial extension of the international registration.* Each designated country then has 18 months to evaluate the application based on its domestic laws and either extend the international registration or issue an office action refusing extension.

   1. **Eligibility:** To apply for Madrid Protocol registration, an applicant must be a national of, be domiciled in, or have a real and effective business or commercial establishment in one of the countries that are members of the Protocol.

   2. **The perceived benefits of the Madrid Protocol:** The Madrid Protocol's centralized filing system is *efficient and saves money*, because it avoids multiple filings and enables U.S. businesses to avoid paying individual filing fees and local attorney fees in each foreign country in which it seeks registration. The Protocol also provides an *efficient, streamlined process for renewing registrations* in multiple countries (registrations must be renewed every ten years) and recording trademark assignments.

   3. **The perceived drawbacks of Madrid Protocol filings:** If a business only seeks to register in a limited number of foreign countries, it may be more cost-efficient to make individual filings, rather than use the Madrid Protocol centralized filing system. Also, it is important to note that *for the first five years, international registrations filed by U.S. businesses will be dependent on the continued validity of their U.S. application and/or registration*. If the U.S. application or registration is rejected, cancelled, or otherwise lapses, then the Protocol registration will no longer be valid in any of the other member countries. (However, the business does have an opportunity, for a limited period, to refile separate national applications in each of those countries, and thereby retain the original Protocol filing date as its priority date against other marks.) A final disadvantage is that *the foreign country registrations achieved through the Madrid Protocol will have the same scope (with regard to the products and services covered) as the U.S. registration*. Since some countries permit registration for a broader range of products and services than the United States does, U.S. businesses may prefer to file individual national applications in order to take advantage of that greater scope.

D. **The Agreement on Trade-Related Aspects of Intellectual Property Rights:** The Agreement on Trade-Related Aspects of Intellectual Property Rights, including Trade in Counterfeited Goods (TRIPs), to which the United States adheres, *builds upon the Paris Convention* and augments international trademark protection. Among other things, the TRIPs Agreement *defines what can* *serve as a trademark*. It also requires that adhering nations provide registration for service marks, as well as trademarks; and requires that adhering nations publish registered marks and provide opportunities for others to oppose or cancel registrations. It prescribes an *international "likelihood of confusion" standard for infringement*, and provides that use of an identical mark for identical goods or services must be presumed to create a likelihood of confusion. The TRIPs Agreement also prohibits the imposition of compulsory licenses for marks, as well as linking requirements (requirements that foreign-owned marks be used only in conjunction with the marks of domestic licensees). The TRIPs Agreement prescribes remedies that must be made available against all kinds of intellectual property infringement, including trademark infringement. The World Trade Organization (which administers TRIPS) also provides more effective mechanisms for *enforcing compliance with the TRIPs provisions* than are available in connection with the Paris Convention.

Quiz Yourself on *TRADEMARK LAW*

59. How might the P.T.O. evaluate an application to register "Mr. Justice" as a mark for study aids for law students? _____

60. How might the P.T.O. evaluate an application to register "Bleachwhite" as a mark for a clothing whitening product to be used in washing machines? The product does not contain bleach. _____

61. How might the P.T.O. evaluate an application to register a stylized graphic representation of a fish as a mark for cat food? The cat food is comprised of horse meat, soy flour, water, and various preservatives and other chemical additives. The company has already registered the word mark "Yummies" for the cat food. _____

62. How might the P.T.O. evaluate an application to register the configuration of a clip, as shown below, that surrounds an ink pen and secures it to the inside of a person's shirt pocket? The evidence indicates that there are numerous alternative designs that would work just as well to clip a pen to the inside of a person's pocket. _____

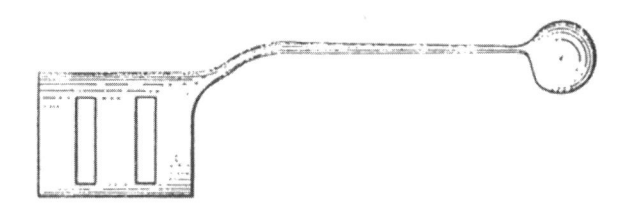

63. How might the P.T.O. evaluate an application to register the words "Apple Sauce" as a mark for children's clothing? _____

290   *Chapter 6   TRADEMARK LAW*

64. How might the P.T.O. evaluate an application to register the words "Champs Elysees" as a mark for luxury automobiles manufactured in Birmingham, England? _____

65. How might the P.T.O. evaluate an application to register the following mark for chairs? _____
_____

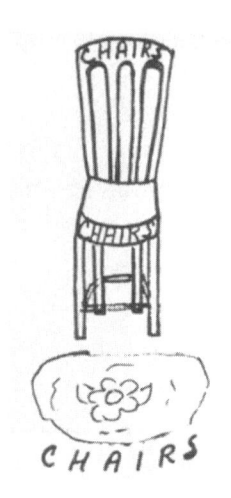

66. How might the P.T.O. evaluate an application to register the color gold for the gilded edges of the pages of a leather-bound diary? _____

67. How might the P.T.O. evaluate an application to register a mark for pickled onions comprised of the words "Super Pickled" superimposed over a cartoon caricature of a well-known former politician who was noted for heavy drinking? The applicant has used this mark continuously and exclusively for the past eight years. _____

68. In March 1995, Ace Corp. filed an "intent-to-use" application to register the mark "Alpine Splendor" for the new carbonated water beverage it intended to introduce to the market. The P.T.O. allowed the application in July, 1995. In January, 1996, Ace filed for an extension of time, which the P.T.O. granted as a matter of course. The following July, Ace filed for another extension, which the P.T.O. granted. In September, 1996, Ace introduced the new carbonated beverage to the market bearing the "Alpine Splendor" mark, filed an affidavit of use with the P.T.O., and obtained registration. Brown Corp. began using the mark "Alpine Splendor" for a new bottled water product in January, 1995. Assuming that the parties are both marketing their products in the same geographic location, which party has priority? _____

69. In 1998, X began manufacturing erasers (to fit on the end of pencils) at its Roanoke, Virginia factory. It marketed the erasers under the unregistered mark "Peccadillo" throughout the State of Virginia. In 2003, X expanded its sales of erasers under the Peccadillo mark to Tennessee. Shortly thereafter, in 2004, X sold his Roanoke factory and assigned the Peccadillo mark to Y. Since then, Y has continued to manufacture and sell erasers, under the Peccadillo mark, in Virginia and Tennessee, and has further expanded sales into parts of North and South Carolina. _____

Z Co., which manufactures various writing accessories in its Texas factory, began preparations to manufacture and sell pencil erasers. It filed an "intent-to-use" application to register the mark "Peck-a-dillo" for the erasers in April, 2000. It first sold erasers under the Peck-a-dillo mark in November, 2002, at which point it filed an affidavit of use and completed its registration of the mark. During the next five years, Z Co. confined its sales activities to Texas and other states west of the Mississippi River. However, in December, 2007, Z Co. completed a new factory to manufacture its erasers and launched a nationwide marketing campaign. Z Co. completed the paperwork necessary to attain incontestable status for its Peck-a-dillo mark, and then brought suit to enjoin Y's use of the Peccadillo mark under Lanham Act §32. What are the respective rights of the parties? _____

70. X Co. decided to adopt the mark "Heckofawallop" for the new fortified wine product it planned to put on the market. It introduced the new fortified wine product (with much advertising and fanfare) to the market in New York in January, 1993, and filed an application to register the mark the following month (in February 1993). The registration was granted in August, 1993.

Meanwhile, in June, 1993, Y Co., a small Mississippi company, began marketing a malt liquor under the mark "Hellofawallop." It sold the malt liquor in Mississippi and parts of western Alabama, but did not register its mark and engaged in relatively little advertising.

X Co. now wants to expand sales of its fortified wine product nationwide under its "Heckofawallop" mark. What are X's and Y's respective rights? _____

71. Assume that, in addition to the facts set forth in Question 70, Z Co., a German Company, decided to adopt the mark "Heckawallap" (a made-up word) for table wines. It applied to register the mark in Germany in December, 1992, was granted registration the following March, 1993, and applied the following month to register the mark in the United States pursuant to Lanham Act §44. It attached a certified copy of its German registration to its application and alleged a *bona fide* intent to use the mark in commerce. However, it had not used the "Heckawallap" mark at the time it applied to register in the United States, and did not do so at any time prior to its ultimate U.S. registration in April, 1994. Z Co. began to use the mark for table wines in the United States in August, 1995, selling its wines throughout the United States under the Heckawallap mark. Germany is a member of the Paris Convention. What are Z Co.'s rights as opposed to X Co. and Y Co.? _____

72. X Co. manufactures and sells widgets under the federally registered mark "Whiz," and has done so throughout the country for many years. Y Co. began selling widgets under the mark "Excelsior." Y then registered "whiz.com" as a domain name and set up a web page under that domain name. The web page extolled the virtues of Excelsior widgets, and explained why Excelsior widgets were better than whiz widgets. The web site made it clear that whiz widgets were manufactured and sold by another company that was unrelated to Y Co. Visitors to the web page could place orders for Excelsior widgets by filling out an electronic form that was provided on the web page, and providing a credit card number. X Co. is unhappy about this. What is the best argument X can make that Y's actions constitute *trademark infringement*? Is X Co. likely to have *any other* cause of action against Y Co.? _____

73. X runs a flower shop in downtown San Francisco, with the trade name and mark "Flower Fracas." Y opened a flower shop in downtown Oakland (which is right over the bridge from San Francisco) under the trade name and mark "Blossom Brawl." At the time he opened his shop, Y had no knowledge of X's preexisting business. X advertises in the San Francisco Chronicle, and does no business in Oakland. Y only advertises in the Oakland Tribune, and does no business in San Francisco. Would X likely have a cause of action for infringement against Y? _____

74. The Rojas Corp., a Mexican Company, owns the mark "Rojas," which it applies to the fine leather goods it produces. Carlos Martinez is the sole shareholder of the Rojas Corp. In 1997, Martinez created a corporation in Delaware, under Delaware law, which he named Segundo Corp. Martinez took ownership of all the Segundo Corp. shares. The Segundo Corp. entered into an agreement with the

Rojas Corp. to become the exclusive distributor of Rojas leather goods in the United States. As a part of the transaction, Segundo Corp. paid Rojas Corp. $100,000 for the exclusive rights to the Rojas mark in the United States, which Rojas Corp. duly assigned over to Segundo. Segundo Corp. began buying leather goods from Rojas and reselling them in the United States under the Rojas mark. It registered the Rojas mark on the Lanham Act Principal Register.

The Rojas Corp. sells its goods, with the Rojas mark, in a number of other countries. Recently, Gregor Ivanov, an international businessman, bought a large shipment of Rojas Corp.'s leather goods in Chile and shipped them to the United States for resale. The goods bear the Rojas mark, which was placed on them at the Rojas factory in Mexico. Segundo Corp., which was tipped off about the shipment, wishes to bring suit against Ivanov to prevent the importation of the leather goods into the United States, or to prevent their resale in the United States. Is it likely to succeed? _____

75. CalPacific sells sweet pickles, with no preservatives, in glass jars under the "Zip" mark. Because the pickles have no preservatives, they need to be kept refrigerated. CalPacific places a notice to that effect on its labels, always delivers wholesale shipments of the pickles in boxes bearing a warning to "refrigerate," and delivers the boxes in refrigerated trucks.

In the middle of summer, 2003, Albertini's, a large grocery store chain, ordered a shipment of 500 boxes of "Zip" pickles, and had them delivered to its Dallas warehouse, planning to divide the boxes up and send them to the 20 retail Albertini's stores in the Dallas area. Due to a mix-up in the paperwork, Albertini's employees let the boxes of Zip pickles stand on the floor of the hot warehouse (unrefrigerated) for several days before shipping them to the retail stores. Several consumers who subsequently bought the pickles from Albertini's stores wrote to CalPacific complaining that the Zip pickles "tasted disgusting." One of them claimed to have "felt sick" after eating eight of the pickles. Does CalPacific have a viable cause of action for trademark infringement against Albertini's?

76. Plaintiff is a European Corporation that operates a chain of high-end restaurants under the name "Bon Bon." The chain consists of five restaurants, located in Paris, London, Madrid, Milan, and Geneva. Plaintiff advertises its restaurants in a number of American magazines and travel guides, and estimates that approximately 5-7 percent of its customers are American tourists. The defendant, which has no relationship with the plaintiff, has just opened a high-end restaurant in New York under the name "Bon Bon." Plaintiff has brought suit to enjoin defendant's use of "Bon Bon" pursuant to Lanham Act §43(a). Assuming that the defendant's use creates a likelihood of consumer confusion about the affiliation of the New York restaurant, is plaintiff likely to succeed? Why or why not? _____

77. The hip musical group "Outtathisworld" wrote and recorded a song entitled "Home from the Star Wars," which has become a top hit. The owner of the "Star Wars" mark for movies, books, video games, and related merchandise has filed suit to enjoin the use, alleging trademark infringement and dilution claims. What is the appropriate standard for evaluating each of these claims? On what ground would the defendant be most likely to prevail? _____

78. Defendant creates a contextual advertising computer program and includes it in a bundle, along with two screen saver programs. Defendant makes the bundle available for Internet users to download free of charge on its web site. The contextual advertising program is installed automatically when a downloader installs one of the free screen saver programs on his or her computer. (Downloaders are notified of the automatic installation feature before they complete their free download of the bundle from the defendant's web site.)

The contextual advertising program contains a directory of terms that are relevant to a range of topics, such as gardening, automobile accessories, and gourmet food items. Whenever the computer user browses the Internet, the program compares the user's search terms and the URL's of the web sites the user visits to the terms in its directory. When it finds a match, it causes the screen display on the user's computer to be completely covered by a new display that advertises a product related to the matched directory term. The advertising display clearly indicates that the advertising is generated by defendant's program, and is not connected in any way with whatever had previously been on the user's screen. When the user clicks the "x" button to get rid of the ad, the user finds himself "mouse-trapped": he must click through a series of five to ten ads before he can exit and return to the previous material he was viewing (search result page or web site). Each ad in the series offers the user the option to "click here" to go to the advertiser's web site. It is made clear in each instance that clicking on the "click here" button will take the user to the web site of the advertiser, and that the advertiser is an entity that is independent of the web site or search result the user was viewing before the advertisements appeared on his screen.

Plaintiff owns the mark "Garden Heaven," which it uses in sales of a range of gardening products, both through its large chain of retail stores and through its Internet site at gardenheaven.com. The defendant's contextual advertising directory includes both "Garden Heaven" and "gardenheaven.com." Thus, whenever users enter either term as a search term for plaintiff's web site or visit the gardenheaven.com web site, defendant's contextual advertising program makes a match and triggers a series of gardening-related advertisements as described above. Does the plaintiff have a viable cause of action for trademark infringement? Please explain your answer. _____

79. Acme Muffler Company seeks to register the unusual, low-pitched "purring" sound that running cars make when equipped with an Acme muffler. The muffler has been on the market for approximately ten years, and is quite popular with drag racing enthusiasts and young men who like to "enhance" their cars. Should the P.T.O. register it? _____

80. John Mallenkrodt seeks to register the word "Mallenkrodt," enclosed in a red circle, as a mark for woven floor mats particularly designed and cut to fit in a Ford Taurus station wagon. Should the P.T.O. accept it for registration? _____

81. Novelties, Inc. has filed an intent-to-use application to register the word "Superior" for its new line of kitchen sponges. Should the P.T.O. allow the application? _____

82. Law, Inc., applies to register the words "Mexican Law Summaries" and "Canadian Law Summaries" on the Principal Register as marks for books summarizing Mexican law and Canadian Law for American lawyers whose practice would be improved by a basic understanding of the law of these countries. This is a use-based application that demonstrates use for over 10 years and heavy advertising in journals and newspapers directed to lawyers. Should the P.T.O. register these marks? _____

Sample Answers

59. "Mr. Justice" for legal study aids: The P.T.O might object that this is primarily merely a surname, within the meaning of Lanham Act §2(e). If it is, then it cannot be registered absent a showing of secondary meaning. Generally, if a word that is a surname also has another well-known meaning in the language, it will not be deemed "primarily merely a surname." Here, however, even though the

word "Justice" alone has a well-known, non-surname meaning, we must evaluate the impact of the mark in its totality. The use of the word "Mr." preceding the word "Justice" emphasizes the surname significance of the mark, and may render the mark as a whole primarily merely a surname.

In arguing against this result, the applicant should point out that to prospective customers (law students), "Mr. Justice" primarily evokes the image of a U.S. Supreme Court justice or state judge—what many law students aspire to become. If that is the case, the mark is suggestive rather than primarily merely a surname, and can be registered without a showing of secondary meaning. It is not descriptive because it requires the exercise of imagination to get a description of the product from the mark (if you use these study aids, you will be so successful that you will become a judge!).

60. "Bleachwhite" as a mark for a clothing whitening product that contains no bleach: It is likely that consumers will assume that this mark is meant to convey information about the product—that the product contains bleach to whiten clothing. Because the product contains no bleach, the mark is either primarily deceptively misdescriptive of the product under Lanham Act §2(e), or is deceptive, under Lanham Act §2(a). In the former case, the mark could still be registered, but only upon a showing of secondary meaning. In the latter case, it could not be registered at all. To decide which it is, the P.T.O. would try to determine whether the presence of bleach in the product would be a material consideration to prospective purchasers. If so, then the mark is deceptive and cannot be registered.

61. The fish mark for cat food comprised of horse meat: This mark may be rejected as deceptive under Lanham Act §2(a). First, since many cat foods contain fish it is likely that consumers would understand the mark to indicate that this product contains fish. Because it does not, it is either primarily deceptively misdescriptive (Lanham Act §2(e), in which case it can only be registered upon a showing of secondary meaning) or deceptive (Lanham Act §2(a), in which case it cannot be registered at all). In deciding whether the mark is primarily deceptively misdescriptive or deceptive, the P.T.O. must determine whether the presence of fish in the product would be a material factor in consumers' purchasing decision. Given the persnickety tastes of cats, it is likely that the presence or absence of fish would be a material consideration for their owners, the prospective purchasers. The mark should be deemed deceptive and refused registration.

62. The configuration of the clip: The appearance of the clip is product feature trade dress. While the Supreme Court's decision in the *Wal-Mart* case addressed protection of unregistered trade dress under Lanham Act §43(a), it seems likely that the *Wal-Mart* reasoning would apply to registration of product configuration trade dress as well. Thus, the clip configuration could not be deemed inherently distinctive, and could only be registered on a showing of secondary meaning.

Moreover, an argument could be made that the clip configuration is functional, under the guidelines set forth in the Supreme Court's *TrafFix* decision. Under *TrafFix*, one must first apply the *Inwood Laboratories* standard for functionality: Is the feature essential to the use or purpose of the article, or does it affect the cost or quality of the article? Here, the finding might depend on the jurisdiction.

Under the Fifth Circuit's construction of this standard, the configuration probably would be deemed functional, because it plays a significant role beyond identifying source: It permits the clip to perform its function of securing a pen to a pocket. The fact that alternative designs are available to perform the same function is irrelevant. The configuration is not an arbitrary, incidental or strictly ornamental element of the product, and therefore it is functional.

Under the Federal Circuit's construction, however, the configuration might not be functional. According to the Federal Circuit, product features are not functional merely because they perform a useful function in a product, other than to indicate source. Rather, product feature trade dress will only be deemed functional if competitors need to copy it in order to compete effectively, because the particular design gives an advantage over alternatives. Four kinds of evidence may be relevant to this inquiry: (1) Is there an expired utility patent that discloses the utilitarian advantage of the design? (2) Does the designer tout the design's utilitarian advantages through advertising? (3) Does the design result from a comparatively simple or cheap method of manufacturing? (4) Since the effect upon competition "is really the crux of the matter," are there other alternatives available to competitors to accomplish the same function? There is no evidence to suggest that competitors need to copy the clip configuration under the first three factors. Under the fourth factor, there are numerous alternative configurations that would work as well, which strongly suggests that the configuration is non-functional under the Federal Circuit's construction of the *Inwood Laboratories* standard.

According to the *TrafFix* decision, even if a product feature is non-functional under the *Inwood Laboratories* standard, one must still apply the *Qualitex* "aesthetic functionality" standard: Would the exclusive use of the feature "put competitors at a significant non-reputation-related disadvantage?" This is a "competitive necessity" inquiry. The presence of numerous alternatives that would give comparable aesthetic satisfaction to consumers makes it likely that the clip configuration would be non-functional under the *Qualitex* standard.

63. "Apple Sauce" for children's clothing: Marks must be evaluated in connection with the particular goods or services they identify. While the words "apple sauce" may be generic for an item of food made of apples, they have no direct relationship to children's clothing, and thus their use is arbitrary. Arbitrary marks are inherently distinctive and can be registered without any showing of secondary meaning. (One might argue that the mark is suggestive of children because most children are fond of apple sauce, and eat a lot of it. Still, the mark would be inherently distinctive and could be registered without a showing of secondary meaning. There is no direct description of the product to support an argument that the mark is merely descriptive.)

64. The words "Champs Elysees" as a mark for luxury automobiles manufactured in Birmingham, England: The Champs Elysees is a world-famous avenue in Paris, lined with exclusive shops, restaurants, theaters, and parks. The words have a strong geographic connotation. Thus, the question arises whether use of the mark for automobiles made elsewhere than the Champs Elysees is primarily geographically deceptively misdescriptive (Lanham Act §2(e)) or deceptive (Lanham Act §2(a)). In either case, the mark cannot be registered.

Since the mark conveys primarily and immediately a geographic connotation to a significant segment of the consuming public, one must ask whether consumers are likely to think that the use of the mark is meant to indicate the geographic origin of the product. Here, most consumers probably *would not think* that the mark was meant to indicate that the cars were *manufactured* on the Champs Elysees because the Paris avenue is not an industrial or manufacturing area. Rather, consumers are likely to take the mark as associating the car with the general qualities of the Champs Elysees—chic, expensive, attractive, and fashionable. This would render the mark suggestive or arbitrary, and inherently distinctive. There would be no bar to registration.

If, on the other hand, consumers would think that the mark indicates that the cars are manufactured on the Champs Elysees (unlikely), then, according to the Court of Appeals for the Federal Circuit, one would have to ask whether the physical place of manufacture would be *a material factor* in consumers' purchasing decision. The Federal Circuit has indicated that the mark will not be deemed either deceptive (under Lanham Act §2(a)) or geographically deceptively misdescriptive (under

Lanham Act §§2(e) and (f)) if the misdescribed geographic origin *would not be a material factor*. In other jurisdictions, the mark might still be found to be disqualified under §§2(e) and (f), even if the place of manufacture would not be a material factor, as long as consumers believed that the cars were manufactured on the Champs Elysees.

65. The illustrated mark for chairs: This is a composite mark, consisting of a simplistic drawing of a chair and hearth rug, and the repeated use of the word "chairs." The overall impact of a mark must be considered in evaluating its distinctiveness. Even though a composite mark contains individual elements that may be deemed generic or merely descriptive of the product, the combination of elements nonetheless may be sufficiently striking and arbitrary to make the composite mark inherently distinctive. In such cases, recognition of rights in the composite mark gives the owner no rights in the individual generic or merely descriptive elements, only in their combined effect.

In the present case, the word "chairs" is the common generic name for the product, and could not be separately recognized or protected as a mark. Likewise, the drawing of a chair could be deemed generic or merely descriptive of the product (although an argument could be made that the drawing is sufficiently whimsical that it is inherently distinctive—for example, cartoon characterizations of products are often found inherently distinctive, if not too realistic). Even if all of the elements are generic or descriptive, however, the use of the drawing of the chair in combination with the hearth rug and the repetitive use of the word "chairs" at arbitrary locations could be deemed inherently distinctive and protected without a showing of secondary meaning. (If not, the overall mark could be deemed descriptive and could be protected with a showing of secondary meaning.)

66. The color gold for page gilding on a leather-bound diary: The Supreme Court has held that colors can be protected as marks. However, color alone is never considered inherently distinctive. Therefore secondary meaning would have to be demonstrated in order to register. That would be hard to do, as gold gilding is very common—even standard—in fine, leather-bound books and diaries. Indeed, gold gilding might be argued to be generic, much as grape leaves are considered generic for wine and the color yellow-green is considered generic for lemon-lime sodas: Consumers may consider it a designation of the product itself (a fine, leather-bound book), rather than a designation of a particular producer.

Moreover, the color gold for gilded pages (a product feature) would likely be deemed functional. First, under the *Inwood Laboratories* test, one could argue that the color gold is not merely arbitrary, incidental, or ornamental. It plays the significant role in accomplishing the purpose of a fine, leather-bound diary, which is to give consumers not just paper to write on, but a fine, opulent, quality journal to display and treasure.

Even if the gold gilding were not deemed functional under the *Inwood Laboratories* standard, it would likely be found functional under the *Qualitex* "aesthetically functional" or "competitive necessity" standard. The color gold carries a special, traditional meaning of luxury and quality to consumers that no other color can emulate. There is no alternative color that would substitute for gold in the binding of a fine leather-bound diary.

67. "Super Pickled" superimposed over a cartoon caricature of a well-known politician who was noted for heavy drinking: This composite mark would need to be evaluated in its entirety. The presence of descriptive elements, in themselves, will not necessarily render the mark "descriptive" of the product (and thus unregisterable under Lanham Act §2(e) absent a showing of secondary meaning). While the words "Super Pickled" might be descriptive of pickled onions, the combination of words and drawing may not. Together they suggest a play on the word "pickled," which, in slang, means "drunk." If that is the meaning that consumers take from the composite mark, it might be suggestive of the product (pickled onions are often placed in cocktails), but not directly descriptive, and thus would be registerable without a showing of secondary meaning. (Even if the mark were deemed primarily descriptive, the applicant may be able to demonstrate secondary meaning, given its eight years of continuous use.)

The applicant might encounter protests under §2(a), however. By invoking the image of the politician, the mark may falsely suggest a connection with a person, living or dead, or bring him into disrepute. Here, the politician's publicity rights are likely violated, as the applicant is using his identity to sell products without his authorization. Section 2(a) can be used to prevent such violations. Moreover, the politician may be deemed to be disparaged by the disrespectful depiction.

68. Brown Corp. has priority because it began its use *before* Ace filed its intent-to-use application. Ace gets the benefit of constructive use as of its application date. Brown, having an earlier use date, prevails because its mark is inherently distinctive, and there is no need to demonstrate acquisition of secondary meaning.

69. The marks, though spelled somewhat differently, sound very similar, and are used for similar products. Their concurrent use in Virginia, Tennessee, and the Carolinas is likely to cause consumer confusion about the source, sponsorship, or affiliation of the parties' products. Z is likely to prevail against Y everywhere except in Virginia.

    X was the first to use the mark. His assignment to Y included the good will represented by the mark because it included the factory, and Y continued to use the mark on similar goods. Thus, the assignment was effective to transfer any geographic or temporal rights X had in the mark to Y. However, X's rights would be limited to Virginia. This is because Z was the first to register, and his mark has now attained incontestable status. This effectively freezes the earlier user's area of priority to the area it occupied on Z's application date. Since X only used the mark in Virginia on that date, Y can only assert superior rights in that portion of its current territory.

70. X Co. has superior rights throughout the country. Even though it only initially used its mark in New York, far from Y Co., and it filed a use application rather than an intent-to-use application, X's registration in August 1993 gave it the benefit of nationwide constructive use of its mark as of its application date (February, 1993). (See Lanham Act §7(c).) Thus, X Co. is officially senior to Y Co. in Mississippi and Alabama and should be able to enjoin Y Co. there if Y's use of the "Hellofawallop" mark creates a likelihood of consumer confusion. Following is a list of factors a court is likely to consider in determining the likelihood of confusion issue, along with an analysis of how each factor weighs.

    a. *Strength of the plaintiff's mark.* "Heckofawallop" is likely to be deemed suggestive of the product, which means that it is inherently distinctive, and thus relatively strong. While the mark is relatively new, the facts state that X introduced the new fortified wine bearing the mark "with much advertising and fanfare," suggesting that it may have acquired secondary meaning as well. Thus, a court is likely to find that the plaintiff's mark is a fairly strong one, which weighs in favor of a finding of confusion.

    b. *Proximity of the goods.* While the goods (fortified wine and malt liquor) do not directly compete, they are related, and consumers thus may think that they come from the same source. This weighs in favor of a finding of confusion, though not as strongly as it would if the products were identical.

c. *Similarity of the marks.* The two marks are similar in sight, sound, and meaning. It should be noted that both words consist of five syllables with the same stress pattern. All of the syllables are the same except for the first one, and the first one is similar (the first syllable of each word begins with "He"). Both words provide the same basic mental image—a drink that hits the user hard—except that the defendant's mark may strike observers as slightly more profound (or profane). This similarity weighs in favor of a likelihood of confusion.

d. *Evidence of actual confusion.* There is none here. However, courts do not require that such evidence be provided. While the presence of such evidence would weigh in favor of a finding for the plaintiff, the lack of it does not necessarily favor the defendant, since actual confusion is not required in order to find infringement.

e. *Marketing channels used.* Here, both parties are likely to use similar marketing channels—retail liquor outlets—and sell to similar or the same customers. They may use similar channels of advertising, but we have no facts on that issue. Similar marketing channels weighs in favor of a finding of likely confusion.

f. *Type of goods and the degree of care likely to be exercised by the purchaser.* Neither of the goods is likely to be expensive or directed to connoisseurs. Customers are likely not to exercise great care. This weighs in favor of a finding for plaintiff.

g. *Defendant's intent in selecting the mark.* Here, it appears that the defendant acted in good faith because it is unlikely that it knew of plaintiff's use at the time that it began its own use. While this will not stop a court from finding a likelihood of confusion, it may motivate the court to tailor the relief it grants as narrowly as possible to permit the defendant to protect its investment in developing good will under the mark.

h. *Likelihood of expansion of the product lines.* We have no facts to suggest that the parties actually plan to expand their lines, but consumers may anticipate that they would, since the products are related.

Given the above analysis, a court would be likely to find that the parties' concurrent use of their marks in Mississippi and Alabama is likely to cause consumer confusion about the source, sponsorship, or affiliation of the parties' goods, and award relief to X Co.

71. Pursuant to the Paris Convention (as implemented in Lanham Act §44(d)), a national of Germany who files an application to register a mark in Germany, and files an application to register the mark in the United States within six months of its German application, gets the benefit of the German application date. Thus, *Z will be treated as having applied to register its mark in the United States in December, 1992, its German filing date.* The P.T.O. acted properly in registering Z's mark without a showing of actual use because Z's mark was registered in Germany, and Z alleged a *bona fide* intent to use the mark in commerce. See Lanham Act §§44(b), (c), and (e). Once Z's mark was registered, it obtained the benefit of *constructive use* dating back to its filing date. *Thus, Z's mark enjoys nationwide priority throughout the United States as of December, 1992. See Lanham Act §7(c).* Z accordingly has priority over both X and Y, and can obtain relief against these parties if their concurrent use of the mark causes a likelihood of consumer confusion.

Applying the factors listed in the answer to Question 70, *supra*, it appears that Z could show a likelihood of confusion, once it begins using the mark throughout the United States on its table wines.

Since "Heckawallap" is a made-up word, it is likely to be deemed fanciful, and thus strong. Z's product does not directly compete with fortified wine and malt liquor, but is a related product, that consumers might expect to come from the same producer. While Z's mark consists of only four syllables, the overall appearance and sound of the mark are highly similar to "Heckofawallop" and "Hellofawallop." The parties' marketing channels are likely to overlap because Z's wines are likely to be sold in retail liquor outlets. While consumers may pay closer attention to the label of a table wine than that of fortified wine or malt liquor, German table wines do not tend to be expensive, and the degree of care is unlikely to be as high, for example, as that paid to the label of an expensive French wine. Thus, while there is no evidence of actual confusion, and the defendants are likely to have acted in good faith, it seems quite possible that Z could make the necessary demonstration of a likelihood of confusion and thus enjoin or limit X and Y's use of their respective marks.

72. X Co. may have a cause of action for trademark infringement, based on an "initial interest confusion" theory. By incorporating X's mark into a domain name and using the domain name for a web site that advertises goods or services, Y uses the "whiz" mark "in connection with" the sale or advertisement of goods that Y is offering for sale. Moreover, that "use" is likely to confuse consumers, at least initially. Internet users often assume that a company will use its trademark in its domain name. Thus, persons wishing to visit X Co.'s web page, to purchase or learn about X's product, may input "whiz.com." Y's use of X's mark in its own domain name will divert those potential customers to Y's web page. While the consumers will learn of their mistake once they read the material on Y's web page, Y will have obtained an opportunity to make its "pitch" to those web site visitors that Y otherwise would not have had, and possibly take sales from X. It is Y's use of X's mark in its domain name, which initially confuses consumers and causes them to *visit* Y's web site, that makes this diversion of sales and interference with X's business good will possible.

X Co. may also have a cause of action for *trademark dilution* under Lanham Act §43(c). To demonstrate dilution, X must show: (1) that its mark is famous; (2) that Y's use qualifies as a use in commerce; (3) that Y's use began after X's "Whiz" mark became famous; and (4) that Y's use "blurs" X's distinctive mark.

The following facts may assist X in establishing the requisite fame: (1) the Whiz mark is inherently distinctive; (2) X has used the mark for a long time; (3) X has used the mark throughout the country; and (4) X has registered the mark.

Use of a mark as a domain name for a commercial web site is clearly a "use in commerce," as required by Lanham Act §43(c). Moreover, it appears that Y's use began *after* X's mark became famous. Accordingly, the remaining question is whether Y's use blurs the distinctive quality of X's mark.

Under the newly revised Lanham Act §43(c), dilution by blurring occurs when the similarity of a famous mark and the defendant's mark causes consumers to associate them, and this association impairs the distinctiveness of the famous mark. Factors that are relevant to this determination include: the degree of similarity between the marks, the degree of the famous mark's inherent or acquired distinctiveness, the extent to which the owner's use of the mark is exclusive, the degree of the famous mark's recognition, whether the defendant intended to create an association with the famous mark, and evidence of actual association of the marks by consumers. Under this standard, X may be able to succeed in demonstrating that Y's actions create a likelihood of dilution by blurring. A number of the statutory factors seem to apply.

First, for all practical purposes, "whiz" and "whiz.com" are virtually identical. To most consumers, the ".com" top level domain just indicates a web presence. Thus, most consumers would assume that the "Whiz" mark would be represented as "whiz.com" on the Internet. Second, "Whiz" is inherently distinctive, and given its long use, probably enjoys wide public recognition. While we have no facts about who else uses "Whiz" as a mark, it probably is not commonly used. Clearly Y intended to cause consumers to associate the "whiz.com" domain name with the plaintiff's mark. One could certainly argue that the use of "whiz.com" as a domain name for a competing web site will dilute the effectiveness of the mark to sell X's products. (Of course, given the content of Y's web site, one could also argue that Y's use is *reinforcing* of the public association of the mark with X as a source of widgets, rather than diminishing.)

Finally, X might bring an anticybersquatting action under Lanham Act §43(d). It appears that X's mark was distinctive at the time Y registered the "Whiz.com" domain name, and arguably was "famous" (for purposes of §43(c)), as well. The key issue is whether Y acted with a *bad-faith intent to profit* from the business good will of the mark. Section 43(d) lists a number of factors to assist in making the bad-faith determination. Looking at these factors, it appears that the following groups of facts would support a finding of bad faith on Y's part. First, Y had no preexisting trademark or other legitimate intellectual property rights in the "Whiz" mark prior to the domain name registration, and "Whiz" was not Y's own legal name or nickname. Y had (so far as we know) never used the "Whiz" mark in connection with the *bona fide* offering of goods or services before. Second, Y's use was strictly commercial. While Y might argue that its use of the Whiz mark was a nominative fair use (because its web site compared Y's product with X's, and needed to refer to X's product by name) this argument is unlikely to prevail. While Y might be privileged to use X's mark on the web site, it was not necessary to place it in the site's domain name. It seems clear that Y registered and used the domain name with the *intent to divert consumers* away from X for commercial gain, and to injure X's business by creating a likelihood of consumer confusion.

73. The first issue is whether "Blossom Brawl" is confusingly similar to "Flower Fracas." The two indications of origin do not sound or look alike, but they have similar meanings, both evoking the image of fighting or chaotic flowers. Both names also employ alliteration as a device to make their names more noticeable and memorable. Similarity of meaning may be sufficient to support a finding of likelihood of confusion, especially if other factors also favor such a finding. Here the parties are in the same business, presumably selling through similar channels of trade to similar consumers. Indeed, some of the consumers may overlap, as many people in Oakland commute to San Francisco to work, shop, or socialize, and thus might buy flowers in either location. While the parties do not advertise in the same newspaper, they both advertise in newspapers, and Oakland residents may subscribe to the San Francisco paper and vise versa. Flowers are not highly expensive items, so consumers might not exercise the same degree of care in ascertaining the source as they might if the items were more expensive. Finally, X's composite mark is inherently distinctive, and arguably a strong mark. While Y did not intentionally adopt a similar name, and there is no evidence of actual confusion, the combination of factors may weigh in favor of a finding of likelihood of confusion.

Since there is no indication in the facts that the parties had registered the names as marks, the common-law rule of geographic rights would apply. The common law provides that a junior user who adopts a confusingly similar mark in good faith in a geographic area that is remote from the senior user's geographic area will not infringe. Defendant in this case probably won't get the benefit of this "remote, good-faith user" defense, however, because his area of use probably was not "remote" for this purpose. Given the close proximity of Oakland to San Francisco, and the likelihood that Oakland residents would encounter plaintiff's shop and its ads in the Chronicle, a court could find that plaintiff had a "presence" in Oakland, so that it was the first user there.

74. The Segundo Corp. is unlikely to succeed in its suit, as long as the goods Ivanov imports are the *same* as those that Segundo sells in the United States. Though Ivanov's imported goods are gray market goods, they will not infringe Segundo's U.S. trademark rights because Segundo and the foreign manufacturer (Rojas) are *related entities*, subject to common ownership and control. Under these circumstances, they will be deemed effectively to be the same person. Under the doctrine of exhaustion, once a trademark owner places its mark on goods and releases them into the stream of commerce, he cannot prohibit their resale with the mark, as long as the use of the mark is truthful and does not cause a likelihood of consumer confusion.

If the goods Ivanov sells are a different grade or quality or have materially different characteristics than those sold by Segundo, then infringement may be found even though Segundo and the manufacturer are related. In that case, sale of Ivanov's goods is likely to mislead consumers, because consumers will assume that the mark on Ivanov's goods indicates that the goods have the same qualities and characteristics as Segundo's goods, when they do not.

75. CalPacific marked the pickles and sold them to Albertini's. The doctrine of first sale (or doctrine of exhaustion) allows Albertini's to resell the goods under the mark, as long as the use of the mark is truthful and not misleading. Here, due to Albertini's failure to refrigerate the pickles, arguably its subsequent resale of them under the Zip mark was misleading and thus infringing. Consumers rely on the mark to indicate quality and the characteristics of goods. When they encounter a jar of pickles bearing the Zip mark, they expect that the pickles will have essentially the same quality and characteristics as prior (properly refrigerated) jars of pickles they bought in the past that bore the same mark. In this case Albertini's has changed the nature of the Zip pickles, so that consumers relying on the mark to indicate quality will be misled, and purchase goods that differ from the goods they meant to buy.

76. The issue is whether the plaintiff meets the "use in commerce" requirement and thus is entitled to protection under the Lanham Act. In *International Bancorp LLC v. Societe Des Bains De Mer Et Du Cercle Des Estrangers A Manaco,* the Fourth Circuit held that a foreign plaintiff could prevail under similar circumstances, even though it only offered its services abroad. The court noted that Lanham Act §45 provides that a mark is used "on services when it is used or displayed in the sale or advertising of services *and* the services are rendered in commerce." The plaintiff used the mark in the U.S. to advertise its services and it rendered its restaurant services "in commerce." "Commerce," for purposes of the Lanham Act, includes foreign trade (trade between subjects of the U.S. and subjects of a foreign nation), and the evidence indicated that the plaintiff's restaurant services were rendered in foreign trade because a number of U.S. citizens patronized the plaintiff's restaurants abroad. The *International Bancorp* case distinguished the Second Circuit's decision in *Buti* (which found no use in commerce because the plaintiff's restaurant services were only rendered abroad) on the grounds that the *Buti* plaintiff conceded that its restaurant services were not a part of U.S.-Italy trade.

77. The defendant is most likely to prevail on the dilution claim because Lanham Act §43(c) expressly provides that the dilution cause of action does not extend to uses of marks in non-commercial speech. A number of courts have held that titles of songs, movies, and books are not core commercial speech, as that concept has been defined by the Supreme Court, and thus that the federal dilution cause of action does not reach unauthorized uses of famous marks in titles.

In the case of infringement claims, the modern trend is to follow the Second Circuit's *Rogers v. Grimaldi* balancing of interests approach in the case of titles of expressive works. The *Rogers* approach balances the public's expressive, First Amendment interests against trademark interests in determining whether to find infringement liability. Under this approach, the unauthorized use of plaintiff's mark in defendant's title will not constitute actionable infringement unless the title has no artistic relevance to the underlying work whatsoever, or if it has some artistic relevance, unless the title explicitly misleads as to the source or the content of the work. While it is not clear what relationship the title has to the song in this case, there does not appear to be any explicit deception in the title.

78. To demonstrate trademark infringement, the plaintiff must demonstrate that the defendant *used the mark in connection with the sale, offering for sale, distribution, or advertising of goods or services.* (Made a "trademark use.") Here, defendant did not make the traditional trademark use, which consists of placing the mark on the goods or the label of goods that it offers for sale. However, in the Internet context, courts have stretched the "use" requirement in a number of ways to encompass non-traditional uses of marks. Thus, there are several precedents that might be used to establish the requisite "use" in this case.

First, the plaintiff might argue trademark "use" by analogy to the metatag cases. As in the metatag cases, defendant is making a hidden replication of the plaintiff's mark (here, in the software directory) that causes a reference to the defendant's clients' goods or services to appear on the screen when Internet users search for plaintiff through use of plaintiff's mark. The defendant is applying the plaintiff's mark in a manner that permits it to advertise its clients' products or services to persons seeking the plaintiff. In this sense, the defendant is (at least indirectly) using plaintiff's mark "in connection with" the advertising of goods or services.

Second, the plaintiff might argue trademark "use" by analogy to the cybersquatting cases. As in the cybersquatting situation, the plaintiff is essentially selling rights in the plaintiff's mark (in this case, it is selling to its advertisers—the right to have their ads associated with the plaintiff's mark). This constitutes "trading on the value" of the plaintiff's mark, as in the cybersquatting cases, and can be characterized as at least an indirect "use" of the plaintiff's mark in connection with the sale of services (defendant's advertising services).

Finally, the plaintiff might argue that the forum domain name line of cases provides precedent for finding the requisite trademark "use." In those cases, courts held that when the defendant used the plaintiff's mark in its domain name, it interfered with the ability of the plaintiff to sell its own goods or services by making it harder for potential customers to find the plaintiff's web site. Thus, the defendant "used" the plaintiff's mark in connection with the *plaintiff's* sale of goods or services. Here, plaintiff might argue that by causing a string of ads to appear on users' screens whenever they input plaintiff's mark in an attempt to find the plaintiff (or whenever they visit the plaintiff's web site), this interferes with plaintiff's ability to sell its goods or services—customers may become angry or frustrated and discontinue their search, or they may get side-tracked and shop at one of the defendant's advertiser's web sites, instead. This constitutes a use of plaintiff's mark in connection with (or in a manner that interferes with) the *plaintiff's* sale of goods or services.

However, the plaintiff in this case would have to overcome the precedent set by the Second Circuit in the *WhenU.Com* case, which had somewhat similar facts. The *WhenU* court found that the contextual advertising defendant did not make an actionable Lanham Act "use" of the plaintiff's mark because reproduction of the plaintiff's mark in the software directory did not expose the mark to consumers in a manner that could enable them to rely on the mark for information about the source of goods or services. Moreover, the defendant did not apply the plaintiff's mark to indicate the source of its or its client's goods or services. It merely used the plaintiffs mark to indicate the proper category of ad to send to the user. The Second Circuit stressed that trademark law is concerned with source identification and is not meant to protect consumer good will in a more general sense. Those same arguments would seem to apply in the present case, and might lead to a finding of no actionable trademark use. (The Second Circuit did, however, distinguish the forum site domain name decisions, on the ground that the defendant's pop-up ads did not interfere with computer users' ability to reach the plaintiff's site. It is not clear that the same distinction would apply in the present case.)

In addition to trademark use, the infringement plaintiff must demonstrate that the defendant's use of its mark causes a likelihood of consumer confusion about the source, sponsorship or affiliation of goods or services. This may prove even more difficult. The facts emphasize that the ads are clearly marked, so that consumers are unlikely to be confused about the source, sponsorship or affiliation either of the ads themselves, or of the goods or services being advertised. While courts have often relied on a "pre-sale" or "initial interest" confusion rationale to find infringement in Internet situations, that argument is less likely to work here. Unlike in the *Brookfield* case, defendant's actions do not present consumers with a potentially confusing choice of sites at which plaintiff might be found, or lead consumers to visit the defendant's web site, thinking it is the plaintiffs'. Rather, inputting the plaintiff's mark leads consumers to plaintiff's web site, but immediately presents an advertisement that is clearly labeled as not affiliated with the plaintiff. Arguably, the consumer never has an opportunity to be confused.

If the *Brookfield* case is construed broadly, it might be read for the proposition that whenever a defendant's application of the plaintiff's mark takes consumers to defendant's site or advertisement, when the consumers intended to go to the plaintiff's site, there is infringement, regardless of the presence of consumer confusion. The key is that the plaintiff's mark has been used to divert consumers from the plaintiff. The dissenting judge in the *Netscape* case read *Brookfield* in this manner, but argued that this result was incorrect and that *Brookfield* should be reversed. According to the dissent, this action is equivalent to stores' common practice of placing house brands alongside or in front of name-brand products, in the hopes of diverting consumers who intended to buy the name brand products. This is simply giving consumers a choice, which has never been deemed to constitute trademark infringement.

Unless the court is inclined to stretch the traditional infringement cause of action as described above, the plaintiff is unlikely to prevail on an infringement cause of action. Note, in addition, that a court may be particularly hesitant to prevent the defendant's use of the words "Garden Heaven," because these are ordinary words in the English language (unlike "gardenheaven"), and prohibiting defendants from including ordinary words in the English language in their directories and metatags would overextend trademark rights.

79. The purring sound of the muffler: Marks can consist of any word, name, symbol or device. A sound may be a symbol or device that indicates source to consumers. Here, however, the purring sound would probably be considered to be a product feature, so that the P.T.O. would want to consider evidence of secondary meaning and non-functionality. The fact that the muffler has been sold with the sound for 10 years, and is popular, would provide some evidence of secondary meaning. However, since consumers are not necessarily accustomed to relying on the sound of a muffler for information about its source, the P.T.O. might require additional evidence. (While Lanham Act §2(f) permits the P.T.O. to presume secondary meaning from the fact that the applicant has made continuous and exclusive use of the alleged mark for 5 years, it does not require it to do so.) The P.T.O. might also take into account the fact that consumers don't normally hear the sound that a muffler makes at the time they purchase it, and thus are more likely to rely on other indications of origin, such as a word mark or packaging, in making their purchase selection.

Functionality would probably turn on whether the purring is a natural by-product of the muffler's functioning or whether the sound has been deliberately manipulated so that it can be characterized as "arbitrary or incidental." If it is the sound that a muffler of that construction necessarily makes, then providing trademark protection in the sound may provide a *de facto* monopoly in the construction of the muffler itself. To extend trademark protection in such a case would be anticompetitive, and would extend trademark protection into the domain of patent law. Under either the Federal Circuit's or the Fifth Circuit's construction of the *Inwood Laboratories* standard, functionality would likely be found: there are no readily available alternative sounds, and the sound is significantly related to the product's function.

80. "Mallenkrodt" enclosed in a red circle as a mark for woven floor mats: Composite marks are considered as a whole. The question for the P.T.O. would be whether this composite mark is primarily merely a surname. The red oval is so commonplace that it may not make enough of an impression on consumers to differentiate the applicant's mark from a plain word mark. If that is the case, then the P.T.O. must determine whether consumers would understand the word "Mallenkrodt" as a surname.

    A word is considered "primarily merely a surname" if consumers are likely to infer a surname meaning, and that is the only well-known meaning the word has. With regard to the first question, the P.T.O. might look to telephone directory listings and do an Internet search to see how widely the name shows up. If it is not a common name, consumers may not associate it with a surname meaning, so that the mark could be registered as inherently distinctive, with or without the red circle. On the other hand, if the public would recognize the word as a surname, and nothing else, and if its combination with the red circle would have the same meaning to consumers, then the P.T.O. would require a showing of secondary meaning.

81. The intent-to-use application to register "Superior" for sponges: The word "superior" is a very common, descriptive (laudatory) term, that would require a showing of secondary meaning. Since the applicant merely intends to use the mark, it cannot have acquired any secondary meaning, and the application should not be allowed. Moreover, the Federal Circuit has held that some marks are so highly descriptive and common that they should be deemed incapable of indicating source, as a matter of law. (They should, in effect, be treated as "generic.") However, this is not the majority rule. Under the majority rule, a descriptive word that is not part of the common name of the product may be registered with a showing of secondary meaning, no matter how common the descriptive word. Thus, once the applicant makes its intended use and acquires secondary meaning, it might be able to register.

82. The words "Mexican Law Summary" and "Canadian Law Summary" for summaries of Mexican and Canadian law. The P.T.O. might object that these marks are generic—the common name of a type or genus of product. The standard for making this determination is whether the primary significance of the mark to consumers is the name of the product or an indication of source. If it is the former, it is generic and cannot be registered, regardless of how long it has been used. Both of these marks are composite marks, which must be evaluated in their entirety. While the words "Law Summary" may be deemed generic, that does not automatically mean that the combination of the terms is. The Ninth Circuit would apply the "Who are you/What are you" test, and look for evidence of how consumers would answer that question. The P.T.O. might do a Google or Nexis search to see if it could find the phrases "Mexican Law Summary" and "Canadian Law Summary" used in a generic sense. The burden would be on the P.T.O. to make a *prima facie* showing of genericness. At that point, the burden would shift to the applicant to overcome the *prima facie* showing.

The *Canfield* decision provides a different approach. In the *Canfield* case, the Third Circuit held that when a producer introduces a product that differs from an established product class in a significant, functional characteristic, and uses the common descriptive word for that characteristic as its name, that new product becomes its own genus, and the term denoting the genus becomes generic if there is no commonly used alternative that effectively communicates the same functional information. In such a case, the court essentially assumes that the primary significance of the alleged mark to the public will be the name of the product itself. Here, the P.T.O. might argue that "Law Summaries" is a class or genus of product, and that the applicant's products differ from that class or genus in a significant, functional characteristic (the summaries are of the law of a particular country). The producer uses the common descriptive word for that characteristic (Mexican, Canadian) as its name. Thus, each of the summaries becomes its own genus, and the term denoting that genus, along with the name denoting the root genus, is generic. There is no commonly used alternative that would effectively communicate the same functional information.

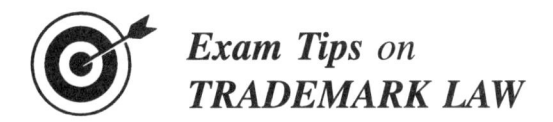

Exam Tips on TRADEMARK LAW

- **Think about the underlying policies:** In the course of analyzing the fact situations in trademark problems, it is useful to *keep the policy concerns underlying trademark protection in mind*, as those policy concerns will often color courts' perception of the facts and influence the courts' analysis and reasoning. Overall, the purpose of trademark protection is to promote competition, but this goal is a complex one and involves a careful balance. On one hand, *strong protection of trademarks promotes competition* by ensuring that consumers can effectively distinguish the goods of one competitor from those of another and exercise their preferences. When consumers are able to exercise their preferences and reward quality with repeat business, businesses are encouraged to strive for better quality and innovative product characteristics, giving consumers more options in the marketplace. On the other hand, *overprotection of marks may impair competition* by depriving competitors of the ability effectively to describe their products to consumers, and by depriving them of access to functional and decorative elements that they legitimately need in order to compete effectively. It may also undermine the First Amendment interests in free speech and commentary and the free flow of useful product-related information to consumers. When these interests are at stake, they may outweigh the interest in avoiding consumer confusion and lead courts to permit an unauthorized use of a word, name, symbol, or device, even though consumers may understand it as indicating source in the plaintiff.

- **Remember that the substantive rules for marks are similar for registered and common-law marks:** While this Outline has discussed the Lanham Act registration provisions at some length, it is important to remember that for the most part (unless the Outline specified otherwise) the substantive rules governing whether a mark can be registered under the Lanham Act are similar to the common-law rules governing whether a mark can be protected. Moreover, the standards for infringement, abandonment, and many other such issues are essentially the same, regardless of whether or not an indication of origin is registered, and whether or not common-law rights are being pursued under Lanham Act §43(a) or state unfair competition law. The Lanham Act registration provisions simply build on the common law by providing some extra benefits to registrants as an incentive to register. Congress wanted to encourage businesses to register their marks for a variety of reasons, including to facilitate nationwide use of marks and to provide a centralized, public record of mark claims.

☛ **Use Lanham Act §2 as a checklist:** In evaluating whether a mark is valid or qualifies for registration or for protection under the common law, it is useful to run through the provisions of Lanham Act §2 (literally, if it is an open book exam, or mentally, if not) to make sure that you have remembered all the possible challenges that might be made to the mark.

☛ **A wide range of things may be protected as indications of origin:** Remember that a wide range of things may be protected as marks ("any word, name, symbol, or device") or as trade dress (including the overall appearance or ambiance of a product or place of business—even including a particular *method of marketing* a product or service). Moreover, on a single package, a number of different elements may qualify for protection as marks besides the brand name, including illustrations, color combinations and designs, slogans, and made-up ingredient names. In addition, the overall combination of these various packaging elements may qualify as trade dress, so that a competitor's packaging may infringe if it creates an overall impression that is similar to the plantiff's and likely to confuse consumers. When you encounter an exam problem, read the question carefully to determine what elements are at issue, and if the question does not specify otherwise, consider all the possibilities for protection.

☛ **Evaluate the distinctiveness of alleged indications of origin:** In many instances, the first issue to consider in a trademark question is whether the mark or trade dress at issue is distinctive. There can be no rights in an indication of origin unless it is either (1) inherently distinctive; or (2) capable of becoming distinctive and has acquired secondary meaning. If the alleged indication of origin is a word mark or a non-abstract illustration, then it is useful to consider the *Abercrombie & Fitch* hierarchy of distinctiveness—(1) arbitrary or fanciful, (2) suggestive, (3) descriptive, and (4) generic—remembering that arbitrary, fanciful, and suggestive indications are inherently distinctive; descriptive indications are capable of becoming distinctive on a showing of secondary meaning; and generic indications can never be distinctive, and thus cannot be protected. When the indication of origin at issue is an *abstract design, a combination of packaging features, or other such nonverbal matter*, it may be easier simply to categorize it as (1) inherently distinctive; (2) merely capable of becoming distinctive; or (3) generic. In these cases, a crucial consideration in distinguishing between inherently distinctive indications and those merely capable of becoming distinctive is whether the indication is commonly used, so that consumers are unlikely initially to perceive it as an indication that the good or service comes from a particular source, and competitors are likely legitimately to need it in their own marketing process.

☛ **Special considerations for product feature trade dress:** Whenever you encounter an exam question involving rights in a feature or combination of features of a product, remember the concerns about trademark protection undermining patents. The Supreme Court has held that product feature (as opposed to product packaging) trade dress can never be deemed inherently distinctive and must always be demonstrated to have secondary meaning. Also remember to evaluate whether the product feature is functional. If it is, it cannot be protected even if it has acquired secondary meaning.

☛ **Timelines can be useful:** Whenever an exam question raises an issue of priority, a timeline can be useful to sort out the facts and keep them straight in your mind. For example, here is a timeline to assist in evaluating the facts in Question 71, above.

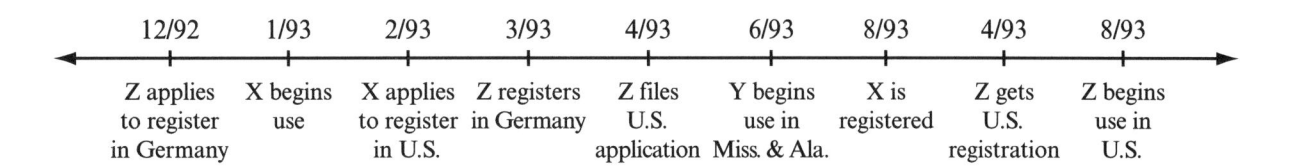

12/92	1/93	2/93	3/93	4/93	6/93	8/93	4/93	8/93
Z applies to register in Germany	X begins use	X applies to register in U.S.	Z registers in Germany	Z files U.S. application	Y begins use in Miss. & Ala.	X is registered	Z gets U.S. registration	Z begins use in U.S.

Chapter 7
UNFAIR COMPETITION

ChapterScope

The law of unfair competition is derived primarily from tort law and consists of several causes of action that redress improper conduct by marketplace actors that may injure others' business good will. This outline addresses the four unfair competition causes of action that are most closely associated with intellectual property interests. These theories arose in the common law, but, as will be discussed, three of them have been liberalized through state and federal statutory enactments.

- **Passing off:** The oldest theory of unfair competition, the passing off cause of action arises when a defendant makes a false representation that suggests to consumers that the defendant's business, goods, or services come from or are sponsored by or affiliated with the plaintiff. The false representation can take a number of forms, including use of a confusingly similar mark, trade dress, or trade name. Section II provides an overview of the common-law and Lanham Act §43(a) versions of passing off, and discusses an important limitation on §43(a) claims recently imposed by the U.S. Supreme Court.

- **Commercial disparagement:** The cause of action for commercial disparagement imposes liability for a defendant's false or deceptive representations about the quality or characteristics of the *plaintiff's* goods or services. As in the case of false advertising, plaintiffs have had difficulty demonstrating the requisite injury in common-law disparagement claims. However, Lanham Act §43(a) makes injunctive relief much more accessible.

- **False advertising:** A cause of action for false advertising arises when a defendant misrepresents the nature or characteristics of *his own* goods to consumers. While this cause of action was long constrained by the common-law requirement that the plaintiff demonstrate lost sales, the Lanham Act §43(a) false advertising cause of action provides the means to enjoin false advertising on a showing that the advertising is *likely* to injure the plaintiff. Section III addresses the false advertising causes of action. Section IV discusses these and related matters.

- **Misappropriation:** A number of states have adopted the misappropriation cause of action from the U.S. Supreme Court's decision in *International News Service v. Associated Press*. This state cause of action provides a plaintiff with redress when the plaintiff has invested to create an intangible trade value, the defendant has appropriated the trade value in a manner that constitutes free riding, and the plaintiff thereby suffers competitive injury. This cause of action is often vulnerable to federal preemption challenges. Section V discusses the misappropriation cause of action.

- **International treaty provisions:** Section VI discusses relevant provisions of the Paris Convention and the TRIPs agreement regarding protection against unfair competition.

I. THE NATURE OF THE LAW OF UNFAIR COMPETITION

A. **The nature of the law of unfair competition:** The term "unfair competition" is an umbrella term that covers a number of different theories of redress for *improper conduct in the marketplace—*

improper conduct by business entities that injures others' business good will or related intangible trade values. The prior chapter discussed trademark and trade dress infringement, which are part of the greater realm of unfair competition. This chapter will address additional unfair competition doctrines.

- B. **The origin of the law of unfair competition:** The law of unfair competition had its origin in the law of torts, but it has since evolved into an independent field of its own, as is demonstrated by the American Law Institute's decision to create a separate Restatement (Third) of Unfair Competition. Nonetheless, the influence of tort doctrine still readily can be seen in many of the unfair competition doctrines. Three of the doctrines discussed below—passing off, false advertising, and commercial disparagement—entail a defendant's *misrepresentations of fact* and draw from the tort doctrine of deceit. The other doctrine—misappropriation—more nearly tracks tort concepts of trespass and conversion. All of these unfair competition doctrines exist in *state law*. However, Lanham Act §43(a) provides *a federal cause of action that parallels three of them*: the doctrines of passing off, false advertising, and commercial disparagement. These federal causes of action have become very popular with plaintiffs because they modernize and expand the original common-law versions and provide the same liberal remedies that are available for infringement of marks.

II. PASSING OFF

- A. **The nature of the "passing off" cause of action:** Passing off (also known as "palming off") is the oldest theory of unfair competition. It is very broad, encompassing a wide range of activity. Essentially, passing off occurs *when the defendant makes some form of false representation that tends to cause consumers to believe that the defendant's business, goods, or services come from or are sponsored by or affiliated with the plaintiff*. Such a false representation may take a number of forms.

    1. **A direct false representation:** The defendant may directly misrepresent the source of its goods or services or the affiliation of its business.

        Example: Defendant, a retailer, specifically tells customers that his goods or services come from plaintiff when in fact they do not.

        Example: Defendant, a retailer, fills customer orders for plaintiff's brand by supplying brand X and not telling the customers of the switch.

    2. **An indirect false representation:** The defendant may indirectly misrepresent the source of its goods or services or the affiliation of its business by adopting a trademark, service mark, trade dress, or trade name that is confusingly similar to the plaintiff's. He might also solicit orders for his own goods by showing customers "samples" or photographs that actually are or depict the plaintiff's goods.

        a. **The requirement of intent:** Under modern law a defendant may be liable for passing off if: (1) he simulates the plaintiff's distinctive mark, trade dress, or trade name; (2) he uses the simulation in connection with the sale or advertising of goods or services; and (3) this causes a likelihood of consumer confusion about the source, sponsorship, or affiliation of businesses, goods, or services. No showing of wrongful intent or of actual consumer confusion need be made if these elements are demonstrated. (See pp. 261-262, *supra*, for a discussion of intent and actual confusion under trademark law.)

b. **Passing off versus trademark infringement:** In the past, courts distinguished between "trademark infringement" and "passing off" (the latter covering a larger range of indications of origin, including trade names and trade dress, and imposing somewhat different rules). Today, however, there are no substantive differences in the common law governing infringement of trademarks, trade names, and trade dress. Each involves a form of misrepresentation about the source of goods or services. The same rules concerning distinctiveness, functionality, ownership, priority, and geographic rights apply, regardless of whether the defendant allegedly infringed the plaintiff's unregistered mark, trade dress, or trade name, and the same "likelihood of confusion" standard will govern.

c. **Terminology:** Terminology in this field has changed over the years, too, and may be confusing to newcomers. At early common law, inherently distinctive marks—arbitrary, fanciful, or suggestive marks—were known collectively as "technical trademarks." Marks that were not inherently distinctive, but were capable of becoming distinctive through acquisition of secondary meaning, were called "trade names." Today all these categories of marks are referred to simply as marks or trademarks. In modern usage the term "trade name" refers not to a mark but to the name of a company, partnership, or other business. Trade names, like marks, may be inherently distinctive or merely capable of becoming distinctive upon a showing of secondary meaning. Trade names will be discussed more fully below.

B. **Lanham Act §43(a):** Lanham Act §43(a), 15 U.S.C. §1125(a), prohibits the use of "false designations of origin" in connection with goods, services, or their containers that are "likely to cause confusion, to cause mistake, or to deceive as to the affiliation, connection, or association of [the user] with another person, or as to the origin, sponsorship, or approval of his or her goods, services, or commercial activities." This provides a federal cause of action for claims of infringement of unregistered marks and other "passing off" types of claims, such as trade name infringement and trade dress infringement. Thus, businesses may bring either a state common-law claim for passing off, or a federal claim under §43(a), or both. Of course, because Congress relied on its Commerce Clause powers in enacting §43(a), plaintiffs bringing §43(a) claims must always establish federal jurisdiction by showing that the prohibited activities they complain of took place in or affected *interstate commerce*.

1. **Relationship to the Lanham Act registration provisions:** In a §43(a) claim regarding infringement of an unregistered mark, trade name, or trade dress, the various benefits of Lanham Act registration will not apply. Thus, for example, there will be *no presumptions of validity* and *no incontestability status*. Similarly, since there is no registration, there can be *no constructive use or notice* resulting from registration. Traditional common-law rules regarding geographic boundaries, ownership of marks, and priority will govern. (See TRADEMARK LAW, *supra*, pp. 244-246, 251-252.) The chief advantages of bringing a passing off type of claim under §43(a), rather than pursuant to state law, is the access that §43(a) gives to federal courts (federal question jurisdiction) and the generous remedies that are available under the Lanham Act. (See TRADEMARK LAW, *supra*, pp. 283-285.)

2. **Construing §43(a):** In the absence of statutory language or legislative history directing otherwise, courts look both to "general principles of common law" and to other Lanham Act trademark provisions for precedent and guidance in construing and applying §43(a) to passing off types of claims. For example, in *Two Pesos, Inc. v. Taco Cabana, Inc.,* 505 U.S. 763 (1992), the Supreme Court relied on Lanham Act §2 registration provisions in finding that §43(a)

protected unregistered, inherently distinctive trade dress, regardless of the existence of secondary meaning. The Court made it clear that *the general principles regarding the qualifications of marks for registration under Lanham Act §2 should apply in determining whether unregistered marks, trade names, or trade dress are entitled to protection under §43(a).*

C. Trade names: Trademarks and trade dress are discussed at length in the prior chapter. While the Lanham Act differentiates trade names (the names of businesses) from marks, and only permits registration of the latter, the common law of passing off has traditionally protected trade names on much the same basis as marks. Lanham Act §43(a) follows this tradition. The rules regarding ownership of trade names and the rights of trade name owners are very similar to those regarding ownership and rights in marks. Thus, for example, trade names must satisfy the same standards of distinctiveness as marks. Ownership of a trade name goes to the first business to use the trade name to conduct business. (Or, if the trade name is not inherently distinctive, ownership goes to the first business to acquire secondary meaning in it.) Infringement occurs if the defendant uses a similar trade name in a way that causes a likelihood of consumer confusion about the identity, sponsorship, or affiliation of the parties' businesses. The trade name owner's geographic rights under the common law are the same as the geographic rights of unregistered mark owners, as described in TRADEMARK LAW, *supra*, pp. 251-252.

1. **Incorporation under a particular trade name:** Rights in trade names arise through use. *Incorporation* under a name, as opposed to *use* of the name in the ordinary course of business, generally gives no rights in the name. Some states alter this rule somewhat by statute, however, prohibiting businesses from incorporating under a name that is confusingly similar to that of a corporation already incorporated and authorized to transact business in that state.

2. **Special sensitivity to use of personal names:** Passing off law traditionally has been sensitive to a person's interest in using his or her own name as a trade name. Early cases suggested that a plaintiff could only enjoin a defendant from using a confusingly similar personal name upon a showing of actual intent to deceive consumers and actual consumer confusion. The modern trend, however, is to provide relief to a plaintiff upon a simple showing of a likelihood of consumer confusion resulting from the defendant's use of a similar name. However, in such cases courts are inclined to tailor injunctive relief narrowly, leaving the defendant as many opportunities to use the name as is possible, while avoiding a likelihood of consumer confusion. Courts sometimes give a person's interest in using his own name less weight when the name is being used for a corporation, rather than a sole proprietorship or partnership, since a corporation is a separate legal entity.

   Example: The plaintiff has superior rights in the trade name "Findlay," by virtue of being the first to use it as a name for an art gallery. The defendant, who is named Findlay, begins using his name as a trade name for an art gallery in the same geographic area and the plaintiff sues, demonstrating that the defendant's use causes a likelihood of consumer confusion about the identity or affiliation of the businesses. The court will probably try to find a way to allow the defendant at least a limited use of his name, if this can be done while avoiding confusion. For example, the defendant may only be enjoined from using the name in certain locations, or he may be permitted to use the name, but only with a disclaimer or in combination with other words, so that the likelihood of confusion is mitigated.

D. Use of the passing off claim to fill the gaps left by other intellectual property doctrines: The cause of action for passing off, particularly under Lanham Act §43(a), is very flexible, and can be used to redress a wide range of alleged wrongs. It has sometimes been used to fill the gaps left by other intellectual property doctrines. For example, while copyright law does not generally extend protection to the titles of books and other works of authorship, these have sometimes been protected as unregistered marks under Lanham Act §43(a). Lanham Act §43(a) may also be extended to provide rights in literary characters whose protection under copyright law has been uncertain. A defendant's unauthorized use of a literary character created by the plaintiff may cause a likelihood of confusion, suggesting to consumers that the plaintiff wrote the defendant's book, or is otherwise affiliated with the defendant. Moreover, as will be discussed in the next chapter, the passing off cause of action is sometimes used as an alternative to a right of publicity claim.

1. **Use of Lanham Act §43(a) to vindicate the moral rights interest in attribution:** Most countries recognize a "right of attribution" and a "right of integrity" in the creators of literary, artistic, musical, and other works of authorship. The *"right of attribution"* recognizes and protects an author's interest in being recognized as the author of his work; in preventing his work from being attributed to someone else; and in preventing the use of his name on works created by others (including distorted editions of the author's original work). The *right of integrity* allows the author to prevent any deforming or mutilating changes to his work that might injure his professional reputation, even after he has transferred title to the work. U.S. international treaty obligations require that the United States protect these interests, but Congress has only provided express rights to attribution and integrity for a very limited class of works—works of visual art—under the Copyright Act. (See COPYRIGHTS, *supra*, pp. 153-156.) Accordingly, authors, artists, and others seeking to vindicate these interests have sometimes turned to Lanham Act §43(a). While §43(a) does not give a right to prevent distortion or mutilation of a work, it might enable the original author to prevent *attribution* of the altered work to himself. Moreover, §43(a) might give the creator the right to prevent misattribution of her work to others, or to avoid having others' work misattributed to her.

    Example: Plaintiff comedians created scripts for 30-minute television programs in which their comedy group performed funny skits. The programs were filmed and broadcast in Britain without commercial interruption. The British broadcaster licensed an American network to broadcast some of the shows in the United States. Without authorization, the U.S. broadcaster edited out almost a third of the programs to make time for advertisements, and to cut out "offensive and obscene matter." The edited versions at times omitted the climax of a skit or deleted essential elements in the schematic development of a story line. Appalled at the garbled, distorted version of their work that ultimately was aired on U.S. television, the comedy group sued, alleging a violation of Lanham Act §43(a). The court enjoined further broadcast of the edited programs, finding §43(a) to be a proper means for vindicating the plaintiffs' moral right interest in preventing presentation of its work to the public in a distorted form. Although it was technically true that the programs came from the comedy group, the programs were so extensively changed that attributing them to the plaintiffs created a false impression of their immediate source. *Gilliam v. American Broadcasting Companies, Inc.*, 538 F.2d 14 (2d Cir. 1976).

    Example: X and Y, as members of the same band, co-authored a song. Later X left the first band and joined a new one. X then published the song, listing himself as the sole author. Y sued, alleging a false indication of the song's origin under Lanham Act §43(a). The court found that the complaint stated a cause of action, characterizing the claim as one for reverse passing off. X had falsely designated the plaintiff's work as his own. This deprived Y of recognition and profits arising from the publication. *Lamothe v. Atlantic Recording Corp.*, 847 F.2d 1403 (9th Cir. 1988).

2. **The Supreme Court limits the scope of §43(a):** In *Dastar Corp. v. Twentieth Century Fox Film Corp.*, 539 U.S. 23 (2003), the plaintiff made a television series about World War II, but failed to renew the copyright in the series, causing it to fall into the public domain. The defendant produced a set of videos that it made from tapes of the plaintiff's public domain series, and sold the set as its own product. The plaintiff sued, alleging that the defendant's sale of its video set without proper credit to plaintiff's television series constituted reverse passing off, in violation of Lanham Act §43(a). (Essentially, plaintiff claimed that the defendant made it likely that consumers would think that plaintiff's product came from the defendant—reverse confusion.) The Supreme Court rejected the claim, reasoning that if the defendant had merely bought copies of the plaintiff's television series and repackaged them as its own, this would constitute a violation of §43(a). However, the defendant had made its own copies of the public domain series, and had made some modifications. The Court reasoned that *the phrase "origin of goods" under Lanham Act §43(a) referred to the manufacturer of the physical goods, not to the person who created the ideas or communications embodied in the goods*. Thus, the defendant was the "origin" of the videos, for purposes of §43(a), and there was no misrepresentation.

   a. **The significance of *Dastar* for other Lanham Act §43(a) claims:** The *Dastar* court reasoned that to find Lanham Act protection in that case would cause the Lanham Act to *conflict with copyright law*, which specifically grants the public the right to copy works of authorship without attribution once their copyright has expired. Moreover, recognizing a §43(a) cause of action in a case such as this would render the limitations Congress placed on the express moral right of attribution in the Copyright Act superfluous. (See COPYRIGHTS, *supra*, pp. 153-156.) On a more general level, the Court cautioned against "misuse or overextension" of trademark and related protections into "areas traditionally occupied by patent or copyright law." Thus, the *Dastar* opinion generally suggested that when a product falls within the subject matter of patent or copyright law, but does not merit protection under patent or copyright law, courts should avoid construing the Lanham act to provide a substitute form of protection.

III. FALSE ADVERTISING

A. **The common-law false advertising cause of action:** Prior to the 1920s, courts hesitated to go beyond the cause of action for passing off to hold a defendant liable for false representations about the *nature*, as opposed to the *source* of his goods or services. However, modern common law recognizes a cause of action for false advertising when a defendant *misrepresents the nature or characteristics of his own goods to consumers*, as long as the plaintiff can demonstrate that the misrepresentation resulted in lost sales.

Example: In *Ely-Norris Safe Co. v. Mosler Safe Co.*, 7 F.2d 603 (2d Cir. 1925), *rev'd on other grounds*, 273 U.S. 132 (1927), the plaintiff, who sold safes with "explosion chambers," sued to enjoin the defendant from falsely representing to customers that its safes had explosion chambers when in fact they did not. There were no allegations that the defendant's misrepresentations led to a likelihood of consumer confusion about the source of its goods, but the court nonetheless found that the complaint stated a cause of action. The court reasoned that the law of unfair competition should provide relief whenever: (1) the plaintiff has in fact lost customers; (2) by means that the law forbids, such as deceit. However, the court stressed that in order to prevail, a plaintiff must prove that *but for the defendant's deceit, customers purchasing from the defendant would have purchased from the plaintiff*. If the plaintiff could not make such proof he could not demonstrate any ascertainable loss or injury, and thus would have no cause of action. He could not sue as a vicarious avenger of the defendant's misled customers. (In *Mosler Safe*, the court of appeals construed the complaint to allege that the plaintiff was the *only* legal source of safes with explosion chambers, and thus found that the plaintiff could make the necessary showing that but for the defendant's false advertising, the defendant's customers would have bought from it. The Supreme Court reversed on the ground that the court of appeals had misconstrued the complaint's allegations. Given the reason for the reversal, the Second Circuit's substantive reasoning continued to be persuasive, and eventually gained general acceptance.)

1. **The difficulty of satisfying the ascertainable loss requirement:** The requirement that the plaintiff demonstrate *actual loss of customers* has limited the common-law false advertising cause of action. For example, suppose that A, B, C, and D all sell widgets in competition with one another. A falsely advertises that its widgets will last ten years. B sues for false advertising. B may be able to convince the court that due to A's false claim, customers bought from A who otherwise would not have. However, in most cases it will be virtually impossible for B to prove that those customers would have bought *from him*, rather than from C or D, in the absence of the deceit. Thus, B will not be able to meet the requirement that he demonstrate an actual loss of customers due to A's false advertising. The modern trend is away from applying the ascertainable loss requirement so strictly.

2. **Additional requirements:** The new Restatement (Third) of Unfair Competition provides that the representation must be *likely to deceive or mislead prospective purchasers*. This is determined by the meaning likely to be attributed to the representation by the audience. Representations that are not literally false may still give rise to liability if they are *misleading or constitute "half-truths" and concern a factor that is material*, or likely to influence the purchasing decision. Although it is not necessary under modern law to prove that the defendant *intended* to deceive, evidence of an intent to deceive may justify an inference that the defendant succeeded in his objective.

B. **State statutes:** Many states have enacted statutory causes of action against false advertising. These statutes differ from one state to the next, and may place the cause of action into the hands of state agencies, consumers, private businesses, or a combination of these entities. Those that place a cause of action into private business' hands usually remove some of the barriers to relief placed on false advertising plaintiffs by the common law. For example, those state statutes patterned after the Uniform Deceptive Trade Practices Act provide injunctive relief to any person "likely to be damaged" by the defendant's false advertising. Thus, competitors may enjoin the false advertising without the necessity of proving an actual loss of customers resulting from the defendant's deceit.

C. **Lanham Act §43(a):** Lanham Act §43(a) prohibits use of a "false or misleading description of fact, or false or misleading representation of fact" in commercial advertising or promotion, which "misrepresents the nature, characteristics, qualities, or geographic origin of . . . goods, services, or commercial activities." The §43(a) cause of action has been construed to extend well beyond the confines of the common law of false advertising. Courts have stated the elements of a §43(a) false advertising claim for injunctive relief to include:

1. a defendant's false or misleading statement of fact in advertising about its own product;
2. the statement actually deceived or had the capacity to deceive a substantial segment of the audience;
3. the deception was material, in that it was likely to influence the purchasing decision;

4. the defendant caused its goods to enter interstate commerce; and
5. the plaintiff has been or is likely to be injured as a result.

1. **Injury:** Section 43(a) was designed to protect consumers, as well as competitors, from a defendant's false representations about his goods or services. Section 43(a) does not give a cause of action directly to consumers, however. Rather, it protects the interests of consumers and competitors simultaneously by making it easier for competitors to enjoin false advertising than has traditionally been possible at common law.

    a. **Injury for purposes of injunctive relief:** To enjoin false advertising under §43(a), the plaintiff need only demonstrate that she is *likely to be damaged* as a result of the defendant's false representations. The plaintiff *need not demonstrate an actual diversion of trade*. The Court of Appeals for the Second Circuit suggested, in *Johnson & Johnson v. Carter-Wallace, Inc.*, 631 F.2d 186 (2d Cir. 1980), that it would be sufficient for the plaintiff to demonstrate:

        1. that the plaintiff and the defendant *compete*, directly or indirectly, in the same market; and
        2. that there is a *logical causal connection* between the alleged false advertising and the plaintiff's sales position—that it is logical, under the circumstances of the case, to believe that the defendant's false advertising will lead to a loss of business for the plaintiff.

        The same court has held that injury will be *presumed*, for purposes of a claim for injunctive relief, when the defendant falsely compares its product with the plaintiff's product by name. The court reasoned that a misleading comparison specifically to the plaintiff's product necessarily would diminish that product's value.

    b. **Injury for purposes of monetary damages:** To obtain money damages for a defendant's false representations about his own goods, the §43(a) plaintiff must meet a higher standard of proof of injury: It must demonstrate *actual consumer reliance* on the false advertisement and *a resulting economic impact on its own business*. However, a plaintiff need not rely entirely on specific proof of lost sales. For example, it might recover damages for profits lost on sales at reduced prices necessitated by the false advertising; for quantifiable injury to the plaintiff's reputation, or for the cost of advertising to repair the damage done by the plaintiff's false advertising.

2. **Falsity and materiality:** The defendant's representation must be material—that is, it must be shown that the representation would be likely to affect an ordinary consumer's purchasing decision. However, §43(a) makes it clear that the defendant's representations need not be false in a literal sense. Representations that are *literally true but misleading*, due to innuendo, omission, or ambiguity, may be deemed "implicitly false" and give rise to liability. When the misrepresentations are implicitly, rather than explicitly false, the plaintiff must prove that consumers in fact understood the advertisement to convey the alleged false message. This evidence may be provided via consumer surveys.

3. **Intent:** Under §43(a), it is *unnecessary* for the plaintiff to demonstrate that the defendant acted with the intent to deceive consumers. However, if the plaintiff does prove deceptive intent, the court may presume that consumers are in fact deceived, thus relieving the plaintiff of the necessity of providing consumer survey evidence on this issue. In such cases, the burden will shift to the defendant to prove an *absence* of consumer deception.

IV. COMMERCIAL DISPARAGEMENT

A. The common-law commercial disparagement cause of action: The cause of action for commercial disparagement has also been called "product disparagement," "trade libel," "slander of title," and "injurious falsehood." It imposes liability for a defendant's false or deceptive representation about the quality or characteristics of the *plaintiff's* goods or services (in contrast to false advertising, which redresses a defendant's false representations about his *own* goods or services). While the elements of this cause of action may vary from one jurisdiction to the next, typical elements include:

1. a false representation;
2. an intent to harm; and
3. specific economic loss, or "special damages."

1. False representation: The defendant's statement may take any number of forms—spoken, written, or nonverbal conduct—as long as the statement directly or indirectly communicates a false and disparaging message to consumers. General comparisons, such as "X's product is not as good as mine," and "puffing," such as "my product is the best," generally do not give rise to liability. Such statements are commonplace, and consumers are unlikely to take them seriously. While some jurisdictions will base liability on a false statement of *opinion* about the plaintiff's product, most require that the defendant's false statement be one of fact. However, this requirement is generally construed broadly. In determining whether a statement is a statement of fact for this purpose, one should ask: Does the statement purport to give specific facts, or at least imply that the maker has specific facts to back up his assertion?

Example: The defendant tells a potential customer that the plaintiff's product will not last for more than two years. This probably would be considered a statement of fact because use of a specific period of time (two years) at least implies that the defendant has specific knowledge of facts, such as formal test results, or prior experience, which lead him to form that conclusion.

2. Intent: There is a split of authority regarding the defendant's intent. Some authorities have stated that the defendant's intent is irrelevant, while others have held that the defendant must have intended to injure the plaintiff, or must at least have acted with reckless disregard of the effect on the plaintiff. The Restatement (Second) of Torts suggests that the defendant must have known that the statement was false or acted in reckless disregard of its truth or falsity.

3. The special damages requirement: The special damages requirement has posed a considerable impediment to plaintiffs in commercial disparagement cases. To satisfy this requirement, a plaintiff must plead and prove actual, specific economic harm resulting from the defendant's disparaging misrepresentation. Traditionally, courts have ruled that this means providing *specific evidence of lost business transactions and customers*. However, the more liberal view allows for some flexibility, for example, when the plaintiff demonstrates that it is impossible to prove specific losses because of the nature of its business. Jurisdictions have also differed over whether special damages must be demonstrated in order to obtain injunctive relief, as well as monetary relief, or whether a lesser showing of injury will be required to support an injunction.

B. State statutory provisions: As in the case of false advertising, the Uniform Deceptive Trade Practices Act provides a more readily available remedy for commercial disparagement in the dozen or so states that have adopted it. The Act provides injunctive relief against false or misleading statements of fact that disparage the goods, services, or business of another, if the plaintiff demonstrates that it is "*likely to be damaged*" by the statements. The Act specifies that proof of specific monetary damage and intent to deceive will not be required.

C. **The Lanham Act §43(a) product disparagement cause of action:** Congress amended §43(a) expressly to extend to disparaging misrepresentations *about a plaintiff's goods or services* in 1988. As amended, §43(a) prohibits a person from making a "false or misleading description of fact, or false or misleading representation of fact" in "commercial advertising or promotion" that "misrepresents the nature, characteristics, qualities, or geographic origin of . . . another person's goods, services, or commercial activities." While this cause of action is similar to a common-law claim for commercial disparagement, it is more liberal. While there have been relatively few opinions construing the new federal disparagement cause of action, the elements are likely to be similar to those for the §43(a) false advertising claim:

1. a defendant's false or misleading statement of fact in commercial advertising or promotion about the plaintiff's product, service, or commercial activities;
2. the statement actually deceived or had the capacity to deceive a substantial segment of the audience;
3. the deception was material, in that it was likely to influence the purchasing decision;
4. the plaintiff caused its goods or services to enter interstate commerce; and
5. the plaintiff has been or is likely to be injured as a result.

1. **Differences between §43(a) and the common law:** Courts are likely to hold, as they have in connection with false advertising types of claims, that the §43(a) disparagement claimant need not prove intent or knowledge on the defendant's part. Likewise, claimants seeking injunctive relief will not have to plead or prove special damages: §43(a) provides a cause of action to persons who are "likely to be damaged" by the false representation. However, as in the case of the §43(a) false advertising claim, a more concrete demonstration of actual economic harm will be needed to support an award of monetary relief.

2. **"Commercial advertising or promotion":** The Lanham Act §43(a) disparagement cause of action is limited to misrepresentations in "commercial advertising or promotion." This limits the cause of action to a defendant's *commercial speech*. (See p. 231, *supra*, for a definition of commercial speech.) Courts have also found that "advertising or promotion," as used in §43(a), entails speech that is intended to influence consumer purchase decisions and that is widely disseminated.

D. **First Amendment considerations in disparagement actions:** The commercial disparagement cause of action bears some similarities to libel, though commercial disparagement vindicates strictly economic interests, while the law of libel primarily vindicates the personal interest in reputation. Because commercial disparagement, like libel, undertakes to regulate speech, First Amendment interests in free speech and press are implicated. In *New York Times v. Sullivan*, 376 U.S. 254 (1964), and succeeding cases, the Supreme Court developed and refined the "*New York Times* rule," which is designed to ensure that First Amendment interests are not unduly abridged in libel actions. Under this rule, plaintiffs who are "public figures" must show with convincing clarity that the defendant's libelous statement was made with *actual malice*—with knowledge that the statement was false or with reckless disregard of whether it was false or not—before they will be permitted to recover. The question arises whether the *New York Times* rule should be applied in commercial disparagement cases, as well.

1. **The *Blue Cross* decision:** In *U.S. Healthcare, Inc. v. Blue Cross of Greater Philadelphia*, 898 F.2d 914 (3d Cir.), *cert. denied*, 498 U.S. 816 (1990), the U.S. Court of Appeals for the Third Circuit held that the *New York Times* rule did not apply to a series of commercial disparagement claims brought pursuant to state common law and Lanham Act §43(a) by two health-care providers. The disparagement claims arose from a series of paid advertisements placed in print and broadcast media.

    a. **Commercial speech:** In finding the *New York Times* rule inapplicable, the Third Circuit emphasized that the advertisements were *commercial speech*, which traditionally has received a lower level of First Amendment protection than other forms of speech. The court defined commercial speech as "expression related to the economic interests of the speaker and its audience, generally in the form of a commercial advertisement for the sale of goods and services." It cited three factors to consider in deciding whether speech is commercial:

        1. is the speech an advertisement;
        2. does the speech refer to a specific product or service; and
        3. does the speaker have an economic motivation for the speech?

        The court held that an affirmative answer to these three questions provides "strong support" for the conclusion that the speech is commercial. The court explained that while the First Amendment protects commercial speech, the level of protection is lower than for other forms of protected speech. This is because:

        1. commercial speech generally makes a lower contribution to the exposition of ideas than other forms of speech;
        2. commercial speakers are less easily dissuaded from their speech because of their economic interest in making it; and
        3. commercial speakers are uniquely situated to evaluate the truthfulness of their speech because of their extensive knowledge of their market and product.

        The court concluded that *when commercial speech is involved, the First Amendment requires no higher standard for liability than that set forth in the elements of the commercial disparagement cause of action.* (Note that the §43(a) cause of action is limited to false representations in "commercial advertising or promotion." Thus, under the Third Circuit's decision, the *New York Times* rule is likely to become an issue only in *state law disparagement cases*, which may provide a cause of action in cases involving speech that is not strictly commercial in nature.)

    b. **Public figure status:** The *New York Times* rule only applies in actions brought by "public figures." The Supreme Court has identified three types of public figures:

        1. those who achieve such stature or notoriety that they are considered public figures in all contexts;
        2. those who become public figures involuntarily (these are exceedingly rare); and
        3. those who are deemed public figures only within the context of a particular public dispute. This last group, called "limited-purpose public figures," have been defined as individuals who voluntarily "thrust themselves to the forefront of particular public controversies in order to influence the resolution of the issue involved."

        Two important factors in determining limited public figure status are whether the person has access to the media and whether the person has voluntarily entered into the controversy.

In *Blue Cross*, even though these two factors seemed to apply to the corporate parties involved in the suit, the court declined to find that the corporate health care providers were public figures for the limited purpose of commenting on health care. The Third Circuit reasoned that although some of the advertisements touched on matters of public concern, their central thrust was commercial. Thus, the parties had acted primarily to generate revenue by influencing customers, not to resolve the issues involved.

V. MISAPPROPRIATION

A. The nature of the misappropriation cause of action: The unfair competition cause of action for misappropriation is broad and flexible, to the point of being amorphous. It had its origin in *International News Service v. Associated Press*, 248 U.S. 215 (1918), a case decided under federal common law prior to *Erie R.R. Co. v. Thompkins*, 304 U.S. 64 (1938). Many state courts found the opinion compelling and adopted the cause of action, giving it a base in state common law. Essentially, the cause of action for misappropriation consists of three elements, as discussed below.

1. **Plaintiff's substantial investment of time, money, skill, or effort to create an intangible trade value:** First, the plaintiff must demonstrate that it has invested a significant amount of time, money, skill, or effort to create something (generally intangible) of commercial value, in which the court can justify finding property rights.

2. **The defendant has appropriated the trade value:** Second, the plaintiff must demonstrate that the defendant has appropriated the intangible trade value in a manner that constitutes "reaping where it has not sown," or free riding.

3. **The plaintiff is thereby injured:** Most courts have also required the plaintiff to demonstrate that it has suffered some form of competitive injury as the result of the defendant's appropriation of the trade value it created. For example, the plaintiff might demonstrate that it lost profits, or concrete opportunities for profit, or advancement in its field. The fact of free-riding, by itself, does not establish injury to the plaintiff. For example, if X creates a highly successful football team, this may give rise to demand for a charter bus company to take fans to X's games. If Y Bus Co. profits by taking advantage of this demand that X has created, X suffers no competitive injury meriting legal redress.

    a. **An exception:** A few opinions have indicated that relief might be granted even in the absence of demonstrable competitive injury, if the public interest would be advanced by granting the plaintiff relief.

    Example: In *Board of Trade of City of Chicago v. Dow Jones & Co., Inc.*, 98 Ill. 2d 109 (1983), Dow Jones sought to prohibit the Board of Trade from using its stock index as the basis for a stock index futures contract. Dow Jones was not itself in the stock index futures contract business, and had no immediate plans to enter it. The court expressly found that Dow Jones could not demonstrate any material injury as a result of the Board's use of its index for this purpose. Nonetheless, the court found that it would be appropriate to enjoin the Board, reasoning that prohibiting the Board from using the Dow Jones index might lead the Board to develop its own index, and that the creation of an additional index would benefit the public. This approach is unusual, and conflicts with the public policy, stressed by the U.S. Supreme Court in numerous cases, that *the ability to copy promotes a competitive* *marketplace,* as long as it does not seriously undercut the incentive to create new products and services.

Example of a misappropriation claim: In the *International News Service* case, in which the misappropriation doctrine was created, plaintiff Associated Press expended considerable time, effort, and money to send its reporters to collect the latest news of World War I in Europe. The plaintiff's reporters wired the news to the plaintiff on the east coast of the United States, and the plaintiff distributed it to its subscribing newspapers. The defendant, a competing news service, bought the early editions of the plaintiff's east-coast subscribing newspapers and visited public bulletin boards maintained by the subscribers, read the news they contained, rewrote it in its own words, and wired it to the defendant's own subscribing newspapers throughout the country. Due to time differences, the defendant's west-coast subscribers could publish the news as early as or earlier than the plaintiff's west-coast subscribers. The Supreme Court expressly found that there was no cause of action for copyright infringement. The Court reaffirmed that news belongs to everybody, but nonetheless recognized limited, "quasi-property" rights in the plaintiff as against the defendant. The Court reasoned that equity required relief, given the plaintiff's effort and expenditure in collecting the news and the fact that the defendant had taken the benefit of that effort and expenditure without making the same kind of investment itself. The defendant was "reaping where it had not sown," or taking a free ride, and the plaintiff suffered competitive injury as a result. In addition, the public would suffer if relief were not granted. If defendants could engage in this form of unfair competition, interfering with the plaintiff's ability to harvest the fruits of its labor, persons in plaintiff's position would have little incentive to invest in bringing the news to the public.

B. **Limitations on the misappropriation cause of action:** The elements of the misappropriation claim can be adapted to fit a great range of situations. In the hands of creative lawyers, misappropriation claims could be used to displace other narrower, more established doctrines of intellectual property law. For example, in the Patent Act, Congress attempted to reach the best possible balance between the conflicting interests of inventors (who may need monopoly rights as an incentive to invent) and the public (which benefits from full access to inventions and strong market competition). To achieve this balance, Congress placed limits on the kinds of inventions that could be the subject of a patent monopoly and the circumstances under which a patent could be granted. If inventors were able to use misappropriation claims to prevent competitors from marketing inventions that Congress declared unpatentable, this would disrupt the careful balance that Congress created under the Patent Act. Likewise, to ensure a competitive marketplace, state and federal courts have both restricted the passing off and trademark causes of action, preventing businesses from enforcing rights in functional product features, or regulating others' collateral use of their marks when the use creates no likelihood of consumer confusion. The courts' efforts would be undermined if businesses could circumvent these restrictions by framing their complaints as misappropriation claims and demonstrating that the defendant's collateral use or use of the functional feature appropriates their hard-earned business good will. For this reason, courts have been conservative in applying the misappropriation doctrine. They have tended to avoid applications that would undermine or circumvent restrictions placed on other intellectual property doctrines. Moreover, as will be discussed in a later chapter, applications of the misappropriation doctrine that would provide rights equivalent to copyright in copyrightable subject matter, or that would frustrate Congress's purposes in enacting federal statutes, will be deemed *preempted*. Indeed, the Court of Appeals for the Second Circuit has relied on preemption grounds to severely limit the misappropriation cause of action. See RELATIONSHIP OF FEDERAL AND STATE LAW, *infra*, p. 344.

VI. INTERNATIONAL TREATIES REGARDING UNFAIR COMPETITION

A. **The Paris Convention:** The Paris Convention for the Protection of Industrial Property (Paris Convention), undertakes to ensure that each of its member nations protects the nationals of its other member countries against unfair competition. (The Paris Convention's provisions regarding patent and trademark protection are discussed *supra* in PATENTS, pp. 80-81, and TRADEMARK LAW, pp. 285-287.)

1. **National treatment:** The Paris Convention is based on the concept of *national treatment*. Each member nation agrees to provide essentially the same protection to nationals of other member nations as it provides to its own nationals. (Nationals of countries outside the Convention who are domiciled or who have real, effective industrial establishments in a member country are entitled to the same treatment as nationals of that member country for purposes of the Paris Convention.) While the principle of national treatment ensures that member nations do not discriminate, it does not in itself undertake to dictate the specifics of members' unfair competition protection. The Paris Convention does, however, impose certain minimum requirements for unfair competition, in addition to its provisions for registration and protection of marks.

2. **Article 10*bis*:** Article 10*bis* of the Paris Convention requires that all member nations provide "*effective protection against unfair competition*." The article defines unfair competition as "any act of competition contrary to honest practices in industrial or commercial matters." Article 10*bis* specifies that, in particular, protection shall be provided against:

    1. "all acts of such nature as to create confusion by any means whatever with the establishment, the goods, or the industrial or commercial activities, of a competitor;"
    2. "false allegations in the course of trade of such a nature as to discredit the establishment, the goods, or the industrial or commercial activities, of a competitor;" and
    3. "indications or allegations the use of which in the course of trade is liable to mislead the public as to the nature, the manufacturing process, the characteristics, the suitability for their purpose, or the quantity, of the goods."

    The United States meets these obligations, respectively, through its causes of action for passing off, disparagement, and false advertising, as described above, and through the provisions of Lanham Act §44, which extent Lanham Act protection to nationals of others parts convention members.

3. **Protection for trade names:** The Paris Convention provides that member nations must protect trade names, but does not impose an obligation to register trade names.

B. **The TRIPs Agreement:** The Agreement on Trade-Related Aspects of Intellectual Property (TRIPs) (see *supra*, pp. 82-83, 197-198, 288-289) incorporates the Paris Convention provisions described above, making them binding on all World Trade Organization members.

Quiz Yourself on
UNFAIR COMPETITION

83. Jacques, a French actor who acted in a supporting role in a French-made movie, learns that the American Company that has obtained the American rights in the movie is distributing the movie on videotape. The videotape credits state that Francois, rather than Jacques, acted in the supporting role. Jacques has asked that the mistake be rectified, but the American Company has refused. Please evaluate whether Jacques might have a cause of action against American Company under the Lanham Act, and explain your answer. _____

84. The Zenpok Corporation manufactures, sells, and services widgets nationwide under the registered mark "Superior." It advertises its widgets heavily, often including the name "Zenpok Corp." in the text of the advertisement. Zenpok also places its name, in small type, at the bottom of its widgets' label. John Jones incorporates a widget repair service under the name Zenpok-Jones, Inc., and begins conducting business under that trade name. Does Zenpok Corp. have a cause of action against Jones? _____

85. Twinkle, Inc., a manufacturer of perfume, advertised that its perfume scent would last for over 48 hours after application to the skin. In fact, no perfume scent will be noticeable more than 24 hours after application. Eau de Waft, Inc., also a manufacturer of perfume, wishes to sue Twinkle for false advertising. What, if any, problems is it likely to encounter? _____

86. Purchasers' Confederation, a nationwide consumer interest group, tests products and publishes the test results in its magazine, entitled "Purchasers' Reports." Purchasers' tested plaintiff's stereo speakers and later published an article falsely stating that individual instruments heard through the plaintiff's speakers "tended to wander about the room." Assuming that this statement is false and disparaging to plaintiff's stereo speakers, would plaintiff have a cause of action under Lanham Act §43(a)? _____

87. Joe and Schmoe own and operate competing carpet installation services. One day Joe tells a customer that he can install carpets "as fast as you can say jackrabbit." In fact, it would take Joe at least an hour to install carpet even in a single small room. Does Schmoe have a cause of action for false advertising against Joe under Lanham Act §43(a)? _____

88. Carla sets up a web site entitled "What's Up in the Entertainment World?" On it, she provides a list of currently popular movie stars, along with a photograph of each star. Next to each star's name and photograph, Carla places a link to another web site that posts a current magazine or newspaper story about the particular star. Her link takes users directly to the story on the other web site, bypassing the other web site's home page (this is known as a "deep link"). When viewers exercise one of the links they see the story in a "frame." The frame divides the viewer's computer screen into sections, one of which shows the story, another of which shows a banner advertisement sold by Carla to an advertiser, and the last of which provides a table of contents and links to other parts of Carla's web site.

Operators of the web sites to which Carla links include a number of entertainment magazines and newspapers, which provide current stories to persons visiting their web sites free of charge. Their hope is that visitors will decide to subscribe to their publications, and they provide the means to do so online. They are displeased with Carla's links, which bypass their subscription information, and would like to prohibit them. Would they have a cause of action for misappropriation? _____

Sample Answers

83. Jacques might allege a "reverse confusion" claim under Lanham Act §43(a). Under this claim, the American Company's actions have led consumers to think that the acting services in the movie come from Francois rather than Jacques. This injures Jacques by depriving him of the credit and good will that would otherwise accrue to him in the acting business, and that is necessary in order to get future acting roles. In effect, Jacques is trying to vindicate his moral right of attribution, which the United States is obligated to protect under international treaty, but which is not expressly protected under the Copyright Act. There have been findings for plaintiffs in Jacques's situation under Lanham Act §43(a) in the past. However, the Supreme Court's recent decision in the *Dastar* case casts doubt on Jacques's chances of success. In *Dastar*, the Court held that Lanham Act §43(a) could not be construed broadly to undercut limitations built into the Copyright Act. There the plaintiff alleged that the defendant's video took most of its material from the plaintiff's earlier video (which had fallen into the public domain), without crediting the plaintiff. The Supreme Court rejected the plaintiff's §43(a) claim on the ground that to allow it would frustrate Congress' purpose in relegating works whose copyright had expired to the public domain, and would undercut Congress's decision to limit the moral right of attribution set forth in the Copyright Act to original works of visual art (which excludes motion pictures).

    Jacques could distinguish *Dastar* on a couple of grounds. First, his movie is not in the public domain, so finding that he has a cause of action will not undermine Congress's purpose of limiting the duration of protection for copyrighted works. However, construing §43(a) to extend to Jacques's situation might still be found to undermine Congress's intent in limiting the Copyright Act's moral right protection to works of visual art. Jacques could also argue that his claim is for *misattribution*, while *Dastar* involved essentially a *lack of attribution*. Misattribution directly deceives the public, and this may be more objectionable from the Lanham Act standpoint. However, the case law to date has not construed *Dastar* to be limited to "lack of attribution" claims.

84. Zenpok is a trade name—the name of a business. Trade names cannot be registered on the Lanham Act Principal Register, but they are indications of origin, and Zenpok Corp. could sue for infringement of its trade name under Lanham Act §43(a) or under state unfair competition (passing off) law. Here, Zenpok appears to be a fanciful name, which is inherently distinctive, and therefore strong. (It is possible that Zenpok is a surname, but because it is so rare, it is unlikely that its meaning would be perceived as "primarily merely a surname" by consumers.) The facts indicate that Zenpok Corp. was the first to use the trade name throughout the country. Therefore it would have priority over Jones and could enjoin Jones's use if Jones's use causes a likelihood of consumer confusion over the identity, source, sponsorship, or affiliation of Jones's business. The court would apply the same factors that are commonly applied to determine the likelihood of consumer confusion in trademark infringement cases.

Here, the plaintiff's name is strong because it is fanciful and probably has significant secondary meaning, by virtue of plaintiff's use of the trade name in advertising and on its labels. The parties both deal with widgets, and their marks are similar (the defendant merely duplicating plaintiff's name and adding his own surname to it). We do not have much information on marketing channels, actual confusion, or the degree of care likely to be exercised by purchasers, or Jones's intent. (Given that Zenpok is nationwide, and Jones is in the same business, he likely was familiar with the Zenpok trade name and may have adopted it for the purpose of suggesting a connection.) However, the first several factors are probably enough to support a finding of likelihood of confusion. Consumers encountering defendant's business are likely to think that it has a connection with the manufacturer of Zenpok widgets—perhaps that defendant is an authorized service provider.

If plaintiff prevails under Lanham Act §43(a), it will be entitled to the same Lanham Act damages that would be available for infringement of a registered trademark.

85. Under the common law, Eau de Waft must demonstrate that it lost customers as a result of Twinkle's false advertising. This might be difficult, since there are many manufacturers of perfume. Even if Eau can show that Twinkle customers would not have bought from Twinkle in the absence of the false advertising, it would be very difficult to prove that they would have bought from Eau rather than from one or more of the other manufacturers.

Eau's best chance is to sue under Lanham Act §43(a). Plaintiffs alleging false advertising under this provision need only show a likelihood of injury in order to enjoin further false advertising. Here, Eau may satisfy this requirement by showing that it competes with Twinkle in the same market and that there is a logical causal connection between Twinkle's false advertising and Eau's sales position—that it is logical to believe that Twinkle's false claims may have lured away Eau customers. (To win damages, Eau would probably still have to demonstrate lost customers.) Other alternatives include suit for an injunction under a state Uniform Deceptive Trade Practices Act or to complain to the F.T.C. in the hopes that the F.T.C. will institute an investigation of Twinkle's advertising practices.

86. No. Lanham Act §43(a) expressly limits false advertising and commercial disparagement claims to misrepresentations of fact made in "commercial advertising or promotion." This limits the cause of action to a defendant's commercial speech. A magazine article such as Purchasers' is not likely to constitute commercial speech, but rather fully protected First Amendment speech. Plaintiff might consider a common-law commercial disparagement claim. However, it might face difficulties satisfying the jurisdiction's requirements for demonstrating damages. Moreover, there is some precedent for finding the *New York Times* rule applicable in a product disparagement case that does not involve commercial speech. If it is applicable, then the plaintiff would have to demonstrate, with clear and convincing evidence, that the defendant acted with actual malice—with knowledge of falsity or reckless disregard for whether the article was false or not.

87. Schmoe has no cause of action for false advertising. First, Joe's statement merely amounts to trade puffery. No consumer would be likely to take his claim literally. They would just take it as a general claim of efficient service. (In legal terms, Schmoe would not be able to demonstrate that Joe's statement "actually deceived or had the capacity to deceive a substantial segment of the audience.") Second, it is not clear that a statement to a single customer, even if a false statement of fact, would fall within §43(a). Some case law indicates that the false claims, which must be made in "advertising or promotion," must be widely disseminated.

88. These facts are somewhat similar to a real case, that raised considerable discussion, but settled before a final resolution from a U.S. court could be obtained. However, the facts are also somewhat similar to those of the *INS* case, which gave rise to the misappropriation cause of action. The misappropriation factors might be evaluated in the following way.

First, the plaintiffs no doubt expended significant time, effort, and expertise to research and write and publish their stories, and the stories have a trade value. Much of the material is time sensitive, and only valuable for a limited time.

Second, by linking to the plaintiffs' sites, Carla is free-riding on the plaintiffs' efforts by incorporating the stories wholesale into her visitors' segmented screens while the stories are still "hot." She does not make the investment in research and writing that the plaintiffs make. Carla profits from providing the stories to her own web site visitors, because the stories attract more visitors, and this enhances her advertising revenues.

Third, the plaintiffs may be injured because, if it were not for Carla's site, Carla's visitors might visit plaintiffs' sites directly, and see the plaintiffs' home pages and the materials that enable visitors to sign up for subscriptions. When visitors read the plaintiffs' stories via Carla's deep links, they bypass the home page and other materials, and may be less likely to sign up for a subscription.

The plaintiffs' misappropriation claim might be preempted by federal law. For information about preemption, see Chapter 9.

Exam Tips on UNFAIR COMPETITION

☞ **Watch out for possible preemption:** Whenever you encounter a problem involving a state cause of action to vindicate intellectual property interests, consider whether the cause of action is vulnerable to a preemption challenge. The law regarding preemption is covered in Chapter 9, *infra*.

CHAPTER 8

THE RIGHT OF PUBLICITY

ChapterScope

The "right of publicity" is *the right to control others' commercial exploitation of one's identity*. A number of states have expressly recognized a cause of action for violation of publicity rights, though early linking of publicity rights to privacy rights has led to some uncertainty and inconsistency in defining the rights. The rights arise from state common law in some jurisdictions and are statutorily created in others.

- **The nature and purpose of publicity rights:** Section I discusses the nature and purpose of the right of publicity. As will be explained, there has been some difference of opinion over what justifies recognizing such a right.

- **The scope of the right—when "identity" is appropriated:** Generally courts have rejected attempts to limit the publicity cause of action to exploitation of *particular aspects of the plaintiff's identity*, such as the plaintiff's likeness or name. As Section II A explains, the plaintiff need only demonstrate that the defendant's actions "evoked" the plaintiff's identity in the minds of a substantial segment of the public, regardless of how the defendant did it.

- **The scope of the right—First Amendment limitations:** States have applied the publicity right broadly to provide a cause of action whenever a defendant makes an unauthorized *commercial* use of a plaintiff's identity. "Commercial use" may be found when the defendant was economically motivated, regardless of whether her use of the plaintiff's identity would be deemed "commercial speech" under First Amendment jurisprudence. However, as Section II B explains, when a plaintiff seeks to enjoin or recover for uses of his identity in *noncommercial speech*, the First Amendment requires a balancing of the publicity interests against the competing First Amendment interests, in light of the particular facts of the case. Relief will be denied when the First Amendment interests outweigh the plaintiff's and the states' interest in enforcing publicity rights.

- **Descendability of the right:** While some early opinions suggested that the right of publicity, like the right of privacy, should end upon death, today the majority opinion is that a decedent's *publicity rights pass to her successors in interest*, just like other economic rights. As Section II C points out, states have differed over the length of time publicity rights endure after death.

- **Preemption and remedies:** Section II E and F point out the vulnerability of publicity rights to federal preemption and discuss the available remedies when a publicity plaintiff is found to prevail.

I. THE NATURE AND PURPOSE OF THE RIGHT OF PUBLICITY

A. **The nature of the publicity cause of action:** The publicity cause of action recognizes that an individual has a *right to prohibit or control others' use of his/her identity for commercial purposes*. This recognition gives the individual a form of property right in his name, likeness, personality, and other aspects of identity. He may license commercial entities to use his identity in selling their products, in return for payment. The right of publicity was first recognized as a distinct cause of action in *Haelan Laboratories, Inc. v. Topps Chewing Gum, Inc.*, 202 F.2d 866, *cert. denied*, 346 U.S. 816 (1953).

1. **Publicity and privacy:** In his famous law review article on privacy rights, Professor William Prosser categorized the substance of the right of publicity as one of four branches of the invasion of privacy tort, which he entitled "appropriation for the defendant's advantage of the plaintiff's name or likeness." The frequent association of the right of publicity with the right of privacy has lead to some confusion, because these two causes of action generally seek to vindicate different interests. Privacy law seeks to protect a personal interest in avoiding the mental anguish that may accompany unwanted publicity or intrusion on one's solitude. In contrast, *the right of publicity primarily vindicates an economic interest.* It is true that mental anguish may be evoked when a defendant uses a photograph of a *private person* without permission in advertising a product. However, when an advertiser uses the photograph of a *celebrity* to promote a product, the injury is more in the nature of appropriating a valuable commodity that the celebrity would like to sell. The large majority of right of publicity claims entail celebrities' interest in vindicating this economic interest. Today, the relationship between the privacy and right of publicity causes of action remains uncertain, varying from one jurisdiction to the next. Some jurisdictions view the right of publicity as a separate cause of action, closely related to unfair competition doctrines, while others continue to view it as one branch of the invasion of privacy tort.

2. **Common law vs. statute:** Many states find the right of publicity cause of action in the common law. Others have enacted statutes authorizing a cause of action for unauthorized commercial appropriation of an individual's identity. The scope of these statutes varies. Some states that have enacted statutory causes of action, such as California, recognize a broader common-law cause of action for the right of publicity, as well. Others, such as New York, have held that the statutory cause of action is exclusive, superseding any common-law claim.

B. **The purpose of the right of publicity claim:** A number of public policies have been invoked to justify the right of publicity cause of action. They include:

1. the need to protect individual privacy (especially in the case of non-celebrity plaintiffs who have been unwillingly thrust into the public arena by the defendant's use of their likeness to advertise products or services);
2. the need to protect against unjust enrichment and defendants' "reaping where they have not sown" by using the plaintiff's hard-earned celebrity status and good will to gain public acceptance for their products;
3. the need to protect against actions likely to lead to consumer confusion about the source, endorsement, or sponsorship of goods and services;
4. the need to provide an incentive to perform, by giving singers, actors, athletes, and other performers property rights in their performances; and
5. an inherent, natural-law sense that one's identity is his personal property.

Some authorities, including the Restatement (Third) of Unfair Competition, have questioned the justification for the right of publicity cause of action, pointing out that most celebrities reap substantial emotional and financial rewards in connection with their celebrity status (for example, as entertainers and sports figures), and do not need the additional incentive that selling their identities for advertising represents. Moreover, other causes of action, including unfair competition, trademark law, and copyright, already provide adequate protection against consumer confusion about the source or sponsorship of products, unjust enrichment, and the unauthorized misappropriation of performances.

II. THE SCOPE OF THE RIGHT OF PUBLICITY

A. **Appropriation of the plaintiff's identity for commercial purposes:** The right of publicity is violated by *unauthorized exploitation of the plaintiff's identity for commercial purposes*. It must be clear that the defendant has *invoked the plaintiff's identity* before a cause of action can be found. For example, the plaintiff must be readily recognizable from the photograph the defendant used. If the defendant used the plaintiff's name, it must appear from the overall context that the plaintiff is being identified, and not someone else who simply happens to have the same or a similar name.

1. **Commercial purposes:** Use of a plaintiff's identity in advertising products or services for sale is clearly a use for "commercial purposes." Incorporating the plaintiff's identity into the product itself (for example, placing the plaintiff's likeness on the exterior surface of children's lunch boxes) is also use for a commercial purpose. A use of the plaintiff's identity may be deemed for "commercial purposes" even if it would not qualify as "commercial speech," as that concept has been developed under the First Amendment. While such cases are subject to careful First Amendment scrutiny, even use of a plaintiff's identity in news reporting or entertainment may qualify as a use for commercial purposes and give rise to a cause of action for violation of the right of publicity. (See pp. 330-332, *infra*, for further discussion of First Amendment scrutiny.)

2. **Ways in which the plaintiff's identity may be appropriated:** Unauthorized commercial exploitation of a plaintiff's identity through use of her name or likeness obviously violates the plaintiff's publicity rights. However, other less direct means of invoking the plaintiff's identity may also give rise to a cause of action.

    a. **Use of the plaintiff's nickname:** In *Hirsch v. S.C. Johnson & Sons, Inc.*, 90 Wisc. 2d 379 (1979), the court found that the famous athlete and team manager "Crazylegs" Hirsch could recover against a cosmetics company for using the name "Crazylegs" to market and promote a shaving cream for women's legs. The fact that the name was a nickname rather than Hirsch's actual name did not preclude a cause of action. According to the court, all that was required was that the nickname clearly identify the plaintiff.

    b. **Use of cartoon images:** In *Ali v. Playgirl, Inc.*, 447 F. Supp. 723 (S.D.N.Y. 1978), the defendant, Playgirl magazine, published a drawing of a nude African-American man sitting on a stool in a corner of a boxing ring with hands taped and arms outstretched on the ropes. An accompanying verse identified the man as "The Greatest." The court found that Muhammad Ali, the former heavyweight champion, stated a cause of action because the drawing, in combination with the verse, clearly identified him.

    c. **Use of phrases associated with the plaintiff:** In *Carson v. Here's Johnny Portable Toilets, Inc.*, 698 F.2d 831 (6th Cir. 1983), the Court of Appeals for the Sixth Circuit found that Johnny Carson, the comedian and television host, could recover against the defendant, who rented "Here's Johnny" portable toilets and advertised itself as "The World's Foremost Commodian." The court reasoned that while Johnny Carson did not create the phrase "Here's Johnny," or even say it in his television show, the phrase was *widely associated* *with* Carson and identified him in the public's mind. By using the phrase, the defendant appropriated the plaintiff's identity to sell its portable toilet rental services.

    d. Use of other devices: In *White v. Samsung Electronics America, Inc.*, 971 F.2d 1395 (9th Cir. 1992), *cert. denied*, 508 U.S. 951 (1993), the defendant electronics company published an advertisement for its video cassette recorders featuring a robot with mechanical features dressed in a blond wig, an evening gown, and jewelry resembling that worn by Wheel of Fortune game show hostess, Vanna White. The robot was posed next to a game board like that used on the Wheel of Fortune game show set. Although the robot did not look like White, the court found that defendant's use of the robot in combination with the wig, clothing, and game board invoked White's identity in viewers' minds. Even though many women have blond hair and wear evening dresses and jewelry, and even though White had not created the game board and had no rights in it, the court found that White had the right to prohibit the defendant's use of these devices in a manner that conjured up her identity. The court explained that *it did not matter how the defendant had appropriated the plaintiff's identity, only that it had done so.* The court noted: "considerable energy and ingenuity are expended by those who have achieved celebrity value to exploit it for profit. The law protects the celebrity's sole right to exploit this value whether the celebrity has achieved her fame out of rare ability, dumb luck, or a combination thereof."

    e. Use of impersonators: Courts have also held that advertisers' *use of individuals who look or sound like the plaintiff* may give rise to a violation of the right of publicity. For example, in *Midler v. Ford Motor Co.*, 849 F.2d 460 (9th Cir. 1988), Ford Motor Company's advertising agency wanted to make an advertisement for Ford automobiles with Bette Midler singing her famous rendition of "Do You Want to Dance" in the background. Ford obtained a license to use the song from the song's copyright owner, but Midler refused to consent to use of her voice. Ford then hired another singer to sing the song, imitating Midler's voice and style as closely as possible. Ford did not use Midler's name or visual image; it merely had another singer imitate her distinctive voice and singing style. The Ninth Circuit found a violation of Midler's right of publicity, reasoning that *imitating Midler's distinctive voice and style had the same effect as directly appropriating it by using a recording of her singing:* In either case Ford was exploiting the value of an attribute of Midler's identity. The court stressed that it did not "go so far as to hold that every imitation of a voice to advertise merchandise is actionable." However, "when a distinctive voice of a professional singer is widely known and is deliberately imitated in order to sell a product, the sellers have appropriated what is not theirs and have committed a tort in California."

B. First Amendment concerns: Unauthorized use of the plaintiff's identity in contexts such as news reporting and entertainment, though "commercial," often will not give rise to a cause of action. First Amendment interests require that persons engaged in political, artistic, and other forms of expression not constituting "commercial speech" have leeway to comment on the characteristics and actions of others. However, *some* limits may be placed on unauthorized use of an individual's identity even in these contexts. In *Zacchini v. Scripps-Howard Broadcasting Co.*, 433 U.S. 562 (1977), the Supreme Court confirmed that the press has a privilege to report matters of legitimate public concern and interest, notwithstanding the subject of the report's state-created right of publicity. But the Court noted that the privilege is not absolute. The individual's personal interest (in *Zacchini*, his ability to earn a livelihood) and the state's interest in providing the publicity cause of action (in *Zacchini*, promoting creativity by protecting an individual's performance) must be taken into account and *balanced against First Amendment interests* in determining how far the press may go.

Example: In *Zacchini*, a local television station filmed the plaintiff's entire 15-second human cannonball act at the county fair, over plaintiff's protests, and played it on the evening news. The Supreme Court held that the First Amendment did not prohibit the plaintiff's suit for damages. The Court considered several factors to be important: (1) the television station had aired the plaintiff's entire act, which impaired his ability to make a living; (2) the station could have accomplished its purpose by airing less than the entire act; and (3) the plaintiff was not trying to *prohibit* the viewing public from seeing his act—he only sought damages, which would allow him to get some payment for his work and control how it was presented to the public.

1. **The transformative nature of the defendant's use:** When a defendant makes an unauthorized use of a plaintiff's identity for commercial purposes, but the use does not constitute commercial speech (speech that does no more than propose a commercial transaction), the court is likely to consider the extent to which the defendant's use of the plaintiff's identity is transformative—whether the work contains significant creative elements beyond the mere celebrity likeness or imitation. The more transformative the work, the more likely the First Amendment interests in a free marketplace of ideas and individual self expression *outweigh* the plaintiff's and state's interest in protecting the plaintiff's economic publicity interest. Thus, as the California Supreme Court has put it, the "inquiry is whether the celebrity likeness is one of the 'raw materials' from which an original work is synthesized or whether the depiction or imitation of the celebrity is the very sum and substance of the work in question"—"whether a product containing a celebrity's likeness is so transformed that it has become primarily the defendant's own expression rather than the celebrity's likeness." *Comedy III Productions, Inc. v. Gary Saderup, Inc.*, 25 Cal. 4th 387 (2001).

   Example: In *Comedy III*, the defendant made and sold lithographs and T-shirts bearing the likeness of The Three Stooges, reproduced from a charcoal drawing he had made. The rendition of the comedians' likeness was an accurate likeness and little more—a conventional portrait made to commercially exploit The Three Stooges' fame. The court found that the First Amendment did not prevent the successors in interest of The Three Stooges from prohibiting the defendant's actions.

   Example: The defendant sports painter created a painting entitled "The Masters of Augusta" (in honor of Tiger Woods's victory at the Masters Golf Tournament in Augusta in 1997) and marketed limited edition prints of the painting. The foreground of the painting featured three views of Woods in different golfing poses. The background featured a clubhouse and likenesses of famous golfers from the past looking at Woods. When Woods sued for violation of his publicity rights, the court found that the painting was not commercial speech, and that it was protected by the First Amendment. The work consisted of more than a literal likeness of Woods, and contained substantial transformative, informational and creative content. *ETW Corp. v. Jireh Publishing, Inc.*, 332 F.3d 915 (6th Cir. 2003).

2. **Other approaches to balancing publicity and First Amendment interests in cases involving noncommercial speech:** The Restatement (Third) of Unfair Competition endorses a "relatedness" test that shelters defendants' use of a plaintiff's identity in a work that is "related to" that person, such as a news report about the person, a biography, or magazine article. Under this approach, use of the identity *solely to attract attention* to a work that is *not related* to the identified person may lead to liability. In *Doe v. TCI Cablevision*, 110 S.W.3d

363 (Mo. 2003), the Missouri Supreme Court rejected both the California "transformative" standard and the Restatement's "relatedness" standard on the ground that they weighed too heavily in favor of First Amendment interests. The Missouri court adopted a "predominant use test" that bases First Amendment protection on whether the defendant's *predominate purpose* is to exploit the commercial value of the individual's identity or to make an expressive comment about the individual.

Example: In *Doe*, a former hockey star sued the publisher of a comic book that had used the star's name as the name of one of the comic's characters. Applying its "predominate purpose" standard, the Missouri Supreme Court found that defendant's use was not protected under the First Amendment. The plaintiff had demonstrated that the defendant had used his name for commercial advantage (to attract hockey fans to buy the comic). The court was unimpressed with the defendant's argument that its use of plaintiff's name was a "metaphorical reference" to suggest that the comic book character was, like the plaintiff, a "tough-guy enforcer." The defendant had conceded that the comic character was not intended to *be* the plaintiff or to constitute a parody or other commentary about the plaintiff.

C. **Descendability of the right of publicity:** Jurisdictions differ about whether and how long a person's right of publicity endures after his death. This is due in part to the association of the right of publicity with the right of privacy. The cause of action for invasion of privacy is highly personal in nature and can only be asserted by the individual whose privacy has been invaded. For this reason, a individual's right of privacy terminates upon his death. The association between the publicity and privacy causes of action has lead some courts to find that the publicity cause of action expires with an individual's death, as well. Most jurisdictions, however, have recognized that the right of publicity is primarily an economic interest, and have found that it *should descend at death to the holder's successors in interest, just like other economic interests, such as trademarks and copyrights.* However, having found that an individual's right of publicity can pass to his successors in interest, courts have hesitated to find that the interest should endure forever, without limit.

   1. **Common-law solutions:** In seeking a rational limit for publicity rights, some courts have looked to copyright law by analogy. Copyright law currently gives authors rights that endure for their lives plus 70 years.

   2. **State statutes:** Some states have enacted statutes that set forth a specific limit for publicity rights. For example, Nevada and Kentucky statutes specify that publicity rights may endure for 50 years after an individual dies. Oklahoma's statute provides that rights may endure for 100 years after death, while Tennessee's statute recognizes a right that lasts for ten years and however long thereafter the right continues to be commercially exploited.

D. **Applicability of the doctrine of first sale:** The doctrine of first sale, which is applicable to patents, trademarks, and copyrights in various forms, is also applicable in connection with the right of publicity. See PATENTS, *supra*, at p. 61; TRADEMARKS, *supra*, at pp. 265-266; COPYRIGHT, *supra*, at pp. 143-145. Thus, for example, if a celebrity authorizes X to produce and sell products incorporating her likeness, subsequent purchasers of the authorized products will have the right to resell them without obtaining X's further authorization.

E. **Remedies for violation of the right:** Preliminary and permanent injunctions are frequently granted for violations of publicity rights. However, First Amendment concerns may limit grants of preliminary injunctions in cases involving noncommercial speech. Monetary damages generally consist of the *fair market value of the defendant's use of the plaintiff's identity.* This may be determined by reference to the charge usually made by the plaintiff or by similarly situated celebrities for a license to make the kind of use that the defendant has made. Any *injury to the plaintiff's reputation,* which may result in lowered demand for her endorsements in the future, may be compensated. Some jurisdictions have permitted the plaintiff to recover the *defendant's profit* attributable to unauthorized use of the plaintiff's identity, as long as it does not lead to double recovery. Punitive damages may be granted in extreme cases.

F. **Possibility of preemption:** Some state actions for violation of the right of publicity may be preempted pursuant to the Constitution's Supremacy Clause or to §301 of the Copyright Act of 1976, which are discussed in the next chapter. For example, in the *Midler* case, if Midler had argued that Ford's use of the particular *song,* "Do You Want to Dance," constituted a violation of her right of publicity (because she is closely identified with that song), that claim might have been preempted under §301 of the Copyright Act. This is because a finding for Midler would give Midler rights equivalent to copyright (e.g., the right to prevent public performance) in copyrightable subject matter (a song). Midler avoided a preemption challenge by arguing that Ford's imitation of her distinctive voice and style (regardless of the song being sung) constituted a violation of her right of publicity. A voice is not copyrightable subject matter.

Quiz Yourself on THE RIGHT OF PUBLICITY

89. The Acme Soap Company places a recognizable image of Demi Moore in a low-cut dress as background on the label of its Acme Beauty Bar, without Moore's authorization. The Acme mark and other printed information is superimposed over the image. Moore's name is not used. Nor is any reference made to her in the printed material on the label. Does Moore have a cause of action for violation of her publicity rights? _____

90. The creators of the weekly comedy program "Friday Night Live" write and perform a skit that satirizes three prominent politicians. The actors performing the skit wear clothes similar to those customarily worn by the politicians, and affect voices, speaking mannerisms, and points of view that effectively bring the politicians to viewers' minds. The comedy show is produced and aired for profit on commercial television stations. (Most of the profits are made by selling advertisements.) Do the three politicians have a cause of action for violation of their publicity rights? _____

Sample Answers

89. Moore is likely to have a cause of action for violation of her right of publicity. By using a recognizable image of her on its label, Acme is appropriating her identity to sell its soap. Use of her image alone is enough, as long as she is recognizable. Since the label of a product is classic commercial speech, Acme is unlikely to have a First Amendment defense.

90. The politicians are unlikely to have a cause of action. The comedy program will not be deemed commercial speech even though aired on commercial television stations and produced for profit. Rather, the show will be deemed fully protected First Amendment expression. Moreover, a satiric comedy skit is likely to be highly transformative, adding significant creative elements of expression, and not merely reproducing the identities of the politicians. The Restatement's "relatedness" standard would dictate a finding for the defendant, because the skit was "about" the identified politicians. Even the Missouri Court's "predominate purpose" standard would likely lead to a finding of First Amendment protection, as the skit appears to have been created "primarily" for expression purposes.

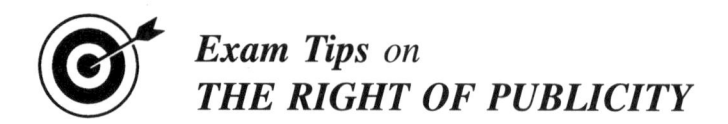

Exam Tips on *THE RIGHT OF PUBLICITY*

☞ **Bear in mind that there is significant overlap:** The right of publicity often overlaps with other causes of action and may be brought as an alternative to those causes of action. For example, unauthorized use of a celebrity's identity in connection with the sale of goods or services may suggest to consumers that the celebrity endorses the goods or services, or is otherwise affiliated with their producer. Therefore, the celebrity may have a cause of action for trademark infringement or passing off, in addition to a cause of action for violation of the right of publicity. Likewise, a famous celebrity plaintiff might allege a cause of action for dilution, to the extent that aspects of his identity are already famous marks for goods or services. (A good example of this might be Paul Newman's image, which he uses as a mark to sell his own line of grocery items. If a defendant uses Newman's image on its own products, this may dilute Newman's mark.)

The cause of action for violation of publicity rights may also overlap with the broad, amorphous cause of action for misappropriation. (See UNFAIR COMPETITION, *supra*, pp. 320-322). Moreover, if the defendant has appropriated the plaintiff's identity by reproducing or disseminating a work of authorship with which she is associated, or her performance of a work of authorship (so that the plaintiff is brought to the public mind) there may be overlap with a cause of action for copyright infringement. Especially in the case of overlap with copyright infringement, be on the lookout for possible arguments that the state publicity cause of action is preempted by federal copyright law.

CHAPTER 9

THE RELATIONSHIP BETWEEN FEDERAL AND STATE LAW

ChapterScope

This chapter examines the tension between federal and state laws that create and protect intellectual property rights. While it is clear that Congress has not undertaken to usurp the field and prohibit *all* state regulation of intellectual property interests (and thus that the states retain the power to regulate these interests under the Tenth Amendment), the states may not regulate in a manner that undercuts or frustrates accomplishment of Congress's purpose in enacting the intellectual property laws that it has. Thus, courts must consider whether a particular state intellectual property cause of action has this effect. If it does, it is preempted, pursuant to the U.S. Constitution's *Supremacy Clause*. In addition, in the course of enacting the Copyright Act of 1976, Congress expressly provided (in §301) that certain kinds of state causes of action that essentially *replicate* a copyright infringement cause of action will be preempted. Thus, courts frequently must determine whether a particular state cause of action falls within those statutory preemption provisions as well.

- **Supremacy Clause preemption:** Section I reviews the standard for Supremacy Clause preemption, and then discusses a line of Supreme Court decisions that have considered Supremacy Clause preemption challenges to state causes of action (including passing off, contract, trade secret, and misappropriation causes of action) that protect intellectual property interests. The section ends with an attempt to reconcile these decisions and with a discussion of the state causes of action that are most at risk of being found preempted.

- **Copyright Act Section 301 preemption:** Section II evaluates the provisions of Copyright Act §301 and two basic elements that must be satisfied before a state cause of action is preempted: The state cause of action must (1) give rights in the *subject matter of copyright*; and (2) provide rights that are *equivalent to the exclusive rights of copyright*. Section II goes on to discuss whether state causes of action giving rights in *facts or ideas* give rights in "the subject matter of copyright," and the various approaches courts have taken to determine whether a state right is *equivalent* to copyright. The section then discusses the typical outcome in cases in which breach of contract, trade secret, passing off, and misappropriation causes of action are alleged to be preempted. The section winds up with discussion of a few express exceptions to §301 preemption.

I. THE SUPREMACY CLAUSE

A. **Federal law prevails over conflicting state law:** Article VI, Clause 2 of the U.S. Constitution provides that "This Constitution, and the Laws of the United States . . . shall be the supreme Law of the Land; and the Judges in every State shall be bound thereby, any Thing in the Constitution or Laws of any State to the Contrary notwithstanding." Pursuant to this clause (known as the "Supremacy Clause"), *state causes of action are preempted if they stand "as an obstacle to the* *accomplishment and execution of the full purposes and objectives of Congress" in enacting a federal statute. Hines v. Davidowitz,* 312 U.S. 52 (1941).

B. Examination of state causes of action in light of the federal Patent and Copyright Acts: On several occasions the U.S. Supreme Court has considered whether a particular state cause of action stands "as an obstacle to the accomplishment and execution of the full purposes and objectives of Congress" in enacting the patent or copyright laws, and thus is preempted. The results have been mixed, and apparent shifts in the Court's perspective from one case to the next have left considerable uncertainty about how strict the test for federal preemption of state intellectual property law is. The relevant line of cases, often called the "*Sears-Compco*" line of cases, is discussed below.

1. The *Sears* and *Compco* cases: *Sears, Roebuck & Co. v Stiffel Co.*, 376 U.S. 225 (1964), and *Compco Corp. v. Day-Brite Lighting, Inc.*, 376 U.S. 234 (1964), were similar claims decided on the same day. In each case the defendant had manufactured and sold a product—in *Sears* a pole lamp and in *Compco* a fluorescent lighting fixture—that a lower court had found confusingly similar in appearance to the plaintiff's product. In each case the plaintiff's product had been awarded a design patent that the lower court found invalid. Nonetheless, the lower court had enjoined the defendant from copying the plaintiff's product on state *unfair competition (passing off) grounds.* In strongly worded opinions the Supreme Court held that the state unfair competition cause of action, as applied in these cases, was *preempted by the federal patent law.*

a. A congressional balance that may not be disturbed: The Court in *Sears* and *Compco* reasoned that in drafting the patent laws, Congress had attempted to balance conflicting public interests: (1) encouraging invention by giving inventors exclusive property rights in their inventions and inventive designs; and (2) promoting a competitive market by leaving ideas in the public domain for others to copy. The *compromise* Congress reached was to provide monopolies of very limited duration for those inventions and inventive designs that were novel and non-obvious, and *to leave all inventions and designs failing to meet those patent standards in the public domain.* Given this understanding, the Court reasoned that Congress had *intended* that all ideas or inventions failing to qualify for patent protection (or for which patent protection had expired) must remain in the public domain. Any state law that permitted an inventor or designer to prevent copying of such an invention or design would frustrate this congressional intent, and thus must be preempted.

b. Copying the product vs. copying marks and trade dress: The Supreme Court qualified its ruling in *Sears* and *Compco* by clarifying that *states may prevent consumer deception about the source of goods by prohibiting the copying of trade marks and trade dress,* as long as they do not, in so doing, prohibit the copying of features of the product itself. Subsequent opinions have construed the Supreme Court's *Sears/Compco* opinions as only prohibiting states from protecting *functional* (as opposed to non-functional) product features.

2. The *Goldstein* case: In the next case in the line, *Goldstein v. California*, 412 U.S. 546 (1973), the petitioner challenged a California criminal statute that prohibited the unauthorized duplication of musical sound recordings. At the time at issue, federal copyright protection was not available for sound recordings. The petitioner argued that under *Sears* and *Compco*, the California statute interfered with Congress's purposes under the Copyright Act: By omitting sound recordings from copyright protection, Congress intended to leave them in the public domain. The California statute, in prohibiting copying, interfered with accomplishment of that purpose and must be preempted. The Court acknowledged its reasoning in *Sears* and *Compco*, but rejected the petitioners' argument. It found that *Congress's intent in enacting the Copyright Act differed* from its intent in enacting the Patent Act. *Congress did not specifically intend that all subject matter excluded from federal copyright protection would remain in the public domain.* "[N]o comparable conflict between state law and federal law arises in the case of recordings of musical performances. In regard to this category of 'writings,' Congress has drawn no balance; rather, it has left the area unattended, and no reason exists why the State should not be free to act."

- a. **No restraint on use of ideas:** In reaching its conclusion, the *Goldstein* Court stressed that under the California statute "[n]o restraint has been placed on the use of an idea or concept; rather, petitioners and other individuals remain free to record the same compositions in precisely the same manner and with the same personnel as appeared on the original recording." The California statute only prohibited taking the actual sounds fixed in the plaintiff's recording.

3. **The *Kewanee* case:** In the next case, *Kewanee Oil Co. v. Bicron Corp.*, 416 U.S. 470 (1974), the defendants argued that state *trade secret laws* were preempted because they frustrated Congress's purpose in enacting the patent laws. The trade secret in this case was a process for growing large crystals. This process was an appropriate subject for a patent but did not qualify for patent protection because the inventor had used it commercially for over one year without filing an application for patent. The challengers argued, pursuant to *Sears* and *Compco*, that Congress intended to relegate the process to the public domain, and state law could not intervene to prohibit copying. However, the Court began its analysis with the statement: "As in the case of the recordings in *Goldstein v. California*, Congress, with respect to non-patentable subject matter, 'has drawn no balance; rather, it has left the area unattended, and no reason exists why the State should not be free to act.' " Thus, *the Kewanee Court seemed to renounce the tough "balancing" and "line-drawing" language of its earlier Sears and Compco opinions.*

- a. **A threefold purpose test:** In place of the "balancing" and "line-drawing" terms of *Sears* and *Compco*, the *Kewanee* Court described the purposes of Congress in passing the patent laws as threefold: (1) *to provide an incentive to invent;* (2) *to promote public disclosure of inventions to inform the public;* and (3) *to ensure that information already in the public domain would remain there.*

- b. **Applying the test to trade secret law:** The Court readily determined that state trade secret protection would not frustrate or interfere with accomplishment of two of these three congressional purposes. First, providing protection for trade secrets *added to business' incentive to invent.* Second, since trade secret information was, by definition, a secret, it was *not in the public domain.* Enforcing trade secret laws could not therefore interfere with Congress's purpose to keep public information in the public domain. The only potential interference that troubled the Court concerned the congressional purpose of encouraging public disclosure of inventions. *The availability of an alternative form of protection might deter inventors from applying for patents and making the public disclosure that is a prerequisite for patent issuance.* Ultimately the Court shrugged this concern away, reasoning that few inventors with inventions that clearly qualified for patent protection would opt for the more limited, weak protection of trade secret law in its place. The minor frustration of congressional purpose that might occur as a result of inventors' choosing trade secret protection over patent protection was *counterbalanced by the interest of the states in exercising their traditional police powers to prohibit commercially unethical behavior and invasions of privacy* through trade secret doctrine.

4. **The *Aronson* case:** In the next case, *Aronson v. Quick Point Pencil Co.*, 440 U.S. 257 (1979), the Court repeated its approach in *Kewanee*. The challenge in *Aronson* went to use of state *contract law to enforce an express contract to pay for use of an idea.* The Patent Office had found the idea/invention that was the subject of the contract (a new kind of key ring) unpatentable. The challenger argued that, under the *Sears/Compco* opinions, Congress had determined that unpatentable inventions must be left freely copyable without state interference, so that use of state law to enforce compliance with a contract to pay for use of the idea interfered with Congress's purpose. Again the Court invoked the *Kewanee* threefold purpose test to determine the preemption question. The Court found that in this case, state *enforcement of the contract furthered the congressional policy of encouraging public disclosure of ideas and inventions,* since the contract led to sale of products that revealed the idea. Moreover, as with trade secret law, enforcement of contracts to pay for ideas would provide *additional incentive to invent.* Enforcement would not withdraw information from the public domain in this case, because the idea that was the subject of the contract at issue *had never been in the public domain:* The contract provided the means by which the product embodying the idea would be manufactured and introduced to the market for the first time. Thus, enforcement of the law would not frustrate or interfere with Congress's purposes in enacting the Patent Act.

   a. **No monopoly in an idea:** In upholding enforcement of the contract in *Aronson*, the Court noted that enforcement would not prevent persons who were not parties to the contract from copying the idea. *In no way could the state doctrine be construed as giving the owner of the idea monopoly rights in it.* Thus, as in *Kewanee*, the Court was tolerant of state rights that it characterized as limited and qualified.

5. **The *Bonito Boats* case:** Finally, in *Bonito Boats, Inc. v. Thunder Craft Boats, Inc.*, 489 U.S. 141 (1989), the Supreme Court examined a Florida statute that prohibited the use of a direct "plug molding" process to duplicate unpatented boat hulls, and forbade the knowing sale of hulls so duplicated. In determining that the statute *was preempted by the Patent Act,* the Court *returned to the view that the Patent Act balances conflicting interests, which it had expounded in Sears and Compco.* The Court acknowledged the "federal policy, found in . . . the Constitution and the implementing federal statutes, of allowing free access to copy whatever the federal patent and copyright laws leave in the public domain." However, *at the same time that the Court reaffirmed its reasoning in Sears and Compco, it also purported to reaffirm its analysis in Kewanee and Aronson.* It portrayed the threefold Congressional purpose considered in those cases—to encourage invention, to promote public disclosure of inventions, and to keep ideas known to the public in the public domain—as part of Congress's overall scheme. The Court concluded that though its more recent cases had taken a "decidedly less rigid view of the scope of federal preemption under the patent laws" than *Sears* and *Compco*, at the bottom line, "the *Sears* Court correctly concluded that the states may not offer patent-like protection to intellectual creations which otherwise remain unprotected as a matter of federal law."

   a. **The Court's analysis:** In assessing the plug molding statute, the Court emphasized that the *statute removed ideas from the public domain,* unlike the trade secret provisions in *Kewanee*. (The protected boat hulls had not been maintained as a secret.) Also, the plug molding statute *gave patent-like protection,* prohibiting all copying of the design idea by use of the highly efficient plug molding process. This, too, differentiated the plug molding statute from the much more limited restrictions on copying imposed under the state trade secret and contract laws. Moreover, in enacting the plug molding statute, the state legislature's purpose was only to encourage invention—it *did not act to promote traditional state police-power goals,* like protecting privacy or preventing commercially unconscionable behavior, that are outside the scope of the patent laws. This was merely an attempt by the state to rearrange the balance Congress had drawn under the patent laws. Such a disruption of Congress's careful plan for a uniform law could not be tolerated. The Court concluded: *"The federal standards, at a minimum, express the Congressional determination that patent-like protection is unwarranted as to certain classes of intellectual property.* The states are simply not free in this regard to offer equivalent protections to ideas which Congress had determined should belong to all."

6. **Where do we stand now?** After *Kewanee* and *Aronson,* many suggested that *Sears* and *Compco,* while not expressly overturned, had been limited to their specific facts and would have little influence on future preemption determinations. However, *Bonito Boats* refutes this. On the other hand, the Court's attempt to reconcile the *Sears/Compco* and *Kewanee* approaches leaves considerable uncertainty about just what the appropriate standard for Supremacy Clause preemption is.

   One way *Bonito Boats* could be read is as follows: In enacting the patent laws, Congress intended that ideas not meeting the high standards for patentability would remain in the public domain free for the public to use. However, a state law that prohibits or restricts copying may be tolerated if:

   1. it is *limited in scope* (provides only limited protection against copying) so that the level of interference with Congress's purpose can be characterized as moderate or slight;
   2. it *does not withdraw ideas that are already within the public domain* or provide a strong disincentive to disclose; and
   3. it is intended to *promote a legitimate state police-power goal* outside the sphere of Congress's concern when it enacted the patent laws.

   a. **State causes of action most open to a Supremacy Clause preemption challenge:** While successful preemption challenges might be made to *specific applications of any* of the state intellectual property causes of action discussed in this outline, the state causes of action *most in danger of preemption* appear to be misappropriation claims and causes of action seeking recovery under the property theory of undeveloped idea law. See UNFAIR COMPETITION, *supra,* pp. 320-322; THE LAW OF UNDEVELOPED IDEAS, *supra,* p. 95.

      i. **Preemption of the misappropriation cause of action:** A preemption challenge is possible whenever a misappropriation claim focuses on the defendant's unauthorized use of an invention, idea, or writing (the subject matter of patent and copyright protection). In such cases it can be argued, under *Sears* and *Compco,* that Congress intended that federal patent and copyright law determine public access to the allegedly misappropriated "thing." Use of state misappropriation law to prohibit copying would interfere with this plan. Moreover, under *Bonito Boats,* the *level of state interference could be great,* since anybody who did not invest the same kind of effort as the plaintiff may be enjoined from copying his intellectual creation on the ground that it constitutes "reaping where he has not sown." In addition, the misappropriation action may *serve little* *purpose other than to provide an incentive to create,* like the plug molding statute in *Bonito Boats.* Finally, if the invention, idea, or writing that the defendant took had already been revealed to the public, enforcement of a misappropriation cause of action might be characterized as *removing ideas from the public domain.*

    ii. **Preemption of the property theory of idea law:** Many of the same arguments made in i., *supra,* would also apply to the property theory of undeveloped idea law, which recognizes *a right in the plaintiff to prevent all unauthorized copying of his idea* if the idea is novel and concrete. Enforcement of the property theory would cause a great interference with the federal plan because, unlike trade secret law, the idea claim would give the plaintiff the right to prohibit all copying and thus possibly give a form of *monopoly* in an idea. Also, there is *no apparent independent state interest* being vindicated by this doctrine, apart from providing an incentive to create, as in *Bonito Boats.*

  b. **Congressional enactment of vessel hull protection:** In 1998, Congress enacted federal law providing a *sui generis* right for designers of "original" boat hulls to prevent the unauthorized making, importation, sale, or distribution of their hulls for ten years. 17 U.S.C. §§1301-1332. This is a form of federal "misappropriation" cause of action. It does not, however, affect the Supreme Court's construction of the law concerning *federal preemption of state rights* in *Bonito Boats.*

II. COPYRIGHT ACT §301

  A. **Uniform system of copyright:** Prior to the Copyright Act of 1976, the United States had a dual system of copyright. State common-law copyright protected unpublished writings. Federal statutory copyright protected writings that were published with proper copyright notice. When Congress enacted the Copyright Act of 1976, it decided to *unify copyright protection and bring it under the exclusive control of Congress.* Congress provided that federal protection would commence as soon as a work of authorship was fixed in tangible form, and expressly provided, in Copyright Act §301, *that state common-law copyright types of claims for fixed works of authorship would be preempted.* In the more recent Visual Artists' Rights Act of 1990, Congress amended §301 to add that state causes of action giving rights equivalent to the moral rights of attribution and integrity in works of visual art, as defined in that Act, would also be preempted. (However, Congress specified that state moral rights extending beyond the life of the author would not be preempted, and that state moral rights *protecting copies outside of the limited editions protected by the Visual Artists' Rights Act* would not be preempted. (Copyright Act §301(f)(2).))

    1. **Preemption reaches beyond literal "copyright" claims:** Congress did not restrict the language of §301 to preempt only state claims *denominated* "copyright," or "rights of attribution or integrity." Rather, §301 provides that *"all legal or equitable rights that are equivalent* to any of the exclusive rights within the general scope of copyright" in "works of authorship that are fixed in tangible form" are preempted. Thus, courts must look to the substance of challenged state claims, and not just to their label, to determine whether they are preempted.

    2. **Dual test for preemption:** Section 301 sets up a dual test for preemption. First, in the particular case at issue, does the state cause of action *protect matter that is "within the subject matter of copyright"* as set forth in Copyright Act §§102 and 103, or is the matter a "work of visual art" as defined in Copyright Act §101? Second, in the particular case at issue, does the

state cause of action *provide rights that are "equivalent" to the rights specified in §§106 or 106A of the Copyright Act?* If both tests are satisfied, then the state-law claim is preempted.

B. **Works of authorship:** The first half of the test for preemption is fairly straightforward. The question is whether the subject matter protected or regulated by the state cause of action in the particular case at issue is a "work of authorship" or a "work of visual art" that is *fixed* in tangible form and comes *within the scope of Copyright Act* §§102, 103, *or* 101. This may be fairly easily ascertained in most cases. Note that it is not necessary that the work *actually qualify* for copyright protection. For example, a compilation that is insufficiently original to qualify for copyright protection under the *Feist* opinion, or that was published without proper notice prior to the Berne Convention Implementation Act, would still be considered a "compilation," and thus a work of authorship under Copyright Act §§103 and 301. One question that has arisen, however, is *whether ideas, procedures, processes, systems, methods of operation, concepts, principles, and discoveries are "within the subject matter of copyright"* as set forth in §102(b), so that state causes of action protecting them may be preempted.

1. **Ideas, procedures, processes, etc. as the subject matter of copyright:** Copyright Act §102(a) provides that copyright protection subsists in "original works of authorship fixed in any tangible medium of expression," and it elaborates that "works of authorship" include literary works, musical works, dramatic works, pantomimes and choreographic works, pictorial, graphic, and sculptural works, motion pictures and other audiovisual works, sound recordings, and works of architecture. *Section 102(b) then provides that "in no case does copyright protection for an original work of authorship extend to any idea, procedure, process, system, method of operation, concept, principle, or discovery, regardless of the form in which it is described, explained, illustrated or embodied in such work."* This language could be interpreted in two ways. There is some support in the case opinions and legislative history for both interpretations.

   a. **Ideas, discoveries, etc. as part of the subject matter of copyright:** Section 102(b) could be interpreted simply to provide that certain elements within an original work of authorship, i.e., ideas, discoveries, etc., *while part of the work of authorship,* will receive no copyright protection. Thus, ideas, discoveries, etc., expressed in original works of authorship are within the subject matter of copyright *because they are part of original works of authorship.* Since §301 preempts state laws that protect the subject matter of copyright, §301 would be interpreted to preempt state laws protecting the ideas, procedures, processes, systems, etc. expressed in works of authorship.

   This is the interpretation adopted by the U.S. Court of Appeals for the Second Circuit in *National Basketball Association v. Motorola, Inc.*, 105 F.3d 841 (2d Cir. 1997). In *NBA v. Motorola*, the court held that NBA's claim for misappropriation against Motorola was preempted. Though Motorola had only taken "real-time" NBA game *scores* and other *factual information* tabulated from copyrightable television and radio broadcasts of NBA games in progress, the court held that the misappropriation claim would provide rights in the subject matter of copyright. Likewise, the Court of Appeals for the Fourth Circuit adopted this interpretation in *U.S. v. Board of Trustees of the University of Alabama*, 104 F.3d 1453 (4th Cir. 1997), when it found plaintiff's conversion claim (alleging that the defendants wrongfully took the ideas and methods expressed in her doctoral dissertation) to be preempted under §301. The Sixth Circuit recently followed the reasoning in the *Board of Trustees* case. *Wrench L.L.C. v. Taco Bell Corp.*, 256 F.3d 446 (6th Cir. 2001).

b. **Ideas, procedures, etc. as outside the subject matter of copyright:** On the other hand, subsection 102(b) could be interpreted to provide that ideas, procedures, etc., are outside the subject matter of copyright—*that by depriving ideas, discoveries, etc., of copyright protection, subsection (b) relieves them of the status of copyrightable subject matter.* In that case, state laws providing rights in such matter would be outside the reach of §301 (although they still might be preempted under the *Sears/Compco* line of cases). This interpretation has been adopted by the Eleventh Circuit in *Dunlap v. G & L Holding Group, Inc.,* 381 F.3d 1285 (11th Cir. 2004), and in several state and district court opinions.

C. **Equivalent rights:** Once it is established that the state cause of action is being applied to the subject matter of copyright (a work of authorship) or a work of visual art, it must be determined *whether the state cause of action provides rights that are "equivalent" to the exclusive rights provided by copyright law*—the rights to reproduce, adapt, distribute copies to the public, publicly perform and publicly display the work, and in the case of works of visual art, the moral rights of attribution and integrity. The meaning of "equivalent" has been the subject of some disagreement in the courts.

1. **The "extra elements" test:** Most courts have adopted an "extra elements" test for determining equivalency. Under this test the court looks to see if the mere act of reproduction, adaptation, distribution to the public, public performance, or public display (or in the case of works of visual art, misattribution or violation of a work's integrity), will in itself give rise to the state cause of action, or *whether some additional element, which is not required for copyright infringement (or violation of the author's rights), must also be alleged.* If no other element must be alleged in order to state the cause of action, then the state cause of action gives rights that are "equivalent" to copyright and (if the subject matter test is satisfied) is preempted. *If other elements are required in order to state a cause of action, most courts will look to see if the additional elements make the cause of action "qualitatively different" from copyright infringement.* If not, preemption may still be found.

2. **The meaning of "qualitatively different":** Courts have suggested several different approaches for determining whether the extra element in a state cause of action makes the cause of action "qualitatively different" from copyright: (1) the "purpose" test; (2) the "scope vs. nature" test; and (3) the "essence of the claim" test.

    a. **The "purpose" test:** In several cases courts have assessed "qualitative difference" by determining whether the extra elements suggest that the state cause of action serves a *different purpose,* or *vindicates a different interest,* than copyright.

    Example: In *Baltimore Orioles, Inc. v. Major League Baseball Players Assn.,* 805 F.2d 663 (7th Cir. 1986), *cert. denied,* 480 U.S. 941 (1987), the players asserted that the team owners' telecast of their games violated their *rights of publicity.* The U.S. Court of Appeals for the Seventh Circuit held that to the extent that there were extra elements in the state common-law right of publicity action, they did not render the cause of action qualitatively different from a claim of copyright infringement. The court reasoned that, unlike a right to privacy action, in which the invasion of privacy element vindicated the personal right to privacy, the right of publicity cause of action *protected economic interests that were essentially the same* as the economic interests protected by copyright. According to the court, "the purpose of federal copyright protection is to benefit the public by encouraging works in which it is interested. To induce individuals to undertake the personal sacrifices necessary to create such works, federal copyright law extends to the authors of such works a limited monopoly to reap the rewards of their endeavors.... Contrary to the players' contention, *the interest underlying the recognition of the right of publicity also is the promotion of performances that appeal to the public.* The reason that state law protects individual pecuniary interests is to provide an incentive to performers to invest the time and resources required to develop such performances."

b. The "scope vs. nature" test: Some courts have, in assessing the impact of an extra element, sought to determine whether the element goes to the "scope" or to the "nature" of the state-created right. *Only if the additional element goes to the nature of the state-created right will it be sufficient to avoid preemption.*

Example: In *Harper & Row Publishers, Inc. v. Nation Enterprises*, 723 F.2d 195 (2d Cir. 1983), *rev'd on other grounds*, 471 U.S. 539 (1985), the plaintiff asserted a state cause of action for *tortious interference with contract,* alleging that the defendant's unauthorized publication of excerpts from its book had lead another publisher to cancel its contract with the plaintiff. In determining whether this claim was "equivalent" to a copyright claim for §301 purposes, the court noted that the plaintiff would have to demonstrate that defendant engaged in unauthorized reproduction and distribution of its copyrighted work, the same as it would if asserting a copyright infringement claim. In addition, *the plaintiff would have to demonstrate awareness and intentional interference on the defendant's part, which would not be required to recover for copyright infringement.* The court declined to find that these elements of awareness and intentional interference were sufficient to save the state claim from preemption, noting that they went "merely to the scope of the right." *They did not "establish qualitatively different conduct on the part of the infringing party, nor a fundamental nonequivalence between the state and federal rights implicated."*

c. The "essence of the claim" test: Some courts have attempted to determine whether, given the plaintiff's specific factual allegations, his claim is "essentially" one for copying, adapting, or publicly distributing, performing, or displaying copyrightable subject matter (or in the case of works of visual art, for violating the author's rights of integrity or attribution). Thus, the *courts focus on the overall impact or "feel" of the claim.* Do extra elements in the specific context of plaintiff's particular factual allegations *in fact* cause the claim to be qualitatively different from a copyright infringement claim?

Example: In *Del Madera Properties v. Rhodes and Gardner, Inc.*, 820 F.2d 973 (9th Cir. 1987), the plaintiff, who owned property to be developed as a subdivision, created a tentative map and supporting documents necessary to develop the subdivision. However, the plaintiff ultimately filed in bankruptcy and was unable to use the map and documents. The defendant later acquired the land and allegedly used the plaintiff's tentative map and documents to make its own development. The plaintiff sued, *alleging unjust enrichment.* The foundation of this claim was that the *defendants violated an implied promise, based on the parties' relationship, not to use the tentative map and supporting documents.* The court found the claim preempted under §301, noting that *"an implied promise not to use or copy materials within the subject matter of copyright is equivalent to the protection provided by §106 of the Copyright Act."* The allegation of an implied contract made no real substantive difference. Thus, the court identified and rejected what it saw as mere maneuvering—an attempt to characterize a claim of unauthorized copying as an implied contract or unjust enrichment claim.

3. **A review of certain state causes of action:** Claims of *breach of contract* involving copyrightable subject matter usually are not preempted because plaintiffs must allege and demonstrate the *qualitatively different extra element of a bargained-for exchange,* which does not need to be demonstrated in copyright infringement actions. *Trade secret claims* involving reproduction or distribution of copyrightable subject matter are similarly rarely preempted under §301, because the plaintiff must demonstrate the *extra elements of trade secret status and either a breach of confidential relationship or "improper conduct."* State *passing off claims* whose facts entail the unauthorized reproduction, adaptation, distribution, public performance, or public display of copyrightable material also generally pass preemption muster, because of the *extra element of likely consumer confusion.* In contrast, *misappropriation claims* entailing the unauthorized reproduction or distribution of copyrightable subject matter frequently have been ruled preempted. While plaintiffs have argued that misappropriation claims entail the extra element of commercial immorality, *most courts have held that commercial immorality is not an actual element of a misappropriation claim, or that if it is an actual element, it does not render the claim qualitatively different from copyright infringement.*

   a. **A special category of misappropriation claims:** In *National Basketball Assn. v. Motorola, Inc.*, 105 F.3d 841 (1997), also discussed *supra*, p. 341, the Court of Appeals for the Second Circuit held that *state misappropriation claims involving the subject matter of copyright are generally preempted, except for a narrow exception, which the court called the "hot-news" exception.* This exception is based on the legislative history of §301, which demonstrates that Congress intended not to preempt state claims that are similar in nature to the claim in *International News Service v. Associated Press*, 248 U.S. 215 (1918), discussed *supra*, pp. 320-322. According to the Second Circuit, a misappropriation claim will fall under the "hot-news" exception when:

      1. a plaintiff generates or gathers information at a cost;
      2. the information is time-sensitive;
      3. a defendant's use of the information constitutes free-riding on the plaintiff's efforts;
      4. the defendant is in direct competition with a product or service offered by the plaintiff; and
      5. the ability of other parties to free-ride on the efforts of the plaintiff or others would so reduce the incentive to produce the product or service that its existence or quality would be substantially threatened.

      In these cases, the Second Circuit reasoned, the following extra elements combine to save the misappropriation claim from preemption by making it qualitatively different from copyright: (1) the time-sensitive value of factual information; (2) the free-riding by a defendant; and (3) the threat to the very existence of the product or service provided by the plaintiff.

D. **Express exceptions to §301 preemption:** Copyright Act §301 expressly leaves state common-law protection intact for some kinds of works. First, it stresses that states remain free to provide *rights in unfixed works.* (Unfixed works are outside of the scope of federally copyrightable subject matter.) Second, it preserves *state and local landmark, historic preservation, zoning, and building codes relating to architectural works.* In addition, §301 expressly permits states to continue protecting *sound recordings fixed prior to February 15, 1972* (the date on which federal copyright became available for sound recordings), as long as the state cause of action arises before February 15, 2067.

E. **The relationship between §301 and Supremacy Clause preemption:** While the Supremacy Clause and its case law focus on whether the state cause of action *conflicts with the purposes* underlying federal law, §301 focuses on whether the state cause of action *replicates* the federal copyright law. (A state cause of action that replicates the federal copyright infringement cause of action would conflict with Congress's purpose to unify copyright protection under federal law.) While a cause of action may be preempted under both provisions, this will not always be the case. (Note that the Patent Act has no express preemption provision. Thus, any claim that a state cause of action is preempted under the patent law can only be asserted directly pursuant to the Supremacy Clause.)

Quiz Yourself on
THE RELATIONSHIP BETWEEN FEDERAL AND STATE LAW

Jeff Jones is a famous country-western singer (known affectionately to his fans as "JJ"), who is known for his deep, husky, gravelly voice, which he accompanies with a banjo. JJ has had a number of hits over the years, but he is probably best known for his rendition of "Lonely, Lonely Me." Although JJ did not compose this song, and does not own copyright in it, the public associates the song with him.

General Products, Inc., which manufactures and sells a line of pickup trucks, wanted to hire JJ to sing in an advertisement for its trucks, but JJ refused to do so. Undaunted, General Products' advertising agency hired David Dursley, a "JJ sound-alike" to sing in the ad, and Bill Brown, a professional banjo player, to accompany him. The advertising agency obtained a license to perform "Lonely, Lonely Me," from the owner of copyright in that song, and instructed David and Bill to perform the song in a manner that sounded as much like JJ's famous rendition as possible. The resulting ad features video shots of a General Products truck traveling up a mountain and through a stream, far from civilization, with David and Bill's performance in the background. The ad does not mention JJ's name or show his image, or say anything expressly to suggest that JJ is singing in the background. Nor does it show or say anything to suggest that he is not.

JJ brings suit to enjoin any further showing of the ad and for damages. Based on these facts, please answer the following questions.

91. JJ's complaint sets forth a state unfair competition (passing off) claim alleging that the public associates him with the song "Lonely, Lonely Me." He further alleges that by playing the song in its advertisement, General Products and its advertising agency falsely represent that JJ endorses or is affiliated with General Products' pickup trucks, leading to a likelihood of consumer confusion. General Products' answer to the complaint alleges that the complaint is preempted under Copyright Act §301 and the Supremacy Clause. How should the court rule on the preemption issue? _____

92. JJ's complaint also sets forth a Lanham Act §43(a) claim to the same effect as the state unfair competition claim set forth above. General Products answers that this claim is preempted under both Copyright Act §301 and the Supremacy Clause. How should the court rule on the preemption issue? _____

93. JJ's complaint also sets forth a state right of publicity claim alleging that by using a singer who imitated Boss's distinctive voice and singing style, and a banjo accompaniment that imitates JJ's distinctive playing style, General Products and its advertising agency made an unauthorized use of JJ's identity for commercial purposes. General Products answers that this claim is preempted under Copyright Act §301. How should the court rule on the preemption issue? _____

94. Finally, JJ's complaint alleges that he has developed an innovative method of playing the banjo with quick, jerky motions with a bamboo pick, which produces a particularly distinctive, unusual "twang." Through the years he has developed a strong public demand for this distinctive form of playing through his own investment of effort and talent. David's use of this unique method of playing constitutes an actionable misappropriation of JJ's innovation and resulting business good will. General Products' answer to the complaint again defends that this claim is preempted under both Copyright Act §301 and the Supremacy Clause. How should the court rule on the preemption issue? _____

Sample Answers

91. The state unfair competition claim may be preempted under Copyright Act §301, because it alleges that a public performance of the copyrighted song violates JJ's rights. The state cause of action claims rights in copyrightable subject matter (the musical composition) and arguably gives rights equivalent to one of the exclusive rights of copyright (control over public performance of the song). Even if JJ were to argue that the state cause of action requires the extra element of distinctiveness, or secondary meaning (that is, a showing that the public understands the use of the song to indicate JJ as a source), that "extra element" arguably would go only to the *scope* of the claim, not the nature of it.

JJ might argue that a further "extra element" in the state cause of action is a likelihood of consumer confusion. In other cases, courts have found that the passing-off cause of action's "likelihood of consumer confusion" element renders the claim "qualitatively different" from a copyright infringement claim, because it demonstrates that the cause of action furthers a state interest (avoiding consumer confusion about the source of goods or services) that differs from the purpose of copyright. However, in this case, a court might evaluate the overall "essence of the claim" and find that, in essence, JJ is just trying to assert a copyright-like interest in a musical composition. Thus, even though the passing off cause of action generally would not be preempted, it may be under the particular facts of this case.

Even if the court found that the passing off claim is not "equivalent" to one of the exclusive rights of copyright, due to the presence of extra elements that render the cause of action "qualitatively different," the court might nonetheless find the claim preempted under the Supremacy Clause. In enacting the Copyright Act of 1976, Congress intended to give composers and their successors in interest the exclusive right to publicly perform their musical compositions. This right enables the composer to exploit the market for his song and profit from his labors. If JJ is able to assert a state right in a manner that prevents others from publicly performing the song, this will interfere with the copyright owner's ability to license public performance of the song, undercutting the value of the right and composers' incentive to create. This would frustrate accomplishment of Congress's purpose in enacting copyright protection for musical compositions. The Court of Appeals for the Ninth Circuit has found that a claim similar to the one described here is preempted under the Supremacy Clause. *Sinatra v. Goodyear Tire & Rubber,* 435 F.2d 711 (9th Cir. 1970), *cert. denied,* 402 U.S. 906 (1971).

92. The Lanham Act §43(a) claim would not be preempted, because it is brought pursuant to *federal,* not state, law. The Supremacy Clause and Copyright Act §301 have no bearing on federal laws, whether they conflict with other federal laws or not. General Products should argue that §43(a) should not be construed to provide a cause of action under the facts of this case, because to do otherwise would create a conflict between the Copyright Act and the Lanham Act. See *Dastar Corp. v. Twentieth Century Fox Film Corp., supra,* at p. 314.

93. The state right of publicity claim is unlikely to be preempted under §301. Under Ninth Circuit precedent, the court would find that the claim concerned defendants' use of JJ's *distinctive voice and performing style, which is not copyrightable subject matter.* Moreover, JJ might argue that he is seeking to protect a personal interest (the interest in controlling commercial use of his identity and the interest in privacy) that differs from the property interest in works of authorship created by copyright law.

94. The misappropriation claim concerning the method of playing a banjo with a bamboo pick is unlikely to be preempted under §301, because a method of playing an instrument is not copyrightable subject matter. (One might argue that the method is nonetheless part of copyrightable works of authorship—JJ's sound recordings—and thus should be considered copyrightable subject matter under the case law holding that facts and ideas expressed in works of authorship are within the subject matter of copyright. However, that line of cases arguably is distinguishable: JJ's sound recordings do not express the method, as such—only sounds resulting from the method.)

It is likely that the misappropriation claim *is preempted under the Supremacy Clause.* JJ's method of playing is a "process," which is patentable subject matter. Under the *Sears/Compco* and *Bonito Boats* decisions, General Products could argue that because the method is within the subject matter of patents, but is unpatented, Congress intended that it remain in the public domain, free to be copied. Removal of the process from the public domain through use of a state misappropriation claim would frustrate Congress's purpose in enacting the Patent Act. None of the special circumstances that the Supreme Court recognized in *Kewanee, Aronson,* or *Bonito Boats* seems to be applicable to excuse the cause of action from preemption. A plaintiff's rights under the misappropriation cause of action are strong and comprehensive—much like the monopoly rights granted by a patent. Indeed, this misappropriation claim, if allowed, would permit JJ to *prevent all other musicians* from employing the method. Nor does it appear that the state would be promoting independent state interests in providing the misappropriation cause of action, apart from the interest in promoting invention. In addition, the cause of action would undermine Congress's intent to leave matter that has already entered the public domain in the public domain.

Exam Tips on
THE RELATIONSHIP BETWEEN FEDERAL AND STATE LAW

☞ **Preemption may be a hidden issue:** Be alert for potential preemption issues whenever an exam question sets forth a state cause of action. Be on *high alert* if the question concerns a misappropriation cause of action, or a "property theory" idea claim. Recognize that even when a state cause of action (such as a breach of contract claim or a passing off or trade secret claim) normally is not preempted, *a particular claim may be,* if the plaintiff is essentially alleging a copyright interest, but is trying to disguise it as something else. Courts will look to the essence of what the plaintiff is seeking, given the facts of the particular case, and the court may examine the state law to determine if the state actually imposes the "extra element" that normally distinguishes the cause of action from a copyright claim.

☞ **Shrink-wrap and click-wrap licenses:** One question that a professor might ask is whether use of state law to enforce the terms of mass market (shrink-wrap or click-wrap) licenses is preempted. (See *supra*, pp. 9, 167, for a discussion of shrink-wrap and click-wrap licenses.) There has been considerable scholarly debate over this issue, and several important court opinions. As a general matter, state breach of contract claims are not preempted under *Copyright Act §301*, even when the alleged breach consisted of an unauthorized reproduction, adaptation, public distribution, performance, or display of a copyrighted work. This is because *plaintiffs in contract cases must allege and prove the "extra element" of a bargained-for exchange,* which is not necessary in copyright infringement actions. Courts have generally found that this extra element renders the contract claim "qualitatively different" from copyright infringement. However, one might argue that, *as a practical matter, there is no meaningful "bargained-for exchange" in the case of shrink-wrap or click-wrap licenses* that restrict what purchasers may do with their copies. *All persons* wishing to purchase and use the works must consent to the terms of the license. Since all users are bound to the same terms, the "contract rights" created by the license look and feel much like a general property right, such as the copyright gives. The Seventh Circuit has nonetheless rejected a §301 preemption challenge to enforcement of a shrink-wrap license. In *ProCD, Inc. v. Zeidenberg*, 86 F.3d 1447 (7th Cir. 1996), the Seventh Circuit equated shrink-wrap licenses with negotiated contracts, reasoning that "[a] copyright is a right against the world. Contracts, by contrast, generally affect only their parties; strangers may do as they please, so contracts do not create 'exclusive rights [that are equivalent to the rights provided by copyright law].' " *Id.* at 1454.

As is demonstrated by the *Aronson* case, courts have not found *Supremacy Clause* preemption of contracts creating rights in intangible creations, in part because enforcement of contract restrictions does not give the plaintiff monopoly rights in the subject matter of the contract. The contract is only enforceable against other parties to the contract, not against the general public. However, in the case of shrink-wrap licenses, the rights created are uniformly created against *all purchasers* so that state enforcement provides a strong, broad, monopoly-like interest in the author. Indeed, these privately created, broad based "property-like" rights threaten to compete with copyright law. Because shrink-wrap licenses can prohibit uses that the copyright law expressly permits (such as fair uses and uses expressly permitted by the other statutory exceptions to infringement liability set forth in Copyright Act §§108-121), authors' widespread reliance on shrink-wrap licenses may frustrate Congress's attempt to balance the competing interests of authors and the general public in drafting the Copyright Act. The Court of Appeals for the Fifth Circuit has held a state statute authorizing enforcement of specified shrink-wrap provisions to be preempted under a Supremacy Clause preemption analysis. *Vault Corp. v. Quaid Software Ltd.*, 847 F.2d 255 (5th Cir. 1988).

ESSAY EXAM QUESTIONS AND ANSWERS

The following are some sample essay exam questions dealing with multiple doctrines of intellectual property law. They will be useful for testing your knowledge and for practicing exam-taking. You should write out your answers fully in essay form and then check them against the sample answers. Note that while the sample answers demonstrate *a good way* to approach the questions, they are *not the only good way.*

Here are some suggestions about how to answer an essay exam question:

1. Remember that you are taking an *essay* examination. The complete essay examination answer must contain not only the "answer" to the question, but of greater importance, must also contain your **analysis**: the applicable **black-letter law**, and an **explanation** of how you have applied the black-letter law to the facts and reasoned to the "answer." It is also important to *consider the policies* underlying the black-letter rules, and discuss them in the course of explaining how the black-letter rules should be applied to the particular facts at hand.

2. Begin by **reading the question** thoroughly.

3. Next, **reread the question;** read it as it is written; try to avoid giving it your own "spin."

4. As you read, spot **key issues** and the applicable principles and concepts they invoke.

5. **Analyze** the fact pattern and the key issues that you have spotted.

6. **Organize your thoughts** into an orderly, logical sequence.

7. **Work out a game plan** for your answer, including the sequence of those things that you are going to write about, the priority for writing, and the general amount of space and time to be allocated to each.

8. Make a brief **word-phrase outline** of your proposed answer.

9. Use at least 25 percent of the time allotted for answering the question to do all of the things outlined above **before you begin to write** the answer. An organized answer can be written quickly. If you are not organized when you begin your answer, time will be wasted adding issues, crossing out the part of your answer that is not relevant, and writing too much about minor issues. Your answer will also be disorganized and hard for the professor to follow.

10. Write your answer in **clear, professional, lawyer-like English prose**, using full and complete **legal terminology**. Remember: This is an essay examination in the English language, at the graduate level, in a learned profession. Use proper grammar and punctuation.

11. Be certain to include **full statements of black-letter law** on each of the key issues. However, *do not write a treatise on the general field* of law involved in the question. *Address the specific issues raised.* If an issue is not fairly raised by a question, do not discuss it.

12. **Do not merely rehash the facts.** A complete answer requires analysis, black-letter law, and a description of how that black-letter law applies to the specific facts set forth in the question, in light

of any relevant policy considerations. Rehashing of the facts is not enough. Nor is it particularly productive.

13. **Use short, complete, simple sentences.** Avoid long, wandering, convoluted sentences that deal with several issues and subjects.

14. **Reason to a lawyer-like conclusion.** If you have time and space, add a wrap-up concluding sentence to your answer.

15. **Reread your answer** to make certain that you have made no unintended errors or omissions, and to ensure clarity and completeness of your answer.

16. **Use the full time allotted** for the question—no more and no less.

Essay Exam Questions

QUESTION 1: Mary, a software engineer with experience in the insurance business, devised a new mathematical algorithm for calculating a customized amount that a customer should be charged for earthquake insurance. The algorithm draws from a number of existing databases containing information about the risk of earthquakes in each part of the United States, the estimated damage that would occur in an earthquake in each of those geographic areas, costs of construction materials and labor in each area, and a range of other geographic and projected financial data. It combines these data with information supplied by the customer concerning the style, age, and environment of the building to be insured, assigns a weighted value to each factor, and then calculates a recommended insurance premium that reflects the precise risk the insurer undertakes to cover.

With the assistance of an old friend who is a patent agent at a law firm, Mary immediately filed patent applications with the U.S. Patent and Trademark Office and the European Patent Office. The patent applications state a single claim for a "method of calculating customized earthquake insurance premiums." The claim describes a series of nine "steps" that the new algorithm takes in selecting the relevant data and calculating the premium.

Mary then began to look for venture capital funding to begin producing and selling a computer program implementing the algorithm. Four months later, having acquired some "seed money" for the venture, Mary formed a corporation, and hired 12 professional programmers to work on creating a commercial embodiment of the program. The programmers were hired under a range of circumstances: Most of them agreed to work for a low wage and no benefits in return for stock options in the new corporation. Some of them only agreed to work for three-month periods, which could be renewed on mutual agreement. Being somewhat new to the role of employer, Mary did not have the programmers sign any written, employment-related, or non-disclosure agreements.

Eight months later, Mary and the programmers completed an early, or "test" version of the program. At that point, Mary called persons she knew at a cross-section of insurance companies, and asked them to try the program free of charge and provide feedback to be used in perfecting the final version. Mary sent disks containing the program to those who agreed. She only distributed the test program in object code, keeping the source code in confidence. Mary did not require the recipients to sign any non-disclosure agreements or other express contractual undertakings.

Five months after that, Mary's new company completed a final version of the program, and began the next phase of launching it on the market. At this point, Mary decided that she should consult with your law firm for expert advice on the best way to protect her rights in the program. Her patent applications are still pending, but she is having some second thoughts about them. She is wondering whether she would be better off retaining the algorithm as a trade secret. After all, her customer pool will be such as to make it possible to negotiate individual licensing agreements with each purchaser, with prohibitions on reverse-engineering, unauthorized uses, etc.

The prospects for the program's success look good. The venture capitalists who examined Mary's proposal were convinced that Mary's product will be well received as a significant breakthrough by the insurance business. What will you advise her? Specifically, please evaluate the likelihood of Mary's obtaining a patent, based on the available information, and the feasibility of protecting the algorithm as a trade secret. What would the relative advantages and disadvantages be to each approach? If Mary decided on trade secret protection, what additional steps should she take to preserve trade secret status? Should Mary also be thinking about copyright? What, if anything, would copyright add to the protection Mary would obtain under patent or trade secret law? Would Mary be likely to encounter any problems with regard to copyright protection?

QUESTION 2: In January, 2004, Alvin, an avid skateboarder, conceived of a new style of skateboard that, rather than being flat on top, would sport an aerodynamically designed fin rising from the middle of the board. The board would be pointed in front rather than rounded, and would have platforms for the rider's feet on either side of the fin, as depicted below. The two front wheels would be placed closer together than the two back wheels.

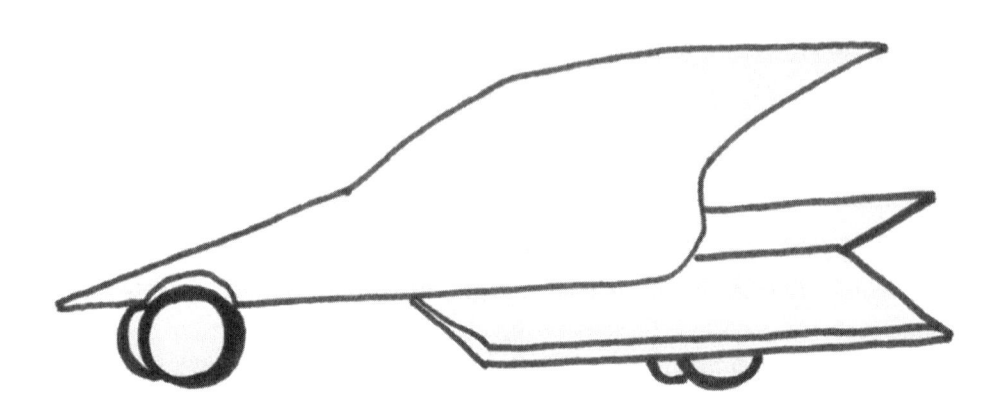

Alvin, who had taken some college courses in engineering, believed that this style of skateboard would provide a faster, more stable ride than other existing skateboard designs. Besides, the fin would look way cool and could be decorated with something awesome like painted orange flames, a skull and crossbones, or eagle wings. While the fin might take any of several shapes and be equally efficient aerodynamically, Alvin believed that the shape he selected was best because of the "retro" look it gave the skateboard.

Alvin believed that the skateboard should be constructed of fiberglass. He did not himself have the means to construct one. However, he made diagrams and drawings to scale that showed the precise shape of the fin and the body of the skateboard, the proper dimensions, the size and placement of the wheels, and all the other information that would be needed to construct a prototype.

In June, 2004, Alvin sent letters of inquiry to five "invention services." Invention services are firms that serve as "middle men," representing independent inventors who are seeking to sell their inventive ideas to companies interested in marketing the inventions. Alvin's letters described his invention as "a breakthrough in skateboard design," but provided no further details. After receiving literature from the five services, Alvin selected one, Invention Brokers Inc. ("Brokers"), to represent him. He and Brokers executed an agreement in July, 2004 in which Alvin agreed to provide Brokers with all the drawings and other information needed to make the skateboard, along with a general written description explaining how the skateboard worked and why it provided advantages over existing skateboard designs. In turn, Brokers promised to use its best efforts to market the new design to skateboard manufacturing companies, and to maintain the confidentiality of the new design.

Brokers received Alvin's information, and approached several manufacturers with Alvin's design during the following year. In each case, it obtained a confidentiality agreement from the manufacturer before disclosing details of the design. Ultimately, none of the manufacturers was interested in pursuing it. Then in August, 2005, Brokers contacted Cool Cat Surfboards, Inc., which was considering branching out into the skateboard business. Cool Cat was intrigued by Alvin's design and agreed to pay Alvin $75,000 for the design concept and to pay Brokers' commission. The same month, Alvin assigned all his rights in the design to Cool Cat and provided Cool Cat with his original drawings and diagrams.

In September, 2005, Diane, an employee of Cool Cat, made an unauthorized set of photocopies of Alvin's drawings and diagrams and took them home with her, without telling anyone about her actions. Shortly thereafter, she gave the photocopies to her boyfriend, Elton, who was an international businessman. Elton was aware that Diane had made the copies without permission. He sent them to a manufacturer in Hong Kong with an order for production of 10,000 skateboards. He directed that the skateboards be produced in a vibrant blue with the word "Elton" in large, bold crimson script running diagonally up the fin. The Hong Kong manufacturer completed the order in January, 2006 and sent the skateboards, pursuant to Elton's direction, to a wholesaler in the European Union, who proceeded to sell all of them in France, Germany, and Great Britain during the next two months.

In December, 2005, Cool Cat began manufacturing the skateboard Alvin had designed. It manufactured the skateboard in a bright yellow enamel paint, with black racing stripes, and two large blocky black "C's" marked prominently on the fin.

The same month (December, 2005), Cool Cat filed an application for a utility patent in Alvin's design. The utility patent application claimed a skateboard with a fin rising from the middle of the board, a pointed front, platforms for the rider's feet on either side of the fin, and front wheels placed more closely together than the back wheels. Cool Cat began marketing the skateboard in the United States in March, 2006, under the "Cool Cat" trademark.

Meanwhile, Elton ordered 20,000 more of the "Elton" skateboards from the Hong Kong manufacturer. He sold them to Freewheelers, Inc., a U.S. sports distributor, in December, 2006. Freewheelers received the shipment of skateboards from Hong Kong in April, 2007, and began selling them in its retail outlets in several states.

The P.T.O. granted a patent to Cool Cat in August, 2007. Cool Cat did not apply for a patent in any country other than the United States.

Cool Cat has become aware of all the facts set forth above and has come to you for legal advice. Please identify and evaluate all the possible causes of action Cool Cat might consider bringing against Diane, Elton, Freewheelers, or any other persons arising out of these facts. In the case of each cause of action you discuss, state whether you would advise Cool Cat to pursue it, and explain your reasoning.

QUESTION 3: Dazzlesmile, Inc., holds a valid, enforceable U.S. patent on a new kind of battery-run, disposable electric toothbrush. Dazzlesmile sells its invention in various forms (including toothbrushes whose plastic handles are shaped and colored like rocket ships and race cars) to appeal to children. The handles hold batteries, and extend to form a shaft with a flat, circular brush attached to the end with three tiny screws. A button on the handle activates the power, which rotates the brush at the end of the shaft and cleans the user's teeth.

Dazzlesmile sells its toothbrushes for $5.00 each. It intends that purchasers use the toothbrush until the bristles on the brush wear down, and then dispose of the toothbrush. It does not market replacement brushes or offer the service of replacing the brush on toothbrushes whose brush has worn down. It advertises and promotes the toothbrushes as "disposable," and on the packaging of each toothbrush, it expressly states that the toothbrush "should be thrown away once the brush bristles have worn down."

In August 2005, Dazzlesmile shipped a large quantity of its patented toothbrushes shaped like rocket ships and race cars to Rojo, Inc., a Brazilian importer, in Rio de Janeiro for sale to Brazilian and other South American consumers. It charged Rojo $2.00 per toothbrush. The package of each toothbrush stated the following (in reasonably conspicuous lettering) in Spanish, Portuguese, and English: "Not for import or resale in the United States."

Rojo resold half of the toothbrushes to Martinez, a Chilean businessman, who resold them to CheepCo Discounters, a large American discount retailer. CheepCo imported the toothbrushes back to the United States and sold them in its stores for $4.00 each.

Rojo resold the other half of the toothbrushes to Blanco, Inc., which resold them to Argentinean consumers. Azul, Inc., advertised to Argentinean consumers that it would pay 50 cents for each discarded Dazzlesmile toothbrush delivered to it. After collecting a large quantity of the discarded toothbrushes, Azul sterilized them, and replaced the worn brush with a new brush that it manufactured itself, and replaced the batteries in each toothbrush. Azul then packaged the refurbished toothbrushes in its own new packaging and sold them to MegaMiddleMan, Inc., which in turn sold them to CheepCo Discounters. CheepCo imported the refurbished toothbrushes into the United States and sold them in its large discount outlets for $3.00 each.

Dazzlesmile would like to sue CheepCo for patent infringement. What is your assessment of this possible cause of action? Please discuss all the issues fairly raised by the facts, even if your disposal of one of them would resolve the case.

QUESTION 4: Both the Dipsy City Post Newspaper Co. and its rival, the Dipsy City Tribune Newspaper Co., maintain web pages on the Internet on which they post national and local news stories. Members of the public are permitted to visit the web sites and read the stories free of charge. The newspaper companies maintain the web sites in order to promote subscriptions to their respective newspapers by showcasing their news reporting.

X maintains a web page that lists the "top 10" news items of the day. X "links" each listing of a "top 10" news item to a relevant news story on the Dipsy City Post's or Dipsy City Tribune's web site. Thus, due to X's actions, visitors to X's web site can click their mouse on a "top 10" news item listed there and be transported immediately to a news story on either the Post's or the Tribune's web site. The link is a "deep" one, so that visitors who use X's link are taken directly to the news story, bypassing the identifying information that each newspaper company puts on the home page of its web site (including subscription forms). X does not expressly notify link users of the identity of the site to which they are linked. In addition, when visitors to X's web site exercise a link to a Post or Tribune news story, and see the story on their computer screen, the news story is "framed" along the top, bottom, and sides of the computer screen with advertisements. The advertisements are placed in the frame by X. X sells the advertising space to a number of entities doing business on the Internet.

Neither the Post nor the Tribune has authorized X to establish the links to its news stories. You should *assume* that in establishing the links, X does not reproduce the Post's or the Tribune's news stories, or any other material on the newspapers' web sites. Given these facts, please answer the following questions.

   a. Has X infringed the Post's or the Tribune's rights of adaptation in the copyrighted news stories to which X has established links? Why or why not?

   b. Is there any other cause of action available to the Post and the Tribune against X, other than copyright infringement? Please describe any possible causes of action and explain why they would or would not be likely to succeed.

QUESTION 5: Smith invented a new kind of widget and filed an application for a U.S. patent on April 20, 2000. The patent was granted for the new widget on January 3, 2002.

In February, 2009, the CEO and various other employees of Jones Co. met with representatives of the Taiwan government at the Jones Co. corporate headquarters in Indianapolis, Indiana. At this meeting, the Jones Co. CEO offered to sell the Taiwanese government 30 widgets that would literally fall within the claims of the Smith patent. The widgets would be manufactured by a Jones Co. subsidiary in South Africa, and shipped from there to Taiwan. The shipment would be delivered in February, 2011. The Taiwanese government representatives agreed to a purchase price of $4,000,000.

Assume the applicable law is the same as in 2007.

a. Smith has learned of all this, and wants to bring a suit for patent infringement. Assume that his patent is valid. Is he likely to have a cause of action? If so, against whom?

b. Instead of agreeing to deliver the widgets to the Taiwanese government in February, 2011, assume that the parties agreed that Jones Co. would deliver the widgets in May, 2020. Would this make any difference in your analysis?

c. Instead of the dates set forth above, assume that the described meeting occurred in April, 2001, with delivery to take place in Taiwan in February, 2004. Would this make any difference in your analysis?

QUESTION 6: Delta Corp. is a Swiss company that is famous for making fine, very expensive watches. It manufactures its watches in Switzerland and sells them under the "Delta" mark through authorized distributors (generally fine jewelry stores) throughout the world. Delta does not place express contractual restrictions on resale of its watches. Although its watches are expensive everywhere, they are sold at lower prices in developing countries than in developed countries. Cheepco, a U.S. wholesale discount chain, has, for the past ten years, frequently purchased Delta watches abroad and resold them in the United States for up to $500 less than the price charged by authorized U.S. Delta distributors. In 2006, at the insistence of its authorized U.S. distributors, who do not like this competition, Delta began engraving a very small design on the back of its watches (referred to herein as "Delta design"):

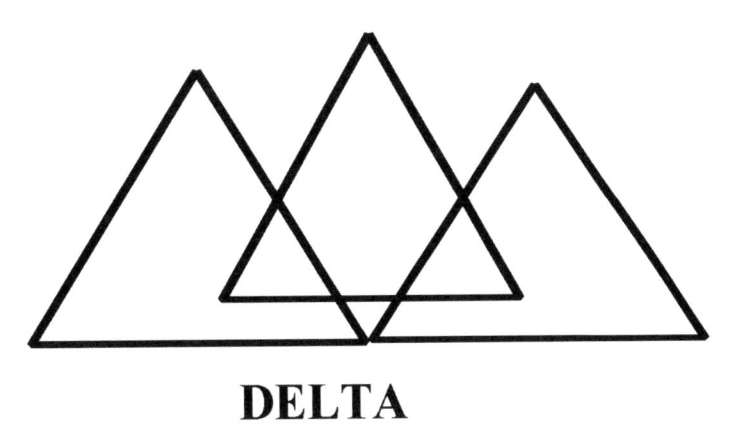

DELTA

The design is so small that most people would not notice it unless they were specifically looking for it. Delta registered the design with the U.S. Copyright Office, but did not publicize its addition of the Delta design onto the back of its watches. It subsequently sold a large quantity of its watches, bearing the design, to a Peruvian company. Cheepco purchased the whole lot from the Peruvian purchaser, shipped them to the United States and offered them for sale through its U.S. stores for $950 each ($550 less than the price charged by authorized U.S. distributors). Upon learning of this from its authorized U.S. distributors, Delta sent Cheepco a letter notifying Cheepco that it claimed copyright in the Delta design, claiming that Cheepco's actions infringed that copyright, and demanding that Cheepco immediately cease selling the Delta watches. Cheepco rejected the demand, and shortly thereafter Delta brought suit against Cheepco in U.S. district court, alleging that its importation and sale of the watches constituted infringement of the Delta design copyright.

Please evaluate the merits of Delta's copyright infringement claim and any defenses that Cheepco might reasonably assert.

An additional fact is that Delta Corp. has registered the word "Delta" as a trademark in every country in which it sells watches. Please discuss briefly whether Delta should amend its complaint to assert a trademark infringement claim as well, and explain your reasoning.

QUESTION 7: In 2000, Bella Bennett, a business efficiency consultant whose hobby was metal sculpture, conceived of and developed a new type of multifunction tool that performed the functions of a wire cutter, pliers, and adjustable wrench, all in one. Bella decided to call the new tool a "plirench." Shortly after making her invention, Bella applied to the U.S. Patent and Trademark Office for a utility patent for the plirench.

The following year, while her patent application was still pending, Bella entered into negotiations with Andrew Anston, President of Anston Tool, Inc. (a tool-manufacturing enterprise) concerning an exclusive license to manufacture the plirench. Andrew was extremely interested in entering into an agreement with Bella, and in order to convince her that Anston Tool was the best company to license, he told her that Anston had a secret process for molding metal objects that was very efficient and inexpensive. Using this secret process, he told Bella, Anston would be able to make the plirench a commercial success. Bella asked him what the secret process was, and Andrew proceeded to tell her.

Of the 35 firms in the tool manufacturing business, six (including Anston Tool) used this particular metal molding process. Four of them—Anston, Duffy Co., Essex Co., and Foley Co.—had developed the process independently. The other two (Gall Co. and Gilson Co.) were licensees of the Essex Co. All of them took reasonable measures to keep the process secret.

As a result of their negotiations, Andrew (acting on behalf of Anston Tool) and Bella entered into an exclusive license agreement for manufacture of the plirench. Their written agreement acknowledged that Bella had applied for a patent for the plirench and provided that she would use her best efforts to obtain a patent. Until the patent was granted, and thereafter, Anston Tool would pay Bella royalties of 50 cents for each plirench that it manufactured and sold. The agreement further provided that if Bella was unsuccessful in obtaining a patent, Anston's royalties would be reduced to 25 cents per plirench effective on the date of the P.T.O.'s rejection. The agreement further provided that Anston would pay either the 50-cent or the 25-cent royalty to Bella for as long as it manufactured the plirench, and that as long as Anston manufactured the plirench, Bella would not license any other company to do so.

Anston Tool began immediately to manufacture and sell the plirench, and to pay royalties to Bella. The following year (2001), despite Bella's best efforts, the P.T.O. denied a patent for the plirench on the grounds that it was neither novel nor non-obvious.

In 2002, two competitors of Anston Tool began manufacturing and selling the plirench, without consulting with either Bella or Anston Tool.

Also in 2002, Bella made a new invention: scissors with a built-in scotch tape dispenser on the handle. She called the new invention "tassers." In the course of negotiating with Tod Taber of the Taber Household Tool Co., regarding a license to manufacture "tassers," Bella asked Tod: "By the way, do you use the special metal molding process?" Tod asked: "What process is that?" Bella proceeded to describe the Anston Tool Company's secret process to Tod. When she had finished, Tod said: "I've been in the business 20 years and I've never heard of that process. How did you learn about it?" Bella replied that she had learned about it from Andrew Anston when negotiating her license agreement with Anston Tool. Tod immediately implemented the new molding process, which saved his company considerable money.

In 2003, Anston Tool was still profitably engaged in manufacturing and selling the plirench, but felt that it was at a disadvantage vis-à-vis its two competitors in the plirench business, who paid no royalties to Bella. Under the circumstances, Anston Tool decided its agreement to pay royalties to Bella was void and unenforceable, and it notified Bella of its intention to continue manufacturing the plirench without paying her any further royalties.

Bella brought suit against Anston Tool Co. for breach of the licensing agreement. Anston filed a counterclaim against Bella, alleging trade secret rights in its metal molding process and seeking damages resulting from Bella's wrongful disclosure of the trade secret to Tod Taber. Anston also sued Tod Taber and Taber Household Tool Co. for damages for misappropriation of its trade secret.

Please evaluate the strength of each claim.

QUESTION 8: In October, 1999, X, an American author living in New York, completed a biography of A, who was a soldier in the American Revolutionary War. The biography was the result of three years of painstaking research. It chronicled A's life from early childhood, but focused particularly on A's enlistment as a foot soldier in the American army and his remarkable rise through the ranks to the position of colonel. The book was entitled *A: The Story of a Remarkable Soldier*. On the cover, under the title, was the statement: "The true story of Colonel A and the battles that made him famous."

In January, 2000, X assigned her copyright in the book to Y Corp., a publisher. Y Corp. printed and sold over 60,000 copies, with proper notice of copyright, during the next several years.

Library records of the Dallas Public Library indicate that in April of 2005, Z, an American living in Dallas, checked out a copy of *A: The Story of a Remarkable Soldier* and kept it for four weeks. The following March, 2006, Z published his own biography of A, entitled *The Life and Times of Colonel A*.

A comparison of the two books reveals the following:

1. Unlike X's biography, Z's biography does not discuss A's childhood, but begins at the time that A enlisted in the American army. While X's book deals equally with all the seven battles in which A was involved, Z's book focuses primarily on the three most important ones. Approximately 80 percent of the facts set forth in Z's book can be found in X's book, although there are a considerable number of facts in X's book that do not appear in Z's, relating mainly to A's childhood and the lesser battles in which A participated. In addition, Z inserted a number of facts about life in colonial America and the drafting of the Declaration of Independence and the Constitution that were not included in X's book.

2. The books are both organized chronologically.

3. In describing A's involvement in one battle, X set forth her own particular theory about A's motivation in choosing the battle strategy that he did. Z's work sets forth a similar theory.

4. X and Z have different writing styles. However, the language in two paragraphs in Z's book, describing A's relationship with his wife, are virtually identical to two paragraphs in X's book.

5. In addition, it appears that X invented a minor character named Corporal Peel, who served as A's messenger in two important battles. X depicts Corporal Peel as a buffoon and descriptions of his "services" to A introduce an element of humor to X's narrative. Even though Corporal Peel was fictional, X said nothing in her book to indicate that this was the case. In his book, Z refers to Corporal Peel as A's messenger three times, and in one place, Z purports to set forth some "facts" regarding Corporal Peel that are the same as "facts" X invented in writing her biography.

Y Corp. became aware of Z's book in January, 2007, and discovered that neither it nor X had registered the copyright in *A: The Story of a Remarkable Soldier*. Y Corp. immediately registered the copyright, recorded the transfer from X to the Y Corp., and then filed a lawsuit against Z alleging copyright infringement.

Please evaluate Y Corp.'s likelihood of success.

QUESTION 9: In February, 1998, X conceived of a new type of widget. He described the new widget and the way to construct it in great detail in a memorandum, which he had witnessed by his secretary and placed in a safe deposit box. He began to construct the new widget the following month. Widgets are fairly intricate machines and require custom-made parts. It took X several months to complete the first one. In May, 1998, the prototype widget was approximately one-third complete, and not yet operable. Nonetheless, during that month X entered into a written contract to sell three of the new widgets to Y. The widgets were to be delivered in March, 2000. X delivered the three completed widgets to Y on schedule. In July, 1999, X filed an application for a patent on his new widget. X was granted a patent on the new widget in April, 2002.

X was primarily in the business of manufacturing metal products, including nails, screws, nuts, and bolts. His New Jersey factory also had a shop for making custom parts for machines. Deciding that he was not well equipped to manufacture his patented widget on a large scale, he entered into an agreement with A in April, 2002. The agreement authorized A, who had a factory in Connecticut, to manufacture a total of 100 of the patented widgets per year, to be delivered to X, who would then sell them to customers. In order to manufacture the widgets, A would need to have gadgets (one of the components of the widget) custom-made. The agreement provided that A must purchase all the custom-made gadgets used in making the patented widgets from X, who would construct them in his New Jersey factory. The agreement further provided that henceforth A must purchase all nails, screws, nuts, and bolts used in his factory from X. The agreement stated that it would last for five years and could be renewed.

A commenced making widgets pursuant to the agreement. In April, 2003, B, who owned an export business in New York, approached A with a proposal. B felt that there would be a strong market for X's widgets in Southeast Asia, but felt that X was charging too high a price. B suggested that A make 50 additional widgets, beyond the 100 per year specified in his license with X, that B would then sell to Southeast Asian buyers. When A protested that he could be held liable for patent infringement, B told him that she had consulted with a patent lawyer, who, upon learning the facts set forth above, had opined that X's patent might be invalid. Upon learning this, A agreed that it would be worth taking the risk.

In order to make the additional widgets, A went to C, who owned a custom machine shop, and placed an order for 50 custom-made gadgets, providing C with the proper specifications. C began work. A couple of weeks later, while at a trade convention, C mentioned her contract with A to a business acquaintance, stating that she had never heard of gadgets of the type ordered by A. The acquaintance told C that the only use for such gadgets was in X's patented widget, but that he thought A was required by license to buy all the gadgets used in the patented widget from X. After returning home from the convention, C completed the custom gadgets and delivered them to A as required by her contract.

When he received the completed custom-made gadgets from C, A incorporated them into the 50 widgets, made the finishing touches, and shipped the completed widgets to B in New York, as agreed.

Once she received the widgets, B negotiated a contract to sell 30 of the widgets to D, a Thai businessman, who would ship them to Thailand for use in that country. B received payment and the widgets were shipped.

The following year X learned all the facts recited above, and communicated them to a senior partner in your law firm. The senior partner has asked you to write a memorandum evaluating all possible causes of action for patent infringement that X might assert against A, B, C, and D, evaluating any potential weaknesses in the case, and discussing what damages X might expect to recover and how they would be measured. Please set forth the substance of your memorandum. Even if you conclude that X's lawsuit would not succeed due to the resolution of one issue, nonetheless discuss all the issues fairly raised by the facts.

QUESTION 10: In 1970, Charles Callum began doing business in San Francisco as a sole proprietorship that he called "Wild West Haberdashery." Wild West Haberdashery manufactured various styles of cowboy hats and sold them wholesale and through a series of retail outlets in Northern California and Oregon. One of Wild West Haberdashery's more popular products was a Stetson hat that it sold under the trademark "Starry Night." In 1972, Callum registered "Starry Night" for hats on the U.S. Patent and Trademark Office's Principal Register. Wild West Haberdashery engaged in sporadic advertising in magazines, newspapers, and on radio stations in California and Oregon, and enjoyed a stable, profitable stream of business.

In 2000, Ted Toben began doing business in Texas as a sole proprietorship called "Wild West Outfitters." Wild West Outfitters sold, through several retail stores in Austin and Dallas, a complete line of cowboy clothing and accessories. One of Wild West Outfitters' most popular products was leather chaps that it sold under its own unregistered trademark, "Starbright." Wild West Outfitters engaged in considerable advertising over the local country and western radio stations in Austin and Dallas, and it also advertised in the local newspapers and through direct mail brochures promoting "Wild West Outfitters" and "Starbright" chaps. When Toben began doing business, he did not know of Wild West Haberdashery or Starry Night Stetsons.

In 2005, Callum decided to expand his business. He opened a new retail outlet of Wild West Haberdashery in Austin and began selling Starry Night Stetsons through that outlet.

Toben learned of Callum's activities two months later and immediately filed suit for Lanham Act §43(a) and state common-law trademark infringement and passing off, seeking to enjoin Callum from doing business under the name "Wild West" and to enjoin Callum's use of the trademark "Starry Night" for hats in the Austin-Dallas area.

Callum filed counterclaims for trademark infringement and passing off to enjoin Toben from operating under the name "Wild West" and to enjoin Toben from using the trademark "Starbright."

Please determine what, if any, relief each is entitled to receive and explain your answer. If you need further facts, state what facts you need and why. Apply federal law and "general common law" as appropriate; you should not try to discuss the specific state law of California or Texas.

QUESTION 11: In 1999, Alpha Co. got a patent for a new chemical compound it had discovered (the "Alpha compound"), that is effective in killing fleas on cats and dogs without injuring the cats or dogs. Alpha markets the patented compound, mixed with water, some preservatives, and a perfume scent, in a spray can under the trademark "Fleasoff." In 2004, Zelda discovered that if she mixed "Fleasoff" with an oil-based paint and painted a wood fence with the mixture, not only fleas, but also flies, ants, and spiders avoided the fenced-in area for up to two years. Zelda would like to apply for a patent on her discovery and exploit it commercially, using the "Fleasoff" mark on her own product label to indicate the key ingredient. Please advise Zelda of her legal rights (and potential liabilities) in this regard.

Sample Essay Exam Answers

SAMPLE ANSWER TO QUESTION 1:

Is Mary's invention patentable? Recent decisions from the Court of Appeals for the Federal Circuit address two questions that arise in connection with the patentability of Mary's invention: First, under what circumstances is a mathematical algorithm patentable as a process and second, is a business method patentable subject matter?

In the *State Street Bank* case, the Federal Circuit held that business methods are patentable subject matter. Thus, Mary's algorithm, which constitutes a method of calculating customized insurance premiums, should not be disqualified by virtue of the fact that it can be described as a business method. Nor is it necessary that the application associate the method with technological elements. Moreover, while a mathematical algorithm in and of itself may be deemed an unpatentable abstract idea or law of nature, in a series of decisions the Federal Circuit has held that mathematical algorithm-related inventions are patentable subject matter as long as the claims are directed to a practical application—a useful, concrete, and tangible result. The patentability determination should focus on the invention's practical utility. In *State Street*, the claimed invention calculated a final mutual fund share price, which the court found to be a useful, concrete, and tangible result that could be used and relied upon by regulatory authorities and securities traders. Thus, it constituted patentable subject matter. Here, as in the *State Street* case, Mary's claimed "process" applies the mathematical algorithm in a practical manner to produce a concrete and useful result: a customized premium to charge insurance customers.

Since Mary's claim is likely to state patentable subject matter, the only other question is whether the claimed invention is novel, non-obvious, and sufficiently disclosed in the patent application. Here, the facts state that Mary's algorithm is "new" and that the venture capitalists who examined Mary's funding proposals were convinced that the invention would be well received as a significant breakthrough by the insurance business. This suggests that the invention is novel and non-obvious. So, based on the facts that are given, it is likely that Mary will be able to obtain a U.S. patent for her invention, if she proceeds with her application.

Is protection as a trade secret feasible? In order to be protectible as a trade secret, Mary's algorithm must be substantially secret and provide a commercial advantage over others who do not know or use it. Here, there is little doubt that the algorithm will provide a commercial advantage, since Mary's corporation will be able to sell the program that incorporates it, and it represents a significant advance over existing programs available to insurance firms.

The main question is whether the algorithm is secret. Mary has undoubtedly revealed the algorithm to the programmers she has hired, but a trade secret owner has leeway to reveal a secret to her employees or agents so that they can perform their duties. Even in the absence of express non-disclosure agreements, the programmers are bound by a duty not to use or disclose the secret in an unauthorized manner. Mary may also disclose the algorithm, if necessary, to the venture capitalists for the purpose of convincing them to provide funding. They, too, are likely to be bound by a duty of confidentiality, since they had notice that the information was being revealed in confidence, and agreed to review it, thus impliedly accepting a duty not to use or disclose the information without Mary's permission.

Mary provided copies of the early version of the program implementing the algorithm to a cross-section of insurance companies to test, without requiring them to sign non-disclosure agreements or other express contractual undertakings. However, there is case authority that distributing a trade secret in object code only does not in itself destroy trade secret status, as long as the source code is kept in confidence, as was done in this case. The fact that the object code is capable of being decompiled will not destroy the trade secret status of the algorithm against persons who learn it through other means. Thus, assuming that Mary's jurisdiction follows that precedent, Mary's acts in distributing disks containing the program to testers should not disqualify the algorithm from trade secret protection.

Mary's main problem with trade secrecy is that her application will be published by the U.S. Patent Office 18 months after it is filed. (The European Patent Office will publish her application 18 months after filing, as well.) Under the facts, Mary filed her application about 18 months ago. Thus, it has already been, or will soon be, published. Once it is published, all the information in the application, including the claim and the specification describing the invention and how to practice it, will lose its trade secret status. If the applications have not already been published, and Mary wants to retain the information as a trade secret, she must move quickly to withdraw her applications. She cannot elect both patent and trade secret protection for the algorithm. She must choose one or the other.

Which form of protection is preferable? A patent is probably preferable because it gives much stronger protection than trade secret law, allowing Mary to prohibit all unauthorized uses, regardless of how the defendant obtained the algorithm. While patents are often more costly to obtain, Mary may already have paid a significant portion of the expense of applying for a patent.

It is true that trade secret protection potentially can last longer than a patent (the period of time the information actually remains secret versus 20 years from application date). However, this advantage is unlikely to carry much weight in this case, since the art in computer science advances so rapidly: Mary's algorithm is likely to become obsolete within the next 18 years. Moreover, while Mary may successfully retain trade secret status through individually negotiated licensing agreements prohibiting reverse engineering and other unauthorized uses, there is still a risk that the trade secret will be lost, either because other firms independently create it and disclose it, or because the information leaks to the rest of the industry. Thus, proceeding with trade secret protection is more risky than relying on a patent, as long as the algorithm does indeed represent novel, non-obvious subject matter.

What would copyright protection add? While a patent will protect the algorithm, and trade secret law will protect the algorithm and any other secret ideas implemented in the computer program, copyright protects the particular expression that Mary and her programmers use to implement the algorithm and ideas. Thus, copyright protects the code used in the program, and original, expressive aspects of the program's structure, including the selection and arrangement of uncopyrightable elements. It might be possible for a competitor to copy portions of the program Mary's corporation creates without infringing the patent on the algorithm, or misappropriating trade secrets. Thus, Mary should claim copyright in the program. This will not be difficult, since copyright arises automatically upon fixation of the program in tangible form. There is no conflict under the law in simultaneously claiming patent or trade secret protection and copyright protection, because the copyright law protects different aspects of the program. Mary should register the program with the Copyright Office and include notice of copyright on the copies she distributes to purchasers and licensees, in order to preserve her opportunity to claim all available infringement remedies.

Potential problems with regard to copyright protection: Mary's corporation may run into difficulties in claiming sole ownership of the copyright in the new program. This is because the status of the programmers she hired is unclear. If they are "employees" within the meaning of Copyright Act §101, then the corporation has the sole ownership of the program by virtue of the work for hire doctrine. However, if they are not "employees," they may have ownership rights in the portions they created, or even qualify as joint authors. The facts suggest that Mary has not obtained any advance assignment of their interest in the copyright to her or the corporation.

In determining whether a work is created by an "employee," and thus is a work for hire, the general law of agency applies, and the ultimate question is whether the hiring party (Mary, or her corporation) had the right to control the process of creating the program. Some of the key factors are discussed below, in light of the facts that are provided.

1. The skill required: programming requires a high level of skill, which weighs in favor of independent contractor status.
2. The source of instrumentalities and tools and the location of the work: Here, presumably the corporation provided the computers, workplace, and other tools used by the programmers, which weighs in favor of employee status.
3. The duration of the relationship between the parties: Here, some of the programmers were only hired for a three-month stint, with the possibility of renewal on mutual consent. This may weigh slightly in favor of independent contractor status, especially since the parties seem to have contemplated that the programmers would only work on one project.
4. The method of payment and the provision of employee benefits: Here, most of the programmers were working without payment of benefits, which suggests independent contractor status.
5. The hired party's role in hiring and paying assistants: Here there is nothing to suggest that the programmers hired their own assistants, such as secretaries or other support staff, which weighs in favor of employee status.
6. Whether the work was part of the regular business of the hiring party, and whether the hiring party is in business: Here, the answer is yes, which weighs in favor of employee status.

It appears that the factors are about equally weighted, so it is hard to predict how a court would rule if one of the programmers were later to assert individual or joint authorship of the program. Mary would be well advised to negotiate for an express assignment, as well as for an agreement that the programmers' work product is a work for hire, when she enters into new employment agreements at the end of the programmers' existing terms of employment, and in hiring new programmers who will work on subsequent versions of the program.

SAMPLE ANSWER TO QUESTION 2:

A. Patent Infringement

Cool Cat obtained a utility patent in August, 2007. It might explore a suit for direct infringement against Freewheelers, and a possible suit for inducement of infringement against Diane and Elton. However, before exploring the specifics of these claims, it is useful to consider whether the patent might be vulnerable to an affirmative defense of patent invalidity, based on the available facts.

1. Patent Invalidity

To be patentable, an invention must be novel, non-obvious, and useful as of its invention date, and fully disclosed as provided in Patent Act §112. There is nothing in the facts to suggest that these requirements are not met. However, Patent Act §102(b) provides that an otherwise patentable invention may be disqualified for a patent if the inventor fails to file his application within a year after the invention is revealed in a printed publication anywhere in the world, or is on sale or in public use in the United States.

The defendants might argue that the Cool Cat patent is invalid under §102(b), on the ground that the invention was on sale, in public use, or the subject of a printed publication prior to the critical date—December, 2004. However, their arguments are unlikely to succeed.

The on-sale bar: Alvin contracted with Brokers to represent him in his attempt to sell his inventive concept, and Brokers undertook sales activities prior to the critical date of December, 2004. In the *Pfaff* case, the Supreme Court held that an invention could be deemed "on sale" for purposes of §102(b) even if it had not yet been reduced to actual practice, as long as the invention was "ready for patenting." Here, Alvin's skateboard could be deemed "ready for patenting" prior to the critical date because he had produced diagrams and drawings that were sufficient to enable a person with ordinary skill in the art to make a physical embodiment without undue experimentation.

However, Alvin's and Brokers' actions would not trigger the §102(b) statute of limitations because their actions did not constitute an offer to sell *the patented invention*. Rather, they were only offering to assign rights in the inventive concept itself, in return for payment. An offer to sell or assign the inventive concept, as opposed to an offer to sell physical embodiments of the invention, will not put the invention "on sale" for purposes of §102(b).

"Printed publication" and "public use": Nor could Alvin's or Brokers' actions amount to a "printed publication" or "public use" within the meaning of §102(b). A "printed publication" requires a fixed description of the invention that is sufficient to enable a person of ordinary skill in the art to make or practice the invention without undue experimentation. While this requirement may be satisfied, it must also appear that the description was available to a person exercising reasonable diligence to find it. Here, Alvin's and Brokers' careful use of confidentiality restrictions make it unlikely that Alvin's drawings and diagrams could be deemed reasonably available to a person exercising reasonable diligence to find them.

A court would be unlikely to find a "public use" prior to the critical date for two reasons: First, the invention itself was not yet reduced to practice and thus could not be put to use; and second, even if Brokers' and the skateboard manufacturers' actions could be deemed a "use" of the patented skateboard, the confidentiality restrictions would likely prevent the use from being deemed "public."

2. Infringement

Direct infringement claims: Patent Act §271(a) provides that it will constitute infringement to make, use, offer to sell, sell, or import the patented invention in the United States during the term of the patent. Cool Cat's patent term began when the patent issued, in August, 2007. [There is nothing to suggest that the patent application was published in the United States, triggering provisional rights against infringement prior to the issuance date. Since Cool Cat only applied in the United States, the application would not be required to be published.] Thus, we can assume that the only actions that would constitute a direct infringement are those that occurred in the United States in or after August, 2007. If Freewheeling continued to sell the skateboards that it acquired through Elton in the United States on or after August, 2007, that would constitute an unauthorized "sale" of the patented invention pursuant to §271 and would constitute infringement. However, only sales that occurred on or after the patent issuance date would be deemed infringing, and subject to injunctive or monetary relief.

Inducement claims: Liability for inducement of patent infringement, under Patent Act §271(b), requires a showing that the defendant actively, intentionally solicited or assisted another to infringe, with knowledge that infringement was likely to occur. Here, Cool Cat might argue that Diane and Elton both induced or assisted Freewheelers' direct infringement. However, this might prove difficult because at the time that Diane and Elton engaged in the acts that induced or assisted Freewheelers' infringement, the

Cool Cat patent had not yet issued. (In Diane's case, the application had not even been filed.) Nor do the facts suggest that Cool Cat notified them of its plan to obtain a patent. Thus, it would be difficult to demonstrate that either Diane or Elton had specific intent to cause infringement, or knowledge that patent infringement was likely to occur as a result of their actions.

3. Conclusion

Thus, while Cool Cat's patent may be valid, its usefulness under the current facts is limited. It can be asserted to *prevent further infringing actions* by Elton and Freewheelers, and to collect damages from any of Freewheelers' sales of infringing skateboards made on or after the patent issuance date. However, the patent will provide no redress for the unauthorized manufacture of the skateboards in Hong Kong, the sales in the European Union, or the importation, sales, or offers to sell in the United States prior to August, 2007.

B. Trade Secret Claims

The inventive concept underlying the skateboard might be deemed a trade secret prior to the skateboard's marketing in the United States, because it was substantially secret and gave Cool Cat a competitive advantage. Alvin and Brokers apparently took reasonable precautions to retain the concept as a secret, requiring all potential assignees to sign confidentiality agreements before receiving the particulars of the inventive design. There is nothing in the facts to suggest that Cool Cat was any less careful in this regard, or that the skateboard design was generally known in the industry or to the general public. Moreover, the new design probably gave Cool Cat a competitive advantage over other skateboard manufacturers/sellers, who did not know or use it. Cool Cat's willingness to pay Alvin $75,000 for rights in the concept, the hot sales in the European Union, and the eagerness of Diane and Elton to take and implement the design concept suggest that the design presented an opportunity for profit. While one might question whether the skateboard design was "continuously used" in Cool Cat's business at the time Diane took it, the Uniform Trade Secrets Act has done away with this requirement, making it possible to claim trade secret status in information that the claimant has yet to put into ongoing use.

As Cool Cat's employee, Diane had a duty not to use or disclose the skateboard design without Cool Cat's permission. She clearly acted in breach of this duty when she made the unauthorized copies and handed them over to Elton. Elton likewise breached a duty to Cool Cat, because he probably had notice (at least inquiry notice) at the time he obtained the secret information that it was a trade secret and was being provided to him in breach of Diane's duty. Thus, his use and disclosure of the design would infringe Cool Cat's rights, as well.

However, Diane and Elton might not be subject to an injunction against further use of the trade secret information at this point. As a general matter, injunctions against trade secret misappropriation are granted only for the time that the information remains secret, or for a reasonable time thereafter (adding the time it would have taken the defendant to obtain and utilize the information once it entered the public domain). Here, the information clearly entered the public domain when the U.S. patent issued and Cool Cat began to market the skateboard itself. Thus, trade secret law might not provide much help in preventing Elton's future marketing of the skateboard design. Likewise, monetary remedies (which would likely take the form of defendants' profits in this case) would only be likely for Elton's use of the trade secret during the time it remained a secret in the United States.

C. Trade Dress Infringement

Cool Cat might claim rights in the mark "Cool Cat," the two large blocky black C's it placed on the fin of the skateboard it marketed, the bright yellow color with black racing stripes, or any combination of these things, as protectible indications of origin. However, the facts do not indicate that Elton copied any of these indications of origin. The only feature of the Cool Cat skateboards that Elton copied was the configuration of the skateboard itself. While it is possible for a producer to claim trade dress rights in the configuration of its product, and thus use Lanham Act §43(a) to prevent competitors from manufacturing knock-offs, Cool Cat would encounter two major problems in taking this approach under the current facts.

First, in the *Wal-Mart* decision, the Supreme Court held that product configuration trade dress cannot be deemed inherently distinctive. Secondary meaning must be demonstrated in all cases before trade dress protection can be afforded under §43(a). This means that the public must have been exposed to the configuration sufficiently to come to think of it as an indication that the skateboard comes from a particular source. Here, it is not clear that the Cool Cat skateboard configuration has had sufficient public exposure and publicity to attain that status. It is highly unlikely that it had in April, 2007, when Freewheeling first began selling skateboards with the same configuration, because it had only been on the market for one month. Presumably, Cool Cat would only be entitled to §43(a) protection as of the date it acquired the necessary secondary meaning in the skateboard configuration.

Second, Elton and Freewheeling will argue that the skateboard configuration is unprotectible as trade dress because it is functional. In the *TrafFix* case the Supreme Court provided that product feature trade dress must be found non-functional under both the *Inwood Laboratories* and the *Qualitex* standards before it can be protected. Under the *Inwood Laboratories* standard, the product configuration is functional if it "is essential to the use or purpose of the article, or if it affects the cost or quality of the article." Under the *Qualitex* standard, the configuration will be functional if exclusive rights would "put competitors at a significant non-reputation-related disadvantage."

It seems likely that the skateboard configuration would be found functional under the first (*Inwood Laboratories*) standard. The facts state that Alvin believed that his particular combination of product features would create a faster, more stable design. Thus, the configuration affects the quality of the skateboard and is directly related to accomplishment of its purpose. Moreover, Cool Cat's utility patent claimed all of the key features of the configuration. Under *TrafFix*, the inclusion of trade dress elements in utility patent claims constitutes strong evidence that the trade dress is functional. To overcome the strong presumption of functionality created by the presence of the features in the utility patent claims, defendants must show that the configuration is merely an ornamental, incidental, or arbitrary aspect of the skateboard. They would be unlikely to be able to do so in this case.

While the facts do suggest that the fin could be shaped in any of several ways and still be efficient aerodynamically, the fin does nonetheless serve a utilitarian function in the product: It adds to the aerodynamic quality of the skateboard. Thus, arguably it would still affect the "quality" of the skateboard, under the *Inwood Laboratories* standard, and thus be found functional. The Court of Appeals for the Federal Circuit has held that the availability of alternatives remains relevant in determining functionality under *TrafFix* and *Inwood Laboratories*, so perhaps that circuit (as opposed to the Fifth Circuit) might consider the particular shape of the fin to be non-functional under *Inwood Laboratories*. However, since the "retro" look is fashionable, the Federal Circuit could find functionality under *Qualitex*, because giving Cool Cat-exclusive rights in the retro design would put other skateboard designers at a significant, non-reputation-related disadvantage.

Accordingly, Cool Cat would have to overcome a functionality challenge and demonstrate secondary meaning before it could assert rights in the skateboard configuration under Lanham Act §43(a). And even assuming that it did, it would still have to demonstrate that the Elton/Freewheeling use caused a likelihood of consumer confusion about the source of the skateboards. This would include showing that the parties marketed the skateboard in the same geographic area, through similar channels, to similar consumers.

Since the products and the fin shapes are identical, the similarity of the configuration itself would weigh in favor of a finding of infringement. The fact that each party clearly placed other identifying information on the fin of each skateboard it sold, on the other hand, would seem to weigh against a finding of likelihood of confusion.

D. Copyright Infringement

Cool Cat might have a cause of action against Diane for copyright infringement because of her unauthorized photocopying of the skateboard diagrams and drawings. The photocopying would infringe Cool Cat's reproduction rights. It might likewise claim that Elton is liable for contributory infringement, if it can demonstrate that he knew of the infringing activity and induced or assisted it. To the extent that Elton made further two-dimensional copies of the skateboard plans in the United States, he might be directly liable for those reproductions.

However, the skateboard itself is a useful article, and under current case law, it generally is not deemed an infringement to produce a useful article from copyrighted plans. So producing the skateboard itself from the plans would not infringe the reproduction or adaptation rights, nor would the subsequent importation or sale of the skateboards made from the plans. The only way that Cool Cat could demonstrate that the Elton skateboards themselves infringed Cool Cat's copyright would be to show that "sculptural" elements of the skateboard design are copyrightable under the "physical or conceptual separability test." Here, the design elements of the skateboard do not appear to be physically separable. They would be deemed conceptually separable under the Second Circuit's standard if the design elements reflect Alvin's artistic judgment exercised independently of functional influences. Here, Cool Cat may argue that the fin was so designed, since there were alternative ways that it could have been designed and still have functioned as well. However, it would probably fail because the facts do indicate that Alvin was influenced by aerodynamic concerns in designing the fin. Under the Second Circuit's decision in *Brandir*, all that is necessary to disqualify a useful article design from copyrightability is a showing that the design was significantly *influenced* by utilitarian concerns. It is not necessary that it be dictated by them.

If Cool Cat could demonstrate that aspects of the skateboard design were copyrighted, then it could hold Elton and Freewheelers both liable for infringement. Elton distributed infringing skateboards to the public (by virtue of his sale to Freewheelers), and may have contributed to Freewheelers' infringement, as well. Freewheelers infringed the right of distribution to the public, and perhaps public display rights, as well. However, it is unlikely that Cool Cat can demonstrate that the skateboard's configuration, or the fin by itself, is copyrightable.

SAMPLE ANSWER TO QUESTION 3:

There are several issues raised by these facts. First, absent the restrictive statement on the labels, would it be infringement for CheepCo to import the new toothbrushes back into the United States for resale? Second, even if new toothbrushes could be imported, could the "refurbished" toothbrushes also be imported? Finally, what, if any, difference does the restrictive statement make?

A. Parallel Imports

Parallel imports are patented goods that were originally made (or authorized to be made) by the U.S. patentee and sold abroad in foreign markets. Until very recently, case precedent allowed persons to import patented goods that they purchased abroad without restriction from the U.S. patentee or its licensee. Essentially, courts applied the doctrine of exhaustion (or the doctrine of first sale) to all goods sold by or under the authority of the U.S. patentee, regardless of whether those goods were first sold domestically or abroad. (This doctrine is known as the doctrine of international exhaustion.) Thus, once the patentee sold the goods without restriction anywhere in the world, the purchaser and/or its successors in interest could resell the goods, in any country they wished, without infringing the U.S. patent.

However, in its recent *Jazz Photo* decision, the Court of Appeals for the Federal Circuit held that the doctrine of exhaustion only applies to the patentee's *domestic* sales. (This doctrine is known as the doctrine of territorial exhaustion.) Thus, under this decision, none of the toothbrushes could be imported into the United States, even in the absence of the restrictive statement on the labels, because the U.S. patentee originally sold them abroad, rather than domestically.

B. The Refurbishment

Even if the new toothbrushes could be imported under *Jazz Photo*, the question arises whether the refurbished ones could be. The answer would turn on whether the refurbishment constituted permissible repair or infringing reconstruction. The refurbishment would constitute reconstruction if it amounted to making a new article after the old one was spent. In the *Sandvik* case, the Federal Circuit listed four factors to consider in making this determination: (1) the nature of the defendant's actions; (2) the nature of the device and how it is designed (namely, whether one of the components of the patented combination has a shorter useful life than the whole); (3) whether a market has developed to manufacture or service the part at issue; and (4) objective evidence of the patentee's intent.

In this case, Azul replaced the brush and batteries, which clearly have a shorter useful life than the plastic handle and motor. Moreover, Azul's actions appear to be fairly simple and straightforward: In replacing the brush, presumably all it did was unscrew the screws holding the first brush to the shaft and screw the new brush in its place. Both these factors seem to weigh in favor of permissible repair. However, the third and forth factors may weigh in favor of infringing reconstruction: There are no facts suggesting the existence of a market to refurbish used disposable toothbrushes. Moreover, the patentee made it clear that it intended that the brushes be discarded after use, and not refurbished. In the *Hewlett-Packard* case, the Federal Circuit refused to permit a patentee's express statements that its product should be discarded determine the outcome of the case. Under this precedent, and given all the evidence, a reasonably good argument could be made that Azul was engaged in permissible repair, which would not infringe in itself if it occurred in the United States, or if the importation of the refurbished brushes was otherwise legal under the laws governing parallel imports. However, even if the refurbishment is legal, the import of the goods is illegal and the legality of the refurbishment in itself cannot change that outcome.

C. The Restrictive Provision

Even if it were not patent infringement for CheepCo to import toothbrushes that the U.S. patentee sold abroad without restriction, it must be determined whether the statement on the toothbrush packaging prohibiting import or resale in the United States would be enforceable against subsequent purchasers. Similar questions arise in connection with shrink-wrap and click-wrap ("mass market") licenses for software. Courts have differed over whether such provisions are enforceable, questioning whether there is adequate consent to the restrictions, whether the restrictions constitute contracts of adhesion or are unconscionable, and whether state enforcement of such provisions might be preempted. Here, given the product and the circumstances, and the fact that alternative toothbrushes are readily available, it seems unlikely that the restriction against import would be deemed anticompetitive, or against public policy. As long as purchasers had clear notice of the restriction, it is likely to be deemed enforceable. It appears that the initial packaging made the restriction reasonably clear.

In the *Mallinckrodt* case, the Federal Circuit upheld a patentee's restriction on the label of a medical product that prohibited reuse of the product. Indeed, the court found that persons reusing the product in violation of the restriction could be liable *either* for breach of contract or for patent infringement. It seems likely that a court would follow this precedent and find the restriction in the present case equally enforceable. Indeed, courts have enforced label restrictions against importation of goods first sold abroad by the U.S. patentee.

Thus, Cheepco would be bound by the restriction on the toothbrushes it purchased from Martinez, and would be liable for importing the toothbrushes into the United States in violation of the restriction, even if parallel imports were otherwise legal. However, the refurbished toothbrushes that CheepCo bought via Azul did not bear the restrictive legend, as they were repackaged in Azul's own packaging. Generally, restrictive legends of this sort will only be binding on those with notice of them. The question would be whether CheepCo had notice from other sources.

SAMPLE ANSWER TO QUESTION 4:

A. A Cause of Action for Infringing the Adaptation Right

Even though facts are uncopyrightable, news articles containing their authors' original expression of the facts are copyrightable subject matter. The newspaper plaintiffs are likely to own copyrights in at least some of the articles by virtue of the work for hire doctrine, or by assignment from the individual authors.

It is not necessary to demonstrate a reproduction in order to demonstrate an infringement of the adaptation right. The Ninth Circuit made it clear, in the *Mirage* case, that one may infringe the adaptation right by recasting or transforming a preexisting, authorized copy of the plaintiff's work. In *Mirage*, the court held that merely cutting authorized reproductions of works of art from books and mounting the works on tiles infringed the adaptation right in the works. The Ninth Circuit rejected the argument that the defendant's action was equivalent to merely changing the frame on a picture (which is generally understood not to constitute an adaptation). However, in the *Lee* case, the Seventh Circuit found that a similar process of mounting works on tiles was an insufficient change to constitute an adaptation as defined in Copyright Act §101.

In the *Galoob* case, the Ninth Circuit held that the defendant must *incorporate* a portion of the copyrighted work into the alleged adaptation in some *concrete or permanent form*. In *Galoob*, the defendant sold a device that permitted users to intercept data bytes flowing from a copyrighted video game cartridge to a central processing unit and substitute other bytes, thus changing the "rules" under which the copyrighted video game was played. This had the effect of altering the screen display when the game was played, but the court held that it did not constitute an infringing adaptation of the copyrighted game. The court reasoned that users did not reproduce the copyrighted game, or incorporate it into a new work in a permanent or concrete way. The device only worked in conjunction with a copyrighted game, and did not replace it or supplant the market for it. Any alterations ceased to exist as soon as the game was complete or the game console was turned off.

Under this precedent, X might argue that it (and persons exercising its link) did not infringe the newspapers' adaptation right. Assuming that X made no infringing reproductions, as specified in the facts, then the facts in this case are somewhat like those in *Galoob*. Due to X's actions, when users exercise a link on X's web site, X's frame is superimposed around the newspaper's copyrighted article on the user's computer. Even if this would otherwise constitute an infringing adaptation under *Mirage* (the articles are placed into a new context, much like the art in *Mirage* after the defendant pasted it on tiles), the combination of frame and article is only temporary, and will vanish once the user moves on to other material on the Internet or turns off his or her computer. Thus, the article is not incorporated into a new framed version in any concrete or permanent way, either by X or by visitors to X's web site.

The plaintiffs might respond that the Ninth Circuit, in the *MAI* case, held that merely taking a work into the random access memory of one's computer constitutes reproduction of the work, notwithstanding the fact that the reproduction will be extinguished as soon as the user moves to another document or turns off his or her computer. The court reasoned that the reproduction is sufficiently "permanent" to be "fixed" and constitutes a "copy" because it is capable of being perceived for more than a transitory period. Under that reasoning, users of X's links, who download the article with frame into their random access memories, reproduce the newspapers' copyrighted articles and the frame. If merely bringing a work into random access memory is sufficiently permanent and concrete to constitute a reproduction, then it should also be sufficiently concrete and permanent to constitute an adaptation, under the Ninth Circuit's decision in *Galoob*. While the newspapers may be found to have impliedly authorized Internet users' RAM reproduction of their articles (by virtue of posting them on their web sites), there is nothing to suggest that they have implicitly authorized adaptation of the articles.

If visitors to X's web site infringe the newspapers' adaptation right, then X may be held liable for their infringement under a contributory infringement theory. (X knew of the visitors' infringing conduct, and induced and materially assisted it.) X might also be liable under a vicarious liability theory. (X was in a position to control his visitors' actions because he controlled the link), and stood to gain direct financial benefit from their infringement (since presumably the availability of the links drew visitors to X's web site, and X was able to charge his advertising clients according to the number of visitors to his site).)

B. Other Possible Causes of Action

X might also be liable under Lanham Act §43(a), under a reverse passing off theory. Under the facts, he arguably is passing off the plaintiff newspapers' articles as his own product. Visitors to X's web site who exercise the links may believe that they are accessing X's own articles, due to the fact that X does not tell them they are being transported to another web site, and the deep link bypasses identifying information on the newspapers' home page. However, if X's actions do not confuse visitors into thinking that the articles come from X, then his failure to credit the proper source may not in itself constitute a §43(a) violation. To constitute passing off under §43(a), X's action must cause a likelihood of consumer confusion about the source, sponsorship, or affiliation of the parties' goods or services. Merely failing to provide information about the source, in itself, is not actionable. If the newspapers enjoyed a moral right of attribution in their articles, then X would be in violation of that right. However, no such right is recognized, as such, in newspaper articles in the United States. The Supreme Court in the *Dastar* case made it clear that Lanham Act §43(a) should not be construed to provide moral rights in works of authorship.

X might also try a state cause of action for misappropriation. The facts in this case are somewhat like those in the *INS* case. The newspapers have invested time, effort, and money to create the stories, and the stories have an economic value. X, in establishing links, can be characterized as reaping where he has not sown, or free-riding, because he did not have to invest the labor, skill, or effort the newspapers did in order to get the stories. Finally, arguably the newspapers are injured, because X's actions may make it unnecessary for Internet users to visit the papers' home pages to obtain the news, and thus may deprive the newspapers of the opportunity to enjoy the advertising and promotional benefits of providing subscription forms to visitors. X's actions may also deprive them of the opportunity to sell advertising in frames of their own devising.

Copyright Act §301 preempts state causes of action that give rights equivalent to the exclusive rights of copyright in copyrightable subject matter. The Court of Appeals for the Second Circuit has held, in the *Motorola* case, that state misappropriation claims are generally preempted under §301 whenever the plaintiff asserts that the defendant misappropriated material that is within the subject matter of copyright. The court reasoned that the rights provided under the misappropriation cause of action in such cases are generally equivalent to the exclusive rights of copyright. Newspaper articles clearly are copyrightable subject matter, so X might argue that the plaintiffs' misappropriation claim is preempted in this case.

However, the *Motorola* court found that Congress intended an exception to the general rule of preemption when a misappropriation claim has facts similar to those in the *INS* case. The newspapers may argue that this exception applies, and thus avoid preemption. The facts here are indeed very similar to those in *INS*. Arguably, in both cases: (1) the plaintiff generates or gathers information at a cost; (2) the information is time-sensitive; (3) the defendant's use of the information constitutes free-riding on the plaintiff's efforts; (4) the defendant is in direct competition with a product or service offered by the plaintiffs; and (5) the ability of other parties to free-ride on the efforts of the plaintiff would so reduce the incentive to produce the product or service that its existence or quality would be substantially threatened. Here, if X is not stopped, the newspapers may lose their incentive to set up web pages to provide free news via the Internet to the public, because X's actions interfere with their ability to obtain advertising value from their work.

SAMPLE ANSWER TO QUESTION 5:

A. Patent Infringement

Patent Act §271(a) grants the patentee the right to prohibit others from making, using, selling, offering to sell, or importing the patented invention in the United States during the patent term. Absent evidence of term extensions, it appears that the patent in this case will be valid until April 20, 2020. The widgets have not been made at the time of the agreement. Since they are to be made in South Africa and shipped directly to Taiwan, there is no instance of making, using, selling, or importing the patented invention in the United States during the patent term.

The only argument for patent infringement under §271(a) is that Jones Co. "offered to sell" the patented invention in the United States during the patent term. Patent Act §271(i) provides that an "offer to sell" is one in which the sale will occur before the expiration of the patent term. The sale arranged in this case will occur during this time frame. However, there is uncertainty in the law about *whether the sale must take place in the United States,* or whether a sale abroad will suffice to trigger liability for an offer to sell made in the United States. Some district courts have held that there can be no liability for offering to sell unless the contemplated sale would itself infringe. Since a sale outside of the U.S. territory will not infringe, an offer to sell outside of the U.S. territory also will not infringe (even if the offer itself took place in the United States). These courts have reasoned that the "offer to sell" provision was meant only to move up the time in which relief can be had against a sale that will infringe the patent.

The Jones Co. did make an offer to sell the patented invention in the United States. Thus, its liability depends on whether the sale must occur in the United States as well. If the offer to sell does infringe, then the Taiwanese government might also be liable for inducing the infringement. However, there are insufficient facts to determine whether the knowledge and intent requirements of Patent Act §271(b) would be satisfied in this case.

B. Delivery in May, 2020

Assuming that the sale occurs on delivery, a delivery date of May, 2020, would occur *after the patent expires.* Jones Co. would not be liable for offering to sell the widgets by virtue of the provisions of Patent Act §271(i), discussed above.

C. Meeting in April 2001 with delivery in February, 2004

If the offer took place in April, 2001, it took place *before the patent term commenced,* and will not infringe. Even if Smith had provisional rights under his patent, those rights would not commence until his patent application was published, which is likely to have been in October, 2001 (18 months after the application was filed), several months after the offer was made. Apart from provisional rights, patents provide no retroactive protection against infringement.

SAMPLE ANSWER TO QUESTION 6:

A. Copyright infringement claim.

The first question that should be addressed is whether the delta design is sufficiently original to constitute copyrightable subject matter. The standard of originality is low: In *Feist*, the Supreme Court suggested that originality requires only that the work not be copied and satisfy a minimum threshold of creativity. One might argue, however, that the second part of the requirement is not met here. The design is of the simplest kind, comprised of three triangles, which are very common geometric figures. The contribution of the single word, which essentially just mimics the shapes, is minimal. The Copyright Office generally refuses to recognize copyright in "words and short phrases such as names, titles, and slogans; familiar symbols or designs, mere variations of typographic ornamentation, lettering or coloring; and mere listings of ingredients or contents" 37 CFR §202.1(a). The design at issue could be deemed a "familiar symbol or design," or in any event, could certainly could be characterized as demonstrating no more originality than the listed examples of uncopyrightable subject matter.

If the delta design were deemed copyrightable subject matter, the next issue would be whether the doctrine of first sale (Copyright Act §109(a)) would apply to authorize Cheepco's importation. In the *L'Anza* case, the Supreme Court held that the Copyright Act §602 importation right was limited by the first sale doctrine, which provides: "Notwithstanding the provisions of section 106(3), the owner of a particular copy or phonorecord lawfully made under this title, or any person authorized by such owner, is entitled, without the authority of the copyright owner, to sell or otherwise dispose of the possession of that copy or phonorecord."

In *L'Anza*, the goods in question had been manufactured in the United States for sale abroad, and the defendant had purchased the goods abroad and imported them back into the United States without the copyright owner's authority, to be sold in competition with the copyright owner's authorized U.S. distributors. The key difference in this case is that the U.S. copyright owner manufactured the watches bearing the delta design abroad, rather than in the United States. While the reasoning in *L'Anza* would seem to fit either situation, Justice Ginsburg, in a concurring opinion, differentiated cases in which the goods were manufactured outside of U.S. territory, suggesting that the doctrine of first sale might not apply to such goods because they were not "lawfully made under this title." There are some lower court decisions that have construed the language of §109(a) to impose a geographical limitation on the doctrine of first sale in this fashion. On the other hand, the Third Circuit in the *Sebastion* case suggested that the doctrine of first sale ought to apply to all goods originally manufactured and sold by or under the authority of the U.S. copyright owner, regardless of where they were manufactured and first sold.

As a matter of policy, this latter approach would make sense because regardless of where the copyright owner manufactured and first sold the goods, the owner got the benefit of the first sale, and should not have a legitimate need to control further sales of the same copies. To permit such control might favor copyright owners who manufacture their goods abroad over those who manufacture them domestically, and sanction the kind of price discrimination against U.S. consumers that we see in this case. (The opposing policy argument would be that copyright law should be used to ensure that copyright owners are able to adopt and enforce the marketing methods they prefer without interference, and thereby maximize their profits.)

The arguments favoring application of the doctrine of first sale to goods manufactured and sold abroad by the U.S. copyright owner are strong, but since there has been no final resolution of the issue, it is useful to consider what, if any, defenses the defendant might have if the doctrine of first sale is found not to apply. First, Cheepco might consider a laches defense since Delta appears to have permitted its actions for a number of years without protest, leading Cheepco to rely on its acquiescence. Given how small and unnoticeable the delta design is, and Delta's silence in adopting it, it would be inequitable to permit Delta to rely on it in an infringement action now.

Cheepco might also consider a copyright misuse defense. The misuse defense is an equitable doctrine that renders a copyright unenforceable if the copyright owner has engaged in misconduct in licensing or enforcing the copyright, impermissibly broadening the scope of his monopoly right, contrary to the policies underlying the copyright law. This defense has primarily been used in cases in which the copyright owner has improperly conditioned a license to reproduce or distribute the copyrighted work. That is not the case here. The argument would simply be that the defendant has created and is asserting the copyright in a manner clearly calculated to extend its monopoly right to an uncopyrightable useful article (the watch). While this argument has some appeal, it may not be accepted, since it is an unorthodox use of the defense and might be hard to contain.

The other possibility might be a fair use defense although, again, the application would be somewhat unorthodox. The argument would be that while the defendant's purpose is commercial and nontransformative, and the defendant distributes the entirety of the copyrighted work (the delta design), distributing the design is necessary in order to obtain the benefit of the useful article on which it is engraved, distribution benefits the public by making the useful article available to a larger range of purchasers, and does not interfere with the market for the work (since the copyright owner has already sold each copy of the work). This argument parallels the reasoning adopted by the Ninth Circuit in the *Sega* case. Moreover, Delta's secrecy in adding the design and the other attendant circumstances suggest inequitable behavior—an attempt to use copyright to prohibit lawful resale of an uncopyrightable useful article.

B. Whether Delta should add a trademark infringement claim.

U.S. trademark law holds that when the foreign manufacturer of goods and the U.S. registrant of the mark under which the goods are sold are related, then the U.S. registrant may not assert trademark law or Tariff Act §556 to prevent goods manufactured and marked abroad by the manufacturer from entering the United States, unless the goods are materially different from those sold domestically under the mark by the U.S. registrant. Here, it appears that Delta is both the foreign manufacturer and the U.S. registrant, so the only way that Delta could prevent the Cheepco import under trademark law would be to demonstrate that the watches imported by Cheepco were materially different from watches Delta (through its authorized distributors) sells in the United States. There is nothing in the facts to suggest that that is so, but it would be worthwhile to determine whether there are material differences in warranty and/or quality control. It would also make sense to see if the written materials accompanying the watches are in the same language, or whether all the watches have multiple-language inserts. If no material difference can be found among the goods, then it would not be useful for Delta to add a trademark infringement claim.

SAMPLE ANSWER TO QUESTION 7:

Bella v. Anston Tool for Breach of License Agreement

The main issue in determining the enforceability of the license is whether state enforcement of a contract to pay indefinitely for use of an unpatentable invention would unduly frustrate Congress's purposes in enacting the patent laws. If so, then the state contract cause of action is preempted and the license is unenforceable. In *Sears, Roebuck & Co. v. Stiffel Co.* and *Compco Corp. v. Day-Brite Lighting, Inc.*, the Supreme Court said that in enacting the patent laws, Congress attempted to accommodate two conflicting interests: (1) providing an incentive to invent by granting property rights in inventions, and (2) promoting free competition by keeping ideas freely available to the public. To do this it drew a line: All those ideas meeting the high standards of federal patent law would qualify for patents, which would give exclusive rights for a limited period of time. Those ideas not meeting these standards would be left in the public domain, free for all to use. Based on these cases, Anston may argue that since the plirench is not patentable it must be freely available to all, including Anston, without the obligation of paying. Anston will probably lose, however. The facts of this case are very similar to those in *Aronson v. Quick Point Pencil Co.*, in which the Supreme Court found that enforcement of a contract to pay for use of an unpatentable idea/ invention was not preempted. The Court reasoned that state enforcement of such contracts poses little real interference with the availability of ideas in the public domain. Only the immediate parties to the contract are bound. Third parties remain free to use the idea. Indeed, enforcement of contracts is consistent with the three purposes of Congress set out in *Kewanee Oil Co. v. Bicron*: (1) enforcement provides further incentive to invent; (2) it promotes public disclosure of ideas (without an enforceable license contract providing for royalties, it is less likely that inventors will make their ideas known and available to manufacturers); and (3) assuming that the idea was not already in the public domain prior to the contract, enforcement of the contract will not withdraw the idea from the public domain. (Of course, the P.T.O.'s finding that the plirench was neither novel nor non-obvious is evidence that it was already in the public domain. However, the Supreme Court has not clarified the meaning of "public domain" in this context. It is possible that evidence that the plirench was not generally known or available on the market may be sufficient to show that it was not "in the public domain.") While the Supreme Court, in *Bonito Boats, Inc. v. Thunder Craft Inc.*, reinforced the *Sears* and *Compco* reasoning, it also appeared to uphold *Kewanee* and *Aronson* as well.

The other issue with respect to the license is whether state law will enforce an express contract to pay for an idea such as the plirench. Some states require that the idea be novel and concrete before they will enforce such a contract. However, even if the state in this case imposes such a requirement, it may be met. The plirench was a completed invention in physical form, and thus was concrete. While the Patent Office did not find it novel under the standards of §102 of the Patent Act, the idea law standard may be lower. The idea of the plirench was original to Bella (she did not copy it from another source) and apparently it was novel enough to be valuable not only to Anston, which has marketed it successfully to the public, but also to two of Anston's competitors. It does not appear to have been widely known by others prior to Bella's invention, or specifically known to Anston.

Thus, Anston probably will not be excused from performing its license agreement, even if it was not an advantageous one.

Anston Tool v. Bella for Trade Secret Misappropriation

In analyzing Anston Tool's case against Bella, two questions must be addressed. First, *was Anston's process a protectible trade secret;* and second, *if it was, did Bella violate a duty in disclosing it to Tabor?*

Trade secret: To prevail, Anston Tool must demonstrate that its process was a secret that gave it a commercial advantage over its competitors. It probably can do this. First, *the process was substantially secret.* Only four companies had managed to develop it themselves (so it must not have been obvious), and only six (out of 35) knew of it. The Restatement specifies that absolute secrecy is unnecessary. The relatively small percentage of firms that knew of the secret process in this case probably is acceptable, since the facts say that all six of the firms took reasonable measures to keep it secret. Thus, it would be difficult for others to acquire knowledge of the secret process. Tod, who had been in the business 20 years, had never heard of it. Second, *it appears that the process gave users a competitive advantage over manufacturers who did not know or use it.* Andrew told Bella that the process was very efficient and inexpensive to use and that he believed that it would help in making the plirench a commercial success. Tod obviously recognized its value, since he implemented it immediately upon learning of it. The facts state that the process saved Tod's company considerable money. While the facts do not indicate precisely what efforts Anston Tool made to keep the process a secret or how much it spent to develop it, the existing evidence indicates that the process was a protectible trade secret.

The violation of a duty: Anston Tool has a good argument that Bella had a duty to maintain the process in confidence. She knew it was a secret (Andrew said so expressly) and yet she specifically asked Andrew to reveal it. Her request to hear the information under these circumstances suggests an implied agreement on her part to keep the secret and use it only for the purpose for which it was revealed: evaluating whether she should contract with Anston. She should refrain from using or divulging it to others without Anston Tool's permission. She breached this duty when she revealed the secret process to Tod, and thus may be liable to Anston Tool.

Anston Tool v. Tod and Tabor Household Tool for Trade Secret Misappropriation

Assuming that Anston Tool's process was a protectible trade secret, it must be determined whether Tod Tabor and his company (hereafter collectively "Tabor") had a duty to refrain from using the process without Anston Tool's permission. The relevant standard is whether a reasonable person in Tabor's situation would know that the process was a trade secret and that Bella was breaching a duty in revealing it to Tabor. If so, Tabor incurred a duty to refrain from disclosing or using the secret without permission. A good argument exists that this standard was satisfied. As to notice that the process was a trade secret, Tod was a professional who had been in the business for 20 years, yet he had never heard of the process. He clearly could see that the process was valuable. These facts arguably should have put him on notice that he was hearing a trade secret, especially given the fact that Bella expressly told him that she had learned it from one of Tabor's competitors in the course of one-on-one business negotiations. In addition, the manner in which Bella learned of the process should have put Tabor on notice that she owed a duty of confidentiality to Anston, which she was breaking. At the very least, a reasonable person in Tabor's position would have made further inquiry, which would have revealed the trade secret status and breach of duty. Since Tabor had the requisite notice, and thus a duty to refrain from use, his subsequent unauthorized use of the process should lead to liability.

SAMPLE ANSWER TO QUESTION 8:

Infringement: In order to prevail on its infringement claim, Y Corp. must demonstrate that Z copied from its copyrighted book and that the copying constituted an unlawful appropriation.

Copying: Copying can be established through circumstantial evidence that the defendant had access to the plaintiff's work and that the two works are sufficiently similar to give rise to an inference that the defendant copied from the plaintiff. Here, Y Corp. has a pretty good case. Access is clear from the Dallas Library records. Moreover, there is considerable similarity between the works. It should be noted that for purposes of the copying issue, all similarities are relevant, even if the similarities do not involve copyrightable elements of the work.

Unlawful appropriation: Under the second part of the *Arnstein v. Porter* test for copyright infringement, it must be determined whether the defendant's work would be deemed "substantially similar" to the plaintiff's copyrightable expression by the average intended reader, based on his or her overall subjective impression. The question is ultimately one for the jury. However, the court must ascertain whether there is sufficient basis for the jury to make a finding of substantial similarity. (Note that in the case of a factual work, such as a biography, the court may apply a more stringent standard than the normal subjective "substantial similarity" standard, described above. For example, the court might apply a "more discerning" or even a "thin copyright" standard, which requires "virtual identicality" or a "bodily appropriation of copyrighted expression.")

(1) Facts: Though Z may have copied a large quantity of facts from X's book, facts are not themselves subject to copyright protection, and thus these similarities cannot themselves support a finding of substantial similarity. Y Corp. might argue that refusal to prohibit the kind of free-riding Z took on X's research will undermine X and other authors' incentive to do original research, to the detriment of the public. However, the Supreme Court rejected such arguments in *Feist Publications, Inc. v. Rural Telephone Service Co., Inc.,* when it rejected the "sweat of the brow" doctrine. Facts are not original to an author. The Constitution's Patents and Copyrights Clause only authorizes Congress to protect the *original writings of an author.*

(2) Selection and arrangement of the facts: While an author's selection and arrangement of facts may be deemed copyrightable expression as a general matter, X's chronological organization is unlikely to be protected. Most works of history and biography are organized chronologically, which suggests that this form of organization may be so common as not to be original. Moreover, the chronological structure of the work may merge with the idea, because there are a limited number of ways effectively to describe the life of a person. While Y Corp. may argue that X's *selection* of facts to report is protectible, nothing in the facts of the question suggests that X engaged in meaningful selection, rather than essentially repeating all the facts she could discover about A. Generally, courts are not generous in finding copyrightable expression in works of non-fiction, apart from the author's literal language. If a court were to find that X's selection judgment constituted copyrightable expression, it might treat the copyright as "thin," and require a showing of "virtual identicality" or "bodily appropriation of expression" before finding that Z infringed it. Given the circumstances of the case, this might be hard to do.

(3) The theory about A's motivation: In the absence of evidence that Z tracked X's language in expressing her theory, a court is unlikely to consider Z's use of the same theory in determining the issue of infringement. The theory is an idea, and copyright does not prevent the copying of ideas.

(4) Similar language in two paragraphs: X's choice of language in the two paragraphs Z copied is protected expression. The similarity in this case is "literal similarity." However, two paragraphs out of an entire book is not very much. These similarities are more likely to lead to a finding of infringement if it can be demonstrated that they are important, in the overall context of X's book, as opposed to mere "filler."

(5) Corporal Peel: Y Corp. may argue that since X's purported "facts" about Corporal Peel are fictitious, they constitute protected expression. However, in this case a court might refuse to consider this argument, based on an estoppel rationale. X represented to the public, both by implication (designating the work a biography—a work of nonfiction) and directly (the subtitle says the work is a true story) that all the information in the book is factual. The law permitted Z to copy facts, and he may reasonably have relied on X's representations, so that X (and as X's successor in interest, Y Corp.) now is estopped to deny that Corporal Peel is factual. Even if a court did not find an estoppel, it might question whether a character in X's work is itself entitled to protection. Y Corp. would have to demonstrate that the character was drawn in considerable detail. Since Corporal Peel was a relatively minor character in X's work, Y Corp. may not be able to do this.

On the whole, since the only copyrightable expression Z took may be the two paragraphs (and possibly selection judgment), Y Corp.'s case for infringement is not a guaranteed winner. Moreover, Z would probably raise a fair use defense.

Fair use defense: Copyright Act §107, which codifies the fair use defense, specifically lists use for purposes of research as an example of a possible fair use. However, this is not in itself determinative. Section 107 lists four factors that should be considered in determining whether an infringing use should be excused from liability:

(1) The purpose and character of the use: In this case, Z's purpose was commercial in nature, because he planned to sell the book commercially. This militates against a finding of fair use. However, since Z added some information and insights of his own to his book, Z's book could be deemed a productive, or transformative use. A finding of a transformative use would weigh in Z's favor.

(2) The nature of the copyrighted work: In this case, X's book was published and it was a work of nonfiction. Courts have found that the public has a greater need to use published works of nonfiction, and a right to copy the uncopyrightable elements, such as facts and ideas. Therefore greater leeway to copy expression may be afforded, to the extent that it is necessary in order effectively to copy the unprotectible facts and ideas. Thus, the nature of the work in this case favors a finding for Z.

(3) The amount and substantiality of the portion used in relation to the copyrighted work as a whole: This factor may favor Z, because the amount of copyrighted expression actually copied in this case is probably relatively small. However, the literal copying of two paragraphs is problematic for Z. Even given Z's legitimate interest in accessing and using uncopyrightable facts from X's book, Z had no need to copy the literal expression of the facts here. As a general matter, the factual nature of the work (factor 2) only permits copying that is necessary to access and use the facts, and no more.

(4) The effect of the use upon the potential market for the work: The Supreme Court has indicated that this is the most important factor. If the defendant's work threatens to serve as a substitute for the plaintiff's work, and thus fill the public demand and undercut the plaintiff's market, then a court is unlikely to find a fair use. In this case, even though the focus of X and Z's biographies differ, persons who otherwise might have bought X's book now may buy Z's instead. Most readers are unlikely to purchase both books.

This is a close case. However, given that Z's use was commercial and may undercut the market for the X book, Y Corp. is likely to prevail on the fair use issue.

Remedies: Because Y Corp. did not register its copyright for several years after X's book was published, its ability to obtain statutory damages and attorney fees will be impaired by Copyright Act §412. Y Corp. might be able to enjoin further reproduction or distribution of Z's book and obtain damages for any lost sales that it can demonstrate are attributable to Z's infringement. It could also recover any of Z's profits that were not attributable to the sales counted in the calculation of Y's lost sales. In the case of Z's profits, Y Corp. need only establish the amount of Z's gross revenues. The burden would then shift to Z to prove what, if any, amounts should be deducted as expenses or costs of producing the infringing book or as attributable to factors other than his infringement.

SAMPLE ANSWER TO QUESTION 9:

A's potential liability: Assuming (for now) that X's patent was valid and enforceable, A should be liable for direct infringement. A was licensed to make 100 widgets yearly, using gadgets supplied by X. However, by making an additional 50 widgets, and without gadgets from X, A engaged in an unauthorized making of the patented invention, in violation of Patent Act §271(a).

B's potential liability: B may also be liable for direct infringement, due to her unauthorized sale of the patented invention to D, the Thai importer. However, this will only be the case if the sale took place in the United States. While more detailed facts are needed in order to determine the location of the sale, it appears that the negotiations, delivery, and payment all may have occurred in the United States, leading to a finding that the sale occurred in the United States. If the sale did not occur in the United States, the question arises whether B nonetheless made an infringing offer to sell in the United States. While the law is not yet settled, some case authority suggests that even if an offer to sell occurs in the United States, it will not infringe unless the contemplated sale would itself infringe. Here, if the sale itself took place outside of the United States, then neither B's offer or sale would directly infringe X's patent under Patent Act §271(a).

Even if B is not directly liable, she is likely to be liable for inducing A to infringe under Patent Act §271(b). B solicited and actively encouraged A's direct infringement, and assisted it by providing a market for the finished infringing widgets. She did so knowing of the existence of X's patent and that (at least if X's patent was valid and enforceable) A's actions would infringe. The only issue might be whether B's belief (based on consultations with her lawyer) that X's patent might be invalid is sufficient to prevent X from demonstrating that B had the necessary knowledge or intent for inducement liability. B might argue that, as a matter of social policy, courts should encourage the testing of patent monopolies by those who have a good-faith, reasonable belief that the patent may be invalid. To do this, the court should construe the knowledge requirement strictly and find that B is not liable because she believed in good faith that there might be no infringement due to patent invalidity.

C's potential liability: C did not actively solicit either A or B to directly infringe, so she is unlikely to be liable under §271(b). However (again assuming that X's patent is valid and enforceable), C probably will be liable for contributory infringement under §271(c). The custom-made gadgets appear to be a material component of X's patented widget. C knew that the gadgets were made for use in an invention that was patented. She knew that the gadgets were not staples, were a material part of the patented invention, and had no substantial noninfringing use. The fact that she may not have known these things when she entered into the contract should not relieve her of liability, since she clearly knew them when she performed the contract of sale to A. To avoid liability, she should have declined to proceed with the transaction.

D's potential liability: D, the Thai businessman, probably is not directly liable to X, because any unauthorized sale, offer to sell, or use of the patented invention that D made probably occurred outside of the United States. X might possibly argue that in buying A's infringing widgets, D rendered himself liable for inducement under §271(b). To fully assess this possibility, more facts are needed regarding D's knowledge and actions at the time the transaction occurred.

Possible defenses: The defendants might raise a couple of defenses in this case. First, they may argue that X's patent is invalid under Patent Act §102(b). Second, A may argue that X's patent is unenforceable under the patent misuse doctrine.

Patent validity—§102 (b): Section 102(b) prohibits a patent if the invention was on sale in the United States more than a year before the application for patent was filed. In this case, X entered into a written contract to sell three widgets to Y in May, 1998, more than a year prior to his application for patent (in July, 1999). X may argue that this should not disqualify him because, at the time of the contract, there was no operable physical embodiment of the widget. However, under the Supreme Court's decision in the *Pfaff* case, the issue is whether, at the time of the contract, the invention was "ready to patent." If the memorandum X wrote in February, 1998 was sufficiently detailed to enable a person with ordinary skill in the art to make or practice the invention, then it is likely that X's later contract will trigger the §102(b) statute of limitations, and that his patent will be invalid for failure to file within the one-year deadline.

Patent misuse: Even if X's patent was not time barred under §102(b), a court might find it unenforceable under the patent misuse doctrine. In this case, X engaged in two instances of "tying" in his contract with A. First, he required that, as a condition of the license, A buy all custom-made gadgets used in the widgets A built from him. This would not constitute patent misuse, because the gadget was a material component of the invention with no substantial noninfringing use. Patent Act §271(d) permits patent owners to tie licenses to an agreement to buy such components from the patentee. Second, X required that, as a condition of the license, A buy all nails, screws, nuts, and bolts used in his factory from X. Nails, screws, nuts, and bolts are staple items with many substantial, noninfringing uses. Under §271(d), this contract condition may constitute patent misuse if X has market power in the widget market. This issue cannot be determined under the facts given. While X has a monopoly in this particular type of widget, it is possible that there are so many other types of widgets (or other noninfringing substitutes) in the market that he actually has no appreciable market power. If he has no market power, then his tying arrangement will not appreciably harm competition and will be permitted. If X does have market power, and thus patent misuse is found, X will be prohibited from enforcing his patent until the misuse stops and X no longer enjoys benefits from it.

Damages: If infringement liability is found, the defendants will be liable for actual damages to X. These damages probably will be measured by the "reasonable royalty" standard, which awards the plaintiff an amount that reasonable parties would have agreed to pay and receive as a royalty for the defendants' use of the invention in an arms-length transaction. The alternative measure of damages—the plaintiff's lost sales—would be difficult to apply in this case because, in order to recover, X must show that "but for" the defendants' actions, X would have sold his own widgets to the defendants' customers.

Here, X did not have the ability to make and sell the 50 widgets himself. In addition, the defendants' sales were all to foreign buyers, who might have bought from others who lawfully made and sold X's invention outside of the United States. Also, there is evidence that X charged significantly more for his widgets than A and B did, which might cast doubt on any assumption that D would have bought from X if the widgets were unavailable from A and B at their lower price.

X might seek punitive damages against A and B for willful infringement. However, B, at least, had consulted her lawyer and had been advised that X's patent might be invalid. When parties consult with qualified lawyers prior to acting, and believe in good faith that the patent is likely to be invalid, courts generally will not impose punitive damages. A may have more difficulty arguing against punitive damages than B because he did not consult a lawyer, but merely accepted B's assurances that she had done so and that an invalidity defense existed.

SAMPLE ANSWER TO QUESTION 10:

Rights in the "Wild West" trade name: Both Toben and Callum are using the "Wild West" designation as a trade name. The Lanham Act does not provide for registration of trade names, and the facts do not indicate that either has registered "Wild West" as a trade or service mark. Thus, the respective rights of the parties must be determined pursuant to Lanham Act §43(a) and/or under the general state common law.

The name "Wild West" would suggest a geographic location in the western United States to most consumers. If consumers would be likely to think that the name indicates that the parties' businesses originate from that place, then the name is geographically descriptive, and the parties must demonstrate secondary meaning. If consumers are not likely to think that the businesses originate from the western part of the country, then the name is suggestive (suggesting the nature of the products, or associating the products with the western lifestyle of cowboy days) and no secondary meaning will be required. Because the outlets consumers would encounter are located in the West, and Western goods like hats and chaps are often made in the West, the name may be deemed geographically descriptive. Assuming that consumers would understand the name to be geographically descriptive of the businesses, we must examine the presence of secondary meaning. Toben has used the name for at least seven years in the Austin and Dallas area, and during that time he has engaged in extensive advertising through the use of that name. Thus, it is fairly likely that he can establish secondary meaning in Austin and Dallas. Callum has used the name for almost 40 years in northern California and Oregon. Though his advertising has been sporadic, the advertising in combination with Callum's steady stream of business under that name is likely to be sufficient to establish secondary meaning in northern California and Oregon. However, there is no evidence that Callum has acquired secondary meaning in Texas. Two months of business under the name is unlikely in itself to be sufficient, and the facts do not suggest that he has engaged in heavy advertising of the name during that time.

Under the common law, the first person to acquire secondary meaning in a descriptive or geographically descriptive trade name acquires superior rights in it. Assuming that Callum acquired secondary meaning in California and Oregon prior to 2000, he was the first to acquire secondary meaning in an absolute sense. However, Toben was the first to acquire secondary meaning in Texas (which is geographically remote from California and Oregon) and he did so in good faith—without notice of Callum's prior use. Thus, Toben should have the benefit of the remote, good faith defense, which not only protects him against Callum's attempt to enjoin his use of "Wild West" in Texas, but also will permit him to enjoin Callum from entering his Austin-Dallas market, if he can demonstrate that Callum's use will cause a likelihood of consumer confusion.

A court would probably find that Callum's use of "Wild West Haberdashery" in Austin and Dallas causes a likelihood of confusion with Toben's "Wild West Outfitters." Only the last word of each name differs, and in this case the first two words probably make the strongest impression on persons viewing or hearing the names. Moreover, while "haberdashery" and "outfitters" do not sound alike, they both suggest a clothier. In determining the issue of confusion, the court will not assume that the consumer has the opportunity to make a side-by-side comparison of the names. In fact, the court should assume that the consumer has only an imperfect memory of one or the other. In addition, in this case, the retail businesses are similar (retail sales of Western-style clothing), and they are likely to attract many of the same customers. These customers may or may not be sophisticated consumers. All these considerations support a finding of a likelihood of confusion and suggest that the court should enjoin Callum from use of the name "Wild West Haberdashery" in the Austin-Dallas area.

Rights in "Starry Night" and "Starbright": Callum's mark, "Starry Night," as applied to hats, appears to be arbitrary. Thus, his rights are not dependent on the existence of secondary meaning. (In any event, given the duration of Callum's registration, the mark probably has become incontestable, thus eliminating a challenge on lack of distinctiveness grounds.)

Callum was the first to use the mark in trade and also the first to register it. Because registration served as constructive notice of prior use, and Toben began his use after Callum's registration, Toben cannot claim the good faith defense. Upon registration, Callum obtained superior rights not only in northern California and Oregon—where he actually had used the mark—but also in all other areas of the United States (including Texas) where the mark was not in use at the time. Thus, if Callum's and Toben's consecutive use of their marks in Austin and Dallas will cause a likelihood of consumer confusion about the source or sponsorship of their respective products, Callum will have, by virtue of his registration, the right to enjoin Toben's further use.

The issue of confusion is a close one; but in the end, the court is likely to find that Toben's use does cause a likelihood of confusion and must be enjoined. While the words "Starry Night" and "Starbright" are different, they sound somewhat similar. The first syllable is the same and the last syllables both have the same vowel sound. Moreover, both marks evoke a similar mental image of a night sky with stars. Although the marks have a different number of syllables and look somewhat different (one word versus two), the similarities outweigh the differences. In addition, while the products the marks identify differ, they are closely related, so that a reasonable consumer might think that they were produced by the same source. Likewise, the outlets at which both products are sold probably are similar, and there will be some overlap in prospective purchasers (Western-wear fans).

Thus, a court is likely to enjoin Toben's use. However, since Toben was in fact unaware of Callum's prior use, and is not selling a directly competitive product, the court probably will decline to award damages. It may even consider ways that Toben could continue to use its mark, with differentiating elements and disclaimers that would avoid confusing consumers.

SAMPLE ANSWER TO QUESTION 11:

Due to Alpha's patent, Zelda cannot manufacture the claimed Alpha compound, or sell paint containing self-manufactured Alpha compound, without a license from Alpha. However, under the doctrine of exhaustion, Zelda can purchase Fleasoff from Alpha or any other lawful distributor, combine it with paint and then resell the combination without liability (as long as Alpha has not placed any enforceable restrictions on use of the Fleasoff it puts on the market). Moreover, Zelda can truthfully advise consumers that her paint contains "Fleasoff," as long as her use of the mark is truthful and not misleading about the immediate source of the paint. Zelda may also apply for a patent on her new composition of matter, and for the process of applying it to wood as a means of keeping bugs away, assuming that her inventions are novel and non-obvious (they clearly are useful). However, even if she obtains a patent, she must obtain a license before she can produce Alpha's patented component.

Table of Cases

Abercrombie & Fitch Co. v. Hunting World,
    Inc. 230, 261
A.J. Canfield Co. v. Honickman 235, 305
Alappat, In re 34
Ali v. Playgirl, Inc. 329
American Fruit Growers, Inc. v. Brogdex Co. 33
American Geophysical Union v. Texaco 167
A & M Records, Inc. v. Napster, Inc. 158, 159
Amsterdam v. Triangle Publications, Inc. 120
Anderson v. Stallone 123
Apple Computer, Inc. v. Franklin
    Computer Corp. 113
Arnstein v. Porter 129, 130, 133
Aro Manufacturing Co. v. Convertible
    Top Replacement Co., Inc. 59, 63
Aronson v. Quick Point
    Pencil Co. 338, 339, 347, 348
AT&T Corp. v. Excel Communications, Inc. 35

Baker v. Selden 110, 113, 121, 206
Bally Total Fitness Holding Corp. v. Faber 257
Baltimore Orioles, Inc. v. Major League
    Baseball Players Assn. 342
Berry Sterling Corp. v. Pescor Plastics, Inc. 77
Bleistein v. Donaldson Lithographing Co. 105
Blue Bell, Inc. v. Farah Manufacturing
    Co., Inc. 245
Board of Trade of City of Chicago v.
    Dow Jones & Co., Inc. 320
Board of Trustees of the University of
    Alabama, U.S. v. 341
Bolger v. Youngs Drug Products Corp. 273
Bonito Boats, Inc. v. Thunder
    Craft Boats, Inc. 338, 339, 340, 347
Borst, In re 36, 37
Bosley Medical Institute, Inc. v. Kremer 257
Brana, In re 52
Brandir International v. Cascade Pacific
    Lumber Co. 118, 119
Brenner v. Manson 52
Bridgeport Music, Inc. v. Dimension
    Films 135, 214
Brookfield Communications, Inc. v.
    West Coast Entertainment Corp. 258, 263, 303
Budge Manufacturing Co., Inc., In re 242

Burrow-Giles Lithographic Co. v. Sarony ... 104, 125
Buti v. Impressa Perosa, S.R.L. 246, 301

California Innovations, Inc., In re 243
Campbell v. Acuff-Rose Music, Inc. 165
Carol Barnhart v. Economy Cover Corp. 118
Carson, In re 246
Carson v. Here's Johnny Portable Toilets, Inc. ... 329
Carter Products v. Colgate-Palmolive Co. 39
Century 21 Real Estate Corp. v.
    LendingTree, Inc. 277
Chamberlain Group, Inc. v.
    Skylink Technologies, Inc. 170, 171, 216
Champion Spark Plug Co. v. Sanders 265
Checkpoint Systems, Inc. v. U.S. Int'l
    Trade Comm. 41
Coca-Cola Co. v. Gemini Rising, Inc. 265
Cochrane v. Deener 32
Columbia Pictures Industries, Inc. v.
    Aveco, Inc. 146, 147
Columbia Pictures Industries, Inc. v. Professional
    Real Estate Investors, Inc. 146, 147
Comedy III Productions, Inc. v. Gary
    Saderup, Inc. 331
Community for Creative Non-Violence v.
    Reid 173, 174
Compco Corp. v. Day-Brite
    Lighting, Inc. 336, 337, 338, 339, 342, 347
Computer Associates International, Inc. v.
    Altai, Inc. 114, 115, 117, 133, 219
1-800 Contacts, Inc. v.
    WhenU.Com, Inc. 258, 259, 302
CoStar Group, Inc. v. Loopnet, Inc. 134

Dastar Corp. v. Twentieth Century
    Fox Film Corp. 314, 324, 347
Dawn Donut Co. v. Hart's Food Stores, Inc. 254
Dawson Chemical Co. v. Rohm & Haas Co. 68
Deepsouth Packing Co., Inc. v.
    Laitram Corp. 58, 60
Del Madera Properties v. Rhodes and
    Gardner, Inc. 343
Diamond v. Chakrabarty 33, 80

Diamond v. Diehr 34
Doe v. TCI Cablevision 331, 332
DSC Communications Corp. v. Pulse
 Communications, Inc. 137
Dunlap v. G & L Holding Group, Inc. 342

E-Bay Inc. v. MercExchange 73
Egbert v. Lippmann 43
E.I. Dupont deNemours & Co. v.
 Christopher 8, 12, 22
Eldred v. Ashcroft 182
Ely-Norris Safe Co. v. Mosler Safe Co. 314, 315
Entertainment Research Group, Inc. v. Genesis
 Creative Group, Inc. 126
Eppendorf-Netheler-Hinz GmbH v.
 Ritter GmbH 241
Erie R.R. Co. v. Thompkins 320
ETW Corp. v. Jireh Publishing, Inc. 331

Feist Publications, Inc. v. Rural Telephone Service
 Co., Inc. 107, 108, 111, 125, 206, 219, 341
Festo Corp. v. Shoketsu Kinozuku Kogyo
 Kabushiki Co., Ltd. 57, 58
Fogarty v. Fantasy, Inc. 195
Fonovisa, Inc. v. Cherry Auction 157, 159, 209
Foster, Application of 51
F.T.C. v. - *See* **Name of party**

Galiano v. Harrah's Operating Co., Inc. 119
Gershwin Publishing Corp. v. Columbia
 Artists Mgt., Inc. 157
Gilliam v. American
 Broadcasting Co. 155, 156, 313
Goldstein v. California 336, 337
Gorham Manufacturing Co. v. White 77
Government Employees Insurance Co. v.
 Google, Inc. 259
Graham v. John Deere Co. 47, 48
Grupo Gigante SA De CV v. Dallo & Co. 247

Haelan Laboratories, Inc. v. Topps Chewing
 Gum, Inc. 328
Hard Rock Cafe Licensing Corp. v. Concession
 Services, Inc. 268
Harper & Row Publishers, Inc. v.
 Nation Enterprises 162, 163, 164, 343
Hazeltine Research, Inc. v. Brenner 48
Herbert Rosenthal Jewelry Corp. v. Kalpakian ... 130

Hines v. Davidowitz 336
Hirsch v. S.C. Johnson & Sons, Inc. 329
Holiday Inns, Inc. v. 800 Reservation, Inc. 256
Hotaling v. Church of Jesus Christ
 of Latter-Day Saints 143, 215
Hupp v. Siroflex of America, Inc. 76

Imazio Nursery, Inc. v. Dania Greenhouses 79
I.M.S. Inquiry Management Systems, Ltd. v.
 Berkshire Information Systems, Inc. 169
In re - *See* **Name of party**
INS 326
International Bancorp, LLC v. Societe des
 Bains de Mer et du Cercle des
 Estrangers a Manaco 247, 301
International News Service v.
 Associated Press 309, 320, 321, 344
Inwood Laboratories, Inc. v. Ives Laboratories,
 Inc. 239, 240, 241, 268, 294, 295, 296, 304
I.P. Lund Trading ApS v. Kohler Co. 274
ITC Ltd. v. Punchgini, Inc. 247

Jazz Photo Corp. v. International Trade
 Commission 61, 62, 89
J.E.M. Ag. Supply, Inc. v. Pioneer Hi-Bred
 International, Inc. 80
Johnson & Johnson v. Carter-Wallace, Inc. 316
Johnson & Johnston Associates, Inc. v.
 R.E. Service Co. 58
Jordache Enterprises, Inc. v. Hogg
 Wyld, Ltd. 264, 265

Kewanee Oil Co. v.
 Bicron Corp. 337, 338, 339, 347
Kieselstein-Cord v. Accessories by Pearl, Inc. 118
Klopfenstein, In re 38
K.P. Permanent Make-Up, Inc. v. Lasting
 Impression I, Inc. 276
KSR International Co. v. Teleflex, Inc. 50

Lamothe v. Atlantic Recording Corp. 313
Lamparello v. Falwell 281
Lasercomb America, Inc. v. Reynolds 167
L. Batlin & Son v. Snyder 125
Lear, Inc. v. Adkins 66
Lee v. A.R.T. Co. 140
Lewis Galoob Toys, Inc. v. Nintendo
 of America, Inc. 140, 141, 208, 210

Lexmark International, Inc. v. Static
  Control Components, Inc. 171, 216
L.L. Bean v. Drake Publishers 270
Lockwood v. American Airlines, Inc. 37, 43
Lotus Development Corp. v. Borland
  International, Inc. 116, 117, 206, 207
Lucas Nursery and Landscaping, Inc. v.
  Grosse 280
Lucent Information Management, Inc. v. Lucent
  Technologies, Inc. 245

Magic Marketing v. Mailing Services of
  Pittsburgh 107
MAI Systems Corp. v. Peak Computer,
  Inc. 134, 136, 137, 210
Manhattan Industries, Inc. v. Sweater Bee
  by Banff, Ltd. 246
Markman v. Westview Instruments, Inc. 54
Masline v. New York, New Haven and
  Hartford Railroad Co. 94
Mattel v. MCA Records 273
McGregor-Doniger, Inc. v. Drizzle, Inc. 261
Mead Data Central, Inc. v. Toyota Motor
  Sales, U.S.A., Inc. 270, 272
MedImmune, Inc. v. Genentech 66
Merck & Co. v. Mediplan Health
  Consulting, Inc. 259
Merck KGAA v. Integra Lifesciences, Ltd. 69
Metro-Goldwyn-Mayer Studios, Inc. v.
  Grokster 102, 159, 160, 209
Microsoft Corp. v. AT&T Corp. 65
Micro Star v. Formgen Inc. 141
Midler v. Ford Motor Co. 330, 333
Mirage Editions, Inc. v. Albuquerque
  A.R.T. Co. 140
Mitek Holdings, Inc. v. Arce Engineering
  Co., Inc. 116
Mitel, Inc. v. Iqtel, Inc. 117
Morrissey v. Procter & Gamble Co. 110
Morton-Norwich 240
Moseley v. V Secret Catalogue, Inc. 271

Nadel v. Play-By-Play Toys & Novelties, Inc. 96
National Basketball Association v.
  Motorola, Inc. 341, 344
Netscape 303
New York Times Co., Inc. v. Tasini 176, 309
New York Times v. Sullivan 318, 319, 325
Nichols v. Universal Pictures Corp. 122, 131, 219

Oddzon Products, Inc. v. Just Toys, Inc. 48
1-800 Contacts, Inc. v.
  WhenU.Com, Inc. 258, 259, 302
Owens-Corning Fiberglas Corp., In re 238

Panavision International, L.P. v.
  Toeppen 256, 274, 281
Paper Converting Machine Co. v.
  Magna-Graphics Corp. 59, 89
People for the Ethical Treatment of Animals,
  Inc. v. Doughney 257
Pepsico, Inc. v. Grapette Co. 278
Pepsico, Inc. v. Redmond 17, 21
Perfect 10, Inc. v. Amazon.com,
  Inc. 143, 150, 163
Pfaff v. Wells Electronics 45, 87
Phillips v. AWH Corp. 55
Pivot Point International, Inc. v.
  Charlene Products, Inc. 119
Playboy Enterprises, Inc. v. Welles 277
ProCD, Inc. v. Zeidenberg 348
Pro-Football, Inc. v. Harjo 242

Qualitex Co. v. Jacobson Products Co., Inc. 238,
  239, 240, 241, 295, 296
Quality King Distributors, Inc. v. L'anza
  Research International, Inc. 144, 145, 215

Rite-Hite Corp. v. Kelley Co., Inc. 71
Rogers v. Grimaldi 301
Ruckelshaus v. Monsanto Co. 14
Russell v. Price 189

Sakraida v. Ag Pro, Inc. 49
Sandvik Aktiebolag v. E.J. Co. 60
Sears, Roebuck & Co. v.
  Stiffel Co. 336, 337, 338, 339, 342, 347
Sega Enterprises v. Accolade, Inc. 166, 214
Shapiro, Bernstein & Co. v. H.L. Green Co. 158
Sid & Marty Krofft Television Prods., Inc. v.
  McDonald's Corp. 132
Sinatra v. Goodyear Tire & Rubber 347
Smith v. Chanel, Inc. 267
Softel, Inc. v. Dragon Medical and Scientific
  Communications, Inc. 115
Sony Corp. of America v. Universal
  City Studios, Inc. 157, 158, 159, 160

State Street Bank & Trust Co. v. Signature
    Financial Group, Inc. 34, 35, 69
State v. - *See* **Name of party**
Steinway & Sons v. Demars & Friends 269
Stewart v. Abend 188
321 Studios v. Metro-Goldwyn-Mayer
    Studios, Inc. 169

Taubman Co. v. Webfeats 257
The New Kids on the Block v. News America
    Publishing, Inc. 277
321 Studios v. Metro-Goldwyn-Mayer Studios,
    Inc. 169
TrafFix Devices, Inc. v.
    Marketing Displays, Inc. 239, 240, 241, 294, 295
Two Pesos, Inc. v. Taco Cabana, Inc. 241, 311

Universal City Studios, Inc. v.
    Corley 170
U.S. Healthcare, Inc. v. Blue Cross of Greater
    Philadelphia 319, 320
U.S. v. - *See* **Name of party** ....

Valu Engineering, Inc. v. Rexnord Corp. 240

Vault Corp. v. Quaid Software Ltd. 348
Veeck v. Southern Building Code Congress
    International, Inc. 127

Wal-Mart Stores, Inc. v. Samara
    Bros., Inc. 238, 294
Warner-Jenkinson Co., Inc. v.
    Hilton Davis Chemical Co. 55, 56, 57
Wedgwood Homes, Inc. v. Lund 270, 272
West Publishing Co. v. Mead Data
    Central, Inc. 125
Whelan Associates v. Jaslow Dental
    Laboratory, Inc. 114
White v. Samsung Electronics America, Inc. 330
Wilson Sporting Goods Co. v. David Geoffrey &
    Associates 56
Wrench L.L.C. v. Taco Bell Corp. 341

Yoder Bros., Inc. v. California-Florida
    Plant Corp. 79

Zacchini v. Scripps-Howard
    Broadcasting Co. 330, 331
Zazu Designs v. L'Oreal, S.A. 245

Table of References to the Copyright Act of 1976 (17 U.S.C. §101 *et seq.*)

§101	108, 109, 112, 117, 120, 122, 124, 125, 126, 128, 133, 134, 139, 146, 150, 153, 154, 172, 173, 175, 178, 182, 183, 207, 208, 210, 217, 340, 341
§102	106, 197, 340, 341
§102(a)	104, 106, 112, 120, 341
§102(b)	109, 111, 112, 113, 116, 341, 342
§103	124, 125, 340, 341
§104A	180, 198
§105	126, 127
§106	127, 144, 145, 148, 150, 215, 216, 341, 343
§106(3)	144
§106(4)	145
§106(6)	145
§106A	128, 154, 155, 182, 185, 341
§107	162, 163, 164, 165, 166
§107-120	144
§107-121	102
§108	138, 166
§108-121	348
§109(a)	143, 144, 145, 215
§109(b)	143, 144
§109(c)	150, 210, 211
§109(e)	152
§110	141, 210
§110(1)	151
§110(2)	152
§110(3)	152, 210
§110(4)	149, 210
§110(5)	150, 151, 210
§110(5)(B)	151
§110(6)	149
§110(7)	149
§110(8)	149
§110(9)	149
§111	152
§112	138
§113	137, 155
§113(b)	119, 207
§113(d)	155
§114	135, 142, 145, 148
§114(b)	207, 214
§115	138, 139
§117	136, 137, 142
§118	153
§118(d)	138
§119	152
§120	137, 142, 211
§121	139
§201	128, 172
§201(c)	176
§202	105
§203	189, 190, 191, 192, 193
§204	105, 177
§205	177
§205(d)	177
§301	106, 109, 333, 335, 340, 341, 342, 343, 344, 345, 346, 347, 348
§302	182, 183, 184, 185, 220, 221
§302(a)	213
§302(c)	183, 213
§303	184, 213, 221
§304	184, 186, 187, 188, 189, 191, 192, 193, 213, 215, 220
§304(a)(4)(A)	189
§304(c)	192
§304(d)	192
§305	185
§401	178, 194
§402	178, 194
§405	179
§406	179
§407	180, 181
§408	181
§410(c)	181
§412	181, 195
§501	156
§502	193
§504	193
§505	195
§506	195
§512	160, 161, 204, 209
§602	144, 156, 215
§602(a)(2)	209
§901-914	124

§1001-1010 138	§1201(a)(2) 171, 216
§1101 148	§1201(a)(3) 169
§1201 . . . . 168, 169, 170, 171, 211, 216	§1201(c)(1) 171
§1201-1205 168	§1204 195
§1201(a) 168, 171	§1301-1332 . . . . 119, 340

Table of References to the Lanham Act (15 U.S.C. §1051 *et seq.*)

§2	241, 244, 250, 306, 311, 312
§2(a)	241, 242, 243, 294, 295, 297
§2(d)	243, 244
§2(e)	231, 242, 243, 293, 294, 295, 296
§2(f)	231, 242, 243, 296, 303
§7(c)	249, 253, 297, 298
§21	227
§22	252, 253
§23	249
§32	291
§32(1)(a)	255
§32(a)(1)	266
§42	266
§43	279
§43(a)	156, 219, 226, 238, 241, 246, 247, 252, 255, 282, 283, 292, 294, 306, 309, 310, 311, 312, 313, 314, 315, 316, 318, 319, 323, 324, 325, 345, 347
§43(c)	224, 244, 271, 272, 273, 274, 275, 281, 282, 283, 299, 300, 301
§43(c)(2)(A)	271, 272
§43(c)(2)(B)	272
§43(c)(2)(C)	272
§43(c)(3)(A)	272
§43(c)(3)(B)	272
§43(c)(4)	274
§43(d)	279, 280, 282, 284, 285, 300
§44	291, 322
§44(b)	298
§44(c)	298
§44(d)	298
§44(e)	298
§45	227, 228, 229, 247, 255, 274, 301
§1051	226
§1052	233, 241, 244
§1057(b)	249
§1057(c)	249
§1064	228, 250
§1071	227
§1072	252
§1091	249
§1114(a)(1)	266
§1124	266
§1125(a)	156, 226, 283, 311
§1125(c)	271
§1125(c)(5)	284
§1127	246, 247, 277
§1129	282
§1225(c)(7)	274

Table of References to the Patent Act
(35 U.S.C. §101 *et seq.*)

§100(b)	86
§101	32, 52
§102	30, 36, 45, 47, 48, 57, 76, 78, 83, 88, 91
§102(a)	27, 36, 37, 38, 39, 40, 42, 46, 47, 48, 51, 86, 87, 88, 91, 92
§102(b)	27, 42, 43, 44, 45, 46, 51, 60, 73, 74, 80, 87, 88, 91, 92
§102(c)	27, 42, 46, 74
§102(d)	27, 42, 46, 76
§102(e)	27, 36, 39, 40, 42, 47, 51, 87, 88, 91
§102(f)	42, 46, 47, 48, 51, 88, 91
§102(g)	27, 36, 40, 41, 42, 47, 48, 51, 70, 87, 88, 91
§103	30, 47, 50, 51, 88, 92
§103(b)	51
§103(c)	51
§104	42
§112	30, 52, 54, 66, 75, 80
§122	30
§122(b)	39
§154	66
§154(d)	66
§162	79
§163	79
§171	75
§173	89
§271	67, 77, 92
§271(a)	58, 60, 64, 65, 89, 90, 92
§271(b)	62, 64, 89, 92
§271(c)	63, 64, 65, 92
§271(d)	67, 68
§271(e)	28, 69
§271(f)	64, 65, 89, 92
§271(g)	63, 64, 92
§271(i)	91
§273	69, 70
§284	70, 72, 73
§285	72
§287	72, 74
§287(b)	64
§289	77
§295	64

Subject Matter Index

ABANDONMENT
Patents, 40–41, 46
Trademark law, 277–279, 287

ADMINISTRATIVE PROCEDURE ACT, 31

AFFIXATION OF MARKS, 246

AFTERMARKET PURCHASES
Copyright law, 170–171

AGREEMENT ON TRADE-RELATED ASPECTS OF INTELLECTUAL PROPERTY RIGHTS (TRIPs), 197–198
Copyright law, 151
Patent protection, 82–83
Trademark law, 288–289
Unfair competition, 322

ANONYMOUS WORKS, 183

ANTICYBERSQUATTING CONSUMER PROTECTION ACT, 225, 279–283

ANTI-TRAFFICKING PROVISIONS
Copyright law, 169–170

ANTITRUST LAW
Infringement, relationship to, 67

APPLICATIONS
Copyright law, 113
Trademark law, 248

ARBITRARY MARKS, 230

ARCHITECTURAL WORKS, 120–122, 137, 142

ARCHITECTURAL WORKS COPYRIGHT PROTECTION ACT OF 1990 (AWCPA), 120, 121

ASEXUAL REPRODUCTION OF PLANTS, 78

ASSIGNMENT
Trade secrets, 15–16

ATTORNEY FEES
Copyright infringement, 195
Patent infringement, 72
Trademark infringement, 284

ATTRIBUTION, RIGHT OF, 153

AUDIO HOME RECORDING ACT OF 1992, 138

BERNE CONVENTION
See INTERNATIONAL TREATIES AND CONVENTIONS

BERNE CONVENTION IMPLEMENTATION ACT OF 1988, 106, 179, 181

BIOTECHNOLOGICAL PROCESS PATENTS, 51

BROADCASTING, NONCOMMERCIAL
Licenses, 153

CERTIFICATION MARKS, 228–229

CHIPS
See COMPUTER CHIPS

CIRCUMVENTION OF TECHNOLOGICAL PROTECTION, 168–172

CLICK-WRAP LICENSES
Trade secrets, law of, 9

COLLECTIVE MARKS, 229

COLLECTIVE WORKS, 124, 175–176

COMBINATION PATENTS, 49–50
Infringement, 58–60

COMMERCIAL DISPARAGEMENT, 317–320
Action, cause of, 317
Blue Cross decision, 319
Commercial speech, 319
False representation, 317
First Amendment considerations, 318–320
Generally, 309
Lanham Act, 318
Public figure status, 319–320
Special damages requirement, 317
State statutory provisions, 317–318

COMMISSIONED WORKS, 175

COMMUNICATIONS OMNIBUS REFORM ACT OF 1999, 69

COMPETITION
Promotion of, 1

COMPILATIONS, 124–125

COMPUTER CHIPS
Copyright law, 113
    Semiconductor chips, 123–124

COMPUTER PROGRAMS
See also SOFTWARE
Copyright law, 112–117
    Adaptation rights and enhancements, 140–141
    Chips, 113, 123–124
    Exclusive right to adapt, exception to, 142
    Rentals, 143–144
    Reproductions, 136–137
    User interface, 115–116
Utility patents, 34–35

COMPUTERS, RANDOM ACCESS MEMORY, 134–135

COMPUTER SYSTEMS, INTERACTIVE
Copyright law, fixation requirement, 109

CONCEALMENT
Patents, 40–41

CONCRETENESS, 93, 96–97

CONFIDENTIALITY
See also TRADE SECRETS, LAW OF
Confidential relationship theory, 95

CONSTITUTIONALITY
Trade secrets, law of
    "Taking," unconstitutional, 14
Utility patents, constitutional limitations
    Appeals, 31
    Enforcing, 30–32
    Generally, 29
    Implementation of, 30
    Reexamination, 31–32
    Reissue, 31

CONTENT OF TRADEMARKS
See TRADEMARK LAW

CONTINUOUS USE, TRADE SECRETS, 7

CONTRIBUTORY INFRINGEMENT
Copyright law, 157–158
Trademark law, 267–268
Utility patents, 62–63

COPIES
Educational copying, 166
Fixation requirement, 108
Library copying, 166
Public display of copyrighted work, 150

COPYRIGHT ACT OF 1909, 177–179, 182, 184

COPYRIGHT ACT OF 1976
See Table of References to the Copyright Act of 1976

COPYRIGHT AMENDMENTS ACT OF 1992, 187, 189

COPYRIGHT LAW, 101–221
Abstraction, filtration, comparison standard, 133
Abstractions test, 131–132
Access plus similarity, 129–130
Anonymous works, 183
Anti-bootlegging provisions, 148
Anti-circumvention provisions, 168–172
Anti-trafficking provisions, 169–170
Applications, 113
Appropriation, unlawful, 129–132
Architectural works, 120–122, 137, 142
Arnstein copying and unlawful appropriation test, 129–132
Attribution, right of, 153–154, 185
Authorship, works of, 104–105, 112–122
Baker v. Selden, 110
Beneficial ownership of copyright, 177
Berne Convention. *See* INTERNATIONAL COPYRIGHT TREATIES
Blank forms, 111
Certification by Copyright Office, 183
Chamberlain decision, 170–171
Circumvention, 168–172
Collective works, 124, 175–176
Commencement of federal copyright, 182
Commercial or noncommercial use, 162–163
Commissioned works, 175
Compilations, 124–125
Computer programs, 112–117
    Adaptation rights and enhancements, 140–142
    Exclusive right to adapt, exception to, 142
    Rentals, 143–144
    Reproductions, 136–137
Computers, random access memory, 134–135
Conceptual separability, 118–119
Congressional extensions of term, 182
Construction of Section 1201(e)(1), 171–172
Copies, fixation requirement, 108
Copyrighted work, exclusive rights and, 128–133
Copyright management information, 172
Copyright Office, 106
Corley decision, 170
Deposit, 180–181
Derivative works, 125–127

Defined, 125
  Exclusive right to prepare, 139–142
  Originality, 125–126
  Renewals of copyright, 188–189
  Termination of transfers, 191
Design patents, overlap, 119
Digital Millennium Copyright Act, 102
Digital Performance Rights in Sound Recordings Act, 148
Digital rights management provisions, 168–172
Direct and indirect infringement, 102, 159–160
Direct evidence of copying, 129
Disabled, special formats for, 139
Display, 150–153
"Distance learning" transmissions, 152
Distribution to the public, exclusive right, 143–145
Divestive vs. investive publication, 178
Divisibility of ownership, 176
Doctrine of first sale, 143–145
  Internet, 145
Droit de suite, 144
Duration of copyright, 103
Duration of protection, 182–185
Economic rights, 105
Educational copying, 166
Electronic video games, 152
Employees, 173–175
Ephemeral recordings, 138
Error in notice of copyright, 179
Exclusion of ideas, procedures, and processes, 109–112
Exclusive economic rights of copyright, 102
Exclusive rights afforded by, 133–142
  Derivative works, right to prepare, 139–142
  Display of copyrighted work publicly, 150–153
  Distribution to the public, 143–145
  Economic rights, 127–133
  Public performance, 145–149
  Reproduction of work, 133–142
Face-to-face nonprofit instruction, 151
Facts, copyrightability, 111–112
Fair use defense, 102
  Market value and, 166–167
  To infringement, 162–167
Family Entertainment and Copyright Act of 2005, 141–142
Federal vs. state law, 106
Fictitious characters, copyright for, 122–123
First sale, doctrine of, 143–145
  Internet, 145
Fixation requirement, 108–109

Foreign copyright restoration, 180
Government works, 126–127
Home audiotaping, 138
Home-style receivers, transmissions received, 150–151
Hotel rooms, public performance, 146–147
Immoral works, 123
Imports, 144–145
Incidental use, 163
Independent contractors, works created for government by, 127
Infringement of copyright, 157–161
  Contributory infringement, 157–158
  Direct infringement, 156–157
  Fair use defense, 162–167
  Grokster, international inducement theory of indirect infringement liability, 159–160
  Innocent infringement, 179, 194–195
  International inducement theory of indirect infringement liability, 159–160
  Internet, 160–161
  Registration as prerequisite to action, 181
  Remedies. *See* REMEDIES FOR COPYRIGHT INFRINGEMENT
  Sale of equipment or products, 157–158
  Sony, interpretation, 158, 160
  Vicarious infringement liability, 158–159
  Willful infringement, 194
Instructional transmissions, 152
Intangible, rights in, 105–106
Integrity, right of, 153–155, 185
Interactive computer systems, 109
International copyright treaties, 103, 195–199
  Agreement on Trade-Related Aspects of Intellectual Property Rights (TRIPs), 197–198
  Berne Convention, 195–196
  WIPO Copyright Treaty, 198–199
International inducement theory of indirect infringement liability, 159–160
Internet, doctrine of first sale, 145
Joint works
  Ownership of copyright, 172–173
  Transfers of copyright, termination, 190
Lanham Act. *See* Table of References to the Lanham Act
Lexmark decision, 171
Libraries and archives, 138
Library copying, 166
Licenses for noncommercial broadcasting, 153
Literal vs. nonliteral similarity, 131–132

COPYRIGHT LAW (*cont.*)
    Literary works, 112–117
    Nonprofit performances, 149
Live musical performances, 148–149
Lotus decision, 116–117
Maps, 120
Market value and fair use, 166–167
Material copy, transfer of, 142–143
Merger doctrine, 110–111
Misuse defenses, 102
Misuse of copyright, 167
Moral rights, 102, 153–156
    Lanham Act, 156
    Registration as prerequisite to action, 182
    Rights of attribution and integrity, 153–155, 185
    State causes of action vindicating, 156
    Visual Artists Rights Act of 1990, 153–155
Moral standpoint, propriety of conduct, 163
"More discerning" standard, 133
Musical works, nondramatic, 138–139, 151
Nature of, 101, 103–106
1909 Act, 177–178
1976 Act, 178–179
1976 Act vs. 1909 Act, 106
Nonprofit instruction, face-to-face, 151
Nonprofit performances of nondramatic literary or musical works, 149
Notice
    Of copyright, 103, 177–180
    Termination of transfers, 190–191, 192
Obscene works, 123
Omissions in violation of express agreement, 179
"Original expression of the facts," scope of in nonfiction literary works, 112
"Originality" requirement, 107–108
Ownership of copyright, 102, 172–177
    Beneficial ownership, 177
    Collective works, 175–176
    Commissioned works, 175
    Common-law agency criteria, 174
    Contribution of copyrightable expression, 173
    Divisibility of ownership, 176
    Employees, 173–175
    Initial owner, 172
    Intent, 172–173
    Joint works, 172–173
    Renewal rights, 186
    Specially ordered works, 175
    Works for hire, 173–175
    Writing requirement to transfer, 177
Parody cases, 165–166
Performing rights societies, 147
Phonorecords
    Distribution to public, exclusive right, 143
    Fixation requirement, 108
    Manufactured outside U.S., 145
    Notice of copyright, 178–179
Pictorial, graphic and sculptural works, 117–120, 137
Privately drafted model codes, 127
Property right vs. personal right, 105
Protectible works of authorship, categories of, 112–122
Protection, nature of, 101
Pseudonymous works, 183
Public display of copyrighted work, 150–153
Publicly perform, right to, 140
Public performance, exclusive right of, 145–149
    Home-style receivers, transmissions received, 150–151
Purpose of, 103
Record rentals, 143–144
Registration, 181–182
Religious services, 152
Renewals of pre-1976 Act copyrights, 185–189
Replacement parts and aftermarket products, 170–171
Reproduction of work, exclusive right of and exceptions, 133–142
    Act of reproduction, 133–134
    Architectural works, 137, 142
    Computer programs, 136–137
    Computers, random access memory, 134
    Definitions, 133–134
    Ephemeral recordings, 138
    Home audiotaping, 138
    Internet copying limitation on reproduction liability, 134–135
    Libraries and archives, 138
    Musical works, nondramatic, 138–139, 151
    Pictorial, graphic and sculptural works, 137
    Sound recordings, 135, 142
    Visually impaired or disabled, special formats for, 139
Research, copyrightability, 111–112
Reverse engineering, 166
Right of attribution, 153–154, 185
Right of integrity, 153–155, 185
Rights afforded by, 127–128
Scenes a faire, 108
Secondary transmissions, 152–153
"Second chance," 189, 192
Section 102 of Copyright Act, 106
Semiconductor chips, 123–124

Separability, 118–119
Short phrases, rules regarding, 107
Slogans, rules regarding, 107
Sonny Bono Copyright Term Extension Act, 192
Sound recordings, 122, 135, 142
    Limited performance rights, 148
Specially ordered works, 175
State and local government works, 127
Subject matter and copyright, 101, 106–127
Substantial similarity, evaluating, 133
"Sweat of the brow," 108
Technical drawings, 119–120
"Technological measures"
    Definitions, 168–169
    Replacement parts and aftermarket products, 170–171
"Thin" copyright protection, 111
Transfers
    Renewal rights, 186–187
    Termination of, 189–193
Transmission, fixation simultaneous with, 109
Typeface, 120
Unauthorized use of copyrighted material, 125
Unfixed works, common-law protection, 109
Unlawful appropriation, 101, 129–132
Useful articles, design of, 117–119
Video games, 152
Video rental and viewing establishments, public performance, 146
Visual arts, rights of attribution and integrity, 185
Visually impaired, special formats for, 139
Visually perceptive copies, notice of copyright, 178
Whelan opinion, 114
WIPO Copyright Treaty, 198–199
Words, rules regarding, 107
Works for hire, 173–175, 183
"Works of authorship," 104–105, 112–122
Writing requirement to transfer, 177

COPYRIGHT OFFICE
See COPYRIGHT LAW

COSTS
Copyright infringement, 195

COUNTERFEITING
Trademarks, 267, 284–285

COVENANT NOT TO COMPETE
Trade secrets, law of, 16–17

CRIMINAL PROSECUTION
Copyright infringement, 195
Trade secrets, misappropriation, 18

CYBERSQUATTING
Bad faith, 283
Remedies and limitation of liability, 282
Remedies for infringement, 285
In rem jurisdiction, 282
Trademark law, 279–283
    Anticybersquatting Consumer Protection Act, 225, 279–282
    Bad-faith intent to profit, 280–282
    Dilution, 274
    Infringement of marks, 256
    Personal names, 282
Uniform Domain Name Dispute Resolution Policy, 282–283

DAMAGES
Copyright infringement, 193–195
Patent infringement, 70–74
    Attorney fees, 72
    Double or treble damages, 72–73
    Entire market value rule, 72
    Lost-profits measure, 71–72
    Measure of damages, 70–73
    Prejudgment interest, 73
    Reasonable royalty measure, 70–71
Trade secrets, misappropriation, 18
Unfair competition, law of
    Commercial disparagement, 317
    False advertising, 316

DECEPTIVE MARKS, 231–232, 242–243, 286

DERIVATIVE WORKS
Copyright law, 125–127
Defined, 125
Exclusive right to prepare, 139–142
Originality, 125–126
Renewals of copyright, 188–189
Termination of transfers, 191

DESCRIPTIVE MARKS, 230–235

DESIGN PATENTS, 75–78
Copyright patents, overlap, 119
Defenses and remedies, 77
Double patenting, 77–78
Duration of, 74–75
Generally, 28
Infringement, 77
Nature of, 75
Non-obviousness standard, 76
Ornamentality standard, 76–77
Prior art, 76

DESIGN PATENTS, (cont.)
Standards for, 75–77
Success of, 78

DIGITAL MILLENNIUM COPYRIGHT ACT, 102, 168–172

DIGITAL PERFORMANCE RIGHTS IN SOUND RECORDINGS ACT, 148

DILUTION, 224–225, 268–275

DISABLED, SPECIAL FORMATS FOR, 139

DISPARAGEMENT
See COMMERCIAL DISPARAGEMENT

"DISTANCE LEARNING" TRANSMISSIONS, 152

DISTINCTIVENESS
Plant patents, 79
Trademark law, 229–236
    Dilution, 224–225, 272
    Infringement of marks, 261–262
    Trade dress, 238–239

DISTRIBUTION TO THE PUBLIC, 142–145

DIVISIBILITY OF OWNERSHIP, 176

DOCTRINE OF EQUIVALENTS, 55–58

DOCTRINE OF EXHAUSTION, 61–62

DOUBLE PATENTING
Design patents, 77–78

DROIT DE SUITE, 144

DURATION OF PROTECTION
Copyright, 182–185
Design patents, 75

ECONOMIC ESPIONAGE ACT OF 1996, 18

ELECTRONIC VIDEO GAMES, 152

EMPLOYEES
See also TRADE SECRETS, LAW OF
Copyright ownership and, 173–175

EPHEMERAL RECORDINGS, 138

EXPERIMENTAL USE DEFENSE, 69

FACE-TO-FACE NONPROFIT INSTRUCTION, 151

FACTS, COPYRIGHTABILITY, 111–112

FAIR USE DEFENSE
Copyright infringement, 162–167
Copyright law, 102
    Market value and, 166–167
Trademark infringement, 275–276
    Nominative fair use, 276–277
Trademark Law
    Dilution, 272

FALSE ADVERTISING, 314–316
Ascertainable loss requirement, 315
Common-law cause of action, 314–315
Injunctive relief, 316
Injury, 316
Intent, 316
Lanham Act. *See* Table of References to the Lanham Act
Materiality, 316
Monetary damages, 316
State statutes, 315

FAMILY ENTERTAINMENT AND COPYRIGHT ACT OF 2005, 141–142

FANCIFUL MARKS, 230

FEDERAL LAW
Overview, 1, 3
Relationship to state law
    Copyright law, 106

FEDERAL TRADEMARK DILUTION ACT OF 1995, 271, 273, 274

FICTITIOUS CHARACTERS, COPYRIGHT FOR, 122–123

FINANCIAL INCENTIVES, 1

FIRST AMENDMENT
Publicity, right of, 327, 330–332
Trademark law and, 265, 270–271
    Infringement of marks, 265
Unfair competition, law of, 318–320

FIRST INVENTOR DEFENSE ACT OF 1999, 69

FIRST SALE, DOCTRINE OF, 143–145
Internet, 145
Publicity, right of, 332

FOREIGN COPYRIGHT RESTORATION, 180

FREEDOM OF INFORMATION ACT
Trade secrets, law of, 13–14

GENERIC MARKS, 235–236

GEOGRAPHICALLY DESCRIPTIVE MARKS, 231–232

GEOGRAPHIC BOUNDARIES. *See* TRADEMARK LAW

GOOD FAITH, 251
Infringement of marks, 262
Lanham Act, 252–253

GOODWILL, ASSIGNMENT OF, 278

GOVERNMENT WORKS
Copyright law, 126–127

GRAY MARKET GOODS, 266–267

HOME AUDIOTAPING, 138

HOME-STYLE RECEIVERS, TRANSMISSIONS RECEIVED, 150–151

ICANN. *See* INTERNET CORPORATION FOR ASSIGNED NAMES AND NUMBERS (ICANN)

IDEAS. *See also* UNDEVELOPED IDEAS, LAW OF
Trade secrets, as, 7–8

IMMORAL OR OBSCENE WORKS, COPYRIGHT LAW, 123

IMPORTS
Copyright law, 144–145
Utility patents, infringement, 61–64

INCONTESTABILITY, TRADEMARKS, 279

INDEPENDENT CONTRACTORS
Works created for government by, copyright law, 127

INDEPENDENT DISCOVERY
Plant patents, 79

INDUCEMENT TO INFRINGE, 62

INEVITABLE DISCLOSURE, DOCTRINE OF, 6, 17

INFRINGEMENT
See also REMEDIES FOR COPYRIGHT INFRINGEMENT; REMEDIES FOR INFRINGEMENT; REMEDIES FOR PATENT INFRINGEMENT; REMEDIES FOR TRADEMARK INFRINGEMENT; TRADEMARK LAW

Design patents, 77
Patents, generally, 28
Plant patents, 79
Utility patents, 54–70
    Active solicitation or assistance, 62
    Antitrust law, relationship to, 67
    Burden of proof, 64
    Claim interpretation, 54–55
    Commercial use, 70
    Component sold, offered for sale, or imported, 63
    "Constructive" making, 59
    Contributory infringement, 62–63
    Corporate officers and directors, 62
    Defenses to claims, 66–70
    Direct infringement, 58–62
    Doctrine of equivalents, 55–58
    Doctrine of exhaustion, 61–62
    Doctrine of prosecution history estoppel, 56
    Estoppel, 56–58, 66
    Experimental use defense, 69
    Importing, 63–64
    Importing patented invention, 61–62
    Inducement to infringe, 62
    Inequitable conduct, 68–69
    Intent, 62
    Invalidity defense, 70
    Knowledge, 62, 63
    Literal infringement, 55
    Majority shareholders, 62
    Material component of U.S.-patented invention, supplying, 64–65
    Offering to sell, 63–64
    Offering to sell patented invention, 60–61
    Patent invalidity, 66
    Patent misuse, 66–68
    Prior use, 69–70
    Provisional rights prior to patent issuance, 65–66
    Publication, 65–66
    Repair vs. reconstruction, 59–60
    Reverse doctrine of equivalents, 56
    Selling, 60–61, 63–64
    Software, supplying, 65
    Sources of evidence for claim construction, 54–55
    Subsection 271(e), 69
    Suits to enforce patents, 54–58
    Supplying components to be assembled abroad, 64–65
    Tying arrangements, 67–68

INJUNCTIONS
Copyright infringement, 193

INJUNCTIONS (*cont.*)
Patent infringement, 73–74
Trade secrets, misappropriation, 17–18

INSTRUCTIONAL TRANSMISSIONS, 152

INTANGIBLES, RIGHTS IN
Copyright law, 105–106
Limited property rights, 1

INTEGRITY, RIGHT OF, 153–155, 185

INTELLECTUAL PROPERTY, OVERVIEW
See also specific topics
Authority, sources, 3
Conflict, potential, 2
Definition of term, 2
Policy issues, 2–3

INTERNATIONAL COPYRIGHT TREATIES, 103
See also INTERNATIONAL TREATIES AND CONVENTIONS
Universal Copyright Convention (U.C.C.), 197
WIPO Copyright Treaty, 198–199

INTERNATIONAL TREATIES AND CONVENTIONS, 80–83
Agreement on Trade-Related Aspects of Intellectual Property Rights (TRIPs), 82–83, 151, 197–198, 288–289, 322
Berne Convention for the Protection of Literary and Artistic Works, 103, 105, 106, 153, 179–181, 187, 195–198, 341
Madrid Protocol, 288
Paris Convention, 80–81, 285–287, 322
Patent Cooperation Treaty, 82
Patent Law Treaty, 29, 83
Telle quelle principle, 286
Trademark Law Treaty, 288

INTERNATIONAL UNION FOR THE PROTECTION OF INDUSTRIAL PROPERTY (PARIS CONVENTION)
See INTERNATIONAL TREATIES AND CONVENTIONS

INTERNET
See also CYBERSQUATTING
Copyright law
  Limitation on reproduction liability, 134–135
Doctrine of first sale, 145
Infringement of copyright, 160–161
Safe harbors, 160–161
Service provider, defined, 161
Trademark law
  Contextual advertising, 258–259
  Cybersquatting, 256, 274
  Dilution, 274–275
  Forum site domain names, 257, 274–275
  Infringement of marks, 256–259
  Metatags, 257–258, 263
  Search engine cases, 259
  WhenU.Com line of cases, 258–259

INTERNET CORPORATION FOR ASSIGNED NAMES AND NUMBERS (ICANN), 282–283

INTERSTATE COMMERCE, 246–247

JOINT INVENTORS
Patents, 47

LANHAM ACT
See also TABLE of REFERENCES TO THE LANHAM ACT
Copyright Law, 156
  Trademark law, 241–244
Dilution, 271–275
Geographic boundaries, 252–254
  Constructive use, 253–254
Registration of marks, 248–250
Trademark law, 226–227
Unfair competition, law of
  Commercial disparagement, 318
  False advertising, 315–316
  Passing off, 311–314

LAW OF NATURE, 33–35

LIBRARIES AND ARCHIVES, 137–138

LICENSES
Noncommercial broadcasting, 153
Trade secrets, 75
Utility patents, 75

LITERARY WORKS, 112–117
Nonprofit performances, 149
"Original expression of the facts," scope of in nonfiction literary works, 112

LIVE MUSICAL PERFORMANCES, 148–149

LOST PROFITS MEASURES, 71–72

MADRID PROTOCOL, 288

MAPS, 120

MARKET VALUE AND FAIR USE
Copyright law, 166–167

MEDICAL PROCEDURES
Utility patents, 35

MISAPPROPRIATION, ACTION FOR
Trade secrets, 5–6, 8–13
Unfair competition, 309, 320–322

MORAL RIGHTS, 153–156
Copyright law, 102

MUSICAL PERFORMANCES, 147

MUSICAL WORKS, NONDRAMATIC, 138–139, 151

NEWSPAPER REPORTING AND NEWS COMMENTARY, 272

NEXUS
Patents, 49

NON-COMMERCIAL BROADCASTING
Licenses, 153

NON-COMPETITION AGREEMENTS, 16–17

NON-OBVIOUSNESS STANDARD
Design patents, 76
Patents, 47–51
    Biotechnological process patents, 51
    Combination patents, 49–50
    Commercial acquiescence, 49
    Commercial success, 49
    Legal determination of obviousness, 48
    Long-felt need, 49
    Nexus, 49
    Pertinent prior art, 47–48
    Skill, level of, 48
Patents, generally, 27
Plant patents, 79

NONPROFIT INSTRUCTION, FACE-TO-FACE, 151

NONPROFIT PERFORMANCES OF NONDRAMATIC LITERARY OR MUSICAL WORKS, 149

NOTICE
Copyright law, 103
Of copyright, 177–180

NOVELTY STANDARD, 36–42
Abandonment, 40–41
Commercializing the invention, 41
Concealment, 40–41
Deemed patented in this or foreign country, 38–39
Failure to file for patent, 41
Interferences, 41–42
Inventive concept, 40
"Known by others," invention as, 36–37
Patents, 27
Plant patents, 78
Printed publication in this or foreign country, invention deemed as prescribed in, 37–38
Printed requirement, 38
Publication requirement, 38
Reasonable diligence, 40
Subsection 102(a), 36–39
Subsection 102(e), 39
Subsection 102(g), 40
Suppression, 40–41
"Used by others," invention deemed, 37

OBSCENE WORKS, COPYRIGHT LAW, 123

OPTIONAL INTER PARTES REEXAMINATION PROCEDURE ACT OF 1999, 32

ORIGINALITY REQUIREMENT, 107–108

ORNAMENTALITY STANDARD, 76–77

PARIS CONVENTION, 80–81, 285–287, 322

PASSING OFF, 309, 310–314
Dastar, significance of, 314
Direct, false representation, 310
Indirect, false representation, 310–311
Intent, 310
Lanham Act, 311–314
Trade names, 312

PATENT ACT. *See* Table of References to the Patent Act

PATENT AND TRADEMARK OFFICE (P.T.O.), 30–32

PATENT COOPERATION TREATY, 82
See also INTERNATIONAL TREATIES AND CONVENTIONS

PATENT LAW TREATY, 83

PATENTS, 27–92
See also DESIGN PATENTS; PLANT PATENTS; UTILITY PATENTS

PATENTS (*cont.*)
    Best mode requirement, 53
Claiming requirement, 52–53
Claim interpretation, 28
Combination patents, non-obviousness standard, 49–50
Commercial use that does not reveal invention to public, 44
Disclosure, 28, 52–53
Enablement requirement, 53
Experimental use, 43–44, 45
Infringement
    Defenses to claims, 28
    Generally, 28
International patent treaties, 80–83
International treaties, 29
Inventive concept, 40, 45–46
Joint inventors, 47
KSR decision, 50–51
Nature of, 27
Non-obviousness standard, 27, 47–51
    Biotechnological process patents, 51
    Combination patents, 49–50
    Commercial acquiescence, 49
    Commercial success, 49
    KSR decision, 50–51
    Legal determination of obviousness, 48
    Long-felt need, 49
    Nexus, 49
    Pertinent prior art, 47–48
    Secret prior art in collaborative situations, 51
    Skill, level of, 48
    Statute of limitations, 51
    Subsection 102(b), 51
    Subsection 103(c), 51
Novelty standard, 27, 36–42
    Abandonment, 40–41
    Commercializing the invention, 41
    Concealment, 40–41
    Deemed patented in this or foreign country, 38–39
    Failure to file for patent, 41
    Interferences, 41–42
    Inventive concept, 40
    "Known by others," invention as, 36–37
    Printed publication in this or foreign country, invention deemed as prescribed in, 37–38
    Printed requirement, 38
    Publication requirement, 38
    Reasonable diligence, 40
    Reduction to practice, 40
    Subsection 102(a), 36–39
    Subsection 102(e), 39
    Subsection 102(g), 40
    Suppression, 40–41
    "Used by others," invention deemed, 37
"On sale" in this country, invention deemed, 45–46
Reduction to practice, 40
Secret prior art in collaborative situations, 51
Statutory bar and inventor requirements, 42–47
    Abandonment, 46
    Commercial use that does not reveal invention to public, 44
    Early disclosure, 42
    Experimental use, 43–44, 45
    "In public use" in this country, invention deemed, 43–44
    Joint inventors, 47
    "On sale" in this country, invention deemed, 45–46
    Over-extended monopolies, prevention of, 43
    Private, personal use, 43
    Statute of limitations, 43–44
    Subsection 102(b), 42–47
    Subsection 102(c), 46
    Subsection 102(d), 46
    Subsection 102(f), 46–47
Statutory bar, generally, 27
Subject matter patentable, 27
Trade secrets, compared, 28
Utility, generally, 28
Written description requirement, 53

PERFORMANCE, LIVE, 148–149

PERFORMING RIGHTS SOCIETIES, 147

PERSONAL NAMES, PROTECTION ON INTERNET, 282

PHARMACEUTICALS
Utility patents, 52

PHONORECORDS
Distribution to public, exclusive right, 108
Fixation requirement, 108
Manufactured outside U.S., 145
Notice of copyright, 178–179

PICTORIAL, GRAPHIC, AND SCULPTURAL WORKS, 117–120, 137

PLANT PATENTS, 78–80
Asexual reproduction, 78

Distinctiveness requirement, 79
Generally, 28
Independent discovery, 79
Infringement, 79
Nature of, 78
Non-obviousness requirement, 79
Novelty and statutory bars, 78
Plant parts, 79
Prior existence in nature, 78
Scope of, 78
Sexual reproduction of plants, 80
Taking seeds, 79
Utility patents for plans, 80

PLANT VARIETY PROTECTION ACT, 80

PREEMPTION, 327, 333

PREJUDGMENT INTEREST, 73

PRINCIPAL REGISTER (LANHAM ACT), 248

PRIVATE OWNERS, INFORMATION SUBMITTED TO GOVERNMENT AGENCIES
Trade secrets, law of, 6, 13–14

PRODUCT DISPARAGEMENT
See COMMERCIAL DISPARAGEMENT

PSEUDONYMOUS WORKS, 183

P.T.O.
See PATENT AND TRADEMARK OFFICE (P.T.O.)

PUBLIC DISPLAY, 150–153

PUBLICITY, RIGHT OF, 327–348
Appropriation of identity, 327, 329–330
Cartoon images, use of, 329
Commercial purposes, 329
Common law vs. statute, 328
Descendability of right of publicity, 327, 332
First Amendment concerns, 327, 330–332
First sale, doctrine of, 332
Impersonators, use of, 330
Nature of, 327–328
Nickname, use of, 329
Phrases, use of, 329–330
Preemption, possibility of, 327, 333
Privacy, publicity and, 328
Purpose of, 327, 328–329
Remedies, 332–333
Scope of, 329–333

PUBLICLY PERFORM, RIGHT TO, 140

PUBLIC PERFORMANCE, 145–149

REASONABLE ROYALTY MEASURE, 70–71

REGISTRATION
Copyright, 181–182
Trademarks, 247–250

RELIGIOUS SERVICES, EXCEPTION TO EXCLUSIVE RIGHTS, 152

REMEDIES FOR COPYRIGHT INFRINGEMENT, 103, 193–195
Attorney fees, 195
Burden of proof, 193–194
Costs, 195
Criminal prosecution, 195
Damages, 193–195
Injunctions, 193
Innocent infringement, 194–195
Willful infringement, 194

REMEDIES FOR INFRINGEMENT
Copyright. See REMEDIES FOR COPYRIGHT INFRINGEMENT
Patents. See REMEDIES FOR PATENT INFRINGEMENT
Publicity, right of, 332–333
Trademark, 283–285

REMEDIES FOR MISAPPROPRIATION OF TRADE SECRETS
Criminal prosecution, 18
Damages, 18
Injunctions, 17–18

REMEDIES FOR PATENT INFRINGEMENT, 70–74
Damages, 70–74
    Attorney fees, 72
    Double or treble damages, 72–73
    Entire market value rule, 72
    Injunctive relief, 73–74
    Lost-profits measure, 71–72
    Measure of damages, 70–73
    "Medical activities," remedies for infringement through, 74
    Prejudgment interest, 73
    Reasonable royalty measure, 70–71
    Utility patents, 70–74
Reasonable royalty measure, 70–71

REMEDIES FOR TRADEMARK INFRINGEMENT, 283–285

RENEWALS OF COPYRIGHT, 185–189

REPLACEMENT PARTS
Copyright law, 170–171

RESTATEMENT OF TORTS, 11

REVERSE ENGINEERING
Copyright law, 166
Trade secrets, law of, 8

SECONDARY TRANSMISSIONS, 152–153

SEEDS, TAKING, 79

SEMICONDUCTOR CHIP PROTECTION ACT OF 1984
Sui generis protection, 123–124

SERVICE MARKS, 228

SEXUAL REPRODUCTION OF PLANTS, 80

SHOP RIGHTS, 15

SHRINK-WRAP LICENSES
Trade secrets, law of, 9

SOFTWARE
See also COMPUTER PROGRAMS
Click-wrap licenses, 9
Shrink-wrap licenses, 9
Utility patents, infringement, 65

SONNY BONO COPYRIGHT TERM EXTENSION ACT, 192

SOUND RECORDINGS, 122, 142
Copyright law, 135
Limited performance rights, 148

STATE LAW, OVERVIEW, 1, 3

STATUTORY BAR AND INVENTOR REQUIREMENTS
See UTILITY PATENTS

SUGGESTIVE MARKS, 230

SUPPLEMENTAL REGISTER, 249–250

SUPPRESSION
Patents, 40–41

SURNAMES, 232–233

TARIFF ACT OF 1930, 54

TARNISHMENT OF MARKS, 269
Dilution, 272

TECHNICAL DRAWINGS, 119–120

TERMINATION OF TRANSFERS OF COPYRIGHT, 189–193

TRADE DRESS, 237–241
Dilution, 273–274

TRADEMARK DILUTION REVISION ACT OF 2006, 271, 274

TRADEMARK LAW, 223–307
Abandonment, 277–279, 287
Abroad, use of mark, 246
Abstract designs, 234–235
Acquiring ownership, 224
    Marks, 244–247
Affixation requirement, 246
Arbitrary marks, 230
Art or design as marks, 237
"Blurring," 268–269
    Dilution by, 272
    Uniqueness of famous mark, 268–269
Certification marks, 228–229
Collateral use of marks, 265–267
Collective marks, 229
Competitors' use of marks for comparison purposes, 267
Composite marks, 237
Concurrent use, 244
Content of marks, 236–241
Contributory infringement, 267–268
"Core" commercial speech, 273
Counterfeiting, 267, 284–285
Cybersquatting, 279–283
    Anticybersquatting Consumer Protection Act, 225, 279–282
    Bad faith, 283
    Bad-faith intent to profit, 280–282
    Dilution, 274
    Infringement of marks, 256
    Personal names, 282
    Remedies and limitation of liability, 282
    Remedies for infringement, 285
    In rem jurisdiction, 282
    Uniform Domain Name Dispute Resolution Policy, 282–283
Deceptively misdescriptive marks, 231–232, 242–243
Deceptive marks, 231–232, 242–243, 286
Descriptive marks, 230–235
    Generic marks versus, 236
Dilution, trademark, 224–225, 268–275

Disparaging matter, 241–242
Distinctiveness of marks, 229–236
    Dilution, 272
    Infringement of marks, 261–262
    Requirement, 223
    Trade dress, 238–239
Drawings as marks, 237
Fair use defense, 275–276
    Dilution, 272
    Nominative fair use, 276–277
False connections with persons living or dead, institutions, beliefs, or national symbols, 242
Fame requirement, 270
Famous marks
    "Blurring" uniqueness of, 268–269
    Dilution, 271–272
Fanciful marks, 230
Federal registration of marks, 247–250
    Cancellation of registration, 250–251
    Certificate of registration, 249
    Constructive use, 249
    Incontestability challenge, 279
    Intent-to-use applications, 248
    Lanham Act Principal Register, 248
    Lanham Act Supplemental Register, 249–250
    Ownership and, 247
    Use applications, 248
First Amendment and, 265, 270–271
Foreign "well-known marks," 247
Foreign words and abbreviations, 234
Functionality doctrine, 224
Generally, 3
Generic marks, 235–236
Geographically deceptively misdescriptive marks, 243
Geographically descriptive marks, 231–232
Geographic boundaries, 251–254
    And majority rule, 254
    At common law, 251–252
    Good faith, 251, 252–253
    Goods or services, source of, 254
    Lanham Act, 252–254
    Of mark owner's rights, 224
    Remote geographical area, 251–252
    Zone of natural expansion, 252
Good faith, geographic boundaries, 251
    Lanham Act, 252–253
Goods, affixation requirement, 246
Goodwill, assignment of, 278
Gray market goods, 266–267
Immoral marks, 241, 286

Infringement of marks, 254–268
    Abandonment, 277–279
    Appearance, similarity of, 260
    Collateral use of marks, 265–267
    Competitors' use of marks for comparison purposes, 267
    Contextual advertising, 258–259
    Contributory infringement, 267–268
    Counterfeiting, 267, 284–285
    Defenses to infringement action, 225, 275–279
    Determination, 255
    Disclaimer, effect of, 262
    Distinctiveness, 261–262
    Fair use defense, 275–276
    Federal registration incontestability status, 279
    First Amendment, 265
    Generally, 224
    Good faith, 262
    Gray market goods, 266–267
    Initial interest (pre-sale) confusion, 263–264
    Injury to be protected against, 254–255
    Internet context, "trademark use" requirement, 256–259
    Knowingly aiding infringement, 268
    Likelihood of confusion requirement, 259–264
    Marketing channels, similarity of, 261
    Meaning, similarity of, 260
    Metatags, 257–258, 263
    Nominative fair use, 276–277
    Ownership rights, challenges to, 279
    Parodies, 264–265
    Passing off vs., 311
    Plaintiff's mark, strength of, 261–262
    Post-sale confusion, 262–263
    Products or services, similarity of, 260
    Purchasers, similarity of, 261
    Remedies, 283–285
    Resale of goods lawfully bearing a mark, 265–266
    Reverse confusion, 264
    Search engine cases, 259
    Secondary meaning, 262
    Similarity of parties' marks, 259–260
    Sound, similarity of, 260
    "Trademark use" requirement, 255–259
    Validity of mark, challenges, 279
    Vicarious liability, 268
    WhenU.Com line of cases, 258–259
Institutions, false connections, 242
International trademark treaties, 285–289
    See also INTERNATIONAL TREATIES AND CONVENTIONS

TRADEMARK LAW (*cont.*)
Internet
    Contextual advertising, 258–259
    Cybersquatting, 256, 274
    Dilution, 274–275
    Forum site domain names, 257, 274–275
    Infringement of marks, 256–259
    Metatags, 257–258, 263
    Search engine cases, 259
    WhenU.Com line of cases, 258–259
Interstate commerce, 246–247
Lanham Act, 226–227, 241–244
    Dilution, 271–275
    Geographic boundaries, 252–254
    Registration of marks, 248–250
Misspellings, 234
National symbols, false connections, 242
Nature of, 225–227
Newspaper reporting and news commentary, 272
Noncommercial use of a mark, 273
Non-functionality requirement, trade dress, 239–241
Nonverbal marks, 234–235, 236
Numbers as marks, 237
Overall commercial impression of marks, 234
Ownership of marks, acquiring, 244–247
Ownership rights, challenges to, 279
Parodies, 264–265
Persons living or dead, false connections, 242
Primarily deceptively misdescriptive marks, 242
Prior use, marks in, 243–244
Purpose of, 225–226
Registration of marks, 247–250
    Cancellation of registration, 250–251
    International treaties, 285–287
Remedies for infringement, 225, 283–285
    Anticybersquatting cases, 285
    Defendant's profits, 284
    Injunction, 283
    Monetary recovery, 283–284
Resale of goods lawfully bearing a mark, 265–266
Scandalous or immoral marks, 241
Scents as trademarks, 237
Secondary meaning, 233
Service marks, 228
Services, affixation requirement, 246
Simultaneous or near-simultaneous use, 245–246
Slogans, 237
Sounds as trademarks, 237
State and federal law, relationship, 226
State dilution claims, 273
Sufficiency, determining for purposes of ownership, 245
Suggestive marks, 230
Surnames, 232–233
Tarnishment, 269
    Dilution, 272
Telle quelle principle, 286
Token uses, insufficiency of, 245
Trade dress, 237–241
    Dilution, 273–274
Trademarks
    Described, 227–228
    Parodies, 264–265
TrafFix decision, 239–241
Types of marks, 223, 227–229
Use in trade, 244–246
Validity of mark, challenges to, 279
Vicarious liability, 268
Words as marks, 237

TRADEMARK LAW TREATY, 288

TRADE NAMES
Passing off, 312

TRADE-RELATED ASPECTS OF INTELLECTUAL PROPERTY
See INTERNATIONAL TREATIES AND CONVENTIONS

TRADE SECRETS, LAW OF, 5–26
Action for misappropriation, 5–6, 8–13
Breach of confidence, disclosure or use of trade secret in, 5, 8–10
Breach of duty, 10–11
Click-wrap licenses, 9
Commercial morality, conduct below, 12
Continuous use, 7
Covenant not to compete, 16–17
Definitions, 5, 7
Employees
    Advance assignment agreements, 15–16
    Creation of trade secret by employee, 14–15
    Doctrine of inevitable disclosure, 6, 17
    Express agreement, absence of, 14–15
    Express agreements, overview, 15–17
    Non-competition agreements, 16–17
    Non-disclosure agreements, 15
    Pre-existing trade secrets, 14
    Shop right in employer, 15
Factors determining status, 7–8
Freedom of information acts, 13–14
"Free ride," defined, 12

Generally, 6
Ideas as trade secrets, 7–8
Illegal conduct, 12
Implied contracts to retain confidentiality, 9–10
Improper means, trade secret acquired by, 11–12
Inevitable disclosure, doctrine of, 6, 17
Information as trade secret, 7–8
Licensing, 75
Mistake, disclosure or use of trade secret learned from with notice, 10, 11
Modification of trade secret, 13
Nature of, 6
Patents, comparison to trade secrets, 28
Private owners, information submitted to government agencies, 6, 13–14
Purpose of, 6
Remedies for misappropriation, 17–18
   Criminal prosecution, 18
   Damages, 18
   Injunctions, 17–18
Reverse engineering, 8
Shrink-wrap licenses, 9
Source of, 6
"Taking," unconstitutional, 14
Third party, disclosure or use of trade secret learned from with notice, 10
Utility patents compared, 74–75
Vulnerability of plaintiff, taking advantage of, 12

TRIPs AGREEMENT
See INTERNATIONAL TREATIES AND CONVENTIONS

TYING ARRANGEMENTS, 67–68

TYPEFACE, COPYRIGHT LAW, 120

UNCONSTITUTIONAL TAKING OF TRADE SECRETS, 14

UNDEVELOPED IDEAS, LAW OF, 93–99
Concreteness requirement, 93, 96–97
Confidential relationship theory, 95
Contract-implied-in-fact theory, 95
Contract-implied-in-law theory, 95
Express contract theory, 94–95
Implied condition, 94–95
Lack of consideration, 94
Miscellaneous accumulation, 93–94
Nature of, 93–95
Novelty requirement, 93, 96–97
Property theory, 95
Recovery, theories of, 93

Value of services rendered, 97

UNFAIR COMPETITION, LAW OF, 309–326
Commercial disparagement, 317–320
   Action, cause of, 317
   Blue Cross decision, 319
   Commercial speech, 319
   False representation, 317
   First Amendment considerations, 319–320
   Generally, 309
   Lanham Act, 318
   Public figure status, 319–320
   Special damages requirement, 317
   State statutory provisions, 317–318
False advertising, 314–316
   Ascertainable loss requirement, 315
   Common-law cause of action, 314–315
   Injunctive relief, 316
   Injury, 316
   Intent, 316
   Lanham Act, 315–316
   Materiality, 316
   Monetary damages, 316
   State statutes, 315
International treaties, 309, 322
Lanham Act. *See also* Table of References to the Lanham Act
   Commercial disparagement, 318
   False advertising, 315–316
   Passing off, 311–314
Misappropriation, 309, 320–322
Nature of law, 309–310
Origin of law, 310
Paris Convention, 322
Passing off, 309, 310–314
   Dastar, significance of, 314
   Direct, false representation, 310
   Indirect, false representation, 310–311
   Intent, 310
   Lanham Act, 311–314
   Trade names, 312
Trademark infringement vs. passing off, 311

UNIFORM DECEPTIVE TRADE PRACTICES ACT, 315, 317-318

UNIFORM DOMAIN NAME DISPUTE RESOLUTION POLICY, 282–283

UNIFORM TRADE SECRETS ACT, 6–7, 11, 17–18

UNIVERSAL COPYRIGHT CONVENTION (U.C.C.), 197

UNLAWFUL APPROPRIATION
Copyright law, 101, 129–132

URUGUAY ROUND AGREEMENTS ACT, 58, 74, 180, 278

USEFUL ARTICLES, DESIGN OF, 117–119

USE IN TRADE, 244–246

UTILITY PATENTS, 29–35
Abstract matter, 33–34
Algorithms and storage medium, 34
AT&T, 35
Benefit to society, 52
Business methods, 35
Combination patents, infringement, 58–60
Composition of matter, 33
Computer programs, 34–35
Constitutional limitations
    Appeals, 31
    Enforcing, 30–32
    Generally, 29
    Implementation of, 30
    Reexamination, 31–32
    Reissue, 31
Generally, 28
Infringement, 54–70. *See also* REMEDIES FOR PATENT INFRINGEMENT
    Active solicitation or assistance, 62
    Antitrust law, relationship to, 67
    Burden of proof, 64
    Claim interpretation, 54–55
    Combination patents, 58–60
    Commercial use, 70
    Component sold, offered for sale, or imported, 63
    "Constructive" making, 59
    Contributory infringement, 62–63
    Corporate officers and directors, 62
    Defenses to claims, 66–70
    Direct infringement, 58–62
    Doctrine of equivalents, 55–58
    Doctrine of exhaustion, 61–62
    Doctrine of prosecution history estoppel, 56
    Estoppel, 56–58, 66
    Experimental use defense, 69
    Importing, 63–64
    Importing patented invention, 61–62
    Inducement to infringe, 62
    Inequitable conduct, 68–69
    Intent, 62
    Invalidity defense, 70
    Knowledge, 62, 63
    Literal infringement, 55
    Majority shareholders, 62
    Material component of U.S.-patented invention, supplying, 64–65
    Offering to sell, 63–64
    Offering to sell patented invention, 60–61
    Patent invalidity, 66
    Patent misuse, 66–68
    Prior use, 69–70
    Provisional rights prior to patent issuance, 65–66
    Publication, 65–66
    Repair vs. reconstruction, 59–60
    Reverse doctrine of equivalents, 56
    Selling, 60–61, 63–64
    Selling components to be assembled abroad, 63–64
    Software, supplying, 65
    Sources of evidence for claim construction, 54–55
    Subsection 271(e), 69
    Suits to enforce patents, 54–58
    Supplying components to be assembled abroad, 64–65
    Tying arrangements, 67–68
Inoperability as lack of utility, 52
Laws of nature, 33–35
Licensing, 75
Live vs. inanimate matter, 33
Machines, 32–33
Manufacture, 33
Medical procedures, 35
Naturally occurring vs. man-made articles, 33
Nature of, 29
Pharmaceuticals, 52
Plants, for, 80. *See also* PLANT PATENTS
Process, 32
State Street, 34–35
Statutory subject matter of patent, 32–35
Surgical procedures, 35
Term of, 29
Trade secret protection, comparison, 74–75
Utility standard, 52

VIDEO GAMES, 152

VISUAL ARTISTS RIGHTS ACT OF 1990, 153–155, 185

VISUALLY IMPAIRED, SPECIAL FORMATS FOR, 139

WIPO COPYRIGHT TREATY, 198–199, 288

WORKS FOR HIRE, 173–175, 183

WORKS OF AUTHORSHIP, 104–105
Categories of, 112–122

WORKS OF VISUAL ART, 153–155, 185

WRITTEN DESCRIPTION REQUIREMENT
Patents, 53

ZONE OF NATURAL EXPANSION, 252

aspenlawstudydesk

It's the best of both worlds – **a print copy** of this *Emanuel Law Outlines* title for your desk reference **and an eBook** version on your laptop to take with you wherever you go. **Plus** a free copy of **AspenLaw Studydesk** productivity software!

BPK83306 — LYHR7FFYX

Use the promotion code above at www.AspenLaw.com to download your pre-paid software and eBook.

Emanuel Law Outlines
Print + eBook BONUS PACK

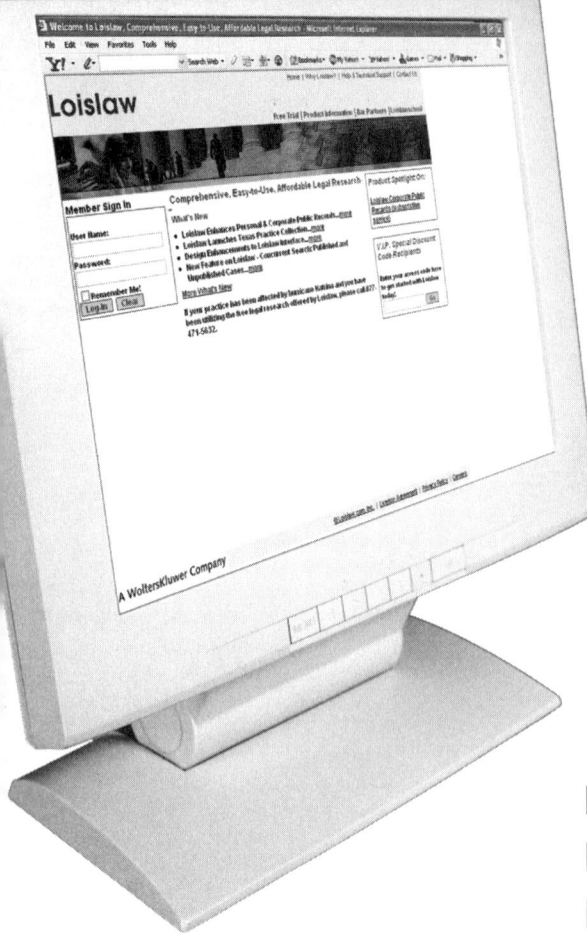

Loislaw

Access to the Critical Information Law Students Need is Just a Click Away

Loislawschool.com is free to all law students. Use www.loislawschool.com at your legal internships, clerkships and summer jobs.

Access includes:

- Up-to-date cases, statutes and other primary law
- National Collection database
- No restrictions or blackout periods – including during the summer
- Six months free after graduation
- Complimentary features: GlobalCite, LawWatch, Find A Case

Loislaw offers subscribers the benefits of:

Saving Time
- Comprehensive database provides up-to-date instant access to state and federal primary law
- Search multiple jurisdictions simultaneously

Gaining Knowledge Easily
- Hyperlink to any cited case, statute or other document
- Save searches and activate LawWatch to notify you of new developments

Trusting Your Source
- Developed specifically for solo practitioners and small firm attorneys
- Provided by Wolters Kluwer Legal, includes Aspen Publishers and CCH

Accessing Assistance
- Research assistance and training by attorneys
- 24/7 technical support

Wolters Kluwer
Law & Business

www.loislawschool.com
See your Librarian for details on your access code.